COLUMBANUS:
STUDIES ON THE LATIN WRITINGS

Columbanus (d. 615), the Irish monk and founder of such important centres as Luxeuil and Bobbio, was one of the most influential figures in early mediaeval Europe. His fiery personality led him into conflict with Gallic bishops and Roman popes, and he defended his position on such matters as monastic discipline in a substantial corpus of Latin writings marked by burning conviction and rhetorical skill. However, the polish of his style has raised questions about the nature of his early training in Ireland and even about the authenticity of the writings which have come down to us under his name. The studies in this volume attempt to address these questions: by treating each of the individual writings comprehensively, and drawing on recently developed techniques of stylistic analysis, new light is shed on Columbanus and his early education in Ireland. More importantly, doubts over the authenticity of certain writings attributed to Columbanus are here authoritatively resolved, so putting the study of this cardinal figure on a sound basis.

Professor MICHAEL LAPIDGE teaches in the Department of Anglo-Saxon, Norse and Celtic, University of Cambridge.

STUDIES IN CELTIC HISTORY

ISSN 0261-9865

For titles already published in this series
see the end of this volume

COLUMBANUS

STUDIES ON THE LATIN WRITINGS

Edited by

MICHAEL LAPIDGE

THE BOYDELL PRESS

First published 1997
The Boydell Press, Woodbridge

ISBN 0 85115 667 3

The Boydell Press is an imprint of Boydell & Brewer Ltd
PO Box 9, Woodbridge, Suffolk IP12 3DF, UK
and of Boydell & Brewer Inc.
PO Box 41026, Rochester, NY 14604–4126, USA

A catalogue record for this book is available
from the British Library

Library of Congress Cataloging-in-Publication Data
Columbanus : studies on the Latin writings / edited by Michael
Lapidge.
    p. cm. — (Studies in Celtic history, ISSN 0261-9865 ; 17)
    Includes bibliographical references and index.
    ISBN 0-85115-667-3 (hc : alk. paper)
    1. Columban, Saint, 543-615—Criticism and interpretation.
2. Christian literature, Latin (Medieval and modern)—History and
criticism. 3. Monasticism and religious orders—History—Middle
Ages, 600–1500. 4. Europe—Civilization—Celtic influences.
5. Europe—Civilization—Irish influences.   I. Lapidge, Michael.
II. Series.
PA8310.C67Z63   1997
270.2′092—DC20   96-38197

The paper used in this publication meets the minimum requirements
of American National Standard for Information Sciences –
Permanence of Paper for Printed Library Materials, ANSI Z39.48–1984

Printed in Great Britain by
St Edmundsbury Press Ltd, Bury St Edmunds, Suffolk

CONTENTS

EDITOR'S PREFACE

During the period which is conventionally known as the Dark Ages, one of the most brilliant lights was the Irish monk and scholar Columba (as he called himself) or Columbanus (as his hagiographer and modern scholars refer to him). The earliest period of christianity in Ireland (that is, the fifth and sixth centuries) is exceptionally dark, and so are the earliest phases of Columbanus's life: his birth, early education and monastic vocation. His career only moves into the light when, in 590 or 591, he arrived in Francia in the company of twelve Irish monks, petitioned the Merovingian king successfully for land on which to establish a monastery for his monks at Annegray, and followed this foundation with another at Luxeuil, where he and his monks followed a régime of extraordinary asperity but succeeded nonetheless in attracting converts to this form of monasticism. The asperity of the régime was in some sense a reflex of Columbanus's fiery and uncompromising personality, and before long he became embroiled in controversy with the Gaulish bishops; he was forced to leave Francia for Italy, where once again with royal patronage he established a monastery at Bobbio and once again became embroiled in controversy, this time with the pope. The nature of Columbanus's personality and his involvement in controversy – on Easter dating, on monastic discipline, on doctrinal issues of various kinds – are known from a small corpus of letters, which reveal him as a Latin stylist of impressive learning and rhetorical skill. Various other writings bearing his name have come down to us alongside the corpus of letters.

As Columbanus during his lifetime was unceasingly involved in controversy, so the legacy of his Latin writings has provoked continuous controversy among modern scholars. It is widely agreed that the small corpus of five *Epistulae* are undoubtedly from the pen of the saint himself (although, interestingly, this corpus is known only from early modern transcripts and is preserved in no mediaeval manuscript). When, in the late nineteenth century, Wilhelm Gundlach was preparing an edition of Columbanus for the Monumenta Germaniae Historica, controversies were raging between various scholars (Albert Hauck, Otto Seebass, August Engelbrecht) about whether a collection of thirteen sermons addressed to a monastic audience – the so-called *Instructiones* – was genuinely the work of Columbanus; between Seebass and others about whether the monastic rules and penitential attributed to Columbanus were his work or that of later followers; between Seebass, Gundlach and Bruno Krusch over the authenticity of various computistical tracts which had been attributed to the saint; and between various scholars (Gundlach, Krusch and Gustav Hertel) on the authenticity of a small group of metrical poems. It cannot be said that any of these controversies was settled definitively, but by 1900 or so they had more or less petered out.

A new phase of controversy was initiated with the publication in 1957 of

G.S.M. Walker's edition of *Sancti Columbani Opera*. For the English-speaking scholarly world, Walker's edition has had the effect of defining the corpus of Columbanus's writings. This edition has the merit of making the saint's writings widely accessible (the Latin text is accompanied by a facing-page translation), but it cannot be described as reliable. Very often the editor's translation reveals that he has failed to understand the Latin text which he has printed, and the text itself is frequently obviously erroneous.[1] Nevertheless, although some reviewers noted various shortcomings, both in the text[2] and in the manuscript-base on which it was constructed,[3] the edition was on the whole received very favourably. In spite of this generally favourable reception, however, the appearance of Walker's edition attracted one particularly virulent review, by Mario Esposito,[4] one of the foremost authorities in the field of Hiberno-Latin studies, and the virulence of his review helped to rekindle the earlier controversies concerning Columbanus's authorship, a situation which was to some degree a result of Walker's uncritical acceptance as genuine of works whose attribution to Columbanus (such as the so-called *Carmen nauale*) depended on pure conjecture. Furthermore, in his citation of sources and parallels, Walker was guided by the presupposition, then prevalent, that sixth-century Ireland, in which Columbanus was educated, had enjoyed unique and privileged access to classical learning, particularly to texts of the classical Latin poets. The result is that Walker's *apparatus fontium* creates the impression that Columbanus had an extraordinarily wide knowledge of classical literature.

This impression was subjected to rigorous scrutiny by J.W. Smit in 1971, who was able to demonstrate beyond doubt that the many quotations cited by Walker as deriving from classical sources were in fact taken by Columbanus at second hand from patristic authors such as Jerome and Gregory. Smit went on to argue that the metrical poems included by Walker in his edition – which do indeed reflect wide knowledge of classical Latin poets – could not on these grounds alone have been composed by the founder of Bobbio, but were probably the product of a later, Carolingian, Columbanus. In an article, first published in 1977, I addressed this same question from various angles and came to conclusions broadly similar to those of Smit: that some of the sources drawn on by the poet of the adonic verses *Ad Fidolium* were composed later than 615, and hence that the poems in question were the product of a Carolingian poet named fortuitously Columbanus, perhaps the shadowy figure of that name who was abbot of Saint-Trond *ca* 800. Some scholars were persuaded by these arguments, some were not.[5] Meanwhile, different kinds of argument were

---

[1] For example, *Sancti Columbani Opera*, p. 40, lines 14–15 ('Attamen deleat Deus tale semen, et nutriat gregem suum teque compungat') is translated as 'But may God destroy such a progeny, and nourish His flock and fight with you', as if *conpungat* in the text were *compugnat* (the subjunctive form apparently passed unnoticed).

[2] See in particular the reviews by Franceschini, Laistner, Löwe and Milburn.

[3] See, for example, Mundó, 'L'édition'; other aspects of Walker's mishandling of manuscript-evidence are noted in the review by Laistner.

[4] Esposito, 'On the new edition'; and cf. the reply to Esposito by Bieler, 'Editing Saint Columbanus'.

[5] See my discussion below, pp. 276–7.

brought from various quarters to suggest that two rhythmical (or rather: non-metrical) poems – *Mundus iste transibit* and *Precamur patrem* – could very probably be attributed to Columbanus of Bobbio.[6]

Given the exceptional importance which Columbanus has for our understanding of Hiberno-Latin culture and for early mediaeval monastic and penitential literature, it is unfortunate that a cloud of doubt should hang over the corpus of his writings. The present book is an attempt to address and resolve this doubt, and to ascertain the corpus of his genuine Latin writing as securely as possible in the present state of our knowledge. Many advances in knowledge have been made since the publication of Walker's edition in 1957. In particular, sophisticated statistical techniques for the analysis of an author's use (or avoidance) of rhythmical *cursus* or sentence-endings have been developed which facilitate the identification of a Latin author's stylistic preferences, and enable us to say with some confidence whether or not two specimens of Latin prose are, or are not, by the same author. Considerable progress has also been made in the study of seventh-century Hiberno-Latin literature. In particular, it is now certain that the *Hisperica famina* and the grammatical works of Virgilius Maro Grammaticus are to be attributed to that century. Much work has been done to elucidate the prose of Adomnán. Substantial corpora of anonymous exegetical and grammatical works produced in seventh-century Ireland have been identified, and the painstaking task of editing these works is underway. In the light of Hiberno-Latin texts such as these, the old notion (which permeated Walker's edition)[7] that the Latin classics were brought to Ireland in the fifth century by scholars fleeing the Germanic invasions of Gaul, has been laid to rest; in its place we have a truer (and in many ways more impressive) understanding of the achievements of Irish scholarship at that time. And although we have far fewer sources for understanding Irish scholarship in the previous century, when Columbanus was a student, the coherent picture of seventh-century Hiberno-Latin culture enables us to make reasonable conjectures about the nature of Latin learning in the sixth.

The underlying intention of the present book is to reassess the arguments for the authenticity of all the Latin writings which have been attributed to Columbanus: to define, once for all as it were, the corpus of his Latin writings. With this aim in view, individual chapters of the book have been allocated to the individual works which have the strongest claim to be considered as authentic; these chapters are prefaced by an account of the career of Columbanus which is intended to provide a context for the individual treatments which follow.

On the question of Columbanus's literary activity and authorship, a number of significant conclusions are reached. The nature of his Latin prose style, and of his monastic discipline, are subjected to new and penetrating analysis. The thirteen *Instructiones*, which in the late nineteenth century attracted the most controversy, are comprehensively analysed and shown beyond reasonable doubt to be the genuine work of Columbanus. The various stages in the genesis and growth of the penitential attributed to Columbanus are elucidated

---

[6] See below, discussion by Schaller (pp. 240–54) and Lapidge (pp. 255–63).
[7] *Sancti Columbani Opera*, ed. & transl. Walker, p. lxvii.

for the first time. Two computistical works printed by Walker are shown conclusively to be spurious, whereas another such treatise (hitherto unnoticed) which passes under the name of Palumbus is shown to be very possibly his. Manuscript evidence adds support to the possibility that a brief *oratio* may also be his. Finally, it is shown that there are no reasonable grounds for attributing any of the metrical verse, which passes in manuscript under the name of Columbanus, to the founder of Bobbio.

Although the chapters of the book are by various hands, a remarkably consistent view of Columbanus's literary activity emerges. Stylistic features which are found to characterise the *Epistulae*, such as the (apparent) avoidance of rhythmical *cursus* and the preference for hyperbaton, are found to be characteristic of the *Instructiones* as well, even though the two works had very different functions and audiences. Many verbal links between the various writings are identified: not only in the major writings, but between *Precamur patrem* and the *Epistulae*, or between *Mundus iste transibit* and the *Instructiones*. The range of reading witnessed in the *Epistulae* – notably of Jerome's *Epistulae*, Rufinus's translations of Gregory of Nazianzus, Gildas and Gregory the Great – is found again in the *Instructiones*, and even (on a more restricted scale) in the monastic rules and penitential, where the influence of Gildas in particular is shown to be decisive. Equally striking is the paucity – one might even say absence – of reminiscences of quantitative Latin verse in general and of classical Latin poets in particular. Such reminiscences amount to the repetition of a single expression from Caelius Sedulius, *Carmen paschale*, in the *Epistulae* and again in the *Instructiones*, and to a single (questionable) debt to Vergil in *Precamur patrem*. It is clear from this evidence that Columbanus had scarcely any knowledge of classical and late Latin metrical (especially hexametrical) verse: a conclusion which squares perfectly with our present-day knowledge of the texts studied in seventh-century Irish schools, but is utterly at odds with the presuppositions prevalent when Walker was preparing his edition.

Although it is the intention of the book to answer questions, not to raise them, there are many ways in which the essays will help to encourage further research. The new understanding of Columbanus's Latin prose style will help to illustrate the achievements and curriculum of sixth-century Irish schools; in particular, certain of his stylistic predilections (such as his preference for agentive nouns in *-or*) will be seen to have a later reflex in the seventh century in the *Hisperica famina* and the prose writings of Adomnán. The attribution of two rhythmical poems to Columbanus may encourage further searches for his authorship in the large corpus of anonymous Hiberno-Latin hymns. Most important, however, is the fact that when the history of Hiberno-Latin literature comes eventually to be written, the Latin writings of Columbanus will be seen to occupy a unique and unparalleled position in that history.

MICHAEL LAPIDGE
January 1996

I

THE CAREER OF COLUMBANUS

Donald Bullough

THE *uita* of Columbanus of Bangor and Bobbio by the north Italian (Burgundian Frank) Ionas of Susa was initiated in the 620s and completed within three decades of its subject's death. Ionas showed a greater interest in the political and social context of his hero's career and included fuller biographical detail than is normally the case in early mediaeval hagiography: but he had only entered Bobbio in 618, and he was inevitably much better informed about Columbanus's later years than about his origins and early life in his native Ireland.[1]

There is no early evidence or acceptable tradition for Columbanus's ancestry, parentage or place of birth: Ionas provides nothing of substance on the matter; and unlike Columba of Iona, Columbanus does not figure in early genealogies.[2] Nor is there incontrovertible evidence from which even an approximate birth-year can be calculated. A widely quoted date in the 540s is derived almost entirely from the six hexameter lines which conclude the adonic verses *Ad Fidolium* in ninth- and tenth-century manuscripts: that these

---

[1] *Vita S. Columbani*: *editio princeps* of *Liber I* by Heerwagen, *Opera Bedae*, III.275–305; critical edition by Krusch, *Ionae Vitae Sanctorum*, pp. 148–224; semi-diplomatic edition (with Italian translation) of the newly discovered Metz, Grand Séminaire, MS. 1, by Tosi, *Vita Columbani et discipulorum eius*. The *terminus post quem* for the completion of the work is provided by the dedication jointly to Abbot Bobolenus of Bobbio, who succeeded Bertulf in 639 or 640. For the author, see *Ionae Vitae Sanctorum*, ed. Krusch, pp. 48–59; for his approach to his subject-matter, see most fully Wood, 'The *Vita Columbani*'. According to Krusch (*Ionae Vitae Sanctorum*, p. 48), Ionas was 'natione neque Scottus neque Francogallus sed in summis Italiae finibus sub ipsis Alpium iugis natus'. But he had obviously forgotten (as Poole, for one, did not: *Studies*, pp. 123–4, 129) that in or shortly after 575 the Imperial (Byzantine) *magister militum* – rather than the Lombards – surrendered Susa to the troops of King Gunthram, after which it remained in the *regnum Francorum* (Burgundia) for centuries: Gregory of Tours, *Historia Francorum*, IV.44; Fredegar, *Chronicon*, IV.45 (ed. & transl. Wallace-Hadrill, pp. 37–8). For the eighth century, see the Novalese documents expounded most recently by Geary, *Aristocracy*, pp. 33–4, 122–3, and also Bullough, '*Albuinus deliciosus regis*', pp. 74–5. But, for Ionas's 'Italian' perspective, cf. his *Vita S. Columbani*, II.5 (ed. Krusch, *Ionae Vitae Sanctorum*, pp. 237–8): 'locus Sigusia, urbs nobilis, quondam Taurinatum colonia, a monasterio [Bobiense] distans .CXL. milibus'.

[2] For Columba and his Cenél Conaill kin, see *Corpus Genealogiarum Sanctorum Hiberniae*, ed. Ó Riain, §§ 8, 327, 336 *et seq.*; cf. Herbert, *Iona, Kells*, pp. 36–7, 310, 311.

were composed by an early seventh-century Columbanus has been seriously challenged but not disproved.[3] No weight can be placed on the statements of the Burgundian Fredegar – the first writer known to have used Ionas's *uita* – that Columbanus died *plenus dierum*, or of the ninth-century Florus of Lyons (in the material which he added to an older Lyons Martyrology) that he died *in senectute bona*, in view of Ionas's own indifference or uncertainty on this point.[4] The assertion in the oldest and best manuscripts of the *uita* (Sankt Gallen, Stiftsbibliothek, MS. 553, of *saec.* ix[2/4]; Metz, Grand Séminaire, MS. 1 of *saec.* ix[3/4]) that Columbanus left Ireland for Gaul *uicensimum aetatis annum agens* (I.4) has been universally rejected; and an early emendation to *tricesimum* is clearly without independent authority.[5]

Ionas had recorded previously that Columbanus was well into his *adulescentiae aetas* if not fully adult (that is to say, twenty-eight or more) before he turned to the monastic life (I.3) and was in his first monastery (Bangor) 'for many years'. Assuming the correctness of the date 590x591 for Columbanus's arrival in Francia,[6] a birth-date in mid-century would be a reasonable deduction: only if his departure from Ireland were ante-dated fifteen/seventeen years would an earlier date be demanded, although not so early as to be incompatible with the beginnings of Bangor (558x559?).[7] Ionas says (I.2) that Columbanus was born *inter primordia fidei* of the inhabitants of the *Lagenorum terra* (Irish *Cóiced Laigen*, Modern English Leinster)[8] and attributes to his mother, whom he does not name, a vision during pregnancy as of a bright sun illuminating the world. The name *Columba* which Columbanus uses of himself in his earliest certainly authentic writing, namely *Epistula I* of 599x600 to Pope Gregory I, and which is his first biographer's preferred usage (the more familiar form being apparently a Latinized Irish diminutive)[9] was probably his name in religion: although it is not absolutely excluded that he had received it at his

---

[3] 'Columbae siue Columbani . . . epistolae', ed. Gundlach, pp. 186–8, Walker, pp. 192–6; cf. Lapidge, 'The authorship of the adonic verses', and Löwe, 'Columbanus und Fidolius'.

[4] Fredegar, *Chronicon*, IV.36 (ed. & transl. Wallace-Hadrill, *The Fourth Book*, p. 29); *Édition pratique*, edd. Dubois & Renaud, p. 211 (*ad XI kal. Decemb.*).

[5] See below, p. 9, n. 31.

[6] See below, p. 10.

[7] The earlier dating was argued for most recently by O'Carroll, 'The chronology'; it seems to create more difficulties than it resolves. For Bangor's foundation, see below, n. 25.

[8] The coastal region south of the lower River Liffey and of the bogs of Offaly, and east of the hills which separated the valley of the River Barrow from the valley of the River Nore: see Byrne, *Irish Kings*, pp. 130–64, with map at p. 133. The passage in Ionas's *Vita S. Columbani* seems to be the earliest evidence of the name.

[9] *Ego Bar-Iona, uilis columba*: *Epistula I*, ed. Gundlach, 'Columbae siue Columbani . . . epistolae', p. 156, Walker, p. 2. In the *uita*, however, the verses which introduce I.2 have *Columbanus qui et Columba*; cf. Smit, *Studies*, pp. 149–51. The Greek as well as the Hebrew equivalent of the Latin *columba* is referred to in *Epistula V* (ed. Gundlach, 'Columbae siue Columbani . . . epistolae', p. 176, ed. Walker, p. 54); for the same play on the name, see the second preface to Adomnán's *Vita S. Columbae* (edd. & transl. Anderson & Anderson, p. 4).

baptism.[10] Ionas's *pubertas nobilis* is a reference to character, not status, and the associated *topoi* characteristic of seventh-century hagiography are avoided. (Textual references to Columbanus's supposed noble or even royal parentage are not older than the twelfth century.)[11] The fact that, in Ionas's concise and elliptical account (I.3), Columbanus is put to study while still young, although apparently without leaving home, argues that he was not of humble origin but also suggests – without proving – that he was not of the social class in which, in the sixth and seventh centuries, 'fosterage' was normal.[12] It is a reasonable inference from the scanty evidence that Columbanus was born shortly after or shortly before 550, into a landowning family of below the highest rank, which may well have been first-generation christian.

Ionas conventionally associates Columbanus's earliest book-learning with his years of boyhood, i.e. seven to fourteen, which made possible a rigorous programme of liberal and divine studies in adolescence. He tells us nothing about Columbanus's first teacher or teachers, although the implication is that (in contrast with the next phase of his career) they were local and non-monastic.[13] His assertion that Columbanus's programme of study at this time consisted of 'grammar, rhetoric and geometry' as well as 'the chain of divine scriptures' may, however, tell us more about his own education than about the young Irishman's.[14] Columbanus's turning to the religious life is attributed to a

---

[10] It seems that *Columb* and diminutive *Columbá* were both current as baptismal names before the end of the sixth century. Columba of Iona, however, may have acquired that name only on his entry into religion: see *Adomnan's Life*, edd. & transl. Anderson & Anderson, p. xxix, where also his distinctive vernacular name, *Colum Cille*, is briefly considered. For the philological aspects, see also Thurneysen, 'Colman Mac Leneni', p. 209.

[11] See Concannon, *Life of St. Columban*, p. 6.

[12] For fosterage, Irish *altur*, and its connotations of status, see *Cáin Iar-raith* (*Ancient Laws*, edd. & transl. O Mahony, Hancock & O'Donovan, II.146–93); *Cáin Lánamna*, §2 (*ibid.*, pp. 344–50); and Thurneysen, *Studies*, pp. 26, 187–8; see also Kerlouegan, 'Essai'. It is clear, however, from early and reliable *uitae sanctorum*, including Adomnán's *Vita S. Columbae*, III.2 (edd. & transl. Anderson & Anderson, pp. 184–5), that the *aite* (Latin *nutritor*) of a *dalta* (Latin *alumnus*) could be a priest or monk; and Ionas – unsurprisingly – could simply have failed to recognise a distinctively Irish social custom. For a different view of Columbanus's origins, see, however, de Vogüé, 'En lisant Jonas', p. 72.

[13] Thirty-plus vernacular inscriptions in the distinctive *ogam*-script, predominantly of the fifth century, are the earliest evidences of a literary culture in Leinster and are claimed to show its derivation from the regions immediately to the west, where such inscriptions are far more numerous: *Corpus Inscriptionum*, ed. Macalister, I, nos 18–51; for the dating, cf. Jackson, 'Notes', pp. 197–202. The christian faith may have come to Leinster by the same route, whether or not Auxilius, who gave his name to Killashee, came from Gaul and was dead as early as 459 (*Annals of Ulster*, edd. & transl. Mac Airt & Mac Niocaill, p. 46).

[14] The singling out of *geometrica*, with *grammatica* and *rhetorica*, from the 'seven liberal arts' seems to be without parallel, and neither the definitions offered by Cassiodorus, *Institutiones*, II.6, nor those of Isidore, *Etymologiae*, III.viii and x–xiii, suggest a convincing explanation. A better pointer is perhaps to be found in late-Imperial legislation, e.g. *Codex Theodosianus*, XIII.iv.3, *Codex Iustinianus*,

determination to resist female attractions and the desire that they provoked in him, and to an encounter with an anchoress who had withdrawn from the world fifteen years previously. Hence, despite his mother's strenuous opposition, he departed for ever – presumably in his late teens or early twenties – from his home and the province of Leinster.

Columbanus took himself first to the 'worthy man' *Sinilis*. The latter has been plausibly identified with Sinell son of Mianiach, abbot of Claen Inis (Cleenish) in Lough Erne, who had a reputation for learning and for heading a community that was subject to a *grauissima regula*, and whose *floruit* was seemingly the later decades of the sixth century.[15] It was while he was this man's pupil that (according to Ionas) Columbanus first displayed his intellectual and literary qualities: thoroughly at home with the Scriptures, he was able to expound the Psalms 'in polished [or: clear] language' and to compose texts to be sung or to be used in teaching. Attempts to identify Columbanus's psalm-commentary with anonymous or doubtfully attributed works in extant manuscripts are generally thought to have failed, and may indeed be misconceived since it is far from certain that Ionas was referring to a *written* exposition: although ninth-century library-catalogues from both Sankt Gallen and Bobbio are evidence that at that date a commentary existed which was credited to Columbanus in the manuscripts.[16] Nor have any other compositions (*dicta*: wrongly *docta* in the Metz manuscript) come down to

---

IX.xviii.2: 'Artem geometriae discere atque exerceri publice intersit; ars autem mathematica damnabilis interdicta est', the first clause apparently covering both those who teach or learn it as a preparation for 'philosophy' and those who train or are trained as surveyors. (Indeed, if it could be shown that the Wolfenbüttel MS. of the *Agrimensores* [Lowe, *Codices*, IX.1374], discovered at Bobbio in 1493, was there throughout the Middle Ages, a connection with Ionas's statement might be supposed.) Alternatively, could Ionas be using *geometrica* exceptionally for 'calendar-calculation'? The familiar term *compotus* seems to have been coined (or first to have gained currency) in seventh-century Ireland (see *Cummian's Letter*, edd. & transl. Walsh and Ó Cróinín, pp. 42, 118 and passim).

15 *Vita altera S. Fintani seu Munnu*, §6: *Vitae Sanctorum Hiberniae*, ed. Plummer, II.228; *Vitae Sanctorum Hiberniae ex codice olim Salmanticensi*, ed. Heist, p. 249. For the historicity of this *uita*, which is predominantly concerned with events in Leinster and adjacent regions of the south, see *Vitae Sanctorum Hiberniae*, ed. Plummer, I.lxxxiv–lxxxvi. Sinilis is said to be *abbas* in Ionas's *uita* only in the – misplaced – *capitulum* to I.4 (*Ionae Vitae Sanctorum*, ed. Krusch, pp. 149, 158), which may not have featured in the original text. Alternative identifications with Sinchell 'the Younger' of *Cell-Achid* (Killeigh, co. Offaly), whose *floruit* is post-549 and the good customs of whose community are recorded in a vernacular text of the eighth (?) century (ed. Meyer, *Hibernica Minora*, pp. 41–2; cf. Kenney, *Sources*, no. 269) or with the ill-documented Sinell, bishop of *Mag Bili* (Moville)(*Annals of Ulster*, edd. Mac Airt & Mac Niocaill, p. 100, s.a. 603), however plausible, or implausible, on other grounds, involve the rejection of Ionas's categoric statement that Columbanus left his native Leinster to pursue his studies under Sinilis.

16 The view that Ionas's phrase 'psalmorum librum elimato sermone exponeret' refers to oral exposition or paraphrase and not to a written commentary has been expressed by Michael Lapidge (pers. comm.), but no supporting argument can be found in the age at which Columbanus is said to have 'expounded' the Psalms, since Ionas clearly credits the achievement to the saint's *adolescentia*, that is, to the

us from this period or from his time at Bangor (on which see below), unless indeed – as has recently been plausibly argued – Columbanus is the author of the Eastertide (?) hymn *Precamur patrem regem omnipotentem*, preserved uniquely in the late-seventh-century 'Antiphonary of Bangor'.[17]

It follows that only the most tentative suggestions can be made about the specific texts read by Columbanus in his boyhood and adolescence. Some or all

---

period between his fourteenth and twenty-eighth years. For the entries in library catalogues, see St Gallen, Stiftsbibliothek, 728, pp. 4–21, ed. Lehmann, *Mittelalterliche Bibliothekskataloge*, I.76; and the ?eighth/ninth century Bobbio catalogue (on its date, see Esposito, 'The ancient Bobbio catalogue', pp. 337–44 and Tosi's edition), preserved only in an early eighteenth-century transcript, now Modena, Biblioteca Estense, Archivio Muratoriano, filza 23, fasc. 3a, ed. Muratori, *Antiquitates*, III.817–23 (reprinted Becker, *Catalogi*, pp. 64–73, at p. 67 [nos. 216–17]) and Tosi, 'Documenti', at p. 140 (nos. 226–7). In the St Gallen catalogue, the entry *Expositi* [sic] *sancti Columbani super omnes psalmos uolumen I* (with a later ninth-century marginal note that it had been taken by an otherwise unknown *Ruodinus*) is immediately followed by *Item eiusdem instructio de fide et alia nonnulla in uolumine I*. An identification with all or part of the Psalm-commentary (with Old Irish glosses) in the one-time Bobbio manuscript, now Milan, Biblioteca Ambrosiana, C.301 inf. (Lowe, *Codices*, III, no. 326) was first proposed by Vallarsi (*apud* Muratori) in the 1730s and was maintained by Germain Morin as late as 1926. Lowe himself supposed that the manuscript was written 'probably at Bangor or possibly in Leinster', but apparently only by identifying the Máil-Gaimrid referred to in the gloss with the *Mael Gaimrid scriba optimus et ancorita abbas Benncair* whose death is recorded in *Annals of Ulster* an. 839 (edd. Mac Airt & Mac Niocaill, p. 297) and, with only some of those attributes, elsewhere: on chronological grounds this is difficult if not impossible to accept, especially if the Milan manuscript is the exemplar of the now fragmentary Turin F.IV.1 Fasc.5 + Fasc.6 (Lowe, *Codices*, IV, no. 452). The work in the two manuscripts is (it is now generally recognised) in part Julian of Eclano's Latin translation of Theodore of Mopsuestia's Psalm-commentary, in part an epitome of that translation (edd. de Coninck & d'Hont, *Theodori Mopsuesteni Expositio in Psalmos*). A more recent alternative identification of the 'lost' commentary by Tosi, 'Il commentario', although supported by Rossi ('Il commento') seems equally mistaken: see Nuvolone, 'Le commentaire'.

[17] *The Antiphonary of Bangor*, ed. Warren, II.5–7; Blume, 'Hymnodia', pp. 271–5; Lapidge, 'Columbanus', pp. 106–10 (and see also below, pp. 255–63). The significance of similar imagery in the Easter Vigil *Benedictio cerei* is unnecessarily diminished by association of that highly distinctive prayer with 'the Gregorian Sacramentary' (Lapidge, 'Columbanus', p. 112). Whatever the authorship or origin of the *Exultet* (on which cf. Capelle, 'L'"Exultet" pascal', Fischer, 'Ambrosius der Verfasser', and Huglo, 'L'auteur de l'Exultet pascal'), it is an unequivocally non-Roman text whose earliest dissemination is in 'Gallican' books, from which it was introduced into the ninth-century 'Gregorian Supplement' (although in fact frequently omitted from early copies, including those of the St Gallen–Reichenau group, namely Oxford, Bodleian Library, Auct. D.1.20, Wien, Österreichische Nationalbibl., lat. 1815, and Donaueschingen, 191 [now Stuttgart, Württembergische Landesbibl.]). Lapidge's further suggestion ('Columbanus', p. 112, n. 38; cf. p. 114, n. 46) that 'Columbanus intended "Precamur patrem" as a replacement for one of the Easter hymns in the "Old Hymnal" ' depends on a concept of the 'Old Hymnal' (i.e. the Office hymns in use in various parts of the West before the Carolingian liturgical 'reforms') which I do not think is sustainable: see Bullough (with A. Harting-Corrêa) 'Texts, Chant and the Chapel', in Bullough, *Carolingian Renewal*, esp. pp. 245–6.

of the Classical quotations and reminiscences in his later writings (which are probably far less numerous than has sometimes been asserted) were presumably taken from the unnamed grammatical texts used in his education.[18] His biblical citations must similarly reflect, in part at least, the character of the text familiar to him in his Irish years: it is noteworthy, therefore, that his quotations from St Matthew's Gospel in unambiguously *Vetus Latina* or 'peculiar' versions never correspond with the readings of the 'African' gospel-text in Torino, Biblioteca Nazionale MS. G.VII.15, a book which is widely regarded as having been carried by Columbanus from Ireland to Bobbio.[19] Columbanus's authorship of *Precamur patrem* entails familiarity with the apocryphal Gospel of Nicodemus, with Venantius Fortunatus's (then recently composed) *Pange lingua*, and more generally with fifth-century hymnography. The single allusion, in his *Epistula I*, to Gildas's *De excidio Britanniae* suggests that this, too, was a work he had read in his homeland.[20] His defence of the Irish ways of calculating Easter in his early letters shows that he was familiar with the sixth-century Irish *Canon paschalis* falsely credited to Anatolius of Laodicea.[21] Moreover, of the writings which he cites in support of this man's authority, namely Eusebius in Rufinus's translation of the *Ecclesiastical History*, Jerome in his *De uiris illustribus* and Gennadius (or pseudo-Gennadius) in the *Liber ecclesiasticorum dogmatum*, the first almost certainly, the second not improbably and the third possibly would have been known to him before he left Ireland. Eusebius-Rufinus is quoted in the *Canon paschalis*, and a mutilated bifolium from a copy written in Ireland in the decades either side of the year 600 has recently come to light.[22] There is other

---

[18] Cf. the discussion of Walker (*Sancti Columbani Opera*, ed. Walker, pp. 221–2) with that of Smit (*Studies*, pp. 167–253), who on this is surely almost wholly correct.

[19] The quotations from Matthew are discussed by Walker (*Sancti Columbani Opera*, pp. 216–18). On the Torino manuscript, see Lowe, *Codices*, IV, no. 465; a complete transcription of the biblical text is given by Wordsworth, Sanday & White, *Old-Latin Biblical Texts*, II.

[20] Curran, *Antiphonary of Bangor*, pp. 53–6, 213–14; Lapidge, 'Columbanus', p. 114, esp. nn. 43, 46. For the allusion to Gildas, see *Epistula I* (§ 6) (ed. Gundlach, p. 158; ed. Walker, p. 8).

[21] *Epistula I* (§ 3) (ed. Gundlach, p. 156–7; ed. Walker, pp. 2–4) quotes Anatolius probably from pseudo-Anatolius, *Canon Paschalis*, ed. Krusch, *Studien*, I.316–27, here 318–19, although the passage in question is taken from that author's genuine writings (see next note); cf. *Epistula II* (§ 7) (ed. Gundlach, p. 162; ed. Walker, p. 18). Krusch's text was based solely on Bucherius's 1633 edition of the *codex Sirmondi* (Oxford, Bodleian Library, Bodley 309) and Köln, Dombibliothek, 83[II], plus the testimonia of Columbanus (!) and Bede, both from unsatisfactory editions: it does not provide, therefore, a trustworthy basis for the detailed comparisons with other computistic texts which have latterly been attempted.

[22] See *Epistulae I, II* (as last note). That the 'Anatolius' passage quoted by Columbanus in his *Epistula I* (last note) is authentic is established by its quotation earlier in Eusebius-Rufinus, *Historia ecclesiastica*, VII.xxxii.14–18 (not VII.28, as Krusch, *ibid.*, p. 319 n., and Walsh & Ó Cróinín, *Cummian's Letter*, p. 33), ed. Mommsen, *Die lateinische Übersetzung*, pp. 723, 725. The recently discovered fragment is ed. Breen, 'A new Irish fragment'. It is generally agreed today that the genuine *Liber ecclesiasticorum dogmatum* of Gennadius is the text edited by Turner, 'The *Liber ecclesiasticorum dogmatum*', whereas the text in *Patrologia Latina*, ed. Migne,

– admittedly scanty – evidence for early Irish familiarity with the *De uiris illustribus*. The extent to which the vocabulary and metaphorics of Columbanus's later writings are dependent on or influenced by Jerome argues, without conclusively proving, that a now-indeterminable range of that Father's works (letters, exegesis etc.) were among his early reading; and Rufinus's translation of the *Orationes* of Gregory of Nazianzus is likewise probably to be reckoned among the latter.[23] The view expressed by the late Professor Mohrmann that the Latinity of Columbanus's extant (post-591) writings is archaic in both style and vocabulary, resembling that of the best fifth-century writers and showing no evident impact of sixth-century writers in Frankish Gaul, although requiring some modification, is still broadly acceptable; and it can therefore be legitimately used as evidence of his linguistic and intellectual formation before he left Ireland.[24]

Ionas records (I.4) that when Columbanus felt the call of the monastic life he took himself to *Bennchor* (Bangor, Co. Down), which owed its high standards to its founder and abbot, Comgell. Columbanus himself never refers to either Comgell or Bangor, unless indeed he is responsible for the late-sixth-century Annals in which they figure.[25] Nor is he named in any of the other sources for Comgell and his monastery, until the strange *Ratio de cursus* (written at an unidentified continental centre in the eighth century) specifically links the spread of the *cursus Scottorum* with Comgell's sending Columbanus to Gaul.[26] Nonetheless, it is generally assumed that both his

---

LVIII.979–100, is an early sixth-century Gallic revision (see *Clavis*, edd. Dekkers & Gaar, nos 958, 958a). But since the majority of witnesses for both versions, including the early Bobbio manuscript, now Milan, Biblioteca Ambrosiana, O.212 sup. (see Lowe, *Codices*, III.361: the authentic Gennadius version?) have the same 'false' reading as the two transcripts of Columbanus's *Epistula I* (ed. Gundlach, p. 157; ed. Walker, p. 4), namely 'ante transgressum uernalis aequinoctii et [*om*. Columbanus] sextae decimae lunae initium' (which according to Walsh & Ó Cróinín, *Cummian's Letter*, p. 28, n. 95, 'we cannot explain'[!]), his source could be either one of them.

[23] Smit, *Studies*, esp. pp. 171–208; Lapidge, 'Columbanus', pp. 107–9.

[24] Mohrmann, 'The earliest continental Irish Latin'; see also Winterbottom, 'Columbanus and Gildas'.

[25] *Annals of Ulster*, s.a. 559 (edd. Mac Airt & Mac Niocaill, p. 80), a presumably non-contemporary entry; 'eclesia Benncair fundata'; cf. *ibid.*, s.a. 602 (edd. Mac Airt & Mac Niocaill, p. 100), a possibly contemporary entry: 'quies Comghaill Bennchair'.

[26] *Ratio de cursus*, ed. Hallinger, *Initia consuetudinis Benedictinae*, pp. 82–91. Comgell's virtues are commemorated without personal detail in the hymn *Audite pantes ta erga* in the 'Antiphonary of Bangor', and the quality of the communal life there is lauded in the hymn *Benchuir bona regula* included in the same collection: *Antiphonary of Bangor*, ed. Warren, II.16–19, 28; Blume, 'Hymnodia', pp. 321–4, 356–7. Comgell is named as *abbas* or *monasterii fundator* three times in Adomnán's *Vita S. Columbae*: I.49, III.13, III.17 (edd. Anderson & Anderson, pp. 88, 200, 206), on the first occasion in connection with events of *ca* 575. His rigorous asceticism is detailed in the later but probably pre-tenth-century *Vita S. Comgalli* (ed. Plummer, *Vitae Sanctorum Hiberniae*, II.3–21; ed. Heist, pp. 332–4).

ordination as priest and his epoch-making acceptance of the concept and practice of private confession and tariffed penance, which had been introduced to Ireland by *Uinnianus*/Finnian (of Clonard? of Moville?), took place in his years at Bangor.[27] Similarly, the discipline and liturgical *cursus* of the community and the ideas of its abbot, less certainly Comgell's actual words, are thought to be embodied in the original (ten-chapter) version of Columbanus's *Regula monachorum* and in the authentically Columbanian sections of the *Regula coenobialis* (see below).[28] In Ionas's account (I.4), Columbanus gave himself to prayer and fasting, imitating Christ on the Cross by his own mortification that he might exemplify to others the demands of christian teaching. In later continental tradition, exemplified first by Wettinus's *Vita S. Galli*, Columbanus was the *magister* who instructed young monks entrusted to the monastery by their parents.[29]

After what Ionas describes as 'many years' spent at Bangor, Columbanus felt the call to 'peregrinate' in the spirit of Abraham: that is, to abandon his native land and kindred.[30] Abbot Comgell eventually gave his reluctant consent because of the benefit which Columbanus's voluntary exile would bring to others. Supported by the prayers of the rest of the community, Columbanus then departed with twelve companions: the names of some of them are supposedly provided by later passages in the *uita*, and Irish 'tradition' eventually

[27] Columbanus is referred to as *sacerdos* in the commemorative verses cited by Ionas (*Ionae Vitae Sanctorum*, ed. Krusch, p. 224). In his earliest extant letter (*Epistula I*), Columbanus reports an exchange of views between *Vennianus auctor* and the British Gildas on monks who abandon their monastic obedience (ed. Gundlach, 'Columbae siue Columbani . . . epistolae', p. 159; ed. Walker, *Sancti Columbani Opera*, p. 8).

[28] A (lost) *regula abbatis Congelli* is among the remarkable collection of Rules listed in the 'lost' section of the ninth-century Fulda catalogue: Schrimpf *et al.*, *Bücherverzeichnisse Fulda*, pp. 64–5. The view of Hertel and Laporte, that the first six chapters of Columbanus's *Regula monachorum* are an abridgement or adaptation of a text by Comgell, lacks supporting evidence. The assertion of Wallace-Hadrill (*The Frankish Church*, p. 65), that in Francia Columbanus 'propagated the idea of monasteries as local centres of aristocratic cultus, *such as he had known in Ireland*' (my italics), seems to be warranted neither by his recorded early life nor by what we know of sixth-century Bangor.

[29] The text of Wettinus is ed. Krusch, *Passiones Vitaeque Sanctorum Aeui Merouingici*, IV.256–80, here p. 257. Wettinus may have been following the corresponding (lost) portion of the *uita uetustissima*: but equally, as the teacher in the monastic school at Reichenau, he could well have 'glossed' his sources in this sense. If recent doubts about Gallus's Irish origins (see below, pp. 19–21) are well founded, such 'evidence' necessarily loses all its force. No support can be claimed from the two poems *Ad Sethum* and *Ad Hunaldum*: even assuming that the poems are authentically Columbanus's and that both the addressees are young monks (which in the case of the second-named is far from certain), their names make it unlikely that they were monks from Ireland.

[30] See Hughes, 'The changing theory'; Leclercq, 'Mönchtum und Peregrinatio'; Angenendt, *Monachi Peregrini*, pp. 124–58; and Charles-Edwards, 'The social background'.

supplied by the rest.[31] The party took ship to Brittany[32] and after a short delay entered Frankish Gaul, where Columbanus and his companions began to preach and live the Gospel.

According to Ionas, their reputation reached the court of one of the Merovingian Frankish kings, whom he names as Sigebert and describes as ruling both the Austrasian and the Burgundian Franks (I.6, similarly I.18): and when they appeared before the king in person they were encouraged to stay. Unwilling to compromise with his call to the simple evangelical life, Columbanus sought out a desolate site and finally settled in a ruined *castrum* at Annegray (dép. Haute-Saône). Ionas describes a life of great austerity and closeness to nature, although very soon when Columbanus wanted true solitude he had to leave Annegray for the surrounding wolf-infested woods: contact with an existing monastery, when Columbanus's community found itself in dire straits, was followed by an afflux of lay people and particularly of the sick, seeking to be healed by prayer. The growing number of vocations to his wilderness community eventually forced Columbanus to seek an alternative site: he found it in the substantial Roman ruins and spa waters of Luxeuil,

---

[31] The textual crux in *Vita S. Columbani* I.4 relating to Columbanus's age when he left Bangor has already been referred to. Whether *uicensimum* is the result of early miscopying or misunderstanding (of his 'age in religion', for example) or false Bobbio or Luxeuil tradition is now indeterminable. Three manuscripts of the tenth to twelfth centuries, beginning with Vatican City, Biblioteca Apostolica Vaticana, Regin. lat. 1025 (Krusch's B2) emend – independently? – to *tricesimum*, apparently in an early attempt to make Ionas's account more consistent with itself. Supposedly among the twelve companions are Gallus (*Vita S. Columbani* I.11 and the *Vita S. Galli* cited above), Domoalis (*Vita S. Columbani* I.9, I.19), Libran(us) and Aid(us)(*Epistula IV*: ed. Gundlach, p. 167; ed. Walker, pp. 28, 30; cf. below, p. 17 and n. 53), another Columban (*Vita S. Columbani* I.17) and, most dubiously, Deicolus, reputed founder of the monastery at Lure (not named by Ionas or any other early source, but the subject of a much later Lotharingian (?) *uita*, listed *Bibliotheca Hagiographica Latina*, no. 2120, on which see most recently Thomas, 'Der Mönch Theoderich').

[32] Ionas, *Vita S. Columbani*, I.4, cf. I.21 (ed. Krusch, *Ionae Vitae Sanctorum*, pp. 160, 198). Nor can the unexpected reference to Columbanus in the unique letter of the southern English bishops to the Irish clergy copied by Bede, *Historia Ecclesiastica*, II.4, be used as evidence of a journey via Britain/England (cf. Wallace-Hadrill, *Commentary*, pp. 56, 220). Indeed, the contrasting references to Bishop Dagan and to Columbanus surely show the opposite; and *uenientem* in relation to the second of these has necessarily to be understood as 'who had come' or 'when he had come'. The real issue of interpretation is seemingly, therefore: on which journey through Gaul had Laurence (or Mellitus or Iustus) encountered Columbanus? The latter's Easter day was almost certainly in conflict with current Roman and Gallic practice already in 597 and not merely in 600 or 603: see Schäferdiek's corrected reconstruction of the 'Irish Easter-table' in München, Staatsbibliothek, Clm. 14456 in 'Der irische Osterzyklus'. It is difficult to believe that this was not part of the customs and *conuersatio* which disturbed the English bishops: Wallace-Hadrill's doubts (*Commentary*, p. 56) about A.A.M. Duncan's assertion ('Bede, Iona and the Picts', pp. 36–7) that Easter observance would *not* have figured in the letter (since 'it was scarcely an issue outside Gaul in 610') are entirely justified.

some eight miles to the south-west, where he re-settled his community and began the construction of a more substantial monastery.[33]

This apparently precise and straightforward narrative raises a whole range of chronological and topographical problems. King Sigebert ruled only over the Austrasians and died in 575. Most scholars since the seventeenth century have therefore supposed that the king who issued the invitation to the Irish pilgrims was either a brother or a son.[34] The Metz manuscript names the king as Childebert (and duly omits the words *cuius superius fecimus mentionem* after the name of Sigebert in I.18) which offers the tempting emendation *Hyldeberti*. King Childebert, however, only added the kingdom of the Burgundians to his kingdom of the Austrasians after the death of Gunthram on 28 March 593: and Ionas twice suggests, although not without ambiguity, that Luxeuil lay within the city-territory of Besançon and therefore presumably within its diocese (as it and Annegray certainly were in later centuries) – which, like Langres to the west, was certainly within the pre-593 Burgundian kingdom. It would still be necessary to suppose, therefore, that before that date the wild country of the upper Sâone (which Ionas, possibly incorrectly, regarded as part of the western Vosges) was either a frontier 'no-man's land' – which is not impossible – or was temporarily within the territory of Toul, the southern boundary of which was adjusted almost immediately afterwards, for which there is not the slightest evidence.[35] The most categoric evidence for the date of the foundation of Annegray and, by extension, of Columbanus's arrival in Gaul is to be found in: first, Ionas's statement (I.20) that Columbanus's expulsion from Luxeuil (which can be dated independently to 610: see below) was *uicesimo anno post incolatum heremi eius*; secondly, Columbanus's assertion in his letter to the bishops and others assembled in council at Chalon-sur-Saône in the summer or autumn of 603 that *usque nunc licuit nobis inter uos uixisse duodecim annis*.[36] The two statements together suggest that Columbanus arrived in Gaul 590x591 and established himself at Annegray in the latter year or 592; and, taken in conjunction with Ionas's earlier (textually

---

[33] Ionas (*Vita S. Columbani* I.6–9) is the only source for the first monastery at Annegray. The late mediaeval priory there which was a dependency of Luxeuil was a later (re-)foundation. For the little that is known of Roman *Luxouium* (*Lussouium*), see Leclercq, 'Luxeuil', cols 2722–87.

[34] In recent decades only O'Carroll ('The chronology', p. 80) has sought to defend the accuracy of the reference to Sigebert and the 'early' chronology which necessarily follows from it.

[35] Fredegar, *Chronicon*, I.14, 15; Ionas, *Vita S. Columbani*, I.10, 14. For the political and ecclesiastical geography of these territories, see Longnon, *Géographie*, pp. 125–6, 220 and map, and Rey *et al.*, *Les diocèses*, pp. 14–16, 43–4, 309 (map).

[36] *Epistula II* (ed. Gundlach, p. 162; ed. Walker, p. 16). For the date, see below. The attempt of O'Carroll ('The chronology', pp. 91–3) to identify the council referred to in the letter with that held at Mâcon in 585 (*Concilia Galliae*, ed. de Clercq, pp. 237–50) must fail, if on no other grounds, because later in the letter Columbanus quotes *sanctus Gregorius* and his *Regula pastoralis* (ed. Gundlach, p. 163; ed. Walker, p. 20), which already in his *Epistula I* he says he has read.

corrupt?) reference to a Frankish king and his kingdom(s), imply that Luxeuil was founded not before 593.[37]

The years at Luxeuil are the most fully documented of Columbanus's life and career, although the absence of dates or independently dated events in the relevant chapters of Ionas's *uita* and the non-existence of early Luxeuil charters make any sort of chronological framework impossible. Ionas records that many men from all parts, including those he describes as *nobilium liberi* (without at this stage giving any names), came to Luxeuil in search of spiritual solace; and that because of the growth of the original community Columbanus had to establish a further one a short distance away at Fontaine (-lès-Luxeuil).[38] It is generally assumed that it was in these years of rapid expansion and of two or three communities under his personal abbacy that Columbanus began to give written form (although apparently never a definitive one) to his two *Regulae*, and to his *Penitential*, with sections respectively for his monks, for secular clerics and for lay penitents.[39] No manuscript of either the *Regula monachorum* or the *Regula coenobialis* is older than the early ninth century. The first of these is transmitted in both a longer version, divided into ten chapters, and a shorter in fourteen chapters; the second similarly exists in both a longer and a shorter version. The longer version of the *Regula monachorum* is the only one provably copied at Bobbio in the ninth and tenth centuries and is generally thought to be Columbanus's own. Much more debatable are the origins of the two versions of the *Regula coenobialis*, the detailed regulation in which nonetheless seems to form a necessary complement to the general principles of the *Regula monachorum*. The most widely held view is that only §§ 1–9 in the shorter (uninterpolated) version are authentically Columban, the additional chapters and the interpolations being the work of unidentified successors. Except for *Regula monachorum* (longer version, § 7) which lays down 'the office of psalms and prayers in canonical manner' or *cursus*, the *Rules* have nothing to say on the organisation of a monastery or its communal life: they are rather exhortations to the heroic pursuit of the monastic virtues, with accompanying penal prescriptions for any lapse of which a monk may be guilty. The *Penitential*, transmitted only in the two Bobbio

---

[37] For a slightly different reconstruction, with additional arguments, see Schäferdiek, 'Columbans Wirken', pp. 174–8.

[38] *Vita S. Columbani* I.10. Ionas (*ibid.* I.17) speaks of sixty monks in this secondary community; and Columbanus himself (*Epistula II*) refers to 'seventeen dead brethren'. Archaeological excavation has not produced any certain evidence for the earliest monastic buildings at Luxeuil, although according to Erlande-Brandenburg, 'Le monastère', pp. 239–43, Merovingian-period tombs have been found under the east end of the subsidiary church of St Martin (which may already have existed in the mid-seventh century: it is recorded as the burial-place of Abbot Waldebert, who died in 670, in his tenth-century *uita*: *Acta Sanctorum*, ed. Bollandists, *Maii* I.280). Ionas refers to the *septa monasterii*, the *ecclesia* (of which the later recorded dedication is to St Peter), an *atrium ecclesiae* in which Columbanus sat reading and which had windows (a narthex or porticus-type construction, therefore?), the *refectorium*, *cellarium* and *horreum*: *Vita S. Columbani*, I.10, 15, 16, 17, 20. Cf. James, 'Archaeology', pp. 43, 45.

[39] Ionas (*Vita S. Columbani*, I.10) specifically links Columbanus's creation of a (written) *rule* with the establishment of Fontaine under a provost.

11

manuscripts that contain the *Regula monachorum* and other works of Columbanus, can be accepted as substantially his work. Many chapters depend heavily on the *Penitential* of Uinnianus, although in a different order; others reflect problems peculiar to Burgundy in the early seventh century.[40] Through it and his personal actions, therefore, Columbanus introduced to continental Europe the hitherto Irish practice of private and frequent confession ('confession of devotion') followed by equally private and reiterated penance ('tariffed penance') as a means to absolution from sins committed since the last confession. The anecdotes recorded by Ionas to illustrate Columbanus's powers over nature, prophetic gifts and healing powers are consistent in emphasising the natural wilderness in which the communities had been established, and the total dependence on the labours of the monks themselves (not on grants of lands, with men to work them) for the necessities of life.[41] Moreover, when every allowance has been made for the requirements of the hagiographic genre, they give a convincing picture of Columbanus's intense spirituality, based on total subjection to the will of God and identification with the Crucified Christ, and of a personal magnetism that inevitably seemed to have a supernatural basis: the moments of percipience and gentleness do much to mitigate the impression of unreasoning and unreasonable harshness given by the disciplinary provisions of Rules and Penitentials. Probably an early instance of the influence exercised by Columbanus on the nobility of northern Burgundy is the appeal to him of the childless *dux* Waldelenus and his wife Flavia (both of whom may have been Gallo-Romans), in consequence of which they entrusted to him their first-born Donatus, future bishop of Besançon; his influence on men of less elevated social position is exemplified by the visits to the community of *Winiocus*, awkwardly described as *presbiter ex parrochianis* and father of a future abbot of Bobbio.[42] Many

---

[40] For the manuscript-tradition of the *Regulae* and Penitential, and for what is, or may be, Columbanus's own part in their composition, see the discussion of Thomas Charles-Edwards, below, pp. 217–39.

[41] Ionas, *Vita S. Columbani*, I.11–12, 16, 17, etc. For the episode of 'the thieving crow' (*ibid.*, I.17, ed. Krusch, *Ionae Vitae Sanctorum*, pp. 178–9), see Schär, 'Der heilige Columban'.

[42] Ionas, *Vita S. Columbani*, I.14, 15, 17. Ionas describes Waldelenus as *dux* over the region between the Alps and the Jura (modern W. Switzerland); but since the succession of *duces Ultraiorani* in this period is well documented by Fredegar, and since Ionas also says that the couple came to Luxeuil *ex Vesontionense oppido*, it seems likely that his duchy was *Cisiuranus*. Since Donatus was bishop by 626x627 (*Concilia Galliae*, ed. de Clercq, p. 296 – assuming that *Donans = Donatus*), his birth and childhood should belong to the early 590s. That Waldelenus was Gallo-Roman in origin in spite of his name is indicated by Fredegar's reference to his second son and successor in the duchy, Chramnelenus, as *ex genere Romano* in contrast with the other dukes *ex genere Francorum*: *Chronicon*, IV.78. A different – but related? – Waldelenus was Columbanus's alternative choice as prior of Luxeuil when he himself was forced to leave the monastery (as recounted in *Epistula IV*); this Waldelenus has been identified with a future abbot of Bèze and as a son of the Frankish *dux* Amalgarius. For the texts and genealogical speculations, see Roussel, *St Columban*, I.128 and de Vogüé, 'En lisant Jonas', p. 75. Surprisingly, the Waldeleni nowhere figure in *Columbanus and Merovingian Monasticism*, edd. Clarke & Brennan, although Donatus does.

others, unrecorded, presumably took advantage of the previously unknown facility of private confession, penance and absolution. Columbanus and his community seem also to have encouraged frequent communion for the laity as well as themselves, which many of the former would have received in the monastic chapels. Ten years after Columbanus's death, a dissident monk of Luxeuil, Agrestius, objected both to some of the devotional practices prescribed in the *Regulae* and to the introduction into the mass of 'superfluous' prayers and collects – actions which were not denied but defended by Columbanus's successor as abbot.[43]

It is not surprising that in Columbanus's own life-time, the monastic and pastoral observances introduced or encouraged by him aroused opposition from some at least of the bishops and other leading ecclesiastics of eastern Francia, although Ionas makes no direct allusion to this; and his continuing use of the 84-year Easter cycle, with the equinox on 25 March and limits of the fourteenth-to-twentieth moon, which he had brought with him from Ireland, sharpened the contrast with local churches which (like most of Gaul) used the tables of Victorius of Aquitaine. Before A.D. 600 Columbanus had apparently sought support for his position from Pope Gregory through his *rector patrimonii* in Gaul, Candidus. In that year or the next, in his first surviving letter (*Epistula I*), he addressed Gregory directly. Acknowledging the special authority of the see of St Peter and indicating his great respect for Gregory personally, he nonetheless argued vigorously for the acceptance of his Easter-calculations as the authentic tradition of the Church; and added, in implied rebuke of many of the leaders of the church in Gaul (some of whose confessions he had heard), queries about simoniac and unchaste bishops and about monks who have left their monastery.[43 bis] Three years later, 603x604, Columbanus was summoned to a council at Chalons-sur-Saône where the assembled bishops were, at Queen Brunechildis's behest, to discipline the bishop of Vienne: Columbanus declined to appear and wrote an exculpatory but also conciliatory letter (*Epistula II*), while denying any inherent conflict with the different 'witness' (*documentum*) of

---

[43] Ionas, *Vita S. Columbani*, II.9, 10. Ionas's phrase 'multiplicationem orationum in sacris officiis' is translated by Riché ('Columbanus', p. 63) as 'the multiplication of prayers outside the mass' (*sic!*). But at this period *sacra officia* meant services in general and the eucharistic celebration in particular, not (as later) 'the office hours': see, for example, the opening words (although not the title!) of Isidore's *De ecclesiasticis officiis* (ed. Lawson, *Sanctus Isidorus*, p. 4), and cf. Gregory of Tours, *Historia Francorum*, VIII.31: 'aduenientem dominicae resurrectionis diae, cum sacerdos ad implenda aeclesiastica officia ad aeclesiam maturius properasset'. No convincing identification of Columbanian *orationes* has been made, although in Agrestius's and Ionas's usage the term might embrace 'office hymns' such as *Precamur patrem* (see above). Indeed, it is precisely in *Vita S. Columbani*, II.10, that Ionas uses the rare word *micrologus* – in the form *migrologa* – which, after Rufinus, is recorded only in *Precamur patrem* and in Columbanus's *Epistulae I* and *V*: see Lapidge, 'Columbanus', pp. 107–8. It has been suggested that Columbanus's critics were also thinking of *loricae* and *lorica*-like prayers: but since these belonged to private devotion, this does not seem very likely.

[43 bis] See now Stanton, 'Letter I'.

secular clergy.[44] Between the dates of the two letters Columbanus had (he records) sent to the pope a three-book work on the errors of the Gallic bishops in relation to Easter and a pamphlet on the subject to Bishop Arigius: neither has survived.[45] A later letter (*Epistula III*) written to Rome, apparently during a papal vacancy and more probably that of 604–5 than that of 607, renewed Columbanus's appeal for his followers to be allowed to continue the observances they had brought with them from Ireland.[46]

Columbanus never mentions a secular ruler in the letters which he wrote while in Francia. His independent conduct towards the Burgundian hierarchy and his seemingly successful resistance to its pressures on him to abandon 'Irish' ways have, however, been taken as evidence that for many years he enjoyed the active support of King Theuderic II or of his grandmother Brunechildis. A formal grant of protection (*mundeburdium*) to him by one of the kings of Burgundy has indeed been inferred from words that Ionas put into the mouths of Theuderic and Columbanus; and a passage in the latter's letter has been interpreted more questionably to mean that his monastic foundations benefited from a royal grant of immunity. Ionas records that the young king Theuderic 'used often to visit Columbanus at Luxeuil humbly to beg the favour of his prayers' and that the abbot rebuked him because he preferred concubines to lawful wedlock – presumably between 603 and 607, therefore.[47]

---

[44] Columbanus's *Epistulae I* and *II* and the allusion in *Epistula III* (§ 2) are the only surviving evidence for the conflict over Easter observance 600–603x604; Fredegar's account (*Chronicon*, IV.24) of the *senodus Cabillonno*, which independently establishes its approximate date, speaks only of the deposition of Desiderius of Vienne; cf. Schäferdiek, 'Der irische Osterzyklus', p. 365 and n. 41. An identification of the *sanctus frater Arigius* named as the recipient of a pamphlet in *Epistula II* (§ 5) with the bishop of Lyon – and therefore Columbanus's metropolitan – who succeeded in 602x603 (Fredegar, *Chronicon*, IV.22, 24) and who in other texts is always named as *Aridius* or *Aredius*, is possible phonologically and historically but cannot be regarded as certain.

[45] The Irish 84-year Easter-cycle and its conflicts with Victorius's 532-year cycle have provoked an extensive scholarly (and unscholarly!) literature, with major contributions from Krusch, MacCarthy, Schwartz, C.W. Jones, Grosjean, and most recently from Schäferdiek ('Der irische Osterzyklus') and Walsh & Ó Cróinín, *Cummian's Letter*. A concise summary of the essential issues with reference to previous literature is provided in the Introduction to Walsh & Ó Cróinín (*ibid.*, pp. 18–51; for the *Epistulae* of Columbanus, see esp. pp. 21–2); unfortunately they have overlooked Schäferdiek's article, which convincingly amends earlier reconstructions of the Irish cycle based on München, Staatsbibliothek, Clm. 14456, and clarifies Columbanus's dates for celebrating Easter (in A.D. 600, *luna xiv* [= 3 April]; in 603, *luna xv* [= 31 March], and in 607, *luna xvi* [= 16 April]. See also my review of Walsh & Ó Cróinín, *Cummian's Letter*.

[46] *Epistula III* (ed. Gundlach, pp. 164–5; ed. Walker, pp. 22–4). For its dating to the vacancy following the death of Pope Gregory I in March 604, see Schäferdiek, 'Der irische Osterzyklus', pp. 365–6.

[47] Threatening Columbanus on his visit to Luxeuil, Theuderic is reported as saying, 'Si largitatis nostrae munera et solaminis supplimentum capere cupis . . .', and Columbanus as replying, '. . . nec tuis muneribus nec quibuscumque subsidiis me fore ad te sustentaturum' (*Vita S. Columbani*, I.19). The words *solamen* and *subsidia*

Either in the same period or possibly during or just after the time of the king's brief marriage to the Visigothic Ermenberga (607/8), Columbanus aroused Brunechildis's bitter enmity by refusing to bless the king's illegitimate sons when he visited a royal villa where they were in her care, and by prophesying that they would never hold the royal sceptre.[48] In retaliation the old queen secured the confinement of the monks of Luxeuil to their monastery: whereupon Columbanus made a successful appeal to the king at the *uilla publica* of Époisses (Côte d'Or), where he was helped by the unexplained shattering of the containers of drink which had been sent out to him when he refused to enter the royal chambers. Subsequently, his renewed rebuke to Theuderic for his adulteries and the threat of excommunication[49] made it easy for Brunechildis and those leading men of the kingdom and court who were under her sway to influence the king against Columbanus and against the communities that followed the Rule which he had laid down. Visiting Luxeuil again, the king objected particularly to the exclusion of others than the monks from the communal buildings in the inner precinct and set foot in the refectory,

---

are acceptable as literary language for '(royal) protection', particularly in conjunction with *munera* (if these are not gifts of property), but there are no obvious parallels for such a usage, and in *Vita S. Columbani*, I.18, Ionas uses *solamina* in the traditional sense of 'consolations'. Formulary examples of royal *carte de mundeburdo* are in *Formularium Marculfi*, I.24 (early to mid-seventh-century) and *Additamenta ad Formularium Marculfi*, no. 2 (ed. Zeumer, *Formulae Merowingici et Karolini Aevi*, pp. 58–111; for the scope of such privileges, see Brunner & von Schwerin, *Deutsche Rechtsgeschichte*, II/2, § 67). Merovingian royal grants of *emunitas* to churches and monasteries go back to at least the first half of the sixth century: see Ganshof, *Les liens de vassalité*, pp. 177, 188–9, and Prinz, *Frühes Mônchtum*, pp. 158–9 (a grant by Chlothar I to *Reomaus* [Moutier Saint-Jean] which was later linked with Luxeuil). But Columbanus's words (*Epistula* III.2), 'constat nos in nostra esse patria, dum nullas istorum suscipimus regulas Gallorum, sed in desertis sedentes', make better sense as an assertion of exemption from *episcopal* authority, which is not the nature of secular *emunitas* and to which at this early date there is no parallel: see McLauglin, *Le très ancien droit monastique*, pp. 153–5; Schwarz, 'Jurisdicio und Condicio', pp. 70–9; and Anton, *Studien*, pp. 49–92. Cf., however, Wood, 'The *Vita Columbani*', pp. 78–9. Note also the view attributed to King Theuderic's courtiers (*auligi*) at the time of Columbanus's first removal to Besançon that 'se habere non uelle his in locis qui omnibus non societur' (Ionas, *Vita S. Columbani*, I.19).

[48] The birth of sons to Theuderic in 602 and 603 is recorded by Fredegar, *Chronicon*, IV.21, 24. The same text (IV.30) reports the brief and unconsummated marriage (with Brunechildis partly to blame). The *Brocariacum uilla* where Columbanus met the queen and her grandsons (Ionas, *Vita S. Columbani*, I.19) is commonly identified with Bruyères-le-Châtel (dép. Seine-et-Oise); but the latter is *Brocaria* in a private charter of ?670 (Wallace-Hadrill, *The Fourth Book*, p. 24, n. 2, confusingly distinguishes the two), which is etymologically far more acceptable. And since Bruyères is over 300 km. in a direct line from Luxeuil, some other place for Columbanus's encounter should be looked for (cf. de Vogüé, 'En lisant Jonas', pp. 78–9). For the whole episode, its background and consequences, see also Schäferdiek, 'Columbans Wirken', pp. 186–9.

[49] On this see de Vogüé, 'En lisant Jonas', p. 79.

only to withdraw when Columbanus threatened him with the destruction of the family and kingdom.[50]

Columbanus had clearly aroused deep antagonisms in at least part of the Burgundian nobility; and whether or not he was conscious of the fact, he was becoming a factor in the internal power-struggles in Burgundia and was perhaps suspected of having allies in the other Frankish kingdoms. By the king's command, Columbanus was removed to Besançon, possibly with the idea that he should be tried, although he was not imprisoned and was accompanied by at least one of his Irish fellow-monks (?609). There he succeeded in delivering from prison, in circumstances which Ionas inevitably treats as miraculous, men who were awaiting execution, and conducting them safely to a church so that they were immune from further punishment.[51] Subsequently finding himself unguarded, Columbanus returned to Luxeuil. Divisions had appeared in the community – whether simply because of the strictness of the régime, of the refusal of Columbanus to adopt the observances customary elsewhere in the region, or for other reasons, is not clear – so that Columbanus could no longer count on the obedience of all its members. When Theuderic and his grandmother again ordered Columbanus's arrest and forcible exile, the officials and soldiers given the task seem to have been upset by Columbanus's courageous obstinacy and the enormity of the deed itself. But rather than imperil the lives of others (according to Ionas, although different explanations are clearly possible), Columbanus agreed to leave. Late but apparently trustworthy evidence suggests that other Luxeuil monks who supported his notions of monastic discipline, including the future abbot Eusthasius, departed at the same time, although they kept in touch with their one-time master.[52]

---

[50] According to Ionas (I.19), the king was persuaded 'de eius [*scil.* Columbani] religione detrahendo et statum regulae quem suis custodiendum monachis indederat macularet'. Columbanus was prepared to admit the king and his followers only to the guest quarters, in contrast with the then apparently widespread practice in Francia of admitting (noble) lay persons to all monastic buildings; see Lesne, *Histoire*, I.398–9.

[51] The *procer* Baudulf took Columbanus to Besançon, 'quandusque ex eo regalis sententia quod uoluisset decerneret' (Ionas, *Vita S. Columbani*, I.19). For the 'freeing of captives' as a hagiographic topos in general, and in Ionas in particular, see Graus, 'Die Gewalt', and Schäferdiek, 'Columbans Wirken', p. 189. But urban prisons and the chaining of prisoners are mentioned many times in Gregory of Tours's *Historia Francorum*, e.g. IV.29 (Marseilles), IV.32 and VIII.29 (Soissons), and IX.6 (Paris), as well as in his *Miracula* IV.26, etc.; and the right of a criminal to asylum within the precincts of a church, already provided for in later Roman law, was specifically confirmed at the First Council of Orleans (§ 1) in 511 (*Concilia Galliae*, ed. de Clercq, pp. 4–5).

[52] *Vita S. Columbani*, I.20; for Columbanus's own testimony to the divisions in the community, see below, p. 17 and n. 54. Eleventh-century evidence for the foundation of the first monastery at Weltenburg (on the Danube west of Regensburg) *ca* 610 by Eusthasius and Agilus (later abbot of Rebais-en-Brie) was put forward by Paringer, 'Das alte Weltenburger Martyrologium', pp. 152–3, and subsequently accepted by Prinz, *Frühes Mönchtum*, pp. 357–8, and 'Columbanus', p. 81, although the founders' stay there must have been very brief.

Columbanus left Luxeuil under escort, his destination evidently the Atlantic coast and a boat thence to his native Ireland. The date was 610 – the twentieth year after he had established his first cell in Francia (or Burgundia) and three years before King Chlothar II 'of Neustria' annexed Austrasia and Burgundy. Surviving an attack on his life by one of his escorts but also finding *en route* hospitality and opportunities for healing miracles and prophecy (notably of Chlothar's future authority over the region, which must have confirmed suspicions that Columbanus was in touch with the court of Soissons), Columbanus was conducted to Auxerre; here, apparently to avoid a dangerous proximity to the boundary with Neustria, the party turned southwest to Nevers where it took a boat down the Loire. At Orleans a starving Columbanus and his party were refused help by everyone, out of fear of the royal wrath, until they were invited into the home of a Syrian woman who knew what it was to be an alien, to whose blind husband Columbanus restored his sight. At Tours his escort tried to stop him landing to visit the tomb of St Martin but the current brought the boat into port and Columbanus was able to spend the night in prayer, to eat next day with the city's bishop and renew his prophecy of the destruction of Theuderic's family.[53]

When he arrived at Nantes, Columbanus was put in the charge of the city's count and bishop until a boat destined for Ireland could be found. He used the delay to write a letter to the monks of the Burgundian communities and more particularly to Attala, a noble-born Burgundian who after a short spell at Lérins sought the monastic regime of Luxeuil and whom Columbanus wanted as his successor (*Epistula IV*). It beautifully reveals his own firmness of purpose in the face of disappointments, including the failure to be welcomed as a missionary to (unidentified) pagans, and his genuine affection for those who shared his notion of the monastic life; it also reveals the divisions which had been developing at Luxeuil even before his departure – probably not merely in matters of observance – which he now expected to worsen and which might only be solved by requiring the dissidents to depart. The unity of the ongoing community was to be expressed through the celebrant at 'the altar which the holy bishop *Aidus* (Aéd?) blessed'.[54]

---

[53] Ionas, *Vita S. Columbani*, I.20–4 (a comparatively detailed account of only a few months in the saint's life, therefore) is the only source for the journey from Besançon to Nantes and thence to Chlothar's court, although the letter written from Nantes (see n. 54) documents some of the background and the delay in finding a ship. The repeated prophecy of Chlothar's victory over the kings and Austrasia 'within three years' provides the date. The Syrian community at Orleans figures in Gregory of Tours's account of King Gunthramn's visit in 585 (*Historia Francorum*, VIII.1). The MS. Metz, Grand Séminaire, 1 (and its copy, A3) correctly names the bishop of Tours as *Leupecharius* (the remaining manuscripts have *Leuparius*), who died 613/14. All manuscripts of Ionas at this point (I.23) give the name of the bishop of Nantes as *Soffronius* (or: *Suffronius*); one *Eufronius episcopus Namnatis* subscribes the Council of Paris in 614 (*Concilia Galliae*, ed. de Clercq, p. 281). De Vogüé ('En lisant Jonas', pp. 81–5) has clarified a number of passages in *Vita*, I.20–4.

[54] *Epistula IV* (ed. Gundlach, pp. 166–9; ed. Walker, pp. 26–36). In the passage recording Columbanus's disappointment at not being able to preach to the *gentes*, the

The boat on which Columbanus finally set sail for Ireland was, however, quickly driven back to the shore and stranded: not until he and his possessions had been unloaded would the boat float. He now found that no-one wished to detain him (as, indeed, he had already hinted at the end of *Epistula IV*) but rather to help him. Before the end of 610 Columbanus had been made welcome at the court of Chlothar II (ruling over a much-reduced Neustria): his complaints against Theuderic and Brunechildis were sympathetically listened to, and according to Ionas the king took his advice to remain neutral in the war that was about to break out between Theuderic II and Theudebert II (611–12).[55] Before that happened Columbanus, now determined to make his way to Italy, had moved on via Paris to Theudebert's kingdom, where his most influential encounters with members of the new Frankish nobility took place. At a villa just outside Meaux he met Chagneric and some of his family; at Ussy, Autharius and his family. From the younger generation came the founders of influential religious communities in north-east France which for many decades continued the Columban monastic tradition.[56] At the court of Theudebert (at Metz?), Columbanus met up with other monks who had abandoned or had been expelled from Luxeuil, including possibly both Athala and

---

two late text-sources have the obviously corrupt *fee.modo* (or: *fel.modo*). Walker (*Opera Sancti Columbani*, pp. 30–1) emended to *Fedolio*, thus providing a link with the questionably attributed poem *Ad Fidolium*; but this emendation (and link) was rejected by Smit, *Studies*, pp. 243–4, and surely rightly, although his claim that in using *gentes* Columbanus 'also thought of Gaul', and not only of true pagans, is less convincing. The reference to 'the altar blessed by Bishop *Aidus*' has inspired some pretty imaginative glossing, especially by art historians but also by historians. Not untypical is the assertion that 'Columbanus records that the altar-board (*sic!*) at Luxeuil had been blessed by Bishop Aéd of Bangor (*sic!*) before his departure from Ireland (!), *and such portable altar-boards* [my italics] are known from other churches in Ireland and England' (quoted from Ó Cróinín, 'Introduction', p. 15, but he has many predecessors). *Aidus* may indeed represent Irish *Aéd*, but alternatives are possible; and there is nothing to show that he had accompanied Columbanus from Bangor.

[55] For the reduction of the kingdom of Chlothar in 600 to *duodecim pagi inter Esara et Secona et mari litores*, i.e. the territories of Beauvais, Amiens and Rouen, and the promise of the return of the lost *ducatus Dentelini*, namely between Boulogne, Cambrai and Tournai, see Fredegar, *Chronicon*, IV.20, 37; see also de Vogüé, 'En lisant Jonas', p. 85.

[56] Ionas (II.7) names the place of the encounter with Chagneric (described as *Theudeberti conuiua*) as *Pipimisiacus*, Poincy. This was almost certainly one of the properties with which his daughter Burgundofara – whom Columbanus had consecrated to God – later endowed her monastic foundation at *Eboriacus*, Faremoutiers; see Guerout, 'Le testament', pp. 807–9, who is very sceptical of Bergengruen's account of the formation of Chagneric's landholdings in *Adel und Grundherrschaft*, pp. 68–76, 81–2. For the rule followed at Faremoutiers, see Ionas, *Vita S. Columbani*, II.11–12 and Prinz, *Frühes Mönchtum*, p. 143. The family connections and possessions of Authar, referred to by Ionas (I.26), are boldly reconstructed by Bergengruen, *ibid.*, pp. 76–80; for his children's religious foundations, see Prinz, *Frühes Mönchtum*, pp. 126–7 and de Maillé, *Les cryptes*, pp. 63–5.

18

Eusthasius. He was now searching for a new permanent home and one from which he could preach the faith to pagans – an aspiration in which he had previously been thwarted; the king and his advisers directed him to the south-eastern corner of the Frankish kingdom proper, where, around Lake Constance, it bordered with semi-independent christian Rhaetia and pagan Germanic Alamannia. Once again Columbanus set out on a river journey, this time up the Rhine, and again he and his party benefited from the (miraculous) hospitality of a bishop, on this occasion at Mainz.[57]

Columbanus can hardly have reached the vicinity of Lake Constance before the spring of 611 at the earliest and he left that area for Italy some time in the summer or early autumn of 612. In Ionas's account (I.27) the saint journeyed directly to Bregenz, a settlement at a formerly-important Roman road-junction at the eastern end of the lake, and now just beyond the south-eastern boundary of territory which King Theuderic had been forced to cede to Theudebert: it has been inferred that the latter hoped to use Columbanus to strengthen his hold on the area.[58] Again according to Ionas, the place did not appeal to Columbanus but had the advantage of being surrounded by Alamans who were either pagan or practised a syncretistic religion with minimal christian elements. In a controversial passage, Ionas describes the local inhabitants' preparations for a sacrifice in honour of 'their god Vodan': but with the help of a miracle, the saint thwarted them in their intention, won converts and re-converted others.[59]

The *uitae* of St Gallus, which for the sections relevant here exist only in ninth-century re-writings, describe an earlier phase of Columbanus's missionary activity in the area to the south of Lake Constance. It began at Tuggen (on

---

[57] That the Luxeuil monks whom Columbanus met again at Theudebert's court (Ionas, *Vita S. Columbani*, I.27) included Athala and Eusthasius (probably a Gallo-Roman from northwest *Burgundia*) can be inferred from their subsequent histories as recorded by Ionas. The latter asserts that Columbanus was directed specifically to Bregenz, *intra Germaniae terminos*, at the eastern end of Lake Constance; but see below. The bishop of Mainz is not named here: Fredegar's account of the war of 612 (*Chronica*, IV.38) refers to Bishop *Lesio* of Mainz (usually identified with the *Leudegasius* of that church's episcopal catalogue) as an admirer of Theuderic and despiser of Theudebert. The so-called *Carmen nauale* (inc. 'En siluis caesa fluctu meat acta carina') was connected by Walker with Columbanus's Rhine journey (*Opera Sancti Columbani*, ed. Walker, p. lviii). Such a connection, and Columbanus's authorship, are most improbable: see Jacobsen, 'Carmina Columbani', pp. 460–3.

[58] Fredegar, *Chronicon*, IV.37; on which see Martin, *Études critiques*, pp. 186–95; Büttner, 'Geschichtliche Grundlagen', pp. 193–4. For *Brigantium*/Bregenz, see Gruber, 'Bregenz', col. 599, and *Das römische Brigantium*.

[59] It would, I think, be generally accepted that in spite of a probable christian Roman survival south and even east of Lake Constance, the Germanic Alamanni who were still expanding into these regions *ca* 600–650 were predominantly pagan in practice and belief; see *Zur Geschichte der Alemannen*, ed. Müller, and Büttner, *Frühmittelalterliches Christentum*, II.74–6. But whether Ionas's story is based on genuine knowledge of Alamannian pagan practice is debatable. No contrary argument, however, can be drawn from the identification of Vodan with Mercury, since this phrase is omitted from the Metz MS. and may not have been part of Ionas's text.

Lake Zürich) which had, however, to be abandoned when the destruction of temples by Columbanus's follower Gallus provoked violent antagonisms; a new base was then found at the *castrum* of Arbon (towards the south-east end of Lake Constance) which had a sub-Roman community and a christian priest. The same *uitae* record a complaint by the inhabitants of the Bregenz region to the Alamannian Duke Gunzo that the incomers were ruining their hunting.[60] Ionas, by contrast, records the generous help of an unidentified neighbouring bishop when Columbanus and his companions were starving.[61]

The historicity of Columbanus's activity in the Tuggen and Arbon regions, of his dealings with Gunzo and of his disagreements with Gallus and their supposed consequences has in recent years been seriously challenged, notably by Professor Jäschke, who has argued that the monastery of St Gallen was founded by inhabitants of the region, led by an otherwise unknown *Gallo*.[62] Other scholars have vigorously defended the essential reliability of the *uitae Galli*.[63] Unfortunately there are no independent sources for this phase of either saint's career, and there are no apparent objective criteria for testing the historical reliability of the *uitae*. (But credence is regularly given to Irish *uitae sanctorum* where the controls

[60] The standard edition of the *uitae* of St Gallus is *Passiones Vitaeque Sanctorum Aeui Merowingici* [IV], ed. Krusch (with the *uita uetustissima* on pp. 251–6; that of Wettinus on pp. 256–80; and that of Walahfrid Strabo on pp. 280–337). Wettinus's account of Columbanus at Tuggen and Arbon are in his *Vita S. Galli*, §§ 4–8, 15 (ed. Krusch, *ibid.*, pp. 257–61, 264–5).

[61] Ionas, *Vita S. Columbani*, I.27 (ed. Krusch, *Ionae Vitae Sanctorum*, p. 215). In the context, *quidam pontifex ex uicinis urbibus* suggests that Ionas knew neither the bishop's name nor his see. Modern scholarship has suggested that the *uicina urbs* was either Constance, Chur or Augsburg. That a bishopric was established in the former *castellum* at Constance as early as the beginning of the seventh century has been argued by several scholars since the 1950s, while others link its foundation with Dagobert: see, e.g., Reiners-Ernst, 'Die Gründing', pp. 17–20; Büttner, *Frühmittelalterliches Christentum*, pp. 55–6; Erdmann & Zettler, 'Zur Archäologie', pp. 19–20; and cf. Keller, 'Fränkische Herrschaft', pp. 7–23. Direct evidence is lacking for either view and no seventh-century bishop of Constance is unequivocally documented. It is very unlikely that there was any bishop 'of Augsburg' in the late sixth and seventh centuries, even if an episcopal presence in the territory of the later diocese was somehow maintained: see Egger, 'Die "ecclesia secundae Rhaetiae" ' and Zoepfl, *Das Bistum Augsburg*, pp. 11–23. The signatory of the Council of Paris in 614 *ex ciuitate Cura Victor episcopus* is almost certainly the bishop of Rhaetian Chur, if only because of his name, although the most recent editor surprisingly favoured an identification with Lectoure (metrop. Eauze): *Concilia Galliae*, ed. de Clercq, pp. 282, 364. If so, he has the best claim (although hardly an overwhelming one) to being Ionas's unnamed bishop.

[62] See Jäschke, 'Kolumban von Luxeuil'.

[63] Berschin, 'Gallus abbas vindicatus'; Schäferdiek, 'Kolumbans Wirken', pp. 194–7; May, *Untersuchungen*, pp. 11–45; Keller, 'Fränkische Herrschaft'; and Hilty, 'Gallus in Tuggen'. Elsewhere Hilty ('Gallus am Bodensee') develops linguistic arguments (some of them very controversial and tenuous) to defend the historicity of Columbanus's and Gallus's contemporaneous missionary activity, but also to propose an Alsace-Vosges origin for the latter.

are not obviously superior.) Archaeological exploration and excavation, predominantly of a very high quality, seem to offer the possibility of revealing at least the context in which these events took place; in fact, to date, its evidence contradicts as often as it supports both Ionas's narrative and that of the *uitae Galli*. The area around Bregenz is completely devoid of Alamannian grave-finds of either the sixth or the seventh century. An early church has been discovered at Tuggen: the presence in it of three Alamannian warrior-graves, the earliest of not before *ca* 650, suggested to the excavator (whose view has been widely adopted) that they were those of the founder and younger relatives; but there are no cemeteries in the surrounding region. Almost nothing certainly post-Roman has been found at Arbon, although one of the few exceptions is a belt-buckle with supposedly christian connotations; and it is difficult to believe that it is anything other than coincidence that the (Germanic) name of the priest at Arbon, Willimar, recurs on a (late-sixth-century?) buckle reliquary found at Yverdon on Lake Geneva.[64]

Even if the conscious design of Ionas's *Vita S. Columbani* is invoked to explain his silence on events that brought Columbanus into conflict with Gallus, and conceding that there is no conclusive reason why the Tuggen and Arbon episodes should not both belong to a very few months in 611 or 611/612, the chronology still creates difficulties. One solution latterly favoured, which seems to fit both with the archaeological evidence for Alamannian expansion southwards and with current views of the development of a native-born aristocracy in Francia and in its dependent territories, is to move the personalities and events recorded in the *uitae Galli* to the middle decades of the century: only the link with Columbanus would be a product of the later *uita*-author's imagination.[65] But if that is accepted, Columbanus's relations with his disciple in the years 611 to 615 remain the prerogative of the hagiographer and are irrecoverable by the historian.

Whatever the true biographical and historical context, Ionas reports (I. 27) that Columbanus flirted briefly with the idea of preaching the Gospel to the wholly pagan Wends or Slavs (the earliest evidence of Western missionary interest in these peoples) but was dissuaded by an angelic vision. His final decision 'to leave Gaul and Germany' was, however, a consequence of the civil war between Kings Theudebert and Theuderic. But before this was forced on him by events, he had (again according to Ionas) left his cell in the 'wilderness' near Bregenz to make a final visit to

---

[64] A convenient map of all find-spots of Alamanian burials to the early 1970s, *except* in Switzerland, is Behr, *Das alemannische Herzogtum*, Appendix IV. For Switzerland, see Moosbrugger-Leu, *Schweiz zur Merowingerzeit*, II.17–29. For the finds at Tuggen and their historical interpretation, see Drack & Moosbrugger-Leu, 'Die frühmittelalterliche Kirche', pp. 183–96; see also Moosbrugger-Leu, *Archäologie der Schweiz*, VI.59–60, 66–9. For the Willimar reliquary, see Moosbrugger-Leu, *Schweiz zur Merowingerzeit*, II.82–4.

[65] Keller, 'Fränkische Herrschaft', esp. pp. 14–26; against this view, see Berschin, 'Gallus abbas vindicatus' and Schäferdiek, 'Kolumbans Wirken', pp. 194–7.

Theudebert's court. There he urged the king to abandon his throne and become a *clericus*: and when the suggestion was rejected as absurd, Columbanus prophesied that Theudebert would soon be compelled to adopt the clerical state.[66] In fact this happened (only to be followed very quickly by his murder) when Theudebert suffered two catastrophic defeats at the hands of Theuderic in the late spring of 612. Columbanus (according to Ionas) had completed his contribution to the king's downfall by declining to pray for his victory over their 'common enemy', Theuderic. The latter's victory deprived the saint of all royal protection in Francia and its border-regions.[67]

Ionas's account (I.30) of Columbanus's last *peregrinatio*, of which several members of the Bobbio community must have possessed detailed knowledge when he joined them, is as succinct as it is possible to be: 'abandoning Gaul and Germany, he entered Italy where he was honourably received by Agilulf, king of the Lombards.' It was left to Wettinus (and the other biographers of St Gallus who built on his account) to record that, while some of Columbanus's original companions from Ireland completed the journey into Italy with him, Gallus gave up because of illness and that an angry Columbanus forbade him to celebrate mass in his own lifetime (*diebus meis missam non celebrabis*).[68] Still later writers purported to know the route that the party followed: in fact the first stage would almost inevitably have been along the old Roman road from Bregenz to Chur, but there the roads divided, and the more favoured western route subsequently divided again, with roads through both the Splügen Pass to Chiavenna and the San Bernardino to Bellinzona. Even if the unnamed individual (*quidam*) who, according to Columbanus, 'almost as soon as I had entered this region' addressed a letter to him criticising the pope is to be identified with

---

[66] Ionas, *Vita S. Columbani*, I.28. For the literal, non-monastic, meaning of *clericus*, see de Vogüé, 'En lisant Jonas', p. 87. Because of the chronological difficulties, some scholars have supposed that Columbanus conveyed his views through a messenger. But this is to suggest a degree of 'literary' invention by Ionas which must throw doubt on the historicity of other episodes in the saint's turbulent relations with Merovingian Frankish monarchs; see Schäferdiek, 'Kolumbans Wirken', pp. 199–201.

[67] Ionas, *Vita S. Columbani*, I.29–30; Fredegar, *Chronicon*, IV.38. Unusually, both sources locate the battles respectively at Toul and at Zülpich; neither enables us to date them more closely than summer/early autumn, 612. (This corrects the statement in 'Colombano', p. 125.) For the political situation in Francia after Theuderic's victories, see the summaries by Wallace-Hadrill, *The Long-Haired Kings*, pp. 204–6, and Ewig, *Die Merowinger*, pp. 51–2; and more fully, with particular reference to the southeast, Martin, *Études critiques*, pp. 195–204.

[68] Wettinus, *Vita S. Galli*, §§ 8–9 (ed. Krusch, *Passiones Vitaeque Sanctorum Aeui Merowingici* [IV], pp. 261–2); Walahfrid Strabo, *Vita S. Galli*, §§ 8–9 (ed. Krusch, *ibid.*, p. 291). For the authenticity or otherwise of this episode, see especially Jäschke, 'Kolumban von Luxeuil' and Berschin, 'Gallus abbas vindicatus'. The effectiveness of 'excommunication' by a monk is discussed by de Vogüé, 'En lisant Jonas', p. 79 (in connection with Ionas, *Vita S. Columbani*, I.19), but he does not refer to the Gallus episode.

a bishop of Como whom he appears to mention by name elsewhere, this can surely tell us nothing about the travellers' route.[69]

It was probably in the autumn of 612 that Columbanus and his party arrived at the Lombard royal court, at that time at Milan.[70] Here they were faced with a disturbing and complex religious situation. The native population and its clergy were divided between those who accepted the 'orthodox' doctrines which were maintained at this time by both Rome and Constantinople, and those who adhered to the doctrines conveniently referred to as 'the Three Chapters' (i.e. inclining towards Nestorianism, with its greater insistence on Christ's real humanity) and were therefore in schism with Rome. The North Italian schismatics were supported by the wife of King Agilulf, Theodelinda, herself a member of the Bavarian ducal dynasty and possibly of mixed Frankish and Lombard ancestry.[71] Agilulf and his leading followers were (in the view of most, although not all, modern scholars: but perhaps not in Columbanus's) Arian christians, whom later evidence suggests had established their own hierarchy in a number of cities; yet the saint was shortly afterwards to record that Agilulf was 'said to have remarked that if he could know for certain he too would believe' (viz. with the orthodox).[72]

The saint's belief in traditional Trinitarianism as the basis of all true Christian faith found expression, according to Ionas (I.30), in 'a treatise of burgeoning learning', written while he was resident in Milan. The work is lost unless – which is not very likely – it is the initial sermon *De fide* in the series of

---

[69] *Epistula V* (ed. Gundlach, pp. 176–7; ed. Walker, p. 54). Walker's translation (p. 55) of the words 'me primo pene ingressu in huius regionis terminos arripuit' as 'with which he greeted me almost on my arrival at the frontiers of this province' (which I adopted in 'Colombano', p. 125) is surely far too specific; even less justified is the confidence of Roncoroni, 'L'epitafio', p. 143 n. 63 that Columbanus's language shows that he followed the left bank of Lake Como. For Agrippinus, bishop of Como, see below, p. 24. For the Roman/early mediaeval roads and routes from Lake Constance to North Italy, see Stähelin, *Die Schweiz*, II.367–8, 380–1, and the very clear map accompanying Martin, *Études critiques*; also relevant is Moosbrugger-Leu, *Schweiz zur Merowingerzeit*, II.45–7.

[70] See Bertolini, 'Agilulfo' (with extensive bibliography); also Hodgkin, *Italy and her Invaders*, V–VI *passim*, and the brief but excellent summary in Wickham, *Early Medieval Italy*, pp. 32–5.

[71] Amann, 'Trois-Chapitres', cols. 1868–924, is still the best general treatment; but for the early canonistic and Italian manuscript-evidence, see Schieffer, 'Zur Beurteilung'. Walker (*Sancti Columbani Opera*, pp. xxix–xxx) is an acceptable English-language summary. Theudelinda's marriage and brothers' names are first reported by Fredegar, *Chronicon*, IV.34; for the (unresolvable?) controversy over her ancestry, see Zöllner, 'Die Herkunft', and Goez, 'Über die Anfänge'.

[72] Wickham, *Early Medieval Italy*, pp. 34–6, and the Italian scholarship (mostly by G.P. Bognetti) referred to in his Bibliography and notes. For an interestingly sceptical view of the evidence for Lombard Arianism, see Fanning, 'Lombard Arianism reconsidered'. Fanning maintains (p. 254) that when in *Epistula V* Columbanus writes 'quando rex gentilis . . . Longobardus . . . rogat' (ed. Gundlach, p. 176; ed. Walker, p. 52) he was categorically labelling Agilulf a pagan, not an Arian; this may be so, but Columbanus's subsequent 'reges namque Arrianam hanc labem . . . firmarunt' (ed. Gundlach, p. 177; ed. Walker, p. 54), immediately after a reference to Agilulf, seems more difficult to explain away.

thirteen *Instructiones* or sermons, the attribution of which to Columbanus is relatively early (ninth-century) and in all probability correct. Scholars since the eighteenth century have seen in the collection as a whole a coherent doctrinal system, a concise and integrated corpus of moral exhortation, proceeding from a single mind, although influences on the thought and language of the sermons as varied as Hilary of Poitiers and Faustus of Riez have been discerned: yet others have tried to transfer several of the *Instructiones* to other (usually southern Gaulish) writers of the sixth or seventh century. Assuming their genuineness, they would have been composed and preached by Columbanus at Milan or at Bobbio.[73]

Perhaps very soon after his arrival at the Lombard court, Columbanus wrote a strongly worded letter to an *Agripp.* (so in the manuscripts) who is usually identified with Bishop Agrippinus of Como. The latter is known from his funerary inscription as an active protagonist of the 'Three Chapters' and could well therefore have been the author of the letter received by the saint in which Pope Boniface (IV) was accused of maintaining heretical doctrines.[74] Both these letters are unfortunately lost: they are known only from the references to them in the saint's longest and most remarkable extant letter (*Epistula V*), which was addressed to Pope Boniface in the course of 613.[75] Writing, as he says, at the behest of the Lombard king and queen, even more concerned than they at the divisions from which the Church in Italy is suffering, and disturbed at the suggestion that the pope himself is favouring heretics, Columbanus apologises for his presumption but feels that his duty is clear – to encourage the pope to call a council at which he can clear himself of the charges against him and, as befits the successor of Peter, lead Italy and its christian inhabitants back into concord and unity. The alternately apologetic and hectoring tone of the letter, the elaborate use of extended metaphors and the rhetorical language generally, the alternation between the single and plural number when the pope is being addressed – from which it has been concluded (unnecessarily) that two originally distinct letters have been conflated – have led to very different interpretations of the writer's attitude to papal authority. Columbanus's central concern, however, is that the church should be united in the belief that 'Christ Our Saviour is true God eternal without time, and true man without sin in time' and that the pope (whom he strangely seems to regard as tainted

[73] The *sermones* are ed. Walker, *Sancti Columbani Opera*, pp. 60–120; see discussion by Clare Stancliffe, below, pp. 93–202.

[74] Columbanus's reference to his own letter *contra Agripp[inum?]* is in *Epistula* V.3 (ed. Gundlach, p. 171; ed. Walker, p. 40). For the letter which he had received, see above, n. 67. The other evidence for the career of Bishop Agrippinus (the Columbanus passages are not referred to!) is summarised by Cerioni, 'Agrippino'. More recently Agrippinus's Funerary inscription (still, *contra* Cerioni, in S. Eufemia ad Isola) has been elaborately but not very illuminatingly discussed by Roncoroni, 'L'epitafio'.

[75] *Epistula V* (ed. Gundlach, pp. 170–7; ed. Walker, pp. 36–56).

[76] See Bardy, 'Saint Colomban', pp. 110–11, and Ryan, 'The early Irish church', pp. 560–6. Schieffer ('Zur Beurteilung', pp. 196–7) has pointed out how ill-informed Columbanus was about the decisions of the Fifth Oecumenical Council (which in 553 first promulgated the 'Three Chapters') and the nature of the subsequent doctrinal divisions.

with Nestorianism) should show the way by a personal reaffirmation of this doctrine: it is this that provokes the nervous passion of his writing.[76] The fact that the letter to Pope Boniface, together with the previous four, was preserved in a single Bobbio manuscript (transcribed by Fleming in the early seventeenth century and subsequently lost) argues that it had almost no mediaeval readers; but it probably brings us as close as we can hope to get to Columbanus's own view of the responsibilities laid on him by God when he chose the way of the *peregrinus* far from his native Ireland.

Columbanus had not lost his earlier desire for the disciplined austerity of a self-sufficient monastic community under his leadership; and the Lombard rulers may have been consciously looking for ways in which his missionary zeal could be directed to the conversion of their followers from Arianism or paganism, or even to wean 'Italians' who still acknowledged the authority of the emperors from that allegiance. According to Ionas (I.30), it was an otherwise unknown *Iocundus* who drew the attention of both parties to a derelict church of S. Pietro, which was on the north slopes of the Apennines about 100 km. from Pavia, near where the River Bobbio flows into the Trebbia; and the same man praised the natural assets of the region. Modern scholars have inevitably discovered 'strategic' reasons for the choice of site – proximity to one of the routes of access from Lombard Emilia to Byzantine Liguria (annexed only in 643); or the presence in this mountain frontier-region of Germanic-speaking pagans or Arians (*arimanni*) whom Columbanus and his monks would be particularly qualified to evangelise.[77] Possibly as early as July

---

[77] For the established trans-Apennine routes which may have influenced the siting of the monastery, cf. *Forma Italiae*, ed. Monaco, esp. p. 115, together with the contributions (not, in fact, of much weight) to *Bobbio e la Val Trebbia*. For 'arimannic' settlement in this region, see Bognetti, 'S. Maria di Castelseprio', with which compare Wickham, *Early Medieval Italy*, pp. 71–2. Bognetti's reconstructions of sixth- and seventh-century history and the place of the *arimanni* in them have subsequently been widely challenged (Wickham, *ibid.*, pp. 200, 204); and, for what the evidence is worth (although given great weight by Hilty, 'Gallus in Tuggen' and 'Gallus am Bodensee'), Wettinus asserts (*Vita S. Galli*, § 6, ed. Krusch, *Passiones Vitaeque Sanctorum Aeui Merowingici* [IV], p. 260) that it was Gallus and not Columbanus who was able to address Germanic pagans in their own language. A modified version of the 'military strategy' theory nonetheless finds some indirect support in the plausible identification of the *uir magnificus Sundrarit* who had previously been granted 'half a well' in the vicinity of Bobbio (see below, n. 78) with the *Sundrarius maxime Langobardorum dux* who won a victory over an Imperial army *ca* 617 ('Continuatio Prosperi Havniensis', ed. Mommsen, p. 339; ed. Cessi, 'Studi sulle fonti', p. 640) and from the probability that the Malaspina castle at Torriglia (close to the watershed at the head of the River Trebbia) incorporated remains of a Byzantine fort (personal observation, 1957; much mutilated by 1980). Ionas's *Iocundus* could be one of the group of *Romani* who were closely associated with Agilulf and his court, although a man with that name in the territory of Sovana in 762 is the father of an *Ermicauso*: *Codice diplomatico Langobardo*, ed. Schiaparelli, II, no. 167. See also Polonio, *Il monastero*.

[78] The reliability or otherwise of King Agilulf's privilege (*Codice diplomatico Langobardo*, ed. Brühl, no. 1) and of King Adaloald's subsequent confirmation transmitted with it (*ibid.*, no. 2) have been long and vigorously debated. The

613 King Agilulf granted to Columbanus and his followers and their successors, as the site for a monastery, the church and an area round about (ostensibly to a distance of four miles) with the exception of 'half a well' which had previously been granted to a prominent layman.[78]

Ionas has a vivid description of the saint's personal contribution to the work of reconstruction, literally if miraculously making light work of the task of moving heavy timber from the barely accessible hillsides. He makes no reference to the internal life of the community, except incidentally in Book II of his work, in connection with the two abbots who followed Columbanus (Athala and Eusthasius); nor does he give the slightest hint of active evangelism.[79] Almost nothing can be inferred from the earliest documents: the probably substantially authentic bull of Pope Honorius I (628) characterises the mode of life in the Bobbio community only in the most general terms.[80] No extant manuscript can be asserted with confidence to have been at Bobbio in Columbanus's lifetime. No manuscript was demonstrably written there until some time after his death. The palimpsesting of Gothic manuscripts *may* already have begun in the time of his immediate successor, the learned Burgundian Athala (616–626/7), but was – to judge from the upper scripts – mostly if not entirely done later: it cannot, therefore, provide the evidence which is otherwise lacking for an active evangelising of locally resident Arians.[81] Some of Columbanus's sermons (*Instructiones*) may have been

---

essential authenticity of the first of these has been established by Brühl (*Studien*, pp. 19–27, and *Codice diplomatico Langobardo*, pp. 4–5: 'Preso nel suo insieme, il diploma non può essere considerato una falsificazione perché, per quanto possiamo capire, il suo contenuto giuridico non ha subito variazioni') and a plausible if not always certain reconstruction of the original wording arrived at. In King Agilulf's privilege, reference is made to the 'medietatem putei quod Sundrarit per nostre donationis preceptum concessum habemus'; in King Adaloald's confirmation (which here seems to be entirely trustworthy), the grant is said to have been made to *Sundrarit uiro magnifico*.

[79] See, e.g., *Vita S. Columbani*, II.1, 2, 5, 7. De Vogüé ('En lisant Jonas', pp. 66–71) has some very interesting comments on the evolution of Ionas's terminology for 'the monastic community'. Note that in *Vita S. Columbani*, II.2, there is a very precise account of a monastic watermill and the natural threats to it.

[80] *Codice diplomatico di Bobbio*, ed. Cipolla, no. x (pp. 102–3); registered: JE. no. 2017; Conte, *Chiese e primato*, pp. 410–12 (no. 50), with references to twentieth-century discussions of its authenticity, to which add Brühl, *Studien*, pp. 33–4.

[81] For a manuscript supposedly brought to Bobbio by Columbanus, see above, p. 6. A fundamental review and revision of the evidence, real and supposed, for the earliest manuscripts written at Bobbio is Engelbert, 'Zur Frühgeschichte', pp. 220–46. For the Bobbio 'Irish' manuscripts (not earlier than the very late seventh century), see *ibid.*, pp. 241–6, 260; for the palimpsests and their upper scripts (not before the second half of the century), see *ibid.*, pp. 227–38 and, for a denial that the palimpsesting reflected Bobbio's anti-Arian policy (as claimed, after others, by Prinz, *Frühes Mönchtum*, pp. 526–7), *ibid.*, p. 246, n. 1. For the date of Athala's death, see *ibid.*, p. 229, n. 4. Bertolini, 'Atala', is more sentimental than scholarly.

[82] But if any of them were *composed* at Bobbio they would presumably throw light on the texts (probably not in fact very many) available there in the first years of the monastery.

preached there.[82] Ionas records only that Eusthasius, who had returned to Luxeuil after his brief sojourn on the Danube and equally brief time with his former abbot at Bregenz, came to Bobbio with an invitation from the recently victorious Chlothar (II) to Columbanus to return to the Frankish kingdom with honour. The saint courteously but firmly declined. Eusthasius was instructed to seek the royal favour for Luxeuil and its monks; and – characteristically, one may think – Columbanus sent with him some admonitory writings to be given to the king, of which (again) no trace survives.[83]

There is no early tradition relating to Columbanus's last months: Ionas is totally silent on the matter. The surviving fragments of the *uita uetustissima* of St Gallus (mid/late eighth century?), however, include the assertion that as he was near death he commanded that his staff (*cambutta*) should be sent to Gallus as a sign of absolution.[84] On 23 November, probably in 615, Columbanus died and was buried at Bobbio.[85] Nothing is certainly known of the site or form of the saint's burial place before the late Middle Ages. Neither the plausibly authentic bull of 628 nor the probably false bull of 643 links Columbanus with Bobbio's original dedication to St Peter in its address

---

[83] For the political background, see Ewig, *Die Merowinger*, pp. 52–4, and (more obliquely) Wallace-Hadrill, *The Long-Haired Kings*, pp. 206–7. For Chlothar's interest in Columbanian monasteries and the advantages to be derived from it, and his indifference to others, see Prinz, *Frühes Mönchtum*, pp. 138–43, 163, and for the possibility that Luxeuil was granted a (lost) privilege, see Wood, 'The *Vita Columbani*', pp. 78–9. For the immediate heritage of Columbanus in the Frankish church generally, cf. Riché, 'Columbanus', pp. 63–4 (negative) and Wallace-Hadrill, *The Frankish Church*, pp. 65–6, 69–70 (optimistic).

[84] *Passiones Vitaeque Sanctorum Aeui Merowingici*, ed. Krusch, pp. 251–2.

[85] The date '.VIIII. kl. Decembris' is that in the majority of manuscripts of Ionas, *Vita S. Columbani*, I.30; it is also the date under which Columbanus's *depositio* is entered in the Echternach and Wissembourg MSS. (Paris, Bibliothèque Nationale, lat. 10837 and Wolfenbüttel, Weissenburgensis 81, listed Lowe, *Codices*, V.606a, IX.1393 – from a common Luxeuil source?) of the *Martyrologium Hieronymianum*, ed. Quentin & Delehaye, *Martyrologium*, p. [146]; and the date under which a proper mass is entered in the tenth/eleventh-century Bobbio *missale plenum*, now Milan, Biblioteca Ambrosiana, D.84 inf., fo 333v. The alternative date, '.XI. kl. Decembris', adopted by the Roman Martyrology, occurs already in ninth-century liturgical manuscripts. (The unfortunate misprint '.VIII. Kl.' in Bullough, 'Colombano', p. 128, adds further confusion to an already confusing situation!) Columbanus's name is not to be found in the *Félire Oengusso* or the *Martyrology of Tallaght*, if the supposed identification with the saint whose *eliuatio* is entered in the latter under the date '27.9' (*The Martyrology*, ed. Best & Lawlor, p. 74) is – surely rightly – rejected.

[86] Brühl, *Studien*, p. 46.

[87] For the various bulls mentioned here, see above, n. 80, for that of Pope Honorius of 628; for that of 643, see *Codice diplomatico di Bobbio*, ed. Cipolla, pp. 108–11, registered JR. no. 2053 (Conte, *Chiese e primato*, pp. 435–6) and Anton, *Studien zu den Klosterprivilegien*, pp. 58–9. According to the second of these bulls, the Bobbio monks 'sub regula sancte memorie Benedicti uel reuerentissimi Columbani fundatoris luci illius conuersari uidentur'. For the royal privileges in question, see *Codice diplomatico Longobardo*, ed. Brühl, p. 108 (no. 22) for that of 747; and for that of 774, see *Diplomata Karolinorum*, ed. Mühlbacher, p. 114 (no. 80).

clause; and Professor Brühl believes that the words *et Christi confessoris Columbani* in King Ratchis's *praeceptum iudicati* of 747 is an interpolation.[86] Charlemagne's privilege of June 774 is the earliest document to refer to the *monasterium Ebobiense ubi sanctus Columbanus corpore requiescit.*[87] Before that date, however, the saint's name had been added to martyrologies in Frankish Gaul, although not (apparently) in his native Ireland.[88]

Ionas avers that 'if anyone wishes to know what Columbanus accomplished, he will find it in his writings' (or 'words': *dictis*). The writings here alluded to may be significantly different from the corpus of texts which since the seventeenth century has been, with Ionas's *uita*, the basis of most accounts of the saint and his achievements. The reduced (and occasionally extended) corpus of probably authentic works has, however, no obvious inconsistencies with the picture of the man and of his earthly activities created by Ionas from information gathered between 618 and *ca* 640 from people who had known him. On the evidence of the *uita* and of the letters, Columbanus in his lifetime earned fame for his intense spirituality and his fearlessness as a critic of even the greatest who failed to match his own high standards of the christian life. If (justifiably) he had critics and made enemies among the contemporary bishops of Frankish Gaul, he forged enduring links between elements in the new Frankish aristocracy and the monastic movement, and through these with bishops of later generations. At least one copy of the *uita* was available in Burgundy only a few years after it had been completed, as its use by Fredegar shows; other early copies were presumably made in or for monastic communities which avowedly based their discipline and observance in part on the *regula Columbani*. Accepting that other texts are substantially the written embodiment of his notions and practices, even if through one or more intermediaries, Columbanus made a unique contribution to the practices of the western church – of lay christians as well as of ecclesiastics – by his extension to Francia of the Irish penitential system. His brief time as a missionary among Germanic pagans and heretics may well have had no enduring consequences. But the monks who followed him from Francia to Bobbio laid the foundations of that monastery's subsequent reputation as a place of book-production and learning, albeit of a somewhat eccentric kind; and Columbanus's posthumous fame, nourished in due course by miracles and then reflected in the multiplication of copies of Ionas's *uita*, were to attract to it later generations of Irish *peregrini*, with well-documented consequences for the *scriptorium* and library. Achievements of such a kind and on such a scale in a harsh and ill-documented age are in no way diminished by acknowledging that the fame inspired by Ionas's *Vita S. Columbani* and the enthusiasm of copyists and editors were probably responsible for spurious extensions of the saint's *curriculum uitae* and of his written *opera*.[89]

---

[88] See above, n. 85.

[89] This present article is a revision and updating of the original English text from which Bullough, 'Colombano', was prepared. It was completed and delivered to the editor in 1989: minor revisions and additions have subsequently been made to the footnotes, but none to the body of the text.

II

COLUMBANUS'S *EPISTULAE*

Neil Wright

THE five *Epistulae* which are our principal concern here were written by Columbanus during the later part of his life, between A.D. 600 and his death in A.D. 615.[1] Before proceeding to a close examination of the latinity and sources of these letters, it will be convenient briefly to summarize their date and contents. The first, *Epistula I*, written probably in 600, is an appeal to Pope Gregory the Great (*ob.* 604) to resolve Columbanus's disputes with the Gallic clergy, primarily over the notorious issue of Easter celebration. The second, one of the most interesting *epistulae*, is a vigorous defence both of Columbanus's paschal position and the monastic way of life in general, sent by the saint in lieu of attendance at a synod called by his opponents in Gaul. Since it is generally agreed that this was the synod of Châlons held in 603, *Epistula II* was probably written in that year.[2] The third *epistula* can be dated to 604, or perhaps 607; it is a short missive, again concerning the paschal controversy, to one of Gregory the Great's immediate successors as pope (either Sabinian or Boniface III; Columbanus does not himself name his addressee). In *Epistula IV*, which was composed in 610 when the saint was about to be driven from Gaul into exile, Columbanus offers advice to his monks about how they are to conduct themselves without him. The last *epistula*, written after his arrival in Italy and probably composed *ca* 613 at the request of the Lombard king Agilulf, is addressed to Pope Boniface IV; this is one of Columbanus's most elaborate compositions, and marks his entry into a different controversy, the so-called 'Three Chapters' schism, which had been troubling western christendom ever since the papacy of Vigilius in the mid-sixth century and was then isolating the Lombard churches from the mother church of Rome.

In addition to these five *epistulae*, a substantial corpus of other writings is

---

[1] The standard edition of the *Epistulae* is *Sancti Columbani Opera*, ed. & transl. Walker, pp. 2–59. The text cited here is Walker's, although, as I have signalled in the notes, I have accepted some of the corrections proposed by Smit, *Studies*; all translations are my own. A summary of the saint's career, our knowledge of which is derived almost entirely from his own writings and the *Vita S. Columbani* by Ionas of Susa (*ca* 634), can be found in Walker, *Sancti Columbani Opera*, pp. ix–xxxiv; see also the discussion by Bullough, above, pp. 1–28. Despite the fact that in the *Epistulae* the saint always calls himself Columba, I have accepted the convention of referring to him as Columbanus (a form which Ionas uses interchangeably with the other), this having the advantage of distinguishing the founder of Bobbio from Columba (or Columcille) of Iona.

[2] Walker, *Sancti Columbani Opera*, p. xxxvi.

also attributed to the Irish saint, but only the authenticy of the *epistulae* described above has never been seriously called into question. These *epistulae* are distinguished from the other works ascribed to Columbanus both by reason of their elaborate literary style, a feature to which we must return later, and also because of their transmission. No early manuscript of *Epistulae I–V* now survives; modern editions rely on two comparatively late sources: first, Patrick Fleming's *editio princeps* of Columbanus's works, published in Louvain in 1667 and based, for these letters at least, on a now lost Bobbio exemplar which Fleming had transcribed in 1623; and second, another transcription, made in the seventeenth century by Judoc Metzler, of a Bobbio manuscript which contained the five *epistulae* as well apparently as other material attributed to Columbanus.[3] Standing apart from *Epistulae I–V*, at least in extant manuscripts, is a number of other works, chiefly comprising the following: a short text which has been printed as another letter (*Epistula VI*), even though it does not travel with the others and entirely lacks a conventional epistolary introduction; thirteen sermons or *Instructiones*; two monastic *regulae*; a penitential; several poems or *carmina*; and certain other *dubia uel spuria*. Of this material, only the so-called *Epistula VI*, the *Instructiones*, the *Regula monachorum* and penitential are transmitted together, in two ninth- to tenth-century Turin manuscripts (although some of these texts are also found separately elsewhere); in contrast, the manuscript tradition for the other works is far less homogeneous.

While our primary concern will naturally be with *Epistulae I–V*, some consideration will also be necessary of the style of '*Epistula VI*' with an eye to the question of its attribution to Columbanus. As for the other works, the problems raised by the *Instructiones*, rules and penitential are examined in detail elsewhere in this volume.[4] However, discussion of the sources of the *Epistulae* will occasionally touch on those of the *Instructiones* and also the implications that this may have for the authorship of the sermons. Conversely, no comparisons will be made with the *carmina* for the following reasons. First, the manuscript evidence for attributing two at least of the poems (the *Carmen nauale* and *Mundus iste transibit*) to Columbanus is weak.[5] Second, serious doubt has long been cast on Columbanus's authorship of these and the remaining *carmina* (*Ad Fidolium*, *Ad Hunaldum*, *Ad Sethum*, and the *Monastica* or *Praecepta uiuendi*), despite the fact that it has been, and continues to be, passionately defended in some quarters; furthermore, the literary case against

---

[3] The transmission of the *Epistulae* (and the other works) is discussed by Walker, *Sancti Columbani Opera*, pp. xxxvi–lxvi, Bieler (*apud* Walker, *ibid.*, pp. lxxiii–viii) and Smit, *Studies*, pp. 33–8, who provocatively suggests that Metzler may in fact have known no more than Fleming's transcription.

[4] See below, pp. 93–202, 203–16, 217–39.

[5] Each poem survives only in a single manuscript: in the case of the first, the author's name is legible only as '. . . banus'; as for the second, *Mundus iste transibit*, the attribution is added in the margin in a modern hand, although it must be conceded that this piece, a rhythmical poem on the transience of the world, is in both form and subject-matter much more in keeping with extant Hiberno-Latin verse of the seventh century than is the metrical poetry ascribed to the saint; see discussion by Schaller, below, pp. 240–54, and Lapidge, pp. 255–63.

the authenticity of these poems has recently been convincingly restated and strongly reinforced by Michael Lapidge.[6]

Mention of the *carmina* brings us up squarely against what has been another highly contentious issue in Hiberno-Latin studies. It used to be fashionable to regard sixth-century Ireland – where Columbanus received his early training, chiefly at the important monastic centre of Bangor – as a storehouse of classical learning, miraculously preserving the study of Latin texts largely neglected on the Continent and enthusiastically continuing that tradition.[7] More recently, the work of scholars such as Mario Esposito and particularly Edmondo Coccia has questioned this view, and more emphasis has quite rightly been placed on the achievement of the Irish in other fields, such as Bible study and exegesis, grammar and computus, hagiography and hymnody.[8] In fact, only a few of the Latin texts written in Ireland in the seventh century reveal any real familiarity with classical sources, and, in those that do, it is not usually extensive.[9] This is not, however, true of the metrical *carmina* discussed above, which contain a plethora of borrowings from, amongst others, Vergil, Horace, Ovid, Lucan, Juvenal, Martial and the *Disticha Catonis*, as well as such rarities as the late Latin poets Tiberianus and Ausonius and the *Anthologia Latina*.[10] The *carmina* have thus attracted a disproportionate share of attention, being seen as a jewel in the crown of early Hiberno-Latin literature, despite the fact that, even if they should prove to have been written by Columbanus, these poems would most likely have been composed during the saint's time on the Continent, not in Ireland itself, where many of the classical texts in question were probably not available to him.

One result of this trend is that Columbanus's *Epistulae*, whose authenticity has never been doubted, have tended to be comparatively neglected by literary critics. This is unfortunate because of their importance not only as some of the earliest Latin prose written by an Irish-speaker but also as the first extant Hiberno-Latin letters. The *Epistulae*, with their elaborate and, as we shall see, often flamboyant style, therefore deserve careful consideration not only in their own right but also for the evidence which they can afford us for Columbanus's reading and for his place in the development of mediaeval prose writing. That said, the pitfall already alluded to in connection with the *carmina* must not of course be forgotten. Columbanus was among the first representatives of another group of Irishmen familiar to all those who study early mediaeval literature, the *peregrini*, and so spent much of his life in Europe in self-imposed exile for Christ. Great care therefore needs to be taken when drawing from the *Epistulae*, which were all written on the Continent, any firm conclusions about the saint's early training at Bangor or about Latin learning more

---

[6] Lapidge, 'The authorship'; see also the discussion by Smit, *Studies*, pp. 209–49.

[7] See, for instance, studies such as Meyer, *Learning*; Bieler, 'The island of scholars'; and *The Miracle of Ireland*, ed. Daniel-Rops.

[8] Coccia, 'La cultura'; relevant articles by Esposito can be found in his collection, *Irish Books and Learning*, ed. Lapidge.

[9] For a survey of the question, see Herren, 'Classical and secular learning'.

[10] See the *fontes* in Walker's edition of the *carmina* (*Sancti Columbani Opera*, ed. & transl. Walker, pp. 182–97); and, for Tiberianus, Lapidge, 'The authorship'.

generally in Ireland at the turn of the sixth century. Indeed, since Colum-banus's surviving correspondence is largely directed to popes and Gallic bishops, it needs also to be studied against the broader background of contem-porary Latin culture. Therefore it is to the immediate continental context of the *Epistulae* that we shall now turn.

The most likely date for Columbanus's arrival in Gaul is A.D. 592.[11] The literary culture of the area at that time is regularly viewed, both by contem-porary witnesses and by modern critics alike, as being at a low ebb. Gregory of Tours, for example, who died in 594, only two years after the probable advent of the Irish saint, had earlier prefaced his best known work, the *Historia Francorum*, with the following disparaging remarks about the state of learning and literature in his day:[12]

Decedente atque immo potius pereunte ab urbibus Gallicanis liberalium cultura lit-terarum, cum nonnullae res gererentur uel rectae uel improbae, ac feretas gentium desaeuiret, regum furor acueretur, eclesiae inpugnarentur ab hereticis, a catholicis tegerentur, ferueret Christi fides in plurimis, tepisceret in nonnullis, ipsae quoque eclesiae uel ditarentur a deuotis uel nudarentur a perfides [*sic*], nec repperire possit quisquam peritus dialectica in arte grammaticus, qui haec aut stilo prosaico aut metrico depingeret uersu: ingemescebant saepius plerique, dicentes: 'Vae diebus nostris, quia periit studium litterarum a nobis, nec repperitur rhetor in populis, qui gesta praesentia promulgare possit in paginis.'

Now it is true that by this date the traditional Roman educational system had in Gaul largely been destroyed, or survived only in a modified and curtailed form.[13] Gregory himself, for instance, does not seem to have had much familiarity with classical authors, beyond Vergil.[14] Nevertheless, Latin texts continued to be studied and written, as the *Historia Francorum* itself bears witness. Furthermore, pessimism such as Gregory's was a literary convention among the cultural elite; his opening remarks represent a rhetorical topos

[11] Walker, *Sancti Columbani Opera*, pp. x–xi.

[12] *Gregorii Episcopi Turonensis libri*, edd. Krusch & Levison, p. 1: 'The practice of literary composition is failing, indeed dying, in the cities of Gaul. Many things were being done, both well and evilly: the savagery of heathens raged, the anger of kings was sharpened; churches were assailed by heretics, but protected by catholics; among very many people the Christian faith burned hot, but for some it was lukewarm; the churches themselves were enriched by the devout, or stripped by the wicked. But no grammarian, skilled in the art of dialectic, could be found to describe this situation in prose or metrical poetry. Many used very often to groan and say: "These are times of woe! The study of letters dies among us, nor can any rhetorician be found in our people to publish these present deeds in his pages." '

[13] For a general survey of the subject, see Riché, *Education et culture*, pp. 220–91, 311–50.

[14] See the discussions of Gregory's education by Bonnet, *Le latin*, pp. 48–76, esp. 49–53, and Kurth, *Etudes franques*, I.1–29, esp. 14–29. It is probably significant that Gregory's two quotations of Sallust's *Catilina* are derived from the preface to that work; and that his borrowings from the *Aeneid* apparently extend no further than the first eight books of the poem (indeed, nearly half come from *Aeneid* I, and many of those are drawn from the storm scene at the beginning of the book); cf. Kurth, *ibid.*, pp. 21–2.

which can frequently be paralleled in prefaces to other Latin texts composed in the sixth and seventh centuries.[15] This is not to say that evidence for the decline in standards bemoaned by Gregory cannot be detected in his *Historia Francorum*, the narrative of which contains a legion of peculiarities of orthography, confusions of case and gender, and errors of syntax, arguably compounded by the early copyists through whose hands the work passed.[16] Yet the preface in particular bears witness to much conscious artistry on Gregory's part, just as might be expected at the opening of an ambitious composition of this sort, and so provides a useful point of comparison with Columbanus's equally elaborate *Epistulae* (although it must be stressed that there is, as yet, no evidence to suggest that the saint was familiar with Gregory's *Historia*).

With such a comparison in view, we must now examine in some detail the initial sentence of Gregory's preface, which is set out in full above. To begin with overall structure, the sentence's careful organisation is immediately apparent. It comprises a single period, which, despite its length, never escapes its author's control.[17] The main clause – 'ingemescebant saepius plerique' – occurs more than two-thirds of the way through the whole; and it is followed by a subordinated participle, *dicentes*, introducing the vivid direct speech which closes the sentence. Before the main verb, *ingemescebant*, Gregory deploys several subordinate clauses: an initial long ablative absolute ('Decedente . . . cultura litterarum') and a complex series of *cum* clauses, which are bound together by a varied selection of conjunctions ('ac . . . quoque . . . uel . . . uel . . . nec') as well as by asyndeton ('feretas gentium . . . regum furor . . . eclesiae . . .'; 'ferueret . . . tepisceret . . .') and also anaphora ('ab hereticis . . . a catholicis'). The majority of these *cum* clauses are short and carefully balanced, but the last ('nec repperire possit . . .') trails a subordinate member of its own, the relative purpose clause 'qui . . . depingeret uersu'. Thus, while Gregory may well lament the lack of *grammatici* and *rhetores* skilled in prose-writing, in so doing he displays a considerable mastery of their supposedly lost art.

To turn from sentence-structure to vocabulary, Gregory does not here employ any particularly unusual or peculiar words.[18] The passage contains, for example, no noteworthy grecisms, archaisms, new coinages or compound words. Poeticisms, which are often used to lend prose an emotive colour, are

---

[15] See, for instance, the examples collected by Winterbottom, 'Aldhelm's prose style'.

[16] In the passage under discussion, such peculiarities are limited to the apparent use of the active infinitive *repperire* (line 5) where the passive *repperiri* is needed; and the seeming confusion of *possit* and *posset* (also line 5). However, both anomalies may be the result of orthographical errors (cf. Bonnet, *Le latin*, pp. 403 and 438 respectively), like the odd spellings *feretas* for *feritas* (line 2) and *perfides* for *perfidis* (line 5); see further below, n. 31. Bonnet's magisterial study remains the standard discussion of the latinity of the *Historia Francorum,* and of Gregory's other works.

[17] Bonnet is thus a little unkind when he comments, 'On ne peut guère parler de périodes chez Grégoire, bien que certaines phrases soient assez longues et compliquées' (*Le latin*, p. 723), although the preface is not of course entirely representative of the *Historia Francorum* as a whole.

[18] For a thorough study of Gregory's vocabulary, see Bonnet, *Le latin*, pp. 191–328; and, on his poeticisms, *ibid.*, pp. 738–41.

not prominent in this passage either, although Gregory does favour vivid verbs in phrases such as 'feretas ... *desaeuiret*' and 'furor *acueretur*', or when he uses the verb *depingere*, literally 'to paint', in the sense of 'to describe in verse'.[19] A certain vividness is similarly imparted by other metaphorical expressions: for example, culture 'is dying' ('pereunte ... cultura'), and faith 'burns' or 'is lukewarm' ('ferueret ... tepisceret').[20] Likewise, a poetic touch can perhaps be felt in the burst of heavy alliteration (in words beginning with *p*) which forms the climax of the sentence: 'qui gesta *p*raesentia *p*romulgare *p*ossit in *p*aginis'.[21]

If Gregory's choice of vocabulary is for the most part conventional in this passage, it is nevertheless with great art that he disposes words within their clauses. In addition to the striking alliteration with which the sentence ends (and the instances of asyndeton and anaphora which we have already noticed), it contains numerous other figures of rhetoric. In particular, antithesis is a recurrent feature within its balanced structure. The figure can, for example, be observed in the paired clauses, 'eclesiae inpugnarentur ab hereticis, a catholicis tegerentur', the contrasting elements there being bound together not only by antithesis but also by chiasmus, so that the verbs *inpugnarentur* and *tegerentur* are made to frame their respective dependent prepositional phrases (*ab hereticis* and *a catholicis*).[22] Similar antithesis occurs in the clauses immediately following, 'ferueret Christi fides in plurimis, tepisceret in nonnullis', where the parallel structure results this time in homoeoteleuton, or rhyme, between the final syllables of the closing word of each member ('plurim*is*, ... nonnull*is*'). Such rhyme is also present (without antithesis) on a larger scale at the end of the sentence, where homoeoteleuton can be observed in the successive clauses, 'Vae diebus nostr*is*, quia periit ... a nob*is*, nec repperitur ... in popul*is*, qui ... possit in pagin*is*.' Indeed, although it is blurred by the unorthodox orthography of *perfides* (for *perfidis*), similar homoeoteleuton is also a feature of our final example of antithesis from the preface, the clauses, 'uel ditarentur a deuotis uel nudarentur a perfides'.[23] In this case, the word-

---

[19] The metaphor is however at least as old as Cicero (see *Thesaurus Linguae Latinae*, V1.572–3). Other examples of Gregory's use of metaphorical language are assembled by Bonnet, *Le latin*, pp. 705–7.

[20] The last of these images is of course biblical; cf. Apocalypse III.16, 'quia tepidus es'.

[21] Less prominent alliteration can be found in the phrases '*p*otius *p*ereunte', '*l*ibera*l*ium cu*l*tura *l*itterarum', '*d*itarentur a *d*euotis' and '*r*epperitur *r*hetor' (lines 1, 2, 7 and 12 respectively). In general, however, Gregory's alliteration is neither frequent nor heavy (Bonnet, *Le latin*, pp. 726–30); his use of insistent alliteration in *p* to round off the opening sentence in his *Historia* may perhaps have been inspired by a similar use of striking alliteration (in *p* and *m*) at the end of the final sentence of Rufinus's *Historia Ecclesiastica*, XI.34, 'ad *m*eliora *m*igrauit cum *p*iissimis *p*rincipibus *p*ercepturus *p*raemia *m*eritorum'. (For Gregory's familiarity with this text, see Bonnet, *Le latin*, p. 64, n. 5.)

[22] A further example of chiasmus appears in lines 4–5, 'feretas gentium ..., regum furor'; elsewhere Gregory seemingly uses this figure only sparingly (Bonnet, *Le latin*, p. 720).

[23] A short list of other examples is provided by Bonnet, *Le latin*, pp. 725–6, though he somewhat underestimates the importance of homoeoteleuton in Gregory's prose.

order of these antithetical clauses is identical, both beginning with *uel*, followed by a verb, preposition and noun. This figure is known as isocolon, a parallelism of structure which is often taken even further, as here: both clauses consist of nine syllables, and in each the words match syllable for syllable, so as to make their correspondence perfect.[24]

Another rhetorical trick prominent in Gregory's preface is the liberal use of hyperbaton, by which term is here meant in particular the separation of adjective and noun in agreement, an element of considerable importance in artistic prose writing.[25] In Latin prose generally, the commonest form of such hyperbaton is usually the division of adjective and noun around a dependent genitive, a type which I have elsewhere termed aBA.[26] However, such patterns are not particularly noteworthy, and there are in fact no examples of this simple hyperbaton in the passage under discussion. Rather more interesting is the expression 'dialectica in arte', where epithet and substantive are positioned so as to frame the preposition which governs them.[27] Moreover, Gregory so constructs his sentence that this prepositional phrase is itself enclosed by another adjective and noun within the elaborate unit 'quisquam peritus dialectica in arte grammaticus' (where the 'natural' word-order might have been 'quisquam grammaticus peritus in arte dialectica').[28] Finally, an example of a different type of more striking hyperbaton is found at the end of the ablative-absolute clause which opens the sentence: there an adjective and noun in the genitive case are split round the noun on which they depend, 'liberalium cultura litterarum', a pattern which I have elsewhere termed bAB;[29] and, on a larger scale, the ablative noun *cultura* is itself separated, by the prepositional phrase *ab urbibus Gallicanis* (and the adjective *liberalium*), from the participles *Decedente* and *pereunte* which qualify it, so that patterns of hyperbaton in effect frame the whole clause. The resultant enclosing word-order is akin to complex, interlaced patterns (in particular that which I have termed abAB) which are frequently used by certain Insular Latin writers, and to which we shall return later.[30] Elsewhere in Gregory's writings, however, such complex patterns are the exception rather than the rule.[31]

To return to simpler forms of separation, another relatively common, but

---

[24] For other, less exactly balanced examples of isocolon (and of antithesis in general), see Bonnet, *Le latin*, pp. 721–2.

[25] See, for example, my discussion in 'Gildas's prose style' in *Gildas: New Approaches*, edd. Lapidge & Dumville, pp. 115–26 (and the references cited there).

[26] *Ibid.*, p. 117 (with examples).

[27] It is surprising that such separation of noun and adjective (or alternatively dependent genitive) around a preposition which governs them – a type of hyperbaton frequent in artistic prose – is elsewhere largely neglected by Gregory (Bonnet, *Le latin*, pp. 722–3).

[28] I have not accepted Bonnet's suggestion (*Le latin*, pp. 16, n. 1 and 216, n. 1) that *aut* (the reading of one manuscript) has been lost between 'peritus dialectica in arte' and 'grammaticus'.

[29] 'Gildas's prose style', p. 117.

[30] See below, p. 54.

[31] A few instances of convoluted word-order are cited by Bonnet, *Le latin*, pp. 720–1 (and see also below, n. 101).

comparatively important, type of hyperbaton is the splitting of adjective and noun around a verb (or aVA), usually at the end of a sentence or clause to give added stress to the delayed final word. In the preface, a good example of this is provided by the phrase 'metrico depingeret uersu' immediately before the main verb of the sentence.[32] Moreover, hyperbaton of this latter sort, occurring as it does at the end of a clause, is closely related to another word-pattern which is found at several points in the preface, and also throughout Gregory's writings.[33] This consists of cases where the verb, normally the last word in its clause, instead precedes a noun, which thus receives rhetorical emphasis, as in the following cases (where the noun concerned is invariably governed by a preposition): 'impugnarentur ab hereticis', 'ferueret . . . in plurimis, tepisceret in nonnullis'; 'ditarentur a deuotis . . . nudarentur a perfides'; and 'repperitur . . . in populis, . . . possit in paginis'. Indeed, clauses such as 'nec repperire possit . . . grammaticus', 'ingemescebant . . . plerique', and 'periit . . . a nobis' (with final pronoun) also exhibit similar construction, making this type of patterning all-pervasive in the sentence.

Gregory does not normally use such word-patterns merely for decoration. On two occasions his use of delayed nouns results, as we have seen, in their respective phrases being linked by rhyme: 'ferueret . . . in plurim*is*, tepisceret in nonnull*is*' and 'repperitur . . . in popul*is*, . . . possit in pagin*is*'. More often, however, Gregory's use of hyperbaton is allied to his interest in prose rhythm, that is fixed rhythmical patterns at sentence- and also clause-endings. Before embarking on an examination of the rhythm of Gregory's opening sentence, some brief introductory remarks are in order. Much work remains to be done on the rhythmical prose of the sixth century, the position being complicated by the fact that Gregory wrote during a period of transition between two kinds of rhythm. On the one hand, we have *clausulae*, a system of fixed metrical patterns (that is, based on syllable-quantity) widely used by classical and late antique authors. For the later period, three types of *clausula* have been identified as being particularly important, namely the cretic and trochee ($-\smile--\overset{\smile}{-}$), the double cretic ($-\smile--\smile\overset{\smile}{-}$), and the cretic and ditrochee ($-\smile--\smile-\overset{\smile}{-}$).[34] In the other system, the *cursus*, it is word-accent rather than syllable-quantity which is important: the three most important rhythmical patterns involved (which loosely correspond to the three metrical types already described) are the *planus* (x́xxx́x), the *tardus* (x́xxx́xx), and the *uelox* (x́xxxxx́x), while another pattern, the so-called *trispondiacus* (x́xxxx́x), is also often included. Use of accentual rhythm is best documented for authors writing in the Middle Ages proper; but it is generally assumed that the *cursus* developed from *clausulae*, by a process similar to that in which some forms of rhythmical verse evolved from metrical

---

[32] Similar hyperbaton perhaps occurs in the clause 'res gererentur uel rectae uel improbae' (line 2), where the noun comes first and it is qualified by two predicative adjectives – unless *rectae* and *improbae* are here unorthodox forms of the adverbs *recte* and *improbe*, as Bonnet argued (*Le latin*, p. 99, n. 6, with parallels).

[33] Cf. Bonnet, *Le latin*, pp. 717–19.

[34] For a fuller description of the late-Antique system, see Hagendahl, *La prose métrique d'Arnobe*; and, for the Classical background, De Groot, *La prose métrique*.

models.[35] The precise relationship between *clausulae* and *cursus* in the sixth century, however, remains imperfectly understood.[36]

When considering Gregory's opening sentence, then, both systems will need to be borne in mind. To begin with what is, in this context, the most important part of the sentence, its final words, we find that it closes with a good metrical *clausula*, the double cretic 'pōssĭt īn pāgĭnīs'. Moreover, if we turn to internal pauses, the same metrical pattern also occurs in the clause-ending 'nudarētŭr ā pērfĭdēs'. Furthermore, in the relative clause which immediately precedes the main verb, the final words scan as a cretic-and-trochee combination, 'depīngĕrēt uērsū', as also do the words closing the main clause itself, 'plerīquĕ dīcēntēs'. However, all four of these endings also constitute accentual *cursus* rhythms, the first two representing the *tardus* form ('póssit in páginis' and 'nudaréntur a pérfides'), and the last mentioned the *planus* ('depíngeret uérsu' and 'pleríque dicéntes').[37] Indeed, if they are considered from the point of view of the *cursus* alone, by far the majority of the clause-endings within our sentence conform to the accentual patterns. Thus, in addition to the examples already considered, the *planus* is found in the ending 'litterárum a nóbis' (with hiatus).[38] The *tardus* is even more frequent, occurring also in the following cases: 'réctae uel ímprobae', 'fídes in plúrimis', 'árte grammáticus', and 'rhétor in pópulis'. Furthermore, the distinctive *uelox* occurs several times: 'pótius pereúnte'; 'géntium desaeuíret' and 'fúror acuerétur'; 'cathólicis tegeréntur'; and 'tepísceret in nonnúllis'. If, as is often done, we also admit the *trispondiacus* to the system, that too can be found in two clause-endings, 'cultúra litterárum', and 'ditaréntur a deuótis'.

In short, of the seventeen clause-endings in the opening sentence, only one does not conform to *cursus*-rhythm, 'inpugnaréntur ab heréticis' (words which are, as we have seen, very closely bound by chiasmus to the following clause, to which they should therefore perhaps be considered as belonging). Even if the somewhat dubious *trispondiacus* form is disregarded, the proportion of unrhythmical endings rises to only three. The remaining fourteen – which represent 82% of the total – comprise three examples of the *planus*, six of the *tardus*, and five of the *uelox* (the majority of these examples, it will have been observed, involving the use of hyperbaton or a delayed final word). It is evident, therefore, that Gregory took great care over the rhythm, as well as the

---

[35] Further details of the *cursus* together with an investigation of its use by later writers can be found in Janson, *Prose Rhythm*.

[36] A useful survey of the problem, including an analysis of Gregory's practice in Book III of the *Historia Francorum*, is provided by Giovanni Orlandi, 'Clausulae', pp.138, 148.

[37] Generally speaking, *cursus*-rhythm is determined by the last two words of a clause; however, in the case of prepositional phrases (such as 'in paginis' and 'a perfides' in the examples cited above), the preposition is conventionally grouped with the noun and its accent ignored, the same principle also being applied to endings such as 'rectae uel improbae' (line 2).

[38] By hiatus is meant the meeting of a final vowel or vowel + *m* with a following initial vowel (viz. 'litterarum a'), where, in metrical verse, that final syllable would be elided. Such hiatus was of course perfectly permissable in the *cursus*-system, but it seems often to have been avoided; cf. Winterbottom, 'Aldhelm's prose style', p. 72.

structure, of the first sentence of his *Historia*, not only at its close but internally too. Moreover, it should not be forgotten that, as we saw at the outset, the accentual patterns which Gregory uses can on four occasions also be scanned according to the rules of prosody. One of the resultant metrical *clausulae* occupies a key position, the close of the sentence, while the other three come at the end of important clauses, including that containing the main verb. It thus seems that Gregory was not only sensitive to the accentual rhythms of the *cursus*, but also to some extent aware of the origins of that system in the metrical *clausulae* of classical prose.[39]

Before we move on to compare the latinity of Columbanus's *Epistulae*, one final stylistic feature of Gregory's preface merits our attention, namely literary allusion. Gregory's favourite works, to judge by the evidence of quotations and echoes, would appear to have been (in verse) Vergil's *Aeneid* and (in prose) the *Vita S. Martini* and *Dialogi* of the christian-Latin author Sulpicius Seuerus.[40] No borrowings from either author have as yet been detected in the preface of the *Historia Francorum*. The opening of the work is not, however, entirely devoid of literary influences. We must not forget the text which Gregory cited most often and undoubtedly knew best, the Bible.[41] For, while there are no explicit quotations of the Bible in Gregory's preface, it has unquestionably left its mark on the language of the sentence which we have been considering. The influence of biblical diction is most readily apparent near the end of the sentence, '*ingemescebant* saepius plerique, *dicentes*: "*Vae* diebus nostris, *quia periit* studium litterarum *a nobis*".' A number of scriptural parallels for Gregory's phraseology can be adduced: compare, for example, I Samuel IV.7, 'et *ingemuerunt* [var. *ingemuerunt dicentes*] uae nobis'; Jeremiah VI.4, '*uae* nobis *quia* declinauit dies'; and Apocalypse XVIII.14, 'omnia pinguia et clara *perierunt a* te'.[42] The effect is primarily one of tone. Gregory does not appear to be using these verbal echoes in such a way as specifically to recall their biblical sources; rather they are an indication of how much his modes of expression had been shaped at a deeper level by his reading of the Scriptures.

To recapitulate: analysis of the opening of the *Historia Francorum* reveals Gregory of Tours as an author whose orthography and morphology may have been shaky, but whose grasp of rhetoric remained strong. His basic vocabulary is relatively unadorned, with a tendency to metaphor and biblical expressions; but his opening sentence at least – admittedly a purple passage – is carefully

[39] Likewise Orlandi has shown that in *Historia Francorum III* metrical patterns, particularly the cretic and trochee and forms of the double cretic, survive alongside their rhythmical equivalents (viz. the *planus* and *tardus*); he concludes that for Gregory 'the ever-increasing tendency towards accentual rhythm has not yet overwhelmed the metrical *clausulae*' ('Clausulae', p. 138).

[40] See the discussions of Gregory's reading cited above, n. 14.

[41] On the complex question of the form in which Gregory knew the Scriptures, see Bonnet, *Le latin*, pp. 53–61.

[42] The same expression is also used in lines 1–2, '*pereunte ab* urbibus Gallicanis' (and for another turn of phrase ultimately indebted to the Apocalypse, see above, n. 20). Other examples of biblical phraseology are given by Bonnet, *Le latin*, pp. 741–2, although his list could be considerably extended.

structured, and abounds in the effective use of rhetorical figures, with consider-able attention being devoted to effects of hyperbaton and prose rhythm, which, for Gregory, are closely interrelated. Our investigation serves, therefore, to demonstrate the tenacity of the rhetorical tradition on the Continent, surviving as it did, in the face of considerable obstacles, to the end of the sixth century and even beyond. Equally, we have also been provided with a useful point of comparison for assessing the style of Columbanus's *Epistulae*. To them we must now apply the same criteria, considering in turn the correctness of the saint's language, his vocabulary, sentence-structure, use of rhetorical figures, the role of hyperbaton and prose rhythm in his letters, and finally the part which literary allusion plays in his writing.

In order to gain an immediate appreciation of Columbanus's style, it will again be best to examine a sample passage, which can then be considered both against the background of the other letters and also in relation to the preface of the *Historia Francorum*. A suitable passage, chosen at random, is the epistolary dedication and first paragraph of *Epistula V* (§§ 1–2), that addressed to Pope Boniface IV. It runs as follows:[43]

1. Pulcherrimo omnium totius Europae Ecclesiarum Capiti, Papae praedulci, praecelso Praesuli, Pastorum Pastori, reuerendissimo Speculatori; humillimus celsis-simo, minimus maximo, agrestis urbano, micrologus eloquentissimo, extremus primo, peregrinus indigenae, pauperculus praepotenti, – mirum dictu, noua res, rara auis – scribere audet Bonifatio Patri Palumbus.
2. Quis poterit glabrum audire? Quis non statim dicat: quis est iste garrulus praesumptuosus, qui non rogatus talia scribere audet? Quis talionis incentor non confestim in illud antiquum probrosum erumpat elogium, quo Moysi Hebraeus ille, qui faciebat iniuriam fratri suo, respondit: 'quis te constituit principem aut iudicem super nos' [Ex II.14]? Cui ego prior respondeo, non esse praesumptionem ubi constat esse necessitatem ad ecclesiae aedificationem; et si in persona cauillatur, non quis dico, sed quid dico, consideret. Quid enim tacebit peregrinus Christianus, quod iam diu declamat uicinus Arrianus? Meliora namque sunt uulnera amici, quam fraudulenta oscula inimici [Prv XXVII.6]. Alii detrahunt laeti in secreto; ego tristis ac dolens arguam in publico, sed schismatis noxii mala, non impiorum pacificorum bona. Non igitur pro uanitate aut procacitate scribere uilissimae qualitatis homunculus tam praecelsis uiris praesumo; dolor enim potius me quam elatio compellit uobis indicare humillima, ut decet, suggestione, quod nomen Dei per uos contendentes utrimque blasphematur inter gentes.

---

[43] *Sancti Columbani Opera*, ed. & transl. Walker, pp. 36–8: '[1.] To Father Boniface, most beauteous head of all the Churches of the whole of Europe, sweetest Pope, mighty Prelate, Shepherd of Shepherds, very reverend Bishop, lofty, most great, urbane, most eloquent, exalted, a native citizen, and most powerful, there dares to write – what an amazing occurrence, what a strange thing, what a rare bird! – the Ring Dove, who is most humble, least of all, unpolished, a pettifogger, insignificant, a foreigner, and a begger.
[2.] Who would listen to the callow? Who would not immediately declare: "Who is this presumptious babbler who dares to write such things unbidden?"? What proponent of exacting justice would not instantly give voice to that old exclamation of rebuke, with which the Jew who was doing wrong to his brother retorted to Moses, "Who set you up over us as lord or judge" [Exodus II.14]? But I pre-empt him by replying that there is no presumption where the maintenance of the church is patently involved; and if his objection is to my person, then let him pay attention not

To begin with language, it is abundantly clear that this passage is marked by none of the irregularities which were apparent in the *Historia Francorum*. Spelling and orthography are correct, although this could of course be the result of editorial intervention. It should not be forgotten the *Epistulae* survive only in transcriptions made in the seventeenth century, in which anomalous forms may well have been suppressed. However, neither in the passage above nor indeed in any of Columbanus's *Epistulae* is there much trace of the kind of case-confusions, errors of accidence, and abnormal syntax which abound in the Latin of Gregory of Tours. Rather, it is grammatical correctness which is characteristic of Columbanus's *Epistulae*.[44]

If we turn to the vocabulary of the passage, it is evident at once that Columbanus is more prone to employing unusual words than was Gregory of Tours. The dedication of the letter, for example, contains the arresting grecism, *micrologus*.[45] Less striking, at least for its Greek origin, is *elogium*, since the word had long been used by Latin authors; nevertheless it is not common.[46] Likewise, Columbanus also favours unusual Latin words and phrases, for example *talionis incentor*, and *glaber*, an adjective which has a distinctly archaic flavour.[47] Columbanus is also interested in employing less usual synonyms alongside common words. Thus Pope Boniface is addressed not

---

to the speaker but to his words. Will a Christian from abroad refrain from saying what nearby Arians have long been declaiming? Wounds from a friend are better than the treacherous kisses of an enemy [Proverbs XXVII.6]. Others are happy to criticize in private; I in my sorrow and pain shall accuse openly the evils of deadly division, and not the advantages won by wicked peacemakers. For it is not through vanity that I, a being of the meanest rank, presume to write to such noble men; it is sorrow, not pride, which forces me to make to you, as is fitting, the humblest of suggestions: that your strife causes the name of God to be blasphemed by heathens on all sides.'

[44] Cf. Winterbottom, 'Columbanus and Gildas', p. 311 (and n. 8). In the passage cited, constructions like 'indicare ... quod ... blasphematur' (lines 25–7, instead of accusative and infinitive) and 'non quis dico sed quid dico consideret' (lines 16– 17, indicatives rather than subjunctives in an indirect question) may surprise the Classicist, but are by no means unusual in biblical and late Latin; some further instances of later-Latin syntax (though not drawn solely from the *Epistulae*) are discussed by Bieler, *apud* Walker, *Sancti Columbani Opera*, pp. lxxix–lxxxi.

[45] The word is ultimately derived from Rufinus's translation of the sermons of Gregory of Nazianzus; see below, n. 69. Columbanus also employs the same expression in *Epistula* I.2 (ed. & transl. Walker, p. 2), where it appears to mean 'one not worthy of mention'; here, however, I have translated it with its correct Greek meaning, a 'pettifogger' or 'hair-splitter', as this seems better suited to its context in the phrase, 'micrologus eloquentissimo' ('a pettifogger to one most eloquent') – indeed, this could also be its meaning in *Epistula I*.

[46] It is used, for example, by Cicero and, among the authors known to Columbanus, Jerome and Sulpicius Seuerus; see *Thesaurus Linguae Latinae*, V/2.404–6, and below, nn. 68, 70.

[47] For *glaber*, see *Thesaurus Linguae Latinae*, VI/2.1998–9 (the word being twice used by Plautus). The literal meaning is 'hairless', but Columbanus employs the word in the extended sense of 'inexperienced' (cf. the origin of 'callow' in English). However, it is also possible that the word may contain an oblique reference to his

only as *Papa*, but also as *Praesul* ('prelate'), *Pastor* ('shepherd') and *Speculator* (literally 'overseer'), this latter term being a calque, frequently used by christian-Latin authors, on the regular term for 'bishop', *episcopus*, which had originally been a loan-word from Greek.[48] Also in the dedication, the saint does not refer to himself as Columba (the regular form of his name in the *Epistulae*).[49] Instead, playing on the meaning of that name, literally 'the dove', he uses the more recherché form *Palumbus* 'a ring-dove', so preferring a rare word, again ultimately of Greek origin.[50] Another noticeable tendency is a fondness for diminutive forms, so that Columbanus, with proper rhetorical humility, terms himself not *pauper* but *pauperculus*, not a *homo* but a *uilissimae qualitatis homunculus*. This passage then, short as it is, highlights the saint's vocabulary as a subject requiring further investigation in the *Epistulae* in general, and one to which we must return later.

By comparison, the sentence-structure of the passage is less elaborate. To begin with the opening paragraph proper of *Epistula V*, its predominant structure is one of rhetorical questions and relatively short units, without any undue emphasis on subordinate clauses. Since Columbanus's primary aim here is to engage the reader's attention, he is concerned not so much with constructing long periods, but rather, as we shall see in a moment, with balance and antithesis. In fact, short sentences such as these regularly form the basic building blocks of Columbanus's prose. This is not, however, to say that he does not also on occasion use longer units, as is demonstrated by the dedication of the letter. The underlying structure of such epistolary dedications is simple, usually consisting of a formula of the following type: '*Bonifacio* [recipient's name in the dative] *Columba* [sender in nominative] *salutem* [scil. *dat* or *mittit*].' The opening of *Epistula V* is at base only slightly more complex, being: 'scribere audet Bonifatio . . . Palumbus'. However, this simple frame is vastly expanded by the addition of many contrasting epithets to the names of both writer and addressee, and of a parenthetic exclamation of amazement ('mirum dictu, noua res, rara auis'). The resultant complex word-order of the dedication will need further consideration later; here, it is sufficient to note that such expansion of a simple framework is another favourite technique with Columbanus, and one which, allied, as here, with the use of synonyms and unusual vocabulary, is characteristic of the rhetorical figure known as amplification.[51]

There is no shortage of other rhetorical figures in our passage, as can be seen in Columbanus's deferential address to the pope – itself a good example of the modesty-topos, the conventions of which are carefully observed throughout the letters. Consider for instance the description of Boniface as 'Papae

---

monastic tonsure (compare the way in which *caluus* can mean 'a monk' in the Carolingian period). If so, it would be, as we shall see, typical of Columbanus's literary practice for an apparent term of rhetorical modesty also to carry the implication that, as a dedicated monastic father, his views are indeed worthy of attention.

[48] See the discussion by Smit, *Studies*, pp. 40–7.

[49] See above, n. 1.

[50] For the saint's word-plays on his name, see also below, p. 48 and n. 77.

[51] Cf. Winterbottom, 'Aldhelm's prose style', pp. 62–70.

praedulci, praecelso Praesuli, Pastorum Pastori, reuerendissimo Speculatori'. The most striking feature is the exuberant alliteration in *p* – which, in a lesser key, is picked up later in the dedication in the phrases 'pauperculus praepotenti' and 'Patri Palumbus' (doubtless supplying another reason why the saint there preferred the form *Palumbus* to *Columba*). Alliteration aside, however, this description of the pope also exhibits an example of chiasmus in the phrase, 'Papae praedulci, praecelso Praesuli', the noun-adjective order of the first element being reversed by that of the second (and indeed those following it). Neither is the chiasmus simply decorative, for it also secures homoeoteleuton, all four elements rhyming in *-i* (and the last two also in *-ori*). Similar homoeoteleuton, this time in *-o*, is present in the succeeding balanced phrases, running from 'humillimus celsissimo' to 'extremus primo'. Columbanus evidently enjoyed the cumulative effect of such rhyme. Further instances can be found later in the passage, such as the clause, 'non esse praesumption*em* ubi constat esse necessitat*em* ad ecclesiae aedification*em*', or the examples of antithesis which we shall consider next.

Antithesis is much in evidence in the passage. It is particularly prominent in the three sentences where Columbanus appears to have followed the lead given by the quotation (of Proverbs XXVII.6) which forms his second sentence, 'Meliora namque sunt uulnera amici, quam fraudulenta oscula inimici.' In this biblical example, the contrasting units both essentially consist – though they contain other words – of an adjective and noun followed by a dependent genitive (the two constituent clauses again, it will be observed, exhibiting final homoeoteleuton, 'am*ici* ... inim*ici*').[52] Antithesis is, however, taken even further in the two sentences which frame this biblical citation. In the first, 'Quid enim tacebit peregrinus Christianus, quod iam diu declamat uicinus Arrianus?', the verbal parallelism is more complete, the contrasted clauses both comprising verb, adjective and noun (again with homoeoteleuton, 'Chris-*tianus* ... Arri*anus*), while 'Quid enim' in the first unit is loosely balanced by 'quod iam diu' in the second. In fact, the sentence constitutes another example of syllabic isocolon: both its clauses are made up of fourteen syllables, which are identically distributed among the constituent words – save that *peregrinus* has four syllables whilst the corresponding adjective *uicinus* has only three, a discrepancy which is neatly offset by the four syllables of 'quod iam diu' in the second clause matching the three of 'Quid enim' in the first. The third sentence of this group is somewhat more complex, being made up of two pairs of antithetical members. In the first pair, 'Alii detrahunt laeti in secreto, ego tristis ac dolens arguam in publico', we again meet the by now familiar homoeoteleuton ('in secret*o* ... in public*o*'), and the careful balancing of constituent words, in this case pronoun, adjective(s), verb and stressed final prepositional phrase. For variety, however, the isocolon is this time not exact. Rather, by a conceit akin to chiasmus, the verb/adjective order of the first

---

[52] Indeed, Columbanus may have slightly improved on his biblical source, since this is one of the borrowings which Walker terms peculiar (see p. 61 below). The Vulgate text is: 'Meliora sunt uulnera diligentis quam fraudulenta odientis oscula [var. oscula odientis].' The edition of the Vulgate cited here is *Biblia Sacra iuxta Vulgatam Versionem*, ed. Weber.

clause, 'detrahunt laeti', is reversed in the second 'tristis ac dolens arguam', where a further adjective has been added; and instead of matching perfectly, the syllable-count of the second clause (fourteen) exceeds that of the first (twelve). The second, shorter pair of antithetical units, 'sed schismatis noxii mala, non impiorum pacificorum bona', which supply objects for the preceding verb, are constructed in a similar way. Both consist of four carefully balanced words with final rhyme ('mal*a* . . . bon*a*'), but the word-order of 'schismatis noxii' in the first clause is inverted by 'impiorum pacificorum' in the second;[53] and the second clause is again somewhat longer (twelve syllables) than the first (nine only). The sentence may thus constitute a double example of the figure known as *climax*, in which successive clauses grow consecutively longer. Both it and the preceding case certainly serve to indicate the skill and care with which antithesis is employed by Columbanus.[54]

The passage also provides an illustration of Columbanus's interest in patterns of hyperbaton, although, perhaps because he is much concerned with shorter, balanced units of the kind we have just been discussing, hyperbaton is here employed only sporadically. There is, for example, only a single instance of the pattern where adjective and noun frame dependent genitive(s), but it is the most complex example of this sort of hyperbaton that we have yet encountered. Instead of a single dependent noun, here there are two, each with their own adjective, the resultant clause owing its shape entirely to the enclosing word-order: 'Pulcherrimo omnium totius Europae Ecclesiarum Capiti' (a pattern which may be represented as abcCBA). It is no accident that this elaborate clause is prominently placed at the very opening of the letter. A more usual pattern of hyperbaton, that where epithet and substantive frame a verb (or aVA), can also be found in our passage. It occurs not, as we might expect, at a sentence-ending but at the close of the clause, 'Quis . . . non confestim in illud antiquum probrosum erumpat elogium', where the basic aVA pattern ('in . . . probrosum erumpat elogium') is slightly complicated by the addition of the further epithets 'illud antiquum'.[55] A related pattern, of adjective and noun framing a short parenthetical verbal clause, can be observed in the phrase 'humillima, ut decet, suggestione', although this is a less striking instance of separation. Finally, a simple type of hyperbaton, which we have not previously considered, is 'dolor enim potius me quam elatio compellit', where the object, the pronoun *me*, is artfully inserted into the middle of the noun-phrase 'dolor . . . elatio' by the splitting of *potius* from *quam*.

The most all-embracing hyperbaton by far, however, is found in the opening address, like the first example of more complex patterning which we observed. As we have seen, the structure of the dedication is at basis very simple – verb(s), dative, nominative, or 'scribere audet Bonifatio . . . Palumbus'.

---

[53] If, that is, *pacifici* should here be understood as a noun and *impii* as an adjective (as I have translated above, n. 43), and not vice versa.

[54] Examples of balance and antithesis from *Epistula V* (including the first of the sentences discussed above) are also cited by Winterbottom, 'Columbanus and Gildas', p. 310, n. 3.

[55] On Columbanus's occasional liking for multiple adjectives, see below, p. 51 (and n. 89).

Columbanus expands this core principally by means of loading both proper nouns with copious epithets, but hyperbaton also plays a vital role in the resulting construct. At its root, the word-order which Columbanus here uses is related to one that is characteristic not so much of Latin prose as of poetry, namely the so-called 'golden line' in which two adjectives are separated from their nouns by a central verb, usually in the pattern abVAB, as in the following example from Vergil (*Aeneid* IV.139):

> Aurea purpuream subnectit fibula uestem.

In the dedication to our letter, the basic structure, which frames the entire sentence, is, 'Pulcherrimo ... humillimus ... scribere audet Bonifatio ... Palumbus' (the order in this case thus being baVBA). This frame is much complicated, however, by further additions. After the verbs, the name *Bonifatius* is qualified by the noun *Pater* in apposition; and before them, the epithets of the pope are by no means limited to simple adjectives, but comprise instead a string of adjective-noun phrases also in apposition. Moreover, the name *Palumbus* has attracted not one but several adjectives, each of which is itself paired with another in the dative (agreeing with *Bonifatio*) which describes a contrasting quality in the pope ('humillimus celsissimo ... pauperculus praepotenti'). The effect of this pairing is, within its clause, to invert the original order of the adjective-noun pairs ('Pulcherrimo ... humillimus ... Bonifatio ... Palumbus' it will be remembered), so that adjectives in the dative no longer precede those in the nominative, but follow them, and thus add a further chiastic element to the dedication. It is thus abundantly clear that complex hyperbaton can be an important structural element in Columbanus's writing.

Discussion of patterns of hyperbaton leads us naturally to the related question of prose rhythm. To commence with the classical system of *clausulae*, the opening of *Epistula V* certainly provides no evidence that Columbanus sought to employ its characteristic metrical patterns (described in detail above). The two paragraphs in question contain seven sentence-endings (excluding, for our present purposes, the two sentences which close with biblical quotations). Not one of them exhibits any of the three *clausulae* regularly favoured by authors writing metrical prose. The position as regards the accentual *cursus* is, however, much less clear. Six of the seven sentences do indeed close with *cursus*-patterns, including three examples of the *planus* (quoted below) and one of the *tardus* ('díco consíderet'), although the *uelox* is entirely absent. The remaining two patterns present are both *trispondiaci*, 'uicínus Arriánus' and 'blasphemátur inter géntes'.[56] However, given the anomalous position of the *trispondiacus* in the *cursus*-system, this is a suspiciously high proportion of such endings in so small a sample. Moreover, of the three *planus* endings – 'Pátri Palúmbus', 'glábrum audíre' and 'scríbere aúdet' – the last two both contain hiatus.[57] Since such hiatus was generally avoided by authors

---

[56] Treating, that is, the prepositional phrase 'inter gentes' in the second example in the manner described above, n. 37.
[57] See above, n. 38.

who employed the *cursus*, its occurrence twice in close succession is also disquieting.[58] It could therefore be argued that of these six instances of *cursus*-rhythm, only two may be accepted without question, namely: the first *planus*, 'Pátri Palúmbus', and the *tardus* 'díco consíderet'. In that case, the proportion of *cursus*-endings would fall from six (or 86% of the total) to no more than two (29%), percentages which are further reduced to only 67% and 22% respectively if the two sentences ending with biblical quotations are taken into account.

The picture is similarly confused if we turn our attention from sentence- to clause-endings, as we did in the case of the opening sentence of the *Historia Francorum*. In the initial dedication of the letter, for instance, which closes with the *planus* 'Patri Palumbus', there are arguably two or three main clause-endings: one of these has a *uelox* rhythm, 'paupérculus praepoténti'; but the others do not conform to the *cursus*, viz. 'reuerendíssimo Speculatóri' and 'Ecclesiárum Cápiti' (if indeed this should be counted as the end of a separate clause). Similarly, to pass on to some examples drawn from the second paragraph, in the sentence beginning 'Alii detrahunt . . .', the closing cadence, 'pacificórum bóna', is not rhythmical, nor is that of the second of its three internal clauses, 'árguam in público' (which moreover exhibits hiatus); but the remaining two comprise a *trispondiacus*, 'láeti in secréto', and a *planus*, 'nóxii mála'. However, in addition to doubts about the validity of the *trispondiacus*, it could further be objected that the first of these clauses again contains hiatus, while the second may be too closely connected to that which follows for its rhythm to be important. In contrast, the sentence 'Quis talionis . . .', even though it ends with a biblical quotation, seems to exhibit internal rhythm: the clause-ending 'súo respóndit' is a *planus*, and that closing 'probrosum erúmpat elógium' forms a *tardus* – where, moreover, the aVA-pattern of hyperbaton (discussed above) may arguably have been employed to secure the *cursus*-rhythm. In the light of all this, two conclusions are possible: either that Columbanus was entirely indifferent to accentual rhythm, and that such *cursus*-endings as we find are the result of chance; or that he was aware of the *cursus*-system, but used it only intermittently and then for motives which remain unclear.

The findings which emerge from our examination of the opening of *Epistula V* may be summed up as follows. Columbanus's prose is grammatically and syntactically correct by the standards of christian-Latin authors, and much more so than that of Gregory of Tours. Many of Columbanus's sentences are short, the longer ones often being expanded by techniques typical of rhetorical amplification. Allied with this amplification is a tendency to the use of synonyms and unusual or striking vocabulary. Moreover, other rhetorical topoi and figures, particularly balance and antithesis, are freely employed. Patterns of hyperbaton, ranging from simple forms to the very complex, also play an important part in the structure of Columbanus's sentences. But contrary to what we observed in the *praefatio* to the *Historia Francorum*, Columbanus, here at least, does not appear to be using such patterns or delayed words so regularly to secure rhythmical effects. Indeed, it is far from clear whether or

[58] See the statistics for early mediaeval prose given by Winterbottom, 'Aldhelm's prose style', pp. 72–3.

not *cursus*-rhythm is being deliberately sought in the passage with which we have been dealing.

Having analysed *Epistula V* (§§ 1–2) in detail, it is now time to set some of our conclusions more firmly against the background of the other *Epistulae* and, indeed, within a wider context. With this in view, Columbanus's vocabulary furnishes a useful point of departure. Up until quite recently, some works written by Insular authors were conventionally labelled 'hisperic', a term which was used to denote amongst other things a concern with arcane vocabulary. Now, however, the term is generally applied only to a more limited range of texts, and chiefly to the *Hisperica Famina* themselves. The *Famina* were probably composed in Ireland around the middle of the seventh century. They exhibit many perplexing features, not least of which is their bizarre vocabulary. In the opening line of the A-text, for example, the relatively simple idea 'I am happy' is expressed by the faminator in the following way:[59]

Ampla pectoralem suscitat uernia cauernam.

One may note here a number of features characteristic of the *Famina*. A preference for less usual synonyms instead of common words is apparent in the use of *amplus* (for *magnus*) and *suscito* (for *moueo*). A penchant for poetic periphrasis can be observed in the substitution of the metaphorical expression *pectoralis cauerna* for *pectus* or *cor*.[60] And finally a taste for strange neologisms is manifest in the elsewhere unparalleled noun *uernia* ('joy'), seemingly derived from the adjective *uernus* ('springtime'). Throughout the text the faminators delight in this sort of abstruse vocabulary. They are fond, for example, of using nouns formed in *-men* or agentives in *-or* and *-trix*, verbs in *-esco* and *-izo*, and adjectives in *-fer* and *-ger*, *-osus* and *-alis* (such as *pectoralis* in the line cited above).[61] Many of these words are extravagant new-coinages, but, not content with that, the faminators also deck out their pages with frequent grecisms and, on occasion, borrowings from Hebrew as well perhaps as Old Irish. As far as vocabulary goes, then, the *Hisperica Famina* are clearly very much *sui generis*, but their interest in the unusual and the recherché immediately raises a question. How far should the similar traits which we have observed in Columbanus's *Epistulae* be seen as foreshadowing the practice of the faminators?

It is immediately evident that Columbanus's interest in unusual vocabulary is neither as extreme nor as continual as that of the faminators. Let us consider, for example, his use of agentive nouns in *-or*. *Epistulae I–V* contain only the following examples: *agitator* (V.11); *bellator* (V.7); *celator* (IV.8); *contemplator* (V.8); *criminator* (V.9); *gubernator* (V.3); *habitator* (V.3); *incentor* (V.2); *reprehensor* (V.14); and *speculator* (I.1). Most of these words are by no

---

[59] *The Hisperica Famina*, ed. Herren, I.64: 'Ample joy excites the cavern of my breast.'

[60] Cf., for instance, the hexameter-ending 'pectoris antro', used by Prudentius and other christian-Latin poets; see Schumann, *Lateinisches Hexameter-Lexikon*, IV.197–8.

[61] See the discussions by Herren, *The Hisperica Famina*, I.45–9; and Niedermann, 'Les dérivés en *-osus*'.

means rare, and all can be paralleled in other late Latin texts.[62] Indeed, of the types of word-formation so favoured by the faminators, only adjectives in *-osus* are relatively frequent in the *Epistulae* (especially *Epistula V*), for example: *clamosus* (V.9); *confragosus* (V.12); *fabulosus* (V.10); *iniuriosus* (V.14); *luxoriosus* (V.7); *oliginosus* (V.14, a variant spelling of *uliginosus*); *praesumptuosus* (V.2); *probrosus* (V.2); *procellosus* (V.3); *spumosus* (V.3); *superciliosus* (V.12); *tumultuosus* (II.2, III.2); and *zelosus* (V.4).[63] Again, the majority of these words are not unusual, and all can be paralleled elsewhere.[64] Likewise, Columbanus employs archaisms and poeticisms only on occasion.[65] Perhaps the most striking strand in his vocabulary is his liking for Greek words. An impressive list of Columbanus's grecisms (drawn from all the works attributed to the saint) has been assembled by Walker.[66] However, as Smit has pointed out (and Walker himself conceded), very many of the words listed – for instance (restricting examples to the *Epistulae*) *agon* (V.6), *brauium* (VI.3), *cenodoxia* (V.16), *dogma* (I.3), *schisma* (V.2), and *zelare* (V.4) – had by Columbanus's time become so frequent in ecclesiastical Latin as no longer to be properly felt as grecisms.[67] Moreover, many more of the saint's less usual Greek words can easily be found in patristic sources likely, as we shall see, to have been known to him: for example, *apologia* (II.6), *calcenterus* (I.3), *catalogus* (I.3), *elogium* (I.2, V.2), *euripus* (I.5), *hyperbolice* (I.5; V.3, 11, 14), and *tomus* (II.5) in Jerome;[68] *apologia* and *micrologus* (I.2, V.1) in Rufinus;[69] *elogium* (I.2, V.2) and *neotericus* (V.12) in Sulpicius Seuerus.[70] In fact, only a small minority of Columbanus's grecisms cannot be paralleled elsewhere.[71] In

[62] The most unusual is *celator*, which is elsewhere used only by Lucan and Cassiodorus (*Thesaurus Linguae Latinae*, III.737); for Smit's proposal to read instead *zelator*, see below, n. 71.

[63] Note too that *Epistula* V.11 (*Sancti Columbani Opera*, ed. & transl. Walker, p. 48) also contains in close proximity two unusual adjectival formations in *-alis*, viz. *transmundialis* and *triundalis*.

[64] On *confragosus*, for example, see below, n. 163.

[65] For a probable archaism (*glaber*), see above, p. 40. Two other words which can be paralleled in Plautus are the grecisms *epicrocus* (V.14) and *proreta* (V.3). As for poeticisms, a verse-word employed by Columbanus is, for example, *trisulcus* (V.14), an adjective used by both Vergil (*Aeneid*, II.475) and the christian-Latin poet Caelius Sedulius (*Carmen Paschale*, I.133) – the latter being an author probably known to Columbanus; see below, pp. 79–82; and the expression *aetheris climata* (V.11) also has a poetic tone (both words again being grecisms).

[66] 'On the use of Greek words'; cf. Bieler's *index grammaticus*, *apud* Walker, *Sancti Columbani Opera*, p. 231.

[67] See Smit, *Studies*, pp. 25–7.

[68] *apologia*, *Aduersus Rufinum* II.1; *calcenterus*, see Smit, *Studies*, pp. 71–2; *catalogus*, *De uiris illustribus*, *praef.*; *elogium*, *Epistulae* X.1.1 and XXXIX.4.5; *euripus*, *ibid.*, III.4.3; *hyperbolice*, *ibid.*, CXXI.8.15; *tomus*, *ibid.*, XXII.38.4.

[69] *apologia*: Gregory of Nazianzus, *Oratio I* (§ 102.1); *micrologus*: *Oratio III* (§ 16.2) and *IV* (§ 7.5).

[70] *elogium*: *Dialogi* III.xviii.2; *neotericus*: *ibid.*, I.vi.2.

[71] In particular, *bubum* (I.4), *castalitas* (I.1), *chilosus* (I.5), *copis* (V.14), and *scynthenium* (I.4). Of these words, *bubum*, *copis*, and *scynthenium* are discussed by Smit, *Studies*, pp. 88– 96, 137–9, and 81–7 respectively (in the last case he proposes reading instead

most respects, therefore, Columbanus's vocabulary more closely resembles that of continental authors than that of the faminators. In this, as in other features of his style, Columbanus for the most part worked within the established tradition of rhetorical amplification, a tradition which the *Hisperica Famina* by contrast pushed to new extremes.[72]

We can, nevertheless, identify some points of contact between Columbanus's *Epistulae*, the *Hisperica Famina* and Irish learning in general. The most important of these is Columbanus's misuse of the word *dodrans*, which occurs in the phrase, 'trans turgescentem dodrantem' (V.11). Correctly, *dodrans* should mean 'three quarters', but context makes it clear that for Columbanus it has the sense of 'wave' or 'flood tide'. In an entertaining article, Alan K. Brown has shown how this meaning of the word stems from a misunderstanding of a passage in the commentary on Job written by one Philippus, supposedly a disciple of Jerome; and that the incorrect usage of this word is limited to certain early Hiberno-Latin texts, including the *Altus Prosator* and particularly the *Hisperica Famina*, as well as being employed by Aldhelm, and sternly censured by Bede.[73] It seems therefore that the original misunderstanding of the word came about in Ireland. The use of *dodrans* in its incorrect 'hisperic' sense in *Epistula V* (which is in fact the earliest attested occurrence of the error) thus provides one very clear link between Columbanus's latinity and that of his homeland. A further verbal parallel with the *Hisperica Famina* has been noted by Michael Winterbottom.[74] Columbanus, again in *Epistula V*, refers to Rome as 'Ausonicum decus', 'the ornament of Italy' (V.11). The odd adjectival form *Ausonicus* is attested only here and in the *Hisperica Famina*.[75] In other words, the coining from the noun *Ausonia* (a poetic expression for 'Italy') of an adjective in *-icus*, a procedure typical of the *Famina*, can be observed already in Columbanus. These parallels are isolated ones, but suggestive nonetheless; as Winterbottom himself concludes, 'it is in Columbanus that we see the first step in a series of steps that were to develop . . . into the bizarrerie of the *Hisperica Famina*.'

In addition to these links with the *Famina*, other traits characteristic of Hiberno-Latin also manifest themselves in the *Epistulae*. In *Epistula V*, for instance, Columbanus refers to himself as follows: 'mihi Ionae hebraice,

---

scynthemam). As for the strange word *castalitas*, Smit maintains that it has arisen through corruption, and would emend Walker's text, 'theoria utpote diuinae castalitatis perito [castulitatis potito MSS.]' to 'theoria utpote diuina ac actuali statu potito' (*Studies*, pp. 39–56). He also suggests (*Studies*, pp. 99–104) that *chilosus* is a hypercorrect spelling of *zelosus* (comparing *Epistula* IV.8, where Metzler has *zelator* as against Fleming's much rarer *celator*), but it should be noted that *chilosus*, 'thick-lipped', makes good sense in its context. On two further unusual grecisms, *epicrocus* (V.14) and *proreta* (V.3), see above, n. 65.

72 Cf. Winterbottom, 'Aldhelm's prose style', pp. 59–62; and, for Columbanus's place in the rhetorical tradition in general, cf. the remarks of Mohrmann, 'The earliest continental Irish Latin'.

73 Brown, 'Bede, a hisperic etymology'.

74 'Columbanus and Gildas', p. 316.

75 *The Hisperica Famina*, ed. Herren, A.40, 58, 92, 117, 273.

Peristerae graece, Columbae latine' (§ 16).[76] This is one of the saint's many plays upon his name, literally 'dove', using in turn the Hebrew, Greek and Latin forms. This passage has been discussed at length by Smit, who quite rightly emphasises its relationship with the concern for the 'tres linguae sacrae' which is so common in early Irish exegesis and learning generally.[77] Columbanus's interest in the Latin, Greek and Hebrew equivalents of his name is thus typical of early Hiberno-Latin scholarship. A further Irish element in the *Epistulae* has recently been identified by Maura Walsh and Dáibhí Ó Cróinín. In *Epistula I* (§ 3) they suggest reading, with Fleming, 'contra Gallicos rimarios' (where Walker prints Metzler's *primarios*); they explain the noun *rimarius* as being derived from Old Irish *rimaire*, and meaning a 'computist', an explanation which is attractive since it could also involve word-play on the Latin verb *rimare* ('to probe' or 'investigate').[78]

Compared with his vocabulary, Columbanus's sentence-structure need not detain us unnecessarily. Examination of *Epistula V* (§§ 1–2) has already shown the saint using a variety of sentence-types, this being in fact quite typical of his practice throughout the letters. However, it remains to show that, like Gregory of Tours, Columbanus could, when he chose, also work with longer periods. A good example of this is afforded by the following passage, also drawn from *Epistula V* (§§ 8–9):[79]

Sed quia fragilis ingenii cumba non tam in altum iuxta uerbum Domini ducta est, quam adhuc in uno haereat loco (non enim charta totum comprehendere potest, quod animus, uariantibus causis, epistolae angustiis concludere uoluit), dum a rege rogor ut singillatim suggeram tuis piis auribus sui negotium doloris (dolor namque suus est schisma populi pro regina, pro filio, forte et pro se ipso; fertur enim dixisse, si certum sciret, et ipse crederet), redeamus ad librum, quem iuxta ripam dimisimus.

Columbanus is here, as so often elsewhere in the *Epistulae*, making a conventional apology, excusing himself, in highly rhetorical language, for dwelling on a subsidiary point, when he ought (to use his own metaphor) to be spreading his sails in order to broach more specifically the problem of the 'Three

---

[76] 'To me, Jonah in Hebrew, Peristera in Greek, Columba in Latin.'

[77] *Studies*, pp. 141–6 (pointing to a number of likely sources for Columbanus, in particular, the prologue to Jerome's *In Ioel*); on the significance of the 'tres linguae sacrae' for the Irish, see McNally, 'The tres linguae sacrae'.

[78] *Cummian's Letter*, edd. & transl. Walsh & Ó Cróinín, p. 33, n. 126; see also pp. 62–3, n. 52, where they support the view that for Columbanus, as for Irish writers generally, *calcenterus* had the meaning 'computist', perhaps by a confusion with *calculenterus* or *calcalenterus* – on which form of the word, cf. Smit, *Studies*, pp. 70–7.

[79] *Sancti Columbani Opera*, ed. & transl. Walker, p. 44: 'Yet, since the unseaworthy boat of my talent has not yet reached, as the Lord says, the high sea, but would still linger in one spot (my missive being unable to encompass everything that my mind, for various reasons, wished to include within the confines of this letter), seeing that I am requested by the king to rehearse the cause of his sorrow point by point to your pious ears (schism among his people is his sorrow, for the sake of his queen, his son, and perhaps himself; for they claim that he said he would believe if he had certain knowledge), let us return to my book, which I left behind by the shore.'

Chapters' controversy, as the Lombard king Agilulf has asked him to. The main clause, near the end of the sentence is jussive, 'redeamus ad librum', followed by a relative clause, 'quem iuxta ripam dimisimus', which picks up the nautical imagery from the beginning of the sentence. Before the main clause, the structure is more complex. The initial subordinate clause, 'Sed quia . . . uno haereat loco' (closing with hyperbaton of the aVA-type), is neatly divided by a pair of correlatives ('non tam . . . quam . . .'). After that, the flow of the sentence is artfully interrupted by one of a pair of explanatory parentheses, 'non enim . . . concludere uoluit', here lamenting Columbanus's inability to adhere to the rules of epistolary brevity. These two members are then balanced by two more subordinate units. First comes a *dum*-clause which itself introduces a final clause, 'dum a rege . . . sui negotium doloris' (this time ending with hyperbaton of the baB-type);[80] and second, there is another parenthetical unit explaining the cause of Agilulf's anxiety, 'dolor namque . . . se ipso' (the closing phrase, 'pro regina, pro filio, forte et pro se ipso' constituting an excellent example of tricolon with anaphora), and offering the further explanation, 'fertur enim . . . ipse crederet' (note Columbanus's varying of the causal connectives, 'namque . . . enim'). Overall, the sentence is carefully crafted; and, even though this particular example relies for its effect almost as heavily upon parenthesis as on subordination, it certainly demonstrates Columbanus's ability to handle larger periodic structures.[81]

Nor need we spend too long considering the importance of rhetorical figures in Columbanus's prose. We have already noted in the opening paragraphs of *Epistula V* examples of antithesis, homoeoteleuton, isocolon and chiasmus, all of which can be paralleled without difficulty throughout the *Epistulae*.[82] Columbanus also employs other figures freely, for instance: tricolon, as in the following balanced clauses – the first simple, the second furnishing an example of tricolon crescendo – 'meum fuit prouocare, interrogare, rogare: tuum sit gratis accepta non negare, foenerari petenti talentum, et panem doctrinae, Christo praecipiente, dare' (I.10);[83] word-play, 'melius uobis erit

---

[80] I have accepted here *dum* (the reading of both Fleming and Metzler) rather than *tum* (Walker's conjecture), and repunctuated the sentence accordingly; otherwise, the period (and Columbanus's nautical imagery) is 'unduly abbreviated', as has been pointed out by Winterbottom, 'Columbanus and Gildas', p. 310, n. 5.

[81] Cf., for instance, the more orthodox period (*Epistula* V.9, ed. & transl. Walker, *Sancti Columbani Opera*, p. 44, immediately following that discussed here), which is analysed by Winterbottom, 'Columbanus and Gildas', p. 315.

[82] For example, *Epistula* I.4 (ed. & transl. Walker, *Sancti Columbani Opera*, p. 6), 'nostrae solemnitatis initium finem solemnitatis eorum non excederet' (chiasmus); *Epistula* I.10 (*ibid.*, p. 10), 'Rescribere te persuadeat ca*ritas*, exponere te non impediat cartae asper*itas*' (antithesis, anaphora, balance and homoeoteleuton); *Epistula* II.5 (*ibid.*, p. 14), 'nocuit nocetque ecclesiasticae paci morum diuersitas et uarietas traditionum' (chiasmus); *Epistula* IV.6 (*ibid.*, pp. 30–2), 'Mirum in modum cernitur in stultitia sapientia innume*rabilis* et in infirmitate fortitudo incompa*rabilis*' (syllabic isocolon and homoeoteleuton).

[83] Also *Epistula* I.9 (*ibid.*, p. 10), 'librum . . . stylo breuem, doctrina prolixum, mysteriis refertum' (again crescendo); *Epistula* V.3 (*ibid.*, p. 38), 'nullus hereticus, nullus Iudaeus, nullus schismaticus fuit' (with anaphora); *Epistula* V.4 (*ibid.*, p. 40),

illos *confortare* quam *conturbare*' (II.6);[84] climax, 'Si tollis hostem, tollis et pugnam; si tollis pugnam, tollis et coronam – si haec sint, ubi fuerint, uirtus, uigilantia, feruor, patientia, fidelitas, sapientia, stabilitas, prudentia sint necesse est, si non, strages – et ut inferam, si tollis libertatem, tollis dignitatem' (IV.6); and, finally, the use of *sententiae*, for example, 'non enim fortis militis est in bello plorare' (IV.6).[85] Columbanus's easy familiarity with the techniques of rhetorical writing is thus everywhere apparent.[86]

More, however, needs to be said about word-order in the *Epistulae*, since it too has a bearing on the 'Irish' quality of Columbanus's Latin. We have already seen how the opening paragraphs of *Epistula V* contained a number of patterns of hyperbaton. That such hyperbaton is central to Columbanus's style is confirmed by an examination of all five *Epistulae*, the results of which are set out below.[87] Since the saint uses hyperbaton of many types, it will be best to consider each in turn. To begin with the simplest form, separation of adjective and noun round a dependent genitive (or aBA), for example, 'caeca prosperitatis securitas' (V.7), this pattern is frequent throughout the *Epistulae*.[88] Columbanus has a tendency to complicate this simple pattern slightly by qualifying the main noun by two adjectives rather than one, for example, *Epistula IV* (§ 2), 'nostroque communi omnium patre' (aaBA);[89]

'confirma testimonio, robora scripto, muni synodo'; *Epistula* V.11 (*ibid.*, p. 48), 'trans euriporum rheuma, trans delphinum dorsa, trans turgescentem dodrantem' (with anaphora and alliteration).

[84] Cf. *Epistula* I.8 (*ibid.*, p. 10), 'licet enim non me *sapientem* sed esse *sitientem* fateor, hoc idem *facerem* si *uacarem*' (a double example); *Epistula* II.2 (*ibid.*, p. 12), 'iusto *iudicio iudicaturi*' (a figure frequent in the Bible); *Epistula* II.6 (*ibid.*, p. 16), 'quam necessitas extorsit non *uanitas*, ut ipsa probat *uilitas*'; *Epistula* V.5 (*ibid.*, p. 40), '*Vigila* itaque, quaeso, papa, *uigila*, et iterum dico, *uigila*; quia forte non bene *uigilauit Vigilius.*'

[85] See also the list of *dicta* collected by Quacquarelli, 'La prosa d'arte', p. 15, examples being drawn from both *Epistulae* and *Instructiones*.

[86] Cf. Winterbottom's examples of rhetorical figures in *Epistula V* ('Columbanus and Gildas', pp. 310–11); Quacquarelli, 'La prosa d'arte'; and also many of the entries in Bieler's *index grammaticus*, in *Sancti Columbani Opera*, ed. & transl. Walker, esp. pp. 239–41. In this respect it is hard to agree with Roger's (otherwise accurate) assessment of Columbanus's prose that, 'Le style est sans art' (*L'enseignement*, p. 231).

[87] See the Appendix, below, pp. 88–92.

[88] I also include in this category (which in the Appendix I have termed 'aBA and similar') patterns in which the noun, not its epithet, comes first, e.g. *Epistula* II.5 (ed. & transl. Walker, *Sancti Columbani Opera*, p. 14), 'tumore superbiae deposito' (ABa, in this case an ablative-absolute phrase with participle rather than an adjective); and also those where the enclosed noun is not in the genitive but governed instead by a preposition, e.g. *Epistula* V.16 (*ibid.*, p. 54), 'prisco inter hebraeos nomine'. In the latter example, I follow Smit (*Studies*, pp. 149–59), at least to the extent of preferring 'inter hebraeos' (Metzler's reading) to 'utor hebraeo' printed by Walker (*utor* being the conjecture of Gundlach, Columbanus's previous editor).

[89] Indeed, Columbanus occasionally loads nouns with adjectives, as for instance in *Epistula* I.4 (*ibid.*, p. 6), 'Hibernicis antiquis philosophis et sapientissimis'; *Epistula* I.5 (*ibid.*, p. 8), 'duorum supradictorum auctorum sibi inuicem contrariorum'; *Epistula* II.2 (*ibid.*, p. 12), 'uniuersis necessariis obseruationibus canonicis'; and *Epistula* III.2 (*ibid.*, p. 24), 'ad istos nostros uicinos fratres.'

and in one particularly complex instance, the adjective/noun pair enclose further words (not in agreement) in addition to the dependent genitive, viz. 'triundialibus saltuatim licet hyperbolice pelagi uorticibus' (V.11). Moving on to the less usual pattern bAB, where a noun is framed by a dependent adjective/noun pair, for example, 'meorum cura peregrinorum' (I.8), it is significant that Columbanus uses this more ornate form of hyperbaton almost as frequently as aBA.[90] This pattern is even more striking if the framing adjective/noun pair are not in the genitive, and hence not grammatically dependent on the enclosed noun. Columbanus most often uses the simpler genitive-form, but in the stylistically elaborate *Epistula V*, which indeed contains just over half the total occurrences of this pattern, there are perhaps three non-genitive examples, as for instance in the phrase, 'tantos Italia lupos habuit' (V.4).[91]

Columbanus's liking for more complex hyperbaton also manifests itself in his use of the pattern abBA, where one adjective/noun pair is framed by another, for example 'ad ueram octaui diei circumcisionem' (II.3). Normally, such patterns would occur less regularly than the simpler aBA, but in the *Epistulae*, it is abBA which is marginally the more frequent.[92] Columbanus does not, however, favour such splitting of adjective and noun round another pair which is not closely grammatically related; in the case of all but one of his abBA patterns the enclosed adjective and noun are genitives (or occasionally ablatives) directly dependent on the words surrounding them.[93] Nevertheless, Columbanus does favour another complex pattern, whereby the two adjective/noun pairs are interwoven to give the order abAB, for instance 'una

[90] Seventeen examples of bAB as against twenty-one of aBA (see Appendix, pp. 88–92). Once again, in the category 'bAB and similar' are included (as in the case of all the types of hyperbaton catalogued in the Appendix) examples where the separated noun precedes its adjective, e.g. 'officii rem legitimi' (*Epistula* IV.6, ed. & transl. Walker, p. 32); similarly, a few examples where noun and dependent genitive (rather than adjective) are split, e.g. 'finem epistula pergaminae' (*Epistula* IV.9, ed. & transl. Walker, p. 34), are incorporated in this category (as also in the case of aVA simple and complex).

[91] The other two examples are 'sulcatis Orco molibus' (*Epistual* V.3, *ibid.*, p. 38) and 'oliginosis celotes paliaribus' (*Epistula* V.14, *ibid.*, p. 52), but both contain textual difficulties. In the case of the first, *Orco* is Gundlach's emendation of *octo*, the reading of both Fleming and Metzler; if, as Smit has argued (*Studies*, pp. 117–26), *octo* should be retained, then hyperbaton is eliminated. In the second phrase the meaning of *celotes* (Fleming's reading) is unclear; Smit (*ibid.*, p. 139) supports accepting *zelotes* (as read by Metzler), which, being a noun, would retain the bAB pattern.

[92] Twenty-five instances of abBA compared with twenty-one of abA. Note that I have included among examples of abBA one related case where the enclosed unit comprises a dependent genitive and a noun governed by a preposition, 'uera in synodo fidei confessione' (*Epistula* V.9, ed. & transl. Walker, *Sancti Columbani Opera*, p. 44); and another where two genitive nouns are involved, 'amputatis dissensionis ac discordiae causis' (*Epistula* II.5, *ibid.*, p. 14).

[93] The single exception is 'simoniacos et Gildas auctor pestes scripsit' (*Epistula* I.6, ed. & transl. Walker, *Sancti Columbani Opera*, p. 8, where *simoniacos* and *pestes* are in apposition).

istorum sententia episcoporum' (I.4). Striking interlace patterns of this kind occur no less than seven times in the *Epistulae*.

In addition to patterns of hyperbaton involving only adjectives and nouns, such as those we have so far been considering, there is also the important class in which verbs are enclosed. This kind of hyperbaton too is fundamental to Columbanus's style. Indeed, the simple pattern in which an adjective/noun pair frame a verb (aVA), usually at the end of a clause, is by far the most frequent type of hyperbaton in the letters, for example, 'horrendam intulit sententiam (I.3).[94] Less frequently Columbanus uses a minor variation on this pattern, whereby it is a noun and its dependent genitive which are separated by the verb, for example, 'mores exponunt infantium' (II.8) or 'a doctrinae recesserunt ueritate' (IV.4).[95] On other occasions Columbanus again makes the basic pattern aVA more complex by adding further words within the adjective/noun frame. In its simplest form, the resultant pattern contains another noun (or prepositional phrase) before or after the internal verb, as in the following examples: 'nostrorum traditionem robores seniorum' (III.2); 'tuae dirige fulcrum sententiae' (I.4); and 'indubitatam in scripturis diuinis accommodant fidem' (I.5).[96] This pattern becomes more complex still if further words (adjectives, adverbs, prepositional or subordinate clauses) are added, as for instance in such cases as '*nulla* sit inter te et Hieronymum in sententia promenda *dissonantia*' (I.5), '*meae* indulge quod sic audacter scripsi rogo *procacitati*' (I.10), or '*inimicis* nostris dum non sensimus circumdati sumus *triplicibus*' (V.7). In these examples, hyperbaton helps to give shape to its cause, adjective and noun providing a neat syntactical frame. Finally, Columbanus on occasion combines the aVA pattern with the interlace abAB, to give the order abVAB (or similar), for example, 'nullas istorum suscipimus regulas Gallorum' (III.2) – a pattern which is, as we have seen, more typical of Latin poetry than prose.

These two tendencies – to expand simpler patterns by the addition of more words, or to combine different patterns – sometimes result in what I have termed complex hyperbaton, where Columbanus delights in word-orders which may at first sight seem highly contorted, but which often under-score a rhetorical point. When, for example, Columbanus wishes to stress his

---

[94] Listed in the Appendix as 'aVA and similar (simple)'. As before, I have included in this class examples where noun precedes adjective, e.g. 'flabris exasperatur feralibus' (*Epistula* V.3, *ibid.*, p. 38); and also cases where a pair of verbs (one usually being an infinitive) are enclosed, e.g. 'tua excusari potest peritia' (*Epistula* I.4, *ibid.*, p. 4, with alliteration).

[95] Such examples are incorporated in my lists of aVA-hyperbaton simple or complex (as appropriate). In the case of aVA simple, a separated adjective and noun can themselves sometimes be followed by a dependent genitive, e.g. 'totam exponas obscuritatem Zachariae' (*Epistula* I.9, ed. & transl. Walker, *Sancti Columbani Opera*, p. 10).

[96] In the Appendix, I have termed this pattern 'aVA (complex)', also including there, as before, those few cases where noun precedes adjective (e.g. 'intra uiscera more Rebeccae discerpitur materna': *Epistula* V.12, *ibid.*, p. 50), or where a further verb in a separate clause is enclosed (e.g. 'miro, ut audiui, elaborasti ingenio': *Epistula* I.9, *ibid.*, p. 10).

amazement that an Arian king of Lombardy should ask him, an untalented Irish *peregrinus*, to write to the pope, he employs complex hyperbaton of the abVAB type to highlight the incongruity of the situation: 'rex gentilis peregrinum scribere Langobardus Scotum hebetem rogat' (V.14; note how the contrasting words 'Langobardus Scotum' are emphatically placed together).[97] Similarly, in *Epistula I* (§ 5), he emphasises the boldness of his position, as an Irishman writing to Gregory the Great, by juxtaposing *te* (the pope) and *mei . . . apices* (his own letters), while at the same time interweaving epithets of both (not to mention a description of St Peter as well): 'ridiculose te mei, nimirum Petri cathedram apostoli et clauicularii legitime insidentem, occidentales apices de Pascha sollicitent'.[98] Both these examples are directly comparable with the complex word-patterning which we observed in the epistolary address which opens *Epistula V*. Such interweaving can also be used for picturesque effect, as for instance in the vivid simile where Columbanus imagines himself as the bloodied beholder of a corpse-strewn battlefield, 'acsi quidam campi bellici roscidus cadauerum ac madidus post pugnam contemplator' (V.14).[99] In this way, complex patterns of hyperbaton are frequently put to good rhetorical effect in Columbanus's *Epistulae*.

This penchant for hyperbaton presents us with a problem similar to that already posed by Columbanus's vocabulary. François Kerlouégan has noted the great frequency with which two of the word-patterns we have been considering, abBA and particularly the interlace abAB, are used by certain Insular authors, such as Gildas, Aldhelm and Adomnán.[100] Moreover, the pattern abVAB with its central verb is characteristic of the *Hisperica Famina* (it can be observed, for example, in line 1 of the A-text, quoted above); the faminators also regularly employed patterns such as aBVA, abBVA, and sometimes simple aVA, the separation of adjective and noun round a verb being a fundamental principle of linear structure in the *Famina*. Kerlouégan would therefore see Columbanus's interest in hyperbaton as a 'celtic' phenomenon. On the other hand, aVA, the pattern most favoured by Columbanus, is very often employed, usually at clause-endings, by the majority of late Latin prose writers. Furthermore, Michael Winterbottom has pointed out that the complex patterns abBA and abAB can often be paralleled in more elaborate continental works.[101] Even interlace patterns with a central verb (abVAB) can occasionally be found, probably in imitation of the golden

[97] 'An Arian Lombard king asks a dull Irish foreigner to write.'
[98] 'And that my western letters should ludicrously trouble you about Easter, seeing that you lawfully occupy the throne of Peter, apostle and key-bearer' (where the expected word-order might have been, 'mei occidentales apices te, nimirum cathedram Petri apostoli et clauicularii legitime insidentem, de Pascha ridiculose sollicitent').
[99] 'Like some observer of the corpses on a field of battle, who is bedewed and bespattered after the engagement.'
[100] Kerlouégan, 'Une mode stylistique'.
[101] Winterbottom, 'A "Celtic" hyperbaton?', including, at p. 209, n. 6, one example of the interlace-pattern from Gregory of Tours's *Historia Francorum*, II.2; see also Winterbottom, 'Aldhelm's prose style', p. 50, n. 2.

line of Latin verse.[102] Thus the basic patterns of hyperbaton favoured by Columbanus are largely those employed by writers of *Kunstprosa* on the Continent. What sets Columbanus apart from most such writers is the great frequency with which he uses these patterns and his readiness to experiment by combining them or by interweaving further words. For Columbanus, separation of adjective and noun is not yet quite the basic structural principle that it became for the faminators, but his interest in hyperbaton and the frequency with which he employs it certainly points in that direction. In this respect then, as with his vocabulary, Columbanus is a writer who looks both forward and back.

Having completed our discussion of hyperbaton in the letters, we must now return to the question of prose rhythm. It will be remembered that, at the beginning of *Epistula V*, it was difficult to determine the extent to which the *cursus* was being deliberately employed by Columbanus. Can a more general examination of the rhythm of all the sentence-endings in the letters help to clarify the situation? The results of such an examination are set out below in Table 1.[103]

Table 1

Cursus in *Epistulae I–V*

Epistula:	I	II	III	IV	V	Total	Percentage
x́xxx́x (*planus*)	13	11	1	19	27	71	28.9
x́xxx́xx (*tardus*)	9	5	3	6	14	37	15.0
x́xxxxx́x (*uelox*)	4	5	–	3	16	28	11.4
Total	26	21	4	28	57	136	55.3
x́xxxx́x (*trispondiacus*)	8	10	–	10	11	39	15.8
others	14	9	2	23	23	71	28.9
Grand total	48	40	6	61	91	246	100
hiatus	9	11	–	6	11	37	15.0

[102] Examples are included in the lists in Winterbottom's two articles (from Augustine, Sedulius and Priscian), and in my 'Gildas's prose style' (Ennodius, Fortunatus and Sedulius). Sedulius's prose certainly seeks to reproduce the intricate word-order of his verse, in which the golden line is very frequent ('Gildas's prose style', pp. 122–5). Indeed, Sedulius's poetry may in this respect have exerted an important influence on the word-order of the *Hisperica Famina* themselves; see Wright, 'The *Hisperica Famina* and Caelius Sedulius'.

[103] The criteria on which this analysis was based are those defined above (pp. 36–7). As before, all sentence-endings have been included, except those closing with quotations (however, isolated cases where Columbanus has added a word or words, thus altering the rhythm, have been counted). Where final and initial vowels meet, I have in all cases assumed hiatus (see above, n. 38) – many of the examples of *cursus*

The statistics presented here do little to solve the difficulties we have already encountered. If we take into account all possible *cursus*-rhythms, then the *Epistulae* contain a grand total of 71.1% of such endings. However, 15.8% of this total is made up of forms of the *trispondiacus*, the place of which within the *cursus*-system remains unclear. For this reason, attention is usually restricted to *planus, tardus* and *uelox* only. These forms account for 55.3% of the sentence-endings in the *Epistulae*. Yet this total presents us with a further difficulty. Generally speaking, polished practitioners of the *cursus* (at least in the later period) use the *planus, tardus* and *uelox* forms in about 70–80% of their sentences, whereas 'unrhythmical' writers usually exhibit totals between 30–40% or lower. Columbanus, with a total of 55.3%, thus falls between the two groups. Evidently the securing of *cursus*-rhythm was by no means an overriding concern for him.

Other factors would support this conclusion. For instance, the proportion of the three main *cursus*-endings varies from letter to letter, falling as low as 45.5% in the least rhythmical, *Epistula IV*. Columbanus also permits a high level of hiatus (15%), a feature which is generally avoided by rhythmical writers. Furthermore, Michael Winterbottom has observed that it is in Latin more usual for the penultimate word of a sentence to have a paroxytone accent than a proparoxytone (respectively *p* and *pp* in Janson's notation). While we should therefore normally expect endings of the type p 4p ('íllum reprehéndit') to be more common than pp 4p ('certántibus coronátur'), writers using the *cursus* in fact tend to favour pp 4p, it being a regular form of the *uelox*. By comparing the relative frequency of these two accentual patterns, Winterbottom has shown that in the case of a number of early Hiberno-Latin texts, including Columbanus's *Epistula I*, there is no preference for pp 4p over p 4p.[104] Examination of all five *Epistulae* yields similar results: twenty-three examples of p 4p as compared with only eleven of pp 4p.[105]

---

rhythm assembled by Quacquarelli ('La prosa d'arte') unfortunately being vitiated by inconsistency on this point. Further, I have, in the circumstances already described, disregarded the accent on prepositions and some other monosyllabes (see above, n. 37), and also on *est* and *sunt* etc. when they form part of a passive or deponent verb. My general categories should thus be understood in the widest sense: *planus* here includes, in terms of Janson's notation (where *p* stands for paroxytone and *pp* for proparoxytone accent), not only the classic p 3p ('mítto salútem'), but also pp 2 ('maióribus scríbi') and by-forms such as p 1 2 ('fáctus sum stúltus'). Likewise, the *tardus* includes p 4pp ('Páscha suffíciant'), pp 3pp ('perículum pértinet'), and also p 1 3pp ('emendáta non fúerint'); and the *uelox* not only pp 4p ('certántibus coronátur') and p 5p ('flli consentiámus'), but also pp 1 3p ('fácerem si uacárem'), p 1 4p ('confortáre quam conturbáre') and occasional types like pp 2 2 ('fécerit saluus érit' – a form certainly permitted in the later middle ages); similarly the *trispondiacus* admits p 4p ('íllum reprehéndit'), pp 3p ('negótium iniúngo'), and also p 1 3p ('orémus ut debémus') and p 2 2 ('blasphemátur inter géntes').

[104] 'Aldhelm's prose style', pp. 71–2 (Table 1). In the forty-eight sentence-endings of *Epistula I*, Winterbottom finds five examples of p 4p as against only 2 of pp 4p (as well as nine cases of hiatus), figures which tally exactly with my own.

[105] Included in these totals are five examples of p 1 3p and four examples of pp 1 3p (see above, n. 103).

The high incidence in the *Epistulae* of hiatus and of p 4p rhythms might therefore indicate that Columbanus – like most other Irish writers, if Winterbottom is right – was not a serious practitioner of the *cursus*; and that the total of 55.3% of such endings in his *Epistulae* could be largely fortuitous. The difficulty with this conclusion lies in ascertaining how likely it is that the *cursus*-rhythms which are present in Columbanus's prose may have arisen through pure chance. One approach to this problem, pioneered by Janson, involves comparing the observed frequency of a rhythmical pattern in a particular author's work with its expected frequency; Janson argues that chance can be ruled out if the observed frequency is found significantly to exceed what is expected.[106] However, the present writer remains sceptical about the validity of calculating expected frequencies, as Janson does, from the *actual* occurrence of all patterns in a work (that is, without any external control); moreover, for authors with a total of approximately 50% *cursus*-endings, like Columbanus, a comparison such as Janson's is often, I have found, inconclusive.

A more promising avenue may perhaps be afforded by considering the relationship of *cursus*-rhythms to patterns of hyperbaton. We have already seen how Gregory of Tours employed delayed final words for the sake of rhythm; and J.N. Adams has observed that the allied aVA pattern of hyperbaton was often similarly used.[107] This pattern is precisely the type of separation of adjective and noun which Columbanus most favours, usually at sentence- and clause-endings. How often does he do so for the purpose of rhythm? Let us examine his practice in *Epistula I*. That letter contains thirty-two examples of hyperbaton of the aVA (and related) variety, both simple and complex.[108] Of these patterns, seven occur at sentence-endings and twenty-two at the ends of clauses (the remaining three being internal). To begin with those patterns at sentence-ends, no fewer than six of the seven exhibit *cursus*-rhythm (viz. two examples of the *planus*, and four of the *tardus*).[109] If, moreover, we turn to the question of rhythm within the sentence (which had perforce to be neglected in Table 1), then we find that the majority of the twenty-two patterns at clause-ends are also so handled: sixteen are rhythmical (six *planus*, nine *tardus* and one *uelox*).[110] So high an incidence of *cursus*-endings combined with hyper-

---

106 The procedure is explained in Janson, *Prose Rhythm*, pp. 10–34.
107 Adams, 'A type of hyperbaton'.
108 See the Appendix, below, pp. 88–92.
109 They are: *planus*, 'hoc imbibit búbum erróris' (*Epistula* I.4), and 'indubitatam . . . accómmodant fídem' (I.5); *tardus*, 'multis comprobátur calcénteris' (I.3), 'errorem . . . confirmáuit inólitum' (I.3), 'non minoris censetur ésse facínoris' (I.6), and 'miro . . . elaborásti ingénio' (I.9) – although note that in the case of the first *tardus*, Columbanus may perhaps have written 'calcalenteris' (see above, n. 78).
110 Namely: *planus*, 'in sancti dogmatis légimus líbro' (*Epistula* I.3), 'suo transgréssus est cýclo' (I.3), 'Victorium non fuísse recéptum' (I.4), 'suum recépit comméntum' (I.4), 'sui rem sustinéret contémptus' (I.8), and 'de tuis transmítte reléctis' (I.9); *tardus*, 'in suo . . . conlaudáuit catálogo' (I.3), 'clarissima . . . diffúsa sunt lúmina' (I.4), 'tua excusari pótest perítia' (I.4), 'tuae dirige fúlcrum senténtiae' (I.4), 'tuum . . aut excusa aut dámna Victórium' (I.5), 'fidei futurum fóre negótium' (I.5), 'Anatolium laudauit húic contrárium' (I.5), 'tua largire . . . précor opúscula'

baton can hardly be fortuitous.[111] It would therefore be a mistake to think that Columbanus wrote in complete ignorance of the *cursus*, or that he was entirely indifferent to rhythm when composing his *Epistulae*. In *Epistula I* at least, Columbanus evidently employed the aVA-pattern of hyperbaton not simply for verbal ornament but also, to some extent like Gregory of Tours, as an adjunct to *cursus*-rhythm. The evidence of Columbanus's hyperbaton thus points clearly towards his having had some understanding of the *cursus*, although the overall total of 55.3% of such endings in his *Epistulae* suggests that he employed rhythm only intermittently there. Beyond that it would be perilous to speculate. It remains unclear whether Columbanus was introduced to the *cursus* during his training in Ireland; or whether his use of hyperbaton in conjunction with rhythm is simply the result of an attentive ear and careful imitation of practices which can regularly be observed in many patristic texts.

We may now recapitulate. Analysis of the *Epistulae* reveals Columbanus as an author with a good grasp of grammar and syntax, and a profound understanding of Latin rhetoric, which he used to good effect in his own writings. Likewise, his taste for varied and unusual vocabulary largely reflects techniques of amplification widely employed in late Latin texts, although a few words do seem to be indicative of the Irish milieu in which he was trained. Elaborate word-order can also be seen as an integral part of the rhetorical tradition in which he worked, but there is in the *Epistulae* a degree of experimentation which can best be paralleled in certain other Insular Latin texts. Finally, Columbanus does not make as extensive a use of prose rhythm as do some continental writers. However, the way in which he employs patterns of hyperbaton in conjunction with accentual rhythm suggests that the saint was not entirely ignorant of the *cursus*, even if he uses it in a seemingly intermittent manner.

Having examined Columbanus's style in detail, it is in order briefly to consider what implications our examination has for the authenticy of the so-called *Epistula VI*. This 'letter', it will be remembered, lacks an epistulary dedication and is transmitted with the *Instructiones* rather than with *Epistulae I–V*. Directed towards a novice, the text primarily consists of a string of moral precepts, as for instance in the following passage (VI.2):[112]

Utilis esto in humilitate infirmusque in auctoritate, simplex in fide, doctus in moribus, mordax in propriis, remissus in alienis, purus in amicitia, callidus in insidiis . . .

The somewhat circumscribed structure of *Epistula VI* thus makes it difficult to draw general conclusions about its style. We may note, however, that such

---

(I.9), 'breuibus . . . trácta senténtiis' (I.9); *uelox*, 'notam subire times Hermagóricae nouitátis' (I.4).

[111] A further indication of this is the preponderance of *tardus*-forms at sentence- (and indeed clause-) ends in *Epistula I*. As Table 1 shows, it is the *planus* which occurs most frequently in all five letters: were the coincidence of hyperbaton and *cursus*-rhythm merely a matter of chance, we should therefore expect the *planus* to be in the majority rather than the *tardus*.

[112] *Sancti Columbani Opera*, ed. & transl. Walker, p. 56: 'Be useful in humility and lowly in authority, simple in faith, learned in character, unrelenting in your own case, lax as regards others, pure in friendship, cunning in traps . . .'.

stringing together of balanced clauses is typical of the rhetorical amplification which we observed at the beginning of *Epistula V*.[113] Moreover, these clauses often exhibit the kind of antitheses so favoured by Columbanus, for instance 'durus in mollibus, mollis in duris' (VI.2, immediately following the passage quoted above). Indeed, *Epistula VI* contains other rhetorical figures which we have met already in the other *Epistulae*: for example, tricolon (with anaphora), 'O te felicem, o te beatum, oque mirabilem te puerum' (VI.3); and word-play, 'Bellum igitur et beluinum uince' (VI.2). The vocabulary of *Epistula VI* also has points of contact with that of *Epistulae I–V*: it contains a sprinkling of agentive nouns in *-or*, viz. *depressor* (VI.2), *negotiator* (VI.3), *publicator* (VI.2), and *quaesitor* (VI.3), as well as one adjectival form in *-osus*, *superciliosus* (VI.2, also used by Columbanus in *Epistula V* (§ 12)). If we turn to prose rhythm, we find that *Epistula VI* contains nine sentence-endings. Of these, seven exhibit conventional *cursus*-rhythm, being three *planus*, two *tardus* and one *uelox*.[114] Clearly this is a higher proportion than in *Epistulae I–V*, but it would be hazardous to base any firm conclusions about authorship on so small a sample of endings. Conversely, hyperbaton is used in *Epistula VI* in a manner strikingly reminiscent of *Epistulae I–V*. As in those letters, the pattern which is found most frequently is the simple aVA.[115] There is also, however, one example of the distinctive interlace-pattern abAB, 'egregius regni negotiator aeterni' (VI.3). Furthermore, on two occasions more complex hyperbaton is in evidence: viz. 'En *tuum*, o puer amande ministerque dulcis, *monimentum*' (VI.1, with two enclosed adjective/noun pairs);[116] and particularly '*suas* uincere possint de intestino *amaritudines* bello' (VI.1, interweaving of adjectives and nouns with enclosed verbs). Stylistic considerations such as these do not, of course, prove conclusively that Columbanus was the author of *Epistula VI*, but viewed as a whole they certainly lend support to the traditional attribution of this work to the saint.

We may now turn our attention to one last, important aspect of Columbanus's style, namely the role of literary reminiscence in his letters. Ludwig Bieler has – with considerable justification in the light of what we have observed in the *Epistulae* – remarked that the saint's writing displays a 'rhetoric elaborate in form but simple and direct in concept – a rhetoric which is the heritage of the great preachers of Christian antiquity and of post-Roman Gaul'.[117] How did Columbanus, an Irishman, achieve such a mastery over late Latin rhetoric?

---

[113] This rhetorical technique is also characteristic of another early Irish product, *De duodecim abusiuis saeculi*, ed. Hellmann, pp. 32–60.

[114] They are: *planus*, 'imbuénde docéri' (*Epistula* VI.1), 'amaritúdines béllo' (VI.1), and 'negotiátor aetérni' (VI.3); *tardus*, 'plúra non próderunt' (VI.1, but as part of a quotation; see p. 76 below), and 'aetérnis stipéndiis' (VI.3); *uelox*, 'ác superciliósum' (VI.2), and 'compléueris uniuérsa' (VI.3). Of the remaining two endings, one is a *trispondiacus* ('profíciens in cérto', VI.2), while the other is unrhythmical ('diuína sítiens', VI.3). There are no cases of hiatus.

[115] Namely: 'perfectio efficitur morum' (*Epistula* VI.1, separation of noun and dependent genitive); 'pro tuis traderis peccatis' (VI.3); 'haec compleueris uniuersa' (VI.3); and 'tuam exercens iuuentutem' (VI.3).

[116] Cf. also 'unius uir uocandus animi' (*Epistula* VI.1).

[117] In *Sancti Columbani Opera*, ed. & transl. Walker, p. lxxxi.

What texts did he read, and how did they influence him when he composed his *Epistulae*? In order to answer these questions, the remainder of this study will be devoted to the borrowings and allusions which can be identified in Columbanus's *Epistulae*. Much work has already been done in this field by Walker and his predecessors, although further reminiscences have come to light since then, some being presented here for the first time. Nevertheless, this survey makes no claim to be comprehensive; Columbanus's borrowings will doubtless repay more study in the future. Certainly we should not assume that Columbanus's reading was necessarily limited to only those works which directly influenced his *Epistulae* (which represent no more than twenty-nine printed pages of Latin in Walker's edition). An analysis of the kind proposed here does, however, have the advantage of showing precisely how the saint drew on his reading as he composed the *Epistulae*, as well as shedding light directly on the ways in which he moulded these sources to his own literary ends.

Columbanus's knowledge of the classics provides us with a convenient starting-point. Only a handful of possible classical borrowings has so far been isolated in the saint's *Epistulae*. These have been submitted to careful scrutiny by J.W. Smit, who rejects some as being too tenuous to bear close examination, while advancing likely intermediate sources for the rest.[118] For example, does the expression 'equitans turbauit aquas multas', which is applied to Christ in *Epistula V* (§ 11), really recall contextually unrelated phrases such as 'per Siculas equitauit undas' (Horace, *Carmina* IV.iv.43), or 'lacrimis turbauit aquas' (Ovid, *Metamorphoses* III.475), particularly when this type of imagery is, as Smit has shown, a commonplace very frequently employed by christian-Latin writers?[119] A similar case can be found in the dedication of *Epistula V*, which we considered above. There, because of his boldness in writing to the pope, Columbanus termed himself a *rara auis*, a 'rare bird.' If a particular source has to be adduced for his employing this quasi-proverbial expression, then that source need not be one of the several classical poets – Horace, Persius, and Juvenal – in whose works it appears; for the same phrase is also used by both Jerome and Augustine, from whom Columbanus is much more likely to have borrowed it.[120] Likewise, in *Epistula VI* (§ 1), the phrase, 'cui nimirum, ut ait quidam, etiam tuta timeo' evidently alludes to Vergil's description of Dido as 'omnia *tuta timens*' (*Aeneid* IV.298); but a much closer parallel to the phrase as it appears in the *Epistula* can be found in one of Jerome's letters, '*huic* ego, *ut ait* gentilis poeta, omnia *etiam tuta timeo*' (*Epistula* VII.iv.1).[121] Smit's reservations about classical borrowings in the *Epistulae* are therefore generally convincing. This does not of course necessarily prove that

---

118 *Studies*, pp. 165–208.

119 *Ibid.*, pp. 188–97.

120 *Ibid.*, pp. 206, 208 and 154, n. 22.

121 *Ibid.*, pp. 202–3, comparing also Jerome, *Epistula* XXX.14.1, '*cui* omnia *etiam* quae *tuta* sunt *timeo*'. A similar case is the Sallustian expression 'contra ius fasque' employed by Columbanus in *Epistula* I.3 (p. 4): to Smit's parallels from Rufinus and Jerome (*Studies*, p. 208), can be added Gildas's use of the same phrase in *De excidio Britannie*, I.15 and II.34 (on which text, see further below, pp. 82–7).

Columbanus had not read any classical authors (for instance Vergil, whose works were apparently known to some writers in seventh-century Ireland); but if he had, they evidently exerted singularly little influence on his *Epistulae*.

Let us move on to the text which Columbanus clearly knew best, the Bible. He quotes from it constantly, the two scriptural borrowings found, it will be recalled, in the opening paragraphs of *Epistula V* being quite typical of Columbanus's practice in this respect.[122] It is, however, less certain in precisely what form or forms he used the Bible-text. His borrowings agree sometimes with the Vulgate, sometimes with the *Vetus Latina*, and often with neither – and include some examples which Walker terms 'peculiar'.[123] For instance, the quotation of Proverbs XXVII.6 in *Epistula V* (§ 2) belongs to this latter group.[124] But whatever his precise sources, there can be no doubt that Columbanus knew the Scriptures intimately, as can be appreciated from the highly allusive way in which he often employs biblical quotations and echoes. This is particularly true of his second letter, as, for example, in the following passage (*Epistula* II.2):[125]

Ecce, inquam, Deo gratias quod uel pro me de Pascha discutiendo occasio uobis sanctae effecta est synodi. Dominus noster Iesus Christus, ille *princeps pastorum*, praestet, ut ad suae ecclesiae utilitatem uestrum prosit concilium; et ipse *Deus*, qui *stare* solet *in synagoga deorum*, praesens inspiret corda suorum ad suam ex integro uoluntatem sequendam ex uirtute mandatorum ut non de solo Paschae negotio, quod iam diu uentilatum ac diu uarie a diuersis auctoribus iudicatum est, tractetis; sed etiam de uniuersis necessariis obseruationibus canonicis, quae a multis, quod grauius est, corruptae sunt.

For Columbanus here, attack is the best form of defence. He thanks God that his dispute with the Gallic clergy over the date of Easter has caused them to call an assembly, and hopes that it will be to the benefit of all, since, as he goes on to point out, there are enough serious irregularities in the church of Gaul to

---

[122] See above, p. 39.

[123] See his useful biblical index (*Sancti Columbani Opera*, ed. & transl. Walker, pp. 216–20), where citations are divided into four classes: Vulgate, *Vetus Latina*, uncertain, and peculiar. Few would now agree with the assertion of Lomiento, 'La Bibbia', that some of the anomalies may be due to direct translation from the Septuagint (p. 25). Rather, it is possible that some of these 'peculiar' borrowings (as well as other citations) may be derived at second hand from patristic sources, as appears to be the case with several of the quotations discussed below (see pp. 73, 75, 79).

[124] See above, n. 52.

[125] *Sancti Columbani Opera*, ed. & transl. Walker, p. 12: 'Behold, I say, thanks be to God, that even on my account you have been afforded the chance of a holy synod to discuss Easter. May our Lord Jesus Christ, the chief of shepherds, permit your meeting to be for the good of His Church. May the presence of God himself, who is accustomed to stand in the assembly of the gods, inspire the hearts of His own people completely to follow His will through the strength of His commands, so that you discuss not only the business of Easter which has already been aired for a long time and for a long time variously decided by different authorities; but also all the necessary canonical observances, seeing that many people have broken them, which is a more serious matter.'

demand a general synod to correct them: in other words, Columbanus implies, the bishops would do better to put their own house in order before criticising himself and his monks. In this passage, Walker notes two borrowings from the Bible (in italics above). The first consists of the reference to Christ as 'ille princeps pastorum', 'the chief of shepherds'. At first sight, this epithet appears relatively commonplace, but in fact it occurs only once in the Bible, in I Peter V.4, 'cum apparuerit *princeps pastorum*'. Columbanus's use of the phrase is of course particularly appropriate for the clergy to whom his letter is directed: they are 'shepherds' and Christ should be their 'chief' and model, a theme which Columbanus will develop later in this same *Epistula*. However, once the context of the biblical allusion is recognised, then I Peter V is also found to contain several points which are germane to the argument of *Epistula II*. Thus, just as Columbanus is writing to the Gallic bishops, so Peter's addressees are the 'seniores\qui in uobis sunt' (V.1). Peter appeals to these *seniores* to 'pascite qui est in uobis gregem, prouidentes non coacto . . . neque ut dominantes in cleris' (V.2–3); but the bishops, far from protecting Columbanus and his monks, are instead highhandedly ('ut dominantes' as it were) threatening to expel them from Gaul, as the saint complains later (*Epistula* II.6–7).[126] In the verse from which Columbanus borrows the phrase 'princeps pastorum' (V.4), Peter promises the *seniores* that if they act as he advises, they will be rewarded with the kingdom of heaven. Conversely, Columbanus will later argue that his opponents are, through their persecution of his monks, jeopardising their own chances of eternal life (*Epistula* II.7–8). Peter then goes on to praise the value of humility, 'omnes autem inuicem humilitatem insinuite' (V.5).[127] Columbanus, as we shall see, is about to recommend humility as a prime christian virtue, one moreover which he sees as being more characteristic of monks than of the secular clergy.[128] It is, therefore, not hard to sense which side Christ would, in Columbanus's opinion, favour were he to be present at the synod of Châlons, particularly when we read in I Peter V.5, 'Deus superbis resistit, humilibus autem dat gratiam.'[129]

It might be objected, however, that, despite I Peter V.4 being the only place in the Bible in which the term 'princeps pastorum' appears, the phrase is too commonplace to trigger the series of associations suggested above. This would, in my opinion, be to underestimate the familiarity of Columbanus and his audience with the Bible. Nevertheless, with this objection in mind, let us consider the second of the biblical echoes in the passage set out above. This occurs in the phrase '*Deus* qui *stare* solet *in synagoga deorum*.' Columbanus's use of the very distinctive expression 'stare . . . in synagoga deorum' here puts

---

126 'Feed God's flock that is amongst you, ministering to it ungrudgingly . . . and not like tyrants among the clergy.' Peter's intervening point, that the *seniores* should act generously and not 'turpis lucri gratia' (I Peter V.2), could also reflect badly on the bishops, to whose simony Columbanus alludes in *Epistula* I.6 (ed. & transl. Walker, *Sancti Columbani Opera*, p. 8).

127 'You should all share humility together'; compare Columbanus's plea for unity at the end of the letter, where *inuicem* becomes a key word (*Epistula* II.9, *ibid.*, p. 22).

128 See especially *Epistula* II.8 (*ibid.*, p. 20), discussed below, pp. 67–8.

129 'God resists the proud, but shows His grace to the humble.'

it beyond doubt that he is alluding explicitly to Psalm LXXXI, which begins, 'Deus stetit in synagoga deorum' (verse 1). Why Columbanus should have employed this very unusual expression is however unclear, until we consider how Psalm LXXXI continues (verses 2–5):[130]

> 2. Usque quo iudicatis iniquitatem
> Et facies peccatorum sumitis?
> 3. Iudicate egenum et pupillum,
> Humilem et pauperem iustificate.
> 4. Eripite pauperem et egenum,
> De manu peccatoris liberate
> 5. Nescierunt neque intellexerunt: in tenebris ambulant.

The body of the psalm is thus an appeal to those who make wicked judgements, inciting them to protect the needy and the poor – advice which, in their benighted condition, they cannot grasp. One can easily appreciate the relevance, in Columbanus's eyes, of this psalm to his own situation. It is the judgements of the Gallic bishops which are wicked, being directed against him and his monks, whose poverty and humility ought rather to be protected. Columbanus therefore invokes God, Who is accustomed to 'stand in the assembly of the gods' in order to signal the injustice which is threatening him. The subtlest allusion, however, is certainly contained in the last of the verses quoted above. The root of Columbanus's difficulties with the ecclesiastical authorities in Gaul lay, it will be recalled, in their dispute over the date of Easter. Now one of Columbanus's objections to the Victorian cycle used by the Gallic church was that (in terms of the phases of the moon) it permitted Easter to be celebrated at a time when darkness prevailed over light – a 'Pascha tenebrosum' as he calls it.[131] As regards their celebration of Easter, he could therefore truly claim that the Gallic clergy, like the wicked in the psalm, walked 'in tenebris'. Citing the opening of Psalm LXXXI enables Columbanus implicitly to link what he perceives as his opponents' blind prejudice against him precisely to their paschal error: they 'walk in the darkness' not only metaphorically, by what he sees as their ungodly judgements, but also literally, by virtue of their espousal of a 'Pascha tenebrosum'. The biblical reference, once it is recognised, is well calculated to place the Gallic bishops, their synod and their paschal practices in the worst possible light.

Columbanus employs the Bible in the same allusive way in the following

---

[130] '[2] How long will you make wicked judgements and assume the appearance of sinners? [3] Make your judgements for the needy and the orphan; support the humble and the poor. [4] Save the poor and the needy; free them from the hand of the sinner. [5] But they know not, nor have they understood: they walk in darkness.'

[131] *Epistula* I.3 (ed. & transl. Walker, *Sancti Columbani Opera*, p. 2), 'Quid ergo dicis de Pascha uigesimae primae aut uigesimae secundae lunae, quod iam, tui tamen pace dictum sit, non esse *Pascha* – nimirum *tenebrosum* – a multis comprobatur calcenteris?'; and I.4 (*ibid.*, p. 4), 'Quare ergo tu, tam sapiens, nimirum cuius clarissima per orbem, ut antiquitus, sacri ingenii diffusa sunt lumina, *Pascha tenebrosum* colis?' (note that in the second passage Columbanus's imagery is more pointed if *lumina*, the reading of Fleming, is preferred to *flumina*, that of Metzler; cf. Smit, *Studies*, pp. 78– 80).

section of the letter (*Epistula* II.3). Picking up the theme that Christ should be a model for all, he advocates humility combined with the eight Beatitudes as the pathway to Heaven, a passage to which we shall need to return in connection with the saint's knowledge of Jerome.[132] He then continues:[133]

Dum ergo sicut scriptum est, '*Qui dicit se in* Christo credere, *debet et ipse ambulare sicut* et Christus *ambulauit*' – id est et pauper et humilis et ueritatem semper cum persecutione hominum praedicans – et iterum, '*Qui uolunt in Christo pie uiuere, persecutionem patientur*'.

This passage contains two biblical quotations, both of which call for comment. The first is a citation of I John II.6: '*qui dicit se in* ipso manere, *debet sicut* ille ambulauit et ipse ambulare.' Columbanus expounds this verse as meaning that the Christian must be poor, humble, and preach the truth even when facing persecution – which is clearly another lightly veiled reference to his own position as a lowly monk upholding the paschal traditions of his fathers in the teeth of opposition from his clerical adversaries. But if we set this biblical verse within its immediate context, as his readers – including the Gallic bishops – surely could, the implications become even more damning for his opponents. Just before the appeal to follow Christ cited by Columbanus, John had affirmed, 'qui dicit se nosse eum et mandata eius non custodit, mendax est: in hoc ueritas non est' (II.4).[134] The bishops' moral laxity, we may therefore infer, makes them deceivers, and so denies the truth of their position. Moreover, John goes on (II.7–11):[135]

> 7. Carissimi, non mandatum nouum scribo uobis,
> Sed mandatum uetus quod habuistis ab initio.
> Mandatum uetus est uerbum quod audistis.
> 8. Iterum mandatum nouum scribo uobis
> quod est uerum et in ipso et in uobis,
> quoniam tenebrae transeunt et lumen uerum iam lucet.
> 9. Qui dicit se in luce esse et fratrem suum odit
> in tenebris est usque adhuc.
> 10. Qui diligit fratrem suum
> in lumine manet et scandalum in eo non est.
> 11. Qui autem odit fratrem suum
> in tenebris est et in tenebris ambulat et nescit quo eat,
> quoniam tenebrae obcaecauerunt oculos eius.

---

[132] See below, pp. 67–8.

[133] *Sancti Columbani Opera*, ed. & transl. Walker, p. 14: 'Seeing then that, as is written, "He who says that he believes in Christ, ought himself to walk as Christ walked" – namely by being both poor and humble and always preaching the truth despite persecution from men – and also that, "Those who wish to live a pious life in Christ, will suffer persecution." '

[134] 'He who says that he knows Him but does not keep his commandments, is deceitful. There is no truth in him.'

[135] '[7] Dearest, I do not write a new instruction for you, but the old instruction which you had from the beginning. The old instruction is the word which you have heard. [8] Again, I write a new instruction for you, which is true in Him and in you, for the darkness is passing and the true light shines. [9] He who says that he is in the light

These verses, and particularly the imagery of dark and light which they contain, can again be interpreted as relating directly to the paschal dispute in which Columbanus was embroiled. Like John (verse 7), Columbanus is championing an old rather than a new instruction: he advocates the traditional Easter cycle of Anatolius, not that of 'Victorius who wrote recently and uncertainly' ('Victorium nuper dubie scribentem': *Epistula* II.7). Furthermore Columbanus's actual 'nouum mandatum' (cf. verse 8) is one which completely discredits his critics: their claim to be in the right (or 'in the light', verse 9) and their subsequent hostility to Columbanus (or 'hating their brother') simply shows that they are really as benighted as their 'Pascha tenebrosum' would suggest; for it is Columbanus, the humble monk who loves his brothers, that 'remains in the light' (verse 10) both in his moral behaviour and (literally) as regards Easter. The very virulence of the Gallic clergy's attack upon him is, Columbanus implies, no more than another proof that they 'walk in darkness' (verse 11; cf. Psalm LXXXI.5), and an example of the sort of persecution which he must be prepared to endure as a true follower of Christ.

A second biblical citation follows almost immediately in the passage under discussion. Columbanus quotes St Paul's Second Letter to Timothy, 'et omnes *qui uolunt pie uiuere in Christo* Iesu *persecutionem patientur*' (II Timothy III.12). He thus reinforces the supposition that antagonism towards him comes as a direct result of his efforts to live the christian life. However, recognition of the biblical context of this quotation again adds a subtext to his assertion. II Timothy, chapter 3, begins with the statement that times will be dangerous in the last days, 'in nouissimis diebus instabunt tempora periculosa' (verse 1). Likewise Columbanus has just reminded his readers that the Day of Judgement grows ever more imminent, 'dies iudicii propior nunc est quam tunc' (*Epistula* II.2). St Paul continues by describing the men of that time (verses 2–9): amongst other things they will be 'elati, superbi' (verse 2), 'sine affectione, sine pace, criminatores' (verse 3), and 'proditores, proterui, tumidi' (verse 4). And if this is not enough for the opponents of the 'humble' Columbanus, we learn that these men will also be 'habentes speciem quidem pietatis, uirtutem autem eius [viz. Dei] abnegantes' (verse 5).[136] As for their teaching, they will be 'semper discentes et numquam ad scientiam ueritatis uenientes' (verse 7); like Jannes and Mambres, 'et hii resistunt ueritati' (verse 8), but in vain, 'insipientia enim eorum manifesta erit omnibus' (verse 9).[137] Those who persecute the true christian will thus be arrogant hypocrites, vainly seeking in their stupidity to suppress the truth. For Columbanus, the implication is once again that the clergy's very opposition to him is in itself sufficient evidence to discredit the Victorian Easter cycle which they were seeking to impose on his monks. Moreover, in the verses that follow (including that quoted by

---

but hates his brother, is still in the darkness. [10] He who loves his brother remains in the light, and there is no stumbling-block in his case. [11] But he who hates his brother, is in darkness, walks in darkness, and does not know where he is going since the darkness has blinded his eyes.'

[136] 'Having the appearance of holiness, yet denying His power.'

[137] 'Always learning, yet never attaining knowledge of the truth'; 'they too resist the truth'; 'for their foolishness will be clear to all'.

Columbanus), Paul praises Timothy for his steadfastness, closing with the injunction, 'tu uero permane in his quae didicisti'.[138] This is precisely what Columbanus is doing, vigorously defending the paschal practices of his Irish teachers against adversaries whom he sees as ignorant, biased and hypocritical. Biblical allusions of the sort we have been discussing show how powerful a weapon the Scriptures could be in Columbanus's conduct of that defence.

In addition to the Bible, Columbanus was also familiar with the works of a number of Church Fathers. The patristic author he most admired was unquestionably Jerome. When writing to Gregory the Great about the paschal question for instance, Columbanus specifically warns the Pope not to contradict Jerome's authority (*Epistula* I.5):[139]

Tua itaque consideret uigilantia, ut in fide supradictorum auctorum sibi inuicem contrariorum probanda, nulla sit inter te et Hieronymum in sententia promenda dissonantia, ne 'nobis undique sint angustiae', ut aut tibi aut illi consentiamus. Parce in hoc infirmis, ne scandalum diuersitatis ostendas. Simpliciter enim ego tibi confiteor, quod contra sancti Hieronymi auctoritatem ueniens apud occidentis ecclesias hereticus seu respuendus erit, quicumque ille fuerit; illi enim per omnia indubitatam in scripturis diuinis accommodant fidem.

Even a pope as prestigious as Gregory, a considerable author and exegete in his own right, is not in Columbanus's opinion to be preferred to Jerome on this issue.

On which of Jerome's writings was Columbanus's admiration based? Certainly he knew parts of the Scriptures in Jerome's Vulgate version, as Walker's list of biblical borrowings shows.[140] He also used Jerome's *De uiris illustribus* as a work of reference, citing on two occasions its favourable assessment of Anatolius of Laodicea.[141] As to exegetical texts, Columbanus mentions at the end of his letter to Gregory the Great having read part at least of Jerome's commentary on Ezekiel; after requesting a copy of the Pope's homilies on the same prophet, he pays Gregory the compliment of stating, 'Legi Hieronymi

---

[138] 'You, however, should stand by what you have learnt.'

[139] *Sancti Columbani Opera*, p. 8: 'You should diligently take care, therefore, that in testing the faith of the two contradictory authorities mentioned above, there should, when you pass judgement, be no discord between yourself and Jerome; otherwise, we should be in difficulties on both sides, as to whether we should agree with you or him. Spare our weakness in this; do not allow disagreement to be a stumbling-block. I tell you simply that anyone who challenges the authority of St Jerome will in the eyes of the western churches be viewed as heretical or worthy of rejection, whoever he may be; for on Jerome they place a reliance unquestioned in all matters of holy scripture' (note that in the last clause I have preferred Metzler's reading *illi* to the emendation *illae* printed by Walker).

[140] Indeed Columbanus's rhetorical questions, '*Quis non statim* dicat ... *Quis ... non confestim in* illud antiquum probosum *erumpat* elogium' (*Epistula* V.2, ed. & transl. Walker, *Sancti Columbani Opera*, p. 36), may be modelled on Jerome's similar conceit in his preface to the Vulgate Gospels (*Biblia Sacra*, ed. Weber, p. 1515), '*Quis* enim ... *non statim erumpat in* uocem.'

[141] The two passages in question are quoted below n. 165; both refer to *De uiris illustribus*, § 73 (*Patrologia Latina*, ed. Migne, XXIII.719).

sex in illum libros; sed nec medium exposuit' (*Epistula* I.9).[142] However, despite knowing Jerome's commentary, Columbanus does not seem to have made any use of it in the surviving *Epistulae*.

The same cannot be said of Jerome's *Commentarii in Matheum*.[143] As Walker has noted, Columbanus draws on this work twice in his letter to the Gallic bishops. On both occasions, moreover, these borrowings play a key role in Columbanus's argument. The first occurs in the passage where he is lecturing his opponents about humility. He offers them the following exposition of the Beatitudes (*Epistula* II.3):[144]

Sed sufficiat significasse unumquemque ad sui redemptoris exemplum ac ueri pastoris formam fore informandum, qui humilitatem primum praedicans, septemque beatitudines primae paupertati spiritus iungens, in tantum docuit hominem sua sequi uestigia, ut ad *ueram* octaui diei *circumcisionem* iustitiam sequendo peruenriet; quia *beatitudo octaua martyrio terminetur*, eo quod non solum agendo iustus, sed etiam pro iustitia sustinendo martyr, regni nimirum caelestis cupidus, et cum similiter certantibus coronatur.

It is significant that Columbanus does not explicitly quote the eighth and last Beatitude here. It runs, 'beati qui persecutionem patiuntur propter iustitiam quoniam ipsorum est regnum caeli' (Matthew V.10).[145] As has often been the case already, Columbanus's allusion is not a flattering one for his Gallic opponents. For it is he and his monks who are, in his view, being 'persecuted for the sake of righteousness'. The implication is therefore that it is they who will receive the kingdom of heaven – and not the Gallic bishops who are persecuting them, a point which we shall see Columbanus making again later. Furthermore, his allegorical description of the eighth Beatitude as a true circumcision of the eighth day terminating in martyrdom constitutes a covert threat of how far he is prepared to go over his differences with the Gallic clergy: in their quest for righteousness he and his monks are ready, if necessary, for martyrdom at the hands of their opponents. Now, it is precisely a reminiscence of Jerome which permits Columbanus to take this stance. In his commentary on Matthew V.10, Jerome too identifies the eighth Beatitude with the true circumcision of the eighth day (viz. of Christ; cf.

---

[142] *Sancti Columbani Opera*, ed. & transl. Walker, p. 10: 'I have read Jerome's six books on the prophet, but he did not expound even half' (apparently Columbanus did not know all fourteen books of Jerome's commentary).

[143] *Sancti Hieronymi Commentarii in Matheum*, edd. Hurst & Adriaen.

[144] 'But let it be sufficient to have shown that each man should be shaped after the model of his redeemer and in the mould of the true shepherd. He preached first humility and added seven beatitudes to poverty of spirit which is the first, teaching man to follow so completely in his footsteps that his quest for righteousness leads him to the true circumcision of the eighth day; for the eighth beatitude ends in martyrdom, because a man is not only righteous through his actions, but also by enduring as a martyr for righteousness' sake, since he is eager for the heavenly kingdom, and so is crowned along with those who strive as he does.'

[145] 'Blessed are those who suffer persecution for righteousness' sake, for theirs is the kingdom of heaven.'

Luke II.21), and, exactly like Columbanus, notes that its culmination is martyrdom:[146]

Simulque considera quod *octaua uerae circumcisionis beatitudo martyrio terminatur.*

Columbanus thus owes directly to Jerome not only the exegetical identification of the eighth Beatitude with Christ's circumcision, but also the ominous observation that it can end in martyrdom.

Columbanus has recourse to Jerome's commentary again later in *Epistula II.* Thus, having commented (§ 7) that only a few choose the narrow path (cf. Matthew VII.13–14), Columbanus warns that such people should find help rather than hindrance from the clergy, lest Christ say to them, 'Woe to you, scribes and Pharisees, since you shut the kingdom of God before men; neither do you enter yourselves nor do you permit those going in to enter' (Matthew XXIII.13). This is an explicit warning to his opponents that by persecuting Columbanus and his monks they are putting their own souls at risk. Immediately after this passage, he introduces an interlocutor who asks if the Gallic bishops are then not entering the kingdom of heaven (*Epistula* II.8):[147]

Sed dicet aliquis: Numquid nos non intramus in regnum caelorum? Quare non potestis iuxta gratiam Domini, si efficiamini sicut paruuli, humiles scilicet et casti, simplices et innocentes in malo, prudentes tamen in bono, placabiles et iram in corde non tenentes? Sed complere haec omnia mulieres saepe uidentes et circa mundi facultates saepius rixantes et irascentes difficillime possunt. Idcirco nostri, semel mundo renuntiantes et causas uitiorum ac fomites iurgiorum in primis amputantes, facilius nudos quam diuites sermonem Domini posse complere arbitrantur. Ante istas etenim quattuor res regnum caelorum non intratur sicut sanctus Hieronymus trium testis est et quarti Basilius, qui iuxta euangelici uim dicti mores exponunt infantium. Infans enim humilis est, *non laesus meminit, non mulierem uidens* concupiscit, *non aliud* ore, *aliud* corde habet.

For Columbanus, the interlocutor's question evokes that of the disciples in Matthew XVIII.1, 'quis putas maior est in regno caelorum?' ('Who do you think is greater in the kingdom of heaven?'); to which Christ replies that, in

---

[146] *Sancti Hieronymi Commentarii in Matheum,* edd. Hurst & Adriaen, p. 25: 'Consider too that the eighth beatitude, that of the true circumcision, ends in martyrdom.'

[147] *Sancti Columbani Opera,* ed. & transl. Walker, p. 20: 'But someone will say: "Are we not then entering into the kingdom of heaven?" And why should you not with the Lord's grace, provided that you become like little children, namely humble, chaste, simple-hearted, guileless in evil yet wise in goodness, forgiving and harbouring no anger in your hearts? But all that can only with difficulty be achieved by those who often view women and more often squabble angrily over the riches of the world. For this reason those of our persuasion, once renouncing the world and cutting off especially everything that causes sins and instigates disputes, think that it is more easy for the naked than the rich to fulfil the Lord's commandment. No-one can gain entry to the kingdom of heaven before acquiring these four attributes, three of which are witnessed by Jerome and the fourth by Basil, who explain the character of children according to the force of the Gospel-saying. For a child is humble, easily forgets an injury, experiences no desire on seeing a woman, and does not say one thing while feeling another in his heart.'

order to enter the kingdom of heaven, they must become humble like little children (Matthew XVIII.3–4). Columbanus skilfully turns this reply against the Gallic clergy. Moreover, to do so, he adapts Jerome's commentary on these verses, where the exegete explains why it is the childlike who will be rewarded with heaven:[148]

Quicumque ergo humiliauerit se sicut paruulus iste, hic est maior in regno caelorum [Mt XVIII.4]. Sicut iste paruulus cuius uobis exemplum tribuo non perseuerat in iracundia, *non laesus meminit, non uidens* pulchram *mulierem* delectatur, *non aliud* cogitat et *aliud* loquitur, sic et uos nisi talem habueritis innocentiam et animi puritatem regna caelorum non poteritis intrare.

From Jerome Columbanus borrowed the definition of a child's character as being forgiving, devoid of lust, and without dissemblance.[149] But he gave the gospel verse a new twist. In his opinion, those who can most easily attain this childlike innocence are monks like himself and his followers who have renounced the world ('Nostri ... mundo renuntiantes'). Not so the secular clergy, who frequently see women, and wrangle angrily over worldly possessions ('mulieres saepe uidentes, et circa mundi facultates saepius rixantes et irascentes' – the latter attribute also contrasting with Jerome's observation that the child does not persist in anger, 'non perseuerat in iracundia'). Once again Columbanus asserts his own moral superiority, by virtue of his status as a monk, while at the same time discrediting his opponents. Moreover, by alluding to Jerome he has effectively answered the objection raised by the interlocutor: to enter the kingdom of heaven the clergy must become as innocent as only children (and monks) can be, for as Jerome says, 'nisi talem habueritis innocentiam et animi puritatem, regna caelorum non poteritis intrare.' It is their own souls that the bishops should therefore be worried about; and, Columbanus implies, if they wish to reform, what better way than to begin by ceasing their unchristian persecution of himself and his monks. Jerome's commentary thus, like the Bible itself, furnishes Columbanus with useful ammunition in his dispute with the clergy.

In addition to the commentary on Matthew, Columbanus also knew Jerome's *Epistulae*, which were clearly an important model for his own letters.[150] The most extensive borrowing occurs in his *Epistula I*, when Columbanus expresses his desire to visit Gregory the Great in Rome (§ 8):[151]

---

[148] *Sancti Hieronymi Commentarii in Matheum*, edd. Hurst & Adriaen, p. 157: 'Whoever humbles himself like this little child, he is greater in the kingdom of heaven [Matthew XVIII.4]. Just as this little child, whom I offer you as a model, does not persist in anger, easily forgets an injury, takes no pleasure in seeing a beautiful woman, and does not think one thing while saying another, so you will not be able to enter the kingdom of heaven unless you possess similar innocence and purity of mind.'

[149] Conversely Columbanus's reference to Basil remains puzzling. I am not convinced by Walker's suggestion that he is alluding to *Interrogationes* §§ 161 and 163 (in Rufinus's translation), for which, see *Basili Regula*, ed. Zelzer, pp. 184–5, 186–7.

[150] *Sancti Eusebii Hieronymi Epistolae*, ed. Hilberg.

[151] *Sancti Columbani Opera*, ed. & transl. Walker, p. 10: 'And, if my body could follow

Et si animum corpus sequeretur, Roma iterum sui rem sustineret contemptus, ut, quomodo docto narrante Hieronymo *legimus, quosdam de ultimis* hyalini littoris *finibus* olim *uenisse* Romam et, mirum dictu, *aliud extra Romam quaesisse*, ita et ego nunc te, non Romam, desiderans, salua sanctorum reuerentia cinerum, expeterem; licet enim non me sapientem, sed esse sitientem fateor hoc idem facerem si uacarem.

Columbanus compliments Gregory by saying that the object of his journey to Rome would be to see the pope rather than the city itself. The reference to Jerome adduces a classical precedent for such an attitude. In one of his letters, Jerome relates the famous story of a Spaniard who journied to Rome not to see the city, but one man famous for his literary endeavours, Livy:[152]

Ad Titum Liuium lacteo eloquentiae fonte manantem uisendum *de ultimo* terrarum orbe uenisse Gaditanum *quendam legimus*; et quem ad contemplationem sui Roma non traxerat, uel unius hominis fama perduxerat. Habuit illa aetas inauditum omnibus saeculis celebrandumque miraculum, ut orbem totum ingressus, *alium extra* orbem *quaereret*.

Despite his explicit citation of Jerome, however, Columbanus's version of this story does not at first sight seem noticeably close to his alleged source. Columbanus refers to several visitors (*quosdam*) rather than the one man from Cadiz (*Gaditanum quendam*) mentioned by Jerome. Neither are the verbal parallels between the two passages particularly compelling. We might there-fore be tempted to think that Columbanus was here citing a passage of Jerome which he only dimly remembered. In fact, this case provides an excellent example of the dangers inherent in using modern editions. The text of Jerome's letter quoted above is that preferred and printed by Hilberg (which rests partially on conjectural emendation).[153] However, a number of manuscripts preserves a somewhat different version of the story:[154]

---

my mind, Rome should again endure the fact of being scorned: just as we read in Jerome's learned account how certain people once came to Rome from the farthest reaches of the green seashore and sought, astonishing to relate, something other than Rome, so would I now seek not Rome but you, excepting only my reverence for the ashes of her saints. For though I avow that I do not have knowledge but rather thirst for it, I would do that same thing were I at liberty.' I have adopted here Smit's emendation *hyalini* (for *Hyelini* printed by Walker); see further Smit, *Studies*, pp. 105–9.

152 *Epistula* LIII.1 (ed. Hilberg, *Sancti Eusebii Hieronymi Epistolae*, I.443–4): 'We read that a certain inhabitant of Cadiz came from the farthest edge of the world to see Titus Livius, who distilled a stream of nourishing elequence; Rome did not draw him to see her, it was the reputation of one single man that had attracted him. That age witnessed a notable miracle, unheard of throughout the centuries: a man travelled the world to see something other than the world.'

153 Cf. Smit, *Studies*, pp. 105–7.

154 'We read that certain nobles came from the farthest reaches of Spain and Gaul to see Titus Livius, who distilled a stream of nourishing eloquence; those whom Rome had not drawn to see her were attracted by the reputation of a single man. That age witnessed a notable miracle, unheard of throughout the centuries: having entered so famous a city, they sought something other than that city.'

Ad T. Liuium lacteo eloquentiae fonte manantem *de ultimis* Hispaniae Galliarumque *finibus quosdam uenisse* nobiles *legimus*; et quos ad contemplationem sui Roma non traxerat, unius hominis fama perduxit. Habuit illa aetas inauditum omnibus saeculis celebrandumque miraculum ut urbem tantam ingressi, *aliud extra urbem quaererent.*

Evidently Columbanus used a similar manuscript, and, as the verbal parallels show (compare in particular *'aliud extra* Romam *quaesisse'* and 'ut . . . *aliud extra* urbem *quaererent'*), worked from it closely. Moreover, this passage shows that he employed Jerome's letter in the same allusive way in which we have seen him borrowing from the commentary on Matthew. When retelling Jerome's story, Columbanus does not mention the precise object of the visitors to Rome, namely to see Livy. He evidently expects the learned pope to whom he addresses the letter to know the details of the story and so to appreciate the graceful tribute that Columbanus is paying him: not only does he, as an Irishman, 'from the ends of the earth' ('de extremo mundo ueniens': *Epistula* V.8), long to go to Rome to see the pope rather than his city, but he also, by means of the reference to Jerome, elegantly implies that Gregory is a writer of the same calibre as a great classical historian, Livy.

A further borrowing from Jerome's *Epistulae* has been identified in Columbanus's letter to the Gallic clergy, *Epistula II.* The reminiscence occurs in a passage particularly rich in literary allusions, that where he contrasts the respective roles of monks and secular clergy. We have already seen how Jerome's commentary on Matthew is used there to highlight the innocence of the monastic life. Columbanus goes on to state that those who remain in the world cannot appreciate the advantages of monastic life, and observes (*Epistula* II.8):[155]

Inde sanctus Hieronymus haec sciens iussit *episcopos imitari apostolos, monachos* docuit sequi *patres perfectos.*

Walker, without comment, identifies as the source of Jerome's teaching the following passage from his *Epistulae* (note that 'Nos' here refers to monks):[156]

episcopi et presbyteri habeant in exemplum *apostolos* et apostolicos uiros, quorum honorem possidentes habere nitantur et meritum. Nos autem habemus propositi nostri principes Paulos, Antonios, Iulianos, Hilarionas, Macarios.

Again it would appear that, although the advice given in both passages is fundamentally the same, Columbanus is paraphrasing Jerome rather than following his wording closely. However, the text quoted above is once more that printed by Hilberg. One early and somewhat eccentric manuscript (Lyon,

---

[155] *Sancti Columbani Opera,* ed. & transl. Walker, p. 20: 'Therefore Jerome, recognising this, instructed bishops to imitate the apostles, but taught monks to follow fathers who were perfect.'

[156] *Epistula* LVIII.5 (ed. Hilberg, *Sancti Eusebii Hieronymi Epistolae,* II.534): 'Let bishops and priests take as models the apostles and apostolic men; since they possess their honour, let them also strive to attain their worth. We have as leaders in our calling the likes of Paul the hermit, Anthony, Julian, Hilarion, and Macarius.'

Bibliothèque de la ville, 600, *saec.* vi) offers the following – completely different – version of Jerome's words:[157]

episcopi imitentur apostolos et monachi perfectos patres ut quorum honorem possident, habere nitantur et meritum.

Columbanus clearly knew Jerome's letter in a similar version, which he quotes here with only a minimum of verbal recasting.

There are, moreover, other, unnoticed borrowings from Jerome's letters in the *Epistulae* of Columbanus. The distinction between monks and the secular clergy is also a central theme in one of Jerome's most famous letters, *Epistula XIV*, addressed to the recalcitrant monk Heliodorus. Since this letter was so well known, we might well expect Columbanus to have had it in mind when discussing the same subject. After the citation of Jerome which we have just been considering, Columbanus continues (*Epistula* II.8):[158]

Alia enim sunt et *alia clericorum* et *monachorum* documenta, ea et longe ab inuicem separata.

The same sentiment is almost identically expressed by Jerome in *Epistula XIV* (§ 8):[159]

Sed *alia*, ut perstrinxi, *monachi* est causa, *alia clericorum*.

One might object that in this case the similarity of diction has arisen through coincidence, since both authors are making the same general point. That this is not so is suggested both by the fact that Columbanus has just cited another of Jerome's letters, and also, as we shall see, by the very density of literary allusion in this section of *Epistula II*.

Furthermore, there is another incontestable reminiscence of Jerome's *Epistula XIV* in Columbanus's *Epistula V*, that to Pope Boniface IV. There, after warning the pope of the dangers of complacency, Columbanus continues (*Epistula* V.4):[160]

Non sufficit tibi, quod pro te ipso sollicitus sis, qui multorum curam suscepisti; *cui* enim *plus creditur, plus ab eo exigitur.*

As a possible source for the *sententia* 'cui ... plus creditur, plus ab eo exigitur' Walker cites Luke XII.48, 'Omni autem cui multum datum est, multum quaeretur ab eo et cui commendauerunt multum, plus petent ab eo.'[161]

---

157 'Let bishops imitate the apostles, and monks fathers who are perfect, so that they strive to attain the worth of those whose honour they possess.'

158 *Sancti Columbani Opera*, ed. & transl. Walker, p. 20: 'For the examples of clerics are one thing and of monks another, being entirely distinct from each other.'

159 *Epistula XIV*.8 (ed. Hilberg, *Sancti Eusebii Hieronymi Epistulae*, I.55): 'The case of the monk, as I said before, is one thing, that of clerics another.'

160 *Sancti Columbani Opera*, ed. & transl. Walker, p. 40: 'It is not sufficient that you look after yourself, since you have undertaken to care for many; for more is required from the man to whom more is entrusted.'

161 'For much will be sought from every man to whom much has been given, and they shall ask more of the man to whom they have entrusted much.'

If that were the case, Columbanus's citation would certainly be 'peculiar', as Walker terms it in his biblical index. In fact, it is Jerome's letter to Heliodorus which is the source. There Jerome utters a similar warning to those who enjoy worldly power (*Epistula* XIV.9):[162]

Cui plus creditur, plus ab eo exigitur. Potentes potenter tormenta patientur.

The second part of Jerome's warning is a quotation (of Wisdom VI.3), but no source has been discovered for the first. Most likely, he is reworking passages like Luke XII.48, expressing the biblical idea in a shorter, more neatly balanced form. Doubtless it was this rhetorical balance that appealed to Columbanus, when he took over Jerome's words verbatim in *Epistula* V.4. Moreover, the borrowing is once again pointed within its context: once Pope Boniface recognised its source, Columbanus's admonition also carried with it the unexpressed but highly apt reminder that, should they fail, 'the mighty will suffer mighty torments'.[163]

Passing on now to a different author, Columbanus was also familiar with the writings of Rufinus, Jerome's erstwhile friend and later literary foe. On several occasions Columbanus makes use of Rufinus's best known work, the translation of Eusebius's *Historia ecclesiastica*.[164] For instance, in both *Epistulae I* and *II*, he cites references to Anatolius of Laodicea in the *Historia ecclesiastica* in conjunction with others from Jerome's *De uiris illustribus*;[165] and, at the end

---

[162] *Sancti Eusebii Hieronymi Epistulae*, ed. Hilberg, I.58: 'More is required from the man to whom more is entrusted. The mighty will suffer mighty torments.'

[163] It is also likely, as Winterbottom has observed ('Columbanus and Gildas', p. 313, n. 16), that in *Epistula* V.3 (ed. & transl. Walker, *Sancti Columbani Opera*, p. 38), the striking expression *'cautis spumosis concauae uorticibus'* is modelled on Jerome's *Epistula* XIV.10 (ed. Hilberg, *Sancti Eusebii Hieronymi Epistulae*, I.59), 'inter *cauas spumeis* [var. *concauas spumosis*] fluctibus *cautes* fragilis in altum cumba processit' (cf. also the phrase *'fragilis* ingenii *cymba* non tam *in altum* . . . ducta est' in *Epistula* V.8 (*ibid.*, p. 44; but see further p. 78 below); and compare the idioms *'epistolaris breuitas'* (*Epistula* I.8, *ibid.*, pp. 8–10) and 'epistolae *angustiis*' (*Epistula* V.8, *ibid.*, p. 44) with the similar literary term *epistularis angustia* used in the letter of Jerome from which Columbanus drew the story about Livy (*Epistula* LIII.6, ed. Hilberg, *Sancti Eusebii Hieronymi Epistulae*, II.452). Finally, Columbanus's apology, 'indulgete mihi talia *confragosa loca* tractanti' (*Epistula* V.11, ed. & transl. Walker, *Sancti Columbani Opera*, p. 48) echoes a favourite Hieronyman metaphor; cf., for instance, 'quoniam iam e cautibus et *confragosis locis* enauigauit oratio', *De perpetua uirginitate beatae Mariae*, § 17 (*Patrologia Latina*, ed. Migne, XXIII.211).

[164] Ed. Mommsen, *Die lateinische Übersetzung*.

[165] *Epistula* I.3 (ed. & transl. Walker, *Sancti Columbani Opera*, p. 2): 'Anatolius "mirae doctrinae uir", ut sanctus ait Hieronymus, cuius Eusebius Caesariensis episcopus in ecclesiastica excerpta inseruit historia'; and *Epistula* II.7 (*ibid.*, p. 18): 'Anatolium ab Eusebio ecclesiasticae historiae auctore episcopo et sancto catalogi scriptore Hieronymo laudatum.' Anatolius's career is recounted in *Historia Ecclesiastica* VII.32.6–20, esp. 14–19 (ed. Mommsen, *Die lateinische Übersetzung*, pp. 719–27). It is also likely that a reference to the views of Bishop Victor in *Epistula* I.4 (ed. & transl. Walker, *Sancti Columbani Opera*, p. 6), 'Cum Iudaeis facere Pascha non debemus. Dixit hoc olim Victor episcopus, sed nemo orientalium suum recepit commentum', is, as Walker suggests, derived from *Historia Ecclesiastica* V.22–3.

of *Epistula III*, Columbanus's allusion to the compromise over the Paschal question between Pope Anicetus and Polycarp (in which, significantly enough, the pope deferred to his opponent) is also very likely derived from Rufinus.[166] Moreover, J.W. Smit has shown that Columbanus also draws on a less familiar work of Rufinus, his translation of a number of sermons by the Greek father Gregory of Nazianzus.[167] In the second letter, again in the passage where he describes the superiority of the monastic life, Columbanus quotes a *dictum* from Gregory (*Epistula* II.8):[168]

Ipsi *non credunt bonis secretis*, ut sanctus ait Gregorius, qui *publica mala non deuitant*.

The allusion is to a passage in the first of the sermons translated by Rufinus:[169]

Paratior namque est inperitorum turba ad derogandum bonis studiis quam ad imitandum ut sit eis omni genere delictum uel dum manifesta et *publica mala non uitant* uel dum *occultis et reconditis non credunt bonis*.

Although Columbanus has slightly modified the language of his source, the similarity of context and the close verbal parallels place his reliance on Rufinus beyond doubt here. Furthermore, recognition of the original context of the borrowing adds a characteristic barb to Columbanus's citation. It implies that the Gallic bishops' antagonism against himself and his monks is the result of their spiritual inexperience, and so enables Columbanus to represent the clergy as an 'inperitorum turba' who are too quick to criticise practices that they should rather be imitating.

---

[166] *Epistula* III.2 (ed. & transl. Walker, *Sancti Columbani Opera*, p. 24), 'sicut sancti patres, Polycarpus scilicet et papa Anicetus, sine scandalo *fidei*, immo cum *integra caritate* perseuerantes – unusquisque quod accepit seruans et "in quo uocatus est permanens" [cf. I Cor. VII.20] – docuerunt'; the story is told in *Historia Ecclesiastica* V.24.16–17 (ed. Mommsen, *Die lateinische Übersetzung*, p. 497), where the two are said to part 'plena *fide* pace *integra* et firma *caritate*.'

[167] Ed. Engelbrecht, *Tyrannii Rufini . . . interpretatio*.

[168] *Sancti Columbani Opera*, ed. & transl. Walker, p. 20: 'But, as St Gregory says, those who do not avoid public sins cannot believe in hidden good deeds.' I have not accepted Walker's unnecessary emendation *creduntur* (for *credunt*, the reading of both Fleming and Metzler), which he made under the mistaken impression that Columbanus was here citing Gregory the Great; Walker compared *Regula pastoralis* III.35 (*Patrologia Latina*, ed. Migne, LXXVII.119), 'Aliter admonendi sunt qui mala occulte agunt, et bona publice; atque aliter qui bona quae faciunt abscondunt, et tamen quibusdam factis publice male de se opinari permittunt' ('Those who commit sins in secret and good deeds in public should be admonished differently from those who hide the good they do, but allow themselves to be badly thought of in some of their public actions'). However, as has rightly been observed by Smit, who first identified Rufinus as the true source of this quotation, Pope Gregory's meaning is there entirely different from the point which Columbanus is making (*Studies*, pp. 112–15).

[169] *Apologeticus* § 7.3 (ed. Engelbrecht, *Tyrannii Rufini . . . interpretatio*, p. 12): 'For the crowd of the inexperienced is more ready to detract from good efforts than to imitate them, so that they err in all cases either by not avoiding open and public sins or by not believing in unseen and hidden good deeds.'

The same strategy lies behind a second borrowing from Rufinus's translation. Earlier in the same letter, Columbanus had conceded that, if the opposition of the clergy is part of God's plan, he is prepared to go into exile (*Epistula* II.7):[170]

Nam si ex Deo est ut me hinc de loco deserti, quem pro domino meo Iesu Christo de trans mare petiui, propellatis, meum erit *illud propheticum dicere, 'Si propter me haec tempestas est super nos, tollite me et mittite me in mare* ut *commotio* haec quiescat *a uobis.'*

The prophet whom Columbanus cites here is, of course, his namesake Jonah, but his apparent quotation of Jonah I.12 agrees with the versions of neither the Vulgate nor the *Vetus Latina*, it being one of the scriptural borrowings termed 'peculiar' by Walker. In fact, Columbanus is not thinking of the biblical text itself, but of a similar allusion to it in the preface to Rufinus's translation. It is there recounted how Gregory of Nazianzus left Byzantium in order to put an end to disunity within the church:[171]

Ubi cum magnificum opus in uerbo Dei ageret et infinitas cottidie paene multitudines ab hereticis ad fidem ueram conuerteret, ut fieri solet, gloriam aemulatio subsecuta est. Ille uero tam erat in timore Dei perfectus ut, cum sensisset causa sui esse inter episcopos disceptationem, statim sponte discederet *dicens illum* tantummodo *propheticum* sermonem: '*Si propter me est tempestas* ista [var. *haec tempestas*], *tollite me et mittite* [var. *mittite me*] *in mare* et desinat *a uobis commotio.*'

As the verbal parallels indicated above show, Columbanus clearly borrowed his quotation of Jonah directly from Rufinus's preface. His reason for so doing, however, is not simply to draw another parallel between himself and Jonah (both their names meaning, it will be remembered, 'dove'). For he is also subtly comparing himself to Gregory of Nazianzus, who was unfairly driven from Constantinople through the envy of his ecclesiatical foes. Columbanus implies that the attacks of his Gallic opponents are similarly motivated by jealousy for his achievements; he, however, is prepared if necessary to embrace exile with as good a christian grace as Gregory once did for the sake of church unity. For an audience that knew Rufinus's version of Gregory's sermons, both Columbanus's borrowings were thus pointedly effective in their context.[172]

---

[170] *Sancti Columbani Opera*, ed. & transl. Walker, p. 18: 'For if it is through God that you drive me from this desert place which I have sought from overseas, I will repeat that saying of the prophet [viz. Jonah]: "If this storm is upon us because of me, take me and cast me into the sea so that this disturbance recedes from you".'

[171] *Praefatio* § 5 (ed. Engelbrecht, *Tyrannii Rufini . . . interpretatio*, pp. 4–5): 'There [viz. Constantinople] he did magnificent work in the word of God and almost daily converted great multitudes of heretics to the true faith. But, as often happens, glory was dogged by envy. Yet he was so perfect in the fear of God that, when he realised that there was strife between the bishops on his account, he immediately left of his own accord, repeating only that saying of the prophet: "If this storm is because of me, take me and cast me into the sea and let this disturbance recede from you." '

[172] Elsewhere, on the purely verbal level, Columbanus's expression 'pro diuersis *huius* aeui *fragoribus* et *tumultuosis* gentium seditionibus interiacentium' (*Epistula* III.2,

Let us move on now to one of the authors most widely read in sixth-and seventh-century Gaul, Sulpicius Seuerus, the biographer of St Martin of Tours. So far, no-one has detected any borrowings from Seuerus's *Vita S. Martini* in Columbanus's writings. However, the situation is different with regard to the same author's *Dialogi*, a continuation of the *Vita* cast in dialogue form.[173] Walker noted a likely borrowing from the *Dialogi* at the beginning of *Epistula VI* (§ 1):[174]

Audisti quid scriptum est: *cui pauca non sufficiunt*, plura *non proderunt*.

This is a clear quotation, with the change of a single word, of *Dialogi* (I.18), '*cui pauca non sufficiunt*, multa *non proderunt*'; moreover, the same Severan *sententia* is also twice cited in the *Instructiones* – on the second occasion in a form identical to that in *Epistula VI*.[175] Since, however, Columbanus's authorship of all these texts has, as we have seen, been a matter of debate, it is important to note a so far unrecorded borrowing from Seuerus's *Dialogi* in one of the first five *Epistulae*. The letter concerned is once again that to the Gallic bishops (*Epistula II*); indeed the reminiscence occurs in the section of the letter which has attracted our attention so often already, that where Columbanus contrasts monks and secular clergy. Having compared their two ways of life, Columbanus asserts that no-one should criticise the monastic vocation, provided that it is embraced wholeheartedly (*Epistula* II.8):[176]

Nullus detrahat silentii bonis; nisi enim tepescant, secreti melius uiuunt quam publici, excepta austeriore adhuc uita quae maiorem habet mercedem; *ubi* enim *durior pugna*, *ibi gloriosior* inuenitur *corona*.

The last clause of this passage constitutes a neatly balanced antithesis of the type common in the *Epistulae*. We have already seen Columbanus borrowing a similarly antithetical *sententia* directly from Jerome; in this case he borrows the pointed phrase directly from Seuerus; compare *Dialogi* I.xii.3, 'sed *ubi durior pugna*, *ibi gloriosior* est *corona*'. The reminiscence is thus a good indication that Columbanus appreciated Seuerus too as a stylistic model; and it

---

ed. & transl. Walker, *Sancti Columbani Opera*, p. 22) is clearly a characteristically elaborate reworking of Rufinus's '*tumultuosis* uitae *huius fragoribus*' (*Apologeticus*, § 6.3, ed. Engelbrecht, *Tyrannii Rufini . . . interpretatio*, p. 11); cf. also 'pro *tumultuosis huius* aeui dissensionibus' (*Epistula* II.2, ed. & transl. Walker, *Sancti Columbani Opera*, p. 12).

173 Both works are ed. Halm, *Sulpicii Seueri libri*.

174 *Sancti Columbani Opera*, ed. & transl. Walker, p. 56: 'You have heard what is written: if a little is not enough, then more will not help.'

175 *Dialogi* I.18 (ed. Halm, *Sulpicii Seueri libri*, p. 170); cf. *Instructio* I.3 (ed. & transl. Walker, *Sancti Columbani Opera*, p. 62), '*cui haec pauca* de Deo Trinitate *non sufficiunt*, plura iuxta scripturam *non proderunt*'; and *Instructio* III.4 (*ibid.*, pp. 76–8), '*Cui pauca non sufficiunt*, plura *non proderunt*.'

176 *Sancti Columbani Opera*, ed. & transl. Walker, p. 20: 'Let no-one criticise the advantages of silence; for, unless they are lukewarm, the secluded live better than do seculars – excepting only that even stricter life which has a greater reward – since where the battle is harder, there a more glorious crown is discovered.'

also provides a further link between *Epistulae I–V*, *'Epistula VI'* and the *Instructiones*, although the great popularity of Seuerus's works should make us wary of basing any firm conclusions on this one parallel.[177]

Moreover, as has already frequently been the case, there is an interesting contextual play involved in this borrowing. At face value, Columbanus is employing the Seueran antithesis simply to assert the superiority of the monastic, and indeed anchoritic, way of life: since it is harder, its rewards will be the more glorious. Seuerus was of course an avid supporter of monasticism like his hero St Martin, and this may well have been one of the chief reasons for Columbanus's familiarity with the *Dialogi*. Nevertheless the original context of the passage borrowed by Columbanus is of a quite different nature. It occurs after the narrator has mentioned an eastern monk whom the sun had never beheld angry. Faced by this marvel, one of the interlocutors, Gallus, interrupts (*Dialogi*, I.xii.2–3):[178]

Ad haec me Gallus intuens: o si uester ille – nolo nomen dicere – nunc adesset, uellem admodum istud audiret exemplum, quem in multorum saepe personis nimium experti sumus uehementer irasci: sed tamen, quia inimicis suis, quantum audio, nuper ignouit, si istud audiret, magis magisque proposito confirmaretur exemplo, praeclaram esse uirtutem iracundia non moueri. Nec uero infitiabor iustas illi causas irarum fuisse: sed ubi durior pugna, ibi gloriosior est corona.

The original context was thus one of anger. Gallus wishes that a man well-known for his anger would be convinced by the example of the even-tempered monk that restraint is an important virtue; not, Gallus concedes, that his anger was not justified, but the harder the struggle to suppress it, the greater the reward. This original context bears on Columbanus's use of Seuerus's *sententia* in two ways. First, it is relevant because, as we have seen, Columbanus has just been attacking the secular clergy for their lack of the childlike qualities characteristic of monks, one of which is not harbouring anger in their hearts ('iram in corde non tenentes'), whereas the clergy very often quarrel and grow angry over the riches of the world ('circa mundi facultates saepius rixantes et irascentes'). This, however, is only part of the resonance of the borrowing. Gallus's irascible man had good cause for his anger, having been provoked by his enemies, but, according to Seuerus, this was all the more reason to suppress it, since the more difficult that was to do the more glorious the reward. This adds a further dimension to Columbanus's words. Ostensibly he is contrasting secular and monastic life, to the detriment of the former; but, if the source of

---

[177] Note too, however, that the probable borrowing from Jerome's letters in *Epistula VI* (above, p. 60 and n. 121) sits well with Columbanus's use of Jerome's correspondence in *Epistulae I–V*.

[178] *Sulpicii Seueri libri*, ed. Halm, p. 178: 'At this, Gallus said, glancing at me: "If only your acquaintance – I don't wish to name him – were here now, the one whose fierce anger against many people we have often experienced only too well: how I would like him to hear of this paragon. He has, as far as I have heard, recently forgiven his enemies, but he would be convinced by this model, if he heard of it, that it is a fine virtue not to be swayed by anger. I shall not deny that the motives behind his anger were just: yet where the battle is harder, there the crown is more glorious." '

his *sententia* is recognised, an important subtext emerges. Like Gallus's angry man, Columbanus has, in his own eyes, a good reason for anger, the jealous criticism and persecution that he and his monks are suffering at the hands of the Gallic bishops. But, unlike them, he as a monk appreciates the value of childlike virtues, such as the humility which he recommends to his readers again and again throughout the letter; and so he has, despite their dire provocation, refused to succumb to anger. The implication is that his restraint will gain him a hard-won victory; for exercising the monastic virtue of patience, Columbanus expects to be rewarded a glorious crown, whilst by their very persecution of him the Gallic bishops are, as he has already pointed out, jeopardizing their own chances of being received into the kingdom of heaven. Columbanus's echo of Sulpicius Seuerus is thus as allusive in its context as were his citations of the Scriptures.

In addition to Sulpicius Seuerus, Columbanus was also familiar with two other authors from a Gallic milieu, although neither need detain us long here. Given Columbanus's enthusiasm for monasticism, it would be surprising if he were not familiar with the ascetic writings of Cassian of Marseilles. So far, however, the *Epistulae* have yielded only a single reminiscence of his works: compare the identical nautical metaphors, '*fragilis ingenii cymba* non tam in altum ... ducta est' (*Epistula* V.8) and Cassian's similar formulation, 'profundioris nauigationis periculis *fragilis ingenii cumba* iactanda est'.[179] This clear echo of the preface to the *Conlationes* may well indicate that further borrowings from Cassian await discovery in Columbanus's letters. The other Gallic author is Gennadius, best known as a continuator of Jerome's *De uiris illustribus*. However, it is from Gennadius's *De ecclesiasticis dogmatibus* (§ 87) that Columbanus quotes, in *Epistula I* (§ 3), a short passage concerning one of his main preoccupations, the dating of Easter.[180] This aside, he does not appear to have made any further use of Gennadius's works.

To move forward in date, the latest writer known to Columbanus is his contemporary, Gregory the Great. Columbanus mentions having read the pope's *Regula pastoralis* at the end of his letter to Gregory (*Epistula* I.9).[181] Moreover, he evidently read the *Regula pastoralis* attentively, since on one occasion, he cites a *sententia* from it verbatim.[182] This quotation occurs in *Epistula IV* (§ 6):[183]

---

[179] *Conlationes, praefatio* § 4 (ed. Petschenig, *Iohannis Cassiani Conlationes*, p. 4): respectively, 'the unseaworthy boat of my talent has not yet reached the high sea'; and 'the unseaworthy boat of my talent is to be tossed by the dangers of sailing a deeper ocean'.

[180] *Patrologia Latina*, ed. Migne, LVIII.1000.

[181] *Sancti Columbani Opera*, ed. & transl. Walker, p. 10: 'Legi librum tuum pastorale regimen continentem.' The *Regula pastoralis* is in *Patrologia Latina*, ed. Migne, LXXVII.13–128.

[182] Walker also proposed a second borrowing from the same text, but, as we have seen, in the passage in question Columbanus is in fact quoting Gregory of Nazianzus (above, n. 168).

[183] *Sancti Columbani Opera*, ed. & transl. Walker, p. 32: 'Because often, as a certain author says, great virtue has for some people been instrumental in their ruin.'

quia *saepe*, ut ait quidam, *magnitudo uirtutis quibusdam fuit occasio perditionis.*

Compare *Regula pastoralis* (§ IV):[184]

Nam *quibusdam saepe magnitudo uirtutis occasio perditionis fuit.*

Indeed, this quotation merits further attention, since it reveals once again that Columbanus's use of his sources is more subtle than Walker's edition would suggest. The passage of *Epistula IV* cited above continues directly:[185]

quia nimirum eo quo pulchriores sunt uirtutibus ab humilitatis gradu descendunt. Inde scriptum est, '*quo pulchrior es, descende*, surge *et dormi cum incircumcisis*' [Ez XXXII.19] *acsi* aliis uerbis *animae diceret superbae, quia* tua sanctitate *te eleuasti* in superbiam, descende inde modo et esto inter peccatores computanda quia nihil apud me est quod cum superbia efficitur.

Columbanus here relates Gregory's warning about the dangers of spiritual pride to a quotation from the prophet Ezekiel (XXXII.19), which he interprets tropologically as being addressed to the proud soul. His inspiration for so doing was undoubtedly provided by the very same passage of the *Regula pastoralis*. Almost immediately after the *sententia* already quoted, Gregory cites exactly the same verse of Ezekiel and offers a similar moral interpretation of it:[186]

Hinc namque *superbienti animae dicitur*: '*Quo pulchrior es descende et dormi cum incircumcisis.*' *Ac si* aperte *diceretur*: *Quia* ex uirtutum decore *te eleuas*, ipsa tua pulchritudine impelleris ut cadas.

Columbanus has considerably recast the passage, but, as the verbal parallels indicated above show, his debt to Gregory remains clear. We are thus presented with another example of Columbanus deriving a biblical citation at second hand from a patristic source, in this case doubtless because he was attracted by the exegetical explanation of the scriptural verse offered by Gregory. In *Epistula IV*, then, Columbanus does more than simply quote a *sententia* from the *Regula pastoralis*; he also at the same time integrates into his argument an element of biblical exegesis directly derived from Gregory the Great.

So far our discussion has been concerned exclusively with christian-Latin prose. Among the poets, the only author from whom Columbanus borrows in

---

[184] *Patrologia Latina*, ed. Migne, LVIII.125.
[185] *Sancti Columbani Opera*, ed. & transl. Walker, p. 32: 'Since assuredly the more beauteous they are in their virtues, the further they descend from the station of humility. Therefore it is written, "The more beauteous you are, come down; arise and sleep with the uncircumcised," [Ezekiel XXXII.19] as if, in other words, Ezekiel were saying to the proud soul, "since through your sanctity you have raised yourself up in pride, now come down from there and be counted among the sinners, because what is done in pride means nothing to me".'
[186] *Patrologia Latina*, ed. Migne, LVIII.125: 'For the proud soul is therefore told, "The more beauteous you are, come down and sleep with the uncircumcised," as if Ezekiel were saying, "since you raise yourself up through the allure of your virtues, by your own very beauty will you be made to fall".'

the *Epistulae* is, according to Walker, the fifth-century writer Caelius Sedulius. Walker's suggestion deserves careful consideration, since Sedulius's *Carmen paschale*, one of the most widely read of christian-Latin poems, was certainly known to other Irish writers in the seventh century.[187] The single Sedulian borrowing advanced by Walker occurs in *Epistula V*, when Columbanus refers as follows to the hopes he places on Pope Boniface's pontifical authority (§ 8):[188]

ad teque tantum, qui *unica spes* de principibus es per honorem potens Petri apostoli sancti, respiciens.

With the phrase italicised, Walker compares the well-known address to God in *Carmen paschale* I.60:[189]

Omnipotens aeterne Deus, *spes unica* mundi.

However, the verbal parallel is limited the phrase *unica spes*, 'sole hope', which is not unduly striking in itself, and is almost a commonplace in Latin poetry.[190] Columbanus may thus have used this expression entirely independently, or alternatively might have been influenced, possibly at second hand, by any one of a number of poetic sources. We cannot on the strength of this passage alone be sure that Columbanus had read the *Carmen paschale*.

It is therefore important to turn our attention to another passage, this time from Columbanus's *Epistula I*, which has not before been considered in connection with his knowledge of Sedulius. The passage occurs after the saint's request that Gregory the Great send him a copy of his commentary on Ezekiel as well as other works. Columbanus continues (*Epistula* I.9):[191]

Importuna postulo et magna sciscitor, quis nesciat? Sed et tu magna habes, quia de paruo minus et de multo plus bene scis esse foenerandum.

We immediately recognise here the sort of modesty topos of which Columbanus is so fond, and also perhaps his taste for biblical borrowings, arguably present, Walker suggests, in an allusion to Luke XII.48 ('et cui commendauerunt *multum*, *plus* petent ab eo'). An intriguing parallel to the passage is, however, afforded by another Sedulian address to the deity, when the poet rounds off a request that he may find a place as a citizen of heaven with a final apology (*Carmen paschale* I.349–50):[192]

---

[187] See Wright, 'The *Hisperica Famina* and Caelius Sedulius'. The *Carmen paschale* is ed. Huemer, *Sedulii Opera Omnia*, pp. 14–146.

[188] *Sancti Columbani Opera*, ed. & transl. Walker, p. 44: 'And looking only to you who are my sole hope among the princes, empowered by the dignity of the holy apostle Peter.'

[189] 'Almighty, eternal God, sole hope of the world.'

[190] It is also used by, among others, Iuuencus, Claudian, Sidonius, Ennodius and Corippus; see Schumann, *Hexameter-Lexikon*, V.236–7.

[191] *Sancti Columbani Opera*, ed. & transl. Walker, p. 10: 'It is clear to everybody that I make inconvenient demands and seek great things; but you also possess great things, since, as you well know, greater interest is raised on much and less on little.'

[192] 'I indeed request vast things; but You know how to give vast things, and are more displeased when someone's hopes grow cool.'

Grandia posco quidem, *sed tu* dare grandia nosti
Quem magis offendit quisquis sperando tepescit.

At first sight, the two passages do not seem closely related, verbal parallels being limited to the phrase 'sed . . . . tu' alone. The similarity is rather one of sense, both passages stressing the magnitude of the favour requested and giving the same reason for it, although in almost entirely different words (compare 'Importuna postulo et magna sciscitor, quis nesciat?' with 'Grandia posco quidem'; and 'Sed et tu magna habes' with 'sed tu dare grandia nosti'). If, then, Columbanus did have Sedulius in mind here, he was certainly very careful to recast the wording of his source.

Indeed, one would be inclined to dismiss this possible reminiscence as coincidental, were it not for a very similar passage in the last of the *Instructiones* attributed to Columbanus. One argument which can be advanced in favour of the saint's authorship of the sermons is the existence of a number of verbal parallels between the *Instructiones* and the *Epistulae*.[193] To these parallels can be added the following, between Columbanus's request to Gregory the Great (*Epistula* I.9, quoted above) and the peroration of the final sermon. There, after asking Christ to grant him and his audience living water from the Living Fountain, Columbanus again apologises for his boldness (*Instructio* XIII.3):[194]

Magna quidem posco quis nesciat? Sed tu, Rex gloriae, magna donare nosti.

It is immediately evident that there is a close link between the sermon and the letter (compare '*Magna* quidem posco, *quis nesciat?*' with '*magna* sciscitor, *quis nesciat?*'; and '*Sed tu . . . magna* donare nosti' with '*Sed* et *tu magna* habes'). But the passage from the sermon bears an even closer resemblance to the line of Sedulius quoted above (compare 'Magna *quidem posco*' with 'Grandia *posco quidem*'; and '*Sed tu . . .* magna donare *nosti*' with '*sed tu* dare grandia *nosti*').

There can be little doubt that the Sedulian line is directly imitated in *Instructio XIII*. The difficulty, given the doubts about Columbanus's authorship of the *Instructiones*, lies in determining the relationship of the passage in *Epistula I* to the other two texts. The parallels between letter and sermon (set out above) seem too close to have arisen through two independent acts of borrowing from Sedulius. At the same time, the imitation of Sedulius is certainly much more readily apparent in *Instructio XIII* than in *Epistula I*. If the *Instructiones* were not written by Columbanus, then this relationship might be explained in one of two ways, neither of which is entirely satisfactory. First, Columbanus's *Epistula* might be the model for the *Instructio*, whose author recognised the (arguably coincidental) similarity to the Sedulian passage and then chose to imitate that source more closely – although it does not explain his motives for so doing. Second, the *Instructio* may be the model for *Epistula I*, Columbanus imitating the

---

[193] See the discussion by Clare Stancliffe, below, pp. 139–74.
[194] *Sancti Columbani Opera*, ed. & transl. Walker, p. 118: 'It is clear to everybody that I indeed request great things; but You, King of Glory, know how to grant great things.'

passage in question perhaps in ignorance of the Sedulian allusion; but this latter hypothesis does not sit well with the care with which we have seen Columbanus using his other christian-Latin sources. Conversely, no difficulties arise if we suppose that Columbanus wrote both the *Epistulae* and the *Instructiones*, as is argued elsewhere in this volume.[195] In that case, the two passages simply represent two different responses by Columbanus to what seems to have been a favourite passage of Sedulius: in the *Instructio*, he used the borrowing in the same context as the poetic original – namely a prayer – and so echoed Sedulius closely, whereas in the *Epistula*, employing it in the modified context of an address to Pope Gregory, he completely recast it and carefully varied its vocabulary. The two passages which we have been considering cannot prove beyond question that Columbanus was the author of both the sermons and letters, but they certainly provide a powerful pointer in that direction; and, by the same token, they afford evidence that Columbanus may indeed have read Sedulius's *Carmen paschale*.

In addition to the continental authors whom we have been considering thus far, Columbanus also knew a number of texts of Insular origin, his reading in this respect mirroring what we have seen of his style in general. In *Epistula I*, for instance, Columbanus quotes, apparently in good faith, from the *De ratione paschae* of pseudo-Anatolius (*Epistula* I.3); this tract purported to be by Anatolius, bishop of Syrian Laodicea in the third century, but was actually a more recent Irish forgery which lent support to Columbanus's paschal position.[196] Likewise, in the field of hymnody, there is a striking parallel between a passage in *Epistula V* (§ 13) and some lines in *Precamur patrem*, an early Hiberno-Latin hymn preserved in the 'Antiphonary of Bangor', which is very likely to have been Columbanus's source.[197] And in the case of the penitential attributed to Columbanus, Jean Laporte has argued that it was strongly influenced by British sources, in particular the Penitential of Uinniau.[198]

The British writer who had the greatest impact on Columbanus, however, was certainly Gildas. Columbanus mentions Gildas by name twice in the course of his *Epistula I*. In this work (§ 7), he refers to the correspondence of Uinniau and Gildas in relation to the problem of monks who, for the best motives, leave their monasteries against the wishes of their abbots: 'Uennianus auctor Gildam de his interrogauit, et elegantissime ille rescripsit.'[199] And, slightly earlier (I.6), he had also cited Gildas's opinion of simoniac bishops, 'Ceterum de episcopis illis quid iudicas, interrogo, qui contra canones

---

[195] See the discussion by Clare Stancliffe, below, pp. 93–202.

[196] This pseudo-Anatolian work is ed. Krusch, *Studien*, I.311–28.

[197] See further Lapidge, below, pp. 255–63.

[198] Laporte, *Le Pénitentiel*, pp. 24, 42–4; see also the discussion by Thomas Charles-Edwards, below, pp. 217–39.

[199] *Sancti Columbani Opera*, ed. & transl. Walker, p. 8: 'The writer Uinniau asked Gildas about such people, and he wrote back most elegantly.' Parts of this 'most elegant' reply may be preserved in the *Epistolarum Gildae deperditarum fragmenta*, printed in the standard edition of Gildas's works by Winterbottom, *Gildas*, pp. 143–5: see Sharpe, 'Gildas as a father', pp. 197–8; and (on Uinniau), Dumville, 'Gildas and Uinniau', pp. 207–14.

ordinantur, id est quaestu; simoniacos et Gildas auctor pestes scripsit.'[200] Columbanus very probably has in mind here Gildas's strictures against simony in his major work, the *De excidio Britanniae* (§ 67). Indeed, Columbanus's familiarity with that text is confirmed by the presence of a number of verbal echoes of it in the *Epistulae*. The most important reminiscences are the following: '*Lacrimis in his opus est magis quam uerbis*' (*Epistula* V.12) and '*In hoc* namque sermone *lacrimis magis quam uerbis opus est*' (*De excidio Britanniae*, § 108);[201] '*uilissimae qualitatis* homunculus' (*Epistula* V.2) and 'licet *uilissimae qualitatis* simus' (*De excidio Britanniae*, § 36);[202] '*ut . . .* uno impetu feruoris nimii *tota ad* caelestia *festinet ecclesia*' (*Epistula* II.8) and 'ita *ut* agmine denso certatim . . . *ad* amoena caelorum regna . . . *tota festinaret ecclesia*' (*De excidio Britanniae*, § 9);[203] '*ille* enim certus *regni caelorum clauicularius* est' (*Epistula* V.11) and '*clauicularius ille caelorum regni*' (*De excidio Britanniae*, § 73);[204] '*salua sanctorum reuerentia* cinerum' (*Epistula* I.8) and '*salua sanctarum* animarum *reuerentia*' (*De excidio Britanniae*, § 24);[205] 'totius exercitus Domini . . . in campo *potius torpentis quam* pugnantis et . . . aduersariis potius *manus dantis* quam resistentis' (*Epistula* V.7) and 'qui *torpetis potius quam* sedetis legitime in sacerdotali sede' (*De excidio Britanniae*, § 73) as well as 'alii . . . *manus* hostibus *dabant*, in aeuum seruituri' (§ 25).[206] In addition to these purely verbal reminiscences, there are also occasions when Columbanus's imagery directly recalls the vivid metaphorical language which is so typical of Gildas. Consider for example the following

---

[200] *Sancti Columbani Opera*, ed. & transl. Walker, p. 8: 'For the rest, what is your opinion of those bishops who are ordained uncanonically, that is for money; the writer Gildas set them down as simoniacs and plagues.'

[201] 'In these matters there is greater need for tears than for words'; and 'In this saying there is greater need for tears than for words.'

[202] 'A being of the meanest rank'; and 'although I am of the meanest rank'.

[203] 'So that with a single impulse of boundless enthusiasm the whole church hastens to heaven'; and 'so that in a dense and vying crowd the whole church hastened to the pleasant kingdom of heaven'.

[204] 'For he is the sure key-bearer of the kingdom of heaven'; and 'the key-bearer of the kingdom of heaven'.

[205] 'Save the reverence due to the ashes of the holy'; and 'save the reverence due to their holy souls'.

[206] Respectively: 'of the whole army of the Lord, dozing rather than fighting in the field and giving in to the foe rather than resisting'; 'you who doze rather than sit lawfully on the priestly seat', and 'others gave in to the enemy, to be slaves forever' (where the expression *manus do* belongs to the high style). With the first of these Gildasian passages (*De excidio Britanniae*, III.73, 'qui torpetis potius quam *sedetis legitime* in sacerdotali sede'), cf. also *Epistula* I.5 (ed. & transl. Walker, *Sancti Columbani Opera*, p. 8), 'te . . . Petri cathedram . . . *legitime insidentem*'. Columbanus and Gildas also share a number of other expressions in common, for example: 'contra ius fasque' (see above, n. 121); 'nos . . ., *uiles licet*' (*Epistula* II.9, *ibid.*, p. 22) and '*uili licet* stylo' (*De excidio* I.1); '*auriga currus* illius' (*Epistula* V.11, *ibid.*, p. 48) and '*auriga currus* receptaculi ursi' (*De excidio*, II.32); 'licet tepide' (*Epistula* II.6, *ibid.*, p. 18 and *De excidio*, I.9); '*laetitia ecclesiae matris*' (*Epistula* V.17, *ibid.*, p 56) and 'quanta *ecclesiae matri laetitia*' (*De excidio*, II.34); see also the following note.

ornate passage in which Columbanus remarks that the fame of the city of Rome was not prevented by the intervening sea from reaching Ireland in the west: 'Ausonici decoris ... urbis ... nomen ... totum per orbem usque in occidua transmundialis limitis loca, triundialibus ... pelagi uorticibus ... non prohibentibus longe lateque uulgatum est' (*Epistula* V.11).[207] Gildas uses a very similar image, expressed in a more concise form, when he pictures Roman expansion as a flame which could not be quenched by the sea in its inexorable progress towards Britain: 'non acies flammae quodammodo rigidi tenoris ad occidentem caeruleo oceani torrente potuit uel cohiberi uel extingui' (*De excidio Britanniae*, § 5).[208]

I have set out these parallels in detail because they corroborate the findings of an important article by Michael Winterbottom.[209] Although his study was confined to *Epistula V*, Winterbottom drew attention to a number of similarites between Columbanus and Gildas which indeed hold good for the *Epistulae* as a whole: similarities of outlook (particularly in the stress that both writers place on the dangers inherent in peace and prosperity); imagery (though the example from *Epistula V* quoted above is not mentioned in this context); style, including word-order (especially interlace-patterns and complex hyperbaton) and alliteration (*Epistula* V.1 being cited in particular); sentence-structure (Columbanus's paean of Rome in *Epistula* V.11 rightly being seen as matching the 'shapeless grandeur' of some of Gildas's bolder efforts); and finally, the two authors' taste for arcane vocabulary.[210] It is impossible to overemphasise the importance of Winterbottom's study for our appreciation of Columbanus's *Epistulae*. In Gildas we encounter a representative of a vital tradition of Insular Latin, working very much within the rhetorical conventions of the fifth-century continental prose, but at the same time foreshadowing many of the peculiarities characteristic of Columbanus's own latinity.[211] It is easy to see

---

[207] *Sancti Columbani Opera*, ed. & transl. Walker, p. 48: 'The renown of the city which is Italy's ornament has been spread far and wide through the whole earth, even to the western regions at the boundary of the world, unhindered by the swelling whirlpools of the deep' (with 'totum *per* orbem ... *longe lateque* uulgatum', cf. also *De excidio*, II.33, 'palata ... *longe lateque per* auras').

[208] 'The keenness of their flame could not in its relentless movement to the west be hindered or put out by the blue flood of the ocean.' For another example, cf. Columbanus's observation, 'dum dies iudicii propior nunc est quam tunc' (*Epistula* II.2, ed. & transl. Walker, *Sancti Columbani Opera*, p. 12) with Gildas's similar question, 'prope est dies Domini (Isaiah XIII.6) – si prope tunc erat, quid nunc putabitur?' (*De excidio*, II.44).

[209] Winterbottom, 'Columbanus and Gildas'.

[210] Cf. discussion above, p. 46.

[211] On the relationship of Gildas's prose to that of the Contintent, see Kerlouégan, 'Le latin', pp. 151–76. It is interesting to note in this connection that, of the continental texts used by Columbanus, Gildas was also familiar with Jerome's *Epistulae* (particularly *Epistula XIV*) and *De uiris illustribus*, Rufinus's translations of Eusebius's *Historia Ecclesiastica* and also probably of the sermons of Gregory of Nazianzus (see my 'Gildas, Rufinus and Gregory of Nazianzus'), Sulpicius Seuerus's *Dialogi*, Cassian's *Conlationes*, and perhaps Sedulius's *Carmen Paschale*; see Wright, 'Gildas's reading'.

how Columbanus's reading of Gildas, alongside his knowledge of the patristic writers whom we have been considering, did much to foster the saint's own style, a style which, like Gildas's, to some degree heralds the developments which would ultimately lead to the *Hisperica Famina*.

As a further illustration of Gildas's influence on Columbanus, one might cite, for example, by the following passage from the opening of *Epistula III* (§ 2):[212]

Iam diu omnes sedi apostolicae praesidentes dulcissimos omnibus praesules fidelibus ac merito apostolici honoris reuerendissimos patres uisitare spiritu et consolare cupiens, nunc usque uotis pro diuersis huius aeui fragoribus et tumultuosis gentium seditionibus interiacentium, acsi marina trabe interclusus, satisfacere non potui, insuaui scilicet intransmeabilique non tam tithis uisibilis quam intelligibilis dorso, quod optime nostis, opposito.

Much in this passage is in the Gildasian manner, particularly the vivid metaphor whereby Columbanus imagines the troubles of the world and the treacherous tribes cutting him off from Rome as an uncrossable sea on which he is tossed in his lonely ship (note that the use of *trabs* in this sense is distinctly poetic). Moreover, the structure of the sentence is relatively complex, closing with an impressive, if somewhat sprawling, ablative-absolute construction. The word-order is ornate, including two examples of the abBa-type pattern ('omnes sedi apostolicae praesidentes' and 'diuersis huius aeui fragoribus'), both immediately followed by abAB-type interlaces ('dulcissimos omnibus praesules fidelibus' and 'tumultuosis gentium seditionibus interiacentium'). Similarly, the final ablative absolute ('insuaui scilicet . . . nostis, opposito') also exhibits verbal interweaving: of its two constituent nouns, the genitive *tithis* is qualified by the clause 'non tam . . . uisibilis quam intelligibilis', while both it and the ablative *dorso*, on which *tithis* depends, are preceded by the adjectives 'insuaui intransmeabilique', and followed by the participle *opposito*, with the subordinate unit 'quod optime nostis' enclosed for good measure.[213] As to vocabulary, many of the less usual words in the passage can be directly paralleled in Gildas, for instance (limiting examples to the closing ablative-absolute clause): *intransmeabilis* also occurs in Gildas's description of Britain as 'oceani . . . diffusiore et, ut ita dicam, *intransmeabili* undique circulo . . . uallata' (*De excidio Britanniae*, § 3); the poeticism *tithis* ('the sea') appears in adjectival form in the Gildasian expression 'trans *Tithicam* uallem' (*De excidio Britanniae*, § 19); *uisibilis* is used by Gildas in a passage similar to the one we are dealing with,

---

[212] *Sancti Columbani Opera*, ed. & transl. Walker, p. 22: 'I have for a long time wished to visit in spirit and to console all those who preside over the papal see, prelates most dear to all the faithful and, by virtue of their apostolic dignity, most reverend fathers, but I have so far been unable to satisfy my wishes because of the various disturbances of this age and the turbulent mutinies of the peoples lying between; I am, as it were, shut up in a sea-going ship, faced, as you well know, by the hostile and uncrossable surface of a sea not so much visible as metaphorical.'

[213] On Gildas's use of the patterns abBA and abAB, and of more complex interweaving, see Wright, 'Gildas's prose style', pp. 115–28.

when he contrasts the visible sun with Christ, whom he metaphorically depicts as the true sun shining on Britain, 'insulae ... soli *uisibili* non proximae, uerus ille non de firmamento solum temporali sed de summa etiam caelorum arce ... praefulgidum sui coruscum ostendens ... Christus' (*De excidio Britanniae*, § 8); *intelligibilis* is employed by Gildas in the phrase, 'affectu saltem *intelligibilis* asinae' (*De excidio Britanniae*, § 15 – although there it means 'intelligent'); and finally Gildas on one occasion uses, as Columbanus does here, the word *dorsum* in the sense of 'the surface' of water, 'ac si montanus torrens ... sulcato *dorso* ... mirabiliter spumans' (*De excidio Britanniae*, § 17). The whole passage is thus in various ways redolent of Gildas.

It is clear that Columbanus possessed an intimate familiarity with the *De excidio Britanniae*. His knowledge of this text moreover also has a bearing on the vexed question of the authorship of the *Instructiones*. While Gildas was widely read by Insular authors, his work seems to have been hardly known on the Continent (with the exception, that is, of Brittany). Imitation of Gildas in a text can thus be taken as a good indication that its author was of Insular origin. It is therefore important to note a seeming echo of Gildas in the *Instructiones*. The phrase, '*Lacrimis in his opus magis quam uerbis est*' (*Instructio* XI.3) evidently recalls '*In hoc* namque sermone *lacrimis magis quam uerbis opus est*' (*De excidio Britanniae*, § 108). As often with the sermons, however, the picture is somewhat complicated. We have seen already that a reminiscence of this same passage of Gildas is also found in *Epistula* V.12, '*Lacrimis in his opus est magis quam uerbis.*' It is immediately apparent that the relationship between *Instructio XI* and *Epistula V* is much closer than with the *De excidio Britanniae* itself. Again this poses no problem if Columbanus wrote both sermon and letter – in that case he would simply be repeating a favourite phrase (and echoing Gildas at the same time). If however Columbanus were not responsible for the *Instructio*, it could be maintained that its author did no more than take over the phrase 'lacrimis in his opus magis quam uerbis est' directly from *Epistula V*, quite likely in complete ignorance that it constituted a Gildasian echo. (Another possibility, that the *Instructio* is the earliest of the three texts and so may be the source both for Columbanus's *Epistula* and for Gildas, seems highly unlikely, especially when weighed against the extensive borrowings which Columbanus made directly from the *De excidio Britanniae* elsewhere in the letters.) That the author of the *Instructiones* was ignorant of the *De excidio Britanniae* seems, however, to be ruled out by another, unnoticed reminiscence of Gildas in the sermons. It occurs in a passage where the audience are warned always to meditate on the Day of Judgement (*Instructio* IX.1):[214]

suspecta semper mente illum tremendum diuini iudicii aduentum indesinenter cogitate.

The unusual expression 'suspecta semper mente' ('with ever foreboding mind') employed here is also used by Gildas in a passsage where he describes

---

[214] *Sancti Columbani Opera*, ed. & transl. Walker, p. 98: 'Ceaselessly consider with ever foreboding mind the terrible arrival of divine judgement.'

the fate of some British survivors of the English onslaught (*De excidio Britanniae*, § 25):[215]

alii montanis collibus minacibus praeruptis uallatis et densissimis saltibus marinisque rupibus uitam *suspecta semper mente* credentes, in patria licet trepidi perstabant.

It is clear that the diction of the sermon has been influenced by that of the *De excidio Britanniae* here (unless it is held that the *Instructio* is Gildas's source, which, as we have seen, appears unlikely in the extreme).[216] It follows from what was said at the outset that author of the sermons was an Insular writer. In short, parallels with Gildas in the *Instructiones* and the *Epistulae* alike can, as in the case of those from Sedulius, be most convincingly and economically explained if both texts were composed by Columbanus, as the traditional attribution of the works suggests.[217]

In conclusion, then, it must be stressed that Columbanus's *Epistulae* should be viewed as important literary works in their own right, which amply repay critical study – more so in many respects than the poetry often assigned to the saint, which has conventionally attracted far greater scholarly attention. These *Epistulae* reveal Columbanus as a painstaking writer who had evidently received in Ireland a thorough training in the basics of Latin. Far from being turgid or simply bombastic, as it is often described, Columbanus's prose displays a mastery of rhetorical technique which can be explained in terms of his attentive reading of patristic texts as well as by his admiration for Gildas, whose style he obviously regarded as most elegant and eminently worthy of imitation; both the continental and Insular traditions thus meet in Columbanus's writing, combining to form a product which indelibly bears the stamp of the saint's forceful personality. For Columbanus makes highly creative use of the texts which he read. In particular, in his letter to the Gallic

---

[215] 'Others, entrusting their lives with ever foreboding mind to the mountain hills, threatening, craggy and isolated, to the densest woods and to sea-cliffs, remained in their homeland in spite of their fear.'

[216] Indeed this possibility is precluded if we accept that the sermons include borrowings from Gregory the Great, as is held by Walker, *Sancti Columbani Opera*, pp. 84, 110–12.

[217] For another Gildasian phrase shared by both the *Instructiones* and the *Epistulae*, cf. 'nos *uiles licet*' (*Instructio* II.1, ed. & transl. Walker, *Sancti Columbani Opera*, p. 68) and 'me, *uilem licet*' (*Instructio* XII.2, *ibid.*, p. 112) with *Epistula* II.9 and *De excidio*, I.1 (quoted above, n. 206). In this connection it is also important to report two Gildasian echoes in the *Regula monachorum* ascribed to Columbanus, respectively: '*in immanem* nominum *siluam creuerunt*' (*Regula monachorum* VIII, ed. & transl. Walker, *ibid.*, p. 136) and '*uirgultis crescentibus* et *in immanem siluam* iam iamque erumpentibus' (*De excidio*, I.13); and secondly, 'quasi in quadam *ponderatrice* discretionis *statera*' (*Regula monachorum* VIII, *ibid.*, p. 136) and 'diuina, ut dicitur, *statera* terrae totius *ponderatrice*' (*De excidio*, I.3), *ponderatrix* (with dependent genitive in both cases) being a particularly distinctive term. Likewise, the word *depressor*, which occurs in *Epistula VI* (VI.2, ed. Walker, *ibid.*, p. 58) is, to my knowledge, elsewhere attested only in *De excidio*, II.32, 'dei contemptor sortisque eius *depressor*'. The influence of Gildas can thus be detected almost everywhere in the prose works attributed to the saint.

clergy, he fuses elements from the Bible and from various christian-Latin authors into a cocktail of allusions which is skilfully designed to discredit his opponents in the subtlest of manners. Grammatically correct, rhetorically effective, stylistically rich, pointedly allusive – Columbanus's *Epistulae* are all these things; it is through them that we can best appreciate what has been termed the 'miracle of Ireland.'

APPENDIX

Hyperbaton in Epistulae I–V

1. aBA and similar

I.3	de hac lunae aetate
I.4	hunc Galliae errorem
I.9	extrema scilicet libri exposita
II.2	de solo Paschae negotio
II.5	tumore superbiae deposito
II.7	sancto catalogi scriptore
III.2	nostros in Christo patres
III.3	dulcissime in Christo papa
IV.2	nostroque communi omnium patre
IV.4	meum ad totos iussum
IV.4	ad firmitatem reguli tenendam
IV.6	cum omni mentis humilitate
IV.6	sola Domini misericordia
IV.6	quibusdam potentiae experimentis
V.6	quanta Gehennae fomenta
V.7	caeca prosperitatis securitas
V.9	hoc fune erroris longissimo
V.11	triundialibus . . . pelagi uorticibus
V.12	communi omnium nonno
V.16	prisco inter hebraeos nomine
V.16	iuxta meam bonam de uobis aestimationem

2. bAB and similar

I.8	meorum cura comperegrinorum
II.8	iuxta euangelici uim dicti
III.2	istorum liber Gallorum
III.2	uestrae . . . punctum auctoritatis
III.2	cum ecclesiasticae pace unitatis
IV.2	sui tenuitate caespitis
IV.6	officii rem legitimi
IV.9	finem epistula pergaminae
V.3	sulcatis Orco molibus
V.3	ultimi habitatores mundi

V.3   necessariae insinuationem praesumptionis meae
V.4   tantos Italia lupos
V.8   sui negotium doloris
V.11   consequentiae ratio historiae
V.12   ecclesiae unitate communis matris
V.14   oliginosis celotes palearibus
V.16   uestrae idiomate linguae

3.   abBA and similar

I.4   sapientissimis componendi calculi computariis
I.6   simoniacos et Gildas auctor pestes scripsit
I.8   illam spiritalem uiui fontis undam
I.8   de ultimis hyalini littoris finibus
II.1   ceterisque sanctae Ecclesiae Ordinibus
II.2   pro tumultuosis huius aeui dissensionibus
II.3   ad ueram octaui diei circumcisionem
II.3   fatuis sola fide contentis
II.5   per uoluntariam euangelicae admonitionis paupertatem
II.5   amputatis dissensionis ac discordiae causis
II.7   Eusebio ecclesiasticae historiae auctore
II.7   in uia huius saeculi spatiosa
III.2 pro diuersis huius aeui fragoribus
III.3 ecclesias Dei in barbaris gentibus constitutas
V.6   ad proposita suggestionis primae genera
V.8   ignita ipsius Domini uerba
V.9   uera in synodo fidei confessione
V.9   ostensa prius uestrae fidei puritate
V.11   in occidua transmundialis limitis loca
V.11   certus regni caelorum clauicularius
V.12   post neotericam orthodoxorum auctorum scripturam
V.14   trisulcus arcuato uulnere scorpius
V.16   haec instantis leuitatis fama
V.17   magnos magni regis duces
V.17   fortissimos campi felicissimi bellatores

4.   abAB and similar

I.1   Romanae pulcherrimo Ecclesiae Decori
I.4   una istorum sententia episcoporum
I.8   salua sanctorum reuerantia cinerum
III.2 dulcissimos omnibus praesules fidelibus
III.2 tumultuosis gentium seditionibus interiacentium
III.2 tuae pium sententiae solatium
V.3   cautis spumosis concauae uorticibus

5.   aVA and similar (simple)

I.3   a multis comprobatur calcenteris
I.3   horrendam intulit sententiam

I.3	in sancti dogmatis legimus libro
I.3	in suo transgressus est cyclo
I.3	errorem . . . confirmauit inolitum
I.4	tua excusari potest peritia
I.4	Victorium non fuisse receptum
I.4	tantos quos legi auctores
I.4	suum recepit commentum
I.4	hoc imbibit bubum erroris
I.5	tuum itaque aut excusa aut damna Victorium
I.5	fidei futurum fore negotium
I.5	Anatolium laudauit huic contrarium
I.5	Tua itaque consideret uigilantia
I.6	quorum in his nouimus conscientias
I.6	non minoris censetur esse facinoris
I.9	totam exponas obscuritatem Zachariae
II.2	tanti congregati sunt sancti
II.2	hoc debuit uobis inesse studium
II.2	ad minorem prouocarentur profectum
II.2	uestrum prosit concilium
II.4	suae agnoscunt oues
II.4	nudo non potest tradere uerbo
II.5	qualis uerior sit traditio
II.6	meam comportetis insipientiam
II.6	unum regnum habemus promissum
II.7	in suo testatus (viz. testatus est) prologo
II.7	utraque bona sit traditio
II.7	libri legantur utrique
II.8	mores exponunt infantium
II.8	maiorem habet mercedem
II.8	potest certa esse unio
III.2	a nostra transmittuntur uilitate
III.2	per tuum possimus iudicium
III.2	in nostra esse patria
III.3	suis uiuere legibus
IV.2	sensum agnoscunt meum
IV.2	suae sit electionis
IV.4	a mea parua declinauerunt firmitate
IV.4	a doctrinae recesserunt ueritate
IV.5	meum tulit inde animum
IV.6	multa perpetrasse iniusta
IV.6	animae diceret superbae
IV.6	Multa cerne pericula
IV.7	quibus circumdamur aduersitatibus
IV.7	meriti est causa
IV.8	nullus uetat custos
IV.8	terrae reddat optatae
IV.9	uotum scit meum
V.2	humillima, ut decet, suggestione

V.3   flabris exasperatur feralibus
V.4   multos sustinet hereticos
V.4   fructus colligendi ueros
V.5   multorum erit uastatio
V.6   totus consistit agon
V.6   tota stat causa
V.6   toti superaedificamur Christiani
V.8   in uno haereat loco
V.9   multas esse causas
V.10   totius, ut aiunt, scandali
V.16   persecutio uenerit ultima
V.16   grauis fuit persecutio
V.17   in sollicitudinem posuit multiplicem
V.17   nostram rogant roborari fidem
V.17   omne nascitur bonum
V.17   tota sequatur ecclesia
V.17   tripudium fiet sempiternitatis

6.   aVA and similar (complex)

I.3   in *ecclesiastica* excerpta inseruit *historia*
I.3   in *suo* hoc idem de Pascha opus conlaudauit *catalogo*
I.4   *clarissima* per orbem . . . sacri ingenii diffusa sunt *lumina*
I.4   notam subire times Hermagoricae nouitatis
I.4   *tuae* dirige fulcrum *sententiae*
I.4   *nullis* diuinae scripturae fulta *testimoniis*
I.5   *nulla* sit inter te et Hieronymum in sententia promenda *dissonantia*
I.5   *indubitatam* in scripturis diuinis accommodant *fidem*
I.8   *sui* rem sustineret *contemptus*
I.9   *tua* largire, per Christum precor, *opuscula*
I.9   *miro*, ut audiui, elaborasti *ingenio*
I.9   aliqua . . . de *tuis* transmitte *relectis*
I.9   *breuibus*, deposco, tracta *sententiis*
I.9   *occidentalis* in his gratias agat *caecitas*
I.10   *meae* indulge quod sic audacter scripsi rogo *procacitati*
II.2   occasio uobis *sanctae* effecta est *synodi*
II.4   uoci *ueri* non concordat *pastoris*
II.5   si *aliqua* sit traditionis *diuersitas*
II.6   *superbam*, ut aiunt quidam, scribendi *praesumptionem*
II.7   sermo *Domini* sugillet *dicentis*
II.8   *quanta* erit dissimilitudinis in actualibus studiis *mensura*
II.8   *tanta* erit pacis et caritatis inter imperfectos *fictura*
II.8   *tota* ad caelestia festinet *ecclesia*
II.9   unius enim sumus corporis commembra
III.2 *nostrorum* traditionem robores *seniorum*
III.2 cum *nostrorum* regulis manemus *seniorum*
III.2 *istas* quas haec cartula tibi commendat *epistolas*
IV.3 *meum* illi da *osculum*

IV.3   indolis inbuendae scis diu uotum meum
IV.3   non *omnia* omnibus conuenire *monita*
IV.4   *diuersa* sensi multorum *uota*
IV.6   *Lacrimosam* tibi uolui scribere *epistolam*
IV.6   *bonorum* tibi conscii sunt *operum*
IV.7   *quibus* circumluimur acsi uorticum *fragoribus*
V.2   in *illud antiquum probrosum* erumpat *elogium*
V.3   *uerba* aut in hac aut in altera . . . epistola inueneritis *incondita*
V.4   *te* ex intergo cognoscant *pastorem*
V.5   de manibus requirendus erit pastorum
V.7   *inimicis nostris* dum non sensimus circumdati sumus *triplicibus*
V.11   orbis terrarum caput est ecclesiarum
V.12   *sancto* priuilegium dedit *clauiculario*
V.12   inter *uiscera* more Rebeccae discerpitur *materna*
V.14   *azima* cum amaritudine non nesciens *comedenda*
V.17   *regis* insistit iussio *Agonis*

7. abVAB and similar

III.2   nullas istorum suscipimus regulas Gallorum
IV.8   quidam felici reuocans remigio tutus celator
V.17   Quam alacer annos superuenit pater post multos

8. Complex hyperbaton

I.2   illud cuiusdam egregium sapientis elogium
I.5   te mei, nimirum Petri cathedram apostoli et clauicularii legitime insidentem, occidentales apices de Pascha sollicitent
I.5   in fide supradictorum auctorum sibi inuicem contrariorum probanda?
II.2   omnes sedi apostolicae praesidentes dulcissimos omnibus praesules fidelibus
II.2   aliquod adhuc districtius euangelicae religionis et apostolicae traditionis consilium
III.2   insuaui scilicet intransmeabilique non tam tithis uisibilis quam intelligibilis dorso, quod optime nostis, opposito
III.2   nostrorum ad beatae memoriae papam conscriptorum Gregorium olim apicum in subiectis positorum
IV.2   semina non potest sui tenuitate caespitis accepta nutrire?
IV.2   iaculatis illis orationum feruentium acsi quibusdam sagittis
V.1   Pulcherrimo omnium totius Europae Ecclesiarum Capiti
V.8   fortiores peritioresque huius sancti conflictus duces
V.8   acsi quidam campi bellici roscidus cadauerum ac madidus post pugnam contemplator
V.11   in duobus illis feruentissimis Dei spiritus equis?
V.11   salua loci dominicae resurrectionis singulari praerogatiua?
V.14   rex gentilis peregrinum scribere Langobardus Scotum hebetem rogat

III

THE THIRTEEN SERMONS ATTRIBUTED TO COLUMBANUS
AND THE QUESTION OF THEIR AUTHORSHIP

Clare Stancliffe

A CENTURY ago Albert Hauck and, more judiciously, Otto Seebass queried whether the series of thirteen sermons (or *Instructiones*) hitherto ascribed to Columbanus was indeed by the Irish saint of that name, the founder of Luxeuil and Bobbio who died in 615.[1] Seebass disposed of all Hauck's objections to Columbanus's authorship save one: that in the second sermon the author of these thirteen sermons names his teacher as one Faustus, and quotes a passage from him. Hauck claimed that he had identified the source of this passage in a sermon by Faustus of Riez, and further pointed out that the ninth sermon of the thirteen ascribed to Columbanus has verbal reminiscences of another Gallic sermon, which he again claimed as a work of Faustus of Riez. This seemed to confirm the second sermon's claim that the author was Faustus's pupil. As Faustus of Riez died *ca* 490, and Columbanus in 615, it seemed obvious that that pupil could not have been Columbanus.

The reference to Faustus had, it is true, been noticed before; but Patrick Fleming, who first edited the thirteen sermons among Columbanus's works in the seventeenth century, had explained it away as an alternative name for Comgall of Bangor, who was indeed Columbanus's teacher; and he had been able to adduce Notker of Sankt Gallen's ninth-century martyrology which supported this identification, mentioning 'Comgellum, latine Fausti nomine illustrem, Praeceptorem B. Columbani' under 9 June.[2] Hauck's positive identification of what appeared to be the source for *Instructio II* (§ 2) as a work of Faustus of Riez undermined Fleming's theory, and appeared to rule out Columbanian authorship of the thirteen sermons.

A few years later Seebass queried and often refuted Hauck's more wide-ranging questions as to whether the manuscript-tradition, the Latin style and the content of the sermons did indeed point to Columbanus as their author. But at the same time he elaborated upon Hauck's argument about Faustus, using August Engelbrecht's new edition of Faustus's works to good effect in tracing

---

[1] The sermons are edited in *Sancti Columbani Opera*, ed. & transl. Walker, pp. 60–120; for the comments in question, see Hauck, 'Ueber di sogenannte *Instructiones*', and Seebass, 'Über die sogenannte *Instructiones*'. In accordance with current practice, I refer to these sermons either by the English term, sermons, or the Latin term, *Instructiones*, the latter being the title given them in the manuscripts and in Walker's edition.

[2] Fleming, *Collectanea Sacra*, p. 48.

sources for several of the thirteen sermons.[3] Seebass, however, was impressed by the manuscript-evidence for the Columbanian authorship of the thirteen sermons, and he noted that two manuscripts included only nos *III* and *XI* of the thirteen, together with two other sermons, so attributing four sermons in all to Columbanus. Since *Instructio XI* has very convincing parallels with some indubitably Columbanian works, and could, Seebass felt, be withdrawn from the series of thirteen *Instructiones* in which *I–II, V–X,* and *XII–XIII* are thematically closely related, without damaging the sequence, Seebass came to the conclusion that *Instructio XI* was indeed a genuine product of Columbanus; and he further argued that we should follow the attribution of the two manuscripts mentioned in accepting *Instructiones III* and *XI* and the two other sermons in those manuscripts as being genuine works of Columbanus, while assigning the rest of the series of thirteen to an anonymous Gallic pupil of Faustus of Riez.

Seebass's arguments seemed convincing, and were canonised in J.F. Kenney's formative guide, *The Sources for the Early History of Ireland*.[4] It is, however, difficult to believe that Seebass said the last word on the subject. Although to allow Columbanian authorship for *Instructiones III* and *XI* does account for some of the strongest evidence for Columbanian authorship of the series as a whole, it is unsatisfactory to abstract these two sermons alone: to an impartial reader, none of the sermons in that series of thirteen seems out of place, and the same characteristic expressions, themes, and images are found throughout.[5]

Further, if we probe into the evidence of their author's sources, we find that Seebass built his arguments on shifting sands. In the very year in which Seebass wrote, Germain Morin published a detailed critique of Engelbrecht's edition of Faustus's works and argued that many of the sermons which Hauck, Seebass, and Engelbrecht had taken as Faustus's were in fact the work of Caesarius of Arles.[6] This does not necessarily invalidate Seebass's thesis: the sermons in question are not those cited in *Instructio II* under the name of Faustus, but others used elsewhere in the series. It does, however, complicate the picture. Now, a century later, some of the essential spade-work has been done, and we are able to build anew on firmer foundations than were available a century ago. In 1937 Morin published his great edition of Caesarius of Arles's sermons, and in 1970/1 François Glorie produced a critical edition of the Gallic Eusebian sermon-collection. This collection is of great importance for present purposes, because it contains the two sermons cited under the name of Faustus by the author of the thirteen sermons. With critical editions of all

---

[3] Seebass, 'Über die sogenannte *Instructiones*'; *Fausti. . . Opera,* ed. Engelbrecht.

[4] Kenney, *The Sources,* pp. 196–7.

[5] Laporte, 'Étude d'authenticité [*Revue Mabillon* 45 (1955)]', pp. 12–15, 17–18, and cf. p. 25 and below, pp. 127–9. Besides the overwhelming verbal parallels for *Instructio XI* in genuine Columbanian works (Seebass, 'Über die sogenannte *Instructiones*', pp. 528–9), note that *Instructio III* (§ 1) includes the passage which is very close to the poem most likely to be the work of Columbanus, namely *Mundus iste transibit*; see discussion by Schaller, below, pp. 240–54.

[6] Morin, 'Critique'.

the crucial sources used in these sermons now available, the time is ripe for a reconsideration of the evidence of the sources used by the sermons' author in a fresh attempt to solve the problem of his identity.

Meanwhile Columbanian scholarship has also made advances. In 1957 G.S.M. Walker produced a critical edition of all the works with any claim to be considered as by Columbanus. Fortified by a helpful contribution from Ludwig Bieler, this edition provides a firm basis for appraising the manuscript-tradition of the thirteen *Instructiones*, and for studying the author's latinity and characteristic turns of phrase and thought alongside those of indubitably Columbanian works. However, it has to be admitted that in some crucial respects Walker's edition has serious defects. The most glaring is that he does not seem to have taken account of Seebass's article of 1892, which set out many verbal parallels between the thirteen *Instructiones* and other works.[7] It is also unfortunate that Walker never systematically marshalled all the evidence for and against Columbanian authorship of these sermons, and that he included no adequate discussion of the Faustus-question. His own approach was to make light of the extensive parallels between Columbanus's *Instructio II* (§ 2) and the sermon(s) ascribed to Faustus, and to suggest that we are here dealing with a 'loose stock of public material which individual preachers used and adapted for their special needs'. As for the reference to Faustus, he reverted to Fleming's explanation that it was an alternative Latin name for Comgall of Bangor.[8]

Walker's somewhat cavalier attitude towards the Faustus-problem was unfortunate, as it has perhaps led some scholars to dismiss rather too swiftly the claims that Columbanus wrote all thirteen sermons. However, just before Walker's edition was published, a major reconsideration of the authorship of the thirteen sermons was undertaken by Jean Laporte, and this dealt in expert fashion with the most crucial question which Walker had sidestepped. Laporte investigated the manuscript-tradition, and he cited stylistic traits and verbal parallels between all thirteen of the sermons and other prose works of Columbanus, making out a strong case for treating the series of thirteen as a whole. Most important of all, Laporte cast new light on the Faustus-problem, dealing a severe blow to the 'Faustus equals Comgall' school of thought, but at the same time offering an alternative solution. Laporte argued that, despite the wording of *Instructio II*, '[Faustus] et nos uiles licet commissos sibi docuit', this might mean no more than that the author had been a student of Faustus's works in the sense of having read them extensively, rather than necessarily meaning that the author was personally entrusted to Faustus. Although this theory may initially strike some scholars as doubtful, the parallels cited by Laporte, particularly that from Venantius Fortunatus's *Vita S. Hilarii Pictauensis*, make it plausible enough. Venantius addressed his contemporary, Pascentius, bishop of Poitiers, as '[te] quem Hilarius ab ipsis cunabulis ante sua uestigia quasi peculiarem

---

[7] Seebass, 'Über die sogenannte *Instructiones*', pp. 522–5. The parallels for *Instructio II* (§ 2) and *Instructio IX* (§ 2) noted by Walker (*Sancti Columbani Opera*, ed. & transl. Walker, pp. 70, 98) had already been noted by Hauck, 'Ueber die sogenannte *Instructiones*'.

[8] *Sancti Columbani Opera*, ed. & transl. Walker, pp. xli–xliv, 69, n. 1.

uernulam familiariter enutriuit', despite the fact that Hilary had lived in the fourth century, while Pascentius belonged to the sixth century.[9]

If the Faustus-question could be resolved along these lines, then the way would lie open to accepting Columbanus's authorship of the whole series of thirteen sermons. Many scholars, however, are still doubtful about assigning the thirteen sermons to Columbanus. Michael Lapidge and Richard Sharpe's *A Bibliography of Celtic-Latin Literature 400–1200*, which bids fair to succeed Kenney's book as a judicious guide to the contemporary scholarly consensus on such matters, has relegated the thirteen *Instructiones* to the status of pseudo-Columbanian 'dubia', suggesting a fifth-century date for them.[10]

In view of the confusion now reigning in scholarly circles about these sermons, I have undertaken a thorough reappraisal of the whole question in the hope that this will at least set the arguments upon a firmer foundation, and may lead to conclusions acceptable to all scholars.[11] I apologise in advance for what some may regard as finicky detail over rhythmical *clausulae* or attribution of sources used by the sermons' author; but, if this study is to carry conviction in a way in which earlier studies apparently have not, then such detail is essential. Rather than writing in a polemical fashion for or against Columbanus's authorship, I shall try to set out the material objectively, first looking at the manuscript-tradition, then passing on to the evidence of the various sources used by the author, and after that examining the sermons themselves, their content and their style, to see whether or not they appear to be by the same author as other prose works accepted as definitely written by Columbanus. We shall then be in a position to discuss what conclusions may be drawn. In order to combine brevity and objectivity of expression, I shall refer to the author of the thirteen sermons as X.

The Manuscript Evidence

One significant source which bears on the question of the sermons' authorship is the manuscript-tradition (see fig. 1, below, p. 104). The series of thirteen *Instructiones* has been handed down as a whole only in manuscripts stemming from Bobbio, where the sermons are associated with other works widely accepted as being by Columbanus. There are two such manuscripts in Torino, each with the fifteenth-century *ex-libris* inscription of Bobbio Abbey. The earlier is Torino, Biblioteca Nazionale Universitaria, MS. G.VII.16, of the second half of the ninth century (Walker's Ti). This contains the *Regula monachorum* (fos 2r–13v), the thirteen *Instructiones* (fos 13v–59r), the tract *De .viii. uitiis*

---

[9] Laporte, 'Étude d'authenticité [*Revue Mabillon* 45 (1955)]', pp. 18–23, esp. 22.

[10] Lapidge & Sharpe, *A Bibliography*, p. 331 (no. 1251).

[11] This present study, begun in late 1985, was nearing completion when the work of Michele Tosi came to my notice. I am very grateful to the author for sending me his 'Arianesimo Tricapitolino' in time for me to take account of it (see below, pp. 194, 196). He provides a helpful review of various contributions to the authorship-question on pp. 12–41.

(fo 59rv), which Walker relegated to his appendix,[12] followed by the exhortatory tract *Cum iam de moribus* (fos 60r–62v: Walker's *Episula VI*), and finally the Penitential, sections A–B (fos 62v–71v). Exactly the same selection of works, in almost the same order, is found in the second Bobbio manuscript, now Torino, Biblioteca Nazionale Universitaria, MS. G.V.38, of *ca* 900 (Walker's T). In this manuscript the Columbanian corpus occupies fos 80v–130v; it is preceded by the *Regula S. Benedicti*, a Benedictine hymnary, and the monastic-reform canons of 816/17, and followed by two unnumbered folios containing hymns.[13] Again, the same Columbanian corpus occurred in the same order in the Bobbio manuscript which Fleming used for his edition in his *Collectanea sacra* published in 1667, although Ludwig Bieler thought that Fleming had used the archetype of Ti, rather than Ti itself.[14] Finally, the seventeenth-century abbot of Sankt Gallen, Jodoc Metzler, used an exemplar from Bobbio when writing Sankt Gallen, Stiftsbibliothek, MS. 1346, which contains our series of *Instructiones I–XIII*, and the dubious *Exhortatoria S. Columbani in conuentu ad Fratres*, followed by *Epistula IV,* then Walker's *Epistula VI* (*Cum iam de moribus*), then the *De .viii. uitiis*, and finally *Epistulae III, II, V,* and *I*.[15] Metzler's transcript (Walker's M) is textually very close to Fleming's edition (Walker's F). To sum up, the series of thirteen *Instructiones* derives from the Bobbio manuscripts Ti and T and from Fleming's and Metzler's exemplar(s), all of which are related – the two former closely so, and the two latter closely so.

The existence of this collection – or at least one containing *Instructiones I* and *XIII* – at Bobbio as early as the late seventh century is indirectly implied by a Bobbio manuscript of that date[16] which contains two anonymous sermons whose author apparently borrowed from X's *Instructiones I* and *XIII*. True, Morin, who edited the anonymous sermons and signalised their parallels with passages in the sermons ascribed to Columbanus, assumed that all should be ascribed to the same author, our X.[17] However, with Laporte, I am convinced that 'ce sont deux âmes différentes, la chose saute aux yeux de qui connaît bien la manière du saint'. Like Laporte, I miss X's 'style énergique et véhément' in Morin's two sermons.[18] Further, the author of Morin's sermons

---

12 See below, n. 43.
13 *Sancti Columbani Opera*, ed. & transl. Walker, pp. xxxv, lxxiii–lxxiv; and Laporte, 'Étude d'authenticité [*Revue Mabillon* 45 (1955)]', pp. 5–8, who confusingly denotes G.V.38 as T¹ and G.VII.16 as T². I have used Walker's sigla for the MSS., and followed Bieler (*apud* Walker, pp. lxxiii–lxxxii and in his review of Laporte, *Le Pénitential de Saint Columban*, p. 111) on the dates, rather than following Laporte and Seebass, 'Ueber die Handschriften'.
14 Fleming, *Collectanea Sacra.* pp. 41–2; Bieler *apud* Walker, *Sancti Columbani Opera*, pp. lxxiii–lxxiv.
15 Bieler, *ibid.*, p. lxːv and n. 4. Cf. Smit, *Studies*, pp. 35 7.
16 Now Milano, Biblioteca Ambrosiana, MS. O.212 sup., dated to *saec.* vii^ex in Lowe, *Codices*, III, no. 361. The MS. was probably written at Bobbio, but script, spelling and syllabification point to an Irish scribe. Morin's two sermons are on fos 15r–16v.
17 Morin, 'Deux pièces'. The two sermons have been reprinted in *Patrologia Latina*, ed. Migne, Supplementum III.709–13. The parallels are too extensive to admit of doubt.
18 Laporte, 'Étude d'authenticité [*Revue Mabillon* 45 (1955)]', pp. 24–5.

liked categorising or listing points, which he later expounded, sometimes figuratively. For instance, as sons of God, we should offer in a mystical sense three gifts – divine, royal, and human. The divine gift is incense, interpreted as prayer; the royal gift is gold, interpreted as knowledge; and the third gift, presumably myrrh, with its connotation of human mortality, is the mortification of our wills.[19] Although the mortification of our wills occurs as a theme in the sermons of X,[20] this categorising tendency and the figurative interpretations have no parallels in any of the thirteen sermons attributed to Columbanus.

Granted, then, that these differences lead us to conclude that we are dealing with two different authors, can we ascertain who was borrowing from whom? I think that we can. The second sermon edited by Morin, on the Trinity, contains amongst many verbal parallels with X's *Instructio I* the following sentence: 'Cui haec pauca de Trinitate non sufficiunt, iuxta Scribturae sententiam, plura non proderunt.' Compare X's *Instructio I* (§ 3): 'Quia cui haec pauca de Deo Trinitate non sufficiunt, plura iuxta Scripturam non proderunt.' The ultimate source of both passages is a tag, perhaps proverbial, 'cui pauca non sufficiunt, plura non proderunt'. This is first found in Sulpicius Seuerus's *Dialogi* I.xviii.1, in the form 'ad incitandam uirtutum aemulationem, cui pauca non sufficiunt, multa non proderunt'.[21] The parallels between X and Morin's author, however, are closer to each other than either is to other citations of this tag; and we should note that both attributed this tag to 'Scripture'. This, together with the other parallels listed by Morin, makes it clear that one sermon-writer derived it from the work of the other, rather than that both cited the same tag independently.[22] Further, this particular tag was a favourite with X who cited it in a less altered form in *Instructio III* (§ 4), 'Audi quid sapiens dixit, Cui pauca non sufficiunt, plura non proderunt'; while it also appears in the work edited by Walker as *Epistula VI* (§ 1): 'Audisti quid scriptum est: cui pauca non sufficiunt, plura non proderunt.'[23] Since, then, we have evidence

---

[19] *Sermo de ascensione*, lines 14–28 (ed. Morin, 'Deux pièces', pp. 162–3 = PL Supp III.710). Cf. also how the author expatiates on the sentence 'resurgentes cum Christo per Christum in Christo ad Christum ascendant' (Morin, lines 33–40 = PL Supp. III.711), which X would surely have left without any such long-winded explanation. Note also the figurative explanation given to Christ's nativity, epiphany, passion, etc. in lines 49–59.

[20] *Instructio* X.2; cf. also Columbanus, *Regula monachorum*, § 9; but it is, of course, a common christian ascetic theme.

[21] *Sulpicii Severi libri*, ed. Halm, p. 170. For other citations of the tag, including the second Council of Orange (A.D. 529) and Gregory of Tours, *Vita patrum*, see Levison, *England and the Continent*, p. 298, n. 6. Both the latter, like the *Instructiones*, have *plura* for Sulpicius's *multa*.

[22] Laporte, 'Étude d'authenticité [*Revue Mabillon* 45 (1955)]', p. 25, had suggested that both sermon writers were drawing upon a common source. But this hypothesis seems unnecessarily complicated, while X's delight in the tag does suggest the course of events which I put forward.

[23] *Epistula VI* has a quite different manuscript-tradition from that of *Epistulae I–V*, occurring in MSS. of the thirteen *Instructiones* after these and the *De octo uitiis*, and before (or in T, amid) the *Penitential*; and it is often headed *exhortatio* rather than

that this tag was already a favourite of X, the likelihood is that X himself applied it to the question of the Trinity, and that Morin's author borrowed it, in its adapted form, from his work.

Thus the series of thirteen *Instructiones* has been handed down in Bobbio manuscripts, and these sermons, or at least the first and last, were seemingly already at Bobbio in the late seventh century. Before we leave the manuscript-tradition of the series as a whole, we should note that in the ninth-century catalogue of the monastery of Sankt Gallen there is the following entry: 'Item eiusdem [*scil.* Sancti Columbani] instructio de fide et alia nonnulla in vol. I.'[24] X's first sermon was entitled 'De Fide' in Ti (and, allowing for a misreading, in T): so Sankt Gallen probably had the whole series of thirteen *Instructiones* in the ninth century; certainly it had *Instructio I* and some other(s). Finally, we should note that a collection of X's sermons which included, at the least, *Instructiones III, VII*, and *IX*, was available to the eighth-century Northumbrian anchorite, Alchfrith, who borrowed extensively from them in composing a letter to a priest and monk named Hyglac.[25]

In addition to the Bobbio manuscripts of the series as a whole there are two further groups of manuscripts which contain only some of the sermons: one group, associated with the abbey of Fleury, contains only *Instructiones III* and *XI*; the other group contains only *Instructio V*, which is here found in association with Columbanus's rules. We will examine these groups in turn.

The earliest manuscript in which *Instructiones III* and *XI* are preserved is Vatican City, Biblioteca Apostolica Vaticana, MS. Regin. lat. 140 (Walker's R), dated by André Wilmart to the early ninth century (*saec. ix in*). This has a Fleury *ex-libris* inscription of the tenth (?) century, and two more of the twelfth century. Wilmart observed that it is written 'iuxta Turonicae artis regulas'.[26] The manuscript contains, first, Cassian's *Conlationes*, and secondly an extensive collection of *ascetica* and *monastica* (fos 27–150): sermons and excerpts from or attributed to Augustine, Jerome, Caesarius, Nilus, Gregory the Great, Isidore, Faustus, Alcuin, and others. The Columbanian section is on fos 78v–83r, under the heading 'Incipit ordo lectionum officii sancti Columbani abbatis'. It comprises the possibly Columbanian sermon, *De homine misero*, which Walker relegated to an appendix; then *Instructio III*; then the tract *De .viii. uitiis* (which again Walker printed in his appendix); and finally *Instructio XI*.[27] Exactly

---

epistula. Perhaps, then, it should be ascribed to X, rather than accepted as Columbanian without any doubts, as are *Epistulae I–V*; see *Sancti Columbani Opera*, ed. & transl. Walker, pp. xxxv, xxxix, lxxiii–lxxv, Smit, *Studies*, pp. 33–5, and the discussion of Neil Wright, above, pp. 58–9. A much attentuated echo of Sulpicius's *Dialogi* I.xviii.1 occurs in Columbanus, *Regula monachorum*, § 8 (ed. Walker, p. 136, line 21).

[24] *Catalogi bibliothecarum antiqui*, ed. Becker, p. 48 (no. 230).
[25] Levison, *England and the Continent*, pp. 295–302; the passage printed by Levison (*ibid.*, pp. 297–8) is from *Instructio IX* (§ 1)(*Sancti Columbani Opera*, ed. & transl. Walker, p. 98). Hughes ('Some aspects', p. 59) notes the parallels to X's *Instructiones III* and *VII*.
[26] Wilmart, *Codices Reginenses* I.337–42.
[27] *Sancti Columbani Opera*, ed. & transl. Walker, pp. 208–10 (for *De homine misero*), 210–12 (for *De .viii. uitiis*).

the same selection of 'Columbanian' works occurs in a seventeenth-century manuscript, Paris, Bibliothèque Nationale, MS. lat. 17188 (Walker's D), under the heading 'Ordo S. Columbani abbatis de uita et actibus monachorum'. This manuscript bears a note saying that it was copied from a Fleury manuscript some 700 years old; but, although it is related to R, it is not a copy of R.[28] Finally we should note that Fleming, also in the seventeenth century, used a third manuscript containing a very similar Columbanian corpus under almost the same title, 'Incipit ordo S. Columbani Abbatis de uita et actione Monachorum'. This comprised *De .viii. uitiis* and X's *Instructiones III* and *XI*, and formed part of a monastic collection containing Cassian's *De institutis coenobiorum*, Effrem *Ad monachos*, twenty-two homilies of Caesarius *Ad monachos*, and an *Admonitio S. Basilii ad monachos*. According to Fleming, the manuscript was 'an ancient parchment-codex' then 'in celebri Monasterio S. Joannis Baptistae Florinensis', viz. Florennes, in Belgium. It seems conceivable that there is some confusion between Florinensis and Floriacensis (of Fleury), and that Fleming's manuscript was the ancestor, perhaps even the exemplar, of Walker's MS. D.[29] At all events, in view of the provenance of R and of D's exemplar, I shall christen these the 'Fleury family'. Their text of *Instructiones III* and *XI* is independent of that of the Bobbio family.

The third group of manuscripts to be considered comprises those where *Instructio V* is found on its own, in association with Columbanus's *Regula coenobialis* and/or *Regula monachorum*.[30] These three texts are found together in at least seven manuscripts, and *Instructio V* occurs with one or the other of Columbanus's rules in at least five others. The earliest manuscript to contain these three works together is Lambach, Stiftsbibliothek, MS. 31, of the first half of the ninth century; and this manuscript may be the ancestor of the whole group. Lambach MS. 31, which may have been written at Münsterswarzach, was originally two separate manuscripts. The three Columbanian works occur on fos 97r–108r amid a *corpus regularum*; *Instructio V* is there headed 'S. Columbani abbatis epistola'. The text of *Instructio V* in this group of manuscripts, where it is associated with Columbanus's rules, is related to the Bobbio family of manuscripts in which all thirteen *Instructiones* are included.[31] One may dub this the 'Rules family'.

In addition to this 'Rules family' of manuscripts containing *Instructio V*, this sermon is copied on its own in various other manuscripts. The most important of these is Paris, Bibliothèque Nationale, MS. lat. 13440 (Walker's H). This manuscript is of particular interest because its text of *Instructio V*

---

[28] *Ibid.*, pp. xl, lxxiv, lxxv; and see Mundó, 'L'édition', p. 290. D may have been copied from a manuscript used by Fleming which also contained this selection of 'Columbanian' works.

[29] Fleming, *Collectanea Sacra*, p. 42; Bieler *apud* Walker, *Sancti Columbani Opera*, p. lxxiv.

[30] In addition to Walker [and Bieler], *Sancti Columbani Opera*, pp. xxxix–xl, lxxvi, n. 3, see the reviews by Mundó, 'L'édition', and Esposito, 'On the new edition', as well as the remarks of Glorie, *Eusebius 'Gallicanus'*, pp. 956–8.

[31] Bieler *apud* Walker, *Sancti Columbani Opera*, p. lxxvi and n. 3. On the MS., see Bischoff, *Die südostdeutschen Schreibschulen*, II.41–2. Its script has traces of Insular influence.

(fos 97r–100r) is both good in itself and also independent of that in the manuscripts already considered.[32] It is written in Corbie 'ab'-script, and was therefore assigned by E.A. Lowe to the second half of the eighth century and the vicinity of Corbie.[33] However, recently it has been noted that this manuscript, which contains various homilies and prayers, includes a series of patristic excerpts directed to virgins which is identical with the excerpts quoted from these Fathers in the legislation promulgated at Aachen in 816/17. On these grounds the manuscript has been dated to *ca* 816/17, and this fits with T.A.M. Bishop's study of Corbie 'ab'-script, in which he argued that it was practised by the nuns of Corbie during Adalhard's abbacy. The attribution to Corbie *ca* 816/17 therefore seems secure.[34] What is particularly interesting is that this manuscript, which on the basis of its text appears to stem from a manuscript-tradition wholly different from the Bobbio-family of the thirteen sermons (or the sub-family where *Instructio V* occurs alongside Columbanus's Rules), like them assigns this sermon to Columbanus: 'Epist. sancti ... bani abbatis de incertitudine (?) mortalium uit(ae).'[35] It may or may not be relevant to recall that Corbie was a daughter-house of Luxeuil, founded by Queen Balthildis to follow the mixed rule of Benedict and Columbanus; and that from Luxeuil came some manuscripts, as well as the first monks.[36] We should not put much weight on this fact, however, for by the early ninth century the library of Corbie was becoming one of the most extensive in Francia, and we have no means of knowing when it acquired the exemplar from which H's text of *Instructio V* was copied.

Since Walker's edition, various other manuscripts of X's *Instructio V* have come to light. The only pre-twelfth-century one which was not taken into account at all by Walker or Bieler is now in München, Bayerische Staats-bibliothek, Clm. 6330. Bernhard Bischoff has dated this to shortly after 800 and, on the basis of its script, he assigned it to the same centre as that which produced the 'Lorsch' annals, somewhere in the Alamannic area not far from Lake Constance: viz. the general vicinity of Reichenau or Sankt Gallen. The manuscript includes excerpts from various Fathers, the *Quicunque uult*, and, at the end, a paraphrase of the Lord's Prayer in the Bavarian dialect of Old High German.[37] X's *Instructio V* occurs on fos 48r–49r under the heading 'humelia sancti Columbani abbatis'. Textually it cannot readily be assigned to any existing family: although at times its readings tally with those of the Bobbio and 'Rules' families over against H, in other places this relationship is

---

[32] Walker [and Bieler], *Sancti Columbani Opera*, pp. xl, lxxv–lxxvi; there are four occasions when H shares a reading with the text of *Instructio V* in Clm. 6330, discussed below.

[33] Lowe, *Codices*, V, no. 662.

[34] Ganz, *Corbie*, pp. 48–56, esp. 51, 55, 143–4; Samaran & Marichal, *Catalogue*, III.656; Bishop, 'The scribes', pp. 523–36, esp. 533.

[35] *Eusebius 'Gallicanus'*, ed. Glorie, p. 958. Hrabanus Maurus, the only other author I can think of whose name ends in *-bani*, did not become an abbot until 822.

[36] Prinz, *Frühes Mönchtum*, p. 173; Ganz, 'The Merovingian library', pp. 154, 156.

[37] Bischoff, *Die südostdeutschen Schreibschulen*, I.144–5. See also *Karl der Grosse*, p. 198 (no. 353). For the content, see Halm *et al.*, *Catalogus*, I/3, p.93, and McKitterick, *The Frankish Church*, p. 109.

reversed, while it also contains a number of idiosyncratic – and unacceptable – readings.[38] The relatively early date of this manuscript gives interest to these textual details and to its unambiguous attribution of the sermon to Columbanus.

The other manuscripts containing *Instructio V* all belong to the twelfth century or later; and, to my knowledge, no work has been done to establish which families they belong to textually. In all cases where the attribution is known, *Instructio V* is ascribed to Columbanus.[39]

Finally, one manuscript formerly at Sankt Emmeram, Regensburg, contains a compilation put together from X's *Instructiones V* and *VI* under the heading, 'Dicta Sancti Ysidori'.[40] This manuscript (München, Bayerische Staatsbibliothek, Clm. 14470) was written *ca* 800, probably in southern Germany, and includes Iustus Urgellensis on the Song of Songs, an anonymous *Expositio IV Euangeliorum*, which may be of Irish origin, as well as much homiletic material.[41] The compilation of X's sermons occurs amongst the latter, on fos 102v–104r. It is the only manuscript known to me where the sermons are not either anonymous or attributed to Columbanus.

The details of the manuscript-evidence for the authorship of X's thirteen sermons may not make easy reading; but it is essential to grasp their implications if we are to form any judgment on the question of the sermons' authorship. First, in only one manuscript is any of these sermons attributed to any named author other than Columbanus: Clm. 14470, of *ca* 800, where an abridged compilation of *Instructiones V* and *VI* is ascribed to Isidore. This near unanimity of the manuscript-tradition in ascribing the sermons to Columbanus is all the more striking[42] as in the Carolingian and later periods, to which our manuscripts belong, Columbanus was not held in particularly high regard: his Rule was then being ousted in favour of that of Benedict, and the practice of private penance which he had encouraged also came under attack from the Carolingian reformers. Thus, while attributions of sermons to revered church fathers like Augustine or Jerome always need to be regarded rather sceptically until further evidence is forthcoming, attributions to Columbanus, a lesser luminary, should be taken seriously. Indeed, excluding the series of thirteen sermons with which we are currently concerned, very little sermon material is

---

[38] These observations are my own, based upon photographs of the MS. kindly supplied by the Bayerische Staatsbibliothek.

[39] Helpful details are given by Glorie, *Eusebius 'Gallicanus'*, pp. 957–8; but note that where Glorie does not quote the attribution, this is because he does not know it: it does not necessarily imply that the sermon is anonymous in the manuscript, as the case of Clm. 6330 shows.

[40] Glorie (*ibid.*), and my own photographs of the MS.

[41] Lowe, *Codices*, IX, no. 1300; Halm *et al.*, *Catalogus*, II/2, pp. 177–8; and Griesser, 'Die handschriftliche Ueberlieferung', pp. 285–6. The *Expositio* is listed by Lapidge & Sharpe, *A Bibliography*, no. 341. Textually, Clm. 14470, fos 102v–104r, is of most interest for preserving the opening sentence of *Instructio V* in full. H was the only MS. used by Walker to contain the sentence in question.

[42] Even Seebass ('Über die sogenannte *Instructiones*', p. 519) recognised 'that the external attestation of the Columbanian origin of our sermon collection scarcely leaves anything to be desired.'

attributed to Columbanus apart from works which in all probability really are by him.[43] Further corroboration comes from the fact that in the Bobbio family of manuscripts, including its extensive sub-group where *Instructio V* is associated with Columbanus's Rules, the sermons are copied alongside works which are now widely accepted by scholars as being genuine works of Columbanus.

The arguments from the manuscript-tradition in favour of Columbanus's authorship do not end here. The series of thirteen *Instructiones* as a whole is preserved only in manuscripts stemming from Bobbio, Columbanus's own foundation where he died in 615. Of course, other manuscripts containing the whole series may have perished; but it is interesting to note that the only other two places for which there is evidence of the whole series being available are eighth-century Northumbria and ninth-century Sankt Gallen, the latter a monastery which looked back to Columbanus's disciple Gallus, and which fostered Columbanus's memory and writings in the Carolingian period.[44] This distribution of X's sermons is interesting in view of the fact that, *Instructio V* apart, the thirteen sermons do not seem to have achieved a wide circulation in the Carolingian period.[45] That makes their preservation at Bobbio, and their apparent presence there as early as the seventh century, the more significant. François Glorie has recently touched on the questions raised by this distribution of evidence. He assumed that, because of the reference to Faustus, these sermons could not be by Columbanus; but, recognising the weight of the manuscript-attributions, he suggested that these could have arisen if the archetype had had an inscription 'liber s. Columbani [abbatiae] de Bobio', which was subsequently, whether knowingly or not, interpreted as the name of the author, 's. Columbani [abbatis]'.[46] This suggestion sounds ingenious, but it will not stand up to close scrutiny. The designation 'liber s. Columbani de Bobio', which is written in a fifteenth-century hand in T and Ti, is the normal fifteenth-century Bobbio *ex-libris* inscription.[47] It is unlikely that such a wording was used for this purpose as early as the ninth century, the date of these two Bobbio manuscripts. In any case, if this had been the normal Bobbio formula of ownership at that date, a Bobbio scribe would not have been

---

[43] Gallic Eusebius no. 38 (= *Hom. III ad monachos*) is erroneously attributed to Columbanus in one sixteenth-century MS., Augsburg, Staats- und Stadtbibliothek, MS. 2° Augsb. 320 (see Glorie, *Eusebius 'Gallicanus'*, pp. 903, 954, and Fleming, *Collectanea Sacra*, p. 85). The sermon beginning *In ecclesia Dei* (printed *Sancti Columbani Opera*, ed. & transl. Walker, pp. 206–8) was attributed to Columbanus by Jodoc Metzler in the seventeenth century on no known authority. It is almost certainly spurious (see Walker, *ibid.*, pp. lxi–lxii). The other two homiletic pieces in Walker's appendix, namely *De homine misero* and *De .viii. uitiis* (*ibid.*, pp. 208–12), may well be by Columbanus: see Seebass, *Über Columba von Luxeuils Klosterregel und Bussbuch*, p. 53, n., and 'Über die sogenannte *Instructiones*', pp. 530–1; *Sancti Columbani Opera*, ed. & transl. Walker, p. lxii; and Bieler, review of Laporte, *Le Pénitentiel*, p. 109.

[44] See Helbling & Helbling, 'Der heilige Gallus', pp. 44–6, 56–8.

[45] Esposito, 'On the new edition', p. 201.

[46] *Eusebius 'Gallicanus'*, p. 959; cf. also pp. xiv–xvii.

[47] Lowe, *Codices*, III, no. 353; cf. Tosi, 'Arianesimo Tricapitolino', p. 39.

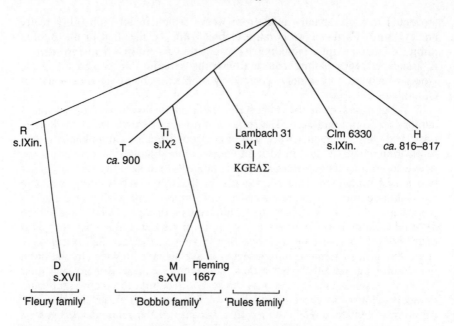

Figure 1. The manuscript tradition of the thirteen *Instructiones* attributed to Columbanus.

confused by it; and if it were not the normal Bobbio formula at that time, then its occurrence in the archetype of T and Ti would itself require explanation. Furthermore, we should expect Bobbio, which had a continuous history from 615 to the Carolingian period,[48] to preserve reliable information about the writings of its founder; and its monks made no attempt to father other *spuria* on him. We should also note that the ninth-century Sankt Gallen library-catalogue corroborates the evidence of the two ninth-century Bobbio manuscripts.

Glorie's case is further weakened by his failure to take fully into consideration the evidence of the separate textual families, additional to the Bobbio family, which are represented by the manuscripts from Fleury on the one hand and H on the other – and arguably also by Clm 6330. What is important is that both the Fleury family (for *Instructiones III* and *XI*) and H (for *Instructio V*) belong to quite different textual traditions from that of the Bobbio family, which itself had already split into sub-groups by the time of its first extant manuscripts, in the ninth century; and the Fleury family, and H, and Clm 6330, and the Bobbio and Rules families *all* ascribe the sermons to Columbanus. A further point is that the Fleury family's selection of sermons appears to have been made for liturgical purposes, viz. to provide lections for the feast of St Columbanus.[49] Liturgical

---

[48] See Polonio, *Il monastero*, pp. 77–80 and *passim*.

[49] Vatican City, Biblioteca Apostolica Vaticana, Regin. lat. 140, fo 78v: 'incipit ordo lectionum officii sancti Columbani abbatis'.

practice is conservative, and this too would argue that these sermons were being ascribed to Columbanus before our first extant manuscripts in the early ninth century. Also, since at Bobbio the lections for St Columbanus's day came from Ionas's *Vita S. Columbani*,[50] this would also imply that the tradition represented by the Fleury family is distinct from that of the Bobbio family, in which case we cannot explain away the attribution of the sermons to Columbanus in the way that Glorie has suggested.

To sum up: the weight of the manuscript-attributions to Columbanus is overwhelming; and, if X were not Columbanus, the attribution remains a very puzzling phenomenon for which no satisfactory solution has yet been offered. The fact that X's *Instructiones* – or *Instructio V* on its own – were so frequently copied with genuine Columbanian works is a further pointer, as is the fact that the series of thirteen sermons has been handed down to modern times only at Columbanus's monastery of Bobbio, where it was apparently to be found already in the late seventh century; and that, of the three places where we have good evidence for the existence of the series as a whole in the early middle ages, two have clear links with Columbanus and his followers.

The Author's Acquaintance with Non-biblical Sources

For the purposes of this paper, our main interest in X's relationship to other writings lies in the light which this may shed upon X's identity. I have therefore not set out to discover further patristic sources in addition to those already noted by other scholars. Instead, for the earlier sources I have generally contented myself with checking the references given by Walker, thus refining his list. Precise references are given in the appendix (below), which omits some of Walker's suggested parallels which I regard as too slight to be significant, while including some other parallels which escaped his eye. We may summarise the findings here. Of Latin works written before A.D. 440, X had apparently read Hilary of Poitiers, *De trinitate*, Jerome's famous *Epistula XXII* to Eustochium (known as *De uirginitate*), and Cassian's *Instituta*. He probably also knew Cassian's *Conlationes*, and may have known Sulpicius Seuerus's *Dialogi*.[51] The last three authors would have been read in ascetic circles everywhere in the Latin-speaking West, although knowledge of Hilary's works was not as common.

The other authors certainly or possibly used by X will require more detailed discussion. They comprise the Greek theologians Origen, Basil and Gregory of Nazianzus, some of whose works were available in Latin translation; the Insular authors Gildas and Uinniaus; the Italian authors Boethius and Gregory the Great; and several Gallic authors, or works emanating from Gaul:

[50] Maestri, 'La prima ufficiatura', pp. 49–50.
[51] For Cassian's *Conlationes*, see the discussion of the words *paracaraximus* and *tristificare*, below, pp. 167, 172. With respect to Sulpicius's *Dialogi*, the doubt arises over whether X drew his favourite tag, 'cui pauca non sufficiunt, plura non proderunt' from the *Dialogi*, or from another source, or whether it was simply a proverbial tag in common use at the time. See above, p. 98 and n. 21.

Gennadius's *Liber ecclesiasticorum dogmatum* and the anonymous *Quicunque uult*, sermons attributed to Caesarius of Arles and to the British-born Faustus of Riez, and finally the anonymous Gallic Eusebian sermon-collection.[52]

1. *Patristic and ascetic authors, Gildas, and credal works*

Let us start with reminiscences of Basil's *Rule*, as translated by Rufinus; and of Origen's *Homilies on Luke*, as translated by Jerome. In the former case there is a brief verbal parallel, and an association with the same biblical passages. In the latter case we are not so much dealing with a verbal parallel, as with an association of two biblical texts together with an interesting metaphor. Both reminiscences occur in the same passage, hence my treatment of them together. X's *Instructio XI* begins with a consideration of Genesis I.27, 'God made man in his image and likeness'. After a discussion of this verse, X tells us that we should render back (*reddere*) to God whatever virtues he first sowed in us ('quascumque ergo Deus in nobis . . . uirtutes serminauit'), as he himself taught us; we should love God and keep his commandments, and his command is, that we should love each other. The wording of God 'sowing virtues' in us, the idea that this should enable us to render them back to him, and the specific instance given of our thus being able to keep the commandments to love God and our neighbour, all this points to a knowledge of Basil's *Rule* – a work which was also known to Columbanus.[53] Equally, however, X's sentence, 'For the love of God is the restoration of his image', and the language of our 'rendering virtues back' to God, is a reference to the gospel story in which Jesus skilfully handled an awkward question about whether it was legitimate to pay taxes to the Roman emperor. Jesus asked to see a coin, with the image of the emperor on it, and said: 'Render therefore to Caesar those things which are Caesar's, and to

---

[52] The opening of the pseudo-Augustinian *Sermones ad fratres in eremo*, no. xlix (*Patrologia Latina*, ed. Migne, XL.1332) is probably drawn from X's *Instructio V* (§ 1), rather than vice versa: see Laporte, 'Étude d'authenticité [*Revue Mabillon* 45 (1955)]', p. 5, and note the use of *baro* for 'noble' in the pseudo-Augustinian *Sermones*, nos xlviii, lxviii (*Patrologia Latina*, ed. Migne, XL.1331, 1355) – though see also Courcelle, review of *Defensoris Locogiacensis Monachi Liber Scintillarum*, ed. Rochais, p. 368. I have therefore omitted it from further consideration. I have also omitted the thematic parallels between X's sermons and the seventh-century Irish work, *De duodecim abusiuis saeculi*, to which Aidan Breen has recently drawn attention ('The evidence', pp. 72–6). They are insufficient to show more than that both authors stood within a similar ascetic tradition.

[53] *Instructio* XI.1 (ed. Walker, p. 106, lines 19–26). Cf. *Basili Regula* 2, 63 (ed. Zelzer, pp. 17–18): 'Quia *ergo* dominus harum *in nobis uirtut*um semina *seminauit*, sine dubio horum etiam fructus requiret et testimonium nostrae erga se dilectionis dilectionem accipiet proximorum.' In 2, 68, some ten lines further on, there follow citations from the same linked passages of John's Gospel as occur in *Instructio* XI.1. For Columbanus's knowledge of Basil's *Regula*, see his *Epist.* II.8 and *Regula monachorum* § 1 (ed. Walker, pp. 20, 124, and cf. p. 146). The parallel between *Instructio* XI.1 and Basil is closer than that with Cassian, *Conlatio* XIII.xii.7 (ed. Petschenig, *Iohannis Cassiani conlationes*, p. 380).

God, the things which are God's.'[54] The reference to the 'image' served to link these two biblical passages in X's mind. After alluding to this story, X extended the metaphor of us bearing the image of God or of Caesar:[55]

Ne simus alienae imaginis pictores; tyrannicae enim imaginis pictor est qui ferus est, qui iracundus est, qui superbus est ... Diuisa est enim ueritas a falsitate, iustitia ab iniquitate ... et utraque imagines quasdam in nobis pingunt sibi inuicem contrarias ... Ne forte itaque nobis tyrannicas introducamus imagines, Christus in nobis suam pingat imaginem.

Let us not be the painters of another's image; for he is the painter of a tyrant's image who is fierce, wrathful, proud. . . . For truth is distinguished from falsehood, justice from unrighteousness, . . . and both paint some images upon us, which are mutually opposed. . . . Then, lest we should import into ourselves tyrannical images, let Christ paint his image in us.

Walker referred to Athanasius's *De incarnatione* for 'the ultimate source of the metaphor'; but that work does not contain the concept of our painting a tyrant's image within us by bad behaviour, but only that of Christ reforming his image in us, a commonplace among Greek authors.[56] Far closer to X is a passage of Origen, which, since it was available in a Latin translation, may well have served as X's source.[57]

Duae sunt imagines in homine: una, quam accepit a Deo factus in principio, sicut in Genesi scriptum est: *iuxta imaginem et similitudinem Dei*, altera *choici* postea, quam propter inoboedientiam atque peccatum eiectus de paradiso assumpsit *principis saeculi huius* suasus illecebris. Scilicet enim nummus siue denarius habet imaginem imperatorum mundi, sic qui facit opera *rectoris tenebrarum* istarum, portat imaginem eius, cuius habet opera: quam praecepit hic Iesus esse reddendam et proiciendam de uultu nostro assumendamque eam imaginem, iuxta quam a principio ad similitudinem Dei conditi sumus. Atque ita fit, ut *quae Caesaris sunt, Caesari et, quae Dei, Deo* reddamus.

There are two images in man: one, which he received in the beginning from God, having been made *after the image and likeness of God*, as it is written in Genesis; the other an earthly one, which he put on later, when, persuaded by the allurements of *the prince of this world*, he was cast out of paradise because of his disobedience and sin. For just as a coin or penny carries the image of the earthly emperors, so he who performs the works of the *ruler of darkness* carries the image of him whose works he does. Jesus here[58] teaches us that this latter image must be given back and cast away from our face and that we must put on that image after which we were created from the beginning in

---

[54] Matthew XXII.15–22; Mark XII.13–17; Luke XX.20–5. Note the use of the verb *reddere*, as in X.

[55] *Instructio XI* (§ 2), ed. Walker, *Sancti Columbani Opera*, pp. 108–9.

[56] *Ibid.*, p. 109. See Ladner, *Images and Ideas*, pp. 73–4, 87–90. In the West, the theme of God as the painter was used by Ambrose, *Hexaemeron*, VI.viii.47 (*Patrologia Latina*, ed. Migne, XIV.260–1).

[57] Origen, *Homilia XXXIX* (§ 5), translated into Latin by Jerome; ed. Crouzel *et al.*, *Origène, Homélies sur S. Luc*, pp. 454–6. Citations from the Bible are italicised. Cf. further *Homilia VIII* (§ 2) (*ibid.*, pp. 164–6); and also Origen, *In Genesim homilia XIII* (§ 4), translated into Latin by Rufinus, ed. Baehrens, *Origenes Werke*, p. 119.

[58] Origen is commenting on Luke XX.25.

the likeness of God. It is thus that we should *give back* (reddamus) *to Caesar those things which are Caesar's, and to God the things which are God's.*

Here, just as in the work of X, we find an exegesis which links together Genesis I.26–7, the passage in the synoptic gospels, and the metaphor of how man carries the image of him whose works he does, either Christ's or the devil's. We may further note that, for Origen, the *imperatores mundi* (the Roman emperors) are the equivalent of the devil. This is typical of Origen's thought, but not of that of most later writers who lived after the conversion of Constantine.[59] Such a source is implied by X's rendering, *tyrannica imago*, for a tyrant is an illegitimate or wrong-doing emperor; and whereas the concept of Christ painting his image in us is widespread in the works of Greek authors, that of the emperor/devil doing the same is much rarer. It is therefore highly likely that this homily of Origen underlies the teaching and the association of ideas in the first half of X's *Instructio XI*.

A text by a third Greek author, Gregory of Nazianzus, was used a little later in the same sermon; for *Instructio XI* (§ 2), 'Nihil enim suauius est hominibus, quam aliena loqui et aliena curare', derives word for word from Rufinus's translation of Gregory's *Apologia*: 'Nihil enim hominibus suauius quam aliena loqui et aliena curare'.[60] Further, the opening of Gregory's *Apologia*, just a few sentences before this more extensive quotation, appears to have influenced the opening sermon of X's series of thirteen. X wrote: 'Cupio, ut . . . ostium[que] nobis sermonis cordis credulitas aperiat', which, with its unusual expression, 'the doorway of our talk', must echo Gregory's 'Dignum enim est, ut mihi beatus Dauid aperiat sermonis ostium'.[61] Again, the passage in *Instructio I*, where X compared God the Trinity to a great sea which cannot be traversed by man, appears to echo a passage in Gregory's discourse *De epiphaniis* – which, like his *Apologia*, was among the nine orations of Gregory translated into Latin by Rufinus. Thus Gregory's statement about God being without a beginning or end, 'insuperabile quoddam ac sine fine substantiae pelagus nullis terminis limitibusque circumdatum . . .', is picked up in *Instructio I* (§ 4): 'quoddam enim insuperabile et inuestigabile pelagus est Deus unus Trinitas'.[62] Further, Gregory went on to say how difficult it is for God to be seen: 'Effugit enim priusquam teneri queat et priusquam adprehendi possit elabitur, tantum se cordi offerens – et hoc si purum sit –, quantum humanos oculos ictus inluminat'. This is much the same argument as X used, although in this case he did not echo Gregory's words, but rather those of Ecclesiastes.[63] Finally, we

---

[59] *Origène, Homélies sur S. Luc*, ed. Crouzel *et al.*, p. 457, n. 1.

[60] Cf. *Sancti Columbani Opera*, ed. & transl. Walker, p. 108, lines 20–1, and Gregory, *Apologeticus* I.3 (ed. Engelbrecht, *Tyrannii Rufini . . . interpretatio*, p. 7, lines 16–17).

[61] *Instructio I* (§ 1), ed. & transl. Walker, *Sancti Columbani Opera*, p. 60, line 5; Gregory, *Apologeticus* I.1 (ed. Engelbrecht, *Tyrannii Rufini . . . interpretatio*, p. 7, lines 4–5).

[62] Gregory, *Oratio II* (*De epiphaniis*) § 7.2 (ed. Engelbrecht, *ibid.*, p. 92, lines 9–11); *Instructio I* (§ 4), ed. & transl. Walker, *Sancti Columbani Opera*, p. 64, lines 20–1.

[63] Gregory, *Oratio II* (*De epiphaniis*) § 7.3 (ed. Engelbrecht, *ibid.*, p. 92, lines 17–20; I have added the comma after *elabitur*); *Instructio I* (§ 5), ed. & transl. Walker, *Sancti Columbani Opera*, p. 64, lines 33–4, and p. 66, lines 1–5.

may note that in the next paragraph, where Gregory wrote that the mind can find no 'edge' to the beginning of God, he (or rather Rufinus) used the expression 'nullam . . . crepidinem'. This figurative use of the word *crepido* ('a foundation', 'raised pavement', 'a retaining wall') is most unusual; but the word was also used figuratively by X at the beginning of *Instructio I*, where he wrote of 'crepido sermonis', 'the foundation of our talk'.[64] Taken together, the evidence indicates that X knew at least the *Apologia* and *De epiphaniis* of Gregory of Nazianzus, in the Latin translation of Rufinus. It is interesting to note that the *Apologia* was certainly known to Columbanus, who echoed it in his *Epistula II*; and almost certainly known to him was Gregory's work *De luminibus*, the third of his discourses to be translated by Rufinus.[65]

Let us now turn to the sixth-century British author, Gildas. Hitherto, it has gone unnoticed that the sentence in X's *Instructio XI* (§ 3), 'lacrimis in his opus magis quam uerbis est', which is also found almost unchanged in Columbanus's *Epistula V*, is drawn straight from Gildas's *De excidio Britanniae* III.108, 'In hoc namque sermone lacrimis magis quam uerbis opus est'.[66] Again, we may compare the passage where Gildas commented on how he was sustained by the prayers of the few faithful christians, 'sacris orationibus . . . quasi columnis quibusdam ac fulcris saluberrimis', with X's comment on how the faith of believers was supported by the twin testimonies of the Old Testament and the Gospel, 'quasi quibusdam fulcris'.[67] Although not an extensive verbal parallel, *fulcrum* is not a particularly common word, especially when used in a metaphorical sense as here.[68] Taken together, these two parallels between Gildas's *De excidio* and X's *Instructiones* prove a direct relationship, and there may be other parallels: the phrase in *Instructio II* (§ 3), 'in aduersarios nostros tela torqueremus' probably echoes Gildas's 'in hunc . . . odia telaque sine respectu contorquebantur' (I.21).

---

[64] Gregory, *Oratio II* (*De epiphaniis*) § 8.1 (ed. Engelbrecht, *ibid.*, pp. 93–4); *Instructio I* (§ 1), ed. & transl. Walker, *Sancti Columbani Opera*, p. 60, line 3. See further below, pp. 167–8.

[65] Smit, *Studies*, pp. 114–15; Lapidge, 'Columbanus', pp. 107–9.

[66] *De excidio*, ed. Winterbottom, p. 140. Cf. *Sancti Columbani Opera*, ed. & transl. Walker, p. 50, lines 20–1, p. 110, line 6. In fact, the ultimate origin of this sentence may lie in Gregory of Nazianzus's *Apologeticus* (§ 51.1): 'Qui languor lacrimis ingentibus et luctu magis quam uerbis indiget' (ed. Engelbrecht, *Tyrannii Rufini . . . interpretatio*, p. 42, lines 13–14). The parallel, however, is not as close as that between Gildas and X; and, given Gildas's opening phrase, 'In hac epistola quicquid deflendo potius quam declamando' (I.1), his predilection for tears (see Kerlouégan, *Le De excidio*, pp. 168–70 and Winterbottom, 'Columbanus and Gildas', p. 313), and the not particularly exceptional nature of the sentiments expressed, it must be an open question whether this passage of Gregory directly influenced Gildas and X. The verbal parallel between Gildas and X, however, is considerably closer; and it is also reinforced by the other two parallels cited, and by the unusual metaphorical use of the word *fulcrum*.

[67] *De excidio* I.26 (ed. Winterbottom, p. 99); *Instructio I* (§ 2), ed. & transl. Walker, *Sancti Columbani Opera*, p. 60, line 21.

[68] The word *fulcrum* is also used in a metaphorical sense in Columbanus's *Epistula I*. See further below, p. 168.

Turning now to Italy, there is an outside chance that X's 'usque ad corrup-
tionem et interitum perpetuum huius uitae' echoes the words of Boethius,
'Estne ... quod ... uenire ad interitum corruptionemque desideret?'[69] If
confirmed, this would be a very interesting borrowing. However, the parallel is
so short that both authors may have hit upon coupling the same two words
independently; and, as Boethius went almost unread before the Carolingian
period, this is probably what happened.

A second author from Italy, Gregory the Great, will require more extended
consideration. Various parallels with his *Homiliae .XL. in euangelia* have
already been noted by X's editors. Fleming singled out a passage where
Gregory emphasised the way in which spiritual (as opposed to physical)
hunger increases, the more it feeds on spiritual delights. This general idea of
still hungering for Christ as we eat of him appears in X's *Instructio XIII* (§ 2),
which may indeed have been inspired by reading Gregory's *Homiliae*; but
there are no verbal parallels close enough to prove it, and X's wording is, if
anything, closer to a passage written by Paulinus of Nola.[70] We should,
however, pay more attention to a possible parallel on the theme of this life as a
uia and ourselves as travellers to our true *patria* above. Walker pointed to the
similarity between X's *Instructio V* (§ 1), 'Quid ergo es, humana uita? Via es
mortalium et non uita', and Gregory's 'Quid est uita mortalis, nisi uia?'[71]
Taken on its own, this is too widespread a theme to prove borrowing; but the
likelihood of a relationship between the two texts is strengthened when we
note that both passages also share the image of this life as a passing cloud.[72]
Also, Gregory's recommendation in this passage that 'calcari mundus ...
debeat' is echoed elsewhere by X.[73] Taken together, these parallels make it
likely, though by no means certain, that X knew Gregory's *Homiliae .XL. in
euangelia*.[74]

More impressive are the parallels between X and Gregory's *Moralia in Iob*.
Not only do both share (with a sermon of Caesarius, as we shall see below) the
theme of ourselves as travellers hastening through this world and not being

---

[69] *Instructio III* (§ 4), ed. & transl. Walker, *Sancti Columbani Opera*, p. 78, line 16;
Boethius, *Consolatio Philosophiae*, III.xi.14, ed. Weinberger, p. 70. Cf. Levison,
England and the Continent, p. 299, n. 3.

[70] *Homiliae .XL. in euangelia* II.xxxvi.1 (*Patrologia Latina*, ed. Migne, LXXVI.1266);
Fleming, *Collectanea Sacra*, p. 76. Cf. Paulinus of Nola, *Epistula XI* (§ 6), ed. Hartel,
Sancti Pontii Meropii Paulini Nolani Epistulae, p. 65. See also below, p. 115.

[71] *Homiliae .XL. in euangelia* I.i.3 (*Patrologia Latina*, ed. Migne, LXXVI.1079); *Sancti
Columbani Opera*, ed. & transl. Walker, p. 84. Cf. also the parallels with Caesarius
discussed below, pp. 115, 116.

[72] Gregory, *ibid.* (LXXVI.1080); *Instructio V* (§ 2), ed. & transl. Walker, *Sancti Columbani Opera*, p. 84, line 29.

[73] *Instructio III* (§ 3), ed. & transl. Walker, *Sancti Columbani Opera*, p. 74, lines 30–1.

[74] Walker also suggests that the *quidam* referred to by X, who compares the terror with
which a man would await being burnt to death tomorrow with what we should feel
at the prospect of the last judgement, may be Gregory the Great (*Instructio XII* [§ 1],
ed. & transl. Walker, *Sancti Columbani Opera*, pp. 110–12). He may be right,
although the passage to which he refers (*Homiliae .XL. in euangelia* II.xxvi.11: ed.
Migne, *Patrologia Latina*, LXXVI.1203) is not very close.

sidetracked by its delights lest we lose our heavenly reward; but for both X and Gregory, it is specifically the *iusti* who will reach the heavenly *patria*,[75] and both share the idea that here on earth we are *in alieno/in alienis* and that we should fix our affections rather on our own *propria* above;[76] and both also use the same three words for us human travellers through life, likening us to *uiatores*, *peregrini*, and *hospites*.[77] Whether such parallels imply that one author read the other, or whether both were drawing upon a common theme of man as a pilgrim on earth, is problematical. This theme has biblical roots, and it was developed by some in the early church, not least by Augustine of Hippo.[78] In view of this we cannot claim with certainty that X had read Gregory's *Moralia in Iob*. I should, however, regard it as very likely.

We turn now to two doctrinal works from southern Gaul, Gennadius of Marseilles, *Liber ecclesiasticorum dogmatum*, and the anonymous *Quicunque uult*. First we may compare *Instructio XI* (§ 1), 'Grandis dignatio, quod Deus suae aeternitatis imaginem et morum suorum similitudinem homini donauit', with Gennadius's 'libere confitemur imaginem in aeternitate similitudinem in moribus inueniri'. It certainly looks as though X is here echoing Gennadius's work, although it is possible that both writers are simply reflecting a general Faustian theological position: this is discussed further below.[79] As regards the *Quicunque uult*, or 'Athanasian Creed', we are on firmer ground. Its use by X was noted a century ago by Albert Hauck and is fairly assured, resting both on the phrase 'qui uult saluus esse' and on the formula 'unitatem in trinitate et trinitatem in unitate'.[80] J.N.D. Kelly has plausibly argued that this creed originated between *ca* 435 and *ca* 535 in southern Gaul, seemingly at Lérins or in an associated milieu.[81] However, the work was included by Caesarius of

---

[75] See below, p. 116. Cf. *Instructio IX* (§ 1), ed. & transl. Walker, *Sancti Columbani Opera*, p. 96, and Gregory, *Moralia in Iob* VIII.liv.92 (ed. Adriaen, *S. Gregorii Magni Moralia in Iob*, p. 454). The *iusti* do not figure as such in Caesarius's *Sermones CLXXXVI* and *CCXV*.

[76] Cf. X, *Instructio V* (§ 2), ed. & transl. Walker, *Sancti Columbani Opera*, p. 86 (also *Instructio X* [§ 3], ed. & transl. Walker, *ibid.*, p. 102, line 33); and Gregory, *Moralia in Iob* VIII.liv.92 (as cited above, n. 75). Again, this particular wording is lacking in Caesarius, *Sermones CLXXXVI* and *CCXV*.

[77] *Sancti Columbani Opera*, ed. & transl. Walker, p. 96, line 11; Gregory, *Moralia in Iob* VIII.liv.92 (ed. Adriaen, *S. Gregorii Magni Moralia in Iob*, p. 454, lines 25, 37–8). Caesarius calls us *peregrini et aduenae* (*Sermo* CLXXXVI.3).

[78] Cf. Claussen, '*Peregrinatio*'; von Campenhausen, *Tradition and Life in the Church*, pp. 231–51; Ladner, '*Homo uiator*', pp. 235–7; Leclercq, *Aux sources*, pp. 35–52. An example of a common expression of this theme is the phrase that we pilgrims *patriam suspiremus*: X, *Instructio VIII* (§ 2), ed. & transl. Walker, *Sancti Columbani Opera*, p. 96, line 2; *Fausti . . . Opera*, ed. Engelbrecht, p. 229, lines 21–3; and Gregory, *Registrum* IX.218 (ed. Norberg, p. 782).

[79] See below, pp. 136–8.

[80] Hauck, 'Ueber die sogenannte *Instructiones*', p. 364; *Instructio I* (§ 2), ed. & transl. Walker, *Sancti Columbani Opera*, p. 60, lines 9, 22–3 (and cf. also Columbanus, *Epistula* III.2, ed. & transl. Walker, *ibid.*, p. 24, lines 13–14). See Kelly, *The Athanasian Creed*, pp. 17, 19. None of the parallels from other sources listed by Kelly (*ibid.*, pp. 24–34) contain both phrases.

[81] Kelly, *The Athanasian Creed*, esp. ch. 7. Tosi's contention ('L'Arianesimo

Arles in one of his homiliaries,[82] and, in view of X's use of other sermons by Caesarius, this might well have been the channel whereby it reached X. But it could equally well be that X knew of it independently from Caesarius. It is perhaps worth noting that both Gennadius's *Liber ecclesiasticorum dogmatum* and the *Quicunque uult* were used by Columbanus in his undoubtedly genuine works[83] and that both occur in the same late seventh-century Bobbio manuscript which contains the two sermons which derive from X's *Instructiones I* and *XIII*.[84]

2. Sermons attributed to Caesarius of Arles

Let us now turn to consider the Gallic sermons used by X in his *Instructiones*. This is a highly complex subject because the nature of the material makes it very difficult to assign authors, or even dates, to the relevant sources. Seebass, following Hauck's lead, clearly showed parallels between X's *Instructio II* and two of the 'Homilies to Monks' in the Gallic Eusebian sermon-collection; and between other of X's sermons and two Gallic sermons which begin *Ad inluminandum humanum genus* and *Modo fratres carissimi*.[85] These last two were claimed for Faustus of Riez by August Engelbrecht, but for Caesarius of Arles by Germain Morin. Discussions about authorship are complicated by the general point that one author could easily adapt and re-use for his own purposes someone else's sermon. I shall defer my discussion of the Gallic Eusebian sermon-collection; first, let us look at those works which are either by Caesarius of Arles, or at least have been claimed for him by some scholars.

We begin with the sermons *Ad inluminandum* and *Modo fratres carissimi*, which were edited by Morin as Caesarius's *Sermones CCXV* and *LVIII*, and by Engelbrecht as Faustus's *Sermones X* and *XII*, respectively. Both sermons occur in the 'Codex Durlacensis 36' (Karlsruhe, Badische Landesbibliothek, MS. 340) of *ca* 900 and also in a Visigothic homiliary from Silos (now London,

---

Tricapitolino', pp. 72–89) that Columbanus himself wrote the *Quicunque uult* is untenable. He dismisses too readily the evidence that it was already known to Caesarius of Arles (cf. Kelly, *ibid.*, pp. 35–7); and, in any case, the striking use of rhythmical clausulae in the *Quicunque uult* is incompatible with Columbanian authorship. Cf. Kelly (*ibid.*, pp. 60–4), and below, pp. 154–61, esp. Table 2, which gives the evidence of clausulae for Columbanus's undoubtedly genuine *Epistulae*.

[82] Kelly, *The Athanasian Creed*, pp. 35–7; Caesarius, *Sermo III* (ed. Morin, *Sancti Caesarii Arelatensis Sermones*, pp. 20–1).

[83] For the *Quicunque uult*, see above, n. 80; for Gennadius, note that Columbanus, *Epistula I* (§ 3), ed. & transl. Walker, *Sancti Columbani Opera*, p. 4, lines 9–11, contains an explicit verbal citation from the *Liber ecclesiasticorum dogmatum*, § 53 (apart from rendering *sextaedecimae lunae* as *decimae quartae lunae*!), ed. Turner, 'The *Liber*', pp. 98–9. Also, the first sentence of the *Penitential* attributed to Columbanus is a word-for-word citation from Gennadius, *Liber ecclesiasticorum dogmatum*, § 23 (ed. Turner, 'The *Liber*', p. 94), although similar expressions are also found elsewhere.

[84] Milano, Biblioteca Ambrosiana, MS. O.212 sup. See above, n. 16, and Tosi, 'L'Arianesimo Tricapitolino', pp. 81–2.

[85] Hauck, 'Ueber die sogenannte *Instructiones*', pp. 363–4; Seebass, 'Über die sogenannte *Instructiones*', pp. 521–7.

British Library, MS. Add. 30853), which contains almost the same collection of homilies. In the Karlsruhe manuscript, which served as the basis for Engelbrecht's edition of Faustus's sermons, the collection of twenty-two homilies has no general heading; but nine of them (including *Modo fratres carissimi*) are there attributed to one 'Faustinus'. Engelbrecht identified this 'Faustinus' with Faustus of Riez; and, on the strength of the attributions at the beginning of *Sermones I, II, IX, XI, XII, XIII, XV, XVI, XX* in the 'Codex Durlacensis', and of attributions in other manuscripts of *Sermones II, VIII, IX, XII* and *XIV* to a Faustus or Faustinus, he took the whole collection to be the work of Faustus of Riez.[86] However, although he spoke of all twenty-two homilies as having the same stylistic features, he nowhere attempted to define these characteristics; and although he spoke of Faustus repeating himself in everything he wrote, he never gave details.[87] So Engelbrecht's attributions to Faustus are based on manuscript-ascriptions rather than on any attempt to identify genuine Faustian sermons on the basis of their style or content. This explains the clash between the views of Engelbrecht and Morin; for Morin, in his great labour of identifying all the sermons of Caesarius of Arles, relied heavily on stylistic parallels with other assured works of Caesarius, although he did not neglect manuscript-attributions.[88] Morin's conclusion was that the homily collection in the 'Codex Durlacensis' is a compilation which makes considerable use of Faustus's sermons, but which was put together in Caesarius's scriptorium at Arles.[89]

Morin was correct in insisting that manuscript-attributions should not be the sole criterion for assigning authorship: such attributions are important, but so too are parallels in content and style with works which can definitely be assigned to the author in question. On the basis of this general principle I have examined the two sermons in question to see whether we can reach any conclusion about the identity of the author(s) whose works X used.

(a) *Modo fratres carissimi.* The sermon beginning *Modo fratres carissimi* was claimed by Engelbrecht for Faustus, principally on the basis of manuscript-attributions, with brief mention also of its verbal parallels to *Homilia IV* of the (arguably Faustian) Gallic Eusebian sermon-collection.[90] However, in 1892 Germain Morin pointed out that, while the whole of the central section was indeed lifted from Gallic Eusebius's *Homilia IV*, its opening and closing sections were in the style of Caesarius. He therefore edited it as *Sermo LVIII* in his *Sancti Caesarii Arelatensis Opera.*[91] Morin further suggested that, in view of the link between Faustus and the Gallic Eusebian collection, this extensive use of Gallic Eusebius's *Homilia IV* might explain the manuscript-attribution of *Modo*

---

[86] Engelbrecht, *Studien*, pp. 96–102; *Fausti . . . Opera*, ed. Engelbrecht; and Morin, 'Critique', pp. 50–8.

[87] Engelbrecht, *Studien*, p. 102; *Fausti . . . Opera*, ed. Engelbrecht, pp. xxvii–xxviii.

[88] Morin, 'Mes principes'.

[89] Morin, 'Critique', pp. 51–8, and 'La collection', p. 102.

[90] Engelbrecht, *Studien*, pp. 83–4.

[91] *Sancti Caesarii Arelatensis Sermones*, ed. Morin, pp. 254–8. The correspondence is between *Sermo LVIII* (§§ 3 and 4) (*ibid.*, pp. 256, lines 3–30, and 257, lines 4–23) and Gallic Eusebius, *Homilia IV* (§§ 6–7) (ed. Glorie, *Eusebius 'Gallicanus'*, pp. 51–3).

fratres carissimi to Faustus.[92] Morin's brief observations were elaborated on by Wilhelm Bergmann, who discussed some of the changes which the adapter of Gallic Eusebius's *Homilia IV* made to the text which he took over.[93] These were of a kind to convince him that the adapter was not the same person as the author of *Homilia IV*. We may note particularly the adapter's use of the phrase *secundum illud quod scriptum est* for introducing biblical citations, and his introduction of the phrase *auxiliante Domino*. Neither of these are Faustus's usages; but both are common in Caesarius's sermons.[94] Thus Bergmann's more detailed study fits well with Morin's views; and we may conclude that *Homilia IV* of the Gallic Eusebian collection was probably one of Faustus's sermons, parts of which were then certainly adapted by Caesarius, and provided with two opening (and one closing) paragraphs to form a sermon of his own, *Sermo LVIII* in Morin's edition.

This explanation is entirely plausible, and Caesarius's role as adapter can be further confirmed by the evidence of the biblical citations and of close parallels between the compiler's opening section and other sermons of Caesarius. On the former point, note particularly the compiler's citation of Matthew XXV.34. According to Morin's index, this verse is found no fewer than forty times in his edition of Caesarius's *Sermones*; further, the text of this verse differs markedly from the Vulgate text, while tallying with the version quoted elsewhere in Caesarius's works.[95]

The textual parallels between the adapter's additional paragraphs and other sermons of Caesarius are even more convincing. Caesarius's *Sermo CLVII* (§ 5), 'Dominus terribiliter nos admonet', parallels *Sermo LVIII* (§ 1), 'apostolum terribiliter nos . . . admonentem', and in both texts II Corinthians V.10 and Matthew XVI.27 are cited alongside each other, and the concept of *rationem . . . reddituri* at the last judgment is encountered.[96] Caesarius's *Sermo CLXXXIV* (§ 7) provides an even closer parallel: again we find the same two biblical texts in association, and the same idea that God will show Himself merciful now on earth, but just at the last judgment: compare *Sermo LVIII* (§ 1), 'quia non dixit . . . secundum misericordiam suam, sed *secundum opera sua*. Hic enim est misericors, ibi iustus', with *Sermo CLXXXIV* (§ 7): 'Deus enim in hoc mundo praerogat misericordiam, in futuro exercet iustitiam. . . . Non dixit, secundum misericordiam, sed *secundum opera sua*.'[97] This close parallel, along with the other evidence adduced, confirms Morin's

---

[92] Morin, 'Critique', p. 55 (no. XII). For the link between Faustus and the Gallic Eusebian collection, see further Morin, 'La collection', pp. 99–108.

[93] Bergmann, *Studien*, pp. 266–75.

[94] *Ibid.*, p. 272. For the phrase *auxiliante Domino*, see the index to *Sancti Caesarii Arelatensis Sermones*, ed. Morin, p. 1068; for *illud quod scriptum est*, see Morin, *ibid.*, p. 804, line 14, and 'Mes principes', p. 74.

[95] *Sancti Caesarii Arelatensis Sermones*, ed. Morin, p. 257, and cf. pp. 76, 641, etc. Note that Faustus used the Vulgate: Souter, 'Observations'. The sermon containing the non-Vulgate version (*Fausti . . . Opera*, ed. Engelbrecht, p. 243) is not by Faustus: see Morin, 'Critique', p. 53.

[96] Cf. *Sancti Caesarii Arelatensis Sermones*, ed. Morin, p. 644, lines 1–2, 31–5, and p. 254, bottom line, to p. 255, line 3 and lines 24–5.

[97] *Ibid.*, pp. 255 and 752. The italicised words are from Matthew XVI.27.

and Bergmann's contention that Caesarius was the adapter or compiler of *Sermo LVIII*; and I find Morin's suggestion that Caesarius was here making use of a sermon by Faustus a convincing explanation for the manuscript-attribution of *Sermo LVIII* to Faustus.

The last textual parallel is also important for making it clear that X was quoting from this compilation of Caesarius, viz. *Sermo LVIII*, and not from *Sermo CLXXXIV*, nor from Gallic Eusebius's *Homilia IV*; for this passage comes in the opening paragraph of *Sermo LVIII*, which is not paralleled in Gallic Eusebius's *Homilia IV*. The parallel to X's *Instructio IX*, however, is convincing: X has '... quia non dixit, secundum misericordiam suam, sed *secundum opera sua unicuique reddet*; hic enim misericors, illic iustus iudex'. The relationship is so close that it admits of no doubt.[98] Further, although Walker elsewhere suggested that X also cited Caesarius's *Sermo CXCVI* (§ 1), 'ipsa nobis medicamenta conuertuntur in uulnera', I would suggest that Caesarius's *Sermo LVIII* (§ 5), 'medicamenta in uulneribus uertens', might again be the source for X's *Instructio II* (§ 3), 'arma uertuntur in uulnera'.[99] Here, however, we should also bear in mind the possibility that a passage from Gregory the Great's *Homiliae* could be the source: 'cuius manus ac pedes ... tumescentes, et uersi in uulneribus fuerant'[100] – if, indeed, we should be thinking in terms of a specific 'source', rather than of a phrase in widespread use. We should further note that Seebass pointed to another probable parallel between Caesarius's *Sermo LVIII* (§ 1) and X's *Instructio IX* (§ 2).[101]

(b) *Ad inluminandum humanum genus.* Let us now turn to the sermon beginning *Ad inluminandum*, which is of considerable importance for X's sermons; for here we meet the theme, which runs right through X's *Instructiones V–IX*, of this life as but a roadway (*uia*) leading to our true *patria* which is above. Seebass traced convincing verbal parallels between *Ad inluminandum* and X's *Instructiones IV, V, VII*, and probably *VIII*, and it is unfortunate that these references are not noted in Walker's edition.[102]

Ad inluminandum bears the heading *De natale sancti Felicis*, but its text makes it clear that the sermon as it now stands was preached at Arles in honour

---

98 *Instructio IX* (§ 2), ed. & transl. Walker, *Sancti Columbani Opera*, p. 98. The parallel with Caesarius is more extensive than Walker indicates, beginning on p. 98, line 13.

99 *Ibid.*, p. 70, line 37 and n. (followed by Glorie, *Eusebius 'Gallicanus'*, p. 955); cf. *Sancti Caesarii Arelatensis Sermones*, ed. Morin, pp. 792, 257.

100 *Homiliae .XL. in euangelia*, II.xxxvi.13 (ed. Migne, *Patrologia Latina*, LXXVI.1274).

101 Seebass, 'Über die sogenannte *Instructiones*', p. 524; see below, p. 200. Seebass also compares Caesarius, *Sermo LVIII* (§ 3) (ed. Morin, *Sancti Caesarii Arelatensis Sermones*, p. 256, lines 15–16), with X, *Instructio IX*.2 (ed. & transl. Walker, *Sancti Columbani Opera*, p. 100, lines 6–7). The parallel suggested by Glorie (*Eusebius 'Gallicanus'*, p. 955) between Caesarius, *Sermo LVIII*.3 and X, *Instructio II*.3, is too slight and commonplace to be significant.

102 Seebass, 'Über die sogenannte *Instructiones*', pp. 524–5, 526–7; see below, p. 200. The sermon *Ad inluminandum* was edited by Engelbrecht as Faustus, *Sermo X* (*Fausti ... Opera*, ed. Engelbrecht, pp. 259–62), and by Morin as Caesarius, *Sermo CCXV* (ed. Morin, *Sancti Caesarii Arelatensis Sermones*, pp. 855–8).

of St Honoratus.[103] It is an interesting sermon, containing both the theme of the ascetic life as a kind of martyrdom and also that of this life as a *peregrinatio* from our true fatherland. Engelbrecht claimed it for Faustus on no more substantial grounds than that it forms part of the collection of homilies in the 'Codex Durlacensis'. But Morin pointed out that it is put together from two other sermons which are in the style of Caesarius, and he claimed that the whole bears obvious traces of Caesarius's hand.[104] Indeed, as has already been mentioned, Morin saw the homily-collection in the 'Codex Durlacensis' as it now stands as a product of Caesarius's workshop.

Elsewhere Morin did something to set the study of Faustus's sermons on a firmer base than Engelbrecht had done, plausibly identifying one sermon in the Gallic Eusebian sermon-collection as the work of Faustus, and striving to show that this sermon-collection represents substantially the work of one man, viz. Faustus.[105] He listed a small number of phrases as being typical of this author,[106] and, for what it is worth, I cannot trace any of these in *Ad inluminandum*. The latter does, however, have a few phrases which Morin has taught us to regard as typical of Caesarius, viz. *cum labore et dolore* and *cum magno lucro*, and also *auxiliante Domino* and *Deo donante*.[107]

These suggestions of Caesarius's authorship can be confirmed by comparisons with other sermons by Caesarius. Thus, for instance, Caesarius's *Sermo CLIV* (§ 1) links the same two quotations from John XVI.33 and XVI.20, and also the same two quotations from II Timothy III.12 and Acts XIV.21, as does *Ad inluminandum*. The biblical text employed also tallies with Caesarius's usage. But the most obvious parallels lie with Caesarius's *Sermo CLXXXVI* (§§ 3–4), which has itself been assigned to Caesarius on good grounds.[108] Both *Sermo CLXXXVI* and *Ad inluminandum* (*Sermo CCXV*) have the theme of our being travellers through this world, *in uia* rather than *in patria*. In both sermons, we should, like travellers, be hastening through to our *patria*; but, *peruerso ordine*, says the preacher, many delight in the things of this world. We may, then, accept that *Ad inluminandum* is a sermon of Caesarius.

(c) *Other Caesarian sermons.* The development of these themes in Caesarius's *Sermo CLXXXVI* not only confirms Morin's attribution of *Ad inluminandum* to the same author; it also raises the question of whether X knew Caesarius's *Sermo CLXXXVI* as well as *Ad inluminandum*. Caesarius's *Sermo CLXXXVI* (§ 3) spells out far more fully than *Sermo CCXV* the theme of our being *peregrini in uia*, not yet in our *patria*, which is so fundamental to X, and there are various other parallels which I have detailed in the appendix, below. However, there are

---

[103] *Sancti Caesarii Arelatensis Sermones*, ed. Morin, p. 855.

[104] *Ibid.* See also Morin, 'Critique', pp. 54–5.

[105] Morin, 'La collection', pp. 92–115.

[106] *Ibid.*, p. 115.

[107] *Sancti Caesarii Arelatensis Sermones*, ed. Morin, p. 856, lines 28–9, p. 857, lines 13, 22. See *ibid.*, p. 1075, s.v. 'donare', and Morin, 'Un écrit', p. 119.

[108] *Sancti Caesarii Arelatensis Sermones*, ed. Morin, p. 757, and Morin, 'Un nouveau recueil', pp. 289–92.

no verbal similarities sufficiently close to prove X's knowledge of *Sermo CLXXXVI*. Again, there is a thematic parallel between Caesarius's *Sermo LXXII* (§ 1) and X's *Instructio IV* (§§ 1–2): both authors argue that if craftsmen and others can endure such hardships as they do in practising their trade, then a monk should be prepared to undergo all the greater hardships for the sake of his eternal goal.[109] This parallel makes it likely that X knew Caesarius's *Sermo LXXII*; but again, the verbal parallels which would clinch the matter are lacking.

We have seen, so far, that X definitely used two of Caesarius's sermons, *Modo fratres* and *Ad inluminandum*, and possibly also his *Sermones LXXII* and *CLXXXVI*. The final sermon of Caesarius to be considered here is his *Sermo IX*.[110] In this we find recognition of faith as the *salutis fundamentum*, and the idea that the mysteries of the Godhead should be believed, not investigated intellectually or discussed: 'credendus est ergo Deus esse Pater unici Filii sui Domini nostri, non discutiendus'. Both expressions are echoed in X's first sermon, where belief is seen as the *fundamentum salutis omnium*, and where X insists that 'pie ergo credenda est, et non impie discutienda est magna Trinitas'.[111] However, the matter is complicated by the fact that similar phrases also occur in *Homiliae IX* and *X* of the Gallic Eusebian sermon-collection.[112] Close perusal reveals that the beginning of Caesarius's *Sermo IX* is related to Gallic Eusebius's *Homilia X* (§ 1), and my impression is that Caesarius is here the borrower. It may even be that the original author of Gallic Eusebius's *Homilia X* was Faustus of Riez: certainly the expression *secundum illud* for introducing a biblical citation, the use of the Vulgate text, and the extensive parallels with Faustus's *De spiritu sancto* all point in this direction, as perhaps does the metaphorical use of the word *ostium*.[113]

---

109 *Sancti Caesarii Arelatensis Sermones*, ed. Morin, p. 303; *Sancti Columbani Opera*, ed. & transl. Walker, pp. 78–82; and Laporte, 'Étude d'authenticité [*Revue Mabillon* 45 (1955)]', p. 27.

110 Glorie's table of parallels to X's *Instructiones* (*Eusebius 'Gallicanus'*, ed. Glorie, pp. 954–6) has been a useful point of reference; but, of his nineteen possible parallels, several are too slight to be of much significance (nos 1, 5, 6, 13, 14, 16, 19); nos 7, 8, 11, 12, 17 and 18 relate to parallels with the Gallic Eusebius series of ten homilies *Ad monachos* which will be discussed below; nos 9, 10 and 15 relate to parallels with Caesarius, and no. 3 to a parallel with the *Quicunque uult*, discussed above. Nos 2 and 4 are under discussion here.

111 Caesarius, *Sermo IX* (*Sancti Caesarii Arelatensis Sermones*, ed. Morin, pp. 46, 48); X, *Instructio I* (§§ 1, 4), ed. & transl. Walker, *Sancti Columbani Opera*, p. 60, line 3, p. 64, lines 19–20.

112 *Sermo IX.3*, 'diuina opera non discutienda sunt sed credenda'; *Sermo X.1*, 'fides religionis catholicae, lumen est animae, ostium uitae, fundamentum salutis aeternae' (*Sancti Caesarii Arelatensis Sermones*, ed. Morin, p. 101, line 94, p. 113, lines 1–2).

113 For the expression *secundum illud*, see Bergmann, *Studien*, p. 90, n. 1; for parallels with *De spiritu sancto*, see Gallic Eusebius, *Homilia X* (§§ 2, 10, 11), ed. Glorie, *Eusebius 'Gallicanus'*, pp. 115, 121, 122). Note Faustus's expression *ostium ueritatis* (*De spiritu sancto* I.5, ed. Engelbrecht, *Fausti . . . Opera*, p. 108, line 4), alongside that in *Sermo X* (§ 1), *ostium uitae*; the latter recurs in Caesarius, *Sermo IX*.

Did X read Caesarius's homilies, or did he read the two Gallic Eusebian homilies which were probably Caesarius's source? We cannot say for certain. The Caesarian hypothesis is the more economical, in that both passages are found in the one sermon. On the other hand, Seebass, who originally pointed out the 'credenda ... non discutienda' parallel, also pointed to a further possible parallel between X's *Instructio I* and Gallic Eusebius's *Homilia IX*: both have the general argument that, if one cannot even understand creation, how much less can one hope to understand the creator.[114] However, there are no real verbal parallels, and the idea is worked out very differently by X and by Gallic Eusebius's *Homilia IX*. As the fundamental idea is found in the Bible, in God's answer to Job, it may well be that the adoption of such an argument by X is wholly independent of that in Gallic Eusebius's *Homilia IX*.[115] It will therefore have to remain an open question whether X had encountered the phrases *fundamentum salutis* and *credenda ... non discutienda* in Caesarius or in Gallic Eusebius's *Homiliae IX* and X.

3. *Faustus, and the Gallic Eusebian Sermon-collection*

Leaving aside some slight and very doubtful suggested borrowings,[116] let us turn instead to a matter of major importance: the relationship between X's sermons and the ten homilies *ad monachos* in the Gallic Eusebian sermon-collection. This collection of some seventy-six sermons has complex origins.[117] The earliest manuscript of the sermon-collection as a whole – although it is defective – is Bruxelles, Bibliothèque royale, MS. 1651–1652 (1316) of the early ninth century, a dating which gives us a *terminus ante quem* for the collection. The sermons themselves probably date back to the fifth century or before, but have been excerpted and rearranged at a later date, in Gaul. One school of thought, represented by Germain Morin, argues that the original author of all the sermons was the fifth-century theologian, Faustus of Riez. But another school of thought, represented by Glorie, the collection's recent editor, holds that the collection was put together from the works of various Fathers, Novatian, Cyprian, Zeno, Ambrose, Augustine, Hilary of Arles, Faustus of Riez, 'Eusebius', and others. At the moment I remain open-minded about which view is more likely to be correct, although I am more inclined to trust the judgment of Morin and Souter than that of Glorie when it comes to identifying authors on the basis of their literary style and

---

[114] Seebass, 'Über die sogenannte *Instructiones*', p. 522.

[115] Cf. Gallic Eusebius, *Homilia IX*.3 (ed. Glorie, *Eusebius 'Gallicanus'*, pp. 101–2); X, *Instructio* I.3–5 (ed. & transl. Walker, *Sancti Columbani Opera*, pp. 62–4); and Iob XXXVIII.

[116] I include here nos 1, 5, 6, 14 and 19 of Glorie's nineteen suggested parallels (see above, n.110), together with Seebass's suggestions ('Über die sogenannte *Instructiones*', p. 525) about *fouea* and the quotation from Matthew XI.12. The former parallel amounts to only one word, and in the latter case this interpretation of Matthew is not unusual: cf. Jerome, *Epistula* XXII.40 (ed. Hilberg, *Sancti Eusebii Hieronymi Epistulae*, I.208–9).

[117] On what follows, see Glorie's introduction to *Eusebius 'Gallicanus'*, ed. Glorie, pp. vii–xxi, and Morin, 'La collection'. Cf. also Souter, 'Observations'.

vocabulary. Both Morin and Glorie agree that Caesarius of Arles made considerable use of the sermons. For Morin, this implied that the collection was then in existence. But Glorie saw Caesarius's activity more as a significant stage in the formation of the collection, while the compiler who created the collection as we now have it in the Brussels manuscript would have been subsequent to Caesarius, working perhaps in the seventh or eighth century.

Given the nature of the Gallic Eusebian sermon-collection as a compilation involving various stages, the difficulty of ascribing author or date to individual sermons within the collection will be readily appreciated. The problem is exacerbated by the constant rehashing of excerpts, sometimes quite long ones, within the collection, so that we find the same passages recurring in various sermons. To give some idea of the complexities involved, one can trace Gallic Eusebius's *Homilia VI* (§§ 6 and 8) lying behind Caesarius's *Sermo CCVI* (§§ 2–3); while this passage of Caesarius is apparently the one which directly influenced the Gallic Eusebian *Homilia XXXIX* [= *Hom. IV ad monachos*], § 1.[118] This in itself disproves the theory that the sermon-collection already existed in precisely its present form before the time of Caesarius.

We do not know how long the sermon-collection had been in existence before its first appearance in the early ninth-century Brussels manuscript; but the collection was formed of various component parts, at least some of which had circulated previously.[119] For us, the relevant component is the series of ten homilies *ad monachos*, Gallic Eusebius *Homiliae XXXVI–XLV* (formerly nos *XXXV–XLIV*). Even here, however, investigation reveals that we are not dealing with a coherent body of ten homilies. *Homiliae I* and *X* were originally not addressed to monks at all,[120] and the ten do not appear together in any manuscript before the early ninth century. At least some of them, however, were already grouped together in earlier manuscripts. Thus a late seventh-century manuscript written at Saint-Médard, Soissons, includes Gallic Eusebius homilies *ad monachos* nos IV, V, VI and IX, together with a sermon beginning *Ad locum hunc*, most of which was recycled to form the opening section of *Homilia ad monachos VII* in the early ninth-century Brussels manuscript, MS. 1651–1652. In the Saint-Médard manuscript, and in later ones containing the same selection of sermons, the Gallic Eusebian homilies appear sandwiched between five Caesarian sermons, and the whole series of ten is attributed to Caesarius.[121] In some manuscripts of this 'Caesarian' collection, *ad monachos III* is also found, albeit not in close association with

---

[118] Cf. *Eusebius 'Gallicanus'*, ed. Glorie, pp. 70–3 (lines 91–136, 159–65) with *Sancti Caesarii Arelatensis Sermones*, ed. Morin, p. 826, line 15 to end of sermon. Note that Gallic Eusebius, *Homilia XXXIX* (lines 6–8) is closer to Caesarius (ed. Morin, p. 826, lines 26–8) than to Gallic Eusebius, *Homilia VI*, lines 98–101.

[119] See *Eusebius 'Gallicanus'*, ed. Glorie, pp. 945–9.

[120] See *ibid.*, p. 946, and de Vogüé, 'Sur une série', p. 122, n. 7.

[121] The Saint-Médard MS. is now Bruxelles, Bibliothèque royale, MS. 9850–9852 (1221): Lowe, *Codices* X, no. 1547a. See *Sancti Caesarii Arelatensis Sermones*, ed. Morin, pp. xxxi–xxxiii; *Eusebius 'Gallicanus'*, ed. Glorie, pp. xxvi, 940–1. *Ad locum hunc* was edited by Engelbrecht, *Fausti . . . Opera*, pp. 314–18, and by Glorie, *Eusebius 'Gallicanus'*, pp. 861–8. Cf. §§ 4–11 in Glorie's edition with *Ad monachos VII* (§§ 1–6)(*ibid.*, pp. 862–7, 497–501).

the others.[122] *Ad monachos II* and *III* are already found in a late seventh-century manuscript, Sankt Gallen, Stiftsbibliothek, MS. 226, and *Ad monachos III* and *IV* in an eighth-century manuscript from Bobbio, now Napoli, Biblioteca Nazionale, MS. Vindobonensis lat. 2. But *ad monachos* nos *I*, *VII* (in its present form), *VIII*, and *X* are not found any earlier than the early ninth-century Bruxelles, Bibliothèque royale, MS. 1651–1652 (1316).

The parallels with X's sermons concern the homilies *ad monachos* nos III, IV, and VIII, particularly the last two. As we have already seen, it was these which led Hauck and Seebass to deny that the author of the thirteen sermons could have been Columbanus; for in *Instructio II*, X says that he has chosen a few words from Faustus, his teacher, with which to start, and he then goes on to give a long passage – introduced by 'inquit' – which is textually very close to the opening section of *Hom. VIII ad monachos* of the Gallic Eusebian collection. The way in which the parallels with X's *Instructio II* change and change again between *Homilia VIII* and *Hom. IV ad monachos* has been illustrated beyond all possible doubt by Seebass, Glorie, and Adalbert de Vogüé, although Walker unfortunately indicated only the opening parallel with *Homilia VIII*.[123] Other parallels worth mentioning[124] have been noted by Glorie: the idea that by backbiting we slay ourselves as with our own sword (*proprio mucrone*), which occurs both in *Homilia VIII ad monachos* and X's *Instructio XI*; and the striking expression, *sera paenitentia*, which occurs both in *Hom. III ad monachos* (§ 4), and also in X's *Instructio III* (§§ 2 and 4).[125] To judge from a rapid reading of Caesarius's *Sermones LVIII–LXVIII*, where we might have expected it, this expression is not found in the work of Caesarius.

Seebass explained the parallels by attributing the Gallic Eusebian homilies *ad monachos* to Faustus of Riez, and arguing that X quoted from these in his sermons; and this, indeed, would seem to be the obvious interpretation, particularly in the light of X's explicit remarks in *Instructio II*. There are, however, various complications. First, can the *Homiliae ad monachos III*, *IV*, and *VIII* in their present form be works of Faustus? And, indeed, were they known in their present form to X? The 'disquieting doublets' and signs of a compiler's hand within these sermons force us to ask these questions, as does the use in *Hom. IV ad monachos* of a sermon by Caesarius. De Vogüé has conjectured that the passages which X apparently borrowed from *Homiliae ad monachos IV* and *VIII* might originally have belonged to just one sermon by Faustus.[126] More

---

[122] E.g. St Gallen, Stiftsbibliothek, MS.194 (*saec.* viii[med]); see further Glorie, *ibid.*, pp. 940–1.

[123] Seebass, 'Über die sogenannte *Instructiones*', pp. 520–1; *Eusebius 'Gallicanus'*, pp. xv–xvii, 955; de Vogüé, 'Sur une série', pp. 119–23; and *Sancti Columbani Opera*, ed. & transl. Walker, pp. 68–70.

[124] I omit Seebass's suggested parallel, *festinare ad mortem* ('Über die sogenannte *Instructiones*', p. 525; cf. X, *Instructio VI.2* and *Hom. ad monachos I.7*) because the sense is so different that I doubt whether the one could have inspired the other.

[125] *Eusebius 'Gallicanus'*, ed. Glorie, pp. 955–6, and cf. below. I omit Glorie's parallel no. 12 (p. 955), which begins *praeparemus animum*, because here Cassian, *Instituta*, IV.38, provides a common source. Similarly, Glorie's suggested parallel no. 17 (p. 956) is explained by Matthew XII.36 serving as a common source.

[126] De Vogüé, 'Sur une série', p. 122.

radically, Glorie (who incidentally had no Columbanian axe to grind) claimed that X does not draw upon *Ad monachos IV* and *VIII*; rather, these latter are dependent upon X.[127] Unfortunately he gave no adequate reasons for his conclusion;[128] and, after comparing the two sets of writings myself, I cannot see how one can ascertain which is dependent on which, on the basis of internal evidence.

The second conundrum is that sometimes where there is a verbal parallel between the work of X and *Ad monachos VIII*, a possible parallel with a Celtic work, the *Penitential* of Uinniaus, can also be suggested.[129] This possibility is sufficiently intriguing to warrant investigation, and I begin by setting out the relevant passages in parallel.

Penitential of Uinniaus (§ 29)[130]	*Instructio II* (§ 2)[131]	Gallic Eusebius, *Hom. VIII ad monachos* (§ 1)[132]
Si quis clericus iracundus aut inuidus aut detractor aut tristis aut cupidus, magna sunt peccata haec . . . Sed haec est penitentia eorum donec euellantur et eradicentur de cordibus	quanto magis nos oportet agrum cordis nostri noxiis uitiorum passionibus emundare, et non sufficere credamus nobis terram corporis nostri ieiuniorum et uigiliarum labore conficere, nisi in primis	non nobis sufficere putemus terram corporis nostri uigiliarum exercitiis edomare uel ieiuniorum labore conficere, sed imprimis mentem exstirpatione uitiorum mundare conemur,

[127] *Eusebius 'Gallicanus'*, ed. Glorie, pp. xiv–xvii, 954. Glorie believed that X's reference to his teacher Faustus precluded the identification of X as Columbanus (*ibid.*, p. xiv, n. 29). Glorie also appears to have believed that X's *Instructio II* was in some sense a product of Caesarius's (*ibid.*, pp. xvii, 954). But, while X made considerable use of some of Caesarius's sermons, the style of the two writers is quite different – to say nothing of the well-nigh impossibility of Caesarius having read Gildas.

[128] Tosi seeks to confirm Glorie's view by claiming that the cursus-endings of *Hom. VIII ad monachos* are poor, and far from Faustus's normally elegant style: 'L'Arianesimo Tricapitolino', p. 50. However, my own analysis of the twenty-four sentence-endings of this sermon hardly bears him out: there are eight instances of the regular *tardus* (p 4pp), five of the regular *uelox* (pp 4p) plus two variants, one of the regular *planus* (p 3p) plus two variants, set over against one instance of the *trispondiacus* p 4p, four definitely non-rhythmical endings, and one doubtful case. There are no instances of hiatus. Thus, judging from both the overal 75% cursus-endings and from the incidence of five pp 4p to one p 4p (Winterbottom's *uelox*-test), *Hom. VIII ad monachos* stands vindicated as conforming to the cursus-norms. For explanation of the terms used here, see below, pp. 150–61, and see Table 2 for an example of Faustus's use of rhythmical *clausulae*.

[129] Cf. *Sancti Columbani Opera*, ed. & transl. Walker, p. 68. The author's name, *Vinnianus* or *Uinniaus*, has traditionally been rendered as Finnian, an Irish name. But recently it has been strongly argued that we should adopt the reading of the earlier and better manuscript, *Uinniaus*, which implies a British name: see *The Irish Penitentials*, ed. Bieler, pp. 17, 74, 94, and Dumville, 'Gildas and Uinniau'. This *Vinnianus/Uinniaus* may well be identical with *Vennianus*, correspondent of Gildas: see below, pp. 179–80, 181 n. 439.

[130] *The Irish Penitentials*, ed. Bieler, p. 84.
[131] *Sancti Columbani Opera*, ed. & transl. Walker, p. 68.
[132] *Eusebius 'Gallicanus'*, ed. Glorie, pp. 511–12.

nostris ... insinuamus
uirtutes caelestes pro illis:
patienta pro ira,
mansuetudo et dilectio Dei
et proximorum pro inuidia,
pro detractione
continentia cordis et
lingue, pro tristitia
gaudium spiritale, pro
cupiditate largitas nasci
debet ... Detractio
anathema, sicut in
scripturis dicitur: Qui
detrahit proximo suo
eradicabitur de terra
uiuentium ...

studeamus uitia corrigere
moresque
componere ... Studeamus
ergo in primis uitia
eradicare, uirtutesque
insinuare; eradicemus
superbiam, plantemus
humilitatem, eruamus
iram, fundemus
patientiam, excidamus
inuidiam, insinuemus
beneuolentiam.

Instructio XI (§ 2)[133]
[beware of backbiting; by
speaking evil we condemn
ourselves] quando enim
unusquisque mentitur,
maledicit, detrahit,
seipsum proprio mucrone
iugulat ... 'Noli
detrahere', ait scriptura,
'ne eradiceris.' ... Caueat
ergo unusquisque, ne sua
radix de terra uiuentium
pro odii detractione
eradicetur.

circumcidere mores,
excidere passiones:
eradicare superbiam,
plantare humilitatem;
effodere iram, fundare
patientiam; amputare
inuidiam, inserere
beneuolentiam ...

Hom. VIII ad monachos
(§ 5)[134]
Apertis interdum a nobis
ipsis scandalorum bellis
collidimur,
obtrectationibus ac
maleloquiis linguae
nostrae uelut proprio
mucrone confodimur ...

Careful comparison of the three writings shows that all share the same general theme of cleansing our hearts from vices and instilling virtues in their place; and *ira*, *patientia*, and *inuidia* are listed by all. If we go beyond these generalities we note that the extended parallel between X and *Hom. VIII ad monachos* is so close as to prove a definite relationship; and, given X's opening words (not reproduced here) introducing this passage as one taken from his master Faustus, we may provisionally assume that X was here dependent on *Hom. VIII ad monachos*.

Whether or not there was a direct relationship between either of these writings and the *Penitential* of Uinniaus is a trickier question. The general theme of driving out vices with virtues was commonplace; and, given that Uinniaus's list of virtues and vices would seem to have arisen directly from his list of clerical sins and is not, in fact, identical with the list given by the other two authors,[135] we should not pay much attention to this generalised parallel. Besides the general theme and the mention of *ira*, *patientia*, and *inuidia*, there are no close parallels between Uinniaus's *Penitential* and *Hom. VIII ad monachos*, which makes it unlikely that these two are directly related.

Uinniaus and X have a little more in common: they both use the expression,

---

[133] *Sancti Columbani Opera*, ed. & transl. Walker, p. 108, lines 25–30.
[134] *Eusebius 'Gallicanus'*, ed. Glorie, p. 515.
[135] Note particularly that he counters *inuidia* with different virtues.

insinua(mus) uirtutes, where *insinuare* is not an obvious verb for X to choose, given the extended agricultural metaphor which he shares with the author of *Hom. VIII ad monachos*. (Uinniaus's lack of this metaphor makes *insinuare* an unexceptional choice for him.) Uinniaus and X also share similarities in their warning against backbiting, although this can probably be explained by their reference to a common biblical source, once we identify this correctly.[136] Thus the link between Uinniaus and X is a little closer than that between Uinniaus and the author of *Hom. VIII ad monachos*, but it does not amount to much, and it is too inconclusive and ambiguous to help us at this stage of our enquiry. It could be purely fortuitous. Or, if X were Faustus's literal pupil, then we could argue that *Instructio II* (§ 2) lies behind the *Penitential* of Uinniaus (although there might be dating problems here, as X used the works of Gildas and of Caesarius, but Gildas was a contemporary of Uinniaus). Or if X were Columbanus, then we could argue that his choice of wording, *uirtutes insinuare*, stemmed from his familiarity with Uinniaus's *Penitential*. But for the moment, at least, we must leave wide open the question of whether there was a direct relationship between X's sermon and Uinniaus's *Penitential*, and, if so, which way round it operated.

Let us now discover what we can of the origins and possible author(s) of *Ad monachos III, IV*, and *VIII. Hom. III ad monachos*[137] is predominantly ascribed to Faustus in the manuscripts, including one of the eighth century and five of the ninth.[138] It was probably written by an abbot for his own house, and it certainly belongs to an age before stability was enforced on monks. In both these respects the attribution to Faustus, abbot of Lérins from *ca* 433 to 449x462, seems eminently suitable.[139] Further, various linguistic and doctrinal traits fit with those of Faustus's authentic works.[140] Against this, Bergmann adduced various usages and words which he thought could not be paralleled in Faustus's works. However, since then Morin has vindicated *Homilia XXXV* of the Gallic Eusebian collection as definitely by Faustus, and several of these usages and words are in fact found in this authentic sermon.[141] The one indication against Faustus's authorship is that the biblical text cited does not

---

[136] This must be a Vetus Latina translation of the Septuagint version of Proverbs XX.13, a passage which does not occur at all in the Hebrew Bible or in the Vulgate. A similar text is found in other Latin authors, including Caesarius of Arles, who usually has, 'Qui detrahit fratri suo, eradicabitur', and once, 'qui detrahit, eradicabitur de terra uiuentium'. See *Sancti Caesarii Arelatensis Sermones*, pp. 71, 640, 700, and cf. p. 89. Cf. Gallic Eusebius, *Homilia* LIII.4 (ed. Glorie, *Eusebius 'Gallicanus'*, p. 618, lines 30–1).

[137] *Eusebius 'Gallicanus'*, ed. Glorie, pp. 435–49 (no. XXXVIII).

[138] For details, see *ibid.*, pp. 937–8. I have counted Vatican City, Biblioteca Apostolica Vaticana, MS. Regin. lat. 140, as ninth-century.

[139] See Bergmann, *Studien*, pp. 201–3, 205.

[140] *Ibid.*, pp. 206–7.

[141] Morin, 'La collection', pp. 104–6. With the allegedly non-Faustian usages adduced by Bergmann (*ibid.*, pp 208–9), cf. *merito* (*Homilia XXXV*, line 79, ed. Glorie, *Eusebius 'Gallicanus'*, p. 404; *digne* (*ibid.*, lines 137–8); *sicut autem legimus* (*ibid.*, line 216); *fastidium* (*ibid.*, line 272); *ut sic dixerim* (*ibid.*, line 121); and *rapere* (*ibid.*, lines 183, 299).

always agree with the Vulgate, as is normal for Faustus. However, variations could have occurred through the author quoting from memory, and it is also possible that not every book of the Bible was available at Lérins in Jerome's Vulgate as early as Faustus's abbacy. Given such strong indications in favour of Faustus's authorship, I am inclined to accept it, despite the biblical citations.

Hom. IV ad monachos, as we have seen above,[142] has been handed down in early manuscripts among a collection of ten homilies attributed to Caesarius, and Defensor of Ligugé also ascribes quotations from it to Caesarius. The only early exception occurs in an eighth-century manuscript, now Napoli, Biblioteca Nazionale, MS. Vindobonensis lat. 2, where it follows immediately on *Hom. III ad monachos*. The latter is there attributed to Faustus, but no attribution is given to *Hom. IV*. Most later manuscripts continue to bear the ascription to Caesarius, although in some it is attributed (as are other Gallic Eusebian homilies *ad monachos*) to 'Eusebius'. I am, however, aware of only one manuscript, Paris Bibliothèque nationale, MS. Latin 13468, of the thirteenth century, where it and two other sermons are attributed to Faustus.[143] In its present state, as we have seen, it depends on Caesarius's *Sermo CCVI*. However, although Glorie saw it as a product of Caesarius, it is not in his style; and the correct explanation of its origin is probably that provided by Morin, who suggested that it was an older sermon touched up and interpolated by Caesarius.[144] That would adequately explain its use of Caesarius's *Sermo CCVI*, and also its ascription to Caesarius by Defensor and in early manuscripts. It has some claim to be considered a work of Faustus on internal evidence, as it certainly contains one usage typical of him.[145] Further, the context in which X used it rather implies that he thought of this sermon, like *Hom. VIII ad monachos*, as one by Faustus; and it could in origin be a sermon by Faustus which was later conflated with some Caesarian material. This hypothesis becomes very plausible if we follow those scholars who see the entire Gallic Eusebian sermon-collection as originating from Faustus's sermons.

The Gallic Eusebian *Homilia VIII ad monachos* (which begins 'Si quando terrae operarius') has, as we have seen in part,[146] extensive parallels with X's *Instructio II*, and is seemingly quoted by him as a work of his teacher, Faustus.

---

[142] *Eusebius 'Gallicanus'*, ed. Glorie, pp. 455–64 (no. XXXIX); see above, p. 119.

[143] For details, see Glorie, *ibid.*, pp. 919–20, 925, 940–2.

[144] *Sancti Caesarii Arelatensis Sermones*, ed. Morin, p. 988 (which begins 'Sicut a nobis'); cf. *Eusebius 'Gallicanus'*, ed. Glorie, p. xvii.

[145] The phrase *Ita, inquam* and variants thereon: *Eusebius 'Gallicanus'*, ed. Glorie, pp. 455, 458, lines 3, 6–7, 48; cf. Morin, 'La collection', pp. 101, 106. This Faustian usage is also common in his letters: *Fausti . . . Opera*, ed. Engelbrecht, p. 208, line 23, p. 211, line 9, etc. I have been struck by the use of the words *superequitare* and *colluctatio* in *Hom. IV* (lines 34–5, 49), and its very frequent use of *prodesse*. The evidence of its biblical citations is not very telling.

[146] *Eusebius 'Gallicanus'*, ed. Glorie, nos. XLIII, XLIIb (see above, pp. 121–2). Glorie breaks off in *Homilia XLIII* at line 120, tacking the remainder of this homily on to *Hom. VII ad monachos* (= no. XLII). However, there appears to be no manuscript authority for this, and in my view the last part of *Hom. VIII ad monachos* fits better where it stands in the manuscripts, namely in *Hom. VIII ad monachos*, than tacked

It is also attributed to Faustus (along with *Hom. III ad monachos*) in an early ninth-century Fleury manuscript, Vatican City, Biblioteca Apostolica Vaticana, MS. Regin. lat. 140 (which we have already discussed apropos of its inclusion of sermons attributed to Columbanus).[147] There is just a slight danger that the attribution to Faustus in this manuscript might be the work of an intelligent scribe who noted the parallel with X's *Instructio II*, where X explicitly names his source as Faustus. However, we should not put too much weight on this, as the manuscript in question only contains *Instructiones III* and *XI*, not *II*, and as it does in any case attribute *Hom. III ad monachos* to Faustus. Although *Hom. VIII ad monachos* is not directly attested in any manuscript earlier than the ninth century, there is indirect evidence of its existence before the end of the seventh century, and possibly even earlier.[148] Bergmann recognised the claims of the manuscript-attribution to Faustus but had qualms similar to those which he expressed concerning *Hom. III ad monachos*, as to whether its style was indeed that of Faustus. However, as with *Hom. III ad monachos*, these reservations are no longer necessary, thanks to Morin's work.[149] Further, Souter felt that the vocabulary of this sermon, along with others in the Gallic Eusebian collection, was fully consonant with Faustus's authorship.[150] The strongest evidence for ascribing it to Faustus is, in fact, its apparent citation as such by X, a citation which Bergmann did not mention. In view of the corroborating evidence from the Vatican manuscript, and the lack of any real evidence against it, we should let this attribution stand.

I should therefore conclude that the homilies *Ad monachos III, IV*, and *VIII* are probably all by Faustus of Riez in origin, although *Hom. IV*, at least, has subsequently been interpolated. X may not have known them in precisely the form in which they have come down to us; but we may accept that he knew something similar to our *Ad monachos IV* and *VIII*, and, probably, *III*.

This conclusion confirms Seebass's view that X's teacher, Faustus, was indeed Faustus of Riez. If we look for further evidence of Faustus's influence on X, we might note that the author of *Modo fratres carissimi*, which was certainly Caesarian in the form in which X knew it, probably made considerable use of a sermon by Faustus, and might have been known to X under the latter's name. We have further seen that X may also have known *Homiliae IX*

---

on to *Hom. VII ad monachos*. By '*Hom. VIII ad monachos*' I shall therefore mean the whole of this sermon as it stands in the manuscripts, namely Glorie's nos XLIII and XLIIb. It is printed as one whole in *Patrologia Latina*, ed. Migne, L.850–5.

[147] Fos 94v–98r; see Wilmart, *Codices Reg.inenses*, I.340, and above, p. 99.

[148] A manuscript of late-seventh-century date, Bruxelles, Bibliothèque royale, MS. 9850–2, contains a sermon beginning *Ad locum hoc*, which is a compilation from the homilies *Ad monachos IV, VII*, and *VIII*, plus Gallic Eusebius no. XXXV (formerly no. XXXIV): Bergmann, *Studien*, pp. 191–8; *Eusebius 'Gallicanus'*, ed. Glorie, pp. 857–68. In fact, it is even possible that Caesarius was adapting *Ad monachos VIII*, lines 20 and 55–7, in his *Sermo CXCVIII* (§ 5), ed. Morin, *Sancti Caesarii Arelatensis Sermones*, p. 801, lines 27–9.

[149] Cf. above, n. 141.

[150] Souter, 'Observations', pp. 47–8, 54–7. The words cited from *Hom. VIII ad monachos* are *extirpatio* and *rancor* (*Eusebius 'Gallicanus'*, ed. Glorie, p. 512, lines 14, 31).

and *X* of the Gallic Eusebian sermon-collection, of which *Homilia X* at least has good claims to be considered as Faustus's.[151] As for stylistic matters, Seebass was probably correct in seeing X's use of the expression *male blandum* as evidence of Faustus's influence.[152] In these respects, then, Seebass's thesis is vindicated.

4. *The reading of the author of the* Instructiones *compared with that of* Columbanus

Let us conclude this section by seeing how far the sources known to X tally with those cited or echoed by Columbanus in his indubitably genuine works. On the negative side, no evidence has been found that Columbanus knew Origen's *Homiliae in Lucam*, Hilary's *De trinitate*, or any of the sermons in the Gallic Eusebian sermon-collection. On the positive side, however, there is a fair amount of overlapping. Columbanus knew various of Jerome's works, including his *Epistula XXII* to Eustochium; he knew Sulpicius Seuerus's *Dialogi*, probably alluding to the very tag of which X was so fond; he knew Cassian's *Instituta*, and probably his *Conlationes* also; and he knew at least one sermon by Caesarius of Arles, *Sermo CXCIV*.[153]

These works by Jerome, Sulpicius Seuerus, Cassian and Caesarius were all widespread, and use of them by both X and Columbanus is therefore not particularly noteworthy. There are, however, some very interesting overlaps. The most striking one concerns Gildas: Columbanus definitely used the *De excidio* in his genuine *Epistulae*, citing the very same passage in *Epistula V* (§ 12) as X used in *Instructio XI*.[154] Columbanus is, in fact, the first author known to have cited Gildas. A second interesting overlap occurs with the *Quicunque uult*; for here, again, one of the passages echoed in *Instructio I* is the same as that quoted by Columbanus in his *Epistula III*.[155] Third, Neil Wright has noted the same phenomenon with regard to a line from Caelius Sedulius's *Carmen paschale*, which is echoed both in *Instructio XIII* and,

---

151 See above, pp. 117–18.
152 *Instructio* X.3 (ed. & transl. Walker, *Sancti Columbani Opera*, p. 104, line 13); Faustus, *Epistulae VII, IX* (ed. Engelbrecht, *Fausti . . . Opera*, p. 207, line 27, p. 212, line 18); see Seebass, 'Über die sogenannte *Instructiones*', p. 525. It figures once in Caesarius: *Sermo* CLXXXIV.3 (ed. Morin, *Sancti Caesarii Arelatensis Sermones*, p. 750, line 13). Cf. also below, n. 227.
153 See Walker's index (*Sancti Columbani Opera*, ed. & transl. Walker, pp. 221–2): here and in the following notes, I cite references only to parallels not listed there. Note that Columbanus, *Epistula* II.8 (*ibid.*, p. 20, lines 24–5), cites Sulpicius, *Dialogi* I.xii.3. The tag from Sulpicius, *Dialogi* I.xviii.1, was, however, widely quoted in sixth-century Gaul: see above, n. 21. Walker gives no verbal parallels extensive enough to clinch Columbanus's knowledge of Cassian's *Conlationes*, but the parallels in content, which he notes, make it likely. For Columbanus's use of Caesarius's *Sermo CXCIV* in his hymn, *Precamur patrem*, see Curran, *The Antiphonary*, p. 53.
154 In addition to the parallels cited above (p. 109 and n. 66), see Winterbottom, 'Columbanus and Gildas'.
155 *Epistula* III.2: 'unum Deum esse in trinitate et trinitatem in unitate' (*Sancti Columbani Opera*, ed. & transl. Walker, p. 24, lines 13–14). Cf. above, pp. 111–12 and n. 80.

very distantly, in Columbanus's *Epistula I*.[156] In addition, it is interesting that Columbanus, like X, knew Rufinus's translation of Basil's *Regula*; and that Columbanus also knew Rufinus's translation of Gregory of Nazianzus's *Apologia* and *De luminibus*, while X knew Rufinus's translation of the *Apologia* and another of Gregory's discourses, *De epiphaniis*.[157] Further, X may well have known Gennadius's *Liber ecclesiasticorum dogmatum*, and may conceivably have known Uinniaus's *Penitential*: both of these works were known to Columbanus.[158] Finally, there is the question of Gregory the Great's works. We have seen that it is likely that X knew Gregory's *Homiliae .XL. in euangelia* and highly likely that he knew the *Moralia in Iob*. We have no evidence that Columbanus knew these two works; but he did know Gregory's *Regula pastoralis* and he was in direct touch with Gregory, asking him for a copy of his work on Ezekiel and for expositions of the Song of Songs and Zechariah.[159] This does at least show that Columbanus was in touch with Gregory, that he was impressed by the latter's works, and that he wished to read more of them.

The Content of the Thirteen Instructiones

1. *Links between the Thirteen Sermons indicating common authorship*

Let us start with the fundamental question: do the thirteen sermons form a coherent series, whose authorship must be ascribed to a single person? Or was Seebass justified in separating out *Instructiones III* and *XI* as being genuine works of Columbanus, while assigning the rest to a pupil of Faustus of Riez? A preliminary read through the sermons suggests that each fits well enough with its neighbours where it is: there are no glaring contradictions, differences in style, or breaks in the general sequence of thought. Within this broad framework, it is clear that *Instructiones I* and *II* belong together, linked by the theme of the impossibility of discussing the mystery of the Trinity; indeed, *Instructio II* begins by referring to a previous sermon on this topic. It is equally clear that the theme of life as a road (*uia, non uita*) links *Instructiones V*, *VI*, *VIII*, *IX*, and *X* closely together.

Detailed study reveals a number of further links between various of the sermons. First, a conclusive parallel between *Instructiones I* and *VIII* shows that the opening two sermons definitely belong with the *uia* series:[160]

---

[156] See above, p. 80. See also below, p. 192.

[157] On Basil's *Regula*, see above, p. 106 and n. 53; on Gregory of Nazianzus, see above, pp. 108–9, and nn. 60–5.

[158] For Columbanus's knowledge of Gennadius, see above, n. 83. Knowledge of Uinniaus's *Penitential* is apparent in many places of Columbanus's *Penitential*; on this and on the question of the latter's authorship, see discussion by Charles-Edwards, below, pp. 220–5.

[159] *Epistula* I.9 (ed. & transl. Walker, *Sancti Columbani Opera*, p. 10).

[160] *Instructio I* (§§ 4, 5)(ed. Walker, *ibid.*, p. 64, lines 21–3), giving the manuscript-reading and ignoring all but one of Walker's emendations (see below, pp. 165–6); *ibid.*, p. 66, lines 4–5, 10–12.

Altum caelum et lata terra et profundum mare longaque saecula; sed altior et latior ac profundior longiorque eius scientia, quia natura ascematus est, qui ea ex nihilo creauit . . . Deus enim credendus est inuisibilis ut est, licet ex parte a mundo corde uideatur . . . Qui est et quantus est, sibi soli notus est. Sed quia noster Deus est, inuisibilis licet nobis, a nobis tamen pulsandus est, saepe pulsandus.

High is the heaven and wide the earth and deep the sea and long the ages; but higher and wider and deeper and longer is the knowledge of Him, because He is in his nature without form, He Who created these things out of nothing . . . for God must be believed invisible as He is, though He may be partly seen by the pure heart . . . Who He is and how great He is, is known to Himself alone. But since He is our God, though invisible to us, He must yet be besought by us, often besought.

The parallel passage in *Instructio VIII* is as follows:[161]

[Deus] quam mare profundior, terra stabilior, mundo latior, aere purior, caelo altior, sole clarior est . . . ac sic omnibus ubique praesens, inconspicabilis Deus est. Plus enim est quam totus conspici queat, et plus omnibus, qui omnia ex nihilo creauit; et ideo cum uidetur inuisibilis est, quia quis sit et quantus sit sibi soli notus est. Pulsemus tamen illum, quia unicuique pro merito puritatis notus adest, inuisibilis licet, inaestimabilis licet, Deus Trinitas. Pulsemus, inquam . . .

He [God] is deeper than the sea, firmer than earth, wider than the world, clearer than air, higher than heaven, brighter than the sun . . . and so, while everywhere present to all, God remains invisible. For He is greater than the totality that could be seen, and greater than all things, He Who created all things out of nothing; and thus when seen, He is imperceptible, since Who He is and how great He is, is known to Himself alone. Yet let us beseech Him, since God the Trinity, though imperceptible and imponderable, is known and present to each one, in proportion to the deserts of our purity. Let us beseech Him, I say . . .

Indeed, if one looks closely, one sees that *Instructio I* itself ends with a reference to our being 'in uia tenebrosa huius mundi'.[162]

Secondly, another phrase, which is found in almost identical form in three different sermons, links *Instructiones III* and *XII* to this same group. *Instructio I* (§ 3) has 'Deum omnia implentem et omnia circumdantem, omnia penetrandum et omnia excedentem'; *Instructio III* (§ 2) refers to the Eternal as 'omnia implente et omnia excedente'; and *Instructio XII* (§ 2) has 'Deum . . . omnia implentem et omnia excedentem'. We might also note that *Instructiones I* and *XII* share the same odd version of I Corinthians XIII. 8, 'caritas, quae nescit cadere'.[163]

Other links are indicated by the use of common sources. Thus *Instructiones IV, V, VII*, and probably *VIII*, all use the same sermon of Caesarius of Arles, *Ad inluminandum*; *Instructiones I* and *III* quote the same tag from Sulpicius Seuerus's *Dialogi*; *Instructiones I* and *XI* use different passages from the same

---

[161] *Instructio VIII*.1 (*ibid.*, p. 94, lines 12–13, 21–6).

[162] *Ibid.*, p. 66, line 16.

[163] *Instructio I*.5 and, slightly altered, XII.3 (ed. & transl. Walker, *Sancti Columbani Opera*, p. 66, line 7, and p. 114, line 9); see Laporte, 'Étude d'authenticité [*Revue Mabillon* 45 (1955)]', p. 17.

chapter of Gregory of Nazianzus's *Apologia*; *Instructiones I* and *XI* (certainly) and *Instructio II* (probably) have verbal parallels with Gildas's *De excidio*; and *Instructio II* (certainly) and *Instructio XI* (probably) quote from the same Gallic Eusebian sermon, *Hom. VIII ad monachos*.[164] Less significant, but worth mentioning as corroborative evidence, are various common themes: *Instructiones II* and *X* both contain the forceful argument that we should fight here so that we may be crowned elsewhere;[165] *Instructiones I* and *III* both share the argument that we should understand those things which we do not see in this life by analogy with those things which we do see; and both of them and also *Instructio II* warn against trying to speak of things beyond our human ken;[166] *Instructiones III, V,* and *VI* all share the theme of our being *alieni* in this world;[167] *Instructiones III* and *VI* both emphasise that we should live as though we died daily;[168] *Instructiones X* and *XI* both contain warnings against speaking as we please, a denial of brotherly love;[169] and *Instructiones II* and *XI* both insist that it is no use our knowing in theory what we should do if we do not put it into practice.[170]

All this means that we have good reason for regarding at least *Instructiones I–XII* as belonging together. For *Instructio XIII*, the evidence is less clear cut; but, such as it is, it indicates that it too should be regarded as belonging with the other sermons. It clearly fits well in its position at the end of the series: it mentions earlier sermons, and its reference to their dealing with 'the wretchedness of human life' and rendering their listeners 'terrified by divine prophecies' tallies aptly with their content.[171] Further, it shares with *Instructio XII* the characteristic of beginning as a sermon but passing over into prayer of an almost mystical nature addressed to God. It also uses some expressions characteristic of the author of the rest of the series, such as his referring to 'paruitas ingenioli nostri' or to 'nostra loquacitas'. We might compare the phrase 'nostra paruitas' in *Instructio II*, although the 'impia loquacitas' of *Instructio I* differs in not being used of the author himself.[172] A further argument in favour of *Instructio XIII* belonging with the rest of the series is the fact that two anonymous sermons in a late seventh-century Bobbio manuscript borrow from X's *Instructiones I* and *XIII*.[173] Both were therefore available at

---

[164] For discussion, see above, pp. 98, 108–9, 115, 120; for references, see the Appendix, below, pp. 200–2.

[165] Cf. *Instructiones* II.3 and X.3.

[166] Cf. *Instructiones* I.4 and III.2; I.3–5, II.1 and III.3.

[167] See below, p. 133 and n. 190.

[168] Cf. *Instructiones* III.3 and VI.2 (ed. & transl. Walker, *Sancti Columbani Opera*, p. 76, lines 3 and 5; p. 88, lines 30–1).

[169] Cf. *Instructiones* X.4 ('si loquamur ut libet') and XI.2 ('loqui ut libet'): *ibid.*, p. 104, lines 27–9, p. 108, lines 16–17. Cf. below, pp. 189–90, and n. 473.

[170] Cf. *Instructiones* II.3 and XI.1 and 2 (*ibid.*, pp. 70– 2, 106, lines 23–7, and 108, lines 10–11).

[171] *Instructio* XIII.1. The phrase *humanae uitae miseria* aptly characterises much of the contents of *Instructio V* and those that follow it, and the phrase *diuinis simul territi oraculis* could well summarise the effects of *Instructio X*.

[172] Cf. *Instructio* XIII.1 with II.1 and I.5 (*Sancti Columbani Opera*, ed. & transl. Walker, pp. 114, 68, line 6, and 64, line 26).

[173] See above, p. 97.

Bobbio by the late seventh century. Similarly, it is worth recalling that *Instructiones III*, *VII*, and *IX* were all laid under contribution by an eighth-century Northumbrian, implying that they were available to him together.[174] Finally, we have the evidence of the extant Bobbio manuscripts, in which the whole series of thirteen sermons is given as the work of Columbanus, with no indication that any of them should be ascribed to another author.

At this point it is worth pausing to look at the arguments which Otto Seebass[175] adduced in support of his contention that *Instructiones III* and *XI* did not originally belong to the series, and that they were by Columbanus, whereas the remaining eleven sermons were by an anonymous pupil of Faustus of Riez. A re-reading of Seebass's article makes it clear that he did not reach these conclusions purely on the basis of the internal evidence of the sermons themselves; for he cited the verbal parallel which I have just given, of God 'omnia implentem et omnia excedentem', to show the link between *Instructiones I* and *XII*.[176] But, although he was aware that *Instructio III* used exactly the same phrase of God – and, indeed, that other passages in *Instructio III* were reminiscent both of other of the thirteen sermons and of the 'Faustus' sources common to these other sermons –, he nonetheless disregarded these parallels, and ascribed *Instructio III* to a different author.[177] Conversely, he offered fewer arguments than I have adduced in favour of *Instructio XIII* belonging with the main series of sermons; but this did not inhibit him from definitely assigning it to this main series.[178] What appears to have happened is that Seebass became convinced by the verbal parallels between *Instructio XI* and other genuine works of Columbanus that *Instructio XI* at least must be a work of Columbanus.[179] But, because of the Faustus reference in *Instructio II*, he assumed that that sermon could not be by Columbanus. He therefore cast around for a means of reconciling his belief that two different authors must have been involved, and the Fleury family of manuscripts came to his aid, containing as they do only *Instructiones III* and *XI* from the series of thirteen, and an attribution of these – with two other short pieces – to Columbanus.

It should now be clear why Seebass and I have come to different conclusions as to whether the whole series of thirteen sermons should be ascribed to a single author. My own approach is to postpone discussion of the authorship-question until all the evidence has been examined, and at this point to let the evidence of the sermons speak for itself. On these grounds, all the indications are that the whole series of thirteen sermons has a single author. Seebass, on the other hand, was marshalling the evidence of verbal parallels and citations from common sources in support of his own theories about the authorship of the sermons. I turn now to his specific arguments. He maintained that *Instructiones III* and *XI* could be withdrawn from the sequence of the thirteen sermons without affecting the general continuity of that series. I accept this point, but it

---

174 See above, p. 99 and n. 25.
175 Seebass, 'Über die sogenannte *Instructiones*', pp. 527–30.
176 *Ibid.*, p. 526.
177 *Ibid.*, p. 530.
178 *Ibid.*, p. 523.
179 *Ibid.*, pp. 528–9.

is not decisive; for the series of thirteen is not such a coherent, interlocking sequence that no sermon can be removed from it. For instance, one could equally well extract *Instructio IV*, or *VII*, or *XII*, from the series without destroying the general coherence of the sequence.

Secondly, Seebass argued that the selection of just *Instructiones III* and *XI* in the Fleury manuscripts was significant. But there is no reason to think that the selection of these two sermons should be regarded any differently from the more frequent copying of *Instructio V* on its own. As we saw above,[180] the evidence for attributing the whole series of thirteen to Columbanus is very strong. Thirdly, Seebass attempted to show that *Instructiones III* and *XI* did not have any significant parallels with *Instructiones I–II*, *IV–X*, and *XII–XIII*. Here, he is at his least convincing; for in effect he had to discount parallels, particularly with *Instructio III*, that were, he admitted, there. Besides this evidence – which Seebass was aware of, but discounted – there is now additional evidence: for the use of Gregory of Nazianzus's *Apologia* and of Gildas's *De excidio Britanniae* is common to *Instructiones I* and *XI*; and it also looks as though parallels with both Gildas's *De excidio* and the Gallic Eusebian *Hom. VIII ad monachos* are to be found both in *Instructio II*, the very one which mentions the author's discipleship of Faustus, and in *Instructio XI*. On top of all this, when one examines *Instructio XI* closely, one finds that it contains parallels with the teaching of Faustus of Riez and his school, most notably with Gennadius.[181] For all these reasons, I regard it as inadmissible to split off *Instructio XI* from *Instructio II* as the work of a different author. Whoever wrote the thirteen sermons, we are dealing with a single individual, not with two separate authors.[182]

2. *The sermons' content, particularly with regard to the author and the circumstances of composition*

Before we go on to examine individual passages in the sermons, it is as well to recall their general scope. The preacher begins with a profession of faith and meditation on the mystery of the Godhead, who created the whole visible universe. Those who are accustomed to speak glibly about the Godhead are invited to contemplate the visible sea: only when they have understood everything that is in it should they be so bold as to hold forth about its Creator. Instead, God should be sought in silence, through faith, through righteous living, and through prayer. The preacher then turns to a subject more amenable to human discourse: the inspiring and teaching of his listeners. He seeks to rouse them from their carefree enjoyment of the present world by presenting it as a transient thing, no more than a road along which they should walk, with their sights set firmly on God, their true goal. The Judgment of a just judge awaits them all, and it is those who have spurned the world's delights in this life who will attain everlasting joy; this world, which is transient, is contrasted to their true homeland, in heaven.

[180] See above, pp. 96–105.
[181] See below, pp. 136–8.
[182] The same conclusion is also implied by the evidence of the sermons' latinity: see below, pp. 139–74, esp. p. 154.

In a sense, the preacher's teaching culminates in *Instructio XI*, where he starts from man's being made in God's image, and goes on to show that love of God and our neighbour is the restoration of that image – and that means a love put into practice through the keeping of God's commandments, and through a refusal even to utter words which may hurt others. In the last two sermons he seeks to stir his hearers from their customary inertia to pay heed to what he has been saying, and in both he passes over into prayer of an almost mystical nature.[183]

Domine, da mihi, rogo te, in nomine Iesu Christi Filii tui, Dei mei, illam quae nescit cadere caritatem, ut mea lucerna accendi sciat, exstingui nesciat, mihi ardeat, aliis luceat . . . Tuum sit, quaeso, te nobis pulsantibus monstrare, amantissime Saluator, ut te intellegentes, tantum te amemus, te solum amemus, te solum desideremus, te solum meditemur die ac nocte, semper te cogitemus . . .

Lord, grant me, I pray you in the name of Jesus Christ your son, my God, that love which knows no fall, so that my lamp may feel the kindling touch and know no quenching, may burn for me and for others give light . . . Be it yours, I beg, most loving Saviour, to show yourself to us who clamour for you, so that knowing you, we may love you only, love you alone, desire you alone, contemplate you alone by day and night, and always think on you . . .

My own reading of the evidence of these sermons is that their author was a man of spiritual stature. He was able to take a theme and to develop it coherently over a series of thirteen sermons, with enough repetition to allow his main points to sink into his hearers,[184] but enough skilfully crafted phrases,[185] vivid images, and moving meditations to hold his audience's attention, to woo, instruct, and inspire them. Though no philosopher, and refusing to be drawn into a discussion of the Godhead, he did not shy away from thinking and concern himself solely with morals. Rather, he turned to metaphor to express what could not otherwise be conveyed – the approach of a poet. Thus, for instance, the Trinity is compared with the depths of the sea and the other marvels of creation: 'For the one God, the Trinity, is an ocean which cannot be traversed or investigated. High is the heaven and wide the earth and deep the sea and long the ages; but higher and wider and deeper and longer is the knowledge of Him, because He is in his nature without form, He who created these things out of nothing.'[186] Or he attempted to convey the insignificance of human life by likening it to a shadow: 'you see, and see it not; itself, and not itself, let us say; what has been you do not see, and cannot even

---

[183] *Instructio* XII.3 (*Sancti Columbani Opera*, ed. & transl. Walker, p. 114). It is difficult to convey the impact of these passages of prayer through brief quotations because the preacher's approach is to pile phrase upon phrase, developing the image of flame and light (or, in *Instructio* XIII.3, that of drinking from the springing fount), and building up an overpowering picture of being surrounded by, and wrapped up in, God's love.

[184] X was fully aware of the importance of repetition in this context: see *Instructio* XII.1.

[185] On which see below, pp. 140–1.

[186] *Instructio* I.4. On the correct reading and interpretation of this passage, see below, pp. 161–7.

see what shall be. You only see what is, while it lasts; take away what is, and you see nothing; it is so unseen, as if it were not.'[187] Or he passed from this image to that of a dream, pondering on the difference between that which we see in our waking hours and that which we see in our sleep. Both perceptions are fleeting, and therefore unreal; and this thought led him on to ponder the transient nature of human life:[188]

Quod enim sum non fui, et non ero, et unaquaque hora aliud sum, et numquam sto. Semper enim curro . . . et per singulos dies uitae meae mutor, et quaecumque mutantur uel quomodo mutantur non uideo; et totam simul in uno uitam meam numquam uidere possum . . .

For what I am I was not and I shall not be, and every hour I am different and never stay. For I am always moving . . . and I change through each day of my life, and what things are changed and how they are changed I do not see; and I am never able to see my whole life all together . . .

Such wrestling with the problems of human existence and transience is more reminiscent of Augustine's *Confessions* than of most early mediaeval sermons. We are a long way from the moralising of a Caesarius of Arles.

The internal evidence of the sermons allows us to glean a little more information about them and their author, although it must be done carefully. For instance, a quick reading of the phrase in *Instructio X*, 'in alienis habitamus', translated by Walker as 'we live in foreign lands', might suggest that the author was not a native of the country in which he was writing.[189] This is true only in the sense that the author regarded his true homeland as heaven.[190] For him, then, to live on earth was to live *in alienis*, and we can draw no deductions of a geographical nature from this passage. Other passages in the sermons can, however, be used to cast at least some light on their original context. A reference to 'the terrible predictions' in the Bible, 'from which we have related a few yesterday and today',[191] clearly refers to the content of that sermon and the preceding one, suggesting that the various sermons in the series were preached on consecutive days. There are indications that they were addressed to monks: the frequent use of *fratres* as an aside,[192] the title of *Instructio III*, 'How a monk ought to please God', the whole tenor of the sermons' content, and the prayers with which the last two sermons end. We might note in particular the reference in *Instructio IV* to 'ha[e]c nostrae scholae disciplina', which is described as 'the training of all trainings, . . . at the price

---

[187] *Instructio VI.1 (Sancti Columbani Opera*, ed. & transl. Walker, pp. 86–9).

[188] *Ibid.*

[189] *Instructio X.3 (Sancti Columbani Opera*, ed. & transl. Walker, pp. 102–3).

[190] This reading is obvious if one compares *Instructio X.3* with *Instructio V.2*, where our life in this world is shown to be a 'road' that leads to our true home (*patria*) in heaven; we are therefore urged, 'aliena terrena deuitemus, ut propria aeterna non perdamus; fideles in alienis inueniamur, ut in propriis ac nostris heredes efficiamur' (ed. & transl. Walker, *Sancti Columbani Opera*, p. 86). Cf. also *Instructiones III.4*, VI.1, VIII.2.

[191] *Instructio X.2.*

[192] *Instructiones* I.5, II.1, IX.1 and 2, XIII.1.

of present sorrow it obtains the pleasure of time without end and the delight of eternal joy'.[193] As for the preacher, he bore responsibility for teaching the monks,[194] whether as abbot or as a respected monk to whom that task had been delegated. His discourse was directed both at expounding what they should do, and, simultaneously, inspiring them to continue striving towards heaven. The works in question are thus very much sermons, rather than theological works: as the preacher put it, he has not attempted to expound the mystery of the Godhead, 'not daring like others, for whom we must feel shame, to seek concerning things too high, . . . but rather preaching on the edification of our souls.'[195]

This is the context for his reference to Faustus of Riez:[196]

non primum nostrae paruitatis fundamenta iacere praesumimus, alicuius maioris doctoris auctoritatem quaerentes, sancti scilicet Fausti luculentissimam elegantissimamque doctrinam, de cuius dictis pauca ad initiandum opus nostrum satis conuenienter elegimus, utpote qui de eisdem monitionibus . . . et nos uiles licet commissos sibi docuit, et quasi tempore et merito et scientia me prior, quasi pro me impugnaturus ignaros quosque et ignauos prius loquatur.

we do not dare at the beginning to lay our own poor foundations, but seek the authority of a greater teacher, I mean the most perspicuous and polished doctrine of St Faustus, from whose words we have chosen a few suitably enough for opening our work; for in fact he taught us when, though unworthy, we were entrusted to his care . . . ; and as he is my senior in time, merit and knowledge, let him speak first as if in my defence to attack all ignorant and degenerate men.

We shall return to the question of Faustus in our final discussion; but here let us note, first, that Faustus is represented as being older than X; and, secondly, that X regarded him as a revered authority.

The first two sermons of X contain interesting hints about the context in which he wrote, quite apart from the reference to Faustus. The first sermon starts with a declaration of faith in God as both Trinity and unity, at times echoing the *Quicunque uult*. The explicit reference, 'Cesset ergo uenenosa et insana omnium hereticorum uesania' confirms the implicit indications given by this Trinitarian emphasis: X was clearly writing in a context where some kind of Trinitarian heresy was current.[197] X contents himself with some fairly general remarks, basing himself firmly on the Bible: 'except for those things which either the Law or Prophets or Gospel or Apostles tell, there should be from others a profound silence on the Trinity'.[198] The identity of those who concern themselves with trying to probe the mystery of the Trinity is unfortunately left studiously vague: there are references to 'illi uani et illi nimis mali et impii', who could be heretics; but X's embarrassment at those who

---

[193] *Instructio* IV.1.
[194] *Instructio* I.1: 'Instructionis ualde necessariae curam gerens'.
[195] *Instructio* II.1; and cf. XIII.1, comparing his audience of 'beginners' to the 'perfectly wise'.
[196] *Instructio* II.1.
[197] *Instructio* I.2.
[198] *Instructio* II.1.

dare to seek things too high for them[199] rather implies that dangerous speculation was not confined simply to those who could be clearly labelled as heretics.

3. *Comparison with the teaching of Faustus of Riez*

In view of X's admiration for Faustus of Riez, it is worth looking closely at his ideas on sin, grace, and free will. One passage is particularly revealing: 'Let man strive to be what he was created, and call God's grace to help his attempt; for it is impossible for anyone to acquire by his own efforts alone what he lost in Adam.'[200] This passage implies some awareness of the Pelagian controversy, and rejects Pelagianism in its crudest form; but it still lends itself to the interpretation that man should take the initiative in asking for God's grace, rather than seeing God's grace as already responsible for his turning to God. It is reasonably consonant with the author being a – not very theologically-minded – disciple of Faustus of Riez.[201] It is, in fact, the sort of attitude which Caesarius was instrumental in getting condemned at the second council of Orange in 529.[202] X's general outlook on the human condition seems bleaker than Faustus's: human nature is 'corrupt' (*uitiata*), and he regards man as 'inwardly rotten', his skin outwardly soiled: 'in vain are you washed that are unclean by nature'.[203] *Voluntas*, the common word for man's will, is virtually always used in a pejorative sense by X. This is most obvious in the outburst which begins *Instructio VII*: 'Blind madness, blind pitfall – human will . . . Pricking, unbearable leech, cruel when sated, fawning when hungry, devouring, shameless, gluttonous . . .'[204] Exactly the same sentiments appear in *Instructio I*, which talks of 'the corruption of our rotten will', while *Instructio XII* tellingly links 'the will of the flesh coupled with the lusts of the world'.[205] All this leads X to call for the mortification of our wills: 'we cannot live to Him [Christ] unless first we die to ourselves, that is, to our wills'.[206] He continues:[207]

---

[199] *Ibid.*: 'non praesumentes ut alii, de quibus erubescendum est, de altioribus quaerere'.

[200] *Instructio* III.2.

[201] For Faustus's own, far more reasoned views, see Tibiletti, 'Libero arbitrio', pp. 265–80, and Smith, 'The *De gratia*', pp. 183–200, esp. 196.

[202] See §§ 3–6, 20 (*Les canons*, edd. & transl. Gaudemet & Basdevant, I.156–8, 166).

[203] *Instructiones* X.3, VII.1. The diatribe in *Instructio* VII.1 begins as an excoriation of the will (*humanam uoluntatem*, ed. Walker, p. 90, line 4), and the will is also named at the end of this paragraph and the beginning of the next (*ibid.*, p. 90, line 33, p. 92, line 2); but much of the blistering attack in *Instructio* VII.1 in fact appears to be directed at humanity and our human condition in general (*te . . ., o misera humanitas*: *ibid.*, p. 90, line 10). Contrast Faustus, *De gratia*, II.9 (ed. Engelbrecht, *Fausti . . . Opera*, p. 80, esp. lines 11–14) and *passim*.

[204] *Instructio* VII.1. On *pertusata*, see below, pp. 171–2.

[205] *Instructio* I.3, *putridae uoluntatis corruptio* (*Sancti Columbani Opera*, ed. & transl. Walker, p. 62, line 24); *Instructio* XII.1 (*ibid.*, p. 110, line 27).

[206] *Instructio* X.2.

[207] *Instructio* X.3, quoting Matthew XI.12.

Mortalis est enim, si uoluntatibus suis uiuit ... non nobis uiuere debemus, et grandis uiolentia est per laborem quaerere, et per studium habere, quod natura uitiata non seruauerit. Sed tamen arbitri electionem, amissa licet beatitudine, non amisit. Inde nunc *Per uim et uiolentiam regnum rapimus caelorum*, et illud quodammodo quasi inter medias hostium manus ... Pugnandum ergo hic est et certandum cum uitiis nostris, ut alibi coronemur.

For he is subject to death, if he lives for his own wishes ... We ought not to live to ourselves, and it requires great violence to seek by toil and to maintain by enthusiasm what a corrupted nature has not kept. But yet, though blessedness is lost, it has not lost the choice of free will. Thence we now *seize the kingdom of heaven by strength and violence*, and this we snatch somehow, as it were, from amidst our enemies' hands ... So here we must fight and struggle with our vices, that we may be crowned elsewhere.

This last passage is important as showing that X does maintain man's freedom of will to overcome his delight in worldly blandishments and to 'seize the kingdom of heaven' through ascetic practices, and this sermon ends on an optimistic note: 'For who is really happier than he ... whose life is Christ, ... to whom heaven is made low and paradise opens, to whom earth is heavenly and hell is closed, ... who obtains ... heaven for earth, and by a happy exchange, God for mortality?'[208] We should also note the opening of the following sermon (*Instructio XI*), which begins with the Genesis account of how 'God made man in His image and likeness'. If man uses wrongly what he has received from God, 'then he perverts the likeness of God and destroys it as far as in him lies; yet if he employs the virtues planted in his soul to a proper end, then he will be like to God'.[209] This shows that man's likeness to God can never be entirely destroyed, while also holding out the possibility of man living in accordance with the gift of God's image and likeness.

Thus X, like his revered teacher Faustus, does maintain a place for the freedom of the will; but his ideas do not altogether tally with those of Faustus. First, there is a difference of atmosphere: Faustus does not emphasise man's fallenness in the way that X does. Secondly, whereas X appears to distinguish between *uoluntas*, which carries all the connotations of man's desires for the wrong thing, and *arbitri[i] electio*, or free will, Faustus appears to use such expressions as *uoluntatis libertas* and *libertas arbitrii* interchangeably, although the latter is his normal term.[210] This is all of a piece with his regarding the human will as 'weakened' by the Fall, rather than being inherently sinful.[211]

A third issue requires close inspection: that is, the views of Faustus and of X on the relationship between man's 'image' and 'likeness' to God. There is a very slight verbal parallel in that both authors talk of God bestowing on man 'the dignity of his image',[212] and both authors quote the same variant form of

---

[208] *Instructio* X.4.
[209] *Instructio* XI.1, quoting Genesis I.27.
[210] Cf. Faustus, *De gratia*, II.9 (ed. Engelbrecht, *Fausti ... Opera*, p. 76, line 28, and p. 78, lines 26–7); Smith, 'The *De gratia*', p. 167, n. 35.
[211] *De gratia*, I.8, II.8; see Smith, 'The *De gratia*', pp. 74–5, and Tibiletti, 'Libero arbitrio', pp. 265–6, 271–4.
[212] Faustus, *De gratia*, II.9: 'una diuinitas primo homini suae imaginis tribuit dignitatem' (ed. Engelbrecht, *Fausti ... Opera*, p. 78, lines 24–5); cf. X, *Instructio*

Genesis I.27: 'Fecit Deus hominem ad imaginem et similitudinem suam.'[213] In his discussion of this verse, Faustus distinguishes between image and likeness: God's gift of His image bestows on man eternity, and freedom of the will, whereas the likeness gives the potentiality for exercising virtue to the man who lives in accordance with grace. Thus even the wicked retain the image of God, but only those who actually pursue good attain to the likeness to God, in varying degrees.[214] Faustus is here in tune with the thought of various Greek theologians, such as Irenaeus and Origen.[215] Does X, like them, distinguish between the 'image' and 'likeness' to God? Walker, his editor, believed that he did, but the evidence is confusing. X writes:[216]

Grandis dignatio, quod Deus suae aeternitatis imaginem et morum suorum similitudinem homini donauit. Magna dignitas homini Dei similitudo, si conseruetur; sed grandis iterum damnatio Dei imaginis uiolatio. Quod enim accepit de flatu Dei, si in contrarium deprauauerit usum, et beneficium naturae contaminauerit, tunc Dei similitudinem corrumpit, et quantum in se est delet; si autem animae insitis uirtutibus usus fuerit in rectum, tunc Deo erit similis ... Dei enim dilectio imaginis eius renouatio.

It is a great dignity that God bestowed on man the image of His eternity and the likeness of His character. A grand distinction for man is the likeness of God, if it be preserved; but again, it is great damnation to defile the image of God. For if he prostitutes for the opposite employment what he has received from the breath of God, and corrupts the blessing of his nature, then he perverts the likeness of God and destroys it as far as in him lies; yet if he employs the virtues planted in his soul to a proper end, then he will be like to God ... For the love of God is the restoration of His image.

The first sentence does indeed tally with Faustus's teaching: as in Faustus, it links the gift of *aeternitas* with man's being made in God's image,[217] and it

---

XI.1: 'Deus . . . de limo hominem fingens, imaginis suae dignitate nobilitauit' (*Sancti Columbani Opera*, ed. & transl. Walker, p. 106).

[213] This particular variant of the Vetus Latina translation is found in a relatively small number of authors; but besides Faustus it occurs in works by Priscillian, Isidore, Eucherius of Lyon, in one of the Pelagian tracts edited by Caspari, and in a few other authors. For details, see *Vetus Latina*, ed. Fischer, II.28–9.

[214] *De gratia*, II.9 (ed. Engelbrecht, *Fausti . . . Opera*, pp. 78–9); Smith, 'The *De gratia*', pp. 167–8.

[215] Walker (*Sancti Columbani Opera*, ed. & transl. Walker, p. 107) cites Irenaeus; but although the distinction first appears in his writings, it was taken up by various other Greek authors, including Origen: Burghardt, *The Image of God*, pp. 1–7, provides a useful overview, and cf. also Ladner, *Images and Ideas*, I.84–93, esp. 87. Of the theologians whom I have looked at, Faustus and Gennadius (see below) come the closest to X: none of these three has the interpretation found in Origen and other Alexandrian theologians, that Christ is the image of the Father, and that we are formed in Christ's image. Arguably, however, another aspect of Origen's doctrine of images does lie behind the following passage of X's *Instructio XI*: see above, pp. 106–8.

[216] *Instructio* XI.1.

[217] Cf. Faustus, *De gratia*, II.9 (ed. Engelbrecht, *Fausti . . . Opera*, p. 78, lines 28–30).

implies a distinction between the image, characterised by man's possession of God-like eternity, and the likeness, characterised by man's behaviour. But the second sentence raises doubts: is X really contrasting *similitudo* and *imago*? Is not the contrast between keeping, or violating, the image/likeness with which God has endowed us, *similitudo* and *imago* here being used as synonyms, and alternated for stylistic reasons?

Further, the text goes on to treat of man's obliterating his likeness to God, as much as that is possible; but for Faustus, man's likeness to God could be totally obliterated – it was his possession of God's image which could not be destroyed. The sentence about using aright the virtues planted in him by God and so becoming similar to God is pure Faustus teaching; but the final sentence again suggests that X was using *imago* and *similitudo* without distinction. The evidence is therefore difficult to interpret: there are some undeniable parallels, but also a basic difference in that X does not continue his initial distinction between image and likeness.

One further point is that, as we saw above,[218] there is a close verbal parallel to X's first sentence in Gennadius's *Liber ecclesiasticorum dogmatum*: 'libere confitemur imaginem in aeternitate, similitudinem in moribus inueniri.'[219] The context is one of upholding Faustus's views on the corporeality of the soul, over against Claudianus Mamertus, who had argued that the human soul must be incorporeal because it was made in the image of God, who is incorporeal.[220] There is thus a strong possibility that X's own words reflect a general Faustian school of thought, which was predominant in southern Gaul in the late fifth century and the beginnings of the sixth, rather than necessarily indicating that he had read Faustus's *De gratia* himself. Whether his wording derived from this general current of thought, or whether it owes something to Gennadius directly, is something best left open for the moment.[221] In the meantime let us note simply that in this instance, as throughout our discussion of the possible parallels between X's and Faustus's theological views, we find some definite points of contact, but also some differences.

---

[218] See above, p. 111.

[219] Gennadius, *Liber ecclesiasticorum dogmatum*, § 54, ed. Turner, 'The *Liber*', p. 99. For the correctness of the attribution to Gennadius of Marseilles, see also the comments of F.W. Puller, reported by Turner, 'The *Liber ecclesiasticorum dogmatum*: Supplenda', pp. 104–7.

[220] Gennadius, *Liber ecclesiasticorum dogmatum*, §§ 54, 11–12. See Mathisen, *Ecclesiastical Factionalism*, ch. 10, esp. pp. 235–44 (but beware his mistranslation of the Gennadius passage on p. 242); cf. also Tibiletti, 'Libero arbitrio', pp. 281–2.

[221] If we conclude that the author of the *Instructiones* was indeed Columbanus, then direct dependence on Gennadius may be assumed, first, because we know that Columbanus did use Gennadius (above, n. 83); and secondly, because Columbanus's access to a Faustian school of thought a century after Faustus's death and eighty years after the second Council of Orange (A.D. 529) is most likely to have been through a book. Cf. below, pp. 182–3, 185.

The Latinity of the Thirteen Sermons

1. General stylistic characteristics

The author of the thirteen sermons wrote a Latin which is basically correct;[222] and, granted that he wrote after Caesarius of Arles, that much needs to be said.[223] But X's Latin is far more than 'correct'. He is not struggling to express himself in a tongue in which he is ill at ease; rather, he is able to forge the language into a fit medium for expressing the concerns which he burns to convey,[224] and his command of the language enables him to vary his style in accordance with what he is saying. Much of the time, as we would expect in sermons intended for oral delivery, the sentences are short and the language is straightforward:[225]

Quid enim diligentius, quidue abundantius lex Dei mandauit quam dilectionem? Et raro inuenis quemquam sic facientem. Quid dicemus pro excusatione? Numquid possumus dicere, laboriosum est, durum est? Non est labor dilectio; plus suaue est, plus medicale est, plus salubre est cordi dilectio. Si enim uitiis languidum non fuerit cor, ipsius sanitas dilectio est, et quod Deo carum sit; nihil autem Deo plus carum est quam dilectio . . .

For what has the law of God commanded more carefully or more fully than love? And seldom do you find any so doing. What shall we say for excuse? Can we really say, It is troublesome, it is hard? Love is no trouble; love is more pleasant, more healthful, more saving to the heart. For if the heart has not become enervated in its vices, love is its own health, besides being what is dear to God; yet nothing is dearer to God than love . . .

---

[222] This is but a sketch of the salient features, together with more detailed treatment of those which may be useful diagnostically: interlaced word-order; rhythmical clausulae; and vocabulary. Hitherto little has been written on the style of the *Instructiones*, although Walker (*Sancti Columbani Opera*, ed. & transl. Walker, pp. lxix–lxx) and Bieler (*apud* Walker, p. lxxxi) are good as far as they go; Walker's *index grammaticus* includes several figures of speech (*ibid.*, pp. 239–41); and Mohrmann includes comments on the *Instructiones* in her remarks on Columbanus's style ('The earliest continental Irish Latin', pp. 219–30). Laporte also makes some pertinent observations ('Étude d'authenticité [*Revue Mabillon* 45 (1955)]', pp. 12–14. I succeeded in obtaining Quacquarelli, 'La prosa di san Colombano', only when this section was completed, and have seen no reason to alter anything. Quacquarelli illustrates several rhetorical usages, and may profitably be read alongside my pp. 139–50. When we differ, on *clausulae* (below, pp. 150–61), I stand by what I had already written: Quacquarelli eschews any kind of statistical study ('La prosa di san Colombano', p. 34); but this is a *sine qua non* for studying *clausulae*, since over 50% of sentence endings can follow regular cursus patterns purely by chance (below, pp. 152–3). Similarly, my study was completed before Neil Wright's on Columbanus's *Epistulae* (above), and I have judged it best to leave my original comparison with Columbanus's *Epistulae* as it is.

[223] Cf. Mohrmann, 'The earliest continental Irish Latin', pp. 216, 219–28, 230, treating both the *Instructiones* and Columbanus's *Epistulae*.

[224] I agree with the comments of Walker (*Sancti Columbani Opera*, ed. & transl. Walker, p. lxx).

[225] *Instructio* XI.3.

One might note the separation of noun and its qualifying adjective in 'languidum . . . cor', and the use of the word *medicale*, which does not figure in most Latin dictionaries. Decorative word-order and elements of the author's vocabulary are both matters to which I shall return. Despite this, however, the main thrust of what the author is saying is clear, and in this respect the passage quoted may be taken as typical of the sermons.

While the sermons in the main are characterised by this general ease, correctness, and simplicity of expression, there are nonetheless frequent rhetorical usages. When he so desired, X could employ these tellingly: 'Vide uicissitudinem rerum, uita ante mortem et post mortem uita; iustus pius duas possidet, et peccator impius unam infeliciter habuit, alteram felicem perdidit.'[226] In the first sentence here, alliteration and chiasmus are used to excellent effect, while in the last sentence there is a play on words and meanings with the antithesis between 'infeliciter habuit' and 'felicem perdidit'. As this quotation suggests, some passages in the sermons employ many of the rhetoricians' techniques: those that play with the sound of words (alliteration, assonance, even rhyme on occasion), and those that tease us with their play on contrasting meanings (oxymoron[227] and antithesis); those that are concerned with the pattern of sentences, and those which build up the structure of whole passages. Our author concerned himself with the whole gamut of the interplay between expression and meaning.

Let us begin by looking at one of his more finely wrought passages, the opening of *Instructio V*:[228]

O tu uita humana, fragilis et mortalis, quantos decepisti, quantos seduxisti, quantos excaecasti! Quae dum fugis nihil es, dum uideris umbra es, dum exaltaris fumus es; quae cottidie fugis et cottidie uenis, ueniendo fugis quae fugiendo uenis, dissimilis euentu, similis ortu, dissimilis luxu, similis fluxu, dulcis stultis, amara sapientibus. Qui te amant non te sciunt, et qui te contemnunt ipsi te intellegunt. Ergo non es uerax sed fallax; te ostendis tamquam ueracem, te reducis quasi fallacem. Quid ergo es, humana uita? Via es mortalium et non uita, a peccato incipiens usque ad mortem perseverans . . . Sic enim subtilis es et sic seductrix, ut paucorum sit te scire uiam. Interroganda ergo es et non credenda nec uindicanda, transeunda, non habitanda, misera humana uita; nullus enim in uia habitat sed ambulat, ut qui ambulent in uia, habitent in patria.

O human life, frail and mortal, how many have you deceived, how many beguiled, how many blinded! While you fly, you are nothing, while you are seen, you are a shadow, while you arise, you are but smoke; daily you fly and daily you return, you fly in returning and return in flying, unequal in outcome, identical in origin, unequal in

---

[226] *Instructio* IX.2 (ed. & transl. Walker, *Sancti Columbani Opera*, p. 100, lines 14–16).

[227] E.g. *Instructio* VII.2: 'o fera, licet domestica'; 'amicus est tibi inimicus tuus'; 'diuitiis pauperes' (ed. & transl. Walker, *Sancti Columbani Opera*, p. 92, lines 5, 16, 35–6); *Instructio* X.3–4: 'ille enim bene diligit, qui seipsum salubriter odit'; 'male blandum'; 'rex humilis' (*ibid.*, p. 104, lines 5, 13, 32); *Instructio* XIII.3: 'sanatur uulnerando' (*ibid.*, p. 120, line 10). The expression *male blandus* is a usage typical of Faustus: see Souter, 'Observations', p. 57; *Fausti . . . Opera*, ed. Engelbrecht, p. 492, s.v. 'male'; cf. Gallic Eusebius, *Hom. VII ad monachos* (§ 8), ed. Glorie, *Eusebius 'Gallicanus'*, p. 503.

[228] *Instructio* V.1 (*Sancti Columbani Opera*, ed. & transl. Walker, p. 84, lines 5–13, 19–23).

pleasure, identical in passage, sweet to the fools, bitter to the wise. Those who love you do not know you, and those who scorn you really understand you. Thus you are not true but false; you show yourself as true, render yourself in falsehood. What then are you, human life? You are the roadway of mortals, not their life, beginning from sin, enduring up till death . . . For you are so wily and so winsome that it is granted to few to know you as a way. Thus you are to be questioned and not believed or warranted, traversed, not occupied, wretched human life; for on a roadway none dwells but walks, that those who walk upon the way may dwell in their homeland.

This passage illustrates X's mastery of the play of sounds, here chiefly assonance, and even full rhyme (*luxu/fluxu*, and *ueracem/fallacem*). We see his use of apostrophe and posing of rhetorical questions – both common enough elsewhere in his sermons, as in the opening section of *Instructio VII*. Further, there is a skilful use of anaphora, with the repetition of *quantos* (thrice), *dum* (thrice), and *cottidie* (twice), while piquancy is added by the neat antithesis, 'dulcis stultis, amara sapientibus'. There is also a playing with words, first of the type called ἀντιμεταβολή (in Latin *conuersio, commutatio*), where the components of the first half of the figure change places in the second half, as here 'ueniendo fugis quae fugiendo uenis';[229] and then of the type called *paronomasia*, where words sounding similar, but with dissimilar meanings, are used, as in *dissimilis luxu/similis fluxu, ueracem/fallacem, uia/uita*, and *habitat/ambulat*.[230] The whole passage illustrates a very nice sense of balance, and the building up, through a number of short phrases, of a powerful evocation of the deceptive impermanence of human life. At the end comes the metaphor of this life as but a road, a metaphor which the author continues to develop in this and the following sermons, and which underlies the neat antithesis with assonance which ends the paragraph, 'nullus enim in uia habitat sed ambulat, ut qui ambulent in uia, habitent in patria'.

This passage, then, can serve as an introduction to X's rhetorical skills; and the fact that it was copied more frequently than any other of X's thirteen sermons shows that these skills were appreciated in the early middle ages. I would reiterate that it is not typical of the style of his sermons as a whole, because for much of the time X wrote in a simpler, less elaborate style. It does, however, show what he was able to produce when he so desired. His use of rhetorical devices can be paralleled from late fifth-century Gaul, and indeed, from the circle of Faustus of Riez;[231]

---

[229] On ἀντιμεταβολή and its use by Ruricius, bishop of Limoges and correspondent of Faustus, see Hagendahl, *La correspondance*, pp. 69–70.

[230] For parallels in Ruricius, see Hagendahl, *ibid.*, pp. 71–5. See also the index in *Fausti . . . Opera*, ed. Engelbrecht, pp. 491–2, s.v. 'lusus uerborum'. Other examples in the *Instructiones* are: *corporis/cordis* (*Instructio II*.2, ed. & transl. Walker, *Sancti Columbani Opera*, p. 70, line 3), 'patria non est, sed poena' (*Instructio IX*.1, ed. *ibid.*, p. 96, line 30), and 'squalentibus atque torpentibus mortiferi teporis torporibus' (*Instructio XII*.2, ed. *ibid.*, p. 112, lines 21–2). For examples from the *Epistulae* of Columbanus, see Walker's *index grammaticus, ibid.*, p. 241.

[231] Hagendahl, *La correspondance*, esp. ch. 5, provides a helpful analysis of the style of one of Faustus's correspondents, Ruricius of Limoges; and this provides us with a yardstick for late fifth-century Gaul against which the *Instructiones* of X can be set. For divergence over treatment of *clausulae*, see below, pp. 150–61.

but, equally, it can be paralleled in the undoubtedly genuine *Epistulae* of Columbanus.[232]

I wish now to consider various features which are characteristic of the sermons as a whole, and not just of a few carefully fashioned passages. First, there is the rhetorical use of words like *inquam* and *quaeso*, as in such expressions as: 'Considerate, quaeso, dicti huius dignitatem.'[233] This is a common rhetorical device, and X might well have learnt it from the sermons of Caesarius and Faustus which he knew;[234] I mention it here only because it is by no means always found in early mediaeval sermons. It is, incidentally, a device which Columbanus uses in his (genuine) *Epistulae*.[235] Exactly the same goes for the expression, 'Cum haec ergo ita sunt' and its variants, which again is a stock expression found in many classical and then christian authors including Faustus and Caesarius, as also in the genuine works of Columbanus.[236] Neither of these usages is helpful for our particular diagnostic purposes, but they are nonetheless worth mentioning because they imply some kind of rhetorical or literary awareness which, in the context of a sixth- or seventh-century author, seems worth remarking on.

Another noteworthy feature of the *Instructiones* is the number of metaphors employed. Of course, metaphors were widely used in late antiquity; and many of them, including several originating in the Bible, were shared topoi amongst christian Latin writers: the vine, the *militia Christi*, the clergy's pastoral task of

[232] See Winterbottom, 'Columbanus and Gildas', pp. 310–11, 314–15 (anaphora, accumulation); cf. Mohrmann, 'The earliest continental Irish Latin', pp. 219–27, esp. 226. Further, for antithesis, see Columbanus, *Epistulae* IV.4 and 6, V.3 (ed. & transl. Walker, *Sancti Columbani Opera*, p. 28, line 29, p. 30, lines 15–16, p. 38, lines 10–11); for oxymoron, see *Epistula* V.3 (*audeo timidus*) and 5 (*ibid.*, p. 38, line 19, p. 42, line 5). Walker's *index grammaticus* (*ibid.*, pp. 239–41) lists examples of hyperbaton, chiasmus, anaphora, paronomasia, and other forms of word-play from Columbanus's *Epistulae* and the thirteen *Instructiones*.

[233] *Instructio* XI.1 (*ibid.*, p. 106, line 9). Further examples of *quaeso* occur *ibid.*, p. 66, line 30, p. 98, line 17; examples of *inquam* occur *ibid.*, p. 62, lines 7 and 28, p. 64, line 31, p. 88, line 19, p. 94, line 26, p. 102, line 7; examples of *rogo* occur *ibid.*, p. 64, line 11, p. 88, line 1, p. 98, line 30, p. 112, line 11.

[234] E.g. Caesarius, *Sermo* LVIII.1, partly quoted in *Instructio* IX.1; cf. *Sancti Caesarii Arelatensis Sermones*, ed. Morin, p. 255, lines 1–8, and *Sancti Columbani Opera*, ed. & transl. Walker, p. 98, lines 13–17. See also Gallic Eusebius, *Homilia XXXIX* (= *Hom. IV ad monachos*): *Eusebius 'Gallicanus'*, ed. Glorie, p. 455, lines 3 and 7, p. 458, line 48.

[235] E.g. *quaeso* in *Sancti Columbani Opera*, ed. & transl. Walker, p. 4, line 30, p. 8, line 29, p. 22, line 20, p. 52, line 20, etc.; *inquam*: *ibid.*, p. 12, line 15; *rogo*: *ibid.*, p. 6, line 12.

[236] *Instructio* VII.2 (*ibid.*, p. 92, line 7; cf. p. 80, lines 35–6). Columbanus, *Epistula* V.12 (*ibid.*, p. 50, line 7) and *Regula monachorum* (*ibid.*, p. 126, line 24, p. 136, lines 3–4, p. 138, line 25). Faustus, *De gratia* (ed. Engelbrecht, *Fausti . . . Opera*, p. 78, line 26, p. 79, line 29), *Epistula V* (ed. Engelbrecht, *ibid.*, p. 189, line 1), and see further examples cited by Engelbrecht in his index (*ibid.*, p. 491), s.v. 'locutiones Fausto peculiares'. Caesarius, *Sermo* LVIII.1 and 3 (ed. Morin, *Sancti Caesarii Arelatensis Sermones*, p. 255, lines 14–15, p. 256, line 3).

protecting Christ's sheep from ravening wolves, and so on.[237] X reproduces several of these: the need to cleanse the field of our hearts from the noxious weeds of vices;[238] the *militia Christi*;[239] Christ painting his image in us;[240] Christ as the giver of light;[241] or Christ as the fountain of life.[242] Some of these metaphors, as we have seen, X develops at length: that of this life as a road,[243] or alternatively, as a shadow or a dream that would pass.[244] But others, including some more original looking ones, X tosses out as he writes, without any attempt to wring the last ounce of meaning from them: 'in uanum ergo laborat qui talia pascit, et in uentum seminat qui uanae uoluntati huic seruit'.[245] Here we see X writing so rapidly that he is in fact mixing his metaphors: first he talks of 'feeding' our wills, and then he suddenly switches to the image of this amounting to 'sowing in the wind'. It is all part of his vivid way of speaking and writing. Earlier in that same sermon he likens the human will to a 'pricking, pitiless leech', battening on mankind[246] – a vivid image drawn, surely, direct from life by the preacher, not a conventional metaphor taken from the common stock. Such graphic images enliven and inform X's sermons in a way which is rather different from the more predictable use of metaphor by, say, Caesarius of Arles, or Ruricius, bishop of Limoges.[247] Much closer are the vivid metaphors in the Gallic Eusebian homilies *Ad monachos IV* and *VIII*, from which X borrowed. Indeed, it is very interesting to set X's borrowings in *Instructio II* (§ 2) alongside his Gallic Eusebian sources. In forty-two lines of Latin he incorporates five metaphors – and almost nothing but the metaphors – drawn from these two homilies, which total 258 lines.[248] A sixth metaphor is

[237] Cf. Kerlouégan, *Le De excidio*, ch. 3, esp. pp. 170–1, 181–4, and cf. p. 122.

[238] *Instructio* II.2.

[239] *Instructio* X.3.

[240] *Instructio* XI.2.

[241] *Instructio* XII.2–3.

[242] *Instructio* XIII.

[243] *Instructiones* V, VI and VIII–IX. The same metaphor is used in Columbanus's (genuine) *Epistula* II.7 (ed. & transl. Walker, *Sancti Columbani Opera*, p. 20, line 2).

[244] See above, pp. 132–3, and below, n. 250.

[245] *Instructio* VII.2 (ed. & transl. Walker, *Sancti Columbani Opera*, p. 92, lines 1–2).

[246] *Instructio* VII.1 (*ibid*, p. 90, line 7); cf. below, pp. 171–2.

[247] The metaphors of both Caesarius and Faustus tend to be either biblical in origin, or ones common in late antiquity, like the metaphor of this life as a voyage across a stormy sea. Those of Ruricius have been studied by Hagendahl, *La correspondance*, pp. 80–9.

[248] Statue gilded without, mud within: cf. *Hom. IV ad monachos* (= Gallic Eusebius, *Homilia XXXIX*), ed. Glorie, *Eusebius 'Gallicanus'*, p. 460, lines 84–5, and *Sancti Columbani Opera*, ed. & transl. Walker, p. 68, lines 30–1; cultivating outside a vineyard, and neglecting the vineyard itself: cf. *Hom. IV ad monachos* (*ibid.*, p. 461, lines 92–5) and Walker, *ibid.*, p. 68, lines 32–3; farmer preparing the ground: cf. *Hom. VIII ad monachos* (= Gallic Eusebius, *Homilia XLIII*), ed. Glorie, *ibid.*, pp. 511–12, lines 1–22, and Walker, *ibid.*, p. 68, lines 14–30; slave-girl and mistress: cf. *Hom. VIII ad monachos*, ed. Glorie, *ibid.*, p. 513, lines 55–7, and Walker, *ibid.*, p. 70, lines 12–14; the pointlessness of waging warfare outside the city walls if subversion within them occurs: cf. *Hom. VIII ad monachos*, ed. Glorie, *ibid.*, p. 514, lines 65–6, and Walker, *ibid.*, p. 68, lines 31–2.

used by him in an altered form,[249] and two more are paralleled elsewhere in the *Instructiones*.[250] In fact, there is only one metaphor in those two homilies which he does not borrow at any point.[251] This graphically illustrates his liking for vivid metaphors. It is a trait which is also shared by Columbanus in his genuine *Epistulae*, where we see him both using sustained metaphors, and also throwing out brief, allusive images.[252]

A third stylistic feature of the sermons taken as a whole is something which I shall describe as 'accumulation'. Occasionally this takes the simple form of a string of adjectives or nouns;[253] but more characteristic is the piling up of parallel phrases to emphasise or develop a point: 'Haec ergo scientes nullis laboribus, nullis tribulationibus deficiamus, nullis meroribus uincamur, nullis bellis fatigemur, nullis displicinarum anxietatibus destituamur, nullis rursum deliciis dissoluamur, nullis blanditiis decipiamur . . .'[254] Winterbottom has noted the same feature in Columbanus's *Epistula V*, and dubbed it 'accumulation with assonance'.[255] Assonance is frequently found in this context in the sermons also, as in *Instructio VIII* (§ 1): 'susum amemus, susum desideremus, susum sapiamus, susum quaeramus patriam'.[256] This, however, may owe as much to the normal system of Latin inflexions as to any deliberate intention on the author's part, although intention could well be involved; and certainly in one instance it looks as though alliteration was deliberately sought: 'Quare horrida non horrescimus? Quare pudenda non detestamur? Quare foetida non

---

[249] Cf. *Hom. IV ad monachos* (ed. Glorie, *ibid.*, p. 460, lines 85–7) and Walker, *ibid.*, p. 70, line 2.

[250] Life as a shadow or smoke: cf. *Hom. IV ad monachos* (ed. Glorie, *ibid.*, p. 460, lines 76–7) and *Instructio V.1* and *VI.1* (ed. Walker, *ibid.*, p. 84, line 7 and p. 86, lines 22–8); the christian militia: *Hom. VIII ad monachos*, ed. Glorie, *ibid.*, p. 516, lines 117–19, and *Instructio II.3* and *X.3* (ed. Walker, *ibid.*, pp. 70–2 and p. 104, lines 1–15).

[251] That of giving the harvest to the birds: *Hom. VIII ad monachos*, ed. Glorie, *ibid.*, p. 514, lines 70–1.

[252] The use of sustained metaphors is noted by Winterbottom, 'Columbanus and Gildas', p. 310 and n. 5, in what is a helpful, but all too brief, analysis of the rhetorical style of Columbanus's *Epistulae*. For metaphors thrown out *en passant*, I looked at *Epistula IV*, in which Columbanus addresses his own monks after he has been exiled from Luxeuil (which means that it would be the best comparison to use in relation to the *Instructiones*, also addressed to monks, if the latter should prove to be genuine works of Columbanus). Besides the somewhat extended biblical metaphors of the stony ground and christian warfare against evil (*Sancti Columbani Opera*, ed. & transl. Walker, p. 26, lines 10–11, 15–20, p. 32, line 35–p. 34, line 8), note those of contention over an inherited estate (*ibid.*, p. 26, lines 15–16), the 'little drop' of his knowledge (*ibid.*, p. 28, lines 19–20), the binding of the branches to the root (*ibid.*, p. 28, line 36; cf. John XV.1–6), and the 'tumultuous eddies' which threaten Columbanus as he writes (*ibid.*, p. 34, lines 9–10).

[253] E.g. *Sancti Columbani Opera*, ed. & transl. Walker, p. 70, lines 17–20; p. 80, lines 29–30; p. 88, lines 26–7; p. 100, lines 11–12.

[254] *Instructio IV.3* (*ibid.*, p. 82, lines 33–7).

[255] 'Columbanus and Gildas', p. 310 and n. 4.

[256] *Sancti Columbani Opera*, ed. & transl. Walker, p. 94, lines 8–10.

fugimus?'[257] Be that as it may, there are, all told, some eleven examples of this type of accumulation spread through eight of the sermons.[258]

A more specific type of accumulation in the sermons was noted by Laporte, who drew attention to the author's habit 'of expressing himself by repeated antitheses',[259] as, for instance: 'nitamur . . . ut . . . de uia huius saeculi ad beatam patriam . . . transire feliciter possimus, de praesentibus ad absentia, de tristibus ad laeta, de caducis ad aeterna, de terrenis ad caelestia, de regione mortis ad regionem uiuorum . . .'[260] A briefer example occurs in *Instructio II* (§ 3): 'crebro offensi, raro patientes, crebro uicti, raro uictores, crebro seducti, raro intellegentes sumus'.[261] We might dub these examples 'accumulation with antithesis', for they are a more specific variant of the general type of accumulation already discussed. All told, there are eleven examples of this type spread through seven of the sermons, including *Instructio XI*.[262] As Laporte pointed out, it is not a literary device unique to the author of the sermons, given that examples can also be found in some of Caesarius of Arles's sermons;[263] it is, however, very characteristic of X. The feature can also be found in Columbanus's genuine works, although it is not common there.[264]

A further characteristic of the thirteen sermons is their use of alliteration. At a modest level, it is found throughout them, as, for instance: 'uera enim religio non in corporis sed in cordis humilitate consistit'.[265] Here it is used skilfully, to point up a contrast. A similar use in *Instructio IV* is interesting because X adapts a quotation from Cassian in order to introduce alliteration: 'praeparemus animum, non ad laetitiam, non ad securitatem, ut Sapiens ait, sed ad tentationes et tribulationes, ac tristitias atque labores'.[266] More extreme forms of alliteration are also found, such as 'quasi quibusdam fulcris firmissimis fides credentium firmata est';[267] 'uitae ad ueritatem uerae uitae;[268] and 'incerti itineris incursus infestat'.[269] Most bizarre of all is the end of *Instructio VIII*, which runs: 'caelestia uidebimus, et Regem regum recto regimine regna

---

[257] *Instructio* VII.1 (*ibid.*, p. 90, lines 23–4).

[258] In addition to the examples quoted, see Walker, *ibid.*, p. 70, lines 32–4, p. 84, lines 5–6, p. 102, lines 20–1, p. 112, line 13, p. 114, lines 3–4 and 19–21, p. 116, lines 15–17, p. 118, lines 16–18, 21.

[259] 'Étude d'authenticité [*Revue Mabillon* 45 (1955)]', pp. 12–13.

[260] *Instructio* VIII.2, ed. & transl. Walker, *Sancti Columbani Opera*, p. 96, lines 19–23.

[261] *Ibid.*, p. 70, lines 34–6.

[262] *Ibid.*, p. 108, lines 3–5; cf. also p. 74, line 6, p. 80, lines 11–12, p. 80, line 36–p. 82, line 1, p. 84, lines 16–17, 20–2, p. 92, lines 17–19, 28–9, p. 104, lines 37–9.

[263] 'Étude d'authenticité [*Revue Mabillon* 45 (1955)]', p. 13.

[264] See *Epistula* V.17 and *Regula monachorum* § 8 (ed. & transl. Walker, *Sancti Columbani Opera*, p. 56, lines 6–7, and p. 136, lines 10–13).

[265] *Instructio* II.2 (ed. & transl. Walker, *ibid.*, p. 70, lines 3–4). It is far too frequent for me to attempt to give full references.

[266] *Instructio* IV.2 (*ibid.*, p. 80, line 36–p. 82, line 1). Cassian, himself incorporating a quotation from Ecclesiasticus (italicised), had written: '*prepara animam tuam* non ad requiem, non ad securitatem, non ad delicias, sed *ad temptationes* et angustias' (*De institutis coenobiorum*, IV.38, ed. Petschenig, p. 74).

[267] *Instructio* I.2 (ed. & transl. Walker, *ibid.*, p. 60).

[268] *Instructio* VI.2 (*ibid.*, p. 88).

[269] *Instructio* IX.1 (*ibid.*, p. 98).

regentem Dominum nostrum Iesum Christum . . .'[270] Alliteration on the initial
letter of two or three words is not uncommon on the Continent; alliteration on
four consecutive words can be found, but exceptionally; while the six alliterating *r*'s at the end of *Instructio VIII* is remarkable.[271] Such alliteration is found
in some Latin texts by Irish authors, a good example being Columbanus's
address of his *Epistula V* to 'Pulcherrimo omnium totius Europae Ecclesiarum
Capiti, Papae praedulci, praecelso Praesuli, Pastorum Pastori, reuerendissimo
Speculatori.'[272] Aldhelm's prose letter to Heahfrith, with fifteen of its first
sixteen words alliterating on *p*, appears to be an extreme form or even a parody
of what was recognised as an Irish trait.[273] However, Winterbottom has reminded
us that Aldhelm could have picked up the habit from his continental reading as
well as from the Irish, and pertinently cites the closing words of Rufinus's
translation of Eusebius's *Historia ecclesiastica*: 'ad meliora migrauit cum piis-
simis principibus percepturus praemia meritorum.'[274] Alongside this we can set
an example from one of Caesarius's sermons used by X: 'in procelloso pelago
nauigamus, ut ad patriam paradisi peruenire possimus.'[275] In view of this we
should recognise that X could have acquired his penchant for extensive alliteration in southern Gaul, and even from Caesarius's sermons, although the extreme
use he makes of it may point rather in the direction of Ireland.

Another feature of the Latinity of the sermons which is worth examining in
some detail is that of word-order, in particular the separation of noun and
qualifying adjective, for deliberate stylistic reasons. This literary usage is
known as hyperbaton, although that term can also be used to cover a far wider
range of unusual word-order than is considered here.[276] The phenomenon is of
particular interest to us because, although it does occur in some continental
prose authors, it is carried to far greater lengths by some Insular authors.
Gildas made remarkably extensive use of elaborately interlaced word-order as
a literary device; and in this he was followed by some Irish authors, including
(to a lesser degree) Columbanus in the letters which he wrote to popes, where
he was deliberately ornamenting his prose.[277]

---

[270] *Instructio* VIII.2 (*ibid.*, p. 96, lines 23–4).
[271] These generalisations are based on Winterbottom, 'Aldhelm's prose style', p. 49
and n. 3, and Kerlouégan, *Le De excidio*, I.520–1, II.189, n. 99.
[272] *Sancti Columbani Opera*, ed. & transl. Walker, p. 36, lines 16–18. Of the alliterative
authors cited by Winterbottom ('Aldhelm's prose style', p. 49 and n. 3), the latinity
of Ionas's *Vita S. Columbani* is arguably Irish-influenced (see Mohrmann, 'The
earliest continental Irish Latin', p. 230), and I accept Michael Herren's arguments
('Some new light') for regarding Virgilius Maro Grammaticus as Irish.
[273] *Aldhelmi Opera*, ed. Ehwald, pp. 488–9.
[274] 'Aldhelm's prose style', p. 49.
[275] *Sermo* LVIII.5 (ed. Morin, *Sancti Caesarii Arelatensis Sermones*, p. 258, lines 7–8).
Other examples from Caesarius, *Sermones LVIII* and *CCXV*, and from the Gallic
Eusebius, *Hom. ad monachos III, IV* and *VIII*, do not exceed three alliterating
letters.
[276] I follow the usage of Wright, 'Gildas's prose style', p. 117.
[277] See Kerlouégan, 'Une mode stylistique' (esp. p. 280, n. 6, p. 285, n. 2 and p. 287,
n. 5 for Columbanus); Winterbottom, 'A "Celtic" hyperbaton?'; Winterbottom,
'Columbanus and Gildas', p. 314; and Wright, 'Gildas's prose style', pp. 115–28.

Reading through the thirteen sermons as a whole, there is no word-order so intertwined or so disconcerting for the reader as one encounters in Gildas's *De excidio*. However, a close examination of a small sample comprising *Instructiones XI* and *XII* does reveal a considerable number of instances where the noun and its qualifying adjective are separated. In seven instances, they are separated by a verb, as in 'tua occupet dilectio': the aVA type, according to Wright's classification;[278] in addition, there is one slightly more complex variant on this type, 'tuum inspirare digneris amorem'.[279] In six instances, they are separated by another noun, nearly always in the genitive, as in 'magna caritatis fiducia': Wright's aBA type.[280] In one related instance the normal order of the nouns is reversed, and we have 'iuxta Salvatoris nostri . . . praeceptum dicentis', Wright's BbAb type, which is much less usual.[281] In three instances, one adjective/noun pair is 'framed' by another, as in 'dictis diuini oraculi testimoniis';[282] 'discussis squalentibus atque torpentibus mortiferi teporis torporibus';[283] and 'illo diuinae caritatis igne':[284] Wright's abBA type.

Hitherto all the instances I have given, with the exception of the BbAb example, are of types of hyperbaton that are relatively common. The sermons do, however, contain some more complex types as well. The only example which I have noticed of a real 'interlacing' occurs not in *Instructiones XI* and *XII*, but in *Instructio VIII* (§ 2): 'ad beatam patriam nostri Patris aeternam aeterni'.[285] This has a pattern of aAbBab, presumably because the author wished to place *aeternam* next to *aeterni*. Even within *Instructiones XI* and *XII*, however, there are four instances where the adjective and noun are rather widely separated:

Quascumque ergo Deus in nobis in prima nostra conditione *uirtutes* seminauit . . .[286]

illam quae nescit cadere *caritatem*. . .[287]

utraque *imagines quasdam* in nobis pingunt sibi inuicem *contrarias* . . .[288]

Sic lumen tuum *meae* largiaris, rogo, Iesu mi, *lucernae* . . .[289]

---

[278] *Sancti Columbani Opera*, ed. & transl. Walker, p. 114, line 23. Wright ('Gildas's prose style') uses 'V' for verb; 'A' for main noun, with 'a' for adjectives qualifying that noun; 'B' and 'b', 'C' and 'c', for further nouns and attendant adjectives.

[279] *Sancti Columbani Opera*, ed. & transl. Walker, p. 114, line 22.

[280] *Ibid.*, p. 112, line 34. The only instance where the 'framed' word is not a genitive governed by the noun framing it is 'dulcissime nobis Saluator' (*ibid*, p. 114, line 11), where again the word-order is relatively natural. However, elsewhere in the *Instructiones* we find instances such as 'nostras tua caritate animas' (*Instructio* XIII.3, ed. & transl. Walker, *ibid.*, p. 120, lines 4–5), where the word-order is far from natural.

[281] *Ibid.*, p. 112, lines 13–14; cf. Wright, 'Gildas's prose style', p. 117.

[282] *Sancti Columbani Opera*, ed. & transl. Walker, p. 110, lines 29–30.

[283] *Ibid.*, p. 112, lines 21–2.

[284] *Ibid.*, p. 112, line 38–p. 114, line 1.

[285] *Ibid.*, p. 96, line 20.

[286] *Ibid.*, p. 106, lines 19–20.

[287] *Ibid.*, p. 114, line 9.

[288] *Ibid.*, p. 108, line 6.

[289] *Ibid.*, p. 114, line 14.

The second example given is still straightforward, the other three cases rather less so.

Let us now try to set the usage of hyperbaton in the sermons in its context. In general, we may say that the quantity of hyperbaton employed is noticeable, but that X normally uses simple kinds that can readily be paralleled in other late Latin authors. Thus the aBA type 'is neither very striking nor very uncommon in Latin prose in general'.[290] Similarly, the aVA type, which had been used as a rhetorical device by Cicero in his ornate speeches, had long since become widespread in other types of prose, also. From Livy onwards, it was used by historians, as, for instance, by Ammianus Marcellinus; and some idea of its generalised spread by late antiquity and the early middle ages may be gleaned from the fact that it also occurs in Jerome's Vulgate Old Testament, and in some Merovingian chancery documents.[291] Finally, as regards the type abBA, it is worth noting that in the three simple examples from X, the enclosed adjective and noun are always in the genitive, and governed by the noun which, with its attendant adjective, surrounds them. As Winterbottom has pointed out, this renders the chosen word order reasonably natural.[292]

In addition to knowing that these types of hyperbaton occurred on the Continent, however, we also need to know how frequently they occurred, and how generalised their spread was. Unfortunately very little work has been done on this problem, although Neil Wright has made a beginning. He has scrutinised short passages from four authors: Saluian's *De gubernatione Dei*, Ennodius's *Vita S. Epifani*, Iordanes's *Getica*, and Venantius Fortunatus's *Vita S. Radegundis*. On his evidence, Saluian used very little hyperbaton at all; Iordanes used it only to a modest extent, with just four instances of the straightforward aVA type being noted from the whole of a long chapter; Venantius had three instances of the aVA type, together with one complex type of interweaving (aBVAb); and Ennodius had five instances including two similarly complex interweavings round a verb, and one bAB type.[293] In order to provide examples more closely comparable with our thirteen sermons, I have analysed one sermon addressed to monks by Caesarius of Arles,[294] and *Hom. IV ad monachos* from the Gallic Eusebian sermon collection.[295] In the Caesarian sermon I found seven examples of the simple aBA type of hyperbaton, together with one variant of the aVA type, and only one other example of hyperbaton: 'Talia enim sunt sine caritate ieiunia, qualis sine oleo lucerna.'[296] In *Hom. IV ad monachos*, I found five

---

[290] Wright, 'Gildas's prose style', p. 117.

[291] Adams, 'A type of hyperbaton', esp. pp. 9–12.

[292] 'A "Celtic" hyperbaton?', p. 207.

[293] Wright, 'Gildas's prose style', pp. 119–21.

[294] Caesarius, *Sermo CCXXXIV* (ed. Morin, *Sancti Caesarii Arelatensis Sermones*, pp. 932–5). Its length is 150 lines, compared with 158 lines for X's *Instructiones XI* and *XII* combined.

[295] Gallic Eusebius, *Homilia XXXIX* (ed. Glorie, *Eusebius 'Gallicanus'*, pp. 455–64). It is 138 lines long.

[296] *Sancti Caesarii Arelatensis Sermones*, ed. Morin, p. 934. The aVA variant is 'exhortatorium debeam proferre sermonem' (*ibid.*, p. 932). In all seven cases of aBA, the sandwiched noun was a dependent genitive.

examples of the aBA type, three of which were not simple dependent genitives; one example of the aVA type; and one of the abBA type: 'aeternum teterrimae noctis exsilium'.[297] Let us now look at Columbanus's *Epistula IV* (§§ 1–7), as the best parallel we can find from Columbanus's genuine works to set alongside the *Instructiones*. Hyperbaton is rather more frequent in this letter, though not of the intricate interlaced types which occur in his more rhetorical letters to popes.[298] It contains eleven examples of the simple aVA type (one of which is a biblical quotation); two examples of the aBA type; one example of the rarer BAb variant;[299] one example of the aBbA type;[300] and eleven more complex examples, ranging in complexity from 'meum illi da osculum' (aBVA) to 'semina non potest sui tenuitate cespitis accepta nutrire' (AVcBCa).[301]

This, then, is the evidence for the use of hyperbaton in the sermons, and the possible context for that use. Before we attempt to draw any conclusions from this evidence, I have one further observation to make: that is, that hyperbaton is not found evenly spaced throughout the sermons. Of the two sermons examined in detail, *Instructio XII* has twice as much as *Instructio XI*, although it is shorter. Indeed, the final paragraph of *Instructio XII*, although consisting of only twenty-two lines of Latin, contains as much hyperbaton as all seventy-eight lines of *Instructio XI*. The reason is that X carefully used it to heighten the beautiful prayer with which he ended *Instructio XII*. This means that X used hyperbaton as a conscious literary device to heighten particular passages. In his deliberate application of it to select passages, we may see a parallel to the splendid rhetorical treatment given to the opening of *Instructio V*, although there the parallel ends: for hyperbaton is used in the prayer in *Instructio XII* to convey a different, more mystical effect, as compared with the more declamatory, even mocking tone of *Instructio V*, where word-play and antithesis are used rather than hyperbaton. In connection with our author's use of hyperbaton in *Instructio XII*, we might rather recall Wright's interpretation of Gildas's extensive use of hyperbaton as 'part of an attempt to lend to his prose style the emotive power of poetry'.[302]

---

[297] The three more complex examples of the aBA type are: 'maiorem nobis metum' (line 35); 'hunc sibi specialiter modum' (line 65); and 'iucundissimos ex se fructus' (line 95); the phrase *aeternum . . . exilium* is in lines 132–3.

[298] For references, see above, n. 277, and the *Index grammaticus* to *Sancti Columbani Opera*, ed. & transl. Walker, pp 239–40, s.v. 'ordo uerborum'. *Epistula IV* (§§ 1–7) contains virtually the same number of lines as *Instructiones XI* and *XII* combined; cf. also above, n. 252. Note, however, that complex hyperbaton could make the comprehension of an orally delivered sermon difficult; and that preachers were therefore likely to be more restrained in their use of hyperbaton than in their use of other rhetorical devices like antithesis or alliteration – a consideration that would not apply in the composition of a letter or other texts designed to be seen as they were being read.

[299] *Sancti Columbani Opera*, ed. & transl. Walker, p. 32, line 34.

[300] *Ibid.*, p. 30, line 22.

[301] *Ibid.*, p. 28, line 6, and p. 26, lines 10–11. The remaining nine instances occur on p. 26, line 20; p. 28, lines 20, 25, 35, 35– 6; p. 30, line 13; p. 32, line 14; p. 34, lines 1–2, 9–10.

[302] 'Gildas's prose style', p. 125; cf. pp. 122–6.

The uneven incidence of hyperbaton in the sermons, combined with the small size of the comparative samples we have looked at, makes me chary of jumping to further conclusions about X's use of hyperbaton. It is certainly tempting to point out that the number of occurrences of hyperbaton in *Instructiones XI* and *XII* is double that in the Caesarian sermon and the Gallic Eusebian homily which we examined, and much closer to that in Columbanus's *Epistula IV*, and to interpret this as evidence pointing more in favour of Columbanus's authorship of the sermons rather than that of a literal pupil of Faustus of Riez. The temptation should, however, be resisted. It is clear that hyperbaton of the relatively restrained type which we encounter in the sermons was used on the Continent, and does not necessarily point to an Insular author; and until far larger samples from many more authors are taken, including emotive passages where hyperbaton is likely to occur, it would be rash to say more than that the evidence could, but need not, point towards Columbanus. What remains noteworthy about the use of hyperbaton in the *Instructiones* is the sheer quantity of it in only 158 lines of Latin, and the fact that some instances are rather complex, a particularly striking feature in sermons intended for oral delivery.

All the features of X's Latinity which we have examined so far can be paralleled in continental authors, as well as in the genuine works of Columbanus. Two specific aspects of our author's Latinity, however, may be more helpful for diagnostic purposes, and will be considered below in some detail: the rhythm of sentence-endings (*clausulae*), and unusual elements in the author's vocabulary.

2. *The evidence of* clausulae

From the first century B.C., some Latin prose authors shaped a considerable proportion of their sentence-endings, or *clausulae*, almost as if they were writing verse. They preferred certain metrical patterns for these endings, 'scanning' them with long and short syllables on the same principles – although seeking different patterns – as the long and short syllables of hexameter verses. Thus whereas historians like Livy and Tacitus wrote ordinary non-metrical prose, Cicero wrote what can be called metrical prose, using a high proportion of sentences ending in a ditrochee ($\bar{}\,\smile\,\bar{}\,\smile$), a cretic trochee ($\bar{}\,\smile\,\bar{}\,\bar{}\,\smile$), or a dicretic ($\bar{}\,\smile\,\bar{}\,\bar{}\,\smile\,\smile$).[303] From the third century A.D., alongside this system, we begin to find a second way of shaping *clausulae*: this was a system based on stress, where the rhythm of sentence-endings depended not on the metrical quantity of the syllables, but rather on where the accents fell in the spoken sentence. The accentual forms which were most cultivated were those which could coincide with the favoured metrical forms, and these came to dominate the rhythmical *cursus*-system of the middle ages: the *uelox*, ó o o o o ó o (e.g. *conuíuiam praeparémus*); the *planus*, ó o o ó o (e.g. *nómen accépit*); and the *tardus*, ó o o ó o o (e.g. *ésse cognóscitur*).[304] Several authors in the fourth and fifth

---

303 Hagendahl, *La prose métrique d'Arnobe*, pp. 18–19. The terminology of Orlandi (*'Clausulae'*, p. 129) differs somewhat, but the metrical patterns are identical with those discussed by Hagendahl.

304 Oberhelman has recently argued that in the fourth and fifth centuries some accentual authors deliberately cultivated other rhythmical forms such as the *trispondaicus*

centuries deliberately sought those *clausulae* which, in metrical terms, fitted with (a restricted number of) the *clausulae* favoured by Cicero, while rhythmically conforming to the *uelox, planus* and *tardus* patterns.[305] This combination of the two systems has been dubbed the *cursus mixtus*. Practice varied, however. Some writings, at least as late as *ca* 400, were written in prose that eschewed any type of *clausulae*; others, from the last part of the fourth century onwards, were written with purely rhythmical *clausulae*. Writings using purely metrical *clausulae* are no longer found by this date. Even so, around A.D. 400 there was considerable variety. Ambrose and Jerome chose to employ the *cursus mixtus* for some of their writings, but for others adopted only the rhythmical *cursus*-endings; Augustine used the *cursus mixtus* for his *De ciuitate Dei*, but wrote his *Confessiones* in non-metrical and non-rhythmical prose;[306] and Sulpicius Seuerus chose to employ the *cursus mixtus* for his Martinian writings, but paid far less attention to *clausulae* in his *Chronicle*, a work influenced by classical historical models.[307]

Much still remains to be discovered about the early history of the rhythmical *cursus*; but it does seem fairly well established that by the end of the fifth century, all continental authors who wrote with any kind of stylistic proficiency used rhythmical *clausulae*, and many used metrical *clausulae* as well. Faustus of Riez and his circle in southern Gaul certainly used the *cursus mixtus*.[308] In the sixth century this tradition of the *cursus mixtus* was continued by various Gallic authors including Caesarius, bishop of Arles 502–542, the anonymous author of the *Vita patrum Iurensium*, writing *ca* 520, and Gregory, bishop of Tours 573–594;[309] but other works, such as the *Vita I S. Genovefae*, disregarded metrical *clausulae* entirely, while favouring certain rhythmical forms, particularly the *planus* and *tardus*.[310] What all these Gallic works have in common, however, is the use of rhythmical *clausulae*. We may therefore be reasonably confident that if the thirteen sermons by X were indeed written by a disciple and younger contemporary of Faustus of Riez in sixth-century Gaul, they will be found to contain a high proportion of rhythmical *clausulae*. For

---

(6 o o o 6 o): 'The *cursus*', and 'The history', pp. 228–42. He may be right, but unfortunately he does not use Janson's more sophisticated method of internal comparison to verify whether or not the patterns which he observes are the result of deliberate choice, rather than reflecting an author's preference for certain types of word; instead he relies on the far less accurate method of comparison with non-rhythmical and non-metrical authors. Cf. below, pp. 152–3.

[305] See Hagendahl, *La correspondance*, ch. 3, and Orlandi, '*Clausulae*', pp. 136–9.

[306] See Oberhelman & Hall, 'Meter', pp. 223, 225; but cf. also Oberhelman's revised views in 'The *cursus*', esp. pp. 143–4, 147–8.

[307] Cf. Hyltén, *Studien*, pp. 31–4, 53–7, with Hagendahl, *Arnobe*, pp. 18–25.

[308] Elg, *In Faustum*, ch. 2, and tables on pp. 139–50; Hagendahl, *La correspondance*, ch. 3, esp. p. 35; and Orlandi, '*Clausulae*', pp. 136–8, 144.

[309] Within this tradition of the *cursus mixtus*, some, like Sidonius Apollinaris and the author of the *Vita patrum Iurensium*, appear to have given relatively greater weight to including metrical *clausulae*, whereas Caesarius and Gregory appear to have been more concerned with rhythmical *clausulae*. See Orlandi, '*Clausulae*', pp. 136–8, 144–8; and *Vie des pères du Jura*, ed. & transl. Martine, pp. 124–5.

[310] Orlandi, '*Clausulae*', pp. 139, 145.

that would be normal for sixth-century Gaul; and we would particularly expect it in view of the literary self-consciousness of our author, who, as we have just seen, indulged in word-play, hyperbaton, and other stylistic devices. If, on the other hand, the *Instructiones* were written by Columbanus, we would almost certainly find no significant incidence of rhythmical *clausulae*; for although the Irish learnt to write correct Latin, they did not – with one apparent exception – employ the rhythmical *cursus* that was seemingly still in use among their contemporaries on the Continent in the seventh century.[311] This was demonstrated by Michael Winterbottom, who sampled six Irish works from the seventh century, including Columbanus's *Epistulae*.[312] It has been further confirmed through Jean-Michel Picard's more detailed studies of the saints' Lives by Cogitosus, Muirchú and Adomnán, while Tore Janson has noted that not even Sedulius Scotus and John Scotus Eriugena, for all their Latin learning and their long stay in Carolingian Francia, employed the rhythmical *cursus*.[313] This distinction between Irish and continental use, then, provides us with a most helpful diagnostic tool for probing the authorship of the thirteen sermons attributed to Columbanus.

Given that even non-rhythmical authors will include a number of rhythmical *clausulae* through pure coincidence, what is the best method of discovering whether a particular author deliberately sought such rhythmical *clausulae*? The approach used until comparatively recently – and still by some scholars today – is to ascertain what percentage of sentence-endings within a work employs the favoured *cursus*-endings, and to compare this percentage with similar evidence drawn from non-rhythmical prose.[314] Besides listing the *uelox*, *planus* and *tardus* endings, it is sensible to look also at the *trispondaicus* endings, with a rhythm of ó o o o ó o (e.g. *repósitum habémus*), since in some periods and places this form was favoured alongside the mainstream *uelox*, *planus* and

---

311 E.g. the letters of Sisebut (king of Spain, A.D. 612–21), use rhythmical *clausulae* (Winterbottom, 'Aldhelm's prose style', p. 72), and Desiderius, bishop of Cahors *ca* 650, has 81.6% rhythmical cursus-endings: Lindholm, *Studien*, pp. 10–11; but Lindholm regards the eighth-century papal chancery as not using the cursus. More authors need to be studied before we can generalise about knowledge of the rhythmical cursus in the seventh and eighth centuries, but Winterbottom's impression is that it was 'prevalent everywhere' on the Continent in the sixth and seventh centuries.

312 Winterbottom, 'Aldhelm's prose style', pp. 72–3. The Irish works are: Columbanus, *Epistulae*; Augustinus Hibernicus, *De mirabilibus sacrae scripturae*; pseudo-Cyprian, *De duodecim abusiuis saeculi*; Cogitosus, *Vita S. Brigitae*; pseudo-Isidore, *Liber de ordine creaturarum*; and Adomnán, *Vita S. Columbae* (Lapidge & Sharpe, *A Bibliography*, nos. 639, 291, 339, 302, 342, 305, respectively). There is, however, one apparent exception. The letter of 'Calmanus' (Colmán)(Lapidge & Sharpe, *ibid.*, no. 290), generally dated to the seventh century, does use the cursus: Winterbottom, 'Aldhelm's prose style', p. 54, n. 5, and cf. p. 72. But this text cannot be securely assigned to seventh-century Ireland: see Sharpe, 'An Irish textual critic', pp. 44–5, and cf. Winterbottom's comment: 'I should like to be sure that it is from the Irish homeland, and early in date.'

313 Picard, 'The metrical prose', pp. 258, 264, 267; Janson, *Prose Rhythm*, p. 39.

314 E.g. Oberhelman & Hall, 'A new statistical analysis', pp. 117–27.

tardus forms;[315] but because the position of the *trispondaicus* is doubtful, its tally should not be counted in with the *uelox*, *planus* and *tardus* endings. As a negative pointer, besides listing the percentage of definitely non-rhythmical forms, it is also helpful to note the percentage of endings involving hiatus between vowels (e.g. *laetitia infinita*), as rhythmical authors tried to avoid such hiatus.[316] This system of comparison with non-rhythmical texts is adequate where the evidence points very clearly in one direction or the other: if the combined total of *uelox*, *planus* and *tardus clausulae* amounts to over 75% of the total number of sentence-endings, one can be reasonably sure that rhythmical *clausulae* were deliberately sought; if the percentage of such endings is less than 50%, it is highly likely that one is dealing with a non-rhythmical author. In between, however, there is a grey area: for non-rhythmical authors like Cicero, Descartes and Calvin score a total of about 56 to 58% of *uelox*, *planus* and *tardus clausulae*,[317] and this makes it difficult to assess whether, for instance, Gildas's score of 63% for these *clausulae* is the result of chance or choice. Further, individual authors can vary considerably in their preferences for certain types of word, as Janson showed in comparing the non-rhythmical Cicero with the equally non-rhythmical Livy.[318]

A far more sophisticated system is that devised by Janson.[319] This involves examining the last two words of the sentence: for the final word, its number of syllables is listed, and the syllable which bears the stress is shown by using the shorthand of p for a paroxytone word (i.e. one where the stress falls on the penultimate syllable), and pp for a proparoxytone word (i.e. one where the stress falls on the antepenultimate syllable). For the previous word, only the whereabouts of the stressed syllable is shown, again using p or pp. Thus, for instance, the *uelox*-ending, *hóminem recepístis*, is written as pp 4p.[320] Other examples are given in Table 3 (below, p. 160). By analysing the number of occurrences of the separate components in these sentence-endings (e.g. the number of times a word ends in 4p, and the number of times the first word is proparoxytone), it is possible to calculate the approximate expected frequency of all types of sentence ending used. By comparing the *observed* frequency of individual sentence endings with their *expected* frequency (and this can be further clarified by use of the χ^2 test), one can discover whether or not a high percentage of any particular rhythmical *clausula* is due to the deliberate intention of the author. This procedure is particularly valuable for examining problematical authors with fairly high – but not conclusively high – tallies of such endings as p 3p and p 4pp, the regular *planus* and *tardus* endings which occur frequently even in unrhythmical prose. Thus, for instance, Giovanni Orlandi has recently used this method to show that Gildas did indeed favour rhythmical *clausulae*.[321] The disadvantage of this method is that one needs to

---

[315] See above, n. 304; and Janson, *Prose Rhythm*, pp. 50–8, 104.

[316] Janson, *ibid.*, p. 32; Winterbottom, 'Aldhelm's prose style', p. 72.

[317] Oberhelman & Hall, 'A new statistical analysis', pp. 118–20.

[318] *Prose Rhythm*, pp. 15–18.

[319] *Ibid.*, pp. 19–32.

[320] *Ibid.*, pp. 13–15.

[321] 'Clausulae', esp. pp. 134–5, 141.

take a large sample if differences between observed and expected frequency are to be accurately calculated, and this, combined with all the calculations involved, makes it a slow procedure, while the mathematics and statistics tend to repel those who do not have particular expertise or interest in this area.[322]

One further method of distinguishing between rhythmical and non-rhythmical prose was suggested by Michael Winterbottom in his review of Janson's *Prose Rhythm*, and applied by him in the article mentioned above where he demonstrates the lack of *cursus*-rhythms in seventh-century Irish works.[323] Winterbottom noticed, from Janson's tables, that Latin appeared to have an innate preference for the penultimate word of a sentence to be paroxytone (i.e. p rather than pp); and that means that unrhythmical prose will have a higher proportion of the *trispondiacus* p 4p ending than of the *uelox* pp 4p. Since, however, the latter was the normal form of the *uelox* employed by writers of rhythmical prose, rhythmical prose will have a higher proportion of pp 4p endings. My own observations and Picard's detailed analysis[324] both suggest that Winterbottom's *uelox*-test is indeed a valuable indicator of *cursus*-forms, and it has obvious advantages in its ease of use.

Let us now apply these methods of analysis to the thirteen *Instructiones* of X. Leaving aside those sentences which end with questions or with quotations from other works, all sentence-endings from the thirteen *Instructiones* were analysed: 263 in all. First, Table 1 (below, p. 157) lists separately the breakdown of the various rhythmical endings for *Instructiones I, II, IV, VI–X, XII–XIII*: all of these are sermons which were definitely written by the person claiming to be a disciple of Faustus. In these sermons, all types of *uelox*, *planus* and *tardus* taken together come to a very low score of 41.7%, which indicates that they were written without regard for rhythmical *clausulae*. The same conclusion is reached if we apply the *uelox*-test: there are only twelve instances of pp 4p as opposed to sixteen instances of the *trispondiacus* p 4p, while in 12.5% of the endings hiatus of vowels occurs. The *clausulae* for *Instructiones III* and *XI* are listed separately, in order further to test Seebass's theory that these sermons were written by a different person from the remaining ones in the series. As can be seen by comparing the relevant figures with those of the main body of sermons, there is no justification for Seebass's view: their 32.3% percentage of rhythmical *clausulae* is even lower than that of the other sermons; but the figures are not sufficiently different to justify the view that a different author was involved.[325] Finally, I analysed *Instructio V* separately, because this is the sermon which begins with a number of rhetorical devices, as we saw above. In its own way, it is a tellingly written piece of Latin; and if the author of the sermons was anywhere going to display a knowledge of the *cursus*-system, one would expect it here. However, as the figure of 38.9% for all *uelox*, *tardus* and *planus* endings, and of

---

[322] Cf. Kerlouégan's comments (in a review of *Gildas: New Approaches*, edd. Lapidge & Dumville) on this article by Orlandi: 'l'exposé devient si technique que, je l'avoue, il m'aurait fallu des heures et des heures pour le traduire dans un langage accessible à un non-métricien' (p. 336).

[323] Review of Janson, *Prose Rhythm*, pp. 298–300; 'Aldhelm's prose style', pp. 71–3.

[324] 'The metrical prose', pp. 258–9.

[325] Cf. below, n. 330.

0 for the *uelox* pp 4p over against 2 for the *trispondiacus* p 4p, both indicate, this sermon is written with as little regard for rhythmical *clausulae* as the others. Two conclusions, then, can be drawn from this table: first, that there is no reason to believe that any of these sermons was written by a different author from the others; and secondly, that the author of the whole series was someone who paid no attention whatever to rhythmical *clausulae*, despite his generally good Latinity and his employment of various literary devices.

Two other exercises seem worthwhile. First, I include as Table 3 a breakdown of all 263 sentence-endings, arranged according to Janson's principles; and for those instances where the number of observed occurrences of any particular combination of words was sufficiently great to make it worthwhile, I have also calculated the expected frequency of such combinations, and applied the χ^2 test.[326] Although one cannot take the χ^2 test to its conclusion without producing a value for every pair of endings considered, and the low figures for a few endings precluded this possibility, the general pattern is nonetheless clear: there is no significant difference between the observed and the expected frequency for any combination, with the possible exception of 1 2: but this is a most unlikely rhythmical ending to have been deliberately favoured, and almost certainly, therefore, the observed frequency of fourteen cases compared with an expected eight is just chance. Even with the resulting 4.5 counted in, the χ^2 total of 12.64 is a long way beneath the critical figure of 35.2, which would indicate that our author was deliberately favouring or rejecting certain sentence-endings. What is helpful about Janson's system is that it reveals that even the relatively high figures of 25 for the regular *tardus*-ending (p 4pp) and 22 for the regular *planus*-ending (p 3p) are co-incidental – they do not indicate that our author deliberately favoured these *cursus* endings. Table 3 therefore confirms the results of Table 1: that the author of the thirteen sermons paid no heed to rhythmical *clausulae*.

Secondly, since the author of the thirteen sermons was presumably either Columbanus or a disciple of Faustus of Riez, which would make him roughly contemporaneous with Caesarius of Arles, I include as Table 2 the figures for *Instructiones I–XIII* combined, and set alongside them figures from Columbanus's undoubtedly genuine *Epistulae*,[327] and figures drawn from eighty sentence-endings of a genuine Faustus sermon,[328] and one hundred sentence-

---

[326] I should like to thank my more numerate husband, Ben de la Mare, for his help with this task. Janson explains the basis of these calculations in *Prose Rhythm*, pp. 20–2. A significant discrepancy between the observed and the expected frequency would show up in the χ^2 test as a relatively high figure: for twenty-four pairs, the number I have taken, a χ^2 total of 35.2 or above would be significant, i.e. would indicate that our author deliberately favoured or avoided certain rhythmical sentence-endings. Where the expected frequency is less than 5, the χ^2 test cannot be accurately applied (Janson, *ibid.*, p. 22).

[327] *Epistulae I–V (Sancti Columbani Opera*, ed. & transl. Walker, pp. 2–56).

[328] Gallic Eusebius, *Homilia XXXV* (formerly *XXXIV*), ed. Glorie, *Eusebius 'Gallicanus'*, pp. 401–12. On Faustus's authorship, see Morin, 'La collection', pp. 104–6. Elg (*In Faustum*, pp. 149–50) gives broadly comparable figures for the percentage of *uelox, planus, tardus* and *trispondaicus* endings in Faustus's *Epistulae, De gratia* and *De spiritu sancto*.

endings from a random selection of five of Caesarius's sermons.[329] In every case, I have excluded quotations and questions, and where there is a clash of vowels, I have assumed hiatus, not elision. The results are strikingly clear: whether we look at the overall percentages of *cursus*-forms or whether we apply Winter-bottom's *uelox*-test, either way it is apparent that whereas Faustus and Caesarius were skilled practitioners of the rhythmical *cursus*, the author of the *Instructiones* paid no heed to *cursus*-endings. Of the four sets of writings given in Table 2, the *Instructiones* are closest to Columbanus's *Epistulae*, with the higher percentage of *cursus*-forms in the latter being largely accounted for by a far higher proportion of *planus*-endings.[330] The percentage of *uelox*-endings, the most critical form of the *cursus*, is almost identical. Thus the evidence of the rhythmical *clausulae* strongly suggests that the *Instructiones* were not written by someone from the same continental cultural milieu as Faustus of Riez and Caesarius of Arles; rather, their lack of attention to rhythmical *clausulae* could most readily be explained by the suggestion that they were written by an Irishman, although a Briton remains a possibility: Gildas did favour regular *cursus*-endings,[331] but we would be rash to generalise from this single case and assume that all sixth-century British authors did so.

---

[329] That is, the first twenty *clausulae*-endings from each of *Sermones IV, XXX, LXXIII, CIV*, and *CLXVI*, in *Sancti Caesarii Arelatensis Sermones*, ed. Morin. Orlandi ('*Clausulae*', p. 147) gives tables based on a more extensive sample.

[330] The range of variation within one author's work is illustrated by the fact that *Epistula IV* has a lower percentage of rhythmical *clausulae*-endings than the other *epistulae*. Its figures of 39% for all *uelox, planus* and *tardus* combined, 14.8% for *trispondiacus*, and 42.5% for definitely non-rhythmical endings, with 3.7% uncertain, is extremely close to the average for X's *Instructiones*. Similarly, Table I below (p. 157) illustrates a comparable difference between the figures for *Instructiones III* and *XI* over against those of the other sermons. Here, also, the difference is almost entirely due to a variation in the proportion of *planus* endings.

[331] Orlandi, '*Clausulae*', esp. pp. 134–5, 141.

Table 1
Rhythmical clausulae *in the thirteen* Instructiones
(For notes to the table, see p. 159)

		Instructiones I–II, IV, VI–X, XII–XIII	*Instructiones* III and XI	*Instructio* V
Velox				
	pp 4p	12 (6.8%)	0	0
	pp 1 3p	0	0	1
	p 5p	3	2	0
	p 1 4p	1	3	0
	other	0	1	0
	All *uelox*	**16** (9%)	**6** (8.8%)	**1** (5.55%)
Planus				
	p 3p	18 (10%)	3 (4.4%)	1
	pp 2	9	0	0
	p 1 2	5	2	0
	other	0	1	0
	All *planus*	**32** (18%)	**6** (8.8%)	**1** (5.55%)
Tardus				
	p 4pp	16 (9%)	5 (7.4%)	4 (22.2%)
	p 1 3pp	2	2	0
	pp 3pp	8	3	0
	other	0	0	1
	All *tardus*	**26** (14.7%)	**10** (14.7%)	**5** (27.8%)
All *uelox, planus & tardus*		74 (41.7%)	22 (32.3%)	7 (38.9%)
Trispondiacus				
	p 4p	16 (9%)	1	2 (11.1%)
	pp 3p	6	3	1
	p 1 3p	2	2	0
	other	2	2	1
All *trispondiacus*		**26** (14.7%)	**8** (11.8%)	**4** (22.2%)
Non-rhythmical		70 (39.6%)	35 (51.5%)	6 (33.3%)
Uncertain		7 (4%)	3 (4.4%)	1 (5.6%)
No. of *clausulae* sampled		177	68	18
Instances of hiatus		22 (12.5%)	3 (4.4%)	4 (22.2%)

Table 2

The clausulae *of the* Instructiones *compared with those of Columbanus, Faustus, and Caesarius*
(For notes to the table, see p. 159)

	Columbanus *Epistulae I–V*	*Instructiones* *I–XIII*	Faustus, Homilia XXXV	Caesarius, Sermones IV, XXX, LXXIII, CIV, CLXVI
Velox				
pp 4p	4 (2%)	12 (4.6%)	13 (16.25%)	23
pp 1 3p	2	1	4	6
p 5p	9	5	0	1
p 1 4p	3	4	0	0
other	0	1	0	2
All *uelox*	**18** (9%)	**23** (8.8%)	**17** (21.25%)	**32**
Planus				
p 3p	28 (14%)	22 (8.4%)	20 (25%)	15
pp 2	16	9	4	3
p 1 2	9	7	1	3
other	2	1	1	0
All *planus*	**55** (27.25%)	**39** (14.8%)	**26** (32.5%)	**21**
Tardus				
p 4pp	16 (8%)	25 (9.5%)	11 (13.75%)	30
p 1 3pp	7	4	10 (12.5%)	4
pp 3pp	3	11	0	0
other	3	1	0	1
All *tardus*	**29** (14.5%)	**41** (15.6%)	**21** (26.25%)	**35**
All *uelox, planus* & *tardus*	**102** (50.75%)	**103** (39.2%)	**64** (80%)	**88**
Trispondiacus				
p 4p	15 (7.5%)	19 (7.2%)	3	2
pp 3p	8	10	0	2
p 1 3p	4	4	0	1
other	5	5	1	0
All *trispondiacus*	**32** (16%)	**38** (14.4%)	**4** (5%)	**5**
Non-rhythmical	65 (32.25%)	111 (42.2%)	12 (15%)	7
Uncertain	2 (1%)	11 (4.2%)	0	0
No. of *clausulae* sampled	201	263	80	100
Instances of hiatus	22 (11%)	29 (11%)	2 (2.5%)	1

Explanatory Notes on Tables 1 and 2

I include all sentence endings, apart from those which are too short or which comprise a quotation from another author, or which consist of a question. Where two vowels occur, I assume hiatus, not elision; and I disregard the possibility that long words may have carried more than one stress. Identifying the *uelox* pp 4p and p 5p, *planus* p 3p and pp 2, *tardus* p 4pp and pp 3pp, and the *trispondaicus* pp 3p and p 4p is relatively straightforward. But problems occur with the by-forms where one or more short words which do not carry a stress of their own take the place of longer words, e.g. *ánimae non negétis* (pp 1 3p), which is a variant on the *uelox* pp 4p, or *dúxit in flúmina* (p 1 3pp), which is a variant on the *tardus* p 4pp. See Janson, *Prose Rhythm*, pp. 10–12 and 28–32, who is inclined to disregard such cases. These by-forms, however, appear to have been used deliberately by Faustus and Caesarius, and it therefore seemed right to include them in my tables; but it is difficult to establish hard-and-fast rules over when short words are stressed or unstressed. In this predicament, I have followed Hagendahl, and posited that relative pronouns, prepositions and conjunctions are unstressed; and that *non* and also personal pronouns can be stressed or not, according to context. (*Arnobe*, pp. 14–17). As regards *est*, *sunt* etc., I have regarded these as unstressed when they form part of a passive or deponent; but when they are free standing, I have classified *clausulae* containing them as uncertain. The only exception is when such *clausulae* are non-rhythmical in any case, regardless of whether or not the *est* or *sunt* is stressed: in that case I classify such *clausulae* as non-rhythmical. Thus I have classified *mórtem mercáti sunt* (Walker p. 86, line 12) as a variant *tardus* (p 3p 1); but *inconspicábilis Déus est* (p. 94, lines 21–2) as uncertain, because it could either be a variant *tardus* or non-rhythmical, depending on whether or not the *est* was accented. Endings like *uoluptátibus mórtuus est* (Walker p. 76, lines 1–2) have been classified as non-rhythmi-cal. *Clausulae* containing uncertain forms of *esse* account for all endings listed as 'uncertain' in Tables 1 and 2, with one exception; that is, *putánda est uíta haec* (Walker p. 86, line 5), where I do not know whether the *haec* should be stressed or not.

Table 3

Clausulae *in the* Instructiones *tabulated according to Janson's system of internal comparison*

Type of cadence		Example	Observed frequency	Expected frequency	χ^2 *test*
	6pp	religiónibus	3		
1	5p	non perueniámus	2		
p	5p	dignitáte nobilitáuit	5	5	0.00
pp	5p	caritáte possideámur	2		
p	5pp	umbráta deprehénditur	8	6	0.67
pp	5pp	imáginis uiolátio	3		
1	4p	in Creatórem	5	7	0.57
p	4p	instrúxit audiéntes	20	21	0.05
pp	4p	uoluntátibus moriámur	12	9	1.00
1	4pp	ut decípias	4	7	1.29
p	4pp	párte uidébitur	25	22	0.41
pp	4pp	irremediábilis deméntia	10	9	0.11
1	3p	non amísit	11	8	0.13
p	3p	númquam senéscit	22	24	0.17
pp	3p	Dóminum honóret	10	10	0
1	3pp	in pátria	9	8	0.13
p	3pp	aetérnum nésciet	23	24	0.04
pp	3pp	intolerábilis caécitas	11	10	0.1
1	2	non sápis	14	8	4.5
p	2	reddéndum ésse	19	24	1.04
pp	2	aetérnitas ágit	9	10	0.1
1	1	in te	3		
p	1	dúlcis est	27	21	1.33
pp	1	dissímilis est	6	9	1.00
Total			**263**		**12.64**

Note on Table 3

The expected frequency and the χ^2 test have been calculated according to Janson, *Prose Rhythm*, pp. 19–21. The critical value for the χ^2 test on 24 pairs, as given here, is 35.2. There is one apparent discrepancy between Table 3's figure of 20 instances of p 4p, and the figure of 19 instances of the *trispondiacus* p 4p, in Tables 1 and 2. This has arisen because Table 3 mechanically logs all sentence-endings according to Janson's system of notation (*ibid.*, pp. 13–15), whereas in Tables 1 and 2 I am concerned to record as *trispondiacus* forms only those instances of p 4p which carry the stress pattern ó o o o ó o. This means that I have excluded from them the sentence-ending 'finem eius audiamus' (Walker, p. 104, line 33), because, in context, the *eius* carries no stress, and the rhythmical pattern is therefore not that of the *trispondiacus*.

3. *Vocabulary*

The final aspect of X's Latinity which requires consideration is his vocabulary. I am not here concerned with giving a general overview of his preferred types of word formation, or with listing such items as all Greek-derived words: these are covered (albeit with some omissions) in Walker's grammatical index. Rather, my concern is with X's use of some unusual or rare words, including some that appear in the *Instructiones* for the first time, as far as our information goes. The following words will be considered in this order: *ascematus, paracaraximus, crepido, fulcrum, antes, caelicola, deicola, cassabundus, peruti, pertusatus, tristificare, edaciter, incompungibilis, medicalis, inconuertibilis, lumentum, nutabundus, praelibare, remordere.*

(a) *Ascematus.* The most intriguing of these is, unquestionably, the word *ascematus.*[332] The final two sentences of *Instructio I* (§ 4) read, in the original Bobbio manuscripts:[333]

Pie ergo credenda est, et non impie discutienda est magna Trinitas; quoddam enim insuperabile et inuestigabile pelagus est Deus unus Trinitas. Altum caelum et lata terra et profundum mare longaque saecula; sed altior et latior ac profundior longiorque est scientia, quia natura ascematus est, qui ea ex nihilo creauit.

Walker drastically altered the last sentence in his edition. As another scholar has pointed out, he was presumably misled by finding the verb *ascemare* given with the meaning 'to diminish' in Du Cange's *Glossarium*, citing a source which is difficult to trace, but appears to come from a context quite different from that of the *Instructiones.*[334] As it is axiomatic to Christian theology that God will never change or be diminished, Walker altered the final passage to read: '. . . sed altior et latior ac profundior longiorque *eius* scientia, *qui a* natura *non* ascematus est, qui ea*m* ex nihilo creauit' (my italics). His translation of the whole runs: 'Therefore the great Trinity is to be piously believed and not impiously questioned; for the one God, the Trinity, is an ocean that cannot be crossed over or searched out. High is the heaven, broad the earth, deep the sea and long the ages; but higher and broader and deeper and longer is the knowledge of Him who is not diminished by nature, Who created it of nought.' There is, however, no manuscript authority for the intrusion of a *non*; the only instance of the verb *ascemare* carrying the meaning 'to diminish' to be cited by

---

[332] I should like to thank my husband, Ben de la Mare, for helpful discussions on *ascematus* and related problems.

[333] *Sancti Columbani Opera*, ed. & transl. Walker, p. 64, lines 19–23, but restoring the readings of the two Bobbio manuscripts given in Walker's *apparatus criticus*, and discarding his conjectural emendations. See the discussion in Smit, *Studies*, pp. 161–3.

[334] Smit, *ibid.*, pp. 161–3. Du Cange (*Glossarium*, I.416) cites a passage from 'Contract. Datior. Bergom. lib. 8, cap. 14', but I cannot trace this in the list of sources given in vol. X, nor was Smit able to trace it.

Du Cange comes from a context so far removed from our sixth- or seventh-century *Instructiones* that one may doubt its relevance – his example is a technical term in viticulture; and in any case, the sentiment, 'who is not diminished by nature', does not seem an apt remark in the context.[335]

In fact, J.W. Smit, who offered these criticisms[336] of Walker, pointed out that Du Cange himself cited this passage from the *Instructiones* not under the verb *ascemare*, but under the noun *scema*, from the Greek σχῆμα. The basic meaning of this word is 'form'; but, like its Greek original, it carries several different meanings, including those of attire, clothing, especially the distinctive dress of priests and the monastic habit, and also equipage, accoutrements, finery. These meanings, which are well attested, led Du Cange to give the meaning of 'to be pleased with one's fine attire' ('ornatu suo oblectari') for the verb *scemari*, which occurs in the sixth-century *Regula magistri*; and *scemari*, in its turn, provides the parallel whereby both Du Cange and Smit interpreted X's *ascematus*.[337] For this reason it is worth our looking more closely at the passage in the *Regula magistri*, which is the only occurrence known to me of the word *scemari*.

The passage occurs in a chapter on the monk's clothing. It reads, 'Si quis uero frater in specie sua sibi uisus fuerit scemari uel satis gauisci, mox a praepositis suis ei tollatur et alio detur et alterius illi.' Its recent editor translates this passage: 'Si un frère fait preuve de coquetterie et de complaisance excessive dans sa mise, aussitôt ses prévôts lui ôteront ce qui'il a et le donneront à un autre, et vice-versa.'[338] There are no notes discussing the word *scemari*, nor how, precisely, one should construe the Latin. There is, however, a problem with this passage: what is it which is taken away from the monk who is so concerned with his appearance? Which Latin word in the first clause is the subject of the verb *tollatur* in the main sentence? The French translation is so free that it glosses over the problem entirely. Obviously, however, something very tangible is intended if it is to be swapped for that used by another brother; and, in the context of a chapter on monastic dress, it is presumably an article of clothing. Now, it may be that Du Cange and the recent translator are right: that the verb *scemari* on its own carries the meaning 'to be pleased with one's dress', and that this means that the subject of *tollatur* can be understood without being expressed. But to jump from the word *scema*,

---

[335] *Sancti Columbani Opera*, ed. & transl. Walker, pp. 64–5; Smit, *Studies*, pp. 161–2. I agree with Smit that Metzler's variant, 'scientia eius qui naturam ex nihilo creauit', witnesses to his bewilderment and attempts to make sense of the reading of the earlier Bobbio manuscripts, and does not imply that the manuscript which he was copying had a different reading from the two Bobbio manuscripts which have come down to us.

[336] Smit, *Studies*, pp. 161–2.

[337] Du Cange, *Glossarium*, VII.344; Smit, *Studies*, pp. 161–3.

[338] *Regula magistri*, § 81, ed. & transl. de Vogüé, *La règle du maître*, II.332–5.

'clothing', to a verb *scemari*, 'to be pleased with one's clothing', is a big jump, unsupported by any other evidence.[339] This being so, it is at least worth raising the question whether the manuscript-reading *scemari* may not stand for an original *scemate*, a normal term – indeed, almost a technical term – for the monastic habit. I do not wish to push this suggestion; the point I seek to make now is simply that the passage in the *Regula magistri* is not a straightforward one to interpret; and therefore, that instead of a verb *scemari* providing a well-established point of reference from which one can reach out towards the puzzling word *ascematus*, we should recognise the need for caution in feeling our way towards the correct interpretation both of the passage in the *Instructiones* and of that in the *Regula magistri*.

After dealing with the word *scemari*, Du Cange passed directly to the *Instructiones* passage which concerns us. I quote the relevant paragraph in full:[340]

ASCEMARE. S. Columbanus instr. 1 de Christo: *Quia naturam Ascematus est, qui eam ex nihilo creauit*, i.e. induit, ea se quasi ornauit.

Note, first, that Du Cange or his source has added an *m* to *natura*, so turning this into the direct object of *ascematus est*; secondly, he has added an *m* to *ea*, so interpreting *natura* as the object of *creauit*, rather than *caelum, terra, mare,* and *saecula* (Walker and Smit make exactly the same unnecessary alteration); and thirdly, oddest of all, he refers the passage to Christ, not God the Trinity.[341] The first and the last of these changes lead me to wonder whether Du Cange understood this passage as referring to Christ putting on our (human) nature. Be that as it may, such an interpretation of this passage is quite untenable, because the immediately preceding passage makes it crystal clear that X was here talking about the *Trinity*, and it was only Christ who 't[oo]k our nature upon him'.[342]

Perhaps, however, Du Cange's reference to Christ was an aberration; and when he wrote '[naturam] induit, ea se quasi ornauit', what he was thinking of was biblical passages like the opening of Psalm CIII (CIV), where the psalmist

---

[339] The passage of Arnobius Iunior (*Commentarii in Psalmos*, ed. Migne, *Patrologia Latina*, LIII.488), referred to by Du Cange and Smit, is irrelevant because the word used is the well attested noun, *scema* – not a verb *scemari*. Also, Arnobius's phrase 'in schematibus mundi' does not mean 'the adornment of the world' (cf. Smit, *Studies*, p. 162, n. 5) according to the normal understanding of that phrase. Arnobius, commenting on Psalm CVI.9–10, was emphasising that the recipient of God's goodness is the man 'sedentem in tenebris et in uinculis, in mendicitate et in ferro', not the man 'sedentem . . . in schematibus mundi, . . . in publico gloriantem'. Blaise, *Dictionnaire*, p. 742, gives 'les parures du monde' – 'the finery of the world', as the translation of this passage. The Greek σχῆμα can also mean 'position', 'rank'.

[340] *Glossarium*, VII.344.

[341] Alternatively one might suppose that Du Cange thought that *De Christo* was the title of *Instructio I*. But this is most unlikely: its manuscript-heading is *De fide*, not *De Christo*; and, if one looks at its content, it is patently not concerned with Christ.

[342] *Book of Common Prayer*, collect for Christmas Day.

sings of God being 'amictus lumine sicut uestimento': God is using the light, the clouds, the wind, with which to surround or clothe himself.[343] But this is a very long shot: why should *ascematus est* mean 'he put on' or 'he adorned himself with'? Even the term *scemari* in the *Regula magistri* does not carry that meaning. Further, I doubt whether *natura* would be used with the generalised meaning, 'the natural world', as the object of a verb meaning God 'put on'.[344] It is one thing for the psalmist, using poetic imagery of God, to represent him as clothed in light, or clouds, or wind: the concrete 'clothed' matches the equally concrete and specific 'light', 'clouds', 'wind', but it would not fit at all with the generalised noun, 'nature'. All this makes me unable to accept Du Cange's interpretation of *ascematus* in this passage.

We turn now to the interpretation of Smit, who takes the entry from Du Cange's *Glossarium* as his starting point, but develops it somewhat differently by assuming that *ascematus* is from the verb *scemari*. He therefore adapts the Latin to read, '. . . sed altior et latior ac profundior longiorque eius scientia, quia natura scematus est qui eam ex nihilo creauit'; and he translates: 'High is the sky and broad the earth and deep the sea and long the ages, but higher and broader and deeper and longer is his knowledge, for He has rejoiced in the beauty of nature, He who created it out of nothing.'[345]

This solution, however, is equally unsatisfactory. First, in order to assimilate the word *ascematus* attested in *Instructio I* to the word *scemari* in the *Regula magistri*, it has to be assumed that the initial *a* of *ascematus* is a manuscript error, 'added from the preceding final -*a*- of *natura*'.[346] In the light of our previous discussion of the passage in the *Regula magistri*, I should regard the word *scemari* itself as too uncertain to provide a basis for altering the reading given in both early manuscripts of the *Instructiones*. Secondly, we have another bewildering shift in the meaning ascribed to the word *scemari*. Smit seemingly interprets the wording in the *Regula magistri*, 'in specie sua . . . scemari', to mean 'to take pleasure in his outward appearance', while ascribing to *scemari* the meaning 'to take pleasure in the appearance of someone or something'.[347] The Greek σχῆμα can mean 'appearance', but this meaning does not seem to have been current in the Latin West, to judge from its absence from Du Cange's entries under *scema*; and in any case, since the passage of the *Regula magistri* includes the words 'in specie sua', it seems unlikely that the postulated verb *scemari* would mean, on its own, 'to take pleasure in the appearance of someone or something'. If we revert to the interpretation 'to take pleasure in' as the primary meaning of a verb *scemari*, then we lose any semantic relationship between *scema* and *scemari*.

Thirdly, I find Smit's suggested translation, 'for He [God] has rejoiced in the beauty of nature', implausible in its general context. Smit's insertion of the

---

343 Psalm CIII.2.
344 For a discussion of the likely meaning of *natura* in *Instructio I*, see below, p. 166.
345 *Studies*, pp. 162–3.
346 *Ibid.*, p. 162.
347 *Ibid.*, pp. 162–3.

words, 'the beauty', smacks of a post-Romantic conception of nature; but even if we translate, 'for He has rejoiced in the natural world', it remains a seemingly meaningless statement within its context; and why the perfect tense?[348] In fact, while the word *natura* occurs thirteen times in the *Instructiones*, it is arguably never used in the sense of 'the natural world'. Rather, it is used of 'the nature' of God, or of man, or of the first heaven;[349] or, in the ablative, in the sense of 'by nature', 'naturally'.[350] Its use in this paragraph of *Instructio I* is rather ambiguous;[351] but certainly in the paragraph of *Instructio VIII* which closely echoes the words and themes of this passage of the first sermon, the word *natura* is used in the sense of God's nature and human nature;[352] and the clause containing *ascematus* would fit much more convincingly in its context if we assumed that X was making a theological statement about God and his nature, rather than an irrelevant comment about God 'rejoicing' in the natural world. Also, had the latter meaning been intended, we might have expected *natura rerum* to be used, rather than *natura* on its own.

My own suggestion as regards the meaning of *ascematus* is that *ascematus* is not part of a verb, but rather an adjective meaning 'without form'. I would argue that it is based on the Greek noun τὸ σχῆμα, genitive σχήματος, 'form'. As we have already seen, this word was known in the Latin-speaking world under the spelling *scema* (genitive *scematis*). I suggest that *ascematus* is formed from the Greek negative prefix *a-* (ἀ-) plus the stem *scemat-* plus a Latin adjectival ending *-us*. It would be a Latin equivalent of the Greek ἀσχημάτιστος, 'without form', which is used by Christian theologians in their discussion of God; indeed, they apply it specifically to God's nature.[353] I would adopt just one of Walker's (and Smit's) emendations to the Latin text of

---

[348] Smit (*ibid.*, p. 163) compares Genesis I.31, 'uiditque Deus cuncta quae fecerat et erant ualde bona'; but the perfect tense is natural there since it is part of the story of creation, not a general statement about God; and God seeing that what he had created was very good is not the same as him rejoicing in the natural world.

[349] *Sancti Columbani Opera*, ed. & transl. Walker, p. 60, line 11; p. 94, lines 16 (twice) and 21; p. 102, line 36; p. 106, line 16; p. 94, line 19.

[350] *Ibid.*, p. 74, line 32; p. 90, lines 14, 15, 16.

[351] The paragraph begins: 'Quis est ergo Deus? Pater, Filius et Spiritus Sanctus, Deus unus est. Amplius non requiras de Deo; quia uolentibus altam scire profunditatem rerum ante natura consideranda est. Trinitatis enim scientia profunditati maris merito comparatur . . .' (*Sancti Columbani Opera*, ed. & transl. Walker, p. 62–5). I would translate the relevant passage: 'Do not demand more concerning God; because those wishing to know the deep profundity of things must first consider their nature.' Walker, however, takes 'rerum . . . natura' together, and translates: 'seek no farther concerning God; for those who wish to know the great deep must first review the natural world' (*ibid.*).

[352] *Instructio* VIII.1 (ed. Walker, *ibid.*, p. 94, lines 16, 21); for the parallels with *Instructio I*, see above, pp. 127–8.

[353] Theodoret of Cyrrus: ἡ θεία φύσις ἀνείδεός τε καὶ ἀσχημάτιστος; Basil of Caesarea, of the divine essence: τὴν . . . ἀνείδεον καὶ ἀσχημάτιστον φύσιν (both passages cited from Lampe, *A Patristic Greek Lexicon*, p. 253, s.v. ἀσχημάτιστος, 4).

the *Instructiones* as transmitted in manuscript, reading with them 'longiorque *eius* scientia' by analogy with 'Trinitatis enim scientia' earlier in the same paragraph,[354] in lieu of the manuscripts' 'longiorque est scientia'. An *est* must be understood in this sentence, as in the preceding one. This gives the following sentence:

Altum caelum et lata terra et profundum mare longaque saecula; sed altior et latior ac profundior longiorque eius scientia, quia natura ascematus est, qui ea ex nihilo creauit.

I would translate this and the preceding sentence (quoted above) as follows:

The great Trinity must therefore be devoutly believed, and not impiously discussed; for the one God, the Trinity, is an ocean which cannot be traversed or investigated. High is the heaven and wide the earth and deep the sea and long the ages; but higher and wider and deeper and longer is the knowledge of Him, because He is in his nature without form, He who created these things out of nothing.

In other words, I take *natura* as an ablative of respect or specification, as we find elsewhere in the sermons, for instance, 'O pullatam pellem, frustra lauaris, quae natura immunda es.' 'Defiled skin, in vain are you washed that are unclean by nature.'[355]

There are, I would suggest, three considerations which favour this interpretation of *ascematus*. First, it accepts and makes sense of the manuscript-reading 'quia natura ascematus est', rather than requiring alterations to the text to produce adequate sense. Secondly, my suggested translation does fit the context. X was arguing that mere mortals should not attempt to discuss the mystery of the Trinity, when it was even more unfathomable to them than the visible ocean which itself lies beyond our ken. That the Godhead was 'without form' is a very good reason for insisting that human beings cannot readily discuss it. Note how X continues his discussion in the following paragraph, referring to God as 'inuisibilem, inaestimabilem, inconspicabilem ... Quia sicut maris profunditas ab humanis est uisibus inuisibilis, ita Trinitatis diuinitas ab humanis similiter sensibus incomprehensibilis deprehenditur.'[356] Thirdly, while there is no solid evidence for a sixth- or seventh-century use of a verb *ascemare* 'to diminish' or 'to put on', or of a verb *scemari*, 'to be pleased with one's clothing' or 'to take pleasure in the appearance of something', I can at least point to western knowledge of *scema*, 'form', at this period: it was used by Cassiodorus in his Tripartite History, and, from the opposite side of Europe, by Adomnán in his *De locis sanctis* and by the Irish author of the *Hisperica Famina*, who used it as the basis for coining a new verb, *scemicare*, 'to form'.[357] As regards the Greek prefix ἀ-, it does not

---

354 *Sancti Columbani Opera*, ed. & transl. Walker, p. 64, line 2. The antecedent of *eius* is also God the Trinity. It is in any case clear from the clause, 'qui ea ex nihilo creauit', that God must be intended.

355 *Instructio* VII.1 (ed. & transl. Walker, *ibid.*, p. 90, lines 13–14, p. 91). Cf. above, n. 350.

356 *Instructio* I.5 (ed. Walker, *ibid.*, p. 64, lines 27– 31).

357 Cassiodorus, *Historia ecclesiastica, uocata tripartita*, X.7 (ed. Migne, *Patrologia Latina*, LXIX.1169–70); Adomnán, *De locis sanctis*, I.25 (ed. & transl. Meehan,

require a profound knowledge of Greek to know that this was how the Greeks negated the meaning of an adjective; it is the sort of information which might well be given in, say, one of Jerome's discussions of the meaning of a biblical passage. As for how the word *ascematus* came to be used by X, there are three possibilities: it could have been taken over by X from an earlier work which has not come down to us; or X might have known the Greek word ἀσχημάτιστος, and either deliberately given it a more normal Latin ending, or else have unintentionally garbled it into *ascematus*; or, thirdly, X might have coined the word *ascematus* himself, on the basis of ἀ- plus *scemat-*, as already suggested. As regards his decision to employ a Greek word, we will see below that X used various Greek-derived words elsewhere in his *Instructiones*, including one that never passed beyond Cassian into common Latin parlance.

(b) *Other unusual words.* The other unusual words used by X can be dealt with more speedily, as none of them poses such problems as *ascematus*. As just mentioned, X uses several Greek-derived words, which are listed by Walker in his edition.[358] Most of these were already in fairly common christian Latin use. Besides *ascematus*, it is worth noting *agon, crepido, ergastulum, hypocrita, paracaraximus,* and *pelagus*. Only *paracaraximus* and *crepido* are unusual enough to warrant discussion.

Paracaraximus is used in the context of the Last Judgment, when we shall be tried in the fire; and then, with the counterfeit metal melted (*paracaraximo liquefacto*), any gold or silver which may be present will be revealed.[359] It was coined directly from the Greek παραχαράξιμος by Cassian, who used it in his *Conlationes* both as an adjective and substantive. Like its Greek original, it means 'counterfeit, debased', as applied to money. We know that X had read Cassian's *Instituta*, and by far the most likely explanation for his use of the word *paracaraximus* is that he also knew Cassian's *Conlationes*, and took it over from there.[360] His readiness to do so despite the fact that, to judge from the lack of other citations, it had not passed into current use, is interesting.

Crepido, from the Greek κρηπίς, genitive κρηπίδος, 'foundation', is a rather different case. Latin dictionaries give various citations from Latin authors including Cicero, Livy, and Vergil, but nearly all with the sense of a

---

Adamnan's De locis sanctis, p. 70, line 11 and n.); *Hisperica Famina*, A, lines 43, 55 etc. (ed. Herren, *Hisperica Famina: the A-Text*, pp. 66, 68, and discussion, pp. 25, 131, and cf. p. 177). The word *schema* is also used by Gildas (*De excidio* 67,6), but with the meaning of 'position' (so Winterbottom in *Gildas*, ed. Winterbottom, pp. 120, 54)) or 'vestments' (cf. the examples cited in Blaise, *Dictionnaire*, p. 742, and Du Cange, *Glossarium*, VII.344). *Schema* can also be used to mean 'a figure of speech', as for example by Cassiodorus and Aldhelm.

[358] *Sancti Columbani Opera*, ed. & transl. Walker, p. 231.

[359] *Instructio* IX.2 (*ibid.*, pp. 98–100).

[360] Cassian, *Conlationes*, I.xx.4, I.xxi.1, I.xxii.1, II.9 (ed. Petschenig, pp. 31, 33, 48). Columbanus's seventeenth-century editor noted Cassian as the source: Fleming, *Collectanea Sacra*, p. 65. See also *Thesaurus Linguae Latinae*, Blaise, *Dictionnaire*, Souter, *Glossary*, and Du Cange, *Glossarium*, all s.v. 'paracaraximus'.

physical foundation, embankment, or the like.[361] What is intriguing about X's use of the word is that he uses it in a metaphorical sense, 'crepido sermonis', 'the foundation of our talk'.[362] The only parallel for such a metaphorical use that I have discovered is in Rufinus's translation of Gregory of Nazianzus's discourse, *De epiphaniis*: 'nullam potest . . . principii Dei inuenire crepidinem', one's mind 'can find no edge to the beginning of God'.[363] Although Rufinus and X were using *crepido* with different shades of meaning, both were using it metaphorically, rather than for a physical object; and, as I have already argued that X knew Gregory's *De epiphaniis* in Rufinus's translation,[364] it seems likely that X got the idea of using it metaphorically from Rufinus.

From *crepido* it is natural to pass on to *fulcrum*, 'support', another word which is not very commonly used in a metaphorical sense, but is used by X of the 'support' given by two biblical texts to the doctrine of God as both one and Trinity simultaneously. This passage has already been quoted and discussed above where I have argued that X was almost certainly borrowing the expression 'quasi quibusdam fulcris' from Gildas.[365] It is interesting to note that Columbanus also uses the word metaphorically in *Epistula I*, asking Gregory the Great for his support in connection with disputes over the date of Easter: 'tuae dirige fulcrum sententiae'.[366]

Next, let us take the word *antibus*. This occurs in the penultimate sermon, where X is praying that by the light given him by Jesus he may be able to see the holy of holies, 'quae te aeternum Pontificem aeternorum in antibus magni illius tui templi illic intrantem habeant'. Jesus is here represented as entering *in antibus* of his temple.[367] There appears to be some confusion here over what are in origin two separate words: *antes*, a plural third-declension noun such as is implied by the ablative *antibus*, means 'files' (of cavalry) or 'rows', especially of vines, while *antae*, a plural first-declension noun, means 'square pilasters'. Walker's translation of the passage in *Instructio XII*, 'entering there in the pillars of that great temple of Thine', shows that he took the word to be derived from *antae*, although the ablative of this would properly be *antis* rather than *antibus*. However, the confusion between *antes* and *antae* probably goes back before X; for, as Du Cange points out,[368] it is found in Seruius's *Commentary on Vergil* of ca A.D. 400. Commenting on a line of the *Georgics* where *antes* is used of vines, Seruius writes:[369]

---

[361] The only quasi-metaphorical use of the word is a quotation from Cicero ('omnia tamquam crepidine quadam comprehensione longiore sustinentur'), cited from Lewis & Short, *A Latin Dictionary*, p. 480.

[362] *Instructio* I.1.

[363] *De epiphaniis*, VIII.1 (ed. Engelbrecht, *Tyrannii Rufini . . . interpretatio*, pp. 93–4); cf. above, p. 109.

[364] See above, pp. 108–9.

[365] See above, p. 109.

[366] *Instructio* I.2 and *Epistula* I.4 (*Sancti Columbani Opera*, ed. & transl. Walker, p. 60, line 21, and p. 6, line 6).

[367] *Instructio* XII.3 (ed. Walker, *ibid.*, p. 114, lines 15–16).

[368] *Glossarium*, I.297, s.v. 'antes'.

[369] Seruius, commenting on Georgics II.417 (ed. Thilo, *Seruii . . . Commentarii*, III.257–8).

Et 'antes' alii extremos uinearum ordines accipiunt, alii macerias, quibus uineta cluduntur, quae maceriae fiunt de assis, id est siccis, lapidibus . . . Dicuntur autem antes a lapidibus eminentioribus, qui interponuntur ad materiem sustentandam: nam proprie antes sunt eminentes lapides uel columnae ultimae, quibus fabrica sustinetur . . .

And some take *antes* to mean the outermost rows of vines, others to be the walls within which the vineyard is enclosed, the walls being made of *assis*, that is, dry-stone walling . . . *Antes* are so named from the projecting stones, which are inserted to hold up the wall; for *antes* are properly the 'projecting stones' or the 'end-columns' by which a structure is supported . . .

There is also a pertinent entry in Paul the Deacon's epitome of Festus's *De uerborum significatu*: '*Antes* sunt extremi ordines uinearum. Unde etiam nomen trahunt *antae* quae sunt latera ostiorum.'[370] It looks as though Seruius drew his information from Festus; but where Festus had kept the distinction (albeit postulating an etymological relationship) between *antes* and *antae*, Seruius had run both meanings together under the single word *antes*.

The meanings of 'end-columns' and 'sides of the doorway' given by Seruius and Festus fit our passage in *Instructio XII* precisely, because X represents Jesus as entering 'in antibus templi', 'in the doorway of the temple'. This makes considerably more sense than Walker's translation, 'entering . . . in the pillars of that great temple'. It looks to me, therefore, as though X did not simply confuse *antes* with *antae*; rather, he would appear to have known the meanings ascribed to *antes* by Seruius, or by another author dependent on Seruius or one who gave a similar exposition of the word *antes*. It is perhaps not irrelevant to add that Seruius's commentary on Vergil appears to have been known in Irish circles at least by the late seventh century, and possibly by Adomnán, abbot of Iona, who may have derived his knowledge of the unusual word *maceria* from precisely this passage of Seruius's commentary on the Georgics.[371]

Next let us look at the words *caelicola* and *deicola*. In both cases the second element is a noun ultimately derived from the verb *colere*, meaning 'to cultivate, cherish, inhabit or worship'. *Caelicola*, an 'inhabitant of heaven', is well attested, principally as a poetic word. Classical poets (and occasionally christians) used the word for a (pagan) god or goddess, and the christian poet Paulinus of Nola used it adjectivally of (christian) angels: *caelicolas ministros*.[372] What is unusual about X's use of the term, however, is that the

---

[370] *Glossaria Latina*, ed. Lindsay, IV.111. Festus, a scholar of the late second century A.D., was himself epitomising a work by Verrius Flaccus. The first half of Festus's work (which was alphabetically arranged) is lost, surviving only in the adaptation made in the late eighth century by Paul the Deacon.

[371] See Bullough, 'Columba, Adomnán' [*Scottish Historical Review* 44 (1965)], pp. 24–6, esp. p. 25, n. 7. Bullough's point, that the insistence in the *Scholia Bernensia* on the distinction between *Picti* and *Cruithni* reflects Adomnán's own usage in a matter on which he differed from other early Irish writers, seems to me a weightier reason for thinking that the Vergil commentary goes back to Adomnán than Bullough allows. On Irish knowledge of Seruius, see also Herren, 'Classical and secular learning', p. 136.

[372] See, e.g., Lewis & Short, *A Latin Dictionary*, p. 262; Blaise, *Dictionnaire*, p. 122; *Thesaurus Linguae Latinae*, s.v. 'caelicola'.

context makes it clear that he is applying it to humans: 'Quis enim intellegit
uel semetipsum uel alterum, florem terrae et terram de terra factum, qua
dignitate Dei filium et caelicolam facit terra et puluis post modicum futurus
. . .?' Walker's translation, 'citizen of heaven', is very apt here.[373] While this is
but an extension of its normal usage, it is an interesting one; and it is also
interesting to find X using what is essentially poetic vocabulary. He could have
encountered the word in Gildas: but there it is explicitly given as a quotation
from a poet, and its meaning is probably the well-attested one of '*supernal*
dwellers in heaven', or 'angels'.[374]

Deicola is a rarer word, which appears to have been coined by christian
authors to express the Greek term θεοσεβής, 'god-fearing man' or 'devout
man'; and it is in that sense that it is used by X in *Instructio II* (§ 2).[375] It is
found in Euagrius's Latin translation of Athanasius's *Vita S. Antonii*, here
rendering θεοφιλής;[376] and I suspect it was chiefly from this application of the
word to Antony that it became known in the West. It has been noted in Jerome
and Cassiodorus; and, while never common, it was used by Martin of Braga
and in an Anglo-Saxon dedicatory poem datable to the episcopate of Hæddi,
bishop of Winchester (676–705).[377] It was also known in Irish circles; for,
according to tradition, Deicolus was the name of one of the monks who
accompanied Columbanus to the Continent.[378] Here, it probably represents a
Latin adaptation of the Irish name *Dicuil* (compare Latin *Virgilius* and OIr
Fergil); but, even so, it does testify to familiarity with the word among the
circle of Columbanus.

While *deicola*, though rare, is at least used by a handful of patristic and early
medieval christian authors, the same can scarcely be said of the word
cassabundus. This word occurs in *Instructio V* (§ 1), where the author
is apostrophising human life as 'cassabunda et mortalis': 'tottering and

---

[373] *Instructio* III.1 (*Sancti Columbani Opera*, ed. & transl. Walker, pp. 74–5). Blaise
(*Dictionnaire*, p. 122) cites an example where the word is used in a Vetus Latina
translation of Acts XVII.4; but there it is used in a different sense (for 'the
godfearing').
[374] *De excidio* II.32: '. . . germanam eius, perpetuam deo uiduitatis castimoniam
promittentem, ut poeta ait, summam ceu teneritudinem caelicolarum . . .' I take the
sense of this to be that, in renouncing a second marriage and resolving to dwell in
chastity, Cuneglas's sister-in-law will be imitating the angels in heaven, who do not
marry (cf. Mark XII.25). The source of the poetical quotation has not been
identified. The word is briefly discussed by Kerlouégan, *Le De excidio*, I.245, II.54.
[375] *Sancti Columbani Opera*, ed. & transl. Walker, p. 70, line 9. See Blaise, *Dictionnaire*,
p. 249.
[376] *Vita S. Antonii*, § 4; both the Greek original of Athanasius and Evagrius's Latin
translation are given in *Patrologia Graeca*, ed. Migne, XXVI.845 (there is now a
critical edition of the Greek text: *Athanase d'Alexandrie*, ed. & transl. Bartelink; the
passage in question is at pp. 140–1). This occurrence appears to have escaped the
notice of the dictionaries which I have consulted.
[377] Blaise, *Dictionnaire*, p. 249; Lapidge, 'Some remnants', p. 817. The Anglo-Latin
poem uses the words *deicola* and *caelicola* of Hæddi in adjacent lines, apparently as
approximate synonyms.
[378] Kenney, *Sources*, p. 208.

mortal'.[379] It is an archetypal glossary-word. Dictionaries cite a vivid phrase, 'cassabundum ire ebrium', from the author Gnaeus Naeuius (third century B.C.); a similar usage in Macrobius's *Saturnalia* of the late fourth or (more probably) early fifth century A.D.;[380] a couple of instances from Aldhelm's prose *De uirginitate*; an occurrence in Paul the Deacon's *Epitoma Festi*; and some glosses.[381] It is certainly not the sort of word which one expects to encounter in a sermon, even one delivered to a moderately educated monastic audience. Our author might have found this word in a glossary; or it might have been gleaned from a source from the same milieu as that whence he derived his understanding of the word *antes*. For Macrobius came from the same circles as Seruius, author of the Vergil commentary, and Festus's *De uerborum significatu* also appealed to such circles.

We pass now to a number of words which again are little attested, or not attested at all, in previous authors, but which strike me as words which could have been coined by our author, or were perhaps already in colloquial use, rather than being obscure words carefully culled from his reading or from glossaries. We start with the verb *peruti*, found in *Instructio V* (§ 2), where X was warning his audience that they must be careful how they live this life if they are to reach their true homeland in heaven. He warns them against those who are carefree, presumptuous: 'Hic enim in uia perusi sunt patria, et de breui uita aeternam mortem mercati sunt.' Walker translates *perusi sunt patria* as 'these have exhausted their home', presumably taking *peruti* as 'to use very much', hence 'exhaust'.[382] But Niermeyer gives the meaning of 'to misuse', and includes an example of this usage from the Merovingian *Passio S. Praeiecti*.[383] More light may be shed on this word when the more detailed dictionaries reach this part of the alphabet, but in the meantime Niermeyer's 'misuse' gives adequate sense.

Next, let us consider our author's apostrophe to the human will in *Instructio VII* (§ 1), 'O pertusata sanguisuga impatiens', which Walker translates as 'insatiable and rabid leech'.[384] *Pertusata*, however, looks like a past participle formed from a verb *pertusare*. Such a verb is used by the twelfth-century author, Guibert of Nogent,[385] with the meaning 'to perforate' – i.e. the same as that for the verb *pertundere* (past participle *pertusus*), whence the word presumably derives. However, while a Latin past participle is normally passive in meaning, the sense of the passage under consideration requires that it here carries an active meaning, 'burrowing', 'pricking' – it is the leech which

---

[379] *Sancti Columbani Opera*, ed. & transl. Walker, p. 84, lines 14–15.

[380] See Cameron, 'The date'.

[381] *Thesaurus Linguae Latinae*; *Dictionary of Medieval Latin from British Sources*, edd. Latham *et al.*

[382] *Sancti Columbani Opera*, ed. & transl. Walker, p. 86, lines 11–12; p. 87, line 13.

[383] Niermeyer, *Mediae Latinitatis Lexicon*. The verb is not listed at all in: Lewis & Short, *A Latin Dictionary*; Glare, *Oxford Latin Dictionary*; Du Cange, *Glossarium*; Souter, *Glossary*; or Blaise, *Dictionnaire*; and the relevant fascicule of the *Thesaurus Linguae Latinae* has not yet been published.

[384] *Sancti Columbani Opera*, ed. & transl. Walker, pp. 90–1, lines 7.

[385] Du Cange, *Glossarium*.

makes the holes. It is a vivid metaphor for the human will, assigning it a very active role, and was perhaps coined by our author on the spur of the moment.

The other words to be dealt with under this heading are more straight-forward: *tristificare*,[386] 'to make sad', appears to have been little used: the dictionaries cite Cassian's *Conlationes*, Adomnán's *Vita S. Columbae*, and a couple of other instances.[387] Our author could well have taken it from Cassian; but, unlike *paracaraximus*, its meaning is obvious even to those meeting it for the first time. The meaning of *edaciter*, 'voraciously', is equally clear, although the word is not attested elsewhere at this date.[388] It is an adverb regularly formed from the adjective *edax*, which was common enough. Again, the meaning of *incompungibilis* would have been clear to X's hearers, particularly in context: 'Dura incompungibilisque ignorantia'.[389] 'Blind' or 'impervious' is perhaps the best rendering into English; but X's hearers would have known the verb *compungi*, 'to feel remorse' (literally, 'to be pricked'); and from this, its literal meaning, 'unable to be pricked', would have been obvious to them. *Medicalis*, 'healthful', is slightly different: it looks like an error for *medicabilis* (or conceivably, for *medicinalis*); and indeed, as the Fleury family of manuscripts reads *medicabile* (in lieu of the Bobbio manuscripts' *medicale*), it is probably an error arising from faulty transcription.[390] However, *medicalis* is found in a ninth-century text.[391]

Finally, it is perhaps worth listing a few other words which, while not rare, are still somewhat unusual: *inconuertibilis*, 'unchangeable' (of God);[392] *lumentum*, for *lomentum*, 'washing, cleansing' – the word is also found in Colum-banus's *Penitential*;[393] *nutabundus*, 'staggering, tottering, uncertain' – a word used by some christian-Latin authors, including Gildas;[394] *praelibare* 'to taste

---

[386] *Instructio* IV.3 (ed. & transl. Walker, *Sancti Columbani Opera*, p. 82, line 28).

[387] Blaise, *Dictionnaire* (but note that his references to the *Vita S. Columbae* should read II.25, II.39, II.45, and III.1); Souter, *Glossary*.

[388] *Instructio* XIII.1 (ed. & transl. Walker, *Sancti Columbani Opera*, p. 116, line 23). The only dictionary in which I have found the word is the *Dictionary of Medieval Latin from British Sources*, edd. Latham *et al.*, citing twelfth- and fourteenth-century examples.

[389] *Instructio* III.4 (*ibid.*, p. 76, lines 30–1).

[390] *Instructio* XI.3 (*ibid.*, p. 110, line 10). The early Fleury manuscript, now Vatican City, Biblioteca Apostolica Vaticana, MS. Regin. lat. 140 (*saec.* ix/x) is of virtually the same date as the Bobbio manuscripts, whose reading *medicale* is that printed by Walker.

[391] *Novum Glossarium*, ed. Blatt, citing Heiric's verse *Vita S. Germani*, where the word means 'curable'. (*Medicabilis* can mean both 'curable' and 'curative', so presumably *medicalis* could too.) Cf. Blaise, *Dictionnaire*, s.v.

[392] *Instructio* I.3 (ed. & transl. Walker, *Sancti Columbani Opera*, p. 62, line 37). See Blaise, *Dictionnaire*, s.v.

[393] *Instructio* VII.1 and *Paenitentiale*, §§ 27, 28 (ed. & transl. Walker, *Sancti Columbani Opera*, p. 90, line 31 and p. 180, lines 3, 6). For comparable examples, see the *Thesaurus Linguae Latinae*, s.v., citing both Augustine and Aponius for the figurative use which we find in *Instructio* VII.1.

[394] *Instructio* VI.1 (ed. & transl. Walker, *Sancti Columbani Opera*, p. 88, line 10); Gildas, *De excidio* I.20 (ed. Winterbottom, *Gildas*, p. 95). Cf. Blaise, *Dictionnaire*, s.v.: Apuleius is the only pagan author cited; but the word was current among christian Latin authors, such as Cyprian, Lactantius, Rufinus and Salvian.

beforehand, sample';[395] *remordere*, 'to torment, vex', used in the expression *animo remordente*, 'with his conscience tormenting [him]': in the classical period this word was largely poetic, but it is used in a sense similar to that under consideration by Jerome, Rufinus, Pelagius, Orosius, and Gildas.[396]

No doubt an exhaustive survey of the vocabulary of X's *Instructiones* would reveal other points of interest, but for present purposes this survey of the more unusual words must suffice. Of the nineteen words listed, five or six are not previously attested, but most of these are not particularly difficult or odd coinings, and would be easy to understand (in the case of *edaciter*, *incompugnibilis*, and *medicalis* – if this rather than *medicabilis* really was the correct reading); or at least, not too difficult (in the case of *peruti* and *pertusatus*). Only *ascematus*, which here makes its sole attested appearance, would be likely to cause serious problems. One word, *tristificare*, is apparently seldom found elsewhere, but its meaning is self-evident. Ten words are 'glossary' words, in the literal sense that they are attested in one or more of the early mediaeval glossaries: *antes*, *crepido*, *caelicola*, *deicola*, *cassabundus*, *nutabundus*, *lomentum*, *paracaraximus*, *praelibare*, and *remordere*. Some of these, however, are much more widespread than others, as is the case with *nutabundus*, *lomentum*, *praelibare*, and *remordere*.[397] Others are very obscure: *antes*, *cassabundus*, and *paracaraximus*. In the case of *antes*, *caelicola*, and *crepido*, as with *fulcrum*, the words are used in an unusual sense. *Inconuertibilis*, however, is not particularly rare.

In what direction do these findings point? At the outset, we should remember that these nineteen words were culled from some thirty printed pages of Latin, which means that the incidence of obscure words is relatively slight – slighter than in Gildas's *De excidio*. Turning now to our author's use of these words, we should note that the rare words seem apt where they occur. They read naturally, as though they were part of our author's vocabulary: they do not give the impression that our author sat down with a glossary in a determined attempt to find and use recherché words, or as though he were ostentatiously showing off his extensive vocabulary. On the other hand, their placing is not haphazard. When one looks at the words in context, it is striking that the most unusual words all seem to occur in heightened, poetical passages: this applies to *ascematus*, *antes*, *cassabundus*, *nutabundus*, *caelicola*; we might add that *pertusatus* and *incompugnibilis* occur in rhetorical contexts, and *crepido* and *praelibare* in the introductions to the first and second sermons respectively. Thus in his use of vocabulary as in other respects, our author shows his literary artistry. We might note that Christine Mohrmann has commented, apropos of

---

[395] *Instructio* II.1 (ed. & transl. Walker, *Sancti Columbani Opera*, p. 66, line 19). It is found in Statius, the *Scriptores Historiae Augustae*, Cassian and Gregory the Great: see Blaise, *Dictionnaire*, s.v.

[396] *Instructio* IX.1 (ed. & transl. Walker, *Sancti Columbani Opera*, p. 96, line 19); cf. Lewis & Short, *A Latin Dictionary*; Blaise, *Dictionnaire*; and Gildas, *De excidio*, II.34 (ed. Winterbottom, *Gildas*, p. 102).

[397] See the Latin index in *Corpus Glossariorum Latinorum*, ed. Goetz, VI–VII. It is only fair to add that there are some words in the glossaries which one would have thought were quite common.

Columbanus's *Epistulae*, upon 'a very particular trait of Columban's style (and of that of others following the same line): the use of exotic words in rhetorical or poetic passages'.[398]

A further impression is that our author enjoyed using unusual words, and that he enjoyed using words of Greek origin. He seems to have culled at least some of these words from his reading: *paracaraximus* and *tristificare* were both surely taken from Cassian, and *praelibare* could have been; *crepido* in its abstract sense was probably taken from Rufinus; *fulcrum* in its abstract sense was definitely culled from Gildas, and *caelicola* and *nutabundus* (and possibly *remordere*) could have come from the same source.

A penchant for using unusual words and Greek-derived words is a well-known trait of many Irish writers, well exemplified by Columbanus's three letters to popes. It was, of course, by no means an exclusively Irish trait, and can readily be paralleled in fifth-century Gaul.[399] What is unusual, however, is the use of recherché words in sermons. For comparison's sake, I re-read the first eight sermons *Ad monachos* from the Gallic Eusebian sermon-collection:[400] they come from the relevant Gallic milieu, and, like the *Instructiones* of X, were addressed to monks, and so might be expected to use more obscure words than a preacher addressing a mixed lay congregation would allow himself. The most unusual words that I noted were *eruum, maleloquus, praegustare*, and *superequitare*.[401] All these, however, are attested in authors of the fourth, fifth or sixth centuries, and they are comparable to *nutabundus, lomentum, praelibare* – not to the rare words used by X. We also have X's very interesting use of the hapax legomenon *ascematus*. If I am right in my suggestion about the origin and meaning of this word, then *ascematus* is a significant pointer: it would fit well with the other Greek-derived words found in Columbanus's *Epistulae*,[402] and point more in the direction of Columbanus than of a Gallic author of these sermons.

The Authorship of the Thirteen Sermons

In this paper I have attempted to let the evidence of the sermons speak for itself: I have set down the details of their manuscript-tradition, the sources used, their content, and their Latinity, rather than selecting and deploying evidence in an argumentative fashion. Through this approach I have tried to avoid the danger of seeing only what I was expecting to see in the sermons. Now, however, that the evidence has been presented in the round, it is time to draw the threads together, and to return to the question from which this paper arose: that of their authorship.

---

[398] 'The earliest continental Irish Latin', p. 223.

[399] Cf. Winterbottom, 'Aldhelm's prose style', p. 52.

[400] *Eusebius 'Gallicanus'*, ed. Glorie, pp. 419–516. These eight sermons taken together are roughly the same length as our thirteen *Instructiones*.

[401] *Ibid.*, p. 477, line 127; p. 499, line 50; p. 502, line 94; p. 515, line 88; p. 491, line 60; p. 457, lines 34–5.

[402] See Walker, 'On the use', and Smit, *Studies*, pp. 25–7, 39–163.

Our detailed examination of the sermons has brought clarification on various points. First, whoever wrote the sermons, he cannot have been a fifth-century Gallic disciple of Faustus of Riez, as Seebass claimed. He did not write in the fifth century, for he uses two sixth-century authors, Caesarius, bishop of Arles from 502 to 542,[403] and Gildas, a sixth-century British writer. Nor was he a Gaul; rather, he must have been either Irish or, conceivably, British/Breton in origin. This is indicated in the first place by his use of Gildas, an author whose works do not appear to have been known on the Continent outside Brittany, let alone at a time so close to that of writing.[404] It is also indicated, quite independently, by the evidence of his latinity; for a continental author of the late fifth or early sixth century, who wrote with the literary skill of our author, would certainly have used rhythmical *clausulae*. Other features of his latinity, such as his readiness to use unusual words, also fit with this conclusion.

Although our author was either Irish or British/Breton, he would nonetheless appear to have written on the Continent. This may be deduced from the fact that he wrote against a background of some kind of trinitarian heresy.[405] There is no evidence that any doctrinal heresy answering to this description was rife in Ireland, Britain, or Brittany at this period. Thanks to the vigilance and the energetic action of Hilary of Poitiers, Arianism, the most likely candidate, never got a hold on northern Gaul. True, Gildas writes that the serpent of Arianism and other heresies reached Britain, apparently around the mid-fourth century;[406] but he was poorly informed about this period, and in any case, Arianism does not figure in his account of Britain in subsequent generations. Indeed, it is noteworthy that while Gildas does not stint his criticism of the christianity of his fellow countrymen, there is no hint in his writings that the British of his day were doctrinally unsound. Again, when the Roman missionaries to Anglo-Saxon England encountered British and Irish christians, there is no indication that they found any trace of doctrinal heresy amongst them. The differences between the christian traditions were over matters of praxis, not belief; and the only exception to this pattern is that of some lingering doubts about Pelagianism, a heresy of a type quite different

---

[403] Klingshirn, 'Church politics'.

[404] Mommsen lists the manuscripts and the authors who cite Gildas by name in the introduction to his edition, *Gildae sapientis De excidio*, pp. 13–17, 21–4. See also Grosjean, 'Notes', pp. 185–9, 212–26; Davies, 'The church in Wales', pp. 138, 147, n. 73; Dumville, 'Sub-Roman Britain', pp. 183–4; Wright, 'Knowledge', pp. 175–81. Grosjean speculated that Einhard might have seen a copy, left in Charlemagne's palace school by Alcuin; but Einhard probably cited the words ascribed to Philo direct from Rufinus's translation of Eusebius, *Ecclesiastical History*, not via Gildas; cf. 'Notes', pp. 193–4, 225–6.

[405] See above, pp. 134–5.

[406] *De excidio* I.12 (ed. & transl. Winterbottom, *Gildas*, p. 93). The supposed reference to a 'dog of Arius' in the so-called letter of Vinisius to Nigra (Thomas, *Christianity*, pp. 126–7; Lapidge & Sharpe, *A Bibliography*, no. 1) is the result of a misunderstanding: in 1904 a Roman cursive inscription was read upside down, and interpreted freely! In reality, the 'letter' is a curse tablet, like many others from Bath. See Tomlin, 'The curse tablets', pp. 236–7 (no. 100).

from that implied by the trinitarian emphasis in *Instructio I*.

As our author was writing against the background of some trinitarian heresy, the likelihood is that he was living in or adjacent to an area of Arian influence: Visigothic Spain and Septimania in the period before 589, when the Arian Visigoths embraced Catholicism; possibly Burgundy prior to its conquest by the Franks in 534;[407] Provence prior to 536, when the Franks took it from the Ostrogoths; or Italy under either the Ostrogoths or Lombards. Of these possibilities, we can dismiss Visigothic Spain as unlikely: there is no evidence of any kind to link our thirteen *Instructiones* with Spain. The two real contenders are southern Gaul in the early sixth century, when Arianism was still current amongst its Gothic (and perhaps its Burgundian) overlords, prior to the annexation of this whole area by the catholic Franks (in 534 and 536); and Lombard Italy. The first would suit the theory that X was a literal pupil of Faustus; the second the theory that X was Columbanus.

Some further clues as to the likely date of writing may be winkled out from our author's use of Caesarius and Gildas, and from his praise of Faustus of Riez as a *doctor*, on whose authority he could lean.[408] Caesarius was bishop of Arles from 502 to 542. We have no means of knowing in what year he wrote or put together the sermons *Modo fratres carissimi* and *Ad inluminandum*, but two points can be made. First, Caesarius laid an immense emphasis on the importance of preaching. This led him not only to launch into sermons to clergy who visited him, and sometimes to deliver sermons even at matins and vespers,[409] but also to take active steps to disseminate his sermons as widely as possible. He had collections of sermons prepared which he pressed onto passing *sacerdotes*, so that they could make use of them in their churches back at home; and by this means collections of Caesarius's sermons found their way, even within his lifetime, to Francia, Gaul, Italy, and Spain.[410]

A second point, however, is that Caesarius had a very chequered career for the first seven, or even eleven, years of his episcopate. There is some evidence that his succession was disputed.[411] But the main problems arose because Arles was then close to the frontier of the area under Visigothic control, and its Gothic rulers felt threatened by the Burgundians ensconced north of the River Durance, within twenty miles of Arles itself. To make matters worse, Caesarius did not originate in Arles, but in Cavaillon, a city under Burgundian control.[412] The Arian Visigothic masters of Arles therefore found it easy to suspect the catholic bishop, who originated in a Burgundian area, of a readiness to hand

---

[407] According to Gregory of Tours, the Burgundians were Arians (apart from King Sigismund): *Historiae*, II.9, III.praef. (edd. Krusch & Levison, pp. 58, 97). But Gregory's accuracy in this respect has been questioned recently by Wood: *The Merovingian Kingdoms*, p. 45, 'Ethnicity', pp. 58–61.

[408] *Instructio* II.1: 'maioris doctoris auctoritatem quaerentes, sancti scilicet Fausti luculentissimam elegantissimamque doctrinam'.

[409] Cyprian *et al.*, *Vita S. Caesarii* I.17, 59 (ed. Krusch, *Passiones uitaeque*, pp. 463, 481).

[410] *Ibid.* I.55 (ed. Krusch, pp. 479–80).

[411] Klingshirn, 'Church politics', pp. 85–8.

[412] *Vita S. Caesarii* I.3 (ed. Krusch, p. 458); Klingshirn, *Caesarius*, pp. 93–7.

the city over to the Burgundians. Caesarius was accused of treason before the Visigothic king, Alaric, and sent into exile in 505. He was reinstated the next year, but in 507 the Franks killed Alaric and decisively defeated the Visigoths at the battle of Vouillé; and in 508 the Franks and their allies, the Burgundians, followed up this victory by laying siege to Arles. Again Caesarius was accused of treachery, and again released.[413] Stability was restored when the Ostrogothic king, Theoderic, came to the relief of Arles and took it under his own rule. The aftermath of war, however, lasted some years: Arles was flooded with captives whom the victorious Goths had seized, and Caesarius used all the church's treasures in an attempt to redeem them. Late in 513 Caesarius was once again accused, and taken under armed guard to Theoderic himself at Ravenna. Theoderic released him with honour, and thereafter Caesarius's loyalty appears to have gone unquestioned.[414] The upshot of all this, however, is that it seems unlikely that Caesarius would have had the time to organise the copying and dissemination of his sermons before 509, if not 513. Nor, interestingly, does the importance of preaching figure among the canons adopted by the council of Agde, over which Caesarius presided in 506. Thus, although the *Vita S. Caesarii* mentions Caesarius's concern with preaching right from the time of his consecration as bishop,[415] I suspect that the systematic dissemination of his sermons did not begin before the second decade of the sixth century was well under way. Of course, one cannot rule out the possibility that the author of the *Instructiones* was able to read two of Caesarius's sermons within a few years of his consecration; but *ca* 514 is probably a more realistic *terminus a quo* than *ca* 502 for the writing of our thirteen *Instructiones*.

On the dating of Gildas and his *De excidio*, much has been written recently – particularly since the realisation that one should not rely upon the *Annales Cambriae*, which date Maelgwyn of Gwynedd's death to 547.[416] Here, there is space for no more than a bald listing of the chief points from which an approximate date can be deduced, together with my evaluation of them, but without any detailed argument. First, I accept the most widely held interpretation of *De excidio* I.26: viz. that Gildas there says that he was born in the same year as the battle of Badon, which took place some forty-three years before the time of writing.[417] I further accept, as a corollary, that Gildas can hardly have written before *ca* 513; for, if he had been born before 470, he would probably have been able to find out from people of his grandparents' generation roughly what had happened at least as far back as 425.[418] As it is, his dating of Hadrian's wall to

---

[413] Klingshirn, *Caesarius*, pp. 106–10.

[414] *Vita S. Caesarii* I.21–4, 28–32, 36–8, II.8–9 (ed. Krusch, pp. 465–72, 486–7). Cf. also Krusch's introduction (*ibid.*, pp. 435–7); Klingshirn, *Caesarius*, pp. 111–32.

[415] *Vita S. Caesarii* I.15–19, 27 (ed. Krusch, pp. 462–4, 466–7).

[416] Dumville, 'Gildas and Maelgwn', pp. 53–4; O'Sullivan, *The De excidio*, pp. 77–86. A good general survey of Gildas and the problems of interpreting his narrative is given by Sims-Williams, 'Gildas and the Anglo-Saxons'.

[417] *Gildas*, ed. & transl. Winterbottom, pp. 98, 28. See Charles-Edwards, review of *Gildas: New Approaches*, edd. Lapidge & Dumville, pp. 118–19. I assume that Gildas, as was normal for Roman writers, counted inclusively.

[418] For this and other reasons, I cannot regard Higham's chronological suggestions (*English Conquest*, pp. 118–45) as feasible.

the period just before the Romans left Britain,[419] and, perhaps, his silence about Pelagianism,[420] suggest his ignorance of the early fifth century. Perhaps more worrying is that there is good reason to think that Gildas was wrong in dating the introduction of Saxon federates to the second half of the fifth century, since a contemporary Gallic chronicle records that Britain fell under Saxon control *ca* 442. It looks as though Gildas has here mistaken the context of the appeal to Aetius (datable to 454 at the latest) as being one when Britain was threatened by the Picts and Irish, rather than the Saxons, as we may surmise.[421] Even if one accepts Gildas's account and places the arrival of the Saxons mentioned by Gildas in the latter half of the fifth century, one can hardly fit in the sequence of events which followed on the failure of the appeal to Aetius, and which Gildas represents as taking place between then and the battle of Badon, in less than thirty years at the least, and this would give a *terminus a quo* of *ca* 523 for the writing of the *De excidio*.[422]

At this point mention should be made of an argument recently advanced, that because Gildas's Latin is more comparable to that of fifth-century than sixth-century Gallic writers, the date of the *De excidio* should be pushed back to *ca* 500.[423] This, however, does not follow: it would be rash to assume that Latin followed precisely the same course in sixth-century Britain as in sixth-century Gaul. In Gaul, Latin was the universal spoken language, and the current spoken forms began to influence the written forms in the sixth century. For Britain, there may well be truth in the traditional view that because Latin was not the everyday *koine*, it would have been learnt, deliberately, by

---

[419] Cf. Thompson, 'Gildas', p. 206. Someone born in A.D. 465 could have been asking intelligent questions at the age of twelve of someone born in A.D. 400, who would, as Thompson notes, have known that the Romans did not build Hadrian's wall when they left Britain *ca* 410.

[420] It is difficult to know how much significance to attribute to Gildas's silence (and so, presumably, ignorance) about Germanus's mission in 429 to combat Pelagianism in Britain; cf. Thompson, 'Gildas', pp. 211–12, and Markus, 'Pelagianism'.

[421] Stevens, 'Gildas Sapiens', pp. 360–3; Sims-Williams, 'The settlement', pp. 6–15. 'Aetio ter consuli' (*De excidio* I.20) should strictly yield a date between 446 and 454, but see Casey & Jones, 'The date'. Thompson, 'Gildas', pp. 214–15, attempts to reconcile Gildas and the Gallic chronicle by assuming that they are talking of different areas of Britain; but this hypothesis is unconvincing: if Saxon federates had just got so out of hand in southern Britain, surely even the 'proud tyrant' would not have introduced them to the north at that very moment.

[422] Cf. Dumville, 'The chronology', esp. pp. 68–76, 83, who assigns a date of *ca* 500 to the battle of *mons Badonicus*. A date of *ca* 480 is, in my view, the earliest one can date it if one accepts Gildas's placing of the arrival of the Saxons after the appeal to Aetius; while *ca* 500 is probably more realistic.

[423] Herren, 'Gildas', pp. 66–7, 77–8, reading a considerably earlier date into Lapidge's conclusions than Lapidge himself: cf. Lapidge, 'Gildas's education', pp. 48–50. Herren also points out that the Gildasian 'Fragments', which he accepts as genuine, imply that monasticism had become more widespread and had developed further as compared with the impression gleaned of it from the *De excidio*. This is a valid point; but one could still place the *De excidio ca* 535, and the 'Fragments' a generation later, *ca* 565; it does not necessarily require that the *De excidio* be placed as early as *ca* 500.

members of a relatively small social class, who would have learned 'correct' Latin. In any case, the example of Columbanus's *Epistulae* gives the lie to the assumption that Latin developed in the same way and at the same time in Britain and Ireland as in Gaul; for his letters, too, are more reminiscent of late fifth- than late sixth-century Gallic writers,[424] and yet we know that Columbanus was writing *ca* 600. On a related matter, it is also unwise to argue that, because Gildas shows signs of having received a professional training in rhetoric, this necessarily implies that a Roman-type government career was still a possibility in his youth.[425] A literary education, including rhetoric, was regarded as a *sine qua non* by the aristocracy of the late Roman Empire, regardless of whether or not its recipients desired an active career in politics or administration, or simply to enjoy a life of *otium* on their own estates. Thus Gildas's training in rhetoric may be evidence of the survival of Roman upper class values, rather than of Roman structures of government.[426]

A more promising source of light on Gildas's *floruit* is, in my view, provided by his *obit* in the Irish annals. The *Annals of Ulster* have the simple entry *sub anno* 570, 'Gillas obiit', and a similar notice occurs in the other main Irish annal-collections around the same date.[427] I accept the view that the regular recording of Irish events began around the middle of the sixth century, and, in particular, that annals appear to have been kept at Iona since its foundation in 563.[428] Of course, this does not mean that any set of Irish annals which we have today reproduces the early annals without alteration. Sets of annals from various centres have been amalgamated, in places expanded with additional material derived from foreign sources or inserted from their own calculations by Irish chronographers, in places abbreviated, and sometimes reworded, to produce the basis common to all the sets of Irish annals that have come down to us – a basis established in its final form only in the early tenth century.

The crucial question, then, is whether the entry recording Gildas's death was a contemporary one, entered in the late sixth century, or whether it is a later addition. Given the textual history of the Irish annals, this question cannot be answered with absolute certainty. There is, however, a high degree of probability that the Gildas *obit* does indeed go back to a sixth-century record. The bulk of early annal-entries comprises obits of kings and prominent churchmen, brief notices of battles, and mentions of unusual natural phenomena: the weather, disease, and scarcity or abundance of food supplies. Now we know that Gildas was highly regarded as a churchman even within his own lifetime. *Vennianus*, who was probably active in Ireland, asked his advice about monks who left the monasteries where they had been professed, and Columbanus records that he

---

[424] Mohrmann, 'The earliest continental Irish Latin', pp. 216, 219–24, 226–7; Winterbottom, 'Columbanus and Gildas', pp. 310–11.

[425] Lapidge, 'Gildas's education', pp. 41–50.

[426] See Matthews, *Western Aristocracies*, pp. 79–80, 84–5. Cf. my review of *Gildas: New Approaches*, edd. Lapidge & Dumville, pp. 609–10.

[427] *Annals of Ulster*, edd. Mac Airt & Mac Niocaill, I.84; 'Annals of Tigernach', ed. Stokes, p. 149; *Annals of Inisfallen*, ed. Mac Airt, p. 74 (s.a. 567).

[428] See Smyth, 'The earliest Irish annals', esp. pp. 4–21, 33–43.

replied *elegantissime*;[429] and Columbanus himself is a witness to the respect in which Gildas was held by the Irish within twenty or thirty years of his death.[430] Since Gildas was thus regarded as so authoritative a figure within the sixth-century Irish church, it would be odd if his death were not recorded in contemporary Irish annals. Although there is nothing to link Gildas with Iona, our best-attested centre of annalistic activity in the sixth century, his fame, and word of his death, would have reached that monastery: for Iona was in regular touch with Ireland, and links between Ireland and Britain were very close at that period. It is not irrelevant to point out that Columbanus, who came from Bangor in north-east Ireland, knew Gildas's work well.

If Gildas died *ca* 570, and wrote the *De excidio* when he was forty-three, then it is likely that the traditional dating of that work to the early 540s is approximately correct. We could push the *terminus a quo* back to *ca* 530, and envisage Gildas dying at the grand old age of eighty-three; but beyond that, we rapidly reach the limits of plausibility, and even possibility. The definite *terminus ad quem* is supplied by Columbanus's entry into Francia *ca* 591:[431] he must have known Gildas's work before then, as it did not circulate on the Continent outside Brittany. Further, if, as seems reasonably assured, Britain was struck by a fatal epidemic at much the same time as Ireland, *ca* 544x550, then we may reasonably take the former year as our *terminus ad quem*.[432] For Gildas wrote in a period of calm, when the warfare that had ravaged Britain in the days of Ambrosius Aurelianus was no longer remembered – hence, in his view, the absence of any moral restraint on his fellow countrymen. Now, although Gildas was thinking of warfare, I do not think he could have written of his own day as 'aetas tempestatis illius nescia et praesentis tantum serenitatis experta' if a major epidemic were then raging, or indeed if a major epidemic had struck within the last twenty years.[433] For him, *famosa pestis* was a disaster that had occurred some two or three generations previously, and there is no hint that he himself had lived through anything comparable.[434] Nor, if such an epidemic had struck shortly

---

[429] *Epistula* I.7 (ed. & transl. Walker, *Sancti Columbani Opera*, p. 8). Gildas's reply has probably been at least partially preserved as the *Fragmenta Gildae*: see Sharpe, 'Gildas as a Father'. This *Vennianus* may well be identical with the *Vinnianus/Uinniaus* of the penitential: above, pp. 121–3.

[430] Columbanus, *Epistula I* (§§ 6, 7)(ed. & transl. Walker, *ibid.*); cf. Winterbottom, 'Columbanus and Gildas'. Columbanus's acquaintance with Gildas probably derives from his time in Ireland, which he had left *ca* 590.

[431] See Walker, *Sancti Columbani Opera*, pp. x–xii.

[432] *Annales Cambriae*, ed. Morris, *Nennius: British History*, p. 85 (s.a. 537, and cf. also s.a. 547); *Annals of Ulster*, edd. Mac Airt & Mac Niocaill, I.74, 76 (s.aa. 545, 549). See Mac Arthur, 'The identification', pp. 170–5; cf. Biraben & Le Goff, 'La peste', pp. 1491–5, 1500, 1508, who deny that the bubonic plague of the 540s reached Britain and Ireland; but this may simply be because they exclude all references to diseases which are not sufficiently precise to prove that they relate to bubonic plague. Cf. Morris, 'The plague', pp. 213–14, who basically follows Mac Arthur, 'The identification', pp. 169–79.

[433] *De excidio*, I.26.

[434] *Ibid.*, I.2, and 22, placed between the appeal to Aetius and the invitation to the Saxons.

before he wrote, can I envisage how Gildas, preacher as he was, would have failed to point up the link between the Britons' sins and the ensuing epidemic as interpreted from an Old Testament stance, where disease could readily be seen as God's punishment for sin.[435] There is also the point that if, as seems likely, the *Fragmenta Gildae* are genuine, various differences in their portrayal of monasticism as compared with that of the *De excidio* imply that they were written some twenty or more years later than it.[436] That also would rule out a date after the mid-sixth century for the *De excidio* if we accept an *obit* of 570 for Gildas.

On the basis of our foregoing discussion, I would regard *ca* 513 as the earliest date at which the *De excidio* could have been written, and *ca* 588 as the latest possible date; but I would add that there is an extremely strong degree of probability that its composition should be placed between *ca* 530 and *ca* 544. I would further point out that this more precise dating is fully consonant with the attempt to date the *De excidio* on the basis of the rulers apostrophised therein;[437] with the *obit* for Maelgwn of 547 in the *Annales Cambriae*; with the internal logic of Gildas's text;[438] and with the Irish annalistic *obit* for a churchman named 'Uinnianus' who may well be identical with Gildas's correspondent, 'Vennianus'.[439]

The relevance of establishing *termini a quo* for sermons by Caesarius and for Gildas's *De excidio* is obvious. A third way of casting some light on the likely date – and therefore author – of X's thirteen *Instructiones* is to consider his explicit appeal to Faustus of Riez as an authority, on whose words he may draw in establishing a firm basis of faith which will confute the ignorant.[440] Clearly, if we were to take X's words – 'et nos uiles licet commissos sibi docuit' – literally, it would mean envisaging that X was born not much later than *ca* 470: that would allow him to be taught by the aged Faustus when the

---

[435] *De excidio*, II.37–III.109, is full of warnings drawn from the Old Testament about the terrible fate that overtakes those who do evil and are deaf to God's commands. For disease as God's retribution, see *De excidio*, II.39. Sims-Williams is at his least convincing in arguing that, if plague were already rife, Gildas 'would not need to spell the point out' ('Gildas and the Anglo-Saxons', p. 19).

[436] See above, n. 423, and below, n. 439. On the *Fragmenta*, see also Sharpe, 'Gildas as a Father'.

[437] See Dumville, 'Gildas and Maelgwn', pp. 52–9, whose study should be preferred to that of O'Sullivan, *The De excidio*, pp. 87–133: the 'ascending pedigrees' are highly suspect, and one should not apply the rule of thirty years to a generation too rigidly.

[438] See Dumville, 'The chronology'.

[439] The *Annals of Ulster* record the death of 'Finnio maccu [Tel]duib' in 549, and of 'Uinnianus episcopus, m. nepotis Fiatach' in 579 (edd. Mac Airt & Mac Niocaill, pp. 76, 90). For Vennianus, see above, n. 429, and cf. n. 129. Given the difference in perspective between the *De excidio* and the *Fragmenta Gildae*, we should envisage the *Fragmenta* – alias Gildas's response to Vennianus's questions – as being *ca* 20–30 years later than the *De excidio* (Herren, 'Gildas', and above, n. 423). This makes the 579 obit more plausible as that of Gildas's correspondent. For arguments that the two annal obits are the result of duplication of one original sixth-century figure, see Dumville, 'Gildas and Uinniau'.

[440] *Instructio* II.1.

latter returned from exile to his see in 485, probably not long before he died.[441] Equally important, however, is the fact that X's appeal to Faustus as a *doctor* on whose *auctoritas* he may lean implies that he wrote either before the storm about Faustus's *De gratia* broke out in the 520s, or else long afterwards, when all the accusations against Faustus had been forgotten.[442]

The posthumous reputation of Faustus's *De gratia* is an interesting one. Written in 474, at the request of his fellow bishops, it seeks to establish an orthodoxy which avoids the pitfalls both of Pelagianism and of predestinationism; and for the later fifth century it may be regarded as succeeding in its aims, at least as far as the Gallic church was concerned.[443] In 519, however, it was brought to the notice of some heresy-hunting Scythian monks in Constantinople by an African bishop, Possessor, in connection with a different theological controversy; and they lost little time in attacking its teaching as heretical.[444] A deputation of them was sent to the pope, and, while in Rome, they appealed to Fulgentius of Ruspe and other African bishops then living in exile in Sardinia (*ca* December 519). They asked the African bishops first about their main preoccupation, the Incarnation; and secondly, about their understanding of the operation of God's grace. They concluded their letter by anathematizing Pelagius, Caelestius, Julian of Eclanum, 'and especially the books of Faustus the Gallic bishop, . . . which, without a doubt, were written against the official view (*sententia*) of predestination.'[445] When Possessor asked Pope Hormisdas himself about Faustus's *De gratia*, he received an equivocal reply: the pope made it clear that he did not regard Faustus's work as having patristic authority, but neither did he condemn it. If its teaching concurred with sound doctrine, it should be accepted; if not, it should be cast aside.[446] Hormisdas's views were speedily attacked by the Scythian monks, who composed a more detailed critique of Faustus's teaching on grace (A.D. 520).[447]

Meanwhile Fulgentius of Ruspe, the theological spokesman for the African bishops in exile in Sardinia, had produced a response more to the liking of the Scythian monks, which reproduced unadulterated Augustinian views on predestination and grace.[448] What is more, Fulgentius (who was appealed to again by two of the Scythians in 523) followed this up with three books *De*

---

[441] *Ibid.* The date of Faustus's death is not known, but as he became abbot of Lérins in 433/4, he was probably born no later than the first decade of the fifth century. See *Fausti . . . Opera*, ed. Engelbrecht, pp. vi, x–xi.

[442] This general point was first made to me, orally, by Ian Wood.

[443] Markus, 'The legacy', p. 222: 'Something like it was the Gallic church's orthodoxy in the last decades of the fifth century.'

[444] Markus (*ibid.*, pp. 223–7) offers a good, but all too brief, survey of the controversy. The 'prolegomena' to *Maxentii . . . Opuscula*, ed. Glorie, is very useful for its listing and dating of the documents; see esp. pp. xxxiii, xxxvi–xxxvii.

[445] *Epistula Scytharum monachorum ad episcopos*, esp. § 28 (ed. Glorie, *Maxentii . . . Opuscula*, pp. 157–72, esp. 172). For its date, see *ibid.*, p. xxxiii.

[446] *Epistula . . . Hormisdae ad Possessorem* II (11), ed. Glorie, *Maxentii . . . Opuscula*, p. 119. The letter is dated to 13 August 520.

[447] *Responsio*, ed. Glorie, *ibid.*, pp. 123–53.

[448] *Epistula XVII* in *Sancti Fulgentii . . . Opera*, ed. Fraipont, II.563–615.

ueritate praedestinationis et gratiae, and seven books against Faustus's *De gratia* (this latter does not survive). These works cannot be dated precisely, but they were written before the African bishops replied to the Scythians' second letter, which they did some time between 523 and 526.[449]

The controversy over Faustus's *De gratia* had repercussions in southern Gaul, as one might expect. Indeed, it provides the background to the decrees passed by the second synod of Orange under Caesarius's presidency in 529.[450] These have traditionally been seen as firmly establishing Augustinianism, and outlawing 'semi-Pelagianism', as represented by Faustus's teaching (although he is never mentioned by name). Recently, R.A. Markus has reinterpreted Caesarius's work more as an attempt to find a new orthodoxy which, while avoiding any teaching that might smack of Pelagianism, at the same time avoided the extreme predestinarian brand of Augustine's teaching represented by Fulgentius and his fellow African bishops.[451] Even on this modified view, however, it is difficult to believe that anyone who was writing in the later 520s or subsequent decades would appeal to 'the authority of a greater teacher, that is the most lucid and polished doctrine of St Faustus'.[452] We do not know when rumours of the attack on Faustus's orthodoxy first reached southern Gaul; but Sardinia was not far away, and there were also close links with Italy at this time; and, certainly from the moment at which Fulgentius's explicit attack on Faustus became known, an appeal to his authority of the kind made by the author of the thirteen *Instructiones* would have been unthinkable.

At this point we have to recognise that Seebass's theory that X was literally a pupil of Faustus has become very much less likely than it first seemed. The manuscript-evidence is overwhelming in its support for the authorship of Columbanus, and quite at variance with the idea that the sermons were by a literal pupil of Faustus of Riez, who may be presumed to have written in southern Gaul. Here, both the explicit attribution of the sermons to Columbanus, and their early – and continued – presence at Bobbio, are in accord.

Almost as striking is the evidence of the sources used by the author of the sermons. The number of Gallic sources is noteworthy, but this does not favour either hypothesis, since Columbanus himself lived in Gaul for nearly twenty years. More significant are, first, the number of sources used in the *Instructiones* which were also used by Columbanus: besides Jerome's *Epistula XXII*, Suplicius Seuerus's *Dialogi*, Cassian's *Instituta*, and Caesarius of Arles's sermons, we find knowledge of Gildas's *De excidio*, the *Quicunque uult*, and of Caelius Sedulius's *Carmen paschale* – for all of which the very phrases echoed in the *Instructiones* are those which are echoed elsewhere by Columbanus. Other common sources include Gregory of Nazianzus's *Apologia*; and, probably, Gennadius's *Liber ecclesiasticorum dogmatum*, and conceivably

---

[449] This reply is *Epistula XV* in *Sancti Fulgentii . . . Opera*, ed. Fraipont, II.447–57, where these works are alluded to as already written (§ 19: ibid. p. 456). For the date of this letter, see *Maxentii . . . Opuscula*, ed. Glorie, p. xxxvii.

[450] Printed in *Les canons*, edd. Gaudemet & Basdevant, I.154–72; see Markus, 'The legacy', pp. 225–7.

[451] Markus, 'The legacy', esp. pp. 226–7.

[452] *Instructio* II.1 (ed. & transl. Walker, *Sancti Columbani Opera*, p. 68).

Uinniaus's *Penitential*. Secondly, there is the fact that Gildas's *De excidio* is not, to my knowledge, known and cited by any non-Insular or non-Breton author in the Middle Ages. Thirdly, there is the likelihood that the author of the *Instrutiones* knew Gregory the Great's *Homiliae .XL. in euangelia*, and the even stronger likelihood that he also knew Gregory's *Moralia in Iob*. Gregory wrote these works during his pontificate, 590–604: it is thus out of the question that anyone born early enough to have been literally a pupil of Faustus of Riez (died *ca* 490) could have known these works, whereas it is entirely plausible for Columbanus to have known them.[453]

As far as the content of the sermons goes, the evidence we have looked at so far does not point particularly in one direction or the other.[454] Their indications of background heresy could fit either a pupil of Faustus of Riez writing in southern Gaul, or Columbanus, writing in Lombard Italy under an Arian king. Similarly, their comments on nature and free will are consonant with their author being, in some sense, a disciple of Faustus of Riez, but they do not reproduce Faustus's own views precisely. We might also note that, in at least one instance, X used a sermon of Faustus as rehashed by Caesarius of Arles, rather than in the original.[455]

Far more striking is the evidence of the author's Latinity: the combination of an ability to handle Latin skilfully, using several rhetorical techniques where appropriate, but, at the same time, an apparent blind spot where rhythmical *clausulae* are concerned, is something which definitely points in the direction of an Irish author; it should probably be seen as ruling out a continental author, although a British/Breton author might conceivably be a possibility. The evidence of the author's liking for abstruse and Greek-derived words would also fit with Irish, or possibly British, authorship.

In addition to all this evidence, which points firmly in favour of Columbanus's authorship of the sermons, we now have an additional challenge to Seebass's hypothesis. Let us suppose, to give Seebass the benefit of the doubt, that a Briton born *ca* 470 might have learnt Latin adequately, but never been introduced to rhythmical *clausulae*. (This is contrary to the evidence of Gildas's Latinity, but it is arguably unfair to generalise about the teaching of Latin in late-fifth and sixth-century Britain on such inadequate evidence.) Let us further suppose that, at the age of fifteen or sixteen, he was entrusted to the care of the aged bishop of Riez. To make this appear not too implausible, we could point out that Faustus was himself British by birth, and remained in contact with Britain at least up to the 470s.[456] Such a Briton could have stayed in southern Gaul after his mentor's death; and, by *ca* 518, he could easily have become acquainted with some of Caesarius's sermons, as well as with some by his master, Faustus; and he could also have become a senior member of a monastic community in southern Gaul, to whom he might have delivered a course of sermons. We further have to suppose that any resemblances between

---

[453] See above, pp. 110–11, 127.
[454] However, cf. below, pp. 186–8.
[455] See above, pp. 113–15.
[456] Chadwick, 'Intellectual contacts', pp. 224–5.

his sermons and the *Homiliae* and *Moralia* of Gregory the Great are entirely fortuitous.

The crux, however, is how such a monk could also have known Gildas's *De excidio* by *ca* 518. My own view of the matter is that the *obit* of 570 assigned to Gildas by the Irish annals should be taken seriously, and that, combined with the information that Gildas wrote when he was aged forty-three, means that the *De excidio* can scarcely be dated much before 530. Given the current controversy over Gildas's *floruit*, there will doubtless be some scholars who will disagree here; but even then, I fail to see how the *De excidio* could have been written before *ca* 513. Now, to allow only five, or even ten, years to elapse before we find someone in southern Gaul quoting from a work written in Britain is, frankly, to push one's credulity to the limits. Of course it is not impossible. Our author might have kept up links with his homeland just as Faustus did, and he might thus have been sent Gildas's work while the ink was still wet on the page. But such a scenario is unlikely. The *De excidio* is an immensely topical work, and arguably a rather unlikely one to have been sent post-haste to a monk living more than five hundred miles away; and, if such a copy were sent to southern Gaul, we have to admit that it then vanished, leaving no evidence of its existence save for the verbal echoes in X's *Instructiones*.

What makes X's knowledge of Gildas in southern Gaul *ca* 518 so very unlikely is that we are asked to accept two hypotheses combined, both of them unlikely enough on their own. The first is that Gildas's *De excidio* should have been transmitted so many miles to southern Gaul at all, when there is no other evidence that it was ever known on the Continent outside Brittany. The second is that we are asked to accept that this transmission occurred, at best, within ten years of its publication – and at worst, ten years or more *before* its publication! This is where the implications of the author's reference to Faustus as a revered authority become so important. If it were not for that reference, one could have pushed the composition of the *Instructiones* well on in the 530s, or even as late as *ca* 540; and that would have made the author's acquaintance with the *De excidio* somewhat more plausible. As it is, however, we can scarcely envisage the *Instructiones* being written much after *ca* 523, or 525 at the latest, for by then someone in southern Gaul would have heard rumours of the attack on Faustus's orthodoxy. The only alternative to dating the *Instructiones* to before 525 is to put their composition at a considerably later date, when no one was around who could remember the attacks on Faustus's *De gratia*.

One last means of saving Seebass's belief that X was literally a pupil of Faustus of Riez may be tried: we could explore the possibility that the verbal parallels between X and Gildas arise not from X having read Gildas, but from Gildas having read X. Purely on the basis of a comparison between the relevant passages of Latin, this hypothesis is perfectly viable: there is no means of telling which author is borrowing from which. We might suggest, then, that X was able to read Caesarius's two sermons in the second decade of the sixth century, and wrote the *Instructiones ca* 519, shortly before the storm broke over Faustus's *De gratia*. As he himself may be assumed (on this chronology) to have been British, and so perhaps to have maintained some contact with his native land, one could then envisage his *Instructiones* being transmitted to Britain and reaching Gildas before he wrote the *De excidio* in, let us say, the early 540s. There is, however, one fatal flaw in this otherwise viable hypothesis: it requires us to believe that the very sentence which Columbanus borrowed from Gildas in his *Epistula V*, 'Lacrimis in his opus est magis quam uerbis',[457] was one of the only two or three verbal borrowings which Gildas (on this hypothesis) made from the *Instructiones*. That Columbanus should have selected just this sentence from the whole of the *De excidio* by coincidence is scarcely likely; and when we recall that all the manuscripts attribute the thirteen *Instructiones* to Columbanus, we have to admit that to continue thus to maintain Seebass's hypothesis is to fly in the face of the evidence.

We therefore leave Seebass's hypothesis that the sermons were written by a pupil of Faustus with the verdict that, while not impossible, it is utterly implausible. Let us turn instead to consider the claims of Columbanus.

As soon as we try out the hypothesis that Columbanus was the author of the thirteen *Instructiones*, we find that we are going with the grain, not struggling against it. The manuscript-evidence could scarcely be more explicit; the evidence of the sources used is, as we have just recalled, exceedingly strong, and the use both of so many Gallic sources and also of Gildas slots into place. Equally important is the evidence of the Latinity; for we know, from his *Epistulae*, that Columbanus was a writer with a sense of style who was well able to deploy the rhetoricians' techniques, but at the same time a writer who showed no interest in rhythmical *clausulae*. On top of this, we know that Columbanus had a liking for abstruse words, and, in particular, for words which were derived from Greek, and were not in normal Latin use.

Let us turn now to give more detailed consideration to the content of the sermons. One small point immediately suggests that we are on the right lines. As we noted above, the author was clearly writing against a background of some kind of trinitarian heresy; but as well as outspoken condemnation of 'those wicked men', who are presumably heretics, there is also a sense of shame at others who are speculating too freely about the nature of God:[458]

Dei enim tantum de Deo ... credendum est testimonium ... Ceterum disputatio seu ingenium humanum aut aliqua superba sapientia ... de Deo magistra esse non potest, sed sacrilega et impia in Deum praesumenda est. Unde enim reuera quaeso, fratres, illi uani et illi nimis mali et impii ... potuissent inuisibilem Deum unum, Trinitatem coaeternam ... uel usque ad tractationis modum scire, ut non loquar definitionis de Deo finem? His itaque quasi inenarrabilibus ... silendis, de manifesta re et ineffabili Deo placita loqui incipiamus, non praesumentes ut alii, de quibus erubescendum est, de altioribus quaerere ... sed potius de aedificatione animarum nostrarum sermocinantes.

For only God's witness is to be believed about God ... Human argument or skill or vainglorious philosophy ... cannot be our teacher about God, but is to be regarded as sacrilegious and impious to God. For indeed I ask, my brethren, whence could those vain, too wicked and impious men ... have known the one invisible God, the

---

[457] *Epistula* V.12. For the parallels between the *De excidio* and the *Instructiones*, see above, p. 109.

[458] *Instructio* II.1 (ed. & transl. Walker, *Sancti Columbani Opera*, pp. 66–9); cf. above, pp. 134–5.

co-eternal Trinity . . . even up to the standard required for discussion, not to say as far as a finished definition of God? Therefore . . . committing these things to silence as they are unspeakable, let us begin to talk about a matter which is clear and pleasing to the ineffable God, not daring like others, for whom we must feel shame, to seek concerning things too high, . . . but rather preaching on the edification of our souls.

Who are these 'others, for whom we must feel shame'? The author does not seem to be equating them precisely with the heretics, about whom he is rather more outspoken: 'those vain, too wicked and impious men', here; and, in the previous sermon, 'the poisonous and mad delirium of all the heretics'.[459]

If we envisage Columbanus preaching these sermons in northern Italy, as Walker suggested, then everything falls into place.[460] The arrant trinitarian heretics are the Arians; and the 'others, for whom we must feel shame', might then be those who continued to split hairs over the Three Chapters controversy. The origins of this dispute lay far back in the sixth century, in Justinian's attempt to reconcile monophysite sympathisers to the faith as defined at Chalcedon by condemning the 'Three Chapters', writings considered somewhat Nestorian in their leanings. Justinian had got his way at the Fifth Oecumenical Council, held at Constantinople in 553. His efforts, however, had brought nothing but division in the West: the pope had been browbeaten into acquiescence by Justinian, only to find his actions disowned by much of the western church. The patriarchates of Aquileia and Milan, which lay beyond the effective control of the Byzantine government in Italy, were prominent in their opposition. By the time that Columbanus arrived at the Lombard court in the early seventh century, the situation was very confused. While the patriarchate of Aquileia remained staunch in its opposition to the condemnation of the Three Chapters, and therefore in schism with Rome, in the neighbouring patriarchate of Milan allegiances were divided. The patriarch and several suffragans had accepted the papal position; but some bishops remained loyal to the Three Chapters, and this group, which included the queen's religious director, enjoyed the support of Queen Theudelinda. On top of this Theudelinda's husband, King Agilulf, was probably an Arian, and Columbanus could write that the Lombard kings had long trampled on catholicism and consolidated a lapse into Arianism.[461]

Columbanus was profoundly perturbed at the fact that, while Arianism remained a constant threat, the two church groups who were orthodox in their belief were in schism with each other.[462] That he had little grasp of the theological niceties of the situation is suggested by his grouping of Nestorius along with Eutyches and Dioscorus as heretics who had allegedly been accepted by the Fifth Oecumenical Council;[463] but this becomes intelligible

---

[459] *Instructio* I.2 (ed. & transl. Walker, *ibid.*, pp. 60–1).

[460] *Ibid.*, p. xliii.

[461] *Epistula* V.17 (ed. & transl. Walker, *ibid.*, p. 54). For the general background, see Walker, *ibid.*, pp. xxix–xxx; Duchesne, *L'église*, chs. 5 and 6; and Bognetti, *L'età Longobarda*, II.184–302.

[462] See *Epistula V* (esp. § 2).

[463] *Epistula* V.10.

when viewed in the context of contemporary presentations of the dispute, whose coded formulations he was employing.[464] Columbanus's own instinctive loyalty lay with the papacy; and he could not understand why those who were orthodox in their beliefs, as both pro-Three Chapters and pro-papal groups were, could not bury the hatchet and unite:[465]

Ideo cito, carissimi, concordate et conuenite in unum et nolite contendere pro antiquis litibus, sed magis tacete et aeterno silentio ac obliuioni eas tradite; et si qua dubia sunt, diuino iudicio reseruate; quae autem manifesta sunt, de quibus homines iudicare possunt, iuste *sine acceptione personarum* iudicate ... et agnoscite uos inuicem ... Quid uobis aliud defendere praeter fidem catholicam, si ueri Christiani estis utrique? Non enim ego possum scire, unde Christianus contra Christianum de fide possit contendere; sed quidquid dixerit orthodoxus Christianus, qui recte Dominum glorificat, respondebit alter, Amen, quia et ille similiter amat et credit.

Then quickly, my dearest friends, agree and meet together and refuse to argue over ancient quarrels, but rather hold your peace and commit them to eternal silence and forgetting; and if any things are doubtful, reserve them for God's judgement; but the things that are clear, on which men can make decision, decide these justly *without respect for persons*, ... and pardon one another. Why should you uphold anything other than the catholic faith if you are true christians on both sides? For I cannot understand for what reason a christian can strive about the faith with a christian; but whatever has been said by an orthodox christian, who rightly glorifies the Lord, another will reply Amen, because he also loves and believes alike.

Here, as in *Instructio II*, we find a distinction between abstruse debates about the theology of the Godhead, which are best passed over in silence by man and left to God's judgement, and, on the other hand, matters which can properly be discussed or decided by men. In addition to this parallel line of reasoning between Columbanus's *Epistula V* and *Instructio II*, we may also recognise that the theological situation implied by the latter fits early seventh-century Lombardy more accurately than early sixth-century southern Gaul.

There are many other parallels in content between the thirteen sermons and assured works of Columbanus. The most prominent theme in the sermons, that of this life as a road leading to our heavenly homeland above, a place of transit to be passed through, not settled in, occurs in Columbanus's *Epistula II*: 'in uia huius saeculi spatiosa et lata multi ambulantes currunt'; and, further on, 'tota ad caelestia festinet ecclesia. Praestet hoc nobis sua gratuita gratia, ut omnes mundum horreamus et illum solum amemus illumque cum patre et spiritu sancto desideremus, cui gloria in saecula saeculorum. Amen.'[466] Compare *Instructio VIII*: 'Mundum festinanter transeamus, ac ... de caelestibus semper cogitantes terrena despiciamus'; and at its end: 'nitamur ... ut ... de *uia huius saeculi* ad beatam patriam ... transire feliciter possimus, ... de terrenis *ad caelestia*, ... ubi facie ad faciem caelestia uidebimus, et Regem regum

---

[464] Gray & Herren, 'Columbanus and the Three Chapters controversy'.

[465] Columbanus, *Epistula* V.13, with minor alterations to Walker's translation (*ibid.*, pp. 50–1).

[466] *Epistula II* (§§ 7, 8), ed. & transl. Walker, *Sancti Columbani Opera*, p. 20, lines 2–3, p. 22, lines 9–12.

... Dominum nostrum Iesum Christum, *cui gloria in saecula saeculorum. Amen.*[467] A further verbal parallel is supplied by *Instructio XII*: 'amantissime Saluator, ... te *solum amemus*, te solum *desideremus*'.[468] Equally interesting are the thematic and verbal parallels on this general theme between the sermons and the poem *Mundus iste transibit*. The most striking parallel is between the beginning of the poem, 'Mundus iste transibit / Cottidie decrescit' (*or* 'Et cottidie transit'), and *Instructio III* (§ 1): 'Mundus enim transibit et cottidie transit'.[469] Additional verbal similarities between the poem and the passage at the end of *Instructio VIII*, just cited, together with further parallels in thought from other passages in the sermons, are set out by Dieter Schaller elsewhere in this volume.[470] Here, I will note only that the appellation of human life as *uia mortalium* occurs both in the poem and in *Instructio V* (§ 1).[471] The verbal parallels to which Schaller has drawn attention serve to confirm the attribution to Columbanus both of the poem, and, equally, of the sermons.

Another theme in the sermons which has parallels in other works by Columbanus is that of the danger of a wagging tongue, and, in particular, of malicious gossip and backbiting – obviously a particular problem for a community:[472]

Cauendum est itaque dilectionem fraternam studentibus complere loqui ut libet ... dum non solum de iniuriosis sed etiam *de otiosis sermonibus rationem reddemus*. Quapropter studendum est in multis sermonibus non immorari, sed necessaria quaeque proloqui. *Nihil enim suauius est hominibus* ... otiosa passim uerba proferre, et de absentibus detrahere; et ideo qui non possunt dicere, *Dominus dedit mihi linguam eruditam, ut possim sustinere eum qui lassus est uerbo*, taceant, et si quid dicant pacificum sit.

Those who practise the consummation of brotherly love must beware of speaking as they please ... when it is not only for hurtful words, but even for idle ones, that we shall render an account. Wherefore we must make it our practice not to linger over much speaking, but to say the barest minimum. For there is nothing more pleasant for men than ... to utter idle words everywhere, and to criticize the absent; and thus those who cannot say, the Lord has given me a discerning tongue, that I can support him who is weary with a word, should keep silence, and if they say anything, let it be peaceable.

With *loqui ut libet* we might compare Columbanus's insistence that one of the main strands of monastic mortification was 'non lingua libita loqui'.[473] With

---

[467] *Instructio VIII* (*ibid.*, p. 94, lines 30–1, p. 96, lines 19–25). I have italicised the verbal parallels with *Epistula II*.

[468] *Instructio XII.3* (*ibid.*, p. 114, lines 19–21).

[469] *Mundus iste transibit*, 1–2 (ed. Walker, *ibid.*, p. 182). Cf. the discussion of Schaller (below, pp. 242–3), who suggests the emendation 'Et cottidie transit', by analogy with *Instructio III.1* (ed. Walker, *ibid.*, p. 72, lines 23–4). Cf. also *Epistula V.4*, 'mundus iam declinat'.

[470] See below, pp. 252–3.

[471] See Schaller, below, pp. 251–4.

[472] *Instructio XI.2* (ed. & transl. Walker, *Sancti Columbani Opera*, p. 108, lines 16–24, italicising quotations from Matthew XII.36, Gregory of Nazianzus, *Apologia* (§ 1), and Isaiah L.4).

[473] *Regula monachorum*, § 9 (ed. & transl. Walker, *Sancti Columbani Opera*, p. 140, lines 15–16). cf. also *Instructio X.4*, 'si loquamur ut libet' (*ibid.*, p. 104, line 28).

the general condemnation of backbiting we might compare the punishable offence of one 'qui detrahit alicui fratri aut audit detrahentem', which occurs in the *Regula coenobialis* and, with little change, in the *Penitential*.[474] And with the general principle that talking should be restricted to saying what is necessary, we might compare the ruling of the *Regula monachorum*: 'exceptis utilitatibus ac necessariis opus est ut taceatur'.[475] Finally we may compare a passage from the additions to the *Regula coenobialis*, where again silence is enjoined, except for constructive speech:[476]

ut ... mundemur uitio,[477] aedificationemque potius proximorum ... quam delacerationem absentium ... et *otiosa* passim *uerba*, de quibus iusto sumus retributori *rationem reddituri*, ore promamus.

that ... we may be cleansed from vice and that we may utter with the mouth some edification for our neighbours ... rather than abuse of the absent ... and altogether idle words, for which we shall render an account to a just Avenger.

Here the parallel is not restricted to one of content together with the same biblical quotation as in *Instructio XI*, for note the presence of *passim* in both passages. Whether this addition to the *Regula coenobialis* is the work of Columbanus or of one of his near followers does not materially affect the significance of the parallel phrasing, *otiosa passim uerba*, as one can reasonably assume that his near followers would be well acquainted with their founder's sermons.

On the themes of grace and free will, and the need for man to strive in his daily life here if he is to be crowned elsewhere, we find a general similarity in thought, but no verbal parallels between the sermons and writings by Columbanus. Both are emphatic on the need for humility and God's grace. Columbanus writes to his monks: 'let each constantly beseech the help of God with all humility of mind; ... for none merit mercy, save those who confess themselves to be wretched before God, and feel themselves unworthy of salvation through themselves. ...'[478] Or again: 'Therefore, in the midst of so great dangers, although to will and to run is yours, yet it is not yours; for human *uirtus* is not enough to win through to what it wills amid so many opposing forces, unless the Lord's mercy should also provide the will.'[479] Alongside this, however, we find an emphasis on the need for ascetic discipline with which to fight one's foes, and an affirmation of man's freedom:[480]

---

[474] *Regula coenobialis*, § 7; *Paenitentiale*, A10 (both ed. & transl. Walker, *ibid.*, p. 150, line 28, and p. 170, line 20).

[475] *Regula monachorum*, § 2 (*ibid.*, p. 124, line 19).

[476] *Sancti Columbani Opera*, ed. & transl. Walker, p. 168, lines 4–10; cf. Seebass, 'Über die sogennante *Instructiones*', p. 529. The Vulgate text of Matthew XII.36 is as follows: 'Dico autem uobis quoniam omne uerbum otiosum, quod locuti fuerint homines, reddent rationem de eo in die iudicii.'

[477] Cf. *Instructio* II.1 (ed. Walker, *ibid.*, p. 70, line 16): 'Mundemus itaque nos ... ab omni uitiorum labe.'

[478] *Epistula* IV.6 (ed. Walker, *ibid.*, p. 32, lines 8–9, 11–13; p. 33, lines 11–12, 15–17).

[479] *Epistula* IV.7 (*ibid.*, p. 34, lines 11–14). *Virtus* here carries the double meaning of 'strength' and 'goodness, virtue'.

[480] *Epistula* IV.6 (*ibid.*, p. 32, line 31–p. 34, line 8, using Walker's translation with some emendation).

Gradiendum igitur est uia regia ad ciuitatem Dei uiuentis per afflictionem carnis et contritionem cordis, per corporis laborem et spiritus humiliationem, per studium nostrum, officii rem legitimi, non meriti dignitatem et, quod his maius est, per Christi gratiam, fidem, spem et caritatem ... non nescias hostem, et libertatem in medio arbitrii ... Si tollis hostem, tollis et pugnam; si tollis pugnam, tollis et coronam ... si tollis libertatem, tollis dignitatem.

Therefore we must pass by the royal road to the city of the living God, through affliction of the flesh and contrition of the heart, through bodily toil and spiritual humility, through the application which is due from us, not through the worth of our merit; and, what is greater than these, through Christ's grace, faith, hope, and love ... Do not ignore the enemy's strength, and free will in between ... If you remove the foe, you remove the battle also; if you remove the battle, you remove the crown as well ...; if you remove the freedom, you remove the worth.

These sentiments, which show an awareness of the need to avoid a Pelagian self-sufficiency and a desire to acknowledge man's dependence on God's grace, at the same time as stressing the importance of man's own fight against sin, are fully consonant with those of the author of the sermons examined above.[481] This leads naturally on to the point that both the *Instructiones* and also Columbanus's *Epistulae* put a great deal of emphasis on the need for us to fight with our vices here if we are to gain the kingdom of heaven and our heavenly crowns.[482] In both we find a use of Matthew XI.12, interpreted as meaning that one must do battle in order to seize the kingdom of heaven.[483] Further, while Columbanus's undoubted writings contain no onslaught against the human will as outspoken as that at the beginning of *Instructio VII*, in both the *Regula monachorum* and in *Instructio X* we find the idea that the mortification of our wills is an equivalent to literal martyrdom, or at least, the next best thing;[484] in both we find the same two biblical citations linked together, Matthew XXVI.39 and John VI.38, in the context of the mortification of ourselves;[485] in both *Epistula IV* and *Instructio X* there is an emphasis on the true disciples of Christ taking up the cross, and following Christ's example;[486] and in both *Epistula II* and in the sermons, following Christ is seen in terms of embracing humility and poverty – sometimes tellingly termed *nuditas*.[487] Indeed, the brief

---

[481] See above, pp. 135–6.

[482] Cf. *Epistula* IV.6 (just quoted) and *Instructio* X.3 (quoted above, p. 136), as well as *Instructio* II.3.

[483] Cf. *Epistula* IV.2 and *Instructio* X.3 (ed. & transl. Walker, *Sancti Columbani Opera*, p. 26, lines 15–20, and p. 102, line 35–p. 104, line 2).

[484] *Regula monachorum*, § 9 (*ibid.*, p. 140, line 8): 'hanc martyrii felicitatem'; *Instructio* X.2 (*ibid.*, p. 102, lines 13–16): 'uita ... pro Christo martyrizantibus perdatur; aut si talis beatitudinis desit occasio, non tamen uoluntatum deerit mortificatio, *Ut qui uiuit, non sibi uiuat, sed ei qui pro ipso mortuus est*'. Cf. also *Instructio* X.3 (*ibid.*, p. 104, lines 13–22) and *Epistula* II.3 (*ibid.*, p. 12, line 31–p 14, line 2).

[485] *Regula monachorum*, § 9, and *Instructio* X.3.

[486] *Epistula* IV.6 and *Instructio* X.3.

[487] Cf. *Epistula II* (§§ 3, 8) and *Instructio* X.4 (Christ as *Rex humilis*); and, on *nuditas*, cf. *Epistula* II.8, *Instructio* III.4, *Regula monachorum* § 4 (ed. & transl. Walker, *Sancti Columbani Opera*, p. 20, lines 16–17; p. 78, line 9; p. 126, line 21).

summary of the monk's task that is given in *Regula monachorum* (§ 4) aptly summarises the basic content of the series of thirteen sermons: 'nakedness and disdain of wealth is the first perfection of monks; the second is the cleansing from vices; the third, the most perfect and perpetual love of God and unceasing affection for things divine, which follows on the forgetfulness of earthly things.'[488]

Another feature in common between the sermons and works that are undoubtedly by Columbanus is that both emphasise the point that it is no use our professing ourselves to be followers of Christ, unless we actually put his commands into practice; and in both we find a linking of John XIV.15, 'If you love me, keep my commandments', and John XV.12, 'This is my commandment, that you love one another, even as I have loved you.'[489]

Other themes common to the sermons and to other genuine works of Columbanus include the need to examine ourselves daily: a need urged in *Instructio IX*, and legislated for in the *Regula coenobialis*;[490] and, linked to that, the idea that one should never need to repent, because one should live the whole time in such a way that one avoids ever committing wrongs in the first place. The basic idea is found in Gennadius's *Liber ecclesiasticorum dogmatum*, whence the first sentence of Columbanus's *Penitential* is lifted bodily: 'Paenitentia uera est paenitenda non admittere'; and this helps one to interpret a passage in *Instructio III* praising the man, 'qui sic uiuit, ut numquam aut paeniteat aut non paenituerit'; 'who lives in such a way that he may never either [have cause to] repent or shall not have [had cause to] repent'.[491]

These are the main themes which are found both in the sermons and in Columbanus's genuine works. We should note both the general congruence of subject matter and approach – so much so that most of the key themes dealt with in the sermons seem to occur in Columbanus's undoubted works; and, secondly, we should note that there are some verbal similarities, and often a preference for the same biblical quotations. The former might be put down to both Columbanus and the author of the sermons sharing in a common western ascetic tradition, nourished on Cassian and Jerome; but the latter cannot be disposed of in that way, and does favour the view that Columbanus himself wrote the sermons.

This view is confirmed when we look at the use of the same expressions recurring both in the sermons and in definite Columbanian works. Compare 'Importuna postulo et magna sciscitor, quis nesciat?', from *Epistula I* of Columbanus, and 'Magna quidem posco, quis nesciat?', from *Instructio XIII*.[492]

---

[488] *Ibid.*, p. 126.

[489] Cf. *Epistula II* (§§ 3, 8) and *Instructio* XI.1; cf. also *Instructio* II.3.

[490] *Instructio* IX.2: 'nosmetipsos cottidie discutiamus' (ed. & transl. Walker, *Sancti Columbani Opera*, p. 100, line 6). *Regula coenobialis*, § 1 (*ibid.*, pp. 142, 144–6). Cf. *Instructiones* III.3 and VI.2, which urge one to live as though one had to die each day.

[491] Columbanus, *Paenitentiale*, A1 (ed. Walker, *ibid.*, p. 168), quoting Gennadius, *Liber ecclesiasticorum dogmatum*, § 23, ed. Turner, 'The *Liber*', p. 94. *Instructio* III.2 (ed. Walker, *ibid.*, p. 74); I cannot follow Walker's translation of this passage.

[492] *Epistula* I.9 and *Instructio* XIII.3 (both ed. Walker, *ibid.*, p. 10, line 21, and p. 118, lines 31–2). As Wright has shown (above, pp. 80–2), Caelius Sedulius's *Carmen*

From the same two writings comes also a very similar use of John IV.14. In his letter to Pope Gregory (*Epistula I*), Columbanus expresses an eagerness to visit him, 'ut illam spiritalem uiui fontis uenam uiuamque undam scientiae caelitus fluentis ac *in aeternam uitam salientis* haurirem'. In *Instructio XIII*, the author is looking forward to heaven: 'fontem uitae, *fontem aquae* uiuae . . . quaeramus, ut ibi bibamus *aquam* uiuam et *salientem in uitam aeternam*'.[493] Similarly compare *Epistula IV* (§ 4), 'angustiae undique sunt', with *Instructio VII* (§ 2), 'angustiae mihi undique', both drawing on Daniel XIII.22, 'angustiae sunt mihi undique'.[494] Again, both *Instructio XI* (§ 1) and *Regula monachorum* (§ 6) cite John IV.24.[495]

A fondness for repeating particular passages is not confined to biblical citations. We have already noted that the phrase in *Instructio XI* (§ 3), 'lacrimis in his opus magis quam uerbis est', which derives from Gildas, recurs in Columbanus's *Epistula V*, 'lacrimis in his opus est magis quam uerbis';[496] that the phrase in *Instructio I* (§ 2), 'unitatem in trinitate et trinitatem in unitate', which derives from the *Quicunque uult*, recurs in *Epistula III* (§ 2) as 'unum Deum esse in trinitate et trinitatem in unitate';[497] and that the tag, 'cui pauca non sufficiunt, plura non proderunt', which occurs in *Instructiones I* and *III* and *Epistula VI*, also occurs in attenuated form in Columbanus's *Regula monachorum*, 'cui sufficientia non sufficiunt.'[498] We may add a number of expressions which can often be found in other authors, but which are still of interest because they recur both in the *Instructiones* and in genuine Columbanian works: *unusquisque se consideret*;[499] *Deo auxiliante* and variants (typical of Caesarius of Arles);[500] *diuisa est* (or *sunt*);[501] and *mirum in modum* (a favourite of Sulpicius Seuerus).[502] The use of intercalated *quaeso* (or variants) and of such phrases as *cum haec ita sunt* has already been noted above as occurring both in Columbanian works and in the sermons.[503]

Pace the Faustus passage in *Instructio II*, it is difficult to see how the thirteen sermons could display their Columbanian authorship more convincingly than they have in the course of this study. Each different angle that we have tried gives the same result: that of the manuscripts, of the sources, of the latinity,

---

paschale lies behind the passage in *Instructio* XIII.3; and, very distantly, behind the other one, although that is far closer to *Instructio* XIII than to Sedulius.

[493] *Epistula* I.8 and *Instructio* XIII.2 (and cf. XIII.3), italicising citations from John IV.14 (ed. Walker, *ibid.*, p. 10, lines 3–4, p. 118, lines 21–3, and cf. lines 27–31).

[494] *Sancti Columbani Opera*, ed. & transl. Walker, p. 28, line 27; p. 92, line 10.

[495] *Ibid.*, p. 106, line 12; p. 128, line 18.

[496] *Epistula* V.12 (*ibid.*, p. 50, lines 20–1); cf. above, p. 109 and n. 66.

[497] See above, p. 111 and nn. 80, 155.

[498] See above, p. 98 and nn. 21, 23.

[499] *Epistula* II.3 and *Instructio* X.4 (*Sancti Columbani Opera*, ed. & transl. Walker, p. 14, lines 10–11, and p. 104, line 23).

[500] *Epistula* IV.2 and *Instructio* II.2 (*ibid.*, p. 26, line 32, and p. 70, line 15; cf. also p. 54, lines 15, 17; p. 60, line 7; and p. 94, lines 4–5).

[501] *Instructio* XI.2 and *Regula monachorum*, § 8 (*ibid.*, p. 108, lines 3–4; p. 134, lines 14–15).

[502] *Epistula* IV.6 and *Instructio* IV.1 (*ibid.*, p. 30, line 29 and p. 80, line 11).

[503] See above, p. 142 and nn. 233–6.

and of parallels, both verbal and in content, with other genuine works by Columbanus. In effect, the Faustus passage is isolated in being the only piece of evidence which favours Seebass's view that the sermons were by a literal pupil of Faustus, and not by Columbanus. What is more, we have seen that various pointers, in particular a combination of the use of Gildas together with the author's respect for Faustus as a theological authority, do in fact render Seebass's theory very improbable. It is, surely, time to return to the Faustus passage and see whether his interpretation of it is the only valid one.

The context of the Faustus reference is set by the passage quoted earlier, insisting that humankind should not speculate about the mysteries of the Godhead.[504] Unlike the 'others, for whom we must feel shame', our author proposes to deal with a more accessible matter, 'the edification of our souls':[505]

non primum nostrae paruitatis fundamenta iacere praesumimus,
alicuius maioris doctoris auctoritatem quaerentes,
sancti scilicet Fausti luculentissimam elegantissimamque doctrinam,
de cuius dictis pauca ad initiandum opus nostrum satis conuenienter elegimus,
upote qui de eisdem monitionibus, de quibus dicere cupimus,
et nos uiles licet commissos sibi docuit,
et quasi tempore et merito et scientia me prior,
quasi pro me impugnaturus ignaros quosque et ignauos
prius loquatur.

At the outset we do not dare, in our insignificance, to lay the foundations,
seeking the authority of a greater teacher,
that is, the most excellent and polished teaching of the holy Faustus,
from whose words we have chosen a few, suitable enough, for beginning our work,
since he, from the same admonitions, from which we wish to speak,
both taught us, who, though worthless, had been entrusted to him,
and also, as he is before me in time, merit and learning,
let him speak first,
as if to fight on my behalf against all heedless and idle people.

The sentence builds towards the third line as printed here: the emphasis falls on the excellence of Faustus and his teaching, not on the relationship of X to his teacher. It is the latter, however, which concerns us here. The problem lies with the clause, 'qui ... nos uiles licet commissos sibi docuit'. The word *docuit* on its own would present no great difficulty: masters are able *docere* through books as well as face to face.[506] It is the *commissos sibi* which makes us assume that the teaching must have been done in person. This, however, is where Laporte's study is so helpful.[507] We live in a world where, if we say that we 'have been entrusted to' a teacher, we probably mean it literally. But literary conventions in late antiquity and the early middle ages were very different from ours; and one way in which scholarship has advanced since the

---

[504] See above, pp. 131, 134, 186–7.

[505] *Instructio* II.1 (ed. Walker, *Sancti Columbani Opera*, p. 68). I have followed the example of Tosi ('Arianesimo Tricapitolino', p. 43) in arranging the quotation in lines, as it helps to clarify a somewhat complex, but skilfully written, sentence.

[506] Cf. Tosi, *ibid.*, pp. 45–6.

[507] 'Étude d'authenticité [*Revue Mabillon* 45 (1955)]', pp. 21–3.

last century is in the realisation that we must not take everything that was written then at face value, but that we must learn to recognise what literary conventions an author of that period followed; only then are we in a position to understand aright what he has written.

Laporte has drawn attention to three cases where it is patently obvious that the author cannot have meant what he said literally.[508] One of these concerns Jerome, who more than once writes such a phrase as 'audiui autem quemdam Hebraeum', when in point of fact he himself had *not* heard what he reports from a Jew in person; all he is doing is relaying to us what he has read in Origen's homilies: it was Origen, not Jerome, who had heard the Jew. A second example comes in a letter from Theoderic (written by Cassiodorus) to Boethius, which says, 'Atheniensium scolas, longe positus, introisti', when actually Boethius never went to Athens in person: it presumably means that he engaged in the sort of scholarship associated with Athens. A third example is the one cited above,[509] where Venantius Fortunatus addresses the contemporary (i.e. sixth-century) bishop of Poitiers, Pascentius, as '[te] quem Hilarius ab ipsis cunabulis ante sua uestigia quasi peculiarem uernulam familiariter enutriuit' – Hilary of Poitiers having lived in the fourth century, over two hundred years before Pascentius. This particular example is very relevant for us, because it does imply that Hilary brought up Pascentius himself, in person; and yet we know that such cannot have been the case. Now Columbanus, at the time when (I would argue) he preached the thirteen sermons, had been living on the Continent for between twenty and twenty-five years. He was an educated man, and there is no reason to suppose that he was ignorant of the literary conventions followed by Venantius Fortunatus, his exact contemporary. What is more, it is certainly possible, perhaps even probable, that Columbanus actually knew Venantius's *Vita S. Hilarii*.[510] Venantius Fortunatus was, after all, the most highly regarded writer in Gaul during Columbanus's sojourn there;[511] Columbanus knew Hilary's *De trinitate*, took a forthright stand against Arianism, and had a high regard for St Martin,[512] all of which might argue for an interest in the life of Hilary, the hammer of Arianism and Martin's mentor. Further, Ionas of Bobbio certainly knew of Venantius's *Vita S. Hilarii* when he came to write his Life of Columbanus and his disciples.[513]

---

[508] *Ibid.*, pp. 21–3.

[509] See above, pp. 95–6.

[510] The case for his having known Fortunatus's hymns while he was at Bangor is, however, unconvincing: see Stancliffe, 'Venantius Fortunatus, Ireland, and Jerome', forthcoming in *Peritia* 10 (1996), pp. 91–7.

[511] Cf. Wallace-Hadrill, *The Frankish Church*, pp. 82–7; George, *Venantius Fortunatus*.

[512] Ionas, *Vita S. Columbani*, I.22 (ed. Krusch, *Ionae Vitae Sanctorum*, p. 95). Note also Columbanus's high regard for those who maintain their asceticism while active in the world: 'excepta austeriore adhuc uita quae maiorem habet mercedem; *ubi* enim *durior pugna, ibi gloriosior* inuenitur *corona*' (*Epistula* II.8, ed. & transl. Walker, *Sancti Columbani Opera*, p. 20, lines 24–5). Since the italicised passage is a verbal quotation from Sulpicius Seuerus, *Dialogi*, I.xii.3 (ed. Halm, *Sulpicii Seueri libri*, p. 164), it is likely that St Martin was in Columbanus's mind.

[513] Ionas, *Vita S. Columbani*, I, praef. (ed. Krusch, *Ionae Vitae Sanctorum*, pp. 65–6).

I would suggest, then, that Columbanus might well have known Venantius Fortunatus's preface, where Pascentius is represented as the nursling of St Hilary; and that even if he did not know this work, as he lived and wrote in the same milieu as Venantius Fortunatus, he might well have used literary conventions similar to his. Certainly, when trying to interpret the words 'nos uiles licet commissos sibi docuit', Venantius Fortunatus's usage should be given precedence over our own *a priori* twentieth-century theories as to what these words must mean.

Besides all the evidence adduced above for holding that *Instructio II* should, like the rest of the series, be ascribed to Columbanus,[514] there are a couple of additional pointers that indicate the correctness of this approach. First, the problem sentence itself, with its reference to Faustus, bears all the marks of Columbanus's hand: *nostra paruitas*, as applied to himself, occurs not just here, but also in his *Epistulae I* and *III*,[515] while *nos uiles licet* is also found in *Epistula II*.[516] Secondly, the author says he is going to quote from the very admonitions (or 'homilies') from which Faustus taught him. This on its own should, perhaps, have put the observant on their guard, and made them wonder whether the teaching did not take place through the medium of the written word, rather than through face to face encounter.[517] It certainly lends itself to that interpretation.

There are other ambiguities in our problem sentence. One point, recently noted by Tosi, is that the author switches from the first person plural to the first person singular in the last three lines. Is this significant? Tosi would interpret it as meaning that the author associated the whole religious community with him in the utterances written in the first person plural, and then turned to the things which concerned him alone.[518] I should be inclined to attribute less importance to the switch from plural to singular, and to see Columbanus speaking for himself throughout. In the sentence just before the extract we are considering, he writes: 'de manifesta re . . . loqui incipiamus . . . de aedificatione animarum nostrarum sermocinantes',[519] when clearly it is he alone who is going 'to begin to speak', and to preach. On the other hand, the use of the plural may be at

---

[514] Note particularly the probable citation of Gildas (and the certain citation of Gildas in the closely linked *Instructio I*), and the lack of rhythmical *clausulae*, which are no more in evidence in *Instructio II* than in any of the others: above, pp. 155–7.

[515] *Epistula* I.6, III.2 (ed. & transl. Walker, *Sancti Columbani Opera*, p. 8, line 24 and p. 24, lines 4–5); cf. Laport, 'Étude d'authenticité [*Revue Mabillon* 45 (1955)]', pp. 13, 23.

[516] *Epistula* II.9 (ed. & transl. Walker, *ibid.*, p. 22, line 13).

[517] Cf. Tosi, 'Arianesimo Tricapitolino', pp. 44–5, who points out that a written text, such as he thinks is implied by the word *doctrina*, would provide an objective basis from which Columbanus could proceed, which could be checked by anyone. This, however, implies that Columbanus was going to write about contentious issues, which is scarcely the case – unless one regards *Instructio II* (§ 2) as 'semi-Pelagian'. After the first section, *Instructio II* does not contain anything against the arrogant theological disputants attacked there. Contrast Tosi, 'Arianesimo Tricapitolino', p. 47.

[518] Tosi, *ibid.*, pp. 44, 45, 47.

[519] *Instructio* II.1.

least partially deliberate, as a way of the preacher identifying with his congregation, not setting himself over against it; and it could be that the whole community had, say, been hearing some of Faustus's homilies (including *Ad monachos IV* and *VIII*) read out loud.

After this lengthy discussion, how should we, then, interpret the Faustus passage in *Instructio II*? It is certain that the Faustus named there is the fifth-century bishop of Riez, and the author of the homilies *Ad monachos* from which our author quotes. Our author clearly views this Faustus as a *doctor*, a teacher of authority, whom he regards with great respect: he is superior in merit and learning, as well as being his senior. Further, he has learnt from the very homilies from which he quotes. But, in view of the overwhelming quantity of evidence that Columbanus was indeed the author of *Instructio II*, and in view of the fact that the Pascentius parallel makes it clear that expressions such as 'quem Hilarius . . . familiariter enutriuit' do not necessarily mean that there was any literal, physical bond between master and disciple, I would argue that Laporte was right in 1955: that Columbanus was himself the disciple of Faustus, but that the bond was forged by Columbanus finding inspiration in his writings, not by a literal, physical discipleship. I would add that this interpretation avoids the problem encountered by Seebass's theory, about how someone writing post-Gildas could have acclaimed Faustus as a *doctor* and authority to be deferred to; for news of the controversy over Faustus's *De gratia* probably never reached Britain and Ireland, and the memory of it would have faded on the Continent by the time that Columbanus was writing.

Why does Faustus seem to have been so much more important to Columbanus than were any of the other authors from whom he quotes? We cannot answer that question with certainty, although we can hazard some suggestions. It may be that Faustus's works were highly valued by Insular monks, and that Columbanus first encountered the homilies *Ad monachos* in Ireland, in his formative years. He might, for instance, have been given them to read by Sinilis or Comgall.[520] Certainly we know that at least some of Faustus's works were transmitted back to Britain (or Brittany) during the fifth century;[521] and also that the British church retained some kind of tradition about Faustus, himself a Briton by birth, however garbled and imaginatively developed that tradition later became.[522] Equally, relations between the British and Irish churches were very close in the fifth and sixth centuries.[523] Given the massive loss of early mediaeval manuscripts from Ireland, we should not be surprised if no works by Faustus have been handed down in an Insular manuscript-tradition. We might, however, expect to be able to trace verbal echoes of Faustus's works in other texts written by Insular churchmen in this period, and I am not aware of any; but this could be because scholars have overlooked

---

[520] Cf. Ionas, *Vita S. Columbani*, I.3–4 (ed. Krusch, *Ionae Vitae Sanctorum*, pp. 69–70).

[521] Chadwick, 'Intellectual contacts', pp. 224–5. Given the close contacts then existing between Britain and Brittany, it makes little difference in which of the two the 'Britannis tuis' were then resident.

[522] *Historia Brittonum*, § 48 (ed. Morris, *Nennius*, p. 74).

[523] Sharpe, 'Gildas as a Father'.

them – something which could easily occur if Faustus's impact was made through sermons, whose original author has often gone unknown.

A slight variation would be to suggest that some of Faustus's sermons were transmitted from Gaul to Ireland in the course of the sixth century in a collection of homilies emanating from Caesarius's Arles – a collection which contained both sermons by Faustus, as revised by Caesarius, and others composed by Caesarius himself. We might then suggest that it was this mixed collection which made such an impact on Columbanus in his formative years. (This would tie in with the fact that Columbanus in the *Instructiones* used a sermon based on one by Faustus not in its original Faustian form, but as edited by Caesarius.[524]) Such collections do exist. One such, discussed above,[525] included four of the Gallic Eusebian homilies *ad monachos* as well as five Caesarian sermons. Another collection, also discussed above, is that contained in the 'Codex Durlacensis';[526] and this particular homiliary is of considerable interest in the present context for two reasons:[527] because of its selection of homilies, and because of its attributions. If we look first at the contents of the 'Codex Durlacensis' homiliary,[528] it is interesting to note that its twenty-two homilies include Caesarius's *Sermo CXCIV*, which was known to Columbanus before he left Ireland,[529] and also Caesarius's *Sermones LVIII* and *CCXV* (*Modo fratres carissimi* and *Ad inluminandum*), which were used extensively in the *Instructiones*. Secondly, this homily-collection attributes nine out of its twenty-two homilies to 'Faustinus', the rest being anonymous.[530] If Columbanus had encountered a similar collection, he could easily have jumped to the conclusion that all the sermons in it were by the same author, Faustinus or Faustus; and if he also knew of the sermons *ad monachos*, which now form part of the Gallic Eusebian homily-collection, as works of Faustus, then we can see why he would have regarded this 'Faustus' so highly. For the combined influence of Caesarius and Faustus, above all of Caesarius's sermon *Ad inluminandum*, made an important contribution to the series of thirteen *Instructiones*.

Columbanus's words in *Instructio II*, however, do not necessarily mean that he encountered Faustus's writings in Ireland, or in his youth; he might have given prominence to Faustus for some reason specifically related to the circumstances under which he preached his series of thirteen sermons, which is

---

[524] The sermon in question is Caesarius's *Sermo LVIII*: see above, pp. 113–15.

[525] See above, p. 119.

[526] Morin, 'Critique', pp. 51–8; Morin, *Sancti Caesarii Arelatensis Sermones*, pp. lxxiii–lxxv. See above, pp. 112–13.

[527] Perhaps one should add a third: that the manuscript of this homiliary, now Karlsruhe, Badische Landesbibiothek, MS. 340, which is written in an Anglo-Saxon script of *ca* 900, may have been copied at Sankt Gallen, a monastery with Columbanian links: see Morin, *Sancti Caesarii Arelatensis Sermones*, p. lxxv.

[528] As n. 526.

[529] See above, n. 153. I regard Columbanus's authorship of *Precamur patrem* as assured (see Lapidge, 'Columbanus', and below, pp. 255–63), and that poem's use of Caesarius's *Sermo CXCIV* as assured (see Curran, *The Antiphonary*, p. 53); cf. Stancliffe, 'Venantius Fortunatus'.

[530] Morin, 'Critique', pp. 52–8.

now irrecoverable: for instance, if his community had recently been reading these sermons, as we mooted above. One point that may be worth making is that early manuscripts of some of the Gallic Eusebian homilies *Ad monachos*, of Faustian origin, survive both from Bobbio and Sankt Gallen; indeed, they are amongst the earliest manuscripts of these sermons in existence.[531] True, Sankt Gallen, Stiftsbibliothek, MS. 226, a seventh-century papyrus manuscript, seems to have been written in southern France; in its present incomplete state it contains the sermons *Ad monachos II* and *III*, but it might once have included others.[532] Two other manuscripts, however, one from Sankt Gallen and one from Bobbio, were probably copied in those monasteries. They are both of eighth-century date: that from Sankt Gallen contains *Ad monachos IV*, *V*, *VI*, *IX*, and (separate from the others) *III*;[533] that from Bobbio, copied in Irish minuscule, contains most of *Ad monachos III* and *IV*.[534]

Whether Columbanus encountered Faustus's sermons in Ireland or in Gaul, however, makes no difference to our conclusion: that Columbanus himself was the author of all the thirteen sermons which we have been considering; and that he composed them, as a series, for his monks in northern Italy towards the end of his life, between his arrival in Lombardy late in 612 and his death in 615. Once correctly attributed, these sermons take their place as the only coherent exposition of Irish ascetic spirituality to have come down to us from the formative period of early Irish monasticism. They also provide us with an insight into the religious inspiration of one of Ireland's greatest and most forceful *peregrini*.[535]

---

[531] But also see above, pp. 119–20.

[532] Lowe, *Codices*, VII, no. 929.

[533] Sankt Gallen, Stiftsbibliothek, MS. 194; see Lowe, *Codices* VII, no. 917.

[534] Napoli, Biblioteca Nazionale, MS. Vindobonensis lat. 2 (formerly 16), fos 71r–75v, from Bobbio; see Lowe, *Codices*, III, no. 394.

[535] I dedicate this study to the memory of Richard Hunt, who generously helped to ground me in some of these areas of scholarship when I was in Oxford. The paper itself is in part the product of an Isabel Fleck Research Fellowship at Durham University, and I would like to thank most warmly Lord Fleck, and the Research Foundation and History Department of Durham University, for thus enabling my research. It has grown out of a lecture to theology students at Durham University, given in 1986, and I am grateful to the Theology Department for thus providing the ultimate stimulus. I would also like to thank Mr Kieran Devine, of Queen's University, Belfast, for providing me with a computer concordance of the works edited in Walker's *Sancti Columbani Opera* and of Gildas's *De Excidio*. After this study was completed in August 1991, there was a delay before it went to press; but some updating was possible in the autumn of 1995.

APPENDIX

Index of non-biblical works cited in the thirteen Instructiones

[NOTE: Reminiscences which seem probable, but where verbal parallels are insufficient to prove a direct citation, have been placed within square brackets; for discussion, see above, pp. 105–26. Page and line numbers for the *Instructiones* refer to *Sancti Columbani Opera*, ed. & transl. Walker; editions of sources are cited in relevant footnotes.]

Basil

Regula (trans. Rufinus)[1]

Regula (trans. Rufinus) 2, 63 (p. 17)	*Instr.* XI.1 (p. 106, lines 19–20)
[*Regula* (trans. Rufinus) 2, 68 (p. 18)	*Instr.* XI.1 (p. 106, lines 23–6)]

Caesarius of Arles

Sermones[2]

Serm. III: see *Quicunque uult*

[*Serm.* IX (pp. 46, 48)	*Instr.* I.1, 4 (p. 60, line 3, p. 64, lines 19–20)][3]
Serm. LVIII.1 (p. 255)	*Instr.* IX.1–2 (p. 98, lines 13–17, 23–5)
[*Serm.* LVIII.1 (p. 255, lines 16–17)	*Instr.* IX.2 (p. 100, lines 5, 9–10)]
[*Serm.* LVIII.3 (p. 256, lines 15–16)	*Instr.* IX.2 (p. 100, lines 6–7)]
[*Serm.* LVIII.5 (p. 257, lines 27–8)	*Instr.* II.3 (p. 70, line 37)]
[*Serm.* CLXXXVI.3 (p. 759, lines 5–7)	*Instr.* V.1 (p. 84, lines 12–13)]
[*Serm.* CLXXXVI.3 (p. 759, lines 9–12); cf. also *Serm.* CCXV.5	*Instr.* VIII.2 (p. 96, lines 7–9)]
[*Serm.* CLXXXVI.4 (p. 760, lines 5–7)	*Instr.* VI.1 (p. 86, lines 19–21); cf. also I Tim. VI.7–8]
Serm. CCXV.2 (p. 856, lines 19–20)	*Instr.* VII.2 (p. 92, line 21)
Serm. CCXV.3 (p. 857, lines 4–5)	*Instr.* V.2 (p. 86, lines 5–6)
Serm. CCXV.4 (p. 857, lines 20–1)	*Instr.* V.2 (p. 86, lines 1–2)
Serm. CCXV.4 (p. 857, lines 25–6)	*Instr.* IV.3 (p. 82, lines 23–4)
[*Serm.* CCXV.5 (p. 858, lines 5–6; cf. also *Serm.* CLXXXVI.3	*Instr.* VIII.2 (p. 96, lines 8–9)]

---

[1] *Basili Regula a Rufino Latine uersa*, ed. Zelzer.
[2] *Sancti Caesarii Arelatensis sermones*, ed. Morin.
[3] Alternatively, these parallels could equally be from Gallic Eusebius, *Homiliae IX* and *X*; cf. above, pp. 117–18.

Cassian

De institutis[4]

De institutis IV.38 (p. 74, lines 21–3)   *Instr.* IV.2 (p. 80, lines 36–7)

Faustus of Riez

See under Gallic Eusebius, and cf. discussion above, pp. 118–26.

Gallic Eusebius

Homiliae[5]

[*Hom.* IX.3 (p. 101, line 94)   *Instr.* I.4 (p. 64, line 19)][6]

[*Hom.* X.1 (p. 113, line 2)   *Instr.* I.1 (p. 60, line 3)][7]

[*Hom.* XXXVIII.4 (p. 443, line 142)   *Instr.* III.2, 4 (p. 74, line 13; p. 78, line 18)]

Hom. XXXIX.4 (p. 460, lines 84–5)   *Instr.* II.2 (p. 68, lines 30–1)

Hom. XXXIX.4 (p. 461, lines 92–3)   *Instr.* II.2 (p. 68, lines 32–3)

Hom. XLIII.1–2 (pp. 511–12, lines 1–22)   *Instr.* II.2 (p. 68, lines 14–30)

Hom. XLIII.4 (p. 513, lines 56–7)   *Instr.* II.2 (p. 70, lines 12–14)

Hom. XLIII.4 (p. 514, lines 65–6)   *Instr.* II.2 (p. 68, lines 31–2)

[*Hom.* XLIII.5 (p. 515, lines 88–9)   *Instr.* XI.2 (p. 108, lines 25–6)]

Gennadius

Liber ecclesiasticorum dogmatum[8]

[*Liber eccles. dog.* § 54 (p. 99)   *Instr.* XI.1 (p. 108, line 13)]

Gildas

De excidio Britanniae[9]

[*De excidio* II.21, 4 (p. 96, lines 14–15)   *Instr.* II.3 (p. 72, line 13)]

De excidio II.26, 4 (p. 99, line 13)   *Instr.* I.2 (p. 60, line 21)

De excidio III.108, 4 (p. 140, lines 26–7)   *Instr.* XI.3 (p. 110, line 6)

Gregory the Great

Homiliae .XL. in euangelia[10]

[*Hom. in euang.* I.i.3 (col. 1079D)   *Instr.* V.1 (p. 84, lines 15–16)]

---

[4] *Iohannis Cassiani, De institutis coenobiorum*, ed. Petschenig.
[5] *Eusebius 'Gallicanus', Collectio Homiliarum*, ed. Glorie.
[6] This parallel could equally well be from Caesarius, *Serm. IX*; above, pp. 117–18.
[7] This parallel could equally well be from Caesarius, *Serm. IX*; above, pp. 117–18.
[8] Turner, 'The *Liber Ecclesiasticorum Dogmatum* attributed to Gennadius'.
[9] *Gildas: The Ruin of Britain and Other Works*, ed. & transl. Winterbottom.
[10] *Patrologia Latina*, ed. Migne, LXXVI.1075–1312.

Moralia in Iob[11]

[*Mor. in Iob* VIII.liv.92 (p. 454)]   *Instr.* V.2 (p. 86, lines 7–16)]

Gregory of Nazianzus

Orationes (transl. Rufinus)[12]

Apol. I.1 (p. 7)   *Instr.* I.1 (p. 60, line 5)

Apol. I.3 (p. 7)   *Instr.* XI.2 (p. 108, lines 20–1)

[*De epiph.* VII.2 (p. 92)   *Instr.* I.4 (p. 64, lines 20–1)]

Hilary of Poitiers

De trinitate[13]

De trinitate II.6 (pp. 42–3)   *Instr.* VIII.1 (p. 94, line 17)

Jerome

Epistulae[14]

Epist. XXII.iii.1 (p. 146)   *Instr.* X.3 (p. 104, line 10)

Origen

Homiliae in Lucam[15]

[*Hom. in Luc.* XXXIX.5 (pp. 454–6)   *Instr.* XI.1–2 (p. 106, lines 8–9, 19–20, 27; p. 108, lines 1–10)]

Quicunque uult[16]

§§ 1, 28   *Instr.* I.2 (p. 60, line 9)

§ 3   *Instr.* I.2 (p. 60, lines 22–3)

Sedulius

Carmen paschale[17]

Carmen paschale I.349   *Instr.* XIII.3 (p. 118, lines 31–2)

Sulpicius Seuerus

Dialogus[18]

[*Dialogus* I.xviii.1 (p. 170, lines 19–20)   *Instr.* I.3 (p. 62, lines 11–12); *Instr.* III.4 (p. 76, line 32–p. 78, line 1)]

---

[11] *S. Gregorii Magni Moralia in Iob*, ed. Adriaen.
[12] *Tyrannii Rufini Orationum Gregorii Nazianzeni nouem interpretatio*, ed. Engelbrecht.
[13] *Hilarii Pictauensis De Trinitate*, ed. Smulders.
[14] *Sancti Eusebii Hieronymi Epistulae*, ed. Hilberg, vol. I.
[15] *Origène, Homélies sur S. Luc*, edd. Crouzel *et al.*
[16] Kelly, *The Athanasian Creed.*
[17] *Sedulii Opera Omnia*, ed. Huemer.
[18] *Sulpicii Seueri libri qui supersunt*, ed. Halm.

IV

THE MONASTIC RULES OF COLUMBANUS

Jane Barbara Stevenson

COLUMBANUS'S *opus geminatum* on the monastic life – that is, his *Regula monachorum* and *Regula coenobialis* – is the principal evidence for the way in which Columbanus spent most of the hours of his long and active life. Whatever else he achieved, whether as writer, controversialist, computist or politician, was fitted into the interstices of the unending cycle of the *opus Dei*, which therefore is of importance in understanding Columbanus himself. Another reason why his rule is important is that it was the instrument of his influence on the monastic life of Merovingian Francia and Lombard Italy. Besides its use in his own foundations, it influenced the practice of pupils such as Gall(us), Burgundofara and Donatus, and other Merovingian saints, for example Ebrulfus (Evroul).[1] His rule was not, as some writers have seen it, a fresh growth of ascetic vigour in an otherwise moribund and corrupt ecclesiastical structure. After all, Caesarius of Arles (470–543) was not long dead when Columbanus appeared in Gaul, and Radegund (518–87) had only recently died.[2] The principal difference between Columbanus and contemporary Gallo-Roman and Frankish ascetics is that Columbanus, by his direct dependence on royal patronage, remained aloof from Gallo-Roman ecclesiastical and monastic power structures.[3] Thus part of the attraction of his form of monasticism lay in its different relationship to the existing powers, sacred and secular. But the absolutism of his rule, even though we cannot legitimately contrast it with an atmosphere of worldly corruption, must have exerted its own appeal for his monasteries to survive.

Columbanus received his monastic training at Bangor, on Belfast Lough:[4]

---

[1] See Chibnall, 'The Merovingian monastery', p. 34: 'et ut omnes cursus compleret, scilicet Romanum Gallicanum Sancti Benedicti, Scotticum seu Sancti Columbani, per diuersa horarum spatia psallebat' ('and so that he might fulfil all the *cursus*, that is, whether the Roman and Gallican [custom] of St Benedict, or the Irish [custom] of St Columbanus, he sang psalms at the various times of the hours') (see also *ibid.*, p. 35).

[2] The Burgundian monastery of Agaune practised the *laus perennis* – perpetual psalm-singing by shifts of monks – in the early sixth century (see Wood, 'A Prelude', pp. 16–17). Gregory of Tours, in his treatise *De cursu stellarum ratio*, similarly describes a monastic office which was by no means lacking in rigour, inasmuch as it included a winter night-hour thirty psalms long (*Gregorii Turonensis Opera*, edd. Krusch & Levison, p. 870).

[3] Wood, 'The *Vita Columbani*', p. 76.

relicto ergo natali solo, quem Lagenorum terram incolae nuncupant, ad uirum uenerabilem nomine Sinilem perrexit ... quem cum uir sanctus ingenii sagacis esse uideret, omnium diuinarum scripturarum studiis inbuit.

This Sinilis is almost certainly the same as the Sinlanus who is mentioned in the seventh-century Bangor poem, *in memoriam abbatum nostrorum* as fourth abbot of the monastery and as 'famosum mundi magistrum'.[5] According to Ionas, Columbanus graduated, as it were, from this period of study, and joined the community of Bangor:[6]

Dedit deinde operam, ut monachorum necteretur societate, ad monasterium cuius uocabulum est Benechor petiit, in quo presul uirtutum ubertate cluebat beatus Commogellus.

The use of pre-syncope forms of the three Irish names – *Sinilis*, *Benechor* and *Commogellus* – used by the Italian Ionas in this section suggests that his source of information on Columbanus's early history was itself written very early; perhaps even contemporary with the saint.[7] The Latin forms of the names used in Ionas's own time, as the 'Antiphonary of Bangor' shows (it contains all three), was *Sinlanus* (Irish *Sillan*), *Benchor*, and *Comgillus*.[8] Thus it is virtually certain that Ionas was right to associate Columbanus with Bangor, and probably that he was broadly correct in his brief account of the saint's early days.

The training which Columbanus received from Comgall must have formed the essential matrix of his own monastic practice. Ionas does not mention that he studied elsewhere, and is likely to have reported it if, for example, his hero had visited Lérins.[9] We have no direct information about Bangor in the

---

[4] Ionas, *Vita S. Columbani*, I.3 (ed. Krusch, *Ionae Vitae Sanctorum*, p. 157): 'having left his native soil, which the inhabitants call the land of the *Lageni* (Leinster), he came to a venerable man by the name of *Sinilis* ... and when the holy man had seen that he was wise and intelligent, he filled him with the knowledge of all the divine writings'.

[5] The 'Antiphonary of Bangor', fo 36v (ed. Warren, *The Antiphonary*, II.33). Sillan is further attested, under the hypocoristic form Mo-sinnu moccu Min, as a scholar interested in computus. See Ó Cróinín, 'Mo-sinnu moccu Min'. Columbanus's own interest in computus is suggested by *Epistulae I* and *II* (§ 5), and by the quotation of 'Palumbus' (a name used by Columbanus) as a computistical authority, on which see Ó Cróinín, 'A seventh-century Irish computus', pp. 426–7, and below, pp. 269–70.

[6] Ionas, *Vita S. Columbani*, I.4 (ed. Krusch, *Ionas Vitae Sanctorum*, p. 158): 'next he was at pains to be bound within a community of monks, and sought out the monastery whose name is *Benechor*, in which the leader, famed for the abundance of his virtues, was the blessed *Commogellus*'.

[7] We may compare Adomnán's *Vita S. Columbae*, which like Ionas's *uita* was written in the seventh century about a sixth-century saint, and which contains evidence that the monks of Iona began to compile a written dossier on the deeds of Columba during his lifetime. See Herbert, *Iona*, pp. 13–26.

[8] See *In memoriam abbatum nostrorum*, in the 'Antiphonary of Bangor', fo 36v (ed. Warren, *The Antiphonary*, II.28 [no. 129]).

[9] A possible pattern for a would-be monastic founder would have been to sample a variety of monastic practices before settling on a rule of his own, as Benedict Biscop (for example) did: Columbanus, by contrast, went straight from Bangor to the 'desert'. Ionas does tell us that Columbanus crossed first to Brittany and spent a little

mid-sixth century. The Hiberno-Latin *Vita S. Comgalli* is considerably later, and of negligible value for the history of its subject. For what it is worth, Comgall left behind him a memory of appalling severity outstanding even for the heroic age of Irish monasticism:[10]

Appropinquans iam tempus exitus beatissimi senis Comgalli, immensis et uariis doloribus ipse torquebatur. . .alii iam dicebant, quod tanti dolores super eum a Deo dati sunt propter duriciam et asperitatem regule eius in monachis suis.

More positively, the *Versiculi familiae Benchuir* describe the rule of Bangor as 'stricta, sancta, sedula / summa, iusta, ac mira'.[11] Both descriptions would, from their different perspectives, characterise Columbanus's practice.

The best evidence for the Office and liturgy of Bangor comes from its famous 'Antiphonary of Bangor', now Milan, Biblioteca Ambrosiana, MS. C.5. inf. The book was put together at the end of the seventh century, at Bangor, although its later journey to Columbanus's foundation of Bobbio is suggested by its eventual appearance in the Biblioteca Ambrosiana which, together with the Biblioteca Nazionale in Turin, contains most of the Bobbio library. The 'Antiphonary' certainly contains material contemporary with Columbanus, in the form of a hymn from his own pen,[12] and it is a useful witness to seventh-century practice at Bangor (though not necessarily to the time of Columbanus himself).

Columbanus's dealings with continental *auctoritates*, sacred or secular, suggest a man of markedly inflexible character, and therefore one who is unlikely to have accepted local monastic practice in preference to his own. His open letter to the bishops and priests of Francia, *Epistula II*, rejects any attempts by the Frankish hierarchy to control his actions. Any influence discernible on his monastic office, therefore, is almost certainly a guide to the monastic office of the 'Age of the Saints' in Ireland itself.

Monasticism in Ireland in the fifth and sixth centuries did not have a single source. It was part of a vast, widespread enthusiasm for coenobitic and eremitic ways of life which can be found all over the christian world at this time. The Egyptians, the Gauls and the Britons could all boast large numbers of strong-minded, charismatic and evangelical thaumaturges who adopted the monastic life and found themselves surrounded by flocks of eager recruits. Any or all of these saints could have given impetus to the monastic movement in Ireland, if only through their writings or their reputation, but the precise balance of influences on the life and practice of any one specific monastery is,

---

time there (*Vita S. Columbani*, I.4, ed. Krusch, p. 160); but if his haven was one of the Breton monasteries, such as Dol, Ionas does not mention it.

[10] *Vita S. Comgalli*, § 56 (ed. Plummer, *Vitae*, II.21): 'when the time of death was approaching for the most blessed old man Comgall, he was tormented by immense and various infirmities . . . some people said that such great infirmities were visited on him by God on account of the rigour and harshness of his rule over his monks'.

[11] *Versiculi Familiae Benchuir*, from the 'Antiphonary of Bangor', fo 30r (ed. Warren, *The Antiphonary*, II.28 [no. 95]): 'strait, holy, zealous; perfection, just and wonderful'.

[12] Lapidge, 'Columbanus', and see below, pp. 255–63.

of course, undiscoverable. There is no reason to suppose much uniformity between churches. Uniformity did not prevail in Francia or Anglo-Saxon England, as we can see, for example, from Bede:[13]

[Benedict Biscop is speaking] Ex decem quippe et septem monasteriis quae inter longos meae crebre peregrinationis discursus optima conperi, haec uniuersa didici, et uobis salubriter obseruando contradidi.

Although the *Regula S. Benedicti* was known unusually early in England, Benedict Biscop, half a century after Columbanus's death, felt free to put together a rule of his own devising. Until the *Regula S. Benedicti* had been widely adopted, there was no central authority to legislate on the monastic life of Western Europe. If monastic uniformity was not sought in Francia or Anglo-Saxon England in the sixth and seventh centuries, both of which had a Roman type of ecclesiastical structure with diocesan bishops answering to archbishops, we would hardly expect to find it in Ireland, a land without a central legislature of any kind, sacred or secular.

Columbanus wrote his *Regula monachorum* and *Regula coenobialis* for the guidance of his own houses, Annegray, Luxeuil, Fontaines, and Bobbio. The two works are complementary. The word *monachos* is from Greek *monos*, 'one'. Columbanus, who favoured Greek words and was sensitive to etymology, would certainly have been aware of this.[14] Thus his *Regula monachorum* is addressed to the individual: it is a series of meditative essays on the control of the self, and the character of the ideal monk. It deals with spiritual, rather than material facts. For instance, both the *Regula coenobialis* and the Penitential lay down rules for the monk's conduct towards women. But rather than going into details on monastic etiquette, the *Regula monachorum* begins its section on the monastic virtue of chastity by saying 'castitas uero monachi in cogitationibus iudicatur', and continues, 'et quid prodest si uirgo corpore sit, si non sit uirgo mente?'[15] The work addresses itself to matching correct action with the correct attitude of mind. Some directions are given, for the monk's diet and for the performance of the Office, but in both cases, the framework of action is sketched out, and the thrust of the thought is towards the inner significance of the action and the all-seeing eye of God.[16] The monk is warned, with regard to diet, that excessive abstinence becomes a vice rather than a virtue – fasting is not performed for fasting's sake – and told, after the discussion of the office, 'ceterum uera, ut dixi, orandi traditio, ut possibilitas ad hoc destinati sine

---

[13] Bede, *Historia abbatum*, § 11 (ed. Plummer, *Venerabilis Baedae Opera*, I.374–5): 'Everything which I learned to be best in the life of the seventeen monasteries I visited during the long excursion of my journeys I stored up in my mind, and I pass them down to you to be followed as most beneficial.'

[14] As his very characteristic use of the word *micrologus* bears witness: see discussion by Lapidge, below, p. 259.

[15] *Regula monachorum*, § 6 (ed. & transl. Walker, *Sancti Columbani Opera*, p. 128): 'The chastity of a monk is truly judged by his thoughts', and 'what good is it if one is virgin in body, if one is not virgin in mind?'

[16] *Regula monachorum*, § § 3, 7 (ed. & transl. Walker, *ibid.*, pp. 124–6, 128–32).

fastidio uoti praeualeat'.[17] Thus, to Columbanus's mind, how the office is performed is not of such great importance; what matters is that it is performed unanimously and in the proper spirit, and that it should form a basis for private prayer and contemplation.

The word *coenobium* means 'the common life'. Columbanus's *Regula coenobialis*, therefore, does not deal with the meaning of the monk's life, but with its conduct. Whereas the first *regula* concerns the monk's relationship with God, the second concerns his relationship with men. It is thus close to a penitential in some respects, though it is more concerned to be directive than it is to impose punishment for faults. The monks' lives are ruled in the most trivial respects. For example, a monk who neglects to say 'amen' after grace has been said is to be corrected with six blows.[18] The structure of this work has lent itself to expansion by later hands, and a variety of elaborations has been added throughout the text. The *Regula coenobialis* tends to support the appearance of unusual austerity and holiness which impressed observers of Columbanus and his followers. The grosser varieties of sin are not even mentioned. The most common problems which the community faced, if this *regula* is anything to go by, were related to anger and failure of absolute obedience. Monks seem to have found it far more difficult to subdue their will absolutely to that of the abbot than to undertake a life of poverty, chastity and physical hardship. They sometimes answered back, bickered, laughed during the Office, or lost their tempers. Other problems which emerge are to do with forgetfulness (due possibly to physical exhaustion), and with unnecessary speech. The standard of conduct implied is staggeringly high. Confession is recommended as an almost continuous activity. The monk reviews his actions several times during the day, and seeks immediate confession and penance.[19] This is early evidence for the characteristic Irish monastic attitude towards penance, which was both more continuous and more directly applied to the minutiae of discipline than its prototypes in other Christian traditions.

Columbanus tells us that he followed the practice of *seniores nostri*, perhaps meaning principally the practice of Bangor, since Ionas associates him with no other house.[20] The evidence of Columbanus's *regulae* is strengthened by two continental *regulae* based on his practice, that of Donatus, who is mentioned in Ionas's *uita* as a younger contemporary of Columbanus,[21] and another known as *Regula cuiusdam patris*.[22] Columbanus's *regulae* are, in effect, the earliest evidence for monastic practice in the Irish church.

Geography alone suggests that the British church exerted an influence

---

[17] *Regula coenobialis*, § 7 (ed. & transl. Walker, *ibid.*, p. 132): 'however, as I have said, the true tradition of praying [is] so that the capability of someone dedicated to this task may prevail without weariness at the vow'.

[18] *Regula coenobialis*, § 1 (ed. & transl. Walker, *ibid.*, p. 146).

[19] *Regula coenobialis*, § 1 (ed. & transl. Walker, *ibid.*, p. 144).

[20] *Regula monachorum*, § 7 (ed. & transl. Walker, *ibid.*, p. 130).

[21] Ionas, *Vita S. Columbani*, I.14 (ed. Krusch, *Ionae Vitae Sanctorum*, pp. 175–6). His rule is a fusion of Columbanian, Benedictine, and Caesarian traditions, on which see Luff, 'A survey', and Wallace-Hadrill, *The Frankish Church*, p. 59.

[22] *Patrologia Latina*, ed. Migne, LXVI.937–94. See in particular § 20, at col. 994.

over the Irish during its formative period.[23] Columbanus was profoundly impressed by the Briton Gildas, who, as Richard Sharpe has argued, was a founding father of Irish asceticism.[24] Gildas is a principal source for Columbanus's outstandingly sophisticated prose style,[25] is directly cited by him as an authority in his *Epistula I*,[26] and may be a source for the somewhat anomalous character of Columbanus's Bible-text.[27] It is not unreasonable to assume that he exerted an influence over Columbanus's theory and practice of monasticism, but unfortunately, we know nothing of Gildas's own practice beyond what is contained in his penitential.

A somewhat clearer source of influence over Columbanus's practice is Egypt, via the *Conlationes* and *Instituta* of Cassian of Marseille (*ca* 360–435), the main source-text for Eastern monasticism in the Latin-speaking West.[28] Cassian spent many years in the East, first at Bethlehem, and then in Egypt. Having sat as an eager disciple at the feet of the great Egyptian founders of monasticism, he settled in Gaul around 415, and began to write on monastic thought and spirituality, and the nature of the monastic life. He succeeded in translating the austere principles of the Egyptian desert into Gaul, sensibly making allowances for the harsher climate in matters of diet and clothing. Cassian's work was read by Columbanus and in seventh-century Iona, as well as by such founding fathers of Gaulish monasticism as Honoratus of Lérins and Caesarius of Arles. The extent of Columbanus's personal debt to Cassian will be discussed a little later in the context of Columbanus's treatment of the Psalter.

Another Gaulish figure who may have influenced Columbanus is St Martin, bishop of Tours. Martin was very highly regarded in early medieval Ireland. He was celebrated by Columba, according to Adomnán, who seems to imply that this was a general practice,[29] and his *uita* appears in the 'Book of Armagh'

---

[23] The later Hiberno-Latin *uitae* printed by Plummer, for what they are worth, associate Irish monastic founders with British masters: Finnian, St David of Wales, Gildas, and others.

[24] Sharpe, 'Gildas'.

[25] Mohrmann, 'The earliest continental Irish Latin'; Winterbottom, 'Columbanus and Gildas'; and discussion by Wright, above, pp. 82–7.

[26] *Epistula* I.6: 'simoniacos et Gildas auctor pestes scripsit eos', and I.7: 'Vennianus auctor Gildam de his interrogauit, et elegantissime ille rescripsit' (ed. Walker, *Sancti Columbani Opera*, p. 8). Gildas and Uinniau are the only *auctoritates* of Insular origin cited by Columbanus.

[27] Lomiento, 'La Bibbia', notes that Columbanus's Bible-text seems at various points closer to the Septuagint than the Vulgate, in both the Old and the New Testaments. The works of Gildas provide evidence of unusual Vetus Latina Bible-texts circulating in the sixth-century British church: see Haddan & Stubbs, *Councils*, I.170–97.

[28] An 'Egyptian' tendency in early Irish monasticism is noted by Bäumer, *Histoire*, I.236–9, who discusses the monasticism of Columbanus. See also Hanssens, *Aux Origines*, pp. 88–90.

[29] Adomnán, *Vita S. Columbae*, III.12 (edd. & transl. Anderson & Anderson, p. 198): 'illa consueta decantaretur deprecatio in qua sancti Martini commemoratur nomen': 'that accustomed prayer was chanted, in which the name of holy Martin is commemorated'. By the twelfth century, the 'gospel of Martin in Derry' was the symbol of office of the coarbs of Columba (Herbert, *Iona*, pp. 190–1). See also Mayr-Harting, *The Coming*, p. 97, Grosjean, 'Gloria postuma', and Gwynn, 'The cult'.

alongside the dossier on St Patrick, the only other *uita* preserved there. Ionas's *Vita S. Columbani* asserts that Columbanus also had a special devotion to him,[30] and Columbanus himself refers to him as 'domnus Martinus'[31] in *Epistula II* (§ 7), setting him alongside St Jerome and Pope Damasus, which suggests that he considered Martin to have a title to unusual respect. Perhaps one of the reasons for the veneration of Martin in Ireland is that he was an ascetic and monk who was also a bishop, and thus provided a model for the Irish combination of the clerical and monastic traditions. This aspect of his career may not have been of direct interest to Columbanus, who was not a bishop,[32] but his notable feats of asceticism and his conduct of community life, as described by Sulpicius, probably were.

The rule of life specified by Columbanus is extremely harsh in all respects. Food, clothing, sleep, and comfort of any kind are all ruthlessly restricted. His Office is in line with this austerity. There are eight services, one every three hours of the twenty-four. They are as follows.

ad secundam	(Prime):	6 a.m.
ad tertiam	(Terce):	9 a.m.
ad sextam	(Sext):	12 noon
ad nonam	(None):	3 p.m.
ad uespertinam	(Vespers):	6 p.m.
ad initium noctis	(1 Nocturn):	9 p.m.
ad medium noctis	(2 Nocturn):	12 midnight
ad matutinam	(Lauds/Matins):	3 a.m.

Columbanus arranged the 150 psalms into groups of three, which he refers to as *chori*. Within each group, variety was achieved by the singing method: the first two were sung straight through, and the third antiphonally, that is, with the congregation divided into two and singing verses alternately.[33] A further elaboration of this service, mentioned in the *Regula coenobialis*, is genuflecting at the end of the service while silently repeating Ps. LXIX.2, 'Deus in adiutorium meum intende, domine ad adiuuandum me festina' ('God make haste to help me, Lord make speed to save me'), three times. This verse

---

[30] Columbanus, with the timely assistance of a miracle, went out of his way to spend a night in prayer at the saint's tomb in Tours. See Ionas, *Vita S. Columbani*, I.22 (ed. Krusch, *Ionae Vitae Sanctorum*, pp. 200–1).

[31] 'Master Martin', or 'Lord Martin'. The syncopated form of *dominus* is common in Church Latin, to differentiate earthly lords from *Dominus*: 'the Lord'. It is a title of the highest respect.

[32] He may have included a bishop, subject to his authority, in the group of monks which he took with him to the Continent: *Epistula IV* (§ 4), mentions that the altar of Luxeuil was blessed by 'sanctus Aidus episcopus' (ed. & transl. Walker, *Sancti Columbani Opera*, p. 30). The name is Irish, unfortunately nearly as common as Columba itself.

[33] Similarly, Caesarius of Arles recommended that some psalms be sung antiphonally, some direct. See his *Regula*, § 21 (ed. Migne, *Patrologia Latina* LXVII.1102).

appears in other monastic *regulae*, but is used at the *beginning* of the Office in both the Roman and the Benedictine tradition.[34]

Columbanus made a distinction between the day hours and the night hours, and another between the holy nights of Saturday and Sunday and the rest of the week. He seems to have been abnormally suspicious of the fleshly relaxation of sleep: '[monachus] lassus ad stratum ueniat ambulansque dormitet, necdum expleto somno surgere compellatur'.[35] In the four day hours, *ad secundam* to *ad nonam*, only three psalms were sung, so as not to interfere unduly with the day's labours, together with a series of short intercessory prayers for various categories of people.[36] The nights were consecrated to divine service rather than refreshing slumber, and twelve psalms were sung at each of the three hours from *ad uespertinam* to *ad medium noctis*. The service *ad matutinam* was invariably the longest and most elaborate of the eight hours. On a weekday night, twenty-four psalms were sung in summer, rising to thirty-six in winter. On Saturdays and Sundays, the minimum was thirty-six, and the maximum seventy-five – half the psalter. The prospect of singing psalms continuously for (at a guess) about two and a half hours in the small hours of a winter's night, with barely time to recover before starting again, is one which only the most fervently religious could bear to contemplate.[37] The success of Columbanian monasticism in Francia is a testimony both to his own character, and to the toughness of his converts. A hymn was also sung, as he tells us in *Regula coenobialis*, on Sundays, and on the first day of Easter.[38] There is some reason to suggest that the context of this hymn-singing might be the Mass rather than the Office, on the basis of the 'Antiphonary of Bangor', but the 'Antiphonary' is not always a reliable guide.

There is a number of seventh-century Irish liturgical manuscripts, and as I have tried to show elsewhere, the material which is held in common between them suggests that the 'hymns' which were widely known and used in sixth-century Ireland were the biblical Canticles, 'Te Deum laudamus', 'Gloria in excelsis', and a long, probably Gallican, hymn, 'Spiritus diuinae lucis'.[39] In addition, Columbanus (as the sources of *Precamur patrem* make clear) was familiar with hymns by Venantius Fortunatus and with a set of hymns for the hours similar, if not identical, to that used by Caesarius and his successor Aurelian at Arles, though his *regulae* offer no direct evidence that he chose to use it in his own foundations. His own hymn, *Precamur patrem*, seems to have

---

[34] See for example, *Regula S. Benedicti*, §§ 17, 18 (ed. Hanslik, *Benedicti Regula*, pp. 65, 68).

[35] *Regula monachorum*, § 10 (ed. & transl. Walker, *Sancti Columbani Opera*, p. 140): 'he should go tired to his bed, sleeping as he walks, and he should be made to get up before his sleep is finished'.

[36] *Regula monachorum*, § 7 (*ibid.*, p. 130).

[37] In the *Regula coenobialis*, § 12, omitting an hour is punished with an imposition of fifteen extra psalms, 'nisi matutina in hiemis', which is punished by only twelve: a tacit admission that the strain imposed by this service was abnormal (*ibid.*, p. 160).

[38] *Regula coenobialis*, § 9 (ed. & transl. Walker, *Sancti Columbani Opera*, p. 158): 'in omnique dominica sollempnitate hymnus diei cantetur dominice et in die inchoante pasche' ('at every Sunday celebration the hymn of the day should be sung, and on the day of the beginning of Easter').

[39] Stevenson, 'Irish hymns'.

been written for Holy Saturday, one of the most special nights of the Christian year, and therefore can tell us nothing about the extent of his commitment to hymnody in the round of an ordinary week.

Columbanus probably celebrated Mass on Sundays at dawn, after *ad matutinam*.[40] There is evidence that this was normal Irish practice in Adomnán's *Vita S. Columbae*,[41] and also in the continental *uita* of St Gall(us), who had come from Ireland with Columbanus, but parted from him in Switzerland.[42] Hymns are not a feature of the office of the Mass in the Roman rite,[43] but the 'Antiphonary of Bangor' includes a syllabic hymn *Sancti, uenite*, headed *ymnus quando commonicarent sacerdotes*, 'a hymn for when the priests communicate', which demonstrates that a eucharistic hymn was part of the Bangor liturgy in the seventh century. It appears to be an elaboration of one of the seven communion-antiphons also found in the 'Antiphonary': 'hoc sacrum corpus Domini et Saluatoris sanguinem sumite uobis in uitam perennem'.[44] The question then is, whether Columbanus made use of *Sancti uenite*, a Eucharistic hymn, or of *Hoc sacrum corpus*, a Eucharistic antiphon, and sang his Sunday hymn in some other circumstance. Some light may be shed on this by the practice of his disciple Burgundofara:[45]

Quadam etenim die dominico cum missarum sollemnia saepefacta Burgundofara cum famularum Dei collegio expectaret, et iam sacri corporis communione participarentur,

---

[40] The *Regula cuiusdam patris*, § 20, which draws on Columbanian tradition, states: 'in his uero conuentibus, id est, sabbati et dominicae, usque ad gallorum cantus, missa celebranda est' ('at these congregations, that is, on Saturday and Sunday at cockcrow, Mass should be celebrated')(ed. Migne, *Patrologia Latina*, LXVI.994).

[41] See, for example, *Vita S. Columbae* III.12 (edd. & transl. Anderson & Anderson, pp. 198–200).

[42] Walahfrid Strabo, *Vita S. Galli*, § 26 (ed. Migne, *Patrologia Latina*, CXIV.999): 'quadam itaque die, dum post laborem matutinalis officii quiescendi gratia lectos suos reuiserent, primo diluculo, uir Dei uocauit Magnoaldum diaconem suum, dicens illi, "instrue sacrae oblationis ministerium" ', etc. ('one day, when after the effort of Matins they were returning to their beds for the indulgence of a rest, at first light, the man of God called his deacon Magnoald, saying to him "begin the office of the holy sacrifice" ').

[43] Duchesne, *Christian Worship*, pp. 186–8, states that it was normal to sing an antiphon during Communion in the Roman mass. The *Expositio antiquae liturgiae Gallicanae*, § 8 (ed. Ratcliffe, p. 6), a guide to early Frankish practice, mentions a *hymnus* as part of the Mass, but means by this the 'Song of the Three Children' (Daniel III.52–90). It is also possible that Columbanus used the word *hymnus* to mean not 'hymn', but 'canticle'.

[44] 'The Antiphonary', fo 33r (ed. Warren, *The Antiphonary*, II.31 [no. 112]: 'take to yourselves this holy body of the Lord and the blood of the Saviour into eternal life').

[45] Ionas, *Vita S. Columbani*, II.16 (ed. Krusch, *Ionae Vite Sanctorum*, pp. 266–7): 'One Sunday, when the ceremony of the mass was being celebrated, Burgundofara was waiting with the community of nuns, and just as they were about to receive the communion of the sacred Body, one of them, called Domma, when she had just taken the body of the Lord, drunk the Blood, returned to the holy choir, and was singing with her companions: "Take this holy body of the Lord and the blood of the Saviour for yourselves into eternal life" ', . . .).

quaedam ex his nomine Domma, cum iam corpus Domini accepisset ac sanguinem libasset, et sacro choro inserta, cum comparibus caneret: 'hoc sacrum corpus Domini et saluatoris sanguinem sumite uobis in uitam perennis'. . . .

The words which Ionas gives Burgundofara's nuns to sing during Communion are absolutely identical with that of the antiphon. Thus the balance of probability is that Columbanus used the antiphon rather than *Sancti uenite*, and the place of hymnody in his liturgical practice is left obscure. The antiphon appears in identical form in the 'Stowe Missal', in the Irish sacramentary-fragment in Sankt Gallen, Stiftsbibliothek, MS. 1394, and in the *Nauigatio S. Brendani*, texts which show no other signs of having a common origin. Thus it appears from the available evidence that it is the antiphon which represents the normal practice of early Irish monasteries, while *Sancti uenite* in the 'Antiphonary of Bangor' represents a local, seventh-century variation.[46] Another thing which is made clear by this Eucharistic antiphon and by Ionas's account is that Burgundofara's nuns and the monks of Bangor communicated in both kinds, so we may deduce that this was also the practice of Columbanus.

The 'Antiphonary of Bangor', as I have mentioned, was compiled at the end of the seventh century. It must be used with caution as a guide to the use of Bangor in the mid-sixth century, since the conduct of the monastic Office is liable to change and accretion over time. Canticles, antiphons, collects, hymns, prayers and other addenda are mentioned in the 'Antiphonary', and obviously reflect something about the use of Bangor in the later seventh century, but that is not necessarily to say that they formed part of the Office of Columbanus a hundred years earlier. One might legitimately wonder when even he would have found the time, given the formidable nature of his commitment to the psalter.

In his *De institutis*, Cassian explains the practice of the Egyptian desert saints.[47] The Egyptians were accustomed to sing twelve psalms at a service, this number having been decreed by an angel. Columbanus refers to the practice of the Egyptians, under the name of 'quidam catholici', and describes this number as 'canonicus duodenarius psalmorum numerus': 'the canonical number of twelve psalms'.[48] He speaks with high approval of the Egyptian fathers, and mentions further that they distinguished the holy nights of Saturday and Sunday by singing thirty-six psalms at each service rather than the usual three. Thus, Columbanus's practice of psalmody seems to be modelled specifically on that of Egypt, as he understood it from his reading. The use of only three psalms at each day-hour is also a practice recorded by Cassian, as occurring in Palestinian, Mesopotamian, and other Eastern monasteries.[49] He gives the same practical reason as Columbanus: not letting the hours of prayer interrupt the day's work excessively. The use of collects after canticles and

---

[46] *The Stowe Missal*, ed. Warner, II.18; Warren & Stevenson, *The Liturgy*, p. 178; and *Nauigatio S. Brendani*, § 17 (ed. Selmer, p. 52). See further the discussion of Stevenson, in Warren & Stevenson, *The Liturgy*, pp. lxii–lxiv.

[47] *De Institutis*, II.4 (ed. & transl. Guy, p. 64). See also Heiming, 'Zum monastischen Offizium', p. 106.

[48] *Regula monachorum*, § 7 (ed. & transl. Walker, *Sancti Columbani Opera*, p. 132).

[49] *De institutis*, III.3 (ed. & transl. Guy, p. 94).

psalms (which is, of course, a salient feature of the 'Antiphonary of Bangor') is also a feature of Eastern practice as reported by Cassian,[50] but there is no evidence for its adoption by Columbanus beyond his use of Ps. LXIX.2 at the end of the service. However, a further indication of Columbanus's modelling himself on Egyptian practice is found in *Regula coenobialis* (§12), where the ban against attending Mass while wearing any part of one's night-clothes may be taken from the *Lausiac History* of Palladius.[51] The use of day-clothes and night-clothes is recommended by Cassian.[52] The Egyptians also used to have two readings (*lectiones*), from the Old and New Testament respectively, but these were regarded as edifying rather than essential.[53] Columbanus's *regulae* do not mention lections, or any other aspect of communal divine service, except for a *cottidianus praeceptus* ('daily exhortation').[54] But another rule influenced by Cassian, that of Caesarius of Arles, has a monastic office composed of psalms and lections;[55] and the Columbanian-influenced *Regula cuiusdam patris* similarly specifies psalms and lections.[56] Thus, despite the evidence of the 'Antiphonary' for a more developed office in the seventh century at Bangor, there are grounds for believing that the monastic office of Columbanus himself was strenuous, but essentially extremely simple. We have clear evidence for psalmody and intercessory prayers, indirect evidence for a Eucharistic service at dawn on Sundays (and perhaps on Saturdays as well), and some reason to suggest that lections from the Old and New Testaments were also in use. We have no evidence for the use of canticles, antiphons, other than a Communion antiphon, collects, or hymns for the hours.

If Columbanus's office is essentially a *cursus psalmorum*, the question which remains is, how was it arranged? The simplest answer is that the psalms were organised as Pss. I–III, IV–VI, VII–IX, and so on, and that whenever CXLVIII–CL were reached, the monks began again at the beginning.

---

[50] *De institutis*, II.8 (*ibid.*, p. 72).

[51] *Regula coenobialis*, § 12 (ed. & transl. Walker, *Sancti Columbani Opera*, p. 160); Palladius, *Lausiac History*, § 32 (transl. Lowther Clarke, pp. 112–13). The practice of Pachomius, as described by Palladius, was that a monk should wear a linen *lebiton* and a girdle at night. When he went to Communion, on Saturday and Sunday, he was to loosen his girdle, take off his cloak, and go in in his cowl (*koukoulion*) only.

[52] Cassian, *Conlationes* IX.5 (ed. & transl. Pichery, II.45).

[53] *De institutis*, II.6 (ed. & transl. Guy, p. 68–70). The *Dicta patrum*, § 2 (transl. Wallis Budge, *The Paradise of the Fathers*, II.16) includes the following episode: 'one of the two said unto his fellow, "shall we sing a part of the service?" And he sang the whole of the Psalms of David, and his companion repeated two books of the Great Prophets.'

[54] *Regula coenobialis*, § 9 (ed. & transl. Walker, *Sancti Columbani Opera*, p. 156). Even this fleeting mention occurs only in a part of the *regula* which is an addendum to the original text of uncertain date and origin.

[55] *Regula Caesarii Arelatensis*, § 25 (ed. Migne, *Patrologia Latina*, LXVII.1103).

[56] *Regula cuiusdam patris*, § 20 (ed. Migne, *Patrologia Latina* LXVI.994): 'orationes uero et duae lectiones, una de Veteri Testamento, et alia de Nouo, in singulis noctis conuentibus dicendae sunt' ('prayers and two lections, one from the Old Testament and one from the New, should be said at the assemblies every night').

Jungmann has noted that praying through the psalms in their biblical sequence rather than with regard to their theme is 'a basic feature of the monastic office'.[57] But it was common to arrange the psalms to some extent thematically: some psalms, by their content, suggest a connexion with one time of day rather than another. Pss. CXLVIII–CL are almost universally sung at Lauds (*ad matutinam*).[58] Columbanus's practice was clearly different from Western norms in a number of ways, but he may have conformed in this respect, since the *collectio post tres psalmos* in the 'Antiphonary of Bangor' shows that these psalms were used at Lauds in seventh-century Bangor.[59]

But the 'Antiphonary of Bangor' is not, I have suggested, an entirely reliable witness to Columbanus's practice. It is interesting that both it and the (possibly eighth-century) *Nauigatio S. Brendani* contain mutually compatible evidence for an Irish *cursus psalmorum*, but this may or may not be relevant to the sixth century. This *cursus*, as it is implied by the 'Antiphonary', is set out in two places in the *Nauigatio*, the chapter on the Island of Birds, and that on the Island of the Three Choirs.[60] Each hour mentioned (all are described except Sext) is given three specific psalms, with, additionally, the Gradual Psalms (CXIX–CXXXIII) at Vespers, and another twelve psalms in the order of the psalter at Matins. Thus, these two night hours are, like those of Columbanus, considerably longer than the day hours. The use of three psalms during the day is also consistent with the practice of Columbanus. It may be that in Columbanus's monasteries the short, three-psalm Offices of the day hours were fixed in form, and the long night Offices were, like *ad matutinam* in the *Nauigatio*, sequential. The early Irish *cursus* of the *Nauigatio* is unlike any found in continental offices such as that of the *Regula S. Benedicti*, so presumably evolved out of earlier Irish practice. And the apparently wide distribution of this Irish *cursus* may also support the idea that it went back to the heroic age of the Irish church.[61]

Besides the psalter, the other feature of Columbanus's Office which is confirmed in his own writings is intercessory prayer:[62]

---

[57] Jungmann, *Pastoral Liturgy*, p. 151. See also Baumstark, *Nocturna Laus*, pp. 156–66.

[58] Jungmann, *Pastoral Liturgy*, pp. 134–5, 144.

[59] The content of collect no. 64 makes it absolutely clear which psalms are meant. See the 'Antiphonary of Bangor', fo 22v (ed. Warren, *The Antiphonary*, II.24 and xi–xii [no. 64]).

[60] *Nauigatio S. Brendani*, §§ 11,17 (ed. Selmer, pp. 22–8, 49–58).

[61] The place of writing of the *Nauigatio S. Brendani* is unknown, but there is absolutely no reason to think that it was Bangor, which is not known to have culted St Brendan (see Dumville, 'Two approaches'). A further clue that this Office was quite widespread is in a story about St Columba in the fifteenth-century 'Great Book of Lecan', in which the celebration of the household of heaven begins with Pss. LXIV, CIV, and CXII. The same psalms, in the same order, are given for Vespers in the *Nauigatio*, § 17 (ed. Selmer, p. 51). I noted, above, the wide distribution of a Communion-antiphon used by Columbanus, which appears in § 17 of the *Nauigatio* as well as elsewhere.

[62] *Regula coenobialis*, § 7, (ed. & transl. Walker, *Sancti Columbani Opera*, p. 130): 'our elders have appointed for us three psalms at each of the day Hours, on account of the interruption of work, together with an addition of versicles of intercession, first for

per diurnas terni psalmi horas pro operum interpositione statuti sunt a senioribus nostris cum uersiculum augmento interuenientium pro peccatis primum nostris, deinde pro omni populo christiano, deinde pro sacerdotibus et reliquis deo consecratis sacrae plebis gradibus, postremo pro elemosinas facientibus, postea pro pace regum, nouissime pro inimicis.

This litany of intercession is supported by the 'Antiphonary of Bangor'.[63] Where Columbanus's monks prayed for six categories of person, the monks of Bangor in the seventh century prayed for sixteen: for 'our own sins', 'baptised Christians', 'priests', 'the abbot', 'the brothers', 'the peace of the people and the kings',[64] 'blasphemers', 'the impious', 'those going on a journey', 'the thankful', 'alms-givers', 'the sick', 'the captive', 'martyrs', and 'those who are suffering'. It may be seen that the list is related to that of Columbanus: it includes all his categories, and adds to them.[65] It is therefore probable that the precise form of the prayer (which Columbanus, writing to his own monks, had no need to specify) was the same in his time as it was in the seventh century, consisting of an anthem and a one-sentence prayer, of which the first, *pro peccatis nostris*, is an example:[66]

[*anthem*] Deus, in adiutorium meum intende. Domine, ad adiuandum me festina.
[*oratio*] Festina, Domine, liberare nos ex omnibus peccatis nostris, Qui regnas, etc.

It is a form of prayer which is naturally and easily liable to revision and addition to fit changing circumstances, since the individual sections are quite discrete. This intercessory litany is apparently unique to Bangor: it is not attested anywhere else in Ireland.[67] It resembles the Roman diaconal litany, which might have provided a model for it, but it has some notable differences.[68] The deacon invited the congregation to intercede for various groups, to which the people responded with *Kyrie eleison* or *Domine miserere*. The Bangor *uersiculi* lack this responsorial structuring, and seem to be offered

---

our own sins, then for all Christian people, then for priests and the other grades of the holy people consecrated to God, then for the alms-givers, then for the peace of the kings, and lastly for our enemies'.

63 Curran, *The Antiphonary*, pp. 106–13.

64 Kings in the plural were a feature both of Ireland, and of Merovingian Gaul.

65 This provides direct evidence that the practice of seventh-century Bangor was more elaborate than that of sixth-century Luxeuil or Bobbio.

66 'Antiphonary of Bangor', fo 20v (ed. Warren, *The Antiphonary*, II.22): 'God, make haste to help us, Lord, make speed to save us', 'Hasten, Lord, free us from all our sins, Who reigns ...' The first verse (Ps. LXIX.2: 'Deus, in adiutorium meum intende') is widely associated with the Office, and specified by Columbanus for silent repetition after the hour's psalms had been said. Its appearance here as the opening words of this cycle of prayers to be said after the psalms may strengthen the thesis that this is the form of the intercessory prayers which Columbanus himself used.

67 The 'Stowe Missal' preserves, under the title 'deprecatio S. Martini pro populo' what seems to have been a more widespread formula of intercession, 'pro ... oramus'. See further Ní Chatháin, 'The liturgical background', p. 135.

68 The diaconal litany is discussed by Callewaert, 'Les étapes', p. 21.

by the whole body of monks. Furthermore, in the diaconal litany, several groups might be named together before a response was sought, and the prayers in the 'Antiphonary' are all quite separate. The groups of people prayed for are similar to the categories for intercession found generally in the liturgy of the Mass. But the prayers *pro blasfemantibus*, *pro impiis* and *pro gratias agentibus* are very difficult to parallel, and the absence of any intercession *pro fidelibus defunctorum* is distinctly surprising. The Bangor *orationes* seem to represent an independent synthesis of inherited motifs and personal taste.

The final impression left by the *regulae* of Columbanus is twofold. First, one is struck by the extraordinary integrity and rigour of his monastic practice – *stricta, sancta, sedula*, indeed. He pays as much attention to the inward movement of the heart and the will as he does to the outward, physical actions, the virtual perfection of which he takes almost for granted. Secondly, one notices the independence of his usage. There are several features of his practice, as we have seen, which are unparalleled in other Western Offices. He seems to have picked and chosen among the sources available to him with remarkable independence of mind; and his preference for imitating the practice of the ascetic heroes of the Egyptian desert rather than that of more accessible models is very clear. His reading was extensive: he seems to have known the *Conlationes* and *Instituta* of Cassian intimately, and may have had access to other writers on Eastern monasticism also, Palladius, perhaps, or to the *Dicta patrum*. In any case, he, or perhaps Comgall,[69] gave much thought to the ways of life described by Cassian, and evolved a highly personal synthesis. The importance to him of the Egyptian standard is made clear in his admiring discussion of their monasteries, which immediately follows his outline of his own office. There may be a certain wistfulness in his remark, 'et cum tanta pluralitas eorum sit, ita ut mille abbates sub uno archimandrita esse referantur, nulla ibi conditione coenobii inter duos monachos rixa fuisse fertur uisa.'[70] *Regula coenobialis* that his attempts to discipline the independent minds and hot tempers of his own monks were assiduous, continuous, and never entirely successful. His standards were the highest possible, and his methods were simple, direct, and sincere.

---

[69] The importance of Egypt as a model for Celtic monasticism, not just that of Columbanus, has often been noticed; so this tendency of Columbanus's rule may well go back to Comgall. See, for example, the authorities listed above, n. 27, and note that the Old Irish treatise on the Canonical Hours (ed. Best), gives hours which correspond with the primitive Eastern Office, and is based on Book II of Cassian's *Instituta*.

[70] *Regula monachorum*, § 7 (ed. & transl. Walker, p. 132): 'even though there is so great a number of them that a thousand fathers are said to be under the control of one monastic leader, no one there from the foundation of the community is said to have seen a quarrel between two monks'.

V

THE PENITENTIAL OF COLUMBANUS

T.M. Charles-Edwards

THE penitential attributed to Columbanus is a text of peculiar difficulty.[1] It is, in the first place, evidently composite. To say this is not to imply that any part is not authentic; it does, however, fall into distinct sections, and these sections were not all written as parts of a single work. There are five such sections:[2]

A (i): a monastic penitential dealing with serious sins (*causae casuales*), A 1–8;

A (ii): a monastic penitential directed at 'small offences arising from disorderly habits' (*minuta morum inconditorum*), A 9–12;

B (i): a penitential for the clergy, B 1–12;

B (ii): a penitential for the laity, B 13–25;

B (iii): a monastic penitential dealing with 'minor sanctions for monks' (*minutae monachorum sanctiones*), B 26–9.

The first problem, then, is to account for the textual complexity of the penitential, a complexity shown, most obviously, by the coexistence of two separate sections dealing with minor monastic offences. A further difficulty is that monastic penitential material is also included in Columbanus's *Regula coenobialis*. While the transmission of the latter is principally Frankish, the two existing manuscript-witnesses to the Penitential both go back to a Bobbio archetype, perhaps no earlier than the ninth century. The Penitential also circulated in Francia as shown by quotations in later texts, but the recoverable transmission of the complete text – limited to only one Columbanian monastery – makes it more difficult to assess its relationship to the *Regula coenobialis*. One noticeable characteristic of the anonymous Frankish penitentials of the eighth and ninth centuries is that they quote from the B but not the A sections of the Penitential.[3]

---

[1] The principal editions are: *The Irish Penitentials*, ed. & transl. Bieler, pp. 96–107; *Sancti Columbani Opera*, ed. & transl. Walker, pp. 168–81; and Laporte, *Le Pénitentiel de S. Colomban*. Walker's discussion of the text in his introduction, pp. lii–lv, is short but excellent. The *Penitential* is listed in Lapidge & Sharpe, *A Bibliography*, no. 640, and in Kenney, *The Sources*, no. 46.

[2] The distinction between the A and B sections was made by Wasserschleben, *Die Bussordnungen*, pp. 353–60, and by Seebass, 'Das Poenitentiale Columbani', pp. 430–48, but abandoned, wrongly in my view, by Laporte, *Le Pénitentiel*, whose numbering thus differs from that of other editors.

[3] As shown by the *Index Fontium* to *Paenitentialia Minora*, ed. Kottje *et al.*, p. 212. The interest of the *Paenitentiale Burgundense* was confined to Columbanus's clerical penitential, B (i), but it also had access to the lay penitential, B (ii). The quotations

The textual history of the Penitential needs to be clarified before it can be a reliable basis for more general historical arguments. This paper is an attempt to tease out the history of the text. Because this is difficult, only a few suggestions are offered about Columbanus's significance in the history of penance.

A more general difficulty is that Columbanus's Penitential stands close to the most fundamental single change in the tradition of the Celtic penitential, a change which may be expressed as the divide between the period before Cummian and the period from Cummian onwards. Penitentials before Cummian were directed at particular groups within the Church, monks or clergy or laity. From Cummian onwards much more systematic penitentials, based on Cassian's eight vices and their opposite virtues, dealt with the Church as a whole and only occasionally turned to consider one group to the exclusion of others.[4] I shall describe these two types of penitential as the 'particular' and the 'comprehensive', the particular before Cummian and the comprehensive from Cummian onwards. The particular penitentials are early and predominantly British; the comprehensive ones are initially Irish and only begin in the mid-seventh century.[5] The Penitential of Columbanus is the final stage among the particular penitentials: while it remains particular in that its different sections are each concerned with one group in the Church, it nevertheless has a more comprehensive character in that it is the first to cover all three such groups – monks, clergy and laity.

Particular Penitentials	Abbrev.[6]	Directed at
Preface of Gildas	(Gi)	monks and clergy
Synod of North Britain	(Aq)	monks
Synod of the Grove of Victory	(Lu)	monks
Excerpts from a Book of David	(Da)	clergy
Vinnian	(Vi)	clergy and laity
Columbanus	(Co)	monks, clergy and laity

came from B (i) with the exception of *Paenitentiale Burgundense*, § 19, from Columbanus, *Poenitentiale*, § 18; here the *laicus* of Columbanus has been replaced with *clericus* in the *Paenitentiale Burgundense*, demonstrating that the text's concern was confined to clerics. For the evidence of the 'Longer Version' of the *Regula coenobialis*, see below, pp. 232–5.

[4] It is argued by Körntgen, *Studien zu den Quellen*, pp. 7–35, that the earliest Irish or British penitential to use Cassian's schema was the *Paenitentiale Ambrosianum*; this conclusion arises out of his redating of the penitential, previously thought to be ninth-century, to a period before Cummian. The argument depends upon a consideration of parallels between (a) Cummian, the Ambrosian penitential, and such sources as the *Excerpta de libro Dauidis*, and (b) Cummian, the Ambrosian penitential and the *Regula coenobialis*. On (a) it seems evident to me that Cummian used the *Excerpta de libro Dauidis* directly and did not derive the relevant material *via* the Ambrosian penitential; (b) is a much more complex issue, partly because there are strong reasons to suppose the existence of a lost text or texts which stand behind all surviving versions (see below, pp. 228–31). It may be that Körntgen's argument will prevail, but the issues undoubtedly need further consideration.

[5] All are edited by Bieler, *The Irish Penitentials*. For a discussion of the origins of the Irish type of penitential discipline, see Dooley, 'From penance to confession', pp. 390–411 (I am indebted to Luned Davies for this reference).

[6] The abbreviations are those used by Bieler, *ibid.*, with the exception that I use 'Bigotian' in place of Bieler's Bi for the Bigotian Penitential.

The wide scope of Columbanus's Penitential is, from one point of view, a consequence of drawing on at least two sources, Vinnian preeminently, but also the British penitentials which seem to have been transmitted as a single group.[7] While Vinnian deals with clergy and laity, the British penitentials are predominantly monastic and do not deal with the laity at all. The scope of Columbanus's Penitential also raises, however, the whole issue of the saint's impact on Frankish society. It might be argued that its coverage is a direct reflection of his penitential practice in Francia. Although the surviving manuscript-transmission stems from Bobbio, the reference to the Bonosiac heresy confirms that the text itself goes back to Columbanus's years in Burgundy.[8] Yet, if we then turn to Columbanus's other work and to Ionas's *uita*, an interesting contrast emerges. Only in the *Regula coenobialis* (which includes a monastic penitential) and in the Penitential itself is much concern shown with penitential discipline.[9] In Ionas's *uita*, however, there is frequent mention of penance. The contrast is further sharpened if we look more closely at Ionas's work: the majority of references to penance and to confession of sins occurs in Book II, Ionas's account of the disciples of Columbanus, rather than in Book I, devoted to the saint himself.[10] It seems that the penitential regime was central to Columbanian monasticism in the generation after his death, whereas in his own writings such themes as the perception of human life as a *peregrinatio* alienated from a heavenly *patria* were more prominent.

There may also have been a shift of emphasis within the penitential regime in the first half of the seventh century. Book I of the *uita* shows a concern with *paenitentia*; but in Book II there are even more references to *confessio*. For Book II, what matters most is that the minds of monks and nuns – especially nuns – should be transparent, first to their superiors, but also to their brethren or sisters. In the monastic *familia* hidden sin is the chief enemy, and such sins are thoughts and desires even more than words or actions. For Columbanus, monks should confess their sins, however venial,

---

[7] Cf. Bieler, *ibid.*, p. 3; on the debt to Vinnian, see Wasserschleben, *Die Bussordnungen*, p. 55.

[8] Columbanus, *Poenitentiale*, B 25. According to Laporte, *Le Pénitentiel*, pp. 62–3, this paragraph is an addition made after Columbanus's death; yet he does not, so far as I can see, advance any good reasons. Even if it is an addition, it shows that the text then existed in Burgundy. On Eusthasius's preaching against the Bonosiacs, see Seebass, 'Das Poenitentiale Columbani', p. 435, on the evidence of the *Vita Eusthasii*, § 3, *Vita Agili*, § 9 and *Vita Selebergae*, § 7.

[9] The exceptions which prove the rule are *Epistula* I.6–7 (by implication) and *Instructio* IX.2.

[10] There are approximately six in Book I of Ionas's *Vita S. Columbani* as against sixteen in Book II: they are (a) *paenitentia, paeniteri*: I. 5 (ed. Krusch, *Ionae Vitae Sanctorum*, p. 161. 5), I. 5 (p. 162.5), I. 10 (p. 170. 1), I. 12 (p. 173. 5), I. 19 (p. 192. 1, 10), II. 1 (p. 232. 1, 10), II. 8 (p. 245. 15), II. 10 (p. 254. 15), II. 13 (p. 263. 1), II. 15 (p. 265. 30), II. 19 (p. 273. 5), II. 25 (p. 290. 15); (b) *confessio, confiteri* (in a penitential sense): II. 1 (p. 232. 5), II. 1 (p. 235. 5), II. 12 (p. 261. 25), II. 13 (p. 263. 15), II. 13 (p. 263. 25), II. 17 (p. 269. 25), II. 19 (pp. 272–275. 5), II. 22 (p. 279. 20), II. 24 (p. 288. 10).

once a day;[11] but for his follower, Waldebert, the third abbot of Luxeuil, the number should be increased to three times a day.[12] On this point, it is Waldebert, not Columbanus, who is echoed in Book II of Ionas's *uita*.[13] In Columbanus's Penitential the triad of sins of thought, word and deed, set out by Vinnian, is reduced to the pair of thought and deed, but the triad is openly reiterated by Ionas.[14] The penitential element in Columbanian monasticism was a developing tradition. It may have remained faithful to the spirit of the master, but it was certainly not held captive by the letter of his teaching.[15] The texts, therefore, must be placed in their proper position within the development of this tradition. The textual problem is inseparable from the historical question of the place of penance in the early Irish Church and among Columbanus's followers in Frankish Gaul and Lombard Italy.

Vinnian and Columbanus

The principal key to Columbanus's Penitential is a detailed comparison with its main source, the Penitential of Vinnian. The latter, however, is a penitential for clergy and laity, not for monks.[16] Moreover, the clerical element in Vinnian's Penitential is more elaborate, whereas his penitential for the laity is the first attempt among British or Irish authors to bring the laity within the scope of penitential discipline. I shall, therefore, begin with Columbanus's clerical penitential and compare its provisions both with those of Vinnian and also with Columbanus's monastic and lay penitentials. By making this comparison we can develop an analysis of the text as well as discovering in what ways Columbanus innovated, and thus the particular contribution he made to penitential teaching. The comparison will start with three specimen cases, homicide, theft and perjury.

(a) *Homicide*

Vinnian's treatment of homicide by clerics distinguishes premeditated (§ 23)

---

[11] *Instructio*, IX.2 (ed. & transl. Walker, *Sancti Columbani Opera*, p. 100), *Regula coenobialis*, § I (*ibid.*, p. 144); Krusch seems to me to misinterpret the latter in suggesting that it implies confession twice a day (*Ionae Vitae Sanctorum*, p. 272, n. 2).

[12] *Regula cuiusdam patris ad uirgines*, § 6 (ed. Migne, *Patrologia Latina*, LXXXVIII.1059); cf. Prinz, *Frühes Mönchtum*, p. 81; also the less clear provisions of Columbanus's disciple, Donatus, bishop of Besançon, *Regula ad uirgines*, §§ 19 and 23 (ed. Migne, *Patrologia Latina*, LXXXVII.281–2).

[13] Ionas, *Vita S. Columbani*, II.18 (ed. Krusch, *Ionae Vitae Sanctorum*, p. 272).

[14] Cf. Co A, 2–3 (thought and deed), with Vinnian, 1–3 (thought), 4–5 (word) and 6 onwards (deed); Ionas, *Vita S. Columbani*, II. 18 (ed. Krusch, *Ionae Vitae Sanctorum*, p. 273). On the underlying triad, see Sims-Williams, 'Thought, word and deed' (but Sims-Williams missed the relevance of Vinnian, and, given the possibility that the latter was a Briton, the triad may not be Irish in origin as Sims-Williams supposed).

[15] Cf. the beginning of Ionas, *Vita S. Columbani*, II.9 (ed. Krusch, *Ionae Vitae Sanctorum*, p. 246.2–5).

[16] Pace Bieler, *The Irish Penitentials*, p. 4.

from unpremeditated killing (§ 24). His treatment of premeditated homicide is as follows:[17]

If any cleric has committed homicide and has struck his neighbour and he has died, it is right that he should become an exile from his country for ten years, and let him do penance for seven years in another 'city', three of these on an allowance of bread and water and salt and for four let him abstain from wine and from meat and fast during the forty day periods on bread and water and salt; and when the ten years have been thus completed, if he has behaved well and is approved by the testimony of the abbot or priest to whom he has been entrusted, let him be received back into his homeland and let him pay compensation to the kinsmen of the man whom he killed and let him discharge in his place the duty of care of the old and of obedience to his father and mother if they are still alive; and let him say: 'Here I am in the place of your son; I will do whatever you tell me.' If, however, he has not paid compensation let him never be received back.

There are three distinct elements in the obligations placed upon the penitent homicide. First, the penance proper is in two forms: fasting on bread, water and salt, and a lesser form, abstinence from wine and meat. If we divide the diet in the way normal in this period, into the three elements of bread, *panis*, what accompanies the bread, *companaticum*, and drink, *potus*, it can be seen that the severer form of fasting prohibited any *companaticum* (apart from salt) and restricted the drink to water; the lesser form removed meat from the allowable forms of *companaticum* and wine from the permitted kinds of drink. Secondly, there are additional penalties, running concurrently with the penance. In this instance, the homicide has to live as an exile for ten years. Thirdly, secular obligations may be specifically asserted in the penitential. Thus the penitent homicide must, on his return from exile, compensate the kinsmen of the slain man and care for his parents (the duty known in Old Irish as *goire*, 'warming').[18] The penitential, then, does not confine itself to penance.

On this basis – by distinguishing the penance proper from further penalties and from secular obligation – we may compare the rulings on homicide in Vinnian and Columbanus:

---

[17] For the Latin text, see Bieler, *The Irish Penitentials*, pp. 80–2; 'Si qui\<s\> clericus homicidium fec\<er\>it \<et occiderit proximum suum et mortuus fuerit,\> .x. annis exterrem fieri de patria sua oportet et agat penitentiam .vii. annorum in alia urbe, tres ex his cum pane et aqua et sale per mensura et .iiii. abstineat se a uino et a carnibus et ieiunet xlmas cum pane et aqua et sale, et sic impletis .x. annis, si bene egerit et comprobatus fuerit per testimonium abbatis siue sacerdotis cui commissus fuerit, recipiatur in patria sua et satis faciat amicis eius quem occiderat et uicem pietatis et obedientie reddat patri et matri eius si adhuc in corpore sunt et dicat: "Ecce ego uobis pro filio uestro: quecumque dixeritis mihi faciam." Si autem non satis egerit, non recipiatur in aeternum.' I have corrected Bieler's translation on a few small points; for example, he translates *homicidium* by 'murder' which in a mediaeval context is used for secret homicide.

[18] Binchy, 'Some Celtic legal terms', pp. 228–31. For the combination of penance and *goire*, see the example of Librán in Adomnán, *Vita S. Columbae*, II.39 (edd. & transl. Anderson & Anderson, *Adomnán's Life of Columba*, pp. 154–8).

Table 1

Vinnian and Columbanus on homicide

Penance = periods of (a) Fasting (b) Abstinence	Further Penalties	Secular Obligations

Vinnian, § 27, premeditated homicide by a cleric

7 years = 3 fasting + 4 of abstinence	10 years exile	wergild and *goire*

Vinnian, § 24, unpremeditated homicide by a cleric

6 years = 3 fasting + 3 of abstinence	6 years exile	

Vinnian, § 35, shedding blood (and fornication) by a layman

3 years = 1 fasting + 2 of abstinence	Abstains from bearing arms and from sex. Monetary payment and a feast.[19]	

Co A 3, homicide by a monk

10 years

Co B 1, homicide by a cleric

10 years = 10 fasting	10 years exile	wergild and *goire*

Co B 13, homicide by a layman

3 years = 3 fasting	3 years exile	wergild and *goire*

Co B 1 and 13 follow Vinnian quite closely but introduce several changes: the periods of exile are now of the same length throughout; all of the penance takes the severer form of a ration of bread, water and salt; no distinction is made between premeditated and unpremeditated homicide; wergild and *goire* are explicitly required of the lay homicide, whereas in Vinnian they were at best implicitly demanded. Columbanus on the layman is also more analytical. Vinnian, § 35, is written in terms of a composite picture of the sinful layman: he has committed 'every form of evil', namely the characteristic sins of the lay world, fornicating and shedding blood. The additional penalties, over and above the penance, of abstinence from use of weapons and from sex, reflect this composite picture – a picture, moreover, which was widespread in early Christianity.[20] From Vinnian's composite layman Co B 13 extracts what is

---

[19] Cf. Old Irish *pennait*, which is used for the monetary payment, e.g. *Bretha Crólige*, § 4, ed. Binchy, 'Bretha Crólige', p. 6 and n. on pp. 56–7.

[20] Cf. Sharpe, 'Hiberno-Latin *Laicus*', pp. 75–92.

relevant at that point: the lay homicide. It is only logical that Co specifies only abstinence from the bearing of weapons for the lay homicide, not abstinence from sex: unrestrained anger, not unrestrained sexual appetite is the issue. So far the treatment is rational and shows a readiness to break with tradition. Co A, the monastic penitential, offers, however, only a period of penance, ten years, the same period as for a clerical homicide. Neither the severity of the penance nor further penalties or obligations are specified. One might have expected more detail and also the period of penance to have been longer for a monk than for a cleric.[21]

(b) *Theft*

The provisions for theft are different in form, in that they only prescribe fasting, without a further period of abstinence from meat and wine (in Co A 4 this is not stated explicitly).[22]

Table 2

Vinnian and Columbanus on theft

Penance	Further Obligations
Vinnian, § 25: cleric commits theft once or twice	
1 year of fasting	fourfold restitution
Vinnian, c.26: cleric commits theft more often 3 years of fasting	
Co A 4: a monk commits thefts	
1 year of fasting	
Co B 7: a cleric commits theft once or twice	
1 year of fasting	
Co B 7, a cleric commits theft more often and cannot make restitution	
3 years of fasting	
Co B 19, a layman commits theft once or twice	
3 × 40 days of fasting	restitution
Co B 19, a layman commits theft more often and cannot make restitution	
1 year + 3 × 40 days	alms to the poor and meal to the priest[23]

[21] Cf. Columbanus, *Poenitentiale*, A 5 with B 9 (both on a blow which sheds blood): the monk's penance is more severe than the cleric's.

[22] A possible reason for the absence of any requirement that the penitent abstain from wine and meat is that ample food, especially meat and alcoholic drink, was thought likely to encourage sexual excess but was not relevant to theft (cf. Gildas, *Praefatio de poenitentia*, § 22). In Columbanus, *Poenitentiale*, B 20, however, the division between fasting and abstinence helps to produce an appropriately lighter penance than the corresponding clerical penance of Columbanus, *Poenitentiale*, B 5.

[23] Cf. *Penitentialis Vinniani*, § 35 and Old Irish *pennait* (see above, n. 19).

223

Vinnian, §§ 25–6, provides the basis of the treatment in Co B, notably in the distinction made between isolated and habitual offences. A ruling solely for clerical theft in the source is thus elaborated to provide both for clerical and for lay theft. Again, however, Co A has only a bare penance, with no distinction between isolated and habitual offences and no mention of restitution. Only when multiple restitution was required, could this silence about any restitution be a consequence of the monk's lack of private property. Co A is not directly inconsistent with Co B, although, again, one might have expected a longer penance for a monk.

(c) *Perjury*
The rules on perjury, however, present a different picture.

Table 3

Vinnian and Columbanus on Perjury

Penance	Further Obligations
Vinnian 22, a cleric swears a false oath	
7 years of fasting	Never swear another oath. Free a slave.
Co A 4a, monk commits perjury	
7 years of fasting	
Co B 5, cleric commits perjury	
7 years of fasting	Never swear another oath.
Co B 20, layman commits perjury through cupiditas	
	Gives all his goods to the poor. Lifelong service in a monastery.
Co B 20, layman commits perjury through fear of death	
5 years = 3 fasting + 2 of abstinence	Exile for 3 years. Frees a slave. Not to bear weapons for three years. Gives alms frequently during the last two years.

Columbanus's rule for clerics corresponds closely to Vinnian's, except for the omission of Vinnian's requirement that the perjured cleric ransom a slave. The omitted requirement, however, reappears in Columbanus's rule for lay people. Yet the latter is, taken as a whole, inconsistent with the provisions for clerical and monastic perjurers. There is no mention of the requirement not to swear another oath; the distinction between perjury arising out of *cupiditas* and perjury arising out of fear of death is only applied to the layman; yet a cleric might have property and thus have just as much scope for *cupiditas* as a layman. With its bare mention of a period of penance, Co A differs markedly from the approach taken by Co B, both for the cleric and for the layman.

The only explanation for the inconsistencies, apart from a serious oversight on the part of the compiler, is that these sections of Columbanus's Penitential were not composed as elements of a single work, but as three separate attempts to produce concise penitentials, one for monks, another for clerics and a third for lay people. Probably all three were dependent upon Vinnian: this is clear for Co B on clerics and likely for Co A on monks; Co B on laymen appears to be a separate adaptation of Vinnian, using his material on both laymen and clerics.

Co A, the penitential for monks, was probably written first. If it had been composed after the penitential for clerics, one would have expected more effort to distinguish the two by stiffening the penances for monks. Also Co A is very brief in style, usually only giving the period of the penance and nothing more. If it had been composed after the penitential for clerics, one would have expected a more expansive style, allowing for more detail on the character of the penance.

It is also possible that the relationship between Co A (for monks), Co B (i) (for clerics) and Co B (ii) (for the laity) may have something to do with the physical form of the original manuscript. The dimensions of Vinnian's penitential suggest that it originally took the form of a single quire;[24] but Co A, B (i) and B (ii) could each have been fitted onto a single folio. Written at different times in a developing penitential tradition, there was no compelling reason why they had to be consistent parts of a single treatise. Only when they were copied, probably onto a single quire, would there have been any reason why they should have begun to seem like a single work. An account of the creation of the Penitential along these lines also makes it possible to explain the existence of two sections – my A (ii) and B (iii) – on minor monastic offences. The second of the two, B (iii), has all the appearance of being a response to a particular question, that of the modesty which a monk should observe when bathing. It does not overlap A (ii) in content and there is no intrinsic reason why it should appear where it does, as an appendix to a penitential for the laity. What may have happened is this: B (ii) already existed, perhaps on its own, perhaps conjoined with B (i); the issue of modesty was raised, and because there was space after the end of B (ii) the appropriate rules were written there. If A (i) was already in what we may call Columbanus's penitential file on a single leaf, that leaf may by this stage have been filled up by A (ii), so pushing B (iii) on to a different folio. If this argument is accepted, it follows that A (i) preceded B (i), and that A (ii) preceded B (iii).

The Penitential and the Regula coenobialis

The idea that Columbanus's Penitential is best understood as a file of documents rather than a single text may help us out of some difficulties, but it

---

[24] Cf. the *libelli, quos paenitentiales uocant, quorum sunt certi errores, incerti auctores* denounced by the Carolingian Council of Chalon-sur-Sâone, A.D. 813, § 25 (*Concilia*, ed. Werminghoff, p. 281).

makes one problem more urgent: the relationship between Columbanus's Penitential and his *Regula coenobialis*. The latter was perceived to be just as much a penitential as a monastic rule.[25] The longer (and later) version makes the same distinction between major and minor offences as is made in the Penitential.[26] The sections on minor monastic offences in the Penitential make use, not of penance in the narrow sense, but of the same penalties – corporal punishment, impositions of silence, *superpositiones* (so many forfeited dinners) – as do large parts of the *Regula coenobialis*. On the other hand, parts of the *Regula coenobialis* (§§ X–XIII, XV) mainly employ periods of penance. There are also a very few rules which occur both in the *Regula coenobialis* and in the Penitential,[27] while two passages from the Penitential are quoted in the longer version of the *Regula coenobialis*. The language of the Rule differs a little from that of the Penitential, but no more perhaps than do different sections of the Penitential from each other.[28]

The links between Rule and Penitential should not obscure more fundamental differences. The Rule begins with minor offences sanctioned by corporal punishment. It progresses to somewhat more serious offences punished by *superpositiones*, and eventually to days of fasting as in the Penitential. The essential concern of the Rule, therefore, is with *minores negligentiae*, also termed *minuta morum inconditorum* or *minutae monachorum sanctiones*, the day-to-day matters of monastic discipline.[29] The Penitential, however, is primarily concerned with major offences, *capitalia crimina* or *causae casuales*.[30] Its penalties are regularly in terms of years of penance and only occasionally descend to *superpositiones* or corporal punishment. It is, therefore, the borderland between monastic rule and monastic penitential which offers the best opportunities of comparison between the *Regula coenobialis* and Columbanus's Penitential.

This borderland is occupied by *Regula coenobialis*, §§ X–XV. Walker has put forward reasons for thinking that these sections are a later addition to an original text which consisted of §§ I–IX.[31] While they may or may not be later, they are likely to have been written at different times. Like the Penitential,

---

[25] *Sancti Columbani Opera*, ed. & transl. Walker, p. 144, line 28 (Longer Version).

[26] *Ibid.*, lines 32–3.

[27] *Ibid.*, p. 166, line 34 (from Co A 11–12).

[28] In the original *Regula coenobialis*, §§ I–IX, the word for a blow is *percussio*, in *Regula coenobialis*, §§ XII–XIV, it is *uerber* (but Columbanus does use *uerber*: *Sancti Columbani Opera*, ed. & transl. Walker, p. 80). In Columbanus, *Poenitentiale*, A 2, there is a single example of *plaga*, in Columbanus, *Poenitentiale*, B 3, one of *percussio* and one of *plaga*. Cf. Walker's use of these differences (*ibid.*, p. li).

[29] *Regula coenobialis*, ed. & transl. Walker, *Sancti Columbani Opera*, p. 144, line 32; Columbanus, *Poenitentiale*, A 8, B 25.

[30] *Regula coenobialis*, ed. & transl. Walker, *Sancti Columbani Opera*, p. 144, line 32; Columbanus, *Poenitentiale*, A 8, B Praef. Cf. Vogel, *La discipline pénitentielle*, pp. 88–101, on Caesarius of Arles.

[31] See the preface to Walker's edition (*Sancti Columbani Opera*, p. li). He points out that the term for a blow changes from *percussio* to *uerber* (but cf. *uerberibus*, p. 80.2), that *abbas* and *oeconomus* are introduced (the abbot in the earlier part is *pater*).

therefore, the existing *Regula coenobialis* may be, in origin, more a file of texts than a single work. As we shall see, §§ X–XV are a set of monastic penitential texts devoted to minor offences. An initial approach to this borderland is a set of rules in § XV.[32] These rules are devoted to a most distasteful topic; but here, again, the readiness to prescribe penances for such matters is a direct consequence of maintaining that they can be forgiven. For the writer of penitentials only the unforgivable is unmentionable. For our purposes, they are important, for they demonstrate, first, the existence of lost sources, and, secondly, a complex network of textual relations between the extant Irish penitentials. From this material, therefore, we are enabled to perceive something of the nature of the Irish penitential tradition.

Regula coenobialis, § XV, has two intersecting concerns. One the one hand, it is a text directed at offences involving the consecrated host. Distinct from these issues arising from the host is a further concern, common to most penitential tests, with over-eating and over-drinking, most obviously demonstrated when excess leads to vomiting. The point of intersection occurs when the offender vomits the host. Most penitentials say something about this offence. We may begin by comparing *Regula coenobialis*, § XV, with an eighth-century text, the Bigotian Penitential. The latter gives two authorities, explicitly distinguished by an 'Aliter alius dicit' and by a direct contradiction: in the case when a person vomits the host by reason of sickness one authority decrees a fast of twenty days, the other one of seven days.[33] I shall call these two authorities Bigotian (a) and Bigotian (b).[34] Bigotian (b) is derived from the-mid seventh-century Penitential of Cummian, but Bigotian (a) corresponds closely to part of *Regula coenobialis*, § XV:[35]

Paenitentiale Bigotianum, I.iii.1–2	*Regula coenobialis*, XV.8.
Qui sacrificium euomit causa uoracitatis, .xl. diebus. Si uero obtentu insoliti cybi pinguioris et non uitio saturitatis sed stomachi, .xxx. Si infirmitatis gratia, .xx. peniteat.	Si autem obtentu insoliti pinguioris cybi et non uitio saturitatis sed stomachi euomit in die sacrificii coenam, .xx. diebus; si infirmitatis gratia, .x. diebus paeniteat in pane et aqua.

It is probable that the *Regula coenobialis* has lost a sentence corresponding to the first sentence of the Bigotian Penitential's text.[36] The clause 'Si autem obtentu insoliti pinguioris ... coenam' requires a contrast with a preceding rule covering the case when the sinner has vomited through *uoracitas* (or *saturitas*). The source of the Bigotian Penitential is not, therefore, the *Regula coenobialis* as we have it, but either a better text of the *Regula coenobialis* or the text from which the latter took this part of § XV.[37]

---

[32] A closely related text is contained in the *Paenitentiale Ambrosianum*, § IX, ed. Körntgen, *Studien zu den Quellen*, pp. 269–70.

[33] 'Bigotian Penitential', I. iii (ed. & transl. Bieler, *The Irish Penitentials*, p. 214).

[34] 'Bigotian Penitential' (a) is I. iii. 1–2; (b) is I. iii. 3–4.

[35] This section is not in the *Paenitentiale Ambrosianum*.

[36] Perhaps by eye-skip from one occurrence of *diebus* to the next.

[37] Cf. the way in which §§ X–XIV tend to introduce rules, 'Si quis . . .' with the formulae used by § XV, 'Si . . .' or 'Qui . . .' It is worth noting that the comparison

One element in the contrast between Bigotian (a) and Bigotian (b) is that the former and the *Regula coenobialis* proceed to allocate their penances on a decimal basis, whereas the latter and Cummian, I. 8–9, operate with a pair of penances, forty days and seven days. The twenty-day penance found in Bigotian (a) and the *Regula coenobialis* reappears, however, in another part of Cummian (§ XI: *De questionibus sacrificii*).[38] As Bieler notes, this part of Cummian is close to the *Regula coenobialis*, § XV. The resemblances are sufficiently close to suggest that they draw on the same text.[39] Yet Cummian § XI is itself a text with a complicated history behind it, as one can see by comparing it with Cummian I. 8–11 (itself one of the sources of the Bigotian Penitential):

Cummian I. 8–11

8. Si uero sacrificium euomerit, .xl. diebus.
9. Si autem infirmitatis causa, .vii. diebus.
10. Si in ignem proiecerit, .c. psalmos cantat.
11. Si vero canes lambuerint talem uomitum, .c. diebus qui euomit peniteat.

Cummian XI. 7–9

7. Sacrificium euomens grauatus saturitate uentris, si in ignem proiecerit, .xx. diebus, sin autem, .xl.
8. Si uero canes comederint talem uomitum, .c.
9. Si autem dolore, et in ignem proiecerit, .c. psalmos canat.

If we put these two texts together, we obtain the following:

i.   Si uero sacrificium euomerit grauatus saturitate uentris, .xl. diebus. (I.8; cf. XI.7)
ii. Si in ignem proiecerit, .xx. diebus. (XI.7)
iii. Si autem infirmitatis causa, .vii. diebus. (I.9)
iv. Si autem dolore, et in ignem proiecerit, .c. psalmos canat. (I.10; XI.a)
v.   Si uero canes lambuerint talem uomitum, .c. diebus. (I.11; XI.8)

---

made by Körntgen, *Studien zu den Quellen*, pp. 19–22, between Cummian, the Ambrosian penitential and the *Regula coenobialis*, § XV, uses text which is not from the original § XV but from what I call the Supplement, that is to say the revision of the entire *Regula*. This thoroughly misleading procedure is justified by the astonishing statement, p. 19, n. 86, that 'Die Unterscheidung verschiedener Rezensionen der Regula coenobialis kann im literarischen Vergleich zunächst unberücksicht verbleiben.' The refusal by Körntgen to provide a detailed analysis of the relationship between the original *Regula coenobialis*, § XV, and the *Poenitentiale Ambrosianum* is based on the claim, *Studien zu den Quellen*, p. 45, that for the parallel passages there is no third witness; this is only acceptable if Körntgen's thesis that Cummian used the Ambrosian penitential is already considered to be well-founded; yet that is one of the issues which he is attempting to determine. It is dangerous to settle a question after a partial consideration of the evidence and then fail to consider the rest because, it is supposed, a firm conclusion has already been obtained.

[38] Ed. & transl. Bieler, *The Irish Penitentials*, pp. 130–2.
[39] Cu XI   *Reg. coen.* § XV
    19 = 2
    20 = 3
    21 = 4–5
    22 = 6

It may well be that Cummian's source had all five clauses.

Before we leave Cummian, we should notice another rule in a different part of the work § IX, *De minutis causis*):[40]

Si casu aliquo neglegens quis sacrificium perdat, relinquens illud feris et alitibus deuorandum, si excusabiliter, tres xlmis, sin uero, anno peniteat.

The origins of this clause lie in the sixth century, in Gildas's *Praefatio*, § 9:[41]

Si casu neglegens quis sacrificium aliquod perdat, per .iii. xlmas, relinquens illud feris et alitibus deuorandum.

Other treatments of this issue, apart from Vinnian, all prescribe a year's penance:

Co A 6:   Si ipsum sacrificium quis perdiderit, anno paeniteat.
Co B 12:   Si quis sacrificium perdiderit, anno paeniteat.
Regula coenobialis, XV.8:   Quicumque sacrificium perdiderit, et nescit ubi sit, annum paeniteat.

It is possible that Cummian's distinction, 'si excusabiliter ... sin uero', was designed to achieve a reconciliation between Gildas and an authority favouring a penance of a year. Cummian never explains *excusabiliter* and it may be a mere device to prevent a direct clash between his authorities. Yet although Columbanus is the only extant written authority earlier than Cummian to prescribe a year's penance, there is no certainty that one of his writings was Cummian's source. Columba of Iona was also probably the author of a penitential which has not survived;[42] also, Cummian's authority for the year-long penance may not have been written at all.

The textual relationships so far appear to be as follows:

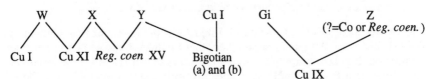

Here W is the source of Cummian I.8–11 and XI.7–9; X = a text on offences involving the host; Y is either a source used by the *Regula coenobialis* and the Bigotian Penitential or a better version of the *Regula coenobialis* than any now existing; Z is the written, or perhaps oral, authority for the year-long penance, an authority which could be Co A, B or the *Regula coenobialis* or some other

---

40 *The Irish Penitentials*, ed. & transl. Bieler, p. 124: 'If by some accident anyone negligently lose the host, leaving it for beasts and birds to devour, if it is excusable he shall do penance for three forty-day periods; if not, for a year.'

41 *Praefatio de poenitentia*, ed. & transl. Bieler, *The Irish Penitentials*, pp. 62–3: 'If someone by a mishap through carelessness loses a host, leaving it for beasts and birds to devour, he shall do penance for three forty-day periods.'

42 See the Old Irish Penitential, III.12 (transl. by Binchy in *The Irish Penitentials*, ed. & transl. Bieler, p. 267).

text which has not survived. The stemma demonstrates how complex the textual tradition of the Irish penitentials had already become by the mid-seventh century. Cummian's Penitential, the next after Columbanus's in the sequence of surviving penitentials, is drawing on different sources for different sections of the text. Most of these sources are lost, but at least it can be shown *via* an analysis of Cummian's Penitential how productive the Irish tradition of penitential writing was in the century between Vinnian and Cummian, a century in which Columbanus occupies a central position. The direct implication is, therefore, that much of the immediate textual setting of Columbanus's Penitential is lost.

Now that the relationships between the penitentials are a little clearer, we can return to Columbanus. There are two clauses in Columbanus's Penitential which prescribe penances for those who vomit the host, Co A 6 and Co B 12, from the monastic and clerical penitentials respectively. We may begin by comparing them with the texts from Cummian, §§ I and XI, and also with a further clause – (iii) below – drawn from the *Regula coenobialis*, § XV, and the Bigotian Penitential. Among the following sentences, some contain reconstructed text. They are not offered as a body of material which existed in any single hypothetical source, but are collected together to give some idea of the range of material on this topic.

i.   Si uero grauatus saturitate uentris sacrificium euomuerit, .xl. diebus. Co A, Co B, Cu I, Cu XI, Bigotian; cf. Gi 7.
ii.   Si in ignem proiecerit, .xx. diebus: Cu XI.
iii. Si uero obtentu insoliti cybi pinguioris et non uitio saturitatis sed stomachi, .xxx./.xx. diebus: *Reg. coen.* XV, Bigotian.
iv.   Si autem infirmitatis causa, .vii. diebus: Co A, Co B, *Reg. coen.* XV, Cu I, Bigotian, cf. Gi 7.
v.   Si in ignem proiecerit, .c. psalmos canat: Cu I, Bigotian.
vi.   Si uero canes lambuerint talem uomitum, .c. diebus: Cu I, Bigotian.

The earliest text, Gildas, *Praefatio*, § 7, agrees with Co A and B in containing only (i) and (iv). We may assume, then, that the texts have grown rather than contracted. It is also quite likely that all the versions of (i) and (iv) subsequent to Gildas stem from a single text, very probably itself a rewritten version of Gildas § 7. This would have been roughly as follows:[43]

Si quis grauatus saturitate uentris sacrificium euomuerit, .xl. diebus paeniteat.
Si autem infirmitatis causa, et non uoracitatis, .vii. diebus.

The clear change to this text, apart from minor rearrangements, is that Co B 12 and the Bigotian Penitential, I.iii.1, prefer *uoracitas* to *saturitas*. It is likely that *saturitas* is the original because it appears in the version of (iii) in *Regula coenobialis*, § XV, and in the Bigotian Penitential, I.iii.2. Support for the notion that all these versions of (i) and (iv) go back to a single original is offered by the agreement of all witnesses, apart from Co B 12, in prescribing

---

[43] This is based mainly on *Poenitentiale Cummeani*, XI. 7, compared with Gildas, *Praefatio*, § 7.

the pair of penances, forty and seven days. On this basis then we may suggest the following stemma:

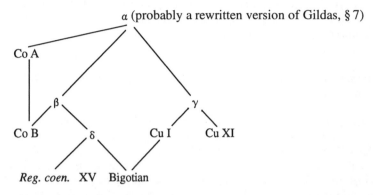

β substituted *uoracitatis causa* for *grauatus saturitate uentris* and omitted *et non uoracitatis*.
γ added (v) and (vi), and possibly (ii).
δ added (iii).

Co A 9 introduced the issue of drunkenness, and this was also inserted into Co B 12, although the latter was derived from β rather than directly from α. In the stemma given above, the left-hand branch is the one which is crucial for the Columbanian penitential tradition. The central position between the two branches of the Bigotian Penitential is also shown by its links both to δ and the Penitential of Cummian.

These conclusions can be checked by comparing Co A 9 and B 12 with a β-version and a γ-version of (i):

Co A 6	Si quis autem inebriauerit se et uomuerit aut saturatus nimis sacrificium per hoc euomuerit, .xl. diebus paeniteat.
Co B 12	Si per aebrietatem aut uoracitatem illud [*sc.* sacrificium] euomuerit et neglegenter illud dimiserit, .iii. quadragisimas in pane et aqua paeniteat.
A β-text	Bigotian Penitential, I.iii.1: Qui sacrificium euomit causa uoracitatis, .xl. diebus.
A γ-text	Cummian, XI.7: Sacrificium euomens grauatus saturitate uentris . . . .xl.

Co A 6 is clumsily expressed: it is unclear whether the drunk, as well as the glutton, has vomited the host. Co B 12 is entirely clear on the question. The clumsiness of Co A 6 may be explained by supposing that a not-too-skilful writer wished to introduce the question of drunkenness. The reason he wished to introduce this further issue is shown by Co B 22, 'Si quis laicus inebriauerit se aut usque ad uomitum manducauerit aut biberit, septimana in pane et aqua peniteat'. This clause does not concern itself with the host, but only with drunkenness and gluttony. Co A 6 has probably tried to combine such a clause with the rule concerning the host and has achieved only confusion. The inconsistency of Co A (i) and Co B (i) is again illustrated: the cleric must do penance for 120 days, the monk only for forty. Such inconsistencies, as well as the different positions in the stemma occupied by Co A and Co B (i) respectively, strongly suggest that they were in origin separate texts. On the other hand, they are both in the same branch of the tradition, and Co B (i) seems to have used Co A (i). The textual history is thus consistent with the idea of a file of penitential texts evolving over time.

The Different Versions of the Regula coenobialis *and their Relationship to the Penitential*

The issue of the position to be assigned to the *Regula coenobialis* remains difficult. The *Regula* itself seems to be a separate file of texts: the original rule (§§ I–IX) is followed by a series of additions. The reason why § XV is contained in the *Regula* rather than in the Penitential may be no more than an accident of filing: it just happened to find a place in the *Regula coenobialis* file rather than in the Penitential file. The stemma indicated that there is a textual relationship between § XV and the Penitential, although it is indirect (*via* δ). So far as the *Regula coenobialis* is concerned, any textual relationship to the penitentials holds good only for § XV. Other chapters might have a quite different set of relationships; indeed, it remains to be seen if there are any textual links at all between the penitentials and chapters of the *Regula* other than § XV.

If we adopt the abbreviation RC^1 for the original rule, namely §§ I–IX, the additional texts can be distinguished as follows:

RC^2 = X–XI	Minor offences mostly punished by so many days on bread and water. This is expressed by the formula '. . . dies una paxmate et aqua'.
RC^3 = XII–XIII	Minor offences, again mostly punished by so many days on bread and water; but this is now expressed by a different formula, '. . . dies in pane et aqua'.
RC^4 = XIV	Even more minor offences punished by so many strokes (*uerbera*).
RC^5 = XV	A text on offences concerning the consecrated host.

Of these RC^{2-3} received very slight additions in the longer version of the *Regula coenobialis*. The latter, however, contains extensive additions after RC^5; these I term the Supplement. The longer version thus revised RC^1 most and is otherwise distinguished mainly by additions rather than revisions.

The first specimen case illustrating the relationship between the Penitential and the Rule, apart from RC^5, is Co A 9 (the beginning of Co A (ii)):

Co A 9	RC^{1-2}*(shorter version)*	*RC (longer version)*
i(a) Qui facit per se aliquid sine interrogatione,	Si quis, quando consummauerit opus suum, non requirit et fecerit aliquid sine iussu, uiginti .iiii. psalmos cantet. XI.2	Operis peculiaris praesumptio .c. plagis. Suppl. 9.

(b)	uel qui contradicit et dicit 'Non facio'.	Si quis dicit 'Non faciam',[44] tres dies uno paxmatio et aqua. X.2.	Qui murmurat, qui dicit 'Non faciam nisi dicit abbas uel secundus', tribus superpositionibus. VII.[6].
(c)	uel qui murmorat, si grande sit, tribus superpositionibus, si paruum, una paeniteat.	Si quis murmurat, duos dies uno paxmatio et aqua. X.3.	Si uel leniter murmurauerit, superpositione. Suppl. 24.
ii(a)	Uerbum uero contra uerbum simpliciter prumptum .l. plagis uindicandum est,	Consilium contra consilium cum simplicitate promens, .l. percussionibus. IV.9	Uerbum contra uerbum simpliciter dictum .vi. percussionibus;
(b)	uel si ex contentione, silentii superpositione.	Si duo fratres contenderint aliquid et ad furorem uenerint, duos dies uno paxmatio et aqua. X.5.	si ex contentione, .c. plagis uel superpositione silentii. Suppl. 16.
(iii)	Nam si rixa, septimana paeniteat.		Qui autem rixam commiserit, septem diebus peniteat. Suppl. 38.

Both the shorter and the longer versions are probably drawing on Co A (ii); yet some of the clearest verbal parallels with clauses of the Penitential occur in the longer version of the *Regula coenobialis*. This is especially clear in ii(a), even though the shorter version retains the same punishment as the Penitential. In other words, the longer version was here using Co A (ii) directly, not *via* the shorter version. The shorter version in this instance, however, is the original Rule, RC^1. As soon as we examine the main source of parallels given above from the shorter version, namely RC^2, it is evident that the penalties, now stated as so many days (*uno*) *paxmatio et aqua*, are quite different from those given in the Penitential:

Penitential	RC^2	*Longer Version*
(i) (b) tribus superpositionibus	tres dies uno paxmatio et aqua	tribus superpositionibustribus
(c) tribus superpositionibus/ una superpositione	duos dies uno paxmatio et aqua	tribus superpositionibus/ (una) superpositione
(ii) (b) superpositione	duos dies uno paxmatio et aqua	.c. plagis uel superpositione silentii

What makes RC^2 look different from Co A (ii) is, therefore, the way in which the clauses prescribing the penances have been rewritten, abandoning the old term *superpositio*. Once that deliberate change has been discounted, the link between the two texts becomes clearer.

---

[44] Cf. Columbanus, *Poenitentiale*, B 1, 'quaecunque uultis faciam uobis'.

The language of the Co A is the most rudimentary among these texts:

(i)	The Penitential uses the present indicative:	Other texts use the future perfect:
	Qui facit . . .	Si quis . . . fecerit . . . XI.2
	Qui murmorat (= si quis murmurat) X.3;	murmurauerit VIII.[6]
	Qui murmurat, VIII.[6])	
(ii)	The Penitential has ellipsis of the verb in the protasis:	Other texts have future perfect verbs:
	si ex contentione . . .	si . . . contenderint . . . X.5.
	si rixa . . .	Qui autem rixam commiserit . . . Supp. 1.38
(iii)	The Penitential uses the present indicative with future meaning:	Other texts do not:
	'Non facio'	'Non faciam', VIII.[6], X.2.
(iv)	Vocabulary: Verbum uero contra	Consilium contra consilium . . . IV.9.

The use of the present indicative *facio* rather than the future *faciam* may be a consequence of the influence of his native language on a speaker of British.[45] If this is the explanation, Co A may be the work of a Briton.[46] It may also be of significance that RC^2 (X.6) contains the clearest example of a calque on Old Irish in the entire corpus of writings attributed to Columbanus: 'si alius contendit mendacium' = 'mad gáu as-mbeir alaile', where *alius* in place of *quis* is very likely to be due to the influence of Irish *alaile*.[47] The first specimen case, therefore, suggests that Co A (ii) was directly available to the author of the original *Regula coenobialis*, namely the shorter version of RC^1, and also both to the Irish author of RC^2 and to the author of the longer version of the entire Rule.

The second specimen example to illustrate the relationship of the *Regula coenobialis* to the Penitential is Co A 10 (also from Co A (ii)). Here the texts to be compared are both from the shorter version, one from the original rule (VII.1), one from RC^2 (X.10):

Co A 10	RC^1	RC^2
(i) Qui autem detrahit aut libenter audit detrahentem, tribus superpositionibus paeniteat;	Qui detrahit alicui fratri aut audit detrahentem, non corrigens eum, tribus superpositionibus. (VII.1)	Si quis detractauerit abbati suo, .vii. dies uno paxmatio et aqua; si quis fratri suo uiginti .iiii. psalmos; si saeculari, duodecim psalmos. (X.10).
(ii) Si de eo qui praeest, septimana paeniteat.		

---

[45] None of the mediaeval or modern Brittonic languages inherited a future tense from the Celtic parent language.

[46] Both Bieler, *The Irish Penitentials*, p. 5, and Körntgen, *Studien zu den Quellen*, p. 46, believe that Columbanus was the author of Co A.

[47] See Bieler *apud Sancti Columbani Opera*, ed. & transl. Walker, p. lxxxii.

The version in RC^1 may well be a slightly expanded, and better written, version of the corresponding sentence in Co A; if the rule in RC^2 also derives from the Penitential, it has been fundamentally rewritten, again abandoning the old term *superpositio*, but also distinguishing the abbot from the other *fratres*.

These comparisons between the Penitential and the *Regula coenobialis* have demonstrated the complexity of the latter. They suggest that some of the closest textual links between the Penitential and the Rule are, first, between Co A (ii) and RC^1, the original version containing nine chapters, and, secondly, between Co A (ii) and the additions made in the longer version of the Rule, perhaps about the middle of the seventh century. There are also probable links with RC^2, but these have been disguised by rewriting. Since the longer version appears to have been written in Francia, it helps to show that Co A was then known north of the Alps, although the indirect tradition of the Frankish anonymous penitentials only attests Co B (the surviving manuscripts, it will be remembered, come from Bobbio, not from Francia).[48] Similarly, the links with the original Rule help to confirm that the monastic penitential, Co A (i) + A (ii), is no later than the early seventh century. The linguistic comparison, however, raises the issue whether Co A was written by Columbanus himself. The rudimentary Latin suggests that the monastic penitential may have been brought from Bangor to Francia as part of a penitential file which also included Vinnian and the British penitentials.

It is very difficult to know whether any of the texts in the monastic penitential in *Regula coenobialis*, §§ X–XV, was the work of Columbanus or, as Walker thought, one of his immediate successors. It antedates the creation of the longer version of the whole rule (itself no later than the second half of the seventh century).[49] The linguistic evidence suggests a plurality of authors, while the rules are consistent, in spirit if not in detail, with the Penitential. As we have seen already in comparing Co A with Co B, it is extremely difficult to settle questions of authorship when texts are compiled from other texts, added to at different times, or combined with other texts by the same or a different author. Two files of, or including, penitential texts were expanding over the century *ca* 550–*ca* 650, and several people and processes of composition were involved. The expansion of the files can, therefore, be plausibly reconstructed in a succession of stages:

(i) The penitential file

(a)   The initial form of the penitential file included the British penitentials and Vinnian. It thus already covered monks, clerics and laity.

(b)   Co A (i) was written to provide an extremely concise monastic penitential, wider in range than the three British penitenitials devoted to monks, and drawn mainly from the clerical section of Vinnian.

(c)   After (b) and before (f) a few rules concerning minor monastic offences, A (ii) were added to (b), probably on the same single folio.

---

[48]   *Paenitentialia Minora*, ed. Kottje *et al.*, p. 212.
[49]   Walker, *Sancti Columbani Opera*, pp. l–lii.

(d)   After (b), Co B (i) was written as a clerical penitential. This was drawn from Vinnian's rules on clerics and also from Co A (i). The quality of the Latin is considerably superior to that of Co A (i).

(e)   Co B (ii) was written as a lay penitential, but was drawn mainly from Vinnian's clerical section. This text was written in Burgundy, probably by the person who wrote Co B (i). These two stages are attested by the indirect tradition of the anonymous Frankish penitentials of the eighth and ninth centuries.[50]

(f)   After (c), Co B (iii), a few rules on minor monastic discipline, was added to B (ii), probably on the same folio and by the same person who wrote B (iii).

(g)   B (i)–(iii) were transcribed onto a quire and provided with preface, connecting passages and conclusion. Again, this may well have been the work of the author of B (i)–(iii). Since the preface was used by the anonymous Frankish penitentials, a text in this form was available to the author of the assumed original, dated to the first half of the eighth century, used by the surviving penitentials.[51]

(h)   A (i)–(ii) and B (i)–(iii) were copied onto a single quire perhaps already before the texts were taken from Burgundy to Bobbio.

(ii) The *Regula coenobialis* file

(i)   The original form of the file consisted of the shorter version of RC^1. This drew on Co A (ii) and therefore postdates stage (c) above.

(j)   After (c) and (i) some minor monastic penitential texts – *Regula coenobialis*, §§ X–XV (RC^2–RC^5) – were added to the shorter version of RC^1, probably by *ca* 650. Of these, RC^2 is likely to have used Co A (ii), while RC^5 drew some of its material from an Irish text also used by the Bigotian Penitential.

(k)   The longer version of the *Regula coenobialis* was written by someone familiar with Co A.

Stage (a) was certainly prior to 591, the probable date of Columbanus's journey to Francia and both (b) and (c) probably so. To judge by their Latinity, neither Co A (i) nor A (ii) are likely to have been written by Columbanus himself. Stages (c) – (f) probably predate the expansion of the *Regula coenobialis* by the addition of §§ X–XV. Otherwise it would be odd, given their penitential nature, that they were not added to Co before the last folio was filled up by (f). They are thus likely to belong to a period no later than the original RC^1. Co B (i)–(iii) are much the most likely to have been done by, or at the behest of, Columbanus. RC^2, however, was the work of one, who, although himself an Irishman, did not show any anxiety to preserve the detailed provisions of Co A. This would not be surprising if the first generation of Columbanus's disciples knew that Co A was not the work of the saint. By the time of the longer version of the *Regula coenobialis*, attitudes had changed:

---

[50] See above, n. 4.

[51] *Paenitentialia Minora*, ed. Kottje *et al.*, pp. xxiv, 212.

the closer verbal resemblance in the quotations from Co A suggests that a higher authority was then ascribed to the text, and it may well have been thought by that stage that Columbanus was himself responsible for the whole of the penitential which now passes under his name.

What is more remarkable, however, is the concentration on clerical and lay sins shown by Co B. Almost all the references in Ionas to penitential discipline concern monks and nuns.[52] The additions to the *Regula coenobialis* demonstrate an active tradition of penitential writing for monasteries in the two generations after Columbanus's death. Their evidence agrees with that of Ionas – not surprisingly, for the *uita* stems from the period in which §§ X–XV were added to the *Regula coenobialis*. One or two of them, especially § XV, may have existed as independent texts before they were incorporated into the Rule; but the very act of incorporating an older text into the Rule demonstrates an interest in its subject matter among the disciples of Columbanus. Yet the almost exclusively monastic orientation of penitential discipline suggested by Ionas and also by the penitential writings composed or edited by Columbanus's disciples is quite different from the concern shown by those texts which are most likely to be his own work, B (i)–(iii). The latter are directed at the world beyond the monastery, both clergy and laity, and only include a very few appended rules on monks. Columbanus's other works, apart from the Penitential and the *Regula coenobialis* contain, as we have seen, very few references to penitential discipline. There are, however, two in the first letter, that to Gregory the Great. The first concerns the clergy, the second monks.[53]

The Reception of Columbanus's Penitential Teaching

One might have supposed that Columbanus's penitential teaching and practice would have aroused the opposition of the leaders of the Frankish clergy, the bishops. The evidence, however, suggests that it was welcomed as much by bishops as by monks and laymen.[54] Because the bishops had controlled the ancient system of penance now challenged by the repeatable Celtic penances administered by priests, so, one might assume, they must have opposed the challenge to their authority posed by Columbanus. Such an interpretation would, however, detect an unavoidable clash of principles where contemporaries saw none. Columbanus's letter to Gregory the Great indeed reveals conflict, but it is over the paschal issue. As far as penitential practice is concerned, he betrays no concern at any onslaught by local bishops on Irish novelties. What he does say is that bishops themselves have sought him out as a spiritual guide.[55] On the issues posed by their confessions Columbanus seeks the pope's advice, apparently without any idea that his practice may be controversial. The paschal issue is again prominent in Columbanus's letter to the

---

[52] The exceptions are: *Vita S. Columbani*, I.19 (ed. Krusch, *Ionae Vitae Sanctorum*, p. 192, lines 1, 10); II.8 (p. 245, line 15; both monastic and lay); II.24 (p. 288, line 10).

[53] *Epistula*. I.6–7 (ed. & transl. Walker, *Sancti Columbani Opera*, p. 8).

[54] See Wallace-Hadrill, *The Frankish Church*, p. 65.

[55] *Epistula*, I.6 (ed. & transl. Walker, *S. Columbani Opera*, p. 8).

Frankish bishops.[56] In the same letter he defends the value of the monastic life itself, but of his activities as a guide of souls he says nothing. Apparently, it was not an issue.

In Ionas's *uita* the paschal dispute is dealt with by silence – he entirely avoids any mention of the issue. This proves most eloquently that it mattered. On the other hand, Ionas also betrays anxiety when he says too much. His elaborate attack on Theuderic and Brunhild was perhaps necessary in order to defend the credentials of a monastic movement whose home was Burgundy.[57] The political catastrophe which allowed Chlothar II to triumph in the feud against Brunhild, the enemy of his mother Fredegund, must have compelled many to change their political allegiances with embarrassing rapidity. Yet Ionas mounts no such elaborate defence of Columbanus's penitential authority over those clerics and laymen who sought his guidance, just as he feels no need to avoid the issue.[58] The one set-piece he allows himself on the subject concerns Columbanus's freeing of prisoners condemned to death and the substitution of penances carried out under the wing of the church and, in part at least, within church sanctuary.[59] The threat is secular, posed by a *tribunus militum*, not a bishop.

The written evidence for the penitential discipline of Columbanus's disciples is, I have argued, almost entirely concerned with monks and nuns. Yet it is unlikely that this implies a withdrawal from claims to offer such a discipline to clergy and laity, for no defensiveness is revealed in the evidence. A better explanation is that Columbanus's own penitential writings, which were directed predominantly at non-monastic clergy and laity, retained so clear an authority that no competing text found favour. Both B (i) and (ii) owe much to Vinnian, yet it is in the lay penitential, B (ii), that Columbanus introduces most change. Vinnian still thinks in terms of a composite lay sinner who 'has wrought every evil deed, by committing fornication, that is, and shedding blood'.[60] Columbanus's demands upon the layman go further than requiring him to abstain from illicit sexual intercourse and violence. The scope of penitential discipline thereby extends over more of the *capitalia crimina* 'which are punished even by the sanction of the law'.[61] The close parallels between the lay and the clerical penitential show that the moral gulf between layman and cleric had narrowed since Vinnian's day. Columbanus thus partially anticipates the decisive step taken by Cummian when he framed a penitential for the entire Church, monastic, clerical and lay. In writing separate penitentials for distinct orders, clerical and lay, Columbanus remained within the tradition of the British penitentials, yet his detailed concern for the spiritual life of the laity was novel and bore fruit.

---

[56] *Epistula*, II.5, 7 (ed.& transl. Walker, *S. Columbani Opera*, pp. 16, 18).

[57] Ionas, *Vita S. Columbani*, I.18–20, 27 (the latter linking the cases of Columbanus and Desiderius of Vienne), 29.

[58] Columbanus's penitential practice was not an issue in the conflict between Eusthasius and Agrestius: see Ionas, *Vita S. Columbani*, II.9 (ed. Krusch, *Ionae Vitae Sanctorum*, pp. 246–51).

[59] Ionas, *Vita S. Columbani*, I.19 (ed. Krusch, *ibid.*, pp. 191–2); cf. I.5 (p. 161).

[60] *Penitentialis Vinniani*, § 35 (ed. & transl. Bieler, *The Irish Penitentials*, p. 86).

[61] Columbanus, *Poenitentiale*, B, Praef.

While Columbanus's influence on the penitential practice of Francia was crucial, there is no clear evidence that he had any influence in Ireland. The text of Columbanus's Penitential may not have been taken back to Ireland. There is no evidence that Cummian had seen it. Admittedly, penitential texts may have moved from Francia to Ireland as well as vice versa. If the Bigotian Penitential was written on the Continent, as Bieler maintained, a copy must have been taken to Ireland within a very few years to be used by the composer of the Old Irish Penitential. If, however, the Bigotian Penitential was written in Ireland, as I think is entirely possible, it also shares material with *Regula coenobialis*, § XV, from a source which may well have been composed on the Continent. Links between the Frankish disciples of Columbanus and Ireland remained strong, as the development of the paschal controversy in the 620s and 630s and Agilbert's period in Ireland illustrates. Penitential texts are at best the guides of practice, and it is possible that Columbanus's practice may have been influential in Ireland, *via* his disciples, even if the Penitential itself never crossed the sea.[62]

[62] I am very grateful to Clare Stancliffe and Luned Davies for commenting on a draft of this paper.

VI

'DE MUNDI TRANSITU': A RHYTHMICAL POEM BY COLUMBANUS?

Dieter Schaller

THE five poems which, in the last complete edition of Columbanus,[1] were printed together as the *Carmina*, do not exist as a collection in any surviving manuscript, and were clearly not collected together by the poet himself as a *Liber carminum*; rather, they have been united by modern editors on the basis of very different criteria of authorship.[2] Accordingly, if someone should wish to affirm or deny the attribution of one or other of these poems either to Columbanus of Bobbio, or to a more recent poet of the same name, his affirmation or denial need have no necessary implications for the collection as a whole: the most that can be said is that the poems *Ad Sethum* and *Ad Hunaldum* apparently belong together.

However, the poem entitled (by Walker, the most recent editor) *De mundi transitu (inc.* 'Mundus iste transibit')[3] occupies a unique position within the corpus, and one which unquestionably justifies its individual treatment,[4] not only because of the arguable grounds for its attribution to Columbanus (which I shall discuss further below), but especially because of its verse-form, inasmuch as it is not metrical (as are the other four poems attributed to Columbanus by Walker) but is constructed on principles of syllable-counting, and is in a strophic form which was characteristically employed by Hiberno-Latin poets of the early Middle Ages.[5] This form consists of stanzas, each

---

[1] *Sancti Columbani Opera*, ed. & transl. Walker. Reference is also made to 'Columbae siue Columbani . . . epistulae', ed. Gundlach; and cf. also the recent edition of the poem *Mundus iste transibit* by Howlett, 'Two works of Columban', pp. 33–46. There is a comprehensive new bibliography of the (much-debated) poems of Columbanus in *Clavis patristica pseudepigraphorum medii aevi* IIA, ed. Machielsen, pp. 728–37; the results of my own research are listed particularly under nos 3215a and 3216d.

[2] See discussion by Jacobsen, 'Carmina Columbani', pp. 434–67.

[3] *Sancti Columbani Opera*, ed. & transl. Walker, pp. 182–5; for additional bibliography, see Schaller & Könsgen, *Initia*, no. 9888, as well as Bulst, 'Hymnologica', pp. 89–91.

[4] The question was addressed in detail by Smit, *Studies*; but Smit's book needs to be read in light of the reviews by Bieler, Vollmann, and Bernt; see also Önnerfors, 'Die Latinität'.

[5] Meyer, *Gesammelte Abhandlungen*, I.223, III.305; see also Meyer, 'Poetische Nachlese', pp. 600–5 and Norberg, *Introduction*, pp. 127, 142. Smit (*Studies*) does not seem to have taken into account these standard treatments of rhythmical form; instead, he went to unnecessary length (p. 212) to refute the inaccurate observation of

comprising four seven-syllable lines, having partly rising, partly falling (paroxytone), cadence. If it is true in general that the Irish were less concerned about the similarity of cadences than with counting syllables,[6] then in the poem under discussion it must be noted that the cadences are mixed to an extent that is elsewhere unparalleled:[7] sixty-three lines end with a 'rising' cadence (e.g. *mors incerta súbripìt*), fifty-six with a falling cadence (e.g. *omnes superbos uágos*). This apparent irregularity nevertheless has a pattern of its own, as Walther Bulst observed in the course of a detailed examination of our poem:[8] the pairs of long lines with which, together with the rhyme scheme,[9] the stanzas are constructed, have either rising or falling cadence, but are never mixed (e.g. stanza 2, *pári / aequáli*; stanza 3, *súbripìt / córripìt*; stanza 6, *ámant / párant*). Furthermore, as these examples show, part of the rhyme is consonantally impure,[10] and therefore should, properly speaking, be classified as assonance. Now the pairs of long lines with rising cadence have trisyllablic rhyme or assonance, those with falling cadence only bisyllabic rhyme or assonance.[11] This rule is apparently broken on only two occasions: *decrescit /*

Manitius (*Geschichte*, I.186) that the poem consists of 'siebensilber trochäischer Struktur'. In this respect Smit revealed that he was not properly in control of research pertaining to metrical matters; what he did say was taken directly from Blume, 'Hymnodia', p. 355. On the problems presented by Hiberno-Latin seven-syllable verse, cf. Herren, 'The stress systems', p. 84.

[6] Meyer, *Gesammelte Abhandlungen*, III.307, 309; Bulst, 'Hymnologica', p. 91.

[7] See below, n. 28.

[8] Bulst ('Hymnologica') concentrated his attention on the problem of long lines in early mediaeval Latin verse that were intended for singing. He did not mention the earlier study by McGann, 'The distribution'. Obviously Bulst (*ibid.*, p. 90, n. 29) did not take notice of Smit's book, which is clear from their differing treatments of lines 111–12 of *Mundus iste transibit*, where the manuscript reads, 'Ubi uita uiridis / ueraque futura est, / quam nec mortis nec meroris / metu consumptura est' (cf. *Sancti Columbani Opera*, ed. & transl. Walker, p. 184: 'quam nec mors nec meroris / metus consumpturus est'):

> Smit: 'quam mortis nec meroris / meta consumptura est'.
> Bulst: 'quam nec mortis meroris / metus consumpturus est'.

Smit's proposed minimal emendation (*metu* to *meta*) has its manuscript support in *consumptura est*.

[9] Meyer, *Gesammelte Abhandlungen*, I.223; Smit, *Studies*, p. 212.

[10] That in this poem the consonants participate more actively in the rhyme-scheme than might at first appear, that is to say, that phonologically similar consonants, such as *r /l* in the above example, correspond in rhyming words, has been shown by Wolff in his review of Pretzel, *Frühgeschichte*, p. 71.

[11] Meyer (*Gesammelte Abhandlungen*, III.317) qualifies this 'rule' by saying that it is 'often' (*oft*) observed, and Bulst ('Hymnologica', p. 91) qualifies Meyer's statement to 'almost entirely'. According to Bulst, Meyer overlooked cases such as *subripit / corripit* (stanza 3), *colligere / credere* (stanza 7), *species / pernicies* (stanza 16), and *libidinem / dulcedinem* (stanza 20) – that is, rhymes consisting of 'three vowels' (*a, e / i*, and *o / u*) which are attested in many other texts. But I am not clear whether Meyer 'overlooked' these instances, or whether he did not draw attention to them because he was unwilling to contradict his earlier assertion (*Gesammelte Abhandlungen*, I.292) that the Irish and Anglo-Saxons seem not to have taken this special liberty with their rhyme-schemes. Note also the important observation by Norberg

remansit (stanza 1) and *uix audent / -is habent* (stanza 5). Do 'the antepenultimate syllables here rhyme instead of the penultimate', as Bulst alleges?[12] It is
difficult to affirm Bulst's allegation, since there is no precise parallel for this
sort of rhyming practice.[13] It is perhaps conceivable that the rhyme *audent /
habent* would have been permitted, since the vowel *a* is one component of the
diphthong *au*.[14] However, it seems to me that the other exception (*decrescit /
remansit*) derives not from the poet, but from faulty manuscript-transmission.
The first stanza of the poem is transmitted as follows in manuscript:

> Mundus iste transiuit / et cotidie crescit
> nemo uiuens manebit / nullus uiuus remansit.

Gundlach and Walker emend the first long line in three places:

> Mundus iste transi*b*it / [. . .] cottidie *de*crescit.

Smit preserves the manuscript-reading in the second half-line (though he
follows Gundlach and Walker in emending the first half-line) –

> Mundus iste transibit / et cottidie crescit –

which he interprets as, 'This world will pass away, and its sinful power
increases daily.'[15] Thus emended, the line contains two familiar, but contradictory, statements, which are inappropriately linked by the copula *et*. Among the
biblical and patristic parallels, which Smit rightly adduces, there is no example
of the combination *mundus crescit*. His eloquent argument, so it might seem,
has the principal aim of diverting the reader's attention from the one obvious
parallel which could link the poem with Columbanus, namely *Instructio III*
(§ 1): 'Mundus enim transibit et cottidie transit et rotatur ad finem'.[16] In Smit's
view, this passage should *not* be compared with the poem's opening, which on
the contrary is said to be inspired by I John II.15–17: 'Nolite diligere mundum
neque ea quae in mundo sunt' (15), 'Et mundus transit et concupiscentia eius'
(17). But there is no specific conception here of a *mundus crescens*,[17] merely

---

(*Les vers latins iambiques et trochaïques*, p. 108, n. 44) concerning Bulst's arguments, namely that rhymes consisting of 'three vowels' are to be posited only for
'syllabes finales dont la prononciation était faible', but not for accented syllables.

[12] Bulst, 'Hymnologica', p. 91.

[13] One could only adduce such a shift of the rhyme back to the antepenultimate syllable
in cases where the antepenultimate syllable bore the stress, that is to say, in cases of
rising cadence; cf. Fickermann, 'Ein frühmittelalterliches Liedchen', pp. 586–7.

[14] Fickermann (*ibid.*, p. 586) draws attention to similar rhyme-combinations (such as
pares / aures, clarus / aurum, and *garritu / auditu*) in his Pirol poem.

[15] Smit, *Studies*, p. 219.

[16] *Sancti Columbani Opera*, ed. & transl. Walker, p. 72, line 23.

[17] Among the various attestations for *crescere* in the Vulgate New Testament, there is
none in which the growth in question has a pejorative connotation. Where the word
is used in contexts other than the purely vegetative, it refers consistently to attributes
of God, as at Act. VI.7 (*uerbum Domini crescebat*). The parallels adduced by Smit
(*Studies*, pp. 220–1) to the Old Testament, such as Gen. XLI.56 (*crescebat . . .
cottidie fames*) are beside the point, as Bieler pointed out in his review of Smit's
book (cited above, n. 4).

the sense of its ending. Smit himself was well aware that the transmitted line-ending *crescit*, which he wished to defend, presented the problems of rhyme which I have already mentioned.[18] Given this awareness, his attempted solution was a most surprising one: since the monosyllabic rhyme *crescit / remansit* did not fit in with the rhyme-scheme of the poem, Smit supposed that the poet must in this first stanza have opted for a rhyme on the first and third short lines (*transibit / manebit*) but then subsequently, from the second stanza onwards, altered this rhyme-scheme 'to the more logical 2–4'.[19] This is indeed a cavalier treatment of metrical form! For rhyme-schemes, in which the final line of the stanza does *not* participate, can scarcely be found anywhere else; that is to say, four-line stanzas without refrain may show the rhyme-schemes *abab, xaxa, aabb, aaaa* or *aaxa*, but never *axax* or *aaax*.

If we may proceed in the opposite direction from Smit, and attempt to relate the poem to the other writings of Columbanus (bearing in mind that in the St Gallen manuscript, in which the poem is uniquely preserved, the poem is attributed *nominatim* to Columbanus), and use the previously mentioned parallel with *Instructio III* as an aid to emendation, it is striking how easily the problem of the rhyme-scheme resolves itself:

> Mundus iste transibit / et cottidie *transit*,
> nemo uiuens manebit, / nullus uiuus remansit.

The question of how the genuine reading *transit* could have been replaced in transmission by *crescit* may be answered by a glance at line 21 (*cottidie decrescit*): an eye-skip from this line could have brought *crescit* to line 2 (there is in any case some palaeographical similarity between the words *transit* and *crescit*).

With respect to the question of how the rhyme-scheme bears on the date of the poem, Smit seriously misapplied the (questionable) rule-of-thumb which was formulated by Blume:[20] namely, that in the sixth century 'impure' rhyme (that is, the simple assonance of vowels) prevailed among Hiberno-Latin poets; in the seventh century the rhyme became entirely 'pure'; and by the eighth century, this 'pure' rhyme had become trisyllabic. While it is true that for many texts this – wholly unreliable – rule-of-thumb may offer the only criterion for dating, we should not overlook the fact that pure trisyllabic rhyme was not always attempted by Irish poets of the eighth century and later,[21] and that, on the other hand, in texts from before A.D. 600 one finds a strikingly large proportion of trisyllabic and bisyllabic rhyme.[22]

In methodological terms, it is evidently wrong to postulate a scale ascending from monosyllabic assonance to pure trisyllabic rhyme, and then to correlate the steps of this scale with century-long periods of time, stretching from the

---

[18] See above, p. 247.
[19] Smit, *Studies*, p. 214.
[20] Blume, 'Hymnodia', p. 355.
[21] Meyer, *Gesammelte Abhandlungen*, III.316–17.
[22] Blume, 'Hymnodia', nos. 216, 217, 218, 219, and 262; listed by Schaller & Könsgen, *Initia*, as nos 685, 3551, 2297, 16128, 10296, and 15745, respective. This last (inc. 'Suffragare trinitatis unitas') is perhaps of seventh-century date; cf. Brunhölzl, *Geschichte*, I.163.

sixth century to the eighth, in order to determine the date of a particular text. Yet this is precisely what Smit did when he argued that *Mundus iste transibit* exhibits an intermediary stage on the scale towards purity of rhyme, and that this stage squares well with a seventh-century date.[23] It is impossible, on the evidence of the rhyme-scheme, to rule out the possibility that the poem was composed sometime 'during the sixth century in Ireland, or by an Irishman'.[24]

To return to the question of the poem's stanzaic form: while it is true that none of the other surviving Hiberno-Latin poems composed in this form may be dated to the sixth century, it is nevertheless significant that three such poems can be securely dated to the seventh century: *Pro peccatis*, *Benchuir bona regula* and *Martine te deprecor*.[25] The last of these three poems (and also probably the least ancient) has only falling cadences; but the other two have pairs of long lines with rising cadence (*Pro peccatis* has two such lines out of twelve; *Benchuir bona regula* has one out of nine). However, there is yet another poem having this stanzaic form preserved in the 'Book of Cerne':[26] that beginning *Ubi resplendent semper*.[27] Given its inclusion in the 'Book of Cerne', this poem can scarcely have been composed later than the eighth century; yet it has a proportion of long lines with rising and falling cadence (12:10) similar to that found in *Mundus iste transibit* (19:11),[28] that is to say, a clear majority of rising cadences.

Unfortunately, this observation has no implication for the dating of *Mundus iste transibit*, since on the one hand *Ubi resplendent* could have been composed earlier than the eighth century, and, on the other, stanzas of seven-syllable lines with mixed cadences were being composed by Irish (or Irish-influenced) poets up until the tenth century.[29] Given this unsatisfactory state of affairs, it may be helpful to consider another text which has not so far figured in our discussion, namely the verses which Ionas of Bobbio[30] added at the end of the first book of

---

23 Smit, *Studies*, p. 215. This objection has already been cogently put by Bernt in his review of Smit's book (cited above, n. 4).

24 Blume, 'Hymnodia', p. 356.

25 *Ibid.*, nos. 258, 260, and 247; listed by Schaller & Könsgen, *Initia*, nos 12625, 1654, and 9333, respectively.

26 *The Prayerbook*, ed. Kuypers.

27 *Ibid.*, fo 53b; listed by Schaller & Könsgen, *Initia*, no. 16681. For an edition and commentary, see Meyer, 'Poetische Nachlese', pp. 602–5.

28 Bulst ('Hymnologica', p. 90) counted seventeen rising cadences in *Mundus iste transibit*; but in addition to these, I should include *bíbere / ridere* (lines 70, 72), because of the shift in stress in Vulgar Latin pronunciation from *ridére* to *rídere*, as well as the stanza in which the original words should have rhymed with the half-line *audíta èst* (line 106) have fallen out and have been replaced with the words *celestis pascitur*, repeated from line 102. The line supplied conjecturally by Esposito ('On the new edition', p. 199) – 'splendet luce superna' – must be rejected in view of the poem's overall rhyme-scheme. I should myself restore the stanza as follows:

> ubi aula regia
> <canticis repleta est>
> in qua male resonans
> nulla uox audita est.

29 Norberg, *Introduction*, p. 128, n. 1.

30 Wattenbach & Levison, *Deutschlands Geschichtsquellen*, pp. 133–4.

his *Vita S. Columbani*, the so-called 'Versus in eius [*scil.* Columbani] festiuitate ad mensam canendi'.[31] This poem (*inc.* 'Clare sacerdos clues') has precisely the same number of stanzas (30) as does *Mundus iste transibit*, and the structure of its stanzas is closely similar, each stanza consisting of four seven-syllable lines. But as the verse technique of *Clare sacerdos clues* differs remarkably from that of *Mundus iste transibit*, Walther Bulst – for whom there was no doubt that Columbanus was the author of *Mundus iste transibit* – only cautiously advanced the opinion that *Mundus iste transibit* was the formal model for the poem composed by Ionas.[32]

While *Mundus iste transibit* displays a thorough mixture of rising and falling cadences, as we have already seen, Ionas clearly preferred falling cadences in his seven-syllable verse.[33] That Ionas's concern was principally with the long lines is clear from the fact that twenty-one of the sixty A-verses (but no B-verse) consist of six rather than seven syllables,[34] a feature which is not found in *Mundus iste transibit*. Furthermore, while the two long lines in any stanza of *Mundus iste transibit* are marked by the regular rhyme of vowels which is at least bisyllabic (a feature lacking in all the A-verses), Ionas merely employs monosyllabic assonance to link the long lines in the first part of his poem (as far as stanza 6); thereafter this feature occurs only sporadically, and is sometimes replaced by sporadic assonances between the A- or B-verses of the first or second long lines of each stanza.

Yet in spite of these noticeable differences, we are nevertheless obliged to ask how the Italian Ionas, writing before the middle of the seventh century, could have come to employ the seven-syllable stanzaic form which is so characteristic of early Hiberno-Latin hymnody. From the historical point of view it has been supposed that such stanzas derive from the (metrical) stanzas consisting of four catalectic iambic dimeters, the unique model for which was the sixth hymn of Prudentius's *Cathemerinon*:[35]

> Ades pater supreme
> quem nemo uidit unquam,
> patrisque sermo Christe
> et spiritus benigne.

---

[31] *Ionae Vitae Sanctorum*, ed. Krusch, pp. 224–7; cf. Schaller & Könsgen, *Initia*, no. 2351.

[32] Bulst, 'Hymnologica', p. 90.

[33] Of the five apparent exceptions in A-verses, two are proper names which evidently could be treated with greater freedom: 17 *Hánnibàl* (but cf. Greek 'Αννίβας) and 18 *Cátulùs* (? – cf. the variant reading *Catullus*!). In line 4 the metrically superfluous *te* in the B-verse should perhaps be treated as an enclitic and attached to the first half-line or A-verse, thus: *prócerès te*. This leaves lines 15 (*símilè*) and 31 (*pósitùs*); but note that in stanza 4 of *Benchuir bona regula* (Blume, 'Hymnodia', no. 260) this same form of the past participle constitutes the only incorrectly falling cadence of a long line.

[34] Meyer, *Gesammelte Abhandlungen*, III.305; Bulst, 'Hymnologica', p. 89.

[35] Schaller & Könsgen, *Initia*, no. 255. One might also include the liturgically separate part (from line 125 onwards) of the poem *Cultor dei memento* (listed *ibid.*, no. 2976).

It is probable that the influence of this hymn led to the production of rhythmical or syllabic counterparts in Visigothic Spain;[36] a similar influence might be posited for Ireland, but cannot be proven. Among the various rhythmical poems in stanzas of seven-syllable lines which belong to the seventh or eighth century, that beginning *Audite omnes gentes*[37] is particularly noteworthy, in that it has an abundance of rhyming patterns similar to those in Ionas, but differs from Ionas in the substantial proportion of multisyllabic rhymes on similar desinences (e.g. stanza 14: *orauit / inuocauit*) as well as in its greater technical licence (instead of lines of seven syllables, some have not only six, but even eight or nine syllables)[38] and its use of the abecedarian form with refrain. On linguistic grounds, this poem appears to have been composed in the Gallo-Roman area in the seventh century (or at latest in the eighth);[39] by the same token, its transmission as part of the great ninth-century Brussels collection of Latin rhythmic verse[40] implies a provenance from the Gallo-Roman area or from northern Italy. One of the texts preserved in this collection has a close link with Bobbio (or, at least, so it has generally been assumed): the *planctus* on the death of Charlemagne.[41] It is difficult to see how the Italian Ionas,

---

[36] Norberg, *Introduction*, p. 111.

[37] MGH, Poetae IV.50 (no. 15); cf. Schaller & Könsgen, *Initia*, no. 1354. The following poems are difficult to classify with regard to stanzaic structure: *Initia*, nos 1355, 4024, 7435. The first two have a West Frankish, the third a Reichenau provenance.

[38] Meyer, *Gesammelte Abhandlungen*, III.294; Norberg, *Introduction*, p. 142, n. 2.

[39] Norberg, *La poésie latine*, p. 9.

[40] The manuscript, Brussels, Bibliothèque royale, 8860–67 (1351), was formerly thought to be of St Gallen origin, and on this assumption Karl Strecker identified St Gallen as the most important mediaeval centre for the production of rhythmical Latin verse. Norberg (*La poésie latine rythmique*, pp. 112–14) argued against this view on linguistic and literary grounds, without however casting doubt on the assumption that the collection was assembled at St Gallen. But Bernhard Bischoff showed on palaeographical grounds that the manuscript was written either at Saint-Bertin (*Mittelalterliche Studien*, II.26, n. 4) or in northeast France (*ibid.*, III.96). But since the manuscript also contains a fragment in Old High German (*Hirsch und Hinde*) and antiphons on Otmar, both of which were added in the tenth century and which undoubtedly stem from St Gallen, Bischoff supposed that in the ninth or tenth century the manuscript must have travelled south. This supposition does not strike me as necessary, however: texts from St Gallen could also have travelled north, like the Notker materials in the Trier manuscript containing Sedulius Scottus and the *Ecbasis captiui*, now Brussels, Bibliothèque royale, 10615–729 (s. xii); and it was a conjecture of Ludwig Traube ('O Roma nobilis', p. 45) that the agent of transmission in this case was that Notker of St Gallen who became bishop of Liège in 972, a conjecture which need not be rejected out of hand, in spite of the views of Düchting, *Sedulius Scottus*, p. 13, n. 2. For further discussion of the Brussels manuscript, see Schaller, *Studien*, pp. 426–7.

[41] Schaller & Könsgen, *Initia*, no. 32 (inc. 'A solis ortu usque ad occidua'); printed MGH, Poetae I.435. Lapidge ('The authorship', pp. 856–9) sees in the wording of stanza 17 ('O Columbane, stringe tuas lacrimas') an self-address by the poet himself, whom he identifies as Columbanus, abbot on Saint-Trond (*ca* 780–820); see also Lapidge & Sharpe, *A Bibliography*, no. 656. However, Löwe ('Columbanus und Fidolius', pp. 1– 6) contests this identification on the basis of various chronological

writing well before the middle of the seventh century, could have been inspired to compose a poem in seven-syllable stanzas, if not through the stimulus of his Irish teachers and informants in Bobbio or Luxeuil. The 'Antiphonary of Bangor',[42] in which the seven-syllable verses *Benchuir bona regula*[43] are preserved, arrived at Bobbio only at the end of the seventh century; and as to whether other seven-syllable Hiberno-Latin verses of the sixth or seventh century were known in Merovingian France or in northern Italy, the record simply does not permit us to say. Only *Mundus iste transibit* remains in question, therefore. Now if this poem really was composed by St Columbanus, then its presence at Bobbio as well as its – for us unique – transmission to St Gallen would be explicable by the saint's cult at both these places: it would have taken the same route as the seven-syllable verses of Ionas, for the transmission of these verses, bound up inevitably with Ionas's *Vita S. Columbani*, is represented primarily by manuscripts from Bobbio and St Gallen (or, more generally, Switzerland).[44]

Accordingly, it is interesting to note that in the two Bobbio manuscripts in question,[45] the text of Ionas's poem is preceded by a rubric[46] – which their editor, Bruno Krusch, regarded as authentic – describing them as *uersus . . . ad mensam canendi*; for, given that Ionas in his *uita* of the saint[47] reports that Columbanus while still a young man had occupied himself with exposition of the psalms and with the composition of texts which were intended either for singing or for purposes of instruction, then it would seem obvious that by the phrases *uersus . . . canendi* and *ad cantum digna*[48] Ionas is describing the same thing, perhaps even seven-syllable verses like *Mundus iste transibit*. This deduction seems obviously preferable to that of Smit,[49] who understands from the phrases in question that Columbanus in his youth composed poems in the Irish language. If so, given the context, Ionas must also have meant that Columbanus composed his psalm-commentary in Irish – a conclusion which is most improbable, for the (lost) psalm-commentary of Columbanus which is traceable in library catalogues from Bobbio and St Gallen was doubtless in Latin.

---

and text-transmissional evidence, and, in line with earlier scholarship, sees the reference to 'Columbane' in stanza 17 as a reference to Columbanus of Bobbio, 'die durchaus etwa dem Ton zeitgenössischer Litaneien entspricht'.

[42] Blume, 'Hymnodia', pp. 259–63; cf. Coccia, 'La cultura irlandese', p. 274, Wattenbach & Levison, *Deutschlands Geschichtsquellen*, I.132, and Lapidge, 'Columbanus'.

[43] See *L'antifonario di Bangor*, ed. Franceschini, p. 67; and cf. Schaller & Könsgen, *Initia*, no. 1654.

[44] *Ionae Vitae Sanctorum*, ed. Krusch, pp. 60–121; see also Duft, 'St Columban', p. 292.

[45] Torino, Biblioteca Nazionale, F.IV.26 (s. x) and F.IV.12 (s. x); cf. *Ionae Vitae Sanctorum*, ed. Krusch, p. 104.

[46] See above, n. 31.

[47] *Vita S. Columbani* I.3 (ed. Krusch, *Ionae Vitae Sanctorum*, p. 158): 'ut intra aduliscentiae aetate detentus psalmorum librum elimato sermone exponeret multaque alia, quae uel ad cantum digna uel ad docendum utilia, condidit dicta.'

[48] Thus Walker in *Sancti Columbani Opera*, ed. & transl. Walker, p. lvi.

[49] Smit, *Studies*, pp. 216, 217, n. 12.

Another criterion, which Smit uses to argue that *Mundus iste transibit* could not have been composed in the lifetime of Columbanus, can be seen on close examination to be inapplicable. As has long been recognized, line 9 of the poem ('Differentibus uitam / mors incerta') seems to show that the poet had access to a collection of *sententiae* which passed under the name of Seneca,[50] perhaps the so-called *Liber de moribus*,[51] in which the heptasyllabic verse 'Multos uitam differentes mors incerta praeuenit' occurs (as no. 10),[52] or perhaps an earlier collection of *Monita*,[53] or one of the interpolated manuscripts of the *Sententiae* of Publilius Syrus, where the same aphorism occurs as follows: 'Omnes (enim) uitam differentes mors incerta praeuenit.'[54] Although in the *acta* of the Council of Tours (A.D. 567) reference was made to two further aphorisms from the pseudo-Senecan *Liber de moribus* (nos. 35–6),[55] this scarcely proves that circulation of the *Liber de moribus* must first have begun at that time;[56] yet Smit took this for granted when he calculated that the *young* Columbanus (whom Walker took to be the author of *Mundus iste transibit*) could scarcely have had knowledge of *De moribus*, and accordingly that we should renounce Columbanus's authorship of *Mundus iste transibit* and place it instead in the mid-seventh century, to which the evidence of the rhyme also allegedly points. But the combination of genuine and dubious aphorisms of Seneca in collections of *sententiae* must go back to well before the sixth century.[57]

While the various considerations bearing on the form and transmission of *Mundus iste transibit* which we have thus far examined point to Columbanus as the poem's author – in spite of Smit's arguments to the contrary – we should

---

[50] Schanz & Hosius, *Geschichte* II.717–20 (§ 471); Nothdurft, *Studien zum Einfluss Senecas*, pp. 30–4.

[51] The edition by Friedrich (cited in MGH, Epistulae III.189) is of little help in matters of textual transmission. A number of manuscripts dating from the ninth century to the fourteenth is listed by Woelfflin in *Publilii Syri Sententiae*, ed. Woelfflin, p. 136. An additional ninth-century manuscript is Vatican City, Biblioteca Apostolica Vaticana, Regin. lat. 191 (Rheims); cf. the comments of Bachman, 'Eine neue Handschrift', cols 1068–72. On fo 102 of this manuscript – and not, as is wrongly stated in MGH, Poetae II.700, in 'Vat. lat. 191' – are found the four verses on Ebo of Rheims (MGH, Poetae II.93); see Schaller & Könsgen, *Initia*, no. 9067.

[52] *Publilii Syri Sententiae*, ed. Woelfflin, p. 137; see also *L. Annaei Senecae Opera: Supplementum*, ed. Haase, p. 60.

[53] Schanz & Hosius, *Geschichte*, IV.719: 'Man muß den liber de moribus als einen Auszug aus den Monita betrachten, und zwar gemacht, als die Sammlung am Anfang noch vollständig war.'

[54] *Publilii Syri Sententiae*, ed. Woelfflin, p. 49.

[55] Instead of citing Mansi, Smit would have done better to cite MGH, Concilia I.125 (§ XV): '. . . sicut ait Senica: Pessimum in eum uitium esse, qui in id, quod insanit, ceteros putat furere . . .'

[56] Woelfflin, in *Publilii Syri Sententiae*, ed. Woelfflin, p. 139, simply stated that by the mid-sixth century at latest the collection of *sententiae* (in the order transmitted to us by later manuscripts) must already have existed: this can therefore provide only a *terminus ante quem*.

[57] Manitius, *Geschichte*, I.112; Rossbach, *De Senecae Philosophi librorum recensione*, p. 85.

not overlook the fact that we would scarcely have arrived at this view of Columbanus's authorship were it not for the fact that he is named as the author of the poem in the unique St Gallen manuscript. But in this very fact lies another basis for doubt, which caused Walker some uneasiness and which naturally did not escape Smit's notice:[58] namely that the attribution of author-ship – *Columbani* –in the St Gallen manuscript (now Zürich, Zentralbibliothek, C. 78: a manuscript of late ninth-century date which was at St Gallen until 1712) is unfortunately an addition made by an early modern hand. As to the evidence of the other, now lost, St Gallen manuscript, we must rely on the trustworthiness of Melchior Goldast,[59] who reported the evidence of Colum-banus's authorship which it contained in words[60] that give a clear impression of antiquity.[61] The question of why the Zürich manuscript originally lacked the indication of authorship is easily answered if one bears in mind the peculiar features of this valuable but somewhat unpredictable miscellaneous codex, whose content has clearly been influenced by the concerns of the monastic school in which it was produced.[62] It contains a jumbled mixture of prose- and verse-texts in various genres, dating both from late antiquity and from the Carolingian period, as well as from all the intervening centuries, many of them lifted arbitrarily out of context and left by the compiler as mere fragments.[63] Especially irksome for us – above all in relation to the 'Aachen Epic' of Charlemagne – is the nonchalance of the various scribes regarding the sources

[58] Smit, *Studies*, p. 216.
[59] In spite of the general warning issued by Ludwig Traube: 'Aber Goldast ist nicht zu trauen' ('O Roma nobilis', p. 43). But in the present instance Goldast seems genuinely to have based his text on the lost manuscript; cf. Blume, 'Hymnodia', p. 354. Goldast's merits as historian and editor have received judicious appraisal by more recent scholarship: cf. Lehmann, *Erforschung*, V.201–2, and Hertenstein, *Joachim von Watt*, p. 117.
[60] *Paraeneticorum Veterum Pars I*, ed. Goldast, p. 153: 'Vidimus duo epistulae huius exempla, utrumque in nostri bibliotheca monasterii, unum bene antiquum, sed ἀνώνυμον, alterum haud magis uetustatis expers, at eo praestabilius, quod suo nobis indice auctorem ostendat.' On Goldast's St Gallen sources, see Hertenstein, *Joachim von Watt*, p. 139.
[61] See also Duft, 'St Columban', p. 290. Gundlach (MGH, Epistolae III.155) under-stood from the quotation of Goldast (cited in the previous note) that the exemplar described by Goldast as ἀνώνυμον – undoubtedly our Zürich manuscript – was older than the other one. However, I suspect myself that the litotes 'haud magis uetustatis expers' must be taken to mean no more than that this manuscript was of the same age as the other.
[62] See Schaller, 'Das Aachener Epos', pp. 159–62 (with further bibliography). I take this opportunity to correct what is said there on p. 161 concerning Augustine, *De ciuitate Dei* XVIII.23: we have not a triple report of the entire chapter, but rather two distinct passages from its latter part (fos 47r, 157r) together with the poem *Iudicii signum* (fo 156r–v); cf. Bischoff, *Mittelalterliche Studien*, I.151, n. 4, together with Schaller & Könsgen, *Initia*, no. 8495. The scribe of fo 157r has copied Lactantius's prose translation of the sibylline text (as quoted by Augustine) so as to give it the appearance of being verse, by using majuscules at the beginning of lines and by dividing the prose into snippets of 12–18 syllables.
[63] For the full list of contents, see Mohlberg, *Katalog*, pp. 43–4.

of their texts, and thus the frequent absence of any indication of author or work. Later users of the manuscript have attempted to remedy this defect in various places, and accordingly the name of Columbanus was added on fo 159r alongside *Mundus iste transibit.*[64] Whoever made this annotation[65] did not invent it out of thin air, but very probably took it from the other manuscript, that known to Goldast, in the same library.

It is surprising that no modern student of Columbanus has noticed that in the same Zürich manuscript there is a second text relevant to Columbanus, namely the two distichs *In mulieres*:

> Omnis mente pius fugiat mortale uenenum,
> quod mulieris habet lingua superba male.
> Conlatum uite distruxit femina culmen;
> femina sed uite gaudia longa dedit.

The most recent editor of Columbanus, who placed these distichs in an *appendix spuriorum*,[66] quoted Goldast[67] – or rather Patrick Fleming,[68] the Franciscan editor who based himself on Goldast – and observed that 'the original manuscript from which the poem was transcribed is lost.'[69] Nevertheless the verses[70] in question can be read in our ninth-century Zürich manuscript on fo 155v in the form in which I have just quoted them.[71] They were

---

[64] The word *Columbani* is placed right beside stanza 1 in a hand probably of the sixteenth century; an obviously more recent hand (seventeenth-century?) placed *S* (= *sancti*) before the name and added the following note: 'Epistola II. in Goldastii Paraeneticis p. 146'. I am grateful to Dr Schönherr of the Zentralbibliothek in Zürich for placing excellent photographs of the relevant folios at my disposal.

[65] Hertenstein (*Joachim von Watt*, p. 100) noted that some of the marginal annotations in Zürich C.78 are in the hand of Bartholomäus Schobinger (1566–1604), the friend of Goldast who was a nobleman and jurist from St Gallen; it remains to be established whether the annotation *Columbani* on fo 159r was made by Schobinger.

[66] *Sancti Columbani Opera*, ed. Walker, p. 214; cf. p. lxiv.

[67] Goldast, *Paraeneticorum Veterum Pars I*, p. 59; cf. Blume, 'Hymnodia', p. 355. The reprint in Patrologia Latina, ed. Migne, LXXX.294 (whence Walther, *Proverbia*, nos 20240a, 2936b) is taken from Galland, *Bibliotheca Patrum* X (1765).

[68] Fleming, *Collectanea Sacra*; on his 'editio princeps' of the letters of Columbanus, see Smit, *Studies*, pp. 33–8.

[69] Ludwig Bieler likewise speaks of 'einer inzwischen verlorenen Handschrift' of Goldast: 'Aduersaria zu Anthologia Latina 676', p. 46.

[70] Cf. Schaller & Könsgen, *Initia*, 11360.

[71] In the manuscript, the two distichs, without being set off in any way, form the conclusion of a school-poem, in bucolic mode, consisting of nineteen rather crude hexameters, inc. 'Quinque puto tremulas'; I hope to return to this poem and the one which precedes it on another occasion (for now, see Schaller & Könsgen, *Initia*, nos. 12965, 13620, 5655). These poems, including *In mulieres*, were transcribed onto the detached leaf (fo 32) of the former St Gallen manuscript, now Vatican City, Biblioteca Apostolica Vaticana, Regin. lat. 421 (s. ix/x) by a hand of the sixteenth or seventeenth century, perhaps by Goldast himself; it may be conjectured that the manuscript in question (on which see Wilmart, *Codices Reginenses*, II.515, and Mundó, 'L'édition des oeuvres', p. 293, who express themselves rather vaguely) is none other than our Zürich manuscript.

previously printed from this manuscript, but with a peculiarity which has prevented them from being recognized, namely that the second distich was printed as no. 689 of the *Anthologia Latina*[72] and the first placed in a footnote with, however, the name of Columbanus alongside it. Though not knowing this edition, others, too, expressed the view that the second distich, which turns on the opposition Eve–Mary, had originally nothing to do with the first, which is couched in general misogynistic terms.[73] For our purposes it is sufficient to note that these verses are transmitted in the Zürich manuscript without any indication of authorship – indeed they are attached unwittingly to an unrelated text – whereas Goldast found them, linked with the name of Columbanus, in another St Gallen source.[74] Is this not the same transmissional history which we have seen with regard to *Mundus iste transibit*? No-one would wish to argue, I take it, that Columbanus's authorship of *Mundus iste transibit* should be brought into disrepute on grounds such as these. Rather, it seems to prove once again that the anonymity of the transmission in Zürich C. 78 is not characteristic of St Gallen manuscripts in general, but is to be blamed on the carelessness of the scribes of this particular manuscript – an unfortunate state of affairs for literary historians! The more reliable sources, which St Gallen once possessed alongside these unreliable ones, are lost, and we are obliged to intermediaries such as Goldast for scattered bits of information such as, for example, the attribution of *Mundus iste transibit* to Columbanus. But to treat such information suspiciously as being the frivolous invention of Goldast or one of his contemporaries poses the question of how such frivolity could have resulted in an opinion which has verisimilitude from the literary-historical point of view: the results of my earlier analysis, that *Mundus iste transibit* is to be seen as an Irish product of the sixth or seventh century, would simply not have been attainable, on methodological or empirical grounds, to a humanist of the seventeenth century.

That the poem has features of style and content which justify an association with the genuine writings of Columbanus, had already been noted by Walker;[75] but unfortunately Walker did not take the trouble to supply the poem with a reliable apparatus of parallels, which in turn enabled Smit[76] to point out that themes such as the frailty of earthly existence and human longing for God are

---

[72] *Anthologia Latina*, ed. Riese, I/2.161. The reference there to fo 153 is no longer correct. In the preface to the first edition of this work (1870), Riese edited from the Zürich manuscript (not, however, without some mistakes) the school-verses mentioned in my previous footnote.

[73] Bieler, 'Adversaria', p. 46, n. 18.

[74] If we are to suppose with Hertenstein (*Joachim von Watt*, p. 146) that it was Goldast himself who transcribed the text of Regin. lat. 421 (see above, n. 72) from the Zürich manuscript, then this must have occurred at an early stage of his work, for he had not yet seen the other St Gallen manuscript mentioned above, which provoked him to ascribe *In mulieres* to Columbanus, and set in train a rather adventurous speculation concerning Queen Brunichildis; cf. *Paraeneticorum Veterum Pars I*, p. 99, and Patrologia Latina, ed. Migne, LXXX.306.

[75] *Sancti Columbani Opera*, ed. & transl. Walker, p. lvi: 'a few of the thoughts and even phrases reappear in Epistle V and Sermon III, and the spirit is closely akin to that of Sermon V.'

[76] Smit, *Studies*, p. 222.

the common coin of monastic literature from late antiquity onwards, so that (for example) any thematic parallels between *Mundus iste transibit* and the *Instructiones* of Columbanus do not justify the assumption of common authorship. But in this case, mere thematic generalities are not in question: close examination of the texts shows instead that there are many striking verbal links between the works.

Let us recall in the first place that a passage from *Instructio III* was useful in reconstructing the corrupt opening lines of our poem.[77] It has not previously been noted, however, that the closing passage of *Instructio VIII* (§ 2) has much in common with the final stanzas of the poem:

Instructio VIII (§ 2)	*Mundus iste transibit*
ut . . . transire feliciter possimus	
de praesentibus ad absentia	uita praesens (22)
de tristibus ad laeta	laeti leto transacto (113)
de caducis ad terrena	
de terrenis ad caelestia	de terrenis eleua tui cordis
	oculos (89)
de regione mortis	ubi uita uiridis ueraque futura
	est (109)
ad regionem uiuorum	quam mortis nec meroris meta
	consumpta est (111)
ubi facie ad faciem caelestia	tunc Rex regum, rex mundus
uidebimus et Regem regum	a mundis uidebitur (119–20)
	laetum regem uidebunt (114)
recto regimine regna regentem	cum regnante regnabunt (115)
Dominum nostrum Iesum	
Christum	

Other trains of thought in the poem have analogues in the *Instructiones*. With lines 34–6 of the poem ('una hora laetantur [*scil.* auari] / sed aeterna tormenta / adhuc illis parantur') compare *Instructio III* (§ 4): 'uide quo amoena diuitum abiit laetitia . . . miserrima anima poenis aeternis reddita'.[78] With lines 37–8 ('caeci nequaquam uident / quid post obitum restat') compare *Instructio III* (§ 3): 'Oculos habens caecus ligaris, libensque morti duceris'.[79] Finally, with lines 5–8 ('totum humanum genus / ortu utitur pari / et de simili uita / fine cadit aequali') compare a sentence from *Instructio IX* (§ 1): 'similiter enim omnes nascuntur, crescunt, decrescunt, infirmantur, tribulantur, moriuntur'.[80]

An apparently insignificant lexical feature assumes striking importance when considered statistically: in the first and sixth stanzas the poet uses the adverb *cot(t)idie* ('Mundus . . . cottidie transit'; 'cottidie decrescit uita praesens'). This adverb occurs, most often doubled, in a number of places in the *Instructiones*: 'cottidie dimicaremus' (*Instructio* II.3); 'Mundus . . . cottidie transit' (III.1); 'uiuere quasi mortui cottidie' (III.3); 'unusquisque sic uiuere

---

[77] See above, n. 18.
[78] *Sancti Columbani Opera*, ed. & transl. Walker, p. 78.
[79] *Ibid.*, p. 76.
[80] *Ibid.*, p. 98.

debet quasi cottidie moriatur' (III.3); 'quae cottidie fugis et cottidie uenis' (V.1); 'quasi cottidie moriendum esset' (VI.1); 'licet cottidie lauaris, cottidie uiolaris' (VII.1); 'dominatio quae cottidie soluitur et cottidie exigitur' (VII.2); and 'nosmetipsos cottidie discutiamus' (IX.2).[81] When one considers that in some 20,000 verses of the first volume of the Monumenta Germaniae Historica's *Poetae Latini Aevi Carolini* the word *cottidie* occurs only four times,[82] in the approximately 23,000 verses of the second volume only once, in Bede's extensive *Historia ecclesiastica* only fifteen times, in the complete *carmina* of Venantius Fortunatus not at all, and in the *Consolatio Philosophiae* and *Opuscula sacra* of Boethius only twice,[83] then the double occurrence of *cottidie* in sixty long lines of *Mundus iste transibit*, in light of Columbanus's unmistakeable preference for the word in his *Instructiones*, is a significant piece of evidence.

Earthly life is referred to as 'uia mortalium' in *Instructio V* (§ 1),[84] exactly as in *Mundus iste transibit*, line 82. It may also be remarked that many of the significant words in the poem also carry significance in the *Instructiones*: *meror* (line 12; cf. *Instr.* III.1–3); *uoluntatis lubricae* (line 67; cf. *Instr.* I.3, *putridae uoluntatis*); *ridere inaniter* (line 74; cf. *Instr.* IV.3, *rideat mundus cum diabolo*); *perge inter laqueos* (line 85; cf. *Instr.* III.3, *laqueus tibi tua uita*); and the word-pair *esuritur / sititur* (line 99; cf. *Instr.* XIII). Of the principal themes of the opening of *Mundus iste transibit*, that of *auaritia* is mentioned twice in the *Instructiones*; on the other hand, the warning against the enticements of *feminarum species* (line 30) is not found there. But worldly wealth and women are not particularly a problem for monks who live in obedience to a rule and have rejected both long since, as they are for young men who are being drawn to the monastic life for the first time. It is my impression that this distinction – between veteran monks and novices – is reflected in the function of the *Instructiones* on one hand, and of *Mundus iste transibit* on the other. The thirteen *Instructiones*, transmitted to us from Bobbio,[85] reveal at every point the features of the monastic sermon, above all in the continually repeated address to 'fratres carissimi' or simply to 'carissimi'. Moreover, these sermons seem to have been composed with the aim of being teaching pieces, by developing step by step and systematically a consistent theological viewpoint.[86] A

---

[81] *Ibid.*, pp. 72, lines 12, 23; 76, lines 3, 5; 84, line 7; 88, line 13; 90, line 13; 92, line 6; 100, line 6.

[82] This point is not vitiated by the fact that *cottidie* as a so-called 'cretic' word is not employable in dactylic verse (Vergil and Ovid, for example, avoided it altogether): medieval Latin poets knew that it could be used with synizesis (*cótidié*), as two examples from Alcuin show: *Carm.* III.117, VIII.2 (MGH, Poetae I.209, 228).

[83] This (apparently random) selection is drawn from texts for which complete word-indices are available.

[84] *Sancti Columbani Opera*, ed. & transl. Walker, p. 84, line 12.

[85] I share the view of Walker (*Sancti Columbani Opera*, p. xliii) and Smit (*Studies*, pp. 33–8) that this group of texts is to be attributed to one author, and that this one author is Columbanus.

[86] The metaphor of the 'way' serves as a stylistic link throughout; cf. *Instructio* VI.1: 'de humana uita diximus, quod uiae similitudo est' (*Sancti Columbani Opera*, ed. & transl. Walker, p. 86, line 19).

monastic audience[87] was clearly envisaged as the recipients of the *Instructiones*, since there is reference throughout to them as being 'de hac nostrae scholae disciplina'.[88] In *Mundus iste transibit*, however, a single person is addressed on three occasions: *amice* (line 42), *filiole* (line 61) and *carissime* (line 77). Nevertheless, the structure of the rhythmic stanzas seems to me to rule out the possibility of seeing the poem as a verse-letter or simply as reading material[89] – as it does in the similar case of the abecedarian, rhythmic poem of Merovingian origin, *Audax es, uir iuuenis*,[90] which in its general tone and its address to *iuuenis* (repeated four times) is comparable to our poem. The refrain of *Audax es, uir iuuenis* suggests that it was poetry intended for singing. Both poems are examples of vocal, collegial songs, manifestly intended for the active instruction of young men being prepared for their spiritual vocation. The language of such poems is necessarily more straightforward, but also more vivid and descriptive, than that of the *Instructiones*, with their theological framework and rhetorical artistry.

If, in spite of their fundamental differences in genre and function, we consider the obvious similarities in content and style between the *Instructiones* and *Mundus iste transibit*, then we have a strong argument in favour of Columbanus as the author of *Mundus iste transibit* which, taken together with our earlier analysis of the poem's form and manuscript-transmission, enables us to state a conclusion with some confidence: there are no reasonable grounds on which to doubt the St Gallen tradition (deriving probably from Bobbio) according to which Columbanus composed *Mundus iste transibit*. On the contrary, such evidence as we have speaks in favour of the saint who died in Bobbio in 615, and from whose pen we also have the *Epistolae* and *Instructiones*.[91]

---

[87] If these texts belong to the last phase of Columbanus's life, then Bobbio – where they were preserved and transmitted in manuscript – has a more pressing claim than Milan, where in Walker's opinion (*Sancti Columbani Opera*, p. xliii) they were delivered as sermons.

[88] *Sancti Columbani Opera*, ed. & transl. Walker, p. 78, line 27.

[89] Thus (hesitantly) Bulst, 'Hymnologica', p. 96.

[90] MGH, Poetae IV.495–500; cf. Schaller & Könsgen, *Initia*, no. 1305.

[91] This article originally appeared as 'Die Siebensilberstrophen "De mundi transitu" – eine Dichtung Columbans?', in *Die Iren und Europa*, ed. Löwe, I.468–83; it was recently reprinted in Schaller, *Studien*, pp. 236–51, with Additamenta at pp. 425–7. These Additamenta have been largely incorporated into the present article, the translation of which was prepared by Michael Lapidge. Concerning the arguments advanced in the original article, cf. the comments of Lapidge ('A new Hiberno-Latin hymn', p. 248): '. . . the poem *Mundus iste transibit*, which Dieter Schaller has recently shown (conclusively, in my opinion) to be the work of Columbanus of Bangor, who died as abbot of Bobbio in 615', and Howlett, 'Two works of Columban', who prints *Mundus iste transibit* as a 'Columbani Carmen' (pp. 33–46).

VII

'PRECAMUR PATREM': AN EASTER HYMN BY COLUMBANUS?

Michael Lapidge

IN his *Vita S. Columbani*, Ionas of Bobbio remarked that Columbanus, while still a young man in his native Ireland, had composed 'a number of pieces which were both suitable for singing and useful for instruction'.[1] Ionas situated this compositional activity during the period of Columbanus's life when he was studying with Sinell, that is, before he became a monk at the monastery of Bangor.[2] It is not wholly clear what these 'pieces' were, nor whether Ionas had anything more than a vague notion of their existence; but if we proceed on the assumption that, when he entered Bangor, Columbanus brought his dossier of compositions with him, then it may in theory be possible to identify some of them among Bangor books. One might look, in particular, to the 'Antiphonary of Bangor', a liturgical manuscript compiled at Bangor by several scribes near the turn of the seventh century (*ca* 700) – that is, approximately a century after Columbanus had left Bangor for the Continent – and containing various prayers and hymns for use in the Divine Office.[3] As usual in liturgical books of this sort, the contents of the 'Antiphonary of Bangor' are presented anonymously; but if any of Columbanus's early compositions, particularly those suitable for singing (by which Ionas presumably understood what we would describe simply as 'hymns') have by chance survived, it is among the anonymous contents of the 'Antiphonary of Bangor' that we might hope to find them. In fact there are compelling reasons for thinking that one such hymn, *Precamur patrem*, is indeed a composition of Columbanus.[4]

---

[1] *Vita S. Columbani*, I.3 (ed. Krusch, *Ionae Vitae Sanctorum*, p. 158): 'multaque alia, quae uel ad cantum digna uel ad docendum utilia, condidit dicta'.

[2] See discussion by Bullough, above, pp. 4–7. On the identity of Sinell, see Ó Cróinín, 'Mo-sinnu moccu Min'.

[3] The 'Antiphonary of Bangor' (not properly an antiphoner – that is, a book containing the chants, antiphons, verses, responsories and invitatories for the Office – but a more random compilation, a sort of commonplace-book containing hymns, collects and prayers, mostly but not entirely for use in the Office) is ed. Warren, *The Antiphonary*; see also Curran, *The Antiphonary*. On the date of the manuscript (now Milano, Biblioteca Ambrosiana, MS. C.5 inf.), see Lowe, *Codices*, III.311, and Brown, 'The Irish element', p. 106.

[4] I repeat here arguments which I earlier presented in 'Columbanus', not only for the sake of completeness of the present volume, but because the earlier form in which the arguments were printed (in *Peritia* for 1985) was drastically mutilated by printer's errors introduced after the proofs had been corrected (affecting Greek words in

Precamur patrem[5] is a hymn consisting of forty-two stanzas; as such it is the longest poem in the 'Antiphonary of Bangor'. In spite of the manuscript-rubric, which describes it as a 'Hymnum apostolorum ut alii dicunt',[6] it is an extensive meditation on the life of Christ and His role in the scheme of salvation, as will be clear from a synopsis of its structure. The poem begins with three stanzas of invocation to the Father, Son and Holy Ghost, who are together addressed as the 'radiance of the fountain of all light' (*uniuersorum fontis iubar luminum*). Following the invocation, the poet turns (in stanzas 4–15) directly to the meaning of Easter day: that on this day Christ shone from heaven on the world (stanza 4); that He as the *lumen aeternum* was made flesh and sent by the Father (stanza 5); that He deprived primordial chaos of its force and so drove night from the world (stanza 6); that He defeated the Enemy so releasing the bonds of death (stanza 7); that He, as First Day, illumined the 'shadows of the abyss' (stanza 8); and that, on the same day, Israel crossed the Red Sea (stanzas 11–13). At this point follow two general stanzas (stanzas 14–15) on the meaning of Easter day in the scheme of salvation, and then the poet turns to the figure of Christ Himself, seen first from the point of view of the end of the world at the Day of Judgment (stanza 16), then from the point of view of the beginning of christian history, with the fact that His Coming was foretold by Old Testament prophets (stanza 17). The major events of Christ's life are then recounted, in chronological order: His Nativity (stanzas 18–20), His miracles (stanzas 21–5), His betrayal (stanzas 26–30) and finally His crucifixion and His Descent into Hell followed by the Resurrection (stanzas 31–9). The hymn closes with a prayer of three stanzas' length (40–2), so balancing the three stanzas of invocation at the beginning, beseeching mercy for the *micrologi* who are unable to describe the indescribable glory of Christ's role in the scheme of salvation.

We shall return to the significance of the word *micrologi* in a moment, once we have considered the function of the hymn as a whole. It is clear, in the first place, that all forty-two stanzas of the hymn are unified by a single theme – that of the meaning of Easter Day. In particular, the imagery – of Christ as Light and Day overcoming darkness and night – which pervades the hymn reinforces the suspicion that it was intended for liturgical use at Eastertide,[7] and it is worthwhile attempting to define more precisely what this use may

---

particular, on which some crucial arguments turn), and because *Peritia* is scarcely available outside of Ireland.

[5] Listed Schaller & Könsgen, *Initia*, no. 12448; ed. Blume, 'Hymnodia', pp. 271–5 (no. 215), and Warren, *The Antiphonary*, II.5–7. Readers who might wish to see the poem rearranged in (allegedly meaningful) geometrical patterns may consult Howlett, 'The earliest Irish writers', pp. 7–9. On *Precamur patrem*, see also Simonetti, 'Studi', pp. 467–9, and Stevenson, 'Irish hymns', pp. 107–8.

[6] The rubric was added by a scribe different from the one who copied the poem; the rubricator's uncertainty concerning the liturgical function of the poem is reflected in his qualification, *ut alii dicunt*.

[7] Cf. the remark of Warren (*The Antiphonary*, ed. Warren, II.39), that 'the language of the Hymn points to its being specially intended as a commemoration of the Resurrection, and therefore for Easter-tide or Sunday use'. Curran (*The Antiphonary*) offers no opinion of the liturgical function of *Precamur patrem*.

have been. In fact much of the imagery of light/darkness in the hymn is paralleled in the service for the vigil of Holy Saturday, when, with the symbolic lighting of the paschal candle, the celebration moves from contemplation of the darkness of a world temporarily vacated by Christ during His Descent into Hell, to rejoicing at the brilliance of the Day brought about by His Resurrection. Thus the poet stresses that 'on this day' (*hic enim dies*)[8] God's First Offspring, Christ, 'shone from the citadel of heaven on the mass of the universe' (stanza 4), having defeated the ancient Enemy and released the chains of death (stanza 7), and 'on the very same day' (*eodem die*) Israel, liberated, left the Red Sea and the Egyptians behind (stanza 10):[9]

> Hic enim dies
>> Velut primogenitus
> Coeli ab arce
>> Mundi moli micuit . . .
>
> Ita ueterno
>> Iste hoste subacto
> Polo nodoso
>> Soluit mortis uinculo . . .
>
> Eodem die
>> Rubrum, ut aiunt, mare
> Post tergum liquit
>> Liberatus Israel.

The same concatenation of ideas, couched in the imagery of light/darkness, is found in the 'Blessing of the paschal candle' (*Benedictio cerei*) in the Gregorian[10] Sacramentary:[11]

---

[8] It is unmistakably clear that *hic dies* refers to the day on which the hymn is to be sung; yet the reference has perennially baffled commentators. Blume ('Hymnodia', p. 274), for example, wrote: 'Str. 4 beginnt nun ganz abrupt mit "Hic enim dies". *Welcher* Tag? Und warum "enim"? Das alles passt schlecht zu der sonst breiten Darstellung. Demnach scheint mir vor Str. 4 etwas zu fehlen, vielleicht der Anfang einer *besonderen* Dichtung. . .' Simonetti ('Studi', p. 468) thought that Blume's remedy was too drastic, and suggested instead – improbably – that *hic dies* refers to *iubar* of stanza 3: 'Resta la difficoltà di *hic* = "questo giorno", laddove nel proemio non è alcuna allusione a tale giorno, ma da sola questa difficoltà non è sufficiente a reggere tutta la costruzione del Blume; potremmo anche pensare ad un riferimento, un po' duro e faticoso, al precedente *iubar*. . .' But these difficulties evaporate as soon as one realizes that *Hic enim dies* refers to the day on which the hymn was appointed for liturgical use.

[9] *The Antiphonary*, ed. Warren, II.5.

[10] I draw this parallel, however, without prejudice to the question of what form of sacramentary would have been known to Columbanus in the late sixth century. Because we do not know what form of sacramentary was then in use, one cannot insist on verbal similarities between (say) the Gregorian Sacramentary and *Precamur patrem*. But the broad outline of the service and its significance (as reflected in the imagery of the prayers) is unlikely to have been substantially different. For example, there can be no doubt that the Crossing of the Red Sea was associated with the liturgy of Holy Saturday in Columbanus's day, for in the

In quo primum patres nostros filios israhel eductos de aegypto, rubrum mare sicco uestigio transire fecisti . . . Haec nox est, in qua destructis uinculis mortis, christus ab inferis uictor ascendit . . . O beata nox, quae sola meruit scire tempus et horam in qua christus ab inferis resurrexit . . .

It is the combination of these elements – the light/darkness imagery, the defeat of the Enemy so releasing the bonds of death, and the Crossing of the Red Sea – which suggests unmistakably that *Precamur patrem* was intended specifically for the vigil of Holy Saturday.[12]

We may now turn to the question of the hymn's authorship. In the final stanza of the hymn, the poet, speaking in the first person plural, had asked why we mortal *micrologi* should attempt to narrate deeds of Christ which no living person could describe:[13]

> Quid tam mortales
> Tentamus micrologi
> Narrare quiuit
> Quae nullus edicere?

The author's reference to himself as a *micrologus* (plural: *micrologi*) is immediately striking, in light of a similar usage by Columbanus. In his *Epistula I*, addressed to Pope Gregory the Great (pope: 590–604) and to be dated probably to 600, Columbanus contrasts his own humble station with the exalted station of Pope Gregory, and in this context refers to himself, employing the striking grecism *micrologus*: 'Licet enim mihi, nimirum micrologo . . .'.[14] He employs the same grecism in a later letter (*Epistula V*), addressed this time to Pope Boniface IV (pope: 608–15) and to be dated to 613. Once again Columbanus employs the word *micrologus* to refer to his own station (in contrast with the pope's exalted station):[15]

Pulcherrimo omnium totius Europae ecclesiarum capiti, papae praedulci, praecelso praesuli, pastorum pastori, reuerendissimo speculatori, humillimus celsissimo, minimus maximo, agrestis urbano, *micrologus* eloquentissimo . . .

---

pre-Gregorian Roman Easter service, which included twelve lections from the Old Testament, one of the lections in question was from Exodus XIV.24–XV.2, which contains the description of the Crossing of the Red Sea. Another of the lections was from Genesis I.1–II.3, concerning the Creation; and note that stanza 8 of *Precamur patrem* contains a reminiscence of Genesis I.2 (see below, n. 27). The twelve pre-Gregorian Old Testament lections have been printed and discussed by Fischer, 'Die Lesungen'. See also the discussion of Bullough, above, p. 5, n. 17.

[11] *Le sacramentaire*, ed. Deshusses, p. 361 (§ 1022a).

[12] It is possible that *Precamur patrem* was composed as a replacement for one of the Easter hymns prescribed in the hymnal then in use in Columbanus's congregation, possibly *Hic est dies uerus*, or *Ad cenam agni prouidi*, or *Aurora lucis rutilat* (but cf. the remarks of Bullough, above, p. 5, n. 17). On the form of hymnal used in sixth-century Ireland, and its Gallican (rather than Roman) antecedents, see the important discussion by Stevenson, 'Irish hymns'.

[13] *The Antiphonary*, ed. Warren, II.7.

[14] *Sancti Columbani Opera*, ed. & transl. Walker, p. 2.

[15] *Ibid.*, p. 36.

The meaning of the word is clear this time from the context. Columbanus is using the word in what he took to be its etymological sense: 'one of little eloquence'.

Where did Columbanus discover this unusual grecism? The answer is not far to seek: in Rufinus's Latin translation of the *Orationes* of the Greek church father, Gregory of Nazianzus.[16] There is independent evidence that Columbanus was familiar with Rufinus's translation of Gregory, for in his *Epistula II* he draws unmistakably on a passage of Rufinus's translation of the *Apologeticus* (= *Oratio I*) of Gregory.[17] In view of Columbanus's familiarity with this translation of Rufinus, it is worth examining in some detail the passage in which the word *micrologus* occurs. The passage in question is in the *De luminibus* (= *Oratio III*); it contains Gregory's refutation of an interlocutor who was arguing that the Holy Ghost is most unlikely to have appeared in the tiny form of a dove:[18]

specie columbae corporalis apparuit [*scil.* spiritus sanctus]; honorat enim corpus per hoc quod et ipsum adsumptum est in deum, sed si in magnitudine et pondere iudicas de diuinitate et propter hoc pusillus tibi uidetur spiritus sanctus, quoniam in specie paruae columbae apparuit, o microloge in rebus magnis, potes tu etiam regnum caelorum putare minimum, quoniam grano sinapis comparatum est.

In translating Gregory, Rufinus apparently did not seek to find an equivalent for the Greek μικρολόγος, which means something like 'captious trifler' or 'pettifogger',[19] but simply transliterated it into Latin. To judge by his own (etymological) use of the word (μικρός, 'small' + λόγος, 'speech'), Columbanus did not understand the precise connotations of the Greek term which lay behind Rufinus's grecism. What drew Columbanus's attention to the word was the context of Gregory's discussion: the parallelism of the small dove (*parua columba*) and the small (μικρός) or ineloquent rhetorician. Columbanus frequently plays on the associations of his own name: *columba* in Latin,[20]

---

[16] *Tyrannii Rufini . . . interpretatio*, ed. Engelbrecht. On this work, see the discussion and bibliography in Di Berardino, *Patrology*, IV.252.

[17] See Smit, *Studies*, p. 115, and discussion by Wright, above, p. 74–5.

[18] *Tyrannii Rufini . . . interpretatio*, ed. Engelbrecht, p. 129: 'The Holy Spirit appeared in the form of a corporeal dove [cf. Luke III.22]; it honours corporeality in that the body itself is taken up into the godhead. But if you judge the godhead on the basis of size and weight and, because of this, the Holy Spirit seems very tiny to you, since it appeared in the form of a tiny dove – o you pettifogger in mighty matters! – you may as well reckon the Kingdom of Heaven to be tiny, since it is compared to a grain of mustard seed [cf. Matthew XIII.31].'

[19] See *A Greek-English Lexicon*, edd. Liddell & Scott, s.v. μικρολόγος 2, 'cavilling about trifles, captious'; cf. *A Patristic Greek Lexicon*, ed. Lampe, s.v. μικρολόγος. Hence the Latin loan-word *micrologus* is defined as follows in the *Thesaurus Linguae Latinae* (s.v.): 'qui paruarum rerum nimis rationem habet, angustus et parcus animo'.

[20] Recall that, although our author's name is conventionally given as *Columbanus*, he referred to himself as *Columba*, as for example in the invocation to his *Epistula II*: 'Dominis sanctis et in Christo patribus uel fratribus . . . Columba peccator salutem in Christo praemitto' (*Sancti Columbani Opera*, ed. & transl. Walker, p. 12); cf. the discussion of Smit, *Studies*, pp. 149–50.

peristera in Greek, *(bar)iona* in Hebrew.[21] It suited Columbanus's literary purposes splendidly that, to a *micrologus*, a small *columba* was the vessel of the Holy Spirit – just as he, literally a *columba* and although a humble *micrologus*, was not to be despised by mighty popes since he was, in effect, a vessel of the Holy Ghost. In other words, Columbanus evidently lifted the word *micrologus* from Rufinus because it had clear, personal associations; it could be used by him as a sort of 'signature tune'.

Outside the writings of Rufinus and Columbanus the word *micrologus* is exceptionally rare.[22] (One may discount an example of the word in Ionas's *Vita S. Columbani*, since he evidently derived it from one of Columbanus's *Epistulae*.[23]) It is therefore striking that the word should occur in the hymn *Precamur patrem*. As we have seen, the author of this hymn, speaking in the first person plural, asks the rhetorical question, why should we mortal *micrologi* attempt to narrate deeds which no living person could describe:[24]

> Quid tam mortales
>   Tentamus micrologi
> Narrare quiuit
>   Quae nullus edicere?

The word *micrologus* is used here in precisely the sense given to it by Columbanus, namely 'one of little speech', rather than the sense it has in Rufinus ('captious trifler', 'pettifogger'). The use of the word to mean 'one of little speech' depends on the personal associations which Columbanus perceived in the passage of Rufinus; and this fact, combined with the extreme rarity of the word, is enough to suggest that Columbanus himself is the author of *Precamur patrem*.

The suggestion that *Precamur patrem* is by Columbanus may be confirmed by a further striking parallel. In his *Epistula V*, Columbanus had occasion to discuss Christology à propos the 'Three Chapters' heresy; and during this discussion he stated the terms of his own belief in Christ:[25]

Christus enim saluator uerus Deus aeternus sine tempore et uerus homo absque peccato ex tempore est, qui iuxta diuinitatem coaeternus est patri et iuxta humanitatem iunior est matre, qui *natus in carne, nequaquam deerat caelo, manens in trinitate*, uixit in mundo.

What is striking is that the italicized words are paralleled closely (and probably drawn directly) from a stanza of *Precamur patrem* (stanza 18):[26]

---

21 See *Sancti Columbani Opera*, ed. & transl. Walker, p. 54; and cf. pp. 2, 34, 36.

22 See *Thesaurus Linguae Latinae*, s.v. 'micrologus' (where only the two passages in Rufinus are cited), and Blaise, *Dictionnaire*, s.v. 'micrologus', who cites the two passages in Rufinus, the two in Columbanus, and one in Ionas (on which see below, n. 23).

23 Ionas, *Vita S. Columbani*, II.10 (ed. Krusch, *Ionae Vitae Sanctorum*, p. 251); cf. Walker, 'On the use of Greek words', p. 122.

24 *The Antiphonary*, ed. Warren, II.7.

25 *Sancti Columbani Opera*, ed. & transl. Walker, p. 52 (italics mine).

26 *The Antiphonary*, ed. Warren, II.6.

Natus ut homo
    Mortali in tegmine
Non deest caelo
    Manens in Trinitate.

The simplest explanation of this verbal debt (in my view) is that Columbanus, attempting to formulate in old age a simple and direct expression of his personal creed, recurred to the very words of a hymn which he had composed in his youth in Ireland. The hymn was subsequently copied at Bangor into the 'Antiphonary of Bangor', approximately a century after Columbanus's departure for the Continent. Two direct verbal links between *Precamur patrem* and the genuine *Epistulae* of Columbanus are unlikely to be a matter of coincidence. As we have seen, the evidence of Ionas indicates that, in his youth, Columbanus composed various *dicta . . . ad cantum digna*, in other words, hymns. I submit that *Precamur patrem* is one such composition, designed by Columbanus for liturgical use during the vigil of Holy Saturday.

By any reckoning *Precamur patrem* is a remarkable composition, but it acquires an especial importance when accepted as an early work of Columbanus, for it reveals its author as a man of impressive literary culture. Taking his inspiration from the liturgy of Holy Saturday, Columbanus amplified his account of the Resurrection by means of numerous allusions to the Bible – which he apparently knew in a Vetus Latina form[27] – as well as to apocryphal works such as the Gospel of Nicodemus.[28] Into this biblical framework he wove allusions to classical poets, such as Vergil,[29] and to patristic authorities, such as Cassian[30] and

---

[27] The wording of stanza 2 ('Tenebrae super / ante erant abyssum') is an unambiguous reminiscence of Genesis I.2, in a Vetus Latina version: 'et tenebrae erant super abyssum' (ed. Sabatier, *Biblorum sacrorum latinae uersiones antiquae*, I.7); cf. the Vulgate reading, 'et tenebrae super faciem abyssi' (ed. Weber, *Biblia Sacra*, I.4). Similarly, stanza 22 ('Tum per profetam / completur ut dictum est / saliet claudus / ut ceruus perniciter') is a reminiscence of Isaiah XXXV.6 in the Vetus Latina version: 'Tunc saliet claudus sicut ceruus' (ed. Sabatier, *ibid.*, II.573); cf. the Vulgate wording, 'tunc saliet sicut ceruus claudus' (ed. Weber, *Biblia Sacra*, II.1131). In both cases the wording and word-order is closer to the Vetus Latina than to the Vulgate. In his later writings Columbanus frequently quotes the Bible in a Vetus Latina version (see Walker, *Sancti Columbani Opera*, pp. 216–20), although for certain books he clearly knew the Vulgate.

[28] See Curran, *The Antiphonary*, pp. 54–6, who demonstrates that the account of the Descent into Hell in stanzas 33–7 is based on §§ 3–10 of the Gospel of Nicodemus (ed. Tischendorf, *Euangelia apocrypha*, pp. 389–416 = Latin A). For knowledge of this text in early Ireland, see Dumville, 'Biblical apocrypha', p. 301, and McNamara, *The Apocrypha*, pp. 68–72.

[29] One assumes that the phrase in stanza 26 ('post tantas moles') is a reminiscence of *Aeneid* I.134: 'et *tantas* audietis tollere *moles*'; but the phrase was common, and Columbanus may have known it from a source closer at hand, such as St Patrick, *Confessio*, § 15 ('Dominus seruulo suo concederet post aerumnas et tantas moles').

[30] Curran (*The Antiphonary*, p. 215, n. 37) demonstrates that stanza 35 ('Quemque antiquum / paradiso incolam / recursu suo / clementer restituit') clearly derives from Cassian, *De institutis coenobiorum*, III.iii.6: 'hora uero nona inferna penetrans . . . *antiquum incolam paradiso* pia confessione *restituit*' (ed. Petschenig, pp. 36–7). It is

possibly Eucherius.[31] Above all, he shows intimate familiarity with the language and diction of Late Latin hymnody, particularly with the hymns of Venantius Fortunatus.[32]

However, in spite of this familiarity with Late Latin hymnody, *Precamur patrem* is cast in an entirely distinct poetic form. Whereas Late Latin hymns are without exception metrical in form (that is, quantitative: their verse-form being based on the length of syllables), that of *Precamur patrem* is apparently based on syllable-counting and stress. Each of its stanzas consists of four lines, or better perhaps, of two couplets each consisting of a five-syllable and a seven-syllable member. By and large the stress-pattern in these lines is arranged so that in the five-syllable member the stress falls on the penultimate syllable (or paroxytone), and in the following seven-syllable member, on the antepenultimate syllable (or proparoxytone), as in the following example (stanza 3):[33]

> Uniuersórum
> Fontis iubar lúminum
> Aethereórum
> Et orbi lucéntium.

This stress-pattern may be described (using Norberg's now-familiar notation) as 5p + 7pp.[34] *Precamur patrem* is one of two hymns in the 'Antiphonary of Bangor' which exhibit this verse-form.[35] However, the stress-pattern is not regularly observed. There are frequent examples of seven-syllable members with stress not on the antepenultimate, but on the penultimate, syllable:

> Precamur patrem
> Regem omnipoténtem;

or again,

> Eodem die
> Rubrum ut aiunt máre.

---

worth adding that Cassian's *De institutis coenobiorum* is a text which Columbanus laid heavily under contribution in his own *Regula monachorum* (see Walker, *Sancti Columbani Opera*, p. xlviii, and notes to the text, *passim*).

[31] It would appear that the name of the pharaoh who was submerged in the Red Sea, which Columbanus gives in stanza 12 as *Cincri*, derives from Eucherius, *Instructiones* (ed. Wotke, p. 142): 'Pharao tamen ille submersus in mare rubrum proprio uocabulo Cenchres uocitatus est.' The identity of this pharaoh is extremely rare in Latin patristic tradition; see Warren, *The Antiphonary*, II.39–40.

[32] See discussion by Stevenson, 'Irish hymns', pp. 107–8.

[33] *The Antiphonary*, ed. Warren, II.5.

[34] Norberg, *Introduction*, p. 111. Bulst ('Hymnologica') discusses the same phenomenon, but in terms of 'rising' and 'falling' stress; on *Precamur patrem*, see esp. p. 94. See also the discussion by Schaller, above, pp. 241–7.

[35] The other is *Sancti uenite, corpus Christi sumite*: listed Schaller & Könsgen, *Initia*, no. 14657; ed. Blume, 'Hymnodia', pp. 298–9 (no. 228) and Warren, *The Antiphonary*, II.10–11.

Here one might think that a regularly observed stress-pattern would require *omnipótentèm* and *ut aiúnt marè*.[36] These apparent departures from a regular stress-pattern have caused earlier commentators to speak of the 'ruggedness' of the metre.[37] But it is not yet clear to what extent such variation was either tolerated or avoided by Hiberno-Latin hymnodists,[38] and hence whether *Precamur patrem* is indeed a piece of rugged (viz. poor) versification, or whether it behaves properly according to rules as yet improperly understood. In other respects, *Precamur patrem* exhibits the features recognized as characteristic of Hiberno-Latin versification: it has sporadic – but not consistent – rhyme, sometimes only between the seven-syllable members, sometimes between all four members of a stanza, sometimes not at all; it has frequent hiatus between vowels but no example of the elision which is almost invariable in Late Latin (quantitative) hymns; and frequent synizesis of *ii*, whereby these two vowels are treated as a single *i* (e.g. stanza 29, 'ut latroni cum gladiis', where *gladiis* is scanned as a bisyllabic word). Why and where and when such metrical conventions were first elaborated remains to be seen.

For the time being, it is sufficient to have identified a new work by the young Columbanus. This identification, when taken together with the compelling arguments of Dieter Schaller, to the effect that the poem *Mundus iste transibit* is by Columbanus,[39] reveals a hitherto unsuspected side of his genius: that he was adept in the composition of rhythmical verse, for both liturgical and admonitory purposes.

---

[36] Bulst ('Hymnologica', p. 94) notes that twenty-three cadences (more than one quarter) are 'fallend' and hence 'falsch' as it were (of these, ten consist of two-syllable words, as *mare* in the present example); cf. Norberg, *Introduction*, p. 128.

[37] Warren, *The Antiphonary*, II.39; the opinion is repeated by Coccia, 'La cultura irlandese', p. 277.

[38] See the discussion by Schaller, above, p. 245.

[39] Above, pp. 240–54.

VIII

THE COMPUTISTICAL WORKS OF COLUMBANUS

Dáibhí Ó Cróinín

IN his *Vita S. Columbani* (I.3), Ionas relates that Columbanus, in the early flush of religious enthusiasm, abandoned his native Leinster and travelled north, first to Crannach at Downpatrick, where he received instruction from a certain Sinilis (*alias* Mo-Sinu maccu Min, d. A.D. 610), 'qui eo tempore singulari religione et scripturarum sacrarum scientiae flore inter suos pollebat'.[1] According to Ionas, the young Columbanus showed such ability that he soon advanced to 'dificilium quaestionum materia', and before his departure he had composed a volume of commentary on the Psalms and many other works which were either suitable for singing or useful for teaching ('multaque alia, quae uel ad cantum digna uel ad docendum utilia, condidit dicta').[2] From Downpatrick Columbanus moved on to Bangor, then still ruled by its founder Comgall (d. A.D. 602), where he spent several years (the exact number cannot be determined). The desire for *peregrinatio* that subsequently possessed him led eventually to his departure, *ca* A.D. 590, with twelve companions for Burgundy.

The evidence for Columbanus's interest in computistical problems is abundantly clear in the letters of his which have survived, and there can be little doubt that the science of computus formed an important part of his early instruction. In fact his earliest teacher Sinilis (*alias* Mo-Sinu maccu Min) is credited by one source as being 'the first of the Irish who learned the computus by heart from a certain learned Greek'.[3] The intricacies of the Easter reckoning may quite conceivably have been among the 'dificilium quaestionum materia' of Columbanus's early years at Downpatrick. There is abundant evidence in the surviving manuscripts to show that in Ireland, as indeed everywhere in western Europe, the computus formed one branch of a trivium with biblical exegesis and Latin grammar in the monastic curriculum. Columbanus's genuine *Epistulae* indicate that he had mastered all three to an exceptional degree.

The first three *Epistulae*, addressed to two popes and to the bishops of Gaul assembled in council, bear witness to a passionate concern with the question of Easter reckoning and an obvious confidence – not to say arrogance – about his abilities in the field. Columbanus shows himself fully conversant with the technical terminology of the subject (e.g. *rimarius*, *calcenterus*, etc.) and he was also familiar with the works of the most eminent computists, such as

---

[1] *Ionae Vitae Sanctorum*, ed. Krusch, p. 69.
[2] *Ibid.*
[3] See Ó Cróinín, 'Mo-Sinu maccu Min'.

pseudo-Anatolius and Victorius.[4] Indeed, he scathingly remarks of Victorius's Easter tables (published in A.D. 457, and from A.D. 541 the official Easter tables of the Gallican churches) that they had long before been scrutinised and found wanting 'by the ancient scholars of Ireland and by learned computists most skilled in reckoning chronology', who thought the work 'more worthy of ridicule or pity than of authority'.[5] Columbanus also states that he had outlined his case for the Irish Easter practices in three letters to Pope Gregory ('de Pascha sancto papae per tres tomos innotui') and again in an abridged pamphlet addressed to Bishop Arigius of Lyons ('et adhuc sancto fratri uestro Arigio breui libello hoc idem scribere praesumpsi').[6]

These 'tres tomos' and the 'breuis libellus' are, unfortunately, lost, but there is a number of computistical texts still extant which are ascribed to Columbanus in some manuscripts, and one at least of these may represent a genuine composition of the saint. The works thus associated with Columbanus are the letter *De sollemnitatibus*, the short tract *De saltu lunae*, and a brief excerpt, apparently from a longer work, ascribed in several manuscripts to 'Palumbus'.

The letter, or *disputatio*, *De sollemnitatibus et sabbatis et neomeniis* is a short treatise on the Jewish festal practices and their relevance to Christian Paschal observances. The work is addressed to a 'uenerabilis papa', whose prayers are requested at the end. If the *disputatio* ever had a superscription it is now lost, and with it the names of both author and recipient. But wherever the work is rubricated in manuscripts it is attributed to Jerome: 'Disputatio (Sancti) (H)Ieronimi de sollemnitatibus'. The letter was first published by Domenico Vallarsi from the Vatican manuscript listed below; Vallarsi's text was subsequently reproduced in Migne's *Patrologia Latina*.[7] A separate edition was published by Jean-Baptiste Pitra from the Paris and London manuscripts.[8] In 1885, strangely unaware of its previous publication (and despite the fact that four years previously he had catalogued the Köln manuscript and correctly identified the work there) Bruno Krusch republished the text from the Paris manuscript (where it has no rubric) and announced it as a 'rediscovered' letter from Columbanus to Gregory the Great.[9] A controversy ensued in German journals, principally between Wilhelm Gundlach and Otto Seebass, with Gundlach supporting Krusch's case and Seebass denying the alleged parallels (chiefly stylistic) between the concluding paragraph of the *De sollemnitatibus* and the opening of Columbanus's *Epistula V*.[10] So confident, in fact, was Gundlach of its

---

[4] Columbanus is, in fact, the earliest witness to the knowledge and use of pseudo-Anatolius in Ireland; see also discussion by Bullough, above, p. 6.

[5] *Sancti Columbani Opera*, ed. & transl. Walker, p. 6: 'Scias namque nostris magistris et Hibernicis antiquis philosophis et sapientissimis componendi calculi computariis Victorium non fuisse receptum, sed magis risu uel uenia dignum quam auctoritate.'

[6] *Ibid.*, p. 16.

[7] *Hieronymi opera omnia*, ed. Vallarsi, I.1114–20 (*Epistula CXLIX*); Vallarsi's text is reprinted in *Patrologia Latina*, ed. Migne, XXII.1220–4.

[8] *Spicilegium Solesmense*, ed. Pitra, I.xi–xiv, 9–13, 565–6.

[9] Krusch, 'Chronologisches aus Handschriften'; see also his earlier description of Köln, Dombibliothek, 83[2] in *Studien*, I.204.

[10] Gundlach, 'Über die Columban-Briefe I' and 'Zu den Columban-Briefen'; Seebass, 'Über die Handschriften' and 'Über dem Verfasser'.

authenticity that he republished Krusch's text as *Epistula VI* in the Monumenta edition of Columbanus's letters.[11] Fernand Cabrol and Henri Leclercq published yet another edition, as an anonymous pre-Nicene tract, in 1913,[12] and Isidor Hilberg then published it as part of his edition of Jerome's letters, again from the Vatican manuscript.[13] The most recent edition is Walker's.[14]

The letter has no salutation, but concludes with the words 'ora pro me, uenerabilis papa'. In the concluding paragraph the author refers to his reader again as 'uenerabilis papa' and describes himself as a 'peregrinus'. He also states that the letter was solicited ('Haec autem et a te postulata sunt'), and the implication is that the writer was requested by higher authority to provide answers to questions on the Easter problem. The use of the word 'papa' need not, of course, mean that the letter was addressed to a pope; Cummian, after all, refers to Patrick as 'papa noster',[15] and the term is frequently used of bishops. Although most modern commentators have dated it in the fifth century or even earlier, and suggested continental origin,[16] there are some indications in the letter that would indicate an Irish milieu and perhaps an Irish author in the seventh century.

The *De sollemnitatibus* is preserved in the following manuscripts:[17]

1. Oxford, Bodleian Library, Bodley 309 (*saec.* xi) fos 82v–84r
2. Paris, Bibliothèque Nationale, lat. 16361 (*saec.* xii) pp. 212–17
3. Köln, Dombibliothek, 83² (*ca* A.D. 805) fos 201r–203r
4. Geneva, Bibliothèque de l'Université, 50 (*saec.* ix¹) fos 121r–123r
5. London, British Library, Cotton Caligula A.xv (*saec.* viii²) fos 86v–90r
6. Vatican City, Biblioteca Apostolica Vaticana, lat. 642 (*saec.* xi) fos 89r–90v
7. Tours, Bibliothèque Municipale, 334 (*ca* A.D. 819) fos 8v–10r

---

[11] 'Columbani . . . epistolae', ed. Gundlach, pp. 177–80. Krusch subsequently retracted his earlier attribution to Columbanus; see *Passiones Vitaeque sanctorum aevi Merovingici* [II], ed. Krusch, p. 20, n. 1.

[12] *Monumenta ecclesiae liturgica*, edd. Cabrol & Leclercq, II.71–3, where the text is printed among 'Pseudepigraphi', although the pseudonymous author is not identified and the manuscript(s) on which the edition is based are not specified.

[13] *Sancti Hieronymi Epistulae*, ed. Hilberg, III.357–63.

[14] *Sancti Columbani Opera*, ed. & transl. Walker, pp. 198–206.

[15] *Cummian's Letter*, edd. Walsh & Ó Cróinín, p. 85.

[16] *Clavis Patrum Latinorum*, edd. Dekkers & Gaar, no. 2278; Zahn, *Forschungen*, pp. 182–5; Blumenkranz, *Die Judenpredigt*, pp. 47–9; and Smit, *Studies*, p. 33, n. 1: 'nowadays the work is usually dated in the fifth century or even earlier' (citing no authority but presumably following the *Clavis*, edd. Dekker & Gaar). The work was first considered as a possible letter of Pelagius by de Plinval, 'L'oeuvre littéraire', p. 40, n. 4, but he subsequently rejected this view in *Pélage*, p. 43. Cf. Grosjean, 'Recherches', p. 240–[1], n. 3: 'La lettre VI . . . reste dans le vague'. For alternative views, see further below.

[17] I have not been able to confirm the existence of further copies in: Einsiedeln, Stiftsbiblibliothek, 263; Münster (Staatsarchiv ?) 198 (508), *saec.* xvi ('deperditus' according to *Clavis*, edd. Dekkers & Gaar, no. 2278, where the catalogue reference is given as: 'Hieronymus de celebratione paschae'); Oxford, Bodleian Library, '56', or Paris, 'Bibl. Univ., 183', all listed by Lambert, *Bibliotheca Hieronymiana Manuscripta*, no. 149; Lambert gives no folio references for these supposed copies.

All these collections contain Irish material and five of them preserve copies of the Irish computus in the 'Sirmond group' of manuscripts first identified by Charles W. Jones, 'a computus used in the school at Jarrow when Bede was teaching there'.[18] The archetype of this group has since been shown to date from A.D. 658 and to have originated in southern Ireland.[19] The evidence of the manuscripts, therefore, speaks strongly for an Irish origin for the *De sollemnitatibus*.[20] The Cotton manuscript, dated *saec.* viii², offers a *terminus post quem non*;[21] the earliest known references to the work are in Irish texts of the seventh century.

The *De sollemnitatibus* is cited, for instance, under Jerome's name, in the seventh-century Irish computus *De ratione conputandi*,[22] a work with clear southern Irish connections and closely related to Cummian's 'Paschal Letter' (A.D. 632/33):[23]

Item HIERONIMUS dicit: 'Cum dominus, uerus agnus, uerum Pascha progreditur', in mundum 'aliqua permanere uolens custodiuit, aliqua non obseruare cupiens motauit'.

The same passage is cited in another well-known Irish work, the 'Munich Computus' (München, Bayerische Staatsbibliothek, Clm. 14456 [*saec.* ix], fo 31v) compiled in A.D. 718 using earlier sources (dated A.D. 689).[24] In the opinion of Charles W. Jones, 'the tract was almost certainly in the Irish *computus* before Cummian',[25] although if the work is contemporary or even slightly later in date it is possible that the *De sollemnitatibus* found inspiration in a curious phrase in Cummian's letter, where he was defending his elders and predecessors: 'Seniores uero nostri, quos in uelamine repulsionis habetis, quod optimum in diebus suis esse nouerunt simpliciter et fideliter sine culpa contradictionis ullius et animositatis obseruauerunt'; compare the *De sollemnitatibus*, where the author refers to his opponents as men who, 'uelamine

---

18 Jones, 'The "lost" Sirmond manuscript', pp. 204–19, and *Bedae Opera de Temporibus*, ed. Jones, pp. 105–10.

19 Ó Cróinín, 'The Irish provenance'.

20 An abbreviated version of the letter, inc. 'De Pascha autem tamquam maximo sacramento' [= *De sollemnitatibus* §§ 2–8] is contained in MSS. 1, 2, 4, 5, 7 listed above, and in Milano, Biblioteca Ambrosiana, H.150 inf. (A.D. 810), printed *Patrologia Latina*, ed. Migne, CXXIX.1361–3, as § CXLIX of the *Liber de computo*. The Milano manuscript is also an Irish collection.

21 Note that Walker's statements concerning manuscript affiliations are completely mistaken; for example, he dated Cotton Caligula A.xv to 'saec. XII/XIII' (*Sancti Columbani Opera*, ed. & transl. Walker, p. lx), whereas Lowe (*Codices*, II.183), gives the date as 'saec. VIII²'. Similarly, the statement that the text in Paris, BN, lat. 16361 'is not related to that of the four previous manuscripts' is equally mistaken. Jones long ago demonstrated that the Paris MS. was derived from the same archetype as the other MSS in the Sirmond group, and in fact it was copied directly, I believe, from Tours 334 (a manuscript not known to Jones).

22 Ó Cróinín, 'A seventh-century Irish computus'.

23 *Cummian's Letter*, edd. Walsh & Ó Cróinín, p. 204.

24 See Ó Cróinín, 'A seventh-century Irish computus', esp. pp. 408–9.

25 *Bedae Opera de Temporibus*, ed. Jones, p. 108.

posito super faciem Moysi spiritus et ueritatis luce illuminari nequeunt'.[26] It is noteworthy also that the *De sollemnitatibus* and Cummian's 'Paschal Letter' are the only known sources for a peculiar reading in Colossians II.16–17: 'nemo uos *seducat* in parte diei festi aut neomenia aut sabbato',[27] thus further strengthening the case for Irish origin. But what of the authorship?

There is nothing definite in the letter to preclude Jerome's authorship, although we know of no circumstances in which he might have composed it. Despite efforts to place it in the fifth century or earlier, its separate circulation and the fact that it first appears in Irish manuscripts whose contents date from the seventh century would seem to argue against the attribution to Jerome, the manuscript rubrics notwithstanding. Jones thought that he noted 'a similarity in the opening paragraph, with its mass of biblical quotation that is only vaguely relevant, to the letter of Cummian to Seghine',[28] but this does scant justice to Cummian and does not advance us very much in our enquiry. It is true that the tone of the letter is forceful, even combative, reminiscent of Columbanus, whom Krusch described as 'homo uehemens feroxque natura'.[29] On the other hand, the author clearly supports the 'orthodox' Easter reckoning rather than that of the Irish 84-year tables,[30] and his thorough advocacy of the Alexandrian Easter obviously precludes Columbanus's authorship, for there is no evidence whatever to show that the saint ever deviated, even in his last days, from the adherence to Irish practices which is such a marked feature of his letters.[31]

There are other possibilities. The name *Columba* and its diminutive form *Columbanus* (cf. Irish Colm/Colmán) were very common Irish names. Ionas, for instance, remarks that one of the saint's companions was 'nomen et ipse Columbanus'[32] and other examples abound. There were countless Irish *peregrini* in England and on the Continent, and Colmanus/Columbanus is a name encountered frequently among them.[33] But since the work is nowhere attributed to Columbanus in the manuscripts we need not restrict the search to

---

[26] *Cummian's Letter*, edd. Walsh & Ó Cróinín, p. 74; *Sancti Columbani Opera*, ed. & transl. Walker, p. 198.

[27] See, however, *Cummian's Letter*, edd. Walsh & Ó Cróinín, p. 225.

[28] *Bedae Opera de Temporibus*, ed. Jones, p. 109.

[29] *Passiones Vitaeque sanctorum aevi Merovingici* [II], ed. Krusch, p. 20. Coming from Krusch, the verdict has a certain piquancy about it!

[30] See, e.g., the following: 'Et hoc etiam intueri debemus, quod non in decima quarta die ad uesperum ... sed decima quinta die, in quo manifestum est diem festum Iudeorum cum suo sacrificio a Domino esse solutum', and 'Unde electa et amica sponsa Christi, uniuersalis ecclesia, anathematizat eos qui cum Iudeis in festiuitate Paschali decimam quartam celebrari diffiniunt' (*Sancti Columbani Opera*, ed. & transl. Walker, pp. 200, 202).

[31] Loofs (*Antiquae Britonum Scotorumque ecclesiae*, p. 93) was of the opinion that Columbanus eventually conformed, but there is no proof, and it seems highly unlikely. The attempt by Jean Laporte to circumvent this problem by claiming the letter for Attala, Columbanus's successor as abbot of Bobbio, is unconvincing; see Laporte, 'Étude d'authenticité' [*Revue Mabillon* 46 (1956)], pp. 9–14 (Appendix: 'Sur la lettre *De Solemnitatibus* ... attribuée à Saint Columban').

[32] *Vita S. Columbani* I.17 (ed. Krusch, *Ionae Vitae Sanctorum*, p. 184).

[33] See, e.g., the index to Lapidge & Sharpe, *A Bibliography*, s.vv. Colmán, Columbanus.

writers of the same name. One who comes to mind as a possible author is the Irishman referred to by Bede (*Historia ecclesiastica* III.25) as 'acerrimus ueri Paschae defensor nomine Ronan', a vigorous supporter of the orthodox Easter reckoning who clashed bitterly with Fínán, bishop of Lindisfarne (d. A.D. 661) on the Paschal question. Rónán might well have been called upon by a bishop ('papa') of the Irish Romanist party to refute the partisans of the 84-year reckoning. But of one thing there can be no doubt: the *De sollemnitatibus* is not a work of Columbanus.

The second computistical work attributed to Columbanus is the short tract *De saltu lunae*, a discussion of the day which the computists omitted at the end of every cycle in order to realign the movements of sun and moon. The work was first printed by Gabriel Meier, librarian of Einsiedeln, from a manuscript in St Gallen;[34] Walker republished it using an additional manuscript in Munich.[35] In fact, however, there are eight complete copies of the text known to me:[36]

1. St Gallen, Stiftsbibliothek, 250 (*saec.* x[1]) pp. 112–14
2. Zürich, Zentralbibliothek, Car. C.176 (*saec.* x/xi) fos 174v–175v
3. Karlsruhe, Landesbibliothek, Ac.132 (*saec.* x) cover (destroyed)
4. München, Bayerische Staatsbibliothek, Clm. 10270 (*saec.* xi) fos 12v–13r
5. München, Bayerische Staatsbibliothek, Clm. 14569 (*saec.* xi) fos 26r–28r
6. St Gallen, Stiftsbibliothek, 459 (*saec.* x) pp. 125–6
7. Malibu, Getty Museum, Ludwig XIII.5 (*saec.* xii[1]), fos 110v–114v
8. Zürich, Zentralbibliothek, C.62 (*saec.* x), fo 217r–v

The work was cited as Columbanus's by Notker Labeo in his computus, and Krusch thought that it dated from the eighth or ninth century.[37] Jones, on the other hand, believed it possibly earlier than Bede.[38] The discussion of the *saltus* is expert and accurate, but Columbanus's authorship must be ruled out, since the tract is clearly based on the 19-year cycle of Dionysius Exiguus and cites that text verbatim.[39] Though Columbanus is named in the superscription, none of the manuscripts offers any indication of the work's age; a pre-Bedan date (as suggested by Jones) seems to me unlikely.

The third computistical tract ascribed to Columbanus occurs in the same Sirmond group of manuscripts which preserves the letter *De sollemnitatibus*,

---

[34] Meier, *Jahresbericht*, Appendix, p. 30.
[35] *Sancti Columbani Opera*, ed. & transl. Walker, pp. 212–14; reprinted *Patrologia Latina*, ed. Migne, Supplementum IV.1609–10.
[36] The work is cited in Paris, BN, lat. 2183, fo 115r, in a miscellany comprising material mostly of Irish origin. It doubtless is cited in other collections as well. I wish to acknowledge the assistance of Dr Cornel Dora and Professor Wesley M. Stevens.
[37] *Passiones Vitaeque sanctorum aevi Merovingici* [II], ed. Krusch, p. 20, n. 1.
[38] *Bedae Opera de Temporibus*, ed. Jones, p. 376.
[39] The words 'Omnis igitur lunaris cursus secundum hebraeorum et egyptiorum supputationem potest facere per singulos menses dies XXVIIII et semissem', 'quia nimis errant, qui lunam peragere cursum sui circuli XXX dierum spaciis aestimant', and 'cum diligens inquisitio ueritatis ostenderet in duobus lunae circulis non LX dies sed LVIIII debere computari', are cobbled together from Dionysius's Prologue; see Krusch, *Studien*, II.65–6.

and it is cited in several others.[40] In every case the attribution is to Palumbus. The only person of such a name in Irish documents, to my knowledge, is Columbanus, who, in his *Epistula V* directed to Pope Boniface, signs himself by that name: 'Rara auis scribere audet Bonifatio Patri Palumbus'.[41] That the text is seventh-century at the latest is proved by its citation in the *De ratione conputandi*, mentioned earlier as being closely related to Cummian's 'Paschal Letter'. The relevant chapter of *De ratione conputandi* (§ 70) is as follows:[42]

Sciendum nobis, cum duae lunae in uno mense inueniuntur, quae est de illis luna ipsius mensis. Quae finitur in mense, ipsa est luna ipsius mensis. Luna uero sequens, si non pertingerit Kalendis mensis sequentis, abortiua luna uocabitur, quam alii dicunt lunam esse embolismi, quod non est uerum, ut PALUMBUS: 'Illi mensi conputa lunam, quae in eo finitur, non quae incipit. Unde, quae primum prioris aut initium sequentis non tenet, abortiua dicitur.'

Manuscripts of the Sirmond group preserve a more complete text:[43]

Palumbus dicit: 'Nunc de luna pauca tractanda sunt. Luna maior lunaque minor in anno sunt, sed uicissim (ut quidam putant) sibi semper alterno succedunt cursu; licet unius temporis alios intellexisse breues. Sciendum est similiter absque una abortiua quae, si tunc illo euenerit tempore, nulla conputanda, ut aiunt: mensi nimirum neutri mensis Kalendis uindicata. Primum scilicet prioris non tenens ac usque ad secundi initium non pertingens e medio quodammodo proiecto deprehenditur. Caeterorum lunas similiter breues esse, id est Iunii et Septembris et Nouimbris, et conputata ratione ab eis. Sed illam mensi conputa lunam quae in eo finitur, non quae incipit. Inde, quae primum prioris aut initium sequentis non tenet, abortiua luna dicitur. †Hoc licet alio lapsu saltus. Omnis enim .xiiii. luna semper facit anno.† Idcirco, dum per menses sex (ut supradictum est), id est aut per tres ueris et alios tres supra iam nominatos, aut (ut plus firmant) per alternos uicis sex lunae .xxviiii. sunt et per sex alios .xxx. inueniuntur.'

The passage occurs usually in relation to discussion of the *abortiua luna* (an Irish technical term)[44] and there is nothing in it – in so far as it can be understood – that would tell against Columbanus's authorship; there is no incompatibility of the doctrine with the workings of the Irish 84-year tables, for instance. But did Columbanus write this text? Of all the works discussed here, this is the only one with a strong claim to be a genuine writing of Columbanus. The work is definitely Irish and was known and cited in Irish texts of the seventh century. Allowing for the same reservations which were voiced above about the frequency of the name Colmanus/Columbanus in an Irish context, the attribution to *Palumbus* would seem to add an extra weight to the case for Columbanus's authorship. More than that, however, it is not possible to say.[45]

---

[40] One sentence is quoted, e.g., in St Dunstan's 'Classbook': Oxford, Bodleian Library, MS. Auct. F.4.32, fo 22v; see Ó Cróinín, 'A seventh-century computus', pp. 426–7. The text occurs in Strasbourg, Bibliothèque Universitaire, 326, fo 150r (not fo 149v, as stated *ibid.*, p. 427).

[41] *Sancti Columbani Opera*, ed. & transl. Walker, p. 36; see Smit, *Studies*, pp. 149–57.

[42] *Cummian's Letter*, edd. Walsh & Ó Cróinín, p. 178.

[43] *Ibid.*, pp. 178–9. The text is based on that in Oxford, Bodleian Library, Bodley 309; the passage is obscure in places and possibly corrupt.

[44] See *Cummian's Letter*, edd. Walsh & Ó Cróinín, pp. 177–8 (§ 69 and discussion).

[45] Research for this study was assisted by a generous grant from the Alexander von Humboldt Stiftung, Bonn.

IX

THE *ORATIO S. COLUMBANI*

Michael Lapidge

AMONG the minor writings which are included by Walker in his appendix of writings doubtfully attributable to Columbanus is a brief prayer in prose which, because of its very brevity, may be quoted here in full:[1]

Domine Deus, destrue quicquid plantat in me aduersarius et eradica, ut destructis iniquitatibus in ore et corde meo intellectum et opus bonum inseras; ut opere et ueritate deseruiam tibi soli, et intellegam implere mandata Christi, et requirere te ipsum. Da memoriam, da caritatem, da castitatem, da fidem, da omne quod scis ad utilitatem animae meae pertinere. Domine, fac in me bonum et praesta mihi quod scis oportere.

Walker, following Otto Seebass,[2] printed the text of the prayer from the only manuscript known to him, namely Turin, Biblioteca Nazionale Universitaria, MS. G.V.2, fo 9r. The principal content of this manuscript is a copy of the Gallican psalter, which is preceded by various prayers attributed to various church fathers (including the one attributed to Columbanus), and followed by hymns and a copy of the Athanasian creed; the manuscript was written at Bobbio sometime in the eleventh century.[3] Perhaps because of the relatively late date of the manuscript, Walker (who was apparently unaware of the Bobbio origin and provenance of the manuscript), was hesitant to attribute the prayer to Columbanus.[4] But in fact the prayer is preserved in several other manuscripts, some of them of ninth-century date, and all of them bearing explicit attribution to Columbanus. One of these is a manuscript written at Nonantola (in northern Italy, not far from Bobbio) in the second half of the ninth century, now in the Fondo Sessoriano in the Biblioteca

---

[1] *Sancti Columbani Opera*, ed. & transl. Walker, p. 214: 'O Lord God, destroy and root out whatever the Adversary plants in me, that with my sins destroyed Thou mayest sow understanding and good work in my mouth and heart; that in deed and truth I may serve Thee only, and understand how to fulfil the commands of Christ and seek Thyself. Grant memory, grant charity, grant chastity, grant faith, grant all that Thou knowest to pertain to the profit of my soul. O Lord, work good in me, and provide me with what Thou knowest that I need.'

[2] Seebass, 'Columba der Jüngere', p. 245.

[3] See Ottino, *I codici Bobbiesi*, pp. 42–3 (no. 47); a Bobbio *ex-libris* inscription is found on fo 13r ('Liber sancti Columbani de Bobio'). The manuscript is mentioned, but not discussed, by Cipolla, *Codici Bobbiesi*, I.16.

[4] *Sancti Columbani Opera*, ed. & transl. Walker, p. lxiii: '. . . the title given in the one manuscript which preserves it may mean no more than that it was intended for Columban's festival or modelled on his style.'

Nazionale Centrale in Rome and having the shelf-mark MS. Sessorianus 71.[5] The manuscript contains various works on the psalter by Jerome, together with pseudo-Alcuin, *De psalmorum usu*, along with a substantial collection of private prayers;[6] the prayer of Columbanus is found on fo 99v, and bears the rubric 'Oratio sancti Columbani'. The prayer (with the same rubric) is also found in a second ninth-century manuscript from Nonantola in the Fondo Sessoriano in the Biblioteca Nazionale Centrale, MS. Sessorianus 95, containing a copy of the pseudo-Egbert Penitential and the private prayerbook of St John Gualbert.[7] In this case, however, the prayer of Columbanus is not part of the original manuscript, but is an addition on fo 166r of *ca* 1300;[8] the likelihood is that this version of the prayer was copied from that in MS. Sessorianus 71.

The existence of these three copies might indicate that the prayer was not known outside northern Italy; but in fact it is also found in a famous ninth-century prayerbook written at Saint-Denis, now Paris, Bibliothèque Nationale, MS. lat. 1153 (*saec.* ix^med^), fo 92r. The prayerbook was first printed in 1617 by André Duchesne, under the title *Officia per ferias*, among the works of Alcuin, whence it was reprinted by Migne.[9] Although the attribution of the prayerbook to Alcuin has been seriously questioned,[10] there seems no reason to question the attribution of the *Oratio S. Columbani* to Columbanus.[11]

The attributions to Columbanus in two ninth-century manuscripts written in different parts of Europe and having no apparent connection, would seem to argue in favour of the prayer's genuineness. Given the brief compass of the prayer, it is difficult to advance comprehensive stylistic arguments in favour of

---

[5] For palaeographical dating of the manuscript, see Morelli & Palma, 'Indagine', pp. 28–9.

[6] For a full list of contents, see Gullotta, *Gli antichi cataloghi*, pp. 121–3; see also Palma, *Sessoriana*, pp. 48–9. For the prayers, see Wilmart, 'Le manuel de prières', esp. p. 292 for the *Oratio S. Columbani*. A number of prayers (for the abbot and the community) thought to have originated in Nonantola are printed and discussed by Leclercq, 'Anciennes prières monastiques', pp. 379–86 (with discussion of Sessorianus 71 at pp. 379–80, 384, but without mention of the prayer of Columbanus). There is a full bibliography pertaining to the manuscript and its contents in Jemolo, Merolla *et al.*, *Bibliografia*, pp. 202–4.

[7] On the manuscript, see Gullotta, *Gli antichi cataloghi*, pp. 304–23, with discussion of the *Oratio S. Columbani* at p. 321; see also Palma, *Sessoriana*, pp. 7–8, Leclercq, 'Anciennes prières monastiques', pp. 379–86, and esp. Wilmart, 'Le manuel de prières'. Bibliography pertaining to the manuscript is found in Jemolo, Merolla *et al.*, pp. 211–12.

[8] See Gullotta, *Gli antichi cataloghi*, p. 321, where it is noted that the prayer was 'scritto da mano del sec. XIII–XIV'.

[9] *Patrologia Latina*, ed. Migne, CI.510–612; the *Oratio S. Columbani* is at col. 604. Note that the first line of the prayer in the Saint-Denis manuscript differs slightly from that in the Turin manuscript as printed by Walker: 'Domine Deus, destrue, et quidquid in me plantat aduersarius, eradica.'

[10] See Wilmart, 'Le manuel de prières', pp. 262–3.

[11] Cf. Bestul, 'Continental sources', p. 105, who notes that, among Hiberno-Latin prayers attributed variously to SS Patrick, Brendan and others, 'the prayer attributed to Columban . . . is the most likely to be genuine'.

Columbanus's authorship, but several points may be mentioned. The list of requests to grant various virtues, including charity (*da caritatem*), has an echo in *Instructio XII*: 'Domine, da mihi . . . illam quae nescit cadere caritatem.'[12] Patrick Sims-Williams has suggested that this type of formulation may have been spread by the Irish, and he points to the prayer of Columbanus as an early Irish example of the type.[13] More importantly, he points out that the metaphor which animates the prayer – that God is to uproot (*eradica*) the vices which the devil has planted in him (*plantat*) – is a reflex of the ascetical principle of 'curing opposites by opposites', first enunciated by Cassian and widely attested in Irish penitentials.[14] As he notes, the same metaphor is found in *Instructio II* (§ 2): 'studeamus ergo in primis uitia eradicare, uirtutesque insinuare; eradicemus superbiam, plantemus humilitatem', and so on.[15] In other words, the spirit of the brief prayer attributed to Columbanus in two ninth-century manuscripts (and two later ones) coincides with that found in the *Instructiones* and more generally in early Irish penitential literature, an indication that the prayer is a genuine composition by the founder of Bobbio.

---

[12] *Sancti Columbani Opera*, ed. & transl. Walker, p. 114.
[13] *Religion and Literature*, pp. 324–5.
[14] *Ibid.*, p. 325.
[15] *Sancti Columbani Opera*, ed. & transl. Walker, p. 68: 'Therefore let us seek above all to root out the vices and plant the virtues; let us root out pride and sow humility . . .'

X

EPILOGUE: DID COLUMBANUS COMPOSE METRICAL VERSE?

Michael Lapidge

AS we have seen, there are compelling reasons for attributing to Columbanus
of Bobbio two rhythmical (or, better: non-metrical) Latin poems, one a hymn,
the other hymn-like in structure: *Precamur patrem* and *Mundus iste transibit*,
respectively. These attributions are enough to show that Columbanus had some
propensity for composing poetry, and help to illustrate a comment by Ionas,
who in his *Vita S. Columbani* (I.3) noted that Columbanus had in his youth
composed works 'suitable for singing', where presumably Ionas had hymns in
mind. Now several poems in metrical (or: quantitative) form have been transmitted under the name of Columbanus: (1) a poem of seventeen hexameters
on the transience of life (*inc.* 'Casibus innumeris decurrunt tempora uitae')
addressed to one Hunaldus, where the authorship of a poet named Columbanus
is confirmed by the first letters of each line, which form an acrostic legend
COLVMBANVS HVNALDO;[1] (2) a poem of seventy-seven hexameters, also on
the transience of life (*inc.* 'Suscipe, Sethe, libens et perlege mente serena')
addressed to one Sethus, where once again the authorship of a poet named
Columbanus is assured by the second line of the poem: '[Suscipe . . .] Dicta
Columbani fida te uoce monentis';[2] and (3) a poem of 159 metrical adonics on
the evils of avarice (*inc.* 'Accipe, quaeso, / Nunc bipedali') addressed to one
Fidolius (line 142: *alme Fidoli*); in this case the author's name is not inserted in
the poem, but manuscript rubrics (the earliest dating from the late eighth
century) are unanimous in attributing it to a poet named Columbanus (*Versus
sancti Columbani ad Fetolium*; *Columbanius Fedolio*; etc.).[3] All three poems[4]
reveal skill in handling quantitative verse. The first two poems (in hexameters)
are impregnated with Vergilian diction, while the third shows an unusual range

---

[1] Listed Schaller & Könsgen, *Initia*, no. 2008; printed *Sancti Columbani Opera*, ed. &
transl. Walker, pp. 184–7.

[2] Listed Schaller & Könsgen, *Initia*, no. 15937; printed *Sancti Columbani Opera*, ed. &
transl. Walker, pp. 186–91.

[3] Listed Schaller & Könsgen, *Initia*, no. 119; printed *Sancti Columbani Opera*, ed. &
transl. Walker, pp. 192–7.

[4] I omit from my discussion the so-called *Carmen nauale* (*Sancti Columbani Opera*, ed.
& transl. Walker, pp. 190–3), since its attribution to a 'Columbanus' depends on a
conjecture of Ernst Dümmler; and in any case Dümmler attributed it to a Carolingian
poet named Columbanus, not to the founder of Bobbio, as Esposito pointed out, 'On
the new edition', pp. 187–8.

of reference to classical mythology and to the diction of Vergil, Horace and
Statius as well as of the late Latin poets Tiberianus and Ennodius. Not
unnaturally, given the state of knowledge of Hiberno-Latin culture which
obtained in the late nineteenth century (and earlier), all three poems were
attributed to Columbanus of Bobbio, and were printed among his works
by Gundlach and subsequently by Walker. On this attribution alone rests
the extravagant picture of Latin culture in early Ireland which permeates
Walker's discussion of Columbanus.[5] I do not believe that the attribution can
be sustained in the late twentieth century, given what we now know of early
Hiberno-Latin culture.[6]

Before addressing the question of attribution, however, several general
points need to be made. In the first place, the name *Columbanus* (a latinisation
of Old Irish *Colum-bán*) is one frequently borne by Irishmen in the early
Middle Ages, in Ireland, England and on the Continent. It is not in any sense a
unique name. Secondly, it should be stressed – as Gustav Hertel had stressed
already in 1875[7] – that in his genuine *Epistulae* the author whom we refer to as
Columbanus referred to himself consistently as *Columba*, never as *Columbanus*. On these grounds alone it would be possible to argue that the three
metrical poems – which are clearly the work of one author and were transmitted together from as early as the ninth century[8] – were the work of an
Irishman named Columbanus who was not identical with the founder of
Bobbio; and this argument would be seen to receive confirmation from the
contrast between the total absence of classical reference or reminiscence in the
genuine prose works of Columbanus of Bobbio, and the abundance of such
reference in the three metrical poems. This was, in effect, the argument

---

[5] *Sancti Columbani Opera*, ed. & transl. Walker, pp. lxvi–lxvii: 'Columban's writings
alone prove that a good number of the best Latin authors were deeply studied in the
schools of Ireland. He is well read in Horace, whose works were practically unknown
on the Continent from the sixth to the eighth centuries; he can quote Virgil readily,
and is familiar also with Ovid, Juvenal, Martial, and Sallust. The Latin Anthology
provides him with a long quotation, and of later writers he knows Prudentius,
Fortunatus, Iuvencus, Sedulius, Ausonius, and Claudian. In the poem to Fidolius he
shows his mastery of a wide tract of classical mythology, and the casual nature of
his references indicates the thoroughness with which his early training had been
imbibed. For Columban classical studies were not merely a graceful accomplish-
ment, but they had exercised a formative power upon his mind. They provided him
with a means of self-expression . . .'

[6] See, for example, the judicious assessment by Rädle, 'Die Kenntnis', who notes (p.
487), 'Desgleichen läßt sich, mit Ausnahme Columbans (unter dem Vorbehalt der
Echtheit seiner Gedichte), bis zur Karolingerzeit kein völlig zweifelsfreier Beleg für
direkte und explizite Kenntnis der profanen lateinischen Literatur bei den Iren
finden', though he immediately adds the qualification, 'Eine Einschränkung ist hier
zu machen in bezug auf Vergil', a qualification which squares well with my discussion below.

[7] 'Über des heiligen Columbas Leben', pp. 427–30.

[8] See Lapidge, 'The authorship', pp. 865–8; Jacobsen, 'Carmina Columbani', pp. 442,
450.

deployed against Columbanus's authorship of the metrical poems by J.W. Smit in 1971.[9]

However, more substantial proof was needed to consolidate the argument against Columbanus's authorship, and some twenty years ago I attempted to supply that proof in an article first published in 1977.[10] My arguments against the authorship of Columbanus of Bobbio can be summarised as follows: (1) the adonic verses *Ad Fidolium* are unmistakably modelled on some similar verses by Ennodius (d. 521), a poet who was wholly unknown until his works were unearthed in Pavia by Paulus Diaconus and brought by him to the court of Charlemagne in the 780s, where the adonic form was avidly imitated by poets such as Alcuin and Paulus himself, as well as by Carolingian poets of the succeeding generation such as Walahfrid Strabo; (2) the sequence of references to classical myths involving gold in *Ad Fidolium* (the Golden Fleece; Amphiaraus; Jupiter and Danaë; etc.) were derived by the poet from the so-called 'First Vatican Mythographer',[11] a work compiled in its turn from various sources including a commentary on Horace (the *Scholia λφψ in Horatium*), a work which in its turn draws on Isidore's *Etymologiae*. Since Isidore's *Etymologiae* were not published until after his death in 636, it follows that the poem *Ad Fidolium* cannot have been composed by Columbanus of Bobbio, who died in 615. And since the three metrical poems (*Ad Hunaldum, Ad Sethum, Ad Fidolium*) are all clearly compositions by one author,[12] this author cannot have been Columbanus of Bobbio. I therefore presented various evidence in favour of a Carolingian poet named Columbanus, who in my view could be identified as an abbot of Saint-Trond of that name. And in order to confirm the identification of this Columbanus of Saint-Trond, I attempted to identify the recipients of his poems (Hunald, Seth, Fidolius) in Carolingian sources of *ca* 800, as well as to attribute to him a *planctus* on the death of Charlemagne (d. 814).

As in all controversial matters, some scholars were persuaded by these arguments,[13] others were not. In particular, Heinz Löwe[14] pointed out a number

---

[9] Smit, *Studies*, pp. 209–53.

[10] Lapidge, 'The authorship'.

[11] See *Mythographi Vaticani*, ed. Kulcsár. Kulcsár argues that the common source of the First and Second Vatican Mythographers depended in its turn on Isidore and on the Horace scholia, although he does not attempt to date either the hypothetical common source or the First Vatican Mythographer. The only serious attempt to date the latter is that by Elliot & Elder, 'A critical edition' (followed by Krill, 'The Vatican mythographers', as well as by Kulcsár), who argue for a date in the seventh or eighth century: a period, that is, well after the death of Columbanus.

[12] See above, n. 8.

[13] See, for example, Contreni, 'The Irish in the western Carolingian empire', p. 760: 'Now, in a recent, detailed, and I think convincing study, Michael Lapidge has re-examined the question . . . of the attribution of several poems to the sixth-century Columbanus, the founder of Bobbio'; Herren, 'Classical and secular learning', pp. 127–8; and cf. Jacobsen, 'Carmina Columbani', p. 457: 'Die Datierung in die frühkarolingische Zeit erscheint verlockend und durch manche Indizien nahegelegt, bleibt aber vorläufig unbewiesen'.

[14] 'Columbanus und Fidolius'.

of chronological difficulties with my reconstruction of the career of Columbanus of Saint-Trond, especially with the identity of Fidolius[15] and with the
attribution of the *planctus* for Charlemagne to the abbot of Saint-Trond.
Michael Herren has also pointed to problems with the supposition of a
Carolingian Columbanus,[16] on grounds which I find unconvincing.

It is important to stress, however, that my original arguments *against*
Columbanus of Bobbio's authorship of the poem *Ad Fidolium* (and, by
implication, of *Ad Hunaldum* and *Ad Sethum*) were two-pronged: (a) the
chronological *impossibility* of Columbanus of Bobbio having composed *Ad
Fidolium*, given that the poem draws on works which in their turn depend on
Isidore's *Etymologiae*; and (b) the *possibility* that the Columbanus in question
was a Carolingian abbot of Saint-Trond. Even were I to grant – as I do not –
that the objections of Löwe and Herren to my argument (b) are valid, the case
against my argument (a) would still need to be addressed. To my knowledge,
no irrefutable case against argument (a) has yet been adduced.[17]

---

[15] A point which no student of Columbanus appears to have noted is that Fidolus was
the name of an early sixth-century saint from Troyes (see *Bibliotheca Hagiographica
Latina*, nos 2974–6). The earliest *Vita S. Fidoli* was edited by Krusch, *Passiones
vitaeque sanctorum* [I], pp. 428–32. According to this *uita*, St Fidolus was captured
in an expedition by King Theuderic against the natives of the Auvergne, an event
which can be dated to before 532 (Gregory of Tours, *Historia Francorum*, III.12).
Once the cult of St Fidolus had been established, his name could have been borne by
any christian.

[16] 'A ninth-century poem'. Herren makes many valuable points about the relationship
of *Ad Sethum* to ninth-century verse composed at Sankt Gallen, and incidentally
adds new evidence – as it seems to me – for the Carolingian origin of that poem (pp.
507–8). But I cannot follow his arguments *against* the supposition of a Carolingian
Columbanus: (1) he argues that the name *Fidolius* is a witty calque on Greek
φειδωλός (p. 516); but see my previous note; (2) he then argues (pp. 517–18) that
'the hypothesis of a late-eighth-century Columbanus raises a peculiar difficulty
vis-à-vis the use of Horace, whose *Epistles* are a prominent source of the "avarice
poems". If our Columbanus was a Carolingian, he *first* wrote his poems before 800
(allowing for some uncertainty with regard to "Ad Hunaldum"). In that case, our
poet would have been a contemporary of Alcuin and Paulus Diaconus. It is now
generally thought that no poet of Alcuin's period possessed a direct acquaintance
with Horace'. But the old argument that the Carolingians were ignorant of Horace
will simply not bear inspection. Alcuin, for example, in his *Carmen LVIII*, based one
of his verses (line 50: 'Uberibus plenis ueniantque ad mulctra capellae') unmistakably on a line of Horace (*Epod.* XVI.49: 'illic iniussae ueniunt ad mulctra
capellae'). This particular line of Horace does not occur in any intermediate source,
such as Jerome, so there are no grounds for doubting that Alcuin took it directly
from Horace; and Alcuin's knowledge of Horace squares well with the mention of a
copy of Horace's *Ars poetica* in the booklist of Charlemagne's palace library: see
Bischoff, *Mittelalterliche Studien*, III.165. If, as I argued in 1977, the Columbanus
who was the author of the three metrical poems was a contemporary and colleague
of Alcuin and Paulus Diaconus, his knowledge of Horace presents no problem,
given Alcuin's undoubted familiarity with the Roman poet.

[17] The only serious attempt to confront this argument is that of Jacobsen, 'Carmina
Columbani', pp. 448–59. Jacobsen confesses himself unpersuaded by my arguments

However, I do not wish here to rehearse the evidence in favour of argument (a). I wish instead to raise certain general considerations which, in my view, tell decisively against the supposition that Columbanus of Bobbio ever composed metrical (quantitative) verse of any kind.

Metrical or quantitative verse-forms in Latin are based on the alternation of long and short syllables. A hexameter, for example, consists of six metrical feet, the first four of which may be either dactyls (each consisting of a long followed by two short syllables: $\bar{\ }\breve{\ }\breve{\ }$) or spondees (each consisting of two long syllables: $\bar{\ }\bar{\ }$); the fifth foot is normally a dactyl, and the sixth foot may be either a spondee ($\bar{\ }\bar{\ }$) or a trochee ($\bar{\ }\breve{\ }$). An adonic verse (that is, the verse-form of *Ad Fidolium*) consists in effect of the final two feet of a hexameter: a dactyl ($\bar{\ }\breve{\ }\breve{\ }$) followed by a spondee ($\bar{\ }\bar{\ }$) or a trochee ($\bar{\ }\breve{\ }$). Of course there are also many subtle rules regarding such things as caesuras (internal pauses) and elision or synizesis, which a competent poet also had to know; but, to put the matter in the simplest terms, an intending poet who wished to compose quantitative verse would have to know the quantities of all the syllables of the words which he wished to employ in his verse. Where would such information be found? A modern student will find the length of syllables, marked by macrons ($\bar{\ }$) or breves ($\breve{\ }$), in a decent Latin dictionary such as that of Lewis & Short, or in a handbook of Latin verse-composition, often called a *gradus*. For an early mediaeval Latin poet, however, matters were not so simple. There was no such thing as a *gradus* in existence,[18] and vowel lengths were not marked in Latin glossaries, the mediaeval equivalents of our Latin dictionaries. Failing these resources, the intending early mediaeval Latin poet could learn the correct quantities of vowels in one of two ways: by studying the placement of words in the quantitative verse of classical and late Latin poets; or by listening to the pronunciation of a native speaker of Latin.

We may begin by considering the first possibility. If we pose the question, which Latin poets (if any) were studied in sixth-century Ireland, the question is impossible to answer for lack of evidence. By the seventh century, however, matters become slightly clearer. In the mid-seventh century, Virgilius Maro Grammaticus evidently had some knowledge of Vergil, for he was able to

---

that the author of *Ad Fidolium* drew on the First Vatican Mythographer, because I provided no convincing verbal links between the two works (p. 452: 'Lapidge hat aber kein Indiz, keine spezifische Formulierung beigebracht, die eine direkte Beziehung, ein Abhängigkeitsverhältnis erweisen könnte'); but my argument ('The authorship', pp. 847–8) was that six of the eight examples of lust for gold in classical myth cited by the poet were to be found in the First Vatican Mythographer in *precisely the same order* as they are found in *Ad Fidolium*, and that the remaining two examples were taken from Tiberianus's poem *De auro*. This provides as close an explanation for the structure of the poem as can be established in the present state of our knowledge; Jacobsen's alternative explanation, that the poet took his examples higgledy-piggledy from various sources, including Augustine's *De ciuitate Dei*, seems to me a much less probable understanding of the working methods of a mediaeval Latin poet.

[18] Aldhelm attempted to compile such a *gradus* in the late seventh century in his treatise *De pedum regulis* (*Aldhelmi Opera*, ed. Ehwald, pp. 150–201); see discussion by Neil Wright, in *Aldhelm: the Poetic Works*, transl. Lapidge & Rosier, pp. 188–9.

paraphrase lines from both the *Eclogues* and the *Aeneid*.[19] There is evidence that the anonymous authors of the *Hisperica famina* (mid-seventh century?) had read Vergil[20] and Caelius Sedulius,[21] but not certainly any other poet. Later in the century Muirchú (*ca* 680) similarly quotes Vergil and Caelius Sedulius, but no other poet.[22] Finally, at the very end of the seventh century, there is reliable evidence, as it seems to me, that Adomnán of Iona was involved in some way in commenting on the poetry of Vergil. In three ninth-century manuscripts are preserved two related commentaries on Vergil's *Eclogues*, known to scholarship as *Explanatio I* and *II*.[23] On the one hand, it is clear that these *Explanationes* incorporate material from late antique commentaries on Vergil, including those by Seruius and also by an obscure grammarian from Milan called Filargyrius. On the other hand, the ninth-century manuscripts show a number of Insular (and specifically Irish) features in their script, and contain substantial numbers of Irish glosses (130 in *Explanatio I*, 32 in *Explanatio II*).[24] It is clear, therefore, that these Vergil commentaries passed at some point through the hands of Irish teachers and scribes; and it is therefore exceptionally interesting to note that *Explanatio I* contains the following comment on *Ecl*. III.90 ('Qui Bauuium non odit, amet tua carmina, Maeui'): 'De Meuio uero nihil reperi ut Adamnanus ait'.[25] The

---

[19] See Herren, 'Classical and secular learning', pp. 124–5. The lines in question are *Ecl*. III.90 ('Qui Bauuium non odit, amet tua carmina, Maeui'), which Virgilius parodies as 'qui fauum mellis non amat, odit tua carmina, Maeui' (*Epistulae* V.6, ed. Polara, *Virgilio Marone grammatico*, p. 300), and *Aen*. VI.724–6 ('Principio caelum ac terram camposque liquentis / lucentemque globum lunae Titaniaque astra / spiritus intus alit'), which Virgilius paraphrases as 'In principio celum terramque mare omniaque astra spiritus intus fouet' (*Epitomae* XV.7, ed. Polara, p. 168). For the date of Virgilius Maro Grammaticus, now securely established, see Ó Cróinín, 'The date, provenance, and earliest verse'.

[20] *Hisperica Famina: the A-Text*, ed. Herren, pp. 24–5; but cf. Herren's qualifications in 'Classical and secular learning', p. 124.

[21] Wright, 'The *Hisperica famina* and Caelius Sedulius'.

[22] See Muirchú, *Vita S. Patricii* II.8 [7](ed. & transl. Bieler, *The Patrician Texts*, p. 118): '. . . nox non inruit et fuscis tellurem non amplexerat alis et pallor non tantus erat noctis et astriferas non induxerat Bosferus umbras'. The first part of the quotation is from *Aen*. VIII.369 ('Nox ruit et fuscis tellurem amplectitur alis'), the second from Caelius Sedulius, *Carmen paschale* III.221 ('Noctis et astriferas induceret hesperus umbras'). On the Vergilian debt, cf. Herren, 'Classical and secular learning', p. 125.

[23] Hagen, 'Iunii Philargyrii Grammatici Explanatio in Bucolica Vergilii', pp. 1–189 (the two *Explanationes* are printed by Hagen in parallel columns). The most recent scholarly discussion of these commentaries, and Adomnán's role in their transmission, is by Daintree, 'Glosse irlandesi', and Daintree & Geymonat, 'Scholia non Seruiana', esp. pp. 711–17.

[24] The Old Irish glosses are edited (incompletely) by Stokes, 'The glosses', and by Stokes & Strachan, *Thesaurus Palaeohibernicus*, II.46–8, 360–3.

[25] Hagen, 'Iunii Philargyrii Grammatici Explanatio in Bucolica Vergilii', p. 66; Stokes & Strachan, *Thesaurus Palaeohibernicus*, II.360: 'Concerning Maeuius I could discover nothing, as Adomnán said'. Given the rarity of the name Adomnán (*Adamnanus*), there is no reason not to identify *Adamnanus* of the gloss with the abbot of Iona. Note that, by chance perhaps, the verse of *Eclogue III* is that which was earlier parodied by Virgilius Maro Grammaticus (see above, n. 19).

279

implication of this remark is that, at late-seventh-century Iona, Adomnán was expounding Vergil's *Eclogues* to his Irish pupils. The results of Adomnán's teaching were subsequently incorporated into *Explanationes I* and *II*; and scholars are no doubt right in distinguishing in these *Explanationes* between the sophisticated and learned scholia, which are the residue of late Latin grammarians such as Seruuius and Filargyrius, and the elementary, christianizing glosses, some of them in Old Irish, which are the contribution of Adomnán and his pupils to the late antique materials which they inherited.[26]

In any event, the evidence seems to suggest that only two quantitative Latin poets were studied in seventh-century Ireland: Vergil and Caelius Sedulius. This extremely small tally is dwarfed by the vast syllabus of Latin poets who were studied and imitated in seventh-century England by scholars such as Aldhelm and Bede.[27] Furthermore, knowledge of a quantitative poet does not in itself carry the implication that the poet's metrical technique was understood. Virgilius Maro Grammaticus had evidently read Vergil, but the verses which he himself composed and which are found scattered throughout his *Epitomae* and *Epistulae*, are without exception ametrical.[28] The authors of the *Hisperica famina* had read Vergil and Caelius Sedulius, and it has been suggested that in their faminations they were attempting to imitate the structure of the so-called 'golden line' (a hexameter in which the centrally placed verb is flanked by nouns and adjectives) as it is found in Caelius Sedulius;[29] but their verse, if such it is, is wholly ametrical. Adomnán attempted to explain the diction and meaning of Vergil's *Eclogues* to his pupils at Iona, but his teaching, as preserved in the *Explanationes*, contains no discussion whatsoever of Vergil's metre,[30] In short, there is no evidence that, even though Vergil and Caelius Sedulius were read and studied in seventh-century Ireland, this study comprised any understanding of the principles of quantitative verse-composition. As far as I am aware, the earliest Hiberno-Latin work which reveals any knowledge of the principles of quantitative verse is the *Letter*

---

[26] Daintree, 'Glosse irlandesi'; cf. Daintree & Geymonat, 'Scholia non Serviana', p. 713.

[27] Aldhelm had demonstrably read the following: of classical Latin poets, Vergil, Persius, Iuuenal, Lucan, Horace, Ovid, Statius, Claudian, Symposius, and possibly Lucretius; of christian-Latin poets, Iuuencus, Cyprianus Gallus, Caelius Sedulius, Arator, Prudentius, Paulinus of Nola, Paulinus of Périgueux, Prosper of Aquitaine, Dracontius, Corippus, Venantius Fortunatus, and anonymous christian poems such as the *Carmen ad Flauium Felicem* and various *tituli* from a *sylloge* of some sort; see Orchard, *The Poetic Art*, pp. 126–238. Bede's range of reading in quantitative verse is less extensive than Aldhelm's, but impressive nonetheless in comparison to what was being studied in Ireland at the time: Aldhelm, Ambrose, Arator, Cyprianus Gallus, Venantius Fortunatus, Iuuencus, Paulinus of Nola, Prosper of Aquitaine, Prudentius, Caelius Sedulius, Vergil, and possibly Alcimus Auitus, Dracontius, Lucan and Ovid.

[28] See Herren, 'The Hiberno-Latin poems'.

[29] Wright, 'The *Hisperica Famina*', pp. 75–6.

[30] Cf. Daintree, 'Glosse irlandesi', p. 774: 'Dove il commento differisce in modo evidente da Servio, mostra una più viva preoccupazione per l'allegoria e un interesse molto più scarso per la metrica'.

of Colmán to Feradach concerning the text of Caelius Sedulius – a work which, in the opinion of its recent editor, may have been composed by 'one of those Irishmen seeking to extend his learning in continental literary circles, especially in the late eighth or early ninth century'.[31] That in the seventh century the Irish were ignorant of the principles of quantitative verse-composition is confirmed by the fact that (leaving aside the three poems attributed to Columbanus, in order to avoid circularity) there is no quantitative verse composed by an Irishman which can be dated certainly to the seventh century;[32] the earliest such verse is that of Josephus Scottus, who apparently learned his verse-composition from the Englishman, Alcuin.[33]

If we project the picture which we have drawn of the study of quantitative Latin verse in seventh-century Ireland back into the sixth century, to the time of Columbanus's schooling, we find remarkable consistency: there is one probable debt to Caelius Sedulius in the *Epistulae* of Columbanus and another in the *Instructiones*,[34] and a possible reminiscence of Vergil in *Precamur patrem*.[35] The implication must be that in the sixth century, as subsequently in the seventh, the only Latin poets who were read (and studied) in Ireland were Caelius Sedulius and Vergil. In the case of Columbanus at least, the verbal debts are so faint and few as to imply that his study of these two poets was anything but intensive, and not sufficient to allow mastery of the technique of quantitative verse composition.

A second way of learning the correct scansion of syllables would be through hearing the pronunciation of a native speaker of Latin, and, in particular, by listening to which syllable(s) in a particular word were accented. It is important to realize that, although they are often conceived as opposites, accent and vowel length are intimately related in Latin. That is to say, all Latin words were stressed on the penultimate syllable unless that syllable was short, in which case the accent was thrown forward onto the antepenultimate syllable. In order to know where in a Latin word to place the stress, therefore, it was necessary to know whether the vowel of the penultimate syllable was long or short; or, put the other way round, once one knows which syllable in a word (of three or more syllables) bears the stress, it is possible to determine whether

---

[31] Sharpe, 'An Irish textual critic', p. 45. I accept Sharpe's approximate dating of the *Letter*. If the *Letter* is left out of consideration, the earliest securely datable treatise on metre by an Irish author is that of Cruindmáel in the first half of the ninth century (see Lapidge & Sharpe, *A Bibliography*, no. 668).

[32] A possible exception might be the verses by Cellanus of Péronne (d. 706), one on a chapel dedicated to St Patrick, the other on another church somewhere in Picardy (Schaller & Könsgen, *Initia*, nos 8406, 13577; Lapidge & Sharpe, *A Bibliography*, no. 644). It is clear from the second of these, however, that the poem was not *composed* by Cellanus, but *commissioned* by him: 'Haec modo Cellanus, uenerandi nominis abbas, / Iussit dactilico discriui carmina uersu'. On the difficulties of accepting these poems as evidence for Irish knowledge of quantitative verse-composition, cf. Lapidge, 'Some remnants', p. 805, and Herren, 'Classical and secular learning', p. 126.

[33] See Lapidge & Sharpe, *A Bibliography*, nos 648–9.

[34] See Wright, above, p. 80–2.

[35] See Lapidge, above, p. 261.

the penultimate syllable is long or short. For example, if one wished to know the quantity of the penultimate vowel in the word *amore* (ablative of *amor*), one would have to know whether it was pronounced as *amóre* or *ámore*; in the case of the word *spiritus*, whether it was pronounced *spíritus* or *spirítus*; or in the case of the word *amicus*, whether it was pronounced *ámicus* or *amícus*. Such knowledge would have been instinctive to a native speaker of Latin (and, in these three examples, is still instinctive for native speakers of Italian, who pronounce the corresponding modern words as *amóre*, *spírito* and *amíco*). For someone who was not a native speaker of Latin, however, the pronunciation would have to be learned. Once learned, however, this pronunciation would give a rough, if necessarily incomplete, guide to the quantities of the vowels of many Latin words.

It has always seemed to me that one of the reasons why in the late seventh century Anglo-Saxon scholars learned the mechanics of quantitative verse-composition so quickly and effectively, was that they had frequent contact with native speakers of Latin. Aldhelm, for example, would have heard Theodore and Hadrian speaking Latin (although neither of these scholars was Italian by birth, they had both lived in Italy long enough to have learned to pronounce the language correctly); and Aldhelm himself travelled at least once to Rome. Similarly, Bede would have heard the Latin pronunciation of John, the archcantor of St Peter's in Rome, who spent some years at Wearmouth-Jarrow; and it might be added that the two abbots of Wearmouth-Jarrow in Bede's time – Benedict Biscop and Ceolfrith – had both spent long periods of residence in Rome and may have mastered the correct pronunciation of spoken Latin. The contrast with Ireland is striking in this respect. Although the Irish church evidently had some sort of contact with Rome at various times in the seventh century,[36] there is no evidence – as far as I am aware – that any native Latin speaker, whether from Rome or more generally from Italy, taught in Ireland during that period. Nor is there evidence for such a person's presence in Ireland during the second half of the sixth century, when the young Columbanus was learning to read and write Latin. There is no doubt that Columbanus managed to acquire amazing fluency in writing Latin, but there is no reason to assume that he knew how to pronounce it correctly (and, by implication, knew the difference between long and short syllables in Latin words).

Certainly the two 'rhythmical' poems which can on reasonable grounds be attributed to Columbanus – *Mundus iste transibit* and *Precamur patrem* – reveal little knowledge of the correct stress-patterns of Latin words. Whereas one might expect consistent patterns of stress to be observed by a poet attempting to write rhythmical verse, these two poems of Columbanus show no such

---

[36] For example, in response to a letter from Pope Honorius (*ca* 629?), several Irish ecclesiastics went to Rome *ca* 631; their experiences are reported by Cummian (*ca* 632) in his letter *De controuersia paschali* (edd. & transl. Walsh & Ó Cróinín, *Cummian's Letter*, pp. 92–5). In 640 John, pope-elect, sent a letter to the churches of northern Ireland, as we know from Bede's *Historia ecclesiastica* II.19 (see discussion by Ó Cróinín, ' "New heresy for old" '). But these meagre points of contact contrast strikingly with the continual intercourse between Rome and Anglo-Saxon England at this time.

consistency. *Mundus iste transibit* is constructed of stanzas of four lines, each having seven syllables; as Dieter Schaller has shown,[37] there is some discernible pattern of rhyme within the poem, but none at all of stress-patterns. Consider the following lines, which have an overall trochaic rhythm, and where the stress apparently falls on the antepenultimate syllable (/x/x/x/: 7pp):

> mórs incérta súbripìt (10)
> méror mórtis córripìt (12)
> cúm dolóre ráditùr (56)
> quám flós cárnis frágilìs (60)
> feminárum spécies (62); etc.

In lines such as these, the pattern of stress falls on correctly stressed syllables within individual words, so that a reader might be led to believe that the poet was trying to achieve a consistent trochaic rhythm. But this illusion is instantly dispelled by other lines in the same poem; consider, for example, the following stanza:

> cógitáre cónuenìt
> té haec cúncta ámice
> ábsit tíbi ámare
> húius fórmulám uitae (41–4)

Here the stresses lie naturally in the first line (41), but in the case of *amice* and *amare* the (supposed) trochaic rhythm would impose stresses on syllables incorrectly: in the case of both *amíce* and *amáre* the penultimate syllable is naturally long, hence stress-bearing. Similar violations of natural stress occur throughout the poem. Modern scholars have therefore concluded that the poet was not attempting to write either metrical or rhythmical verse, but was simply counting syllables.[38] Such a procedure is the natural resort of a poet ignorant of the true rhythm (and, *ipso facto*, quantity) of Latin words.

A similar point can quickly be demonstrated in the case of *Precamur patrem*.[39] Once again the poem consists of four-line stanzas, in which the first and third consist of five syllables, the second and fourth of seven. Sometimes the natural stress patterns of the words produce a trochaic rhythm, as in the last lines of each of the first two stanzas:

> sánctum quóque spíritum
> únum ín esséntia.

However, if we look to the second lines of each of these same two stanzas, the supposition of a trochaic rhythm would impose incorrect stress on half of the words in question:

---

[37] See above, p. 241.

[38] See the remarks of Schaller, above, p. 240: 'it is not metrical . . . but is constructed on principles of syllable-counting'; and Bieler's comment, in *Sancti Columbani Opera*, ed. & transl. Walker, p. lxxxii: 'The verse of *De mundi transitu* is neither metrical nor rhythmical; its principle is a simple count of syllables'.

[39] Cf. my discussion above, pp. 262–3.

régem ómnipótentem
pérfectúm substántia.

The natural stress in *omnipotentem* falls on the penultimate syllable, not the antepenult (which in any case is short, not long), as it does in *perfectum*. Once again Columbanus was apparently concerned simply with syllable-counting, in disregard of the natural stress of the Latin words (and, by implication once again, their quantity). I submit that Columbanus avoided writing rhythmical – or metrical – verse because he did not know the relevant quantities or stress patterns. Such ignorance would disqualify him from composing hexameters or adonics.

It might be argued, however, that these two hymns are early products of the saint, and that the hexameter poems (*Ad Hunaldum, Ad Sethum*) and adonics (*Ad Fidolium*) were composed at a late point in Columbanus's life, when he had lived on the Continent for a decade or more, and had had the opportunity of hearing native speakers pronounce Latin in Francia or in Italy itself, where he spent the last years of his life.[40] There is decisive evidence against such an argument, however. We know that the *Epistulae* can be dated securely to the period *ca* 600 x 613, and that the *Instructiones* were very probably composed at Bobbio. Now one of the stylistic features which characterises much Latin prose at this time is the use of rhythmical *cursus*, that is, the arrangement of words in various conventional patterns of stressed and unstressed syllables, so as to conclude sentences (or clauses) with a flourish. The most frequently used patterns of *cursus* were the *planus* (/xx/x), *tardus* (/xx/xx) and *uelox* (/xxxx/x). In order to compose sentences with rhythmical *cursus*, however, an author would have to know the length of syllables in order to determine whether stress fell on the penultimate or antepenultimate syllable of a word. However, since all Latin words have natural stress, it is possible that a wholly random choice of two or three Latin words might on occasion result in one of the aforementioned *cursus*. Sophisticated statistical tests have therefore been devised to distinguish between random patterns of stress and patterns of *cursus* which have been sought by a particular author. In articles printed elsewhere in this volume, these tests have been applied to the *Epistulae* and *Instructiones* of Columbanus, by Neil Wright and Clare Stancliffe respectively. Neil Wright shows that it is highly unlikely that Columbanus sought the unusually low percentage of rhythmical *cursus* which occurs in his *Epistulae*;[41] Clare Stancliffe demonstrates conclusively that the *Instructiones* show no use of *cursus*.[42]

The absence of *cursus* in Columbanus's two principal prose works – which, it will be remembered, are the products of his late years on the Continent – squares precisely with our earlier conclusions concerning the ignorance of natural stress, and *ipso facto* of quantity, in the 'rhythmical' (or: non-metrical) poems *Mundus iste transibit* and *Precamur patrem*. And if he had no knowledge of stress or quantity, it is inconceivable that he could have composed the three

---

[40] This argument is made by Herren, 'A ninth-century poem', pp. 518–19.

[41] Above, pp. 55–8.

[42] Above, pp. 150–61.

metrical poems which have been transmitted in the name of Columbanus, a conclusion which squares precisely with my arguments (first published in 1977) that one of these poems at least – that addressed *Ad Fidolium* – depends ultimately on texts such as Isidore's *Etymologiae* which were not composed until after the death of the founder of Bobbio in 615. The Columbanus who composed the metrical poems *Ad Hunaldum*, *Ad Sethum* and *Ad Fidolium* remains to be identified convincingly, but of one thing we can be quite sure: the Columbanus in question was not the founder of Bobbio. Nor need this conclusion surprise anyone who will reflect for a moment on the extreme harshness of the monastic régime stipulated by Columbanus's *Regula coenobialis* and practised in the monasteries which he founded.[43] Such a régime, with its nearly interminable hours of psalmody, would not have allowed spare time for the concentrated study of classical and late Latin poetry which would be necessary for someone like Columbanus of Bobbio who, in his earlier studies in Ireland, had not mastered the complexities of Latin quantity, stress and metre. But to say that this Columbanus was not knowledgeable enough in such matters to compose quantitative verse is in no sense to diminish the magnificent achievement which his surviving corpus of Latin prose writings represents.

[43] Cf. the remarks of Jane Stevenson, above, pp. 209–10.

BIBLIOGRAPHY

ADAMS, J.N.   'A type of hyperbaton in Latin prose', *Proceedings of the Cambridge Philological Society* 197 [= new series 17] (1971) 1–16

ADRIAEN, M. (ed.)   *S. Gregorii Magni Moralia in Iob* (3 vols, Turnhout 1979/85)

AMANN, E.   'Trois-Chapitres' in *Dictionnaire de théologie catholique*, XV.1868–924

ANDERSON, A.O. & ANDERSON, M.O. (edd. & transl.)   *Adomnán's Life of Columba* (2nd edn, Oxford 1991)

ANGENENDT, Arnold   *Monachi peregrini* (München 1972)

ANTON, H.H.   *Studien zu den Klosterprivilegien der Päpste im frühen Mittelalter* (Berlin 1975)

BACHMANN, H.   'Eine neue Handschrift des Liber de moribus Senecas' *Philologische Wochenschrift* 50 (1930) 1068–72

BAEHRENS, W.A. (ed.)   *Origenes Werke*, VI: *Homilien zum Hexateuch in Rufins Übersetzung*, 1, *Die Homilien zu Genesis, Exodus und Leviticus* (Leipzig 1920)

BAMMESBERGER, Alfred & WOLLMANN, A. (edd.)   *Britain 400–600: Language and History* (Heidelberg 1990)

BARDY, G.   'Saint Colomban et la papauté', in *Mélanges colombaniens*, pp. 103–18

BARLEY, M.W. & HANSON, R.P.C. (edd.)   *Christianity in Britain 300–700* (Leicester 1968)

BARTELINK, G.J.M. (ed. & transl.)   *Athanase d'Alexandrie, Vie d'Antoine* (Paris 1994)

BÄUMER, Suitbert   *Histoire du Bréviaire* (2 vols, Paris 1905)

BAUMSTARK, Anton   *Nocturna Laus: Typen frühchristlicher Vigilienfeier und ihr Fortleben vor allem im römischen und monastischen Ritus* (Münster in Westfalen 1957)

BECKER, Gustav (ed.)   *Catalogi bibliothecarum antiqui* (Bonn 1885)

BEHR, B.   *Das alemannische Herzogtum bis 750* (Bern 1975)

BEHRENS, G. & WERNER, J. (edd.)   *Festschrift zum 75. Geburtstag von P. Reinecke am 25. September 1947* (Mainz 1950)

BERGENGRUEN, A.   *Adel und Grundherrschaft im Merowingerreich* (Wiesbaden 1958)

BERGMANN, W.   *Studien zu einer kritischen Sichtung der südgallischen Predigtliteratur des fünften und sechsten Jahrhunderts* (Leipzig 1898)

BERNT, G.   [review of Smit, *Studies*], *Gnomon* 45 (1973) 90–3

BERNT, G., RÄDLE, F. & SILAGI, G. (edd.)   *Tradition und Wertung. Festschrift für Franz Brunhölzl zum 65. Geburtstag* (Sigmaringen 1989)

BERSCHIN, Walter   'Gallus abbas vindicatus', *Historisches Jahrbuch* 95 (1975) 257–75

BERTOLINI, O.   'Agilulfo' in *Dizionario biografico degli Italiani*, ed. Ghisalberti *et al.*, I.389–97

BERTOLINI, P.   'Atala' in *Dizionario biografico degli Italiana*, ed. Ghisalberti *et al.*, IV.495–7

BEST, R.I. (ed.)   'The Canonical Hours', *Ériu* 3 (1907) 116

BEST, R.I. & LAWLOR, H.J. (edd.)   *The Martyrology of Tallaght* (London 1931)

BESTUL, T.H.   'Continental sources of Anglo-Saxon devotional writing', in *Sources of Anglo-Saxon Culture*, ed. Szarmach, pp. 103–26

287

Bibliography

Bibliotheca Hagiographica Latina (2 vols, Bruxelles 1899/1901; with *Supplementum* by H. Fros, 1986)

BIELER, L.   'The island of scholars', *Revue du moyen âge latin* 7 (1952) 213–31

BIELER, L.   'Notes on the text tradition and latinity of St. Columban's writings', in *Sancti Columbani Opera*, ed. & transl. Walker, pp. lxxiii–lxxxii

BIELER, L.   'Aduersaria zu Anthologia Latina 676. Mit einer Anhang über die Columbanus-Gedichte' in *Antidosis*, edd. Hanslik, Lesky & Schwabl, pp. 41–8

BIELER, L.   'Editing Saint Columbanus. A reply', *Classica & Mediaevalia* 22 (1961) 139–50

BIELER, L. (ed. & transl.)   *The Patrician Texts in the Book of Armagh* (Dublin 1979)

BIELER, L.   [review of J. Laporte (ed.), *Le Pénitentiel de Saint Colomban*], *Journal of Theological Studies*, new series, 12 (1961) 106–12

BIELER, L.   [review of Smit, *Studies*], *Latomus* 31 (1971) 896–901

BINCHY, D.A.   'Bretha Crólige', *Ériu* 12 (1938) 1–77

BINCHY, D.A.   'Some Celtic legal terms', *Celtica* 3 (1956) 228–31

BIRABEN, J.-N. & LE GOFF, J.   'La peste dans le haut moyen âge', *Annales: Économies, Sociétés, Civilisations* 24 (1969) 1484–510

BISCHOFF, Bernhard   *Die südostdeutschen Schreibschulen und Bibliotheken in der Karolingerzeit* (2 vols, Wiesbaden 1940/80)

BISCHOFF, Bernhard   *Mittelalterliche Studien* (3 vols, Stuttgart 1966/81)

BISHOP, T.A.M.   'The scribes of the Corbie *a–b*', in *Charlemagne's Heir*, edd. Godman & Collins, pp. 523–36

BLAISE, Albert   *Dictionnaire latin-français des auteurs chrétiens* (Strasbourg 1954)

BLUME, Clemens   'Hymnodia Hiberno-Celtica saeculi V.–IX.' in *Analecta Hymnica Medii Aevi*, edd. Blume & Dreves, LI.259–365

BLUME, Clemens & DREVES, G.M. (edd.)   *Analecta Hymnica Medii Aevi* (55 vols, Leipzig 1886/1922)

BLUMENKRANZ, Bernard   *Die Judenpredigt des Augustins* (Basel 1946)

Bobbio e la Val Trebbia (Piacenza 1963)

BOGNETTI, G.P.   *L'età longobarda* (4 vols, Milano 1966/8)

BONNET, Max   *Le latin de Grégoire de Tours* (Paris 1890)

BORST, A. (ed.)   *Mönchtum, Episkopat und Adel zur Gründungszeit des Klosters Reichenau* (Sigmaringen 1974)

BRAUNFELS, W. (ed.)   *Karl der Grosse* (5 vols, Düsseldorf 1965)

BREEN, A.   'The evidence of antique Irish exegesis in pseudo-Cyprian, *De duodecim abusivis saeculi*', *Proceedings of the Royal Irish Academy* 87 C (1987) 71–101

BREEN, A.   'A new Irish fragment of the *Continuatio* to Rufinus-Eusebius *Historia ecclesiastica*', *Scriptorium* 41 (1987) 185–204

BROWN, A.K.   'Bede, a hisperic etymology, and early sea poetry', *Mediaeval Studies* 37 (1975) 419–32

BROWN, T.J.   'The Irish element in the Insular system of scripts to circa A.D. 850', in *Die Iren und Europa*, ed. Löwe, I.101–19

BRÜHL, Carlrichard   *Studien zu den langobardischen Königsurkunden* (Tübingen 1970)

BRÜHL, Carlrichard (ed.)   *Codice diplomatico Langobardo* III (Roma 1973)

BRUNHÖLZL, Franz   *Geschichte der lateinischen Literatur des Mittelalters* (2 vols, München 1975/92)

BRUNNER, H. & VON SCHWERIN, C.   *Deutsche Rechtsgeschichte* (2nd edn, 2 vols, München 1906/28)

BULLOUGH, D.A.   'Columba, Adomnan and the achievement of Iona', *Scottish Historical Review* 43 (1964) 111–30 *and* 44 (1965) 17–33

BULLOUGH, D.A.   'Colombano', *Dizionario biografico degli Italiani*, edd. Ghisalberti *et al.*, XXVII.113–29

BULLOUGH, D.A.   *Carolingian Renewal: Sources and Heritage* (Manchester 1991)

BULLOUGH, D.A.   'Albuinus deliciosus Karoli regis. Alcuin of York and the shaping of the early Carolingian court' in *Institutionen*, ed. Fenske *et al.*, pp. 73–92

BULLOUGH, D.A.   [review of *Cummian's Letter*, edd. Walsh & Ó Cróinín] *Deutsches Archiv für Erforschung des Mittelalters* 46 (1990) 235–6

BULLOUGH, D.A. & HARTING-CORRÊA, A.L.   'Texts, chant and the chapel of Louis the Pious' in *Charlemagne's Heir*, edd. Collins & Godman, pp. 489–508

BULST, W.   'Hymnologica partim Hibernica' in *Latin Script and Letters*, edd. O'Meara & Naumann, pp. 83–100

BURGHARDT, Walter J.   *The Image of God in Man according to Cyril of Alexandria* (Woodstock, MD 1957)

BÜTTNER, H.   'Geschichtliche Grundlagen zur Ausbildung der alamannischen-romanischen Sprachgrenze im Gebiet der heutigen Westschweiz', *Zeitschrift für Mundartforschung* 28 (1961) 193–206

BÜTTNER, H.   *Frühmittelalterliches Christentum und fränkischer Staat zwischen Hochrhein und Alpen* (Darmstadt 1961)

BYRNE, F.J.   *Irish Kings and High-Kings* (London 1973)

CABROL, F. & LECLERCQ, H. (edd.)   *Monumenta ecclesiae liturgica. II. Reliquiae liturgicae vetustissimae ex SS. patrum necnon scriptorum ecclesiasticorum monumentis selectae* (Paris 1913)

CABROL, F. & LECLERCQ, H. (edd.)   *Dictionnaire d'archéologie chrétienne et de liturgie* (15 vols in 30, Paris 1907/53)

CALLEWAERT, C.   'Les étapes de l'histoire du kyrie: S. Gélase, S. Benoît, S. Grégoire', *Revue d'histoire ecclésiastique* 38 (1942) 20–45

CAMERON, Alan   'The date and identity of Macrobius', *Journal of Roman Studies* 56 (1966) 25–38

CAPELLE, B.   'L' "Exultet" pascal, oeuvre de Saint Ambroise' in *Miscellanea Giovanni Mercati* I (Città del Vaticano 1946) pp. 219–46

CASEY, P.J. & JONES, M.G.   'The date of the letter of the Britons to Aetius', *The Bulletin of the Board of Celtic Studies* 37 (1990) 281–90

CERIONI, L.   'Agrippino' in *Dizionario biografico degli Italiani*, edd. Ghisalberti *et al.*, I.504

CESSI, R. (ed.)   'Studi sulle fonti dell'età gotica e longobardica II. Prosperi Continuatio Hauniensis', *Archivio Muratoriano* 22 (1922) 585–641

CHADWICK, N.K.   'Intellectual contacts between Britain and Gaul in the fifth century', in *Studies in British History*, ed. Chadwick, pp. 189–253

CHADWICK, N.K. (ed.)   *Studies in Early British History* (Cambridge 1954)

CHARLES-EDWARDS, T.M.   [review of *Gildas: New Approaches*, edd. Lapidge & Dumville], *Cambridge Medieval Celtic Studies* 12 (1986) 115–20

CHARLES-EDWARDS, T.M.   'The social background of Irish *peregrinatio*', *Celtica* 11 (1976) 43–59

CHIBNALL, M.   'The Merovingian monastery of St Evroul', *Studies in Church History* 8 (1972) 31–40

CIPOLLA, C. (ed.)   *Codice diplomatico di Bobbio* I (Roma 1918)

CIPOLLA, C.   *Codici Bobbiesi della Biblioteca Nazionale Universitaria di Torino* (2 vols, Milano 1907)

CLARKE, H.B. & BRENNAN, Mary (edd.)   *Columbanus and Merovingian Monasticism* (Oxford 1981)

CLAUSSEN, M.A.   ' "Peregrinatio" and "peregrini" in Augustine's "City of God" ', *Traditio* 46 (1991) 33–75

COCCIA, Edmondo   'La cultura irlandese precarolina – miracolo o mito?', *Studi medievali*, 3rd series, 8 (1967) 257–420

COLLINS, R.J.H. & GODMAN, P. (edd.) *Charlemagne's Heir. New Perspectives on the Reign of Louis the Pious (814–840)* (Oxford 1990)

Colombano, pioniere di civilizzazione cristiana europea. Atti del convegno internazionale di studi colombaniani, Bobbio, 28–30 agosto 1965 (Bobbio 1973)

CONCANNON, H. *Life of St Columban* (Dublin 1915)

CONTE, P. *Chiese e primato nelle lettere dei papi del secolo VII* (Milano 1971)

CONTRENI, John J. 'The Irish in the western Carolingian empire (according to James F. Kenney and Bern, Burgerbibliothek 363', in *Die Iren und Europa*, ed. Löwe, II.758–98

COURCELLE, P. [review of *Defensoris Locogiacensis Monachi Liber Scintillarum*, ed. Rochais], *Revue des études latines* 36 (1958) 367–9

CROUZEL, Henri, *et al.* (edd.) *Origène, Homélies sur S. Luc* (Paris 1962)

CUNLIFFE, Barry (ed.) *The Temple of Sulis Minerva at Bath* II. *The Finds from the Sacred Spring* (Oxford 1988)

CURRAN, M.E. *The Antiphonary of Bangor and the early Irish Monastic Liturgy* (Blackrock 1984)

DAINTREE, D.C.C. 'Glosse irlandesi', in *Enciclopedia Virgiliana*, edd. Della Corte *et al.*, II.774–6

DAINTREE, D.C.C. & GEYMONAT, M. 'Scholia non Serviana', in *Enciclopedia Virgiliana*, edd. Della Corte *et al.*, IV.707–20

DANIEL-ROPS, H. (ed.) *The Miracle of Ireland* (Dublin 1959)

Das römische Brigantium. Ausstellungskatalog des Vorarlberger Landesmuseums (Bregenz 1985)

DAVIES, W.H. 'The church in Wales', in *Christianity in Britain, 300–700*, edd. Barley & Hanson, pp. 131–50

DAVIS, R.H.C. & WALLACE-HADRILL, J.M. (edd.) *The Writing of History in the Middle Ages. Essays presented to Richard William Southern* (Oxford 1981)

DE CLERCQ, C. (ed.) *Concilia Galliae A. 511–A. 695* (Turnhout 1963)

DE CONINCK, L. & D'HONT, M.J. (edd.) *Theodori Mopsuesteni Expositio in Psalmos Iuliano Aeclanensi interprete* (Turnhout 1977)

DE GROOT, A.W. *La prose métrique des anciens* (Paris 1926)

DE MAILLÉ, M. *Les cryptes de Jouarre* (Paris 1971)

DE PLINVAL, G. 'L'oeuvre littéraire de Pélage', *Revue de philologie, de littérature et d'histoire anciennes* 60 (1934) 9–42

DE PLINVAL, G. *Pélage, ses écrits, sa vie et sa réforme* (Lausanne 1943)

DEKKERS, E. & GAAR, A. (edd.) *Clavis patrum Latinorum* (2nd edn, Steenbrugge 1961)

DELLA CORTE, F., *et al.* (edd.) *Enciclopedia Virgiliana* (5 vols in 6, Roma 1984/91)

DESHUSSES, J. (ed.) *Le sacramentaire grégorien* (2nd ed, Fribourg-en-Suisse 1979)

DE VOGÜÉ, Adalbert 'Sur une série d'emprunts de saint Colomban à Fauste de Riez', *Studia Monastica* 10 (1968) 119–23

DE VOGÜÉ, Adalbert 'En lisant Jonas de Bobbio', *Studia Monastica* 30 (1988) 63–103

DE VOGÜÉ, Adalbert (ed. & trans.) *La Règle du Maître* (2 vols, Paris 1964)

DI BERARDINO, Angelo (ed.) *Patrology IV. The Golden Age of Latin Patristic Literature from the Council of Nicea to the Council of Chalcedon*, transl. Placid Solari (Westminster, MD 1986)

Dictionnaire de théologie catholique, edd. A. Vacant, E. Mangenot & E. Amann (15 vols, Paris, 1903/50)

Dizionario biografico degli Italiani, edd. Alberto M. Ghisalberti *et al.* (Roma, 1960–)

DOOLEY, K. 'From penance to confession: the Celtic contribution', *Bijdragen* 43 (1982) 390–411

DRACK, W. & MOOSBRUGGER-LEU, R. 'Die frühmittelalterliche Kirche von Tuggen', *Zeitschrift für schweizerische Archäologie und Kunstgeschichte* 20 (1960) 176–207

DU CANGE, Carolus Du Fresne *Glossarium mediae et infimae latinitatis* (2nd edn, 10 vols, Niort 1883/7)

DUCHESNE, Louis *Christian Worship, its Origin and Evolution. A Study of the Latin Liturgy up to the Time of Charlemagne* (London 1903 and successive editions)

DUCHESNE, L., *Fastes épiscopaux de l'ancienne Gaule* (2nd edn, 3 vols, Paris 1907/15)

DUCHESNE, L. *L'Église au VIe siècle* (Paris 1925)

DÜCHTING, Reinhard *Sedulius Scottus. Seine Dichtungen* (München 1968)

DUBOIS, J. & RENAUD, G. (edd.) *Édition pratique des martyrologes de Bède, de l'Anonyme lyonnais et de Florus* (Paris 1976)

DUFT, Johannes 'St Columban in der St Galler Handschriften', *Zeitschrift für schweizerische Kirchengeschichte* 59 (1965) 285–96

DUMVILLE, D.N. 'Biblical apocrypha and the early Irish: a preliminary investigation', *Proceedings of the Royal Irish Academy* 73C (1973) 299–338

DUMVILLE, D.N. 'Gildas and Maelgwn: problems of dating', in *Gildas: New Approaches*, edd. Lapidge & Dumville, pp. 51–9

DUMVILLE, D.N. 'Gildas and Uinniau', in *Gildas: New Approaches*, edd. Lapidge & Dumville, pp. 207–14

DUMVILLE, D.N. 'Sub-Roman Britain: history and legend', *History*, new series, 62 (1977) 173–92

DUMVILLE, D.N. 'The chronology of *De excidio Britanniae*, Book I', in *Gildas: New Approaches*, edd. Lapidge & Dumville, pp. 61–84

DUMVILLE, D.N. 'Two approaches to the dating of *Nauigatio Sancti Brendani*', *Studi Medievali*, 3rd series, 29 (1988) 87–102

DUNCAN, A.A.M. 'Bede, Iona and the Picts' in *The Writing of History*, edd. Davis & Wallace-Hadrill, pp. 1–42

EGGER, R. 'Die "ecclesia secundae Rhaetiae" ', in *Festschrift zu 75. Geburtstag von P. Reinecke*, edd. Behrens & Werner, pp. 51–60

EHWALD, R. (ed.) *Aldhelmi Opera* (Berlin, 1919)

ELG, Arvid Gison *In Faustum Reiensem Studia* (Uppsala 1937)

ELLIOTT, K. & ELDER, J.P. 'A critical edition of the Vatican mythographers', *Transactions of the American Philosophical Association* 78 (1947) 189–207

ENGELBRECHT, August *Studien über die Schriften des Bischofes von Reii Faustus* (Wien 1889)

ENGELBRECHT, Augustus (ed.) *Fausti Reiensis praeter sermones pseudo-Eusebianos opera; accedunt Ruricii epistulae* (Wien 1891)

ENGELBRECHT, Augustus (ed.) *Tyrannii Rufini Orationum Gregorii Nazianzeni novem interpretatio* (Wien 1910)

ENGELBERT, P. 'Zur Frühgeschichte des Bobbieser Skriptoriums', *Revue Bénédictine* 78 (1968) 220–60

ERDMANN, W. & ZETTLER, A. 'Zur Archäologie des Konstanzer Münsterhügels', *Schriften des Vereins für Geschichte des Bodensees* 95 (1977) 19–134

ERLANDE-BRANDENBURG, A. 'Le monastère de Luxeuil au IXe siècle. Topographie et fragments de sculpture', *Cahiers archéologiques* 14 (1964) 239–43

ESPOSITO, M. 'The ancient Bobbio catalogue', *Journal of Theological Studies* 32 (1931) 337–44

ESPOSITO, M. 'On the new edition of the *Opera Sancti Columbani*', *Classica & Mediaevalia* 21 (1960) 184–203

ESPOSITO, M. *Irish Books and Learning in Mediaeval Europe*, ed. M. Lapidge (Aldershot 1990)

EWIG, E. *Die Merowinger und das Frankenreich* (Stuttgart 1988)

FANNING, S.C. 'Lombard Arianism reconsidered', *Speculum* 56 (1981) 241–58

FENSKE, L. *et al.* (edd.) *Institutionen, Kultur und Gesellschaft im Mittelalter. Festschrift für Josef Fleckenstein* (Sigmaringen 1984)

FICKERMANN, Norbert 'Ein frühmittelalterliches Liedchen auf den Pirol', *Neues Archiv* 50 (1935) 582–7

FISCHER, B. 'Ambrosius der Verfasser des österlichen Exultet?', *Archiv für Liturgiewissenschaft* 2 (1952) 61–74

FISCHER, B. 'Die Lesungen der römischen Ostervigil unter Gregor der Grosse', in *Colligere fragmenta*, edd. Fischer & Fiala, pp. 144–59

FISCHER, Bonifatius (ed.) *Vetus Latina: die Reste der altlateinischen Bibel*, II: *Genesis* (Freiburg 1951/4)

FISCHER, Bonifatius and FIALA, V. (edd.) *Colligere fragmenta: Festschrift Alban Dold* (Beuron 1952)

FLEMING, Patricius *Collectanea Sacra seu S. Columbani Hiberni abbatis . . . necnon aliorum aliquot e Veteri itidem Scotia seu Hibernia antiquorum sanctorum acta et opuscula* (Louvain 1667)

FOX, C. & DICKINS, B. (edd.) *The Early Cultures of Northwest Europe (H.M. Chadwick Memorial Studies)* (Cambridge 1950)

FRAIPONT, J. (ed.) *Sancti Fulgentii episcopi Ruspensis Opera* (2 vols, Turnhout 1968)

FRANCESCHINI, E. (ed.) *L'antifonario di Bangor* (Padova 1941)

FRANCESCHINI, E. [review of *Sancti Columbani Opera*, ed. & transl. Walker], *Aevum* 31 (1957) 281–3

GANSHOF, F.L. *Les liens de vassalité et les immunités* (2nd edn, Bruxelles, 1958)

GANZ, David *Corbie in the Carolingian Renaissance* (Sigmaringen 1990)

GANZ, D. 'The Merovingian library of Corbie', in *Columbanus and Merovingian Monasticism*, edd. Clarke & Brennan, pp. 153–72

GAUDEMET, Jean & BASDEVANT, B. (edd. & transl.) *Les Canons des conciles mérovingiens (VIᵉ–VIIᵉ siècles)* (2 vols, Paris 1989)

GEARY, P. *Aristocracy in Provence* (Stuttgart 1985)

GEORGE, Judith W. *Venantius Fortunatus. A Latin Poet in Merovingian Gaul* (Oxford 1992)

GLARE, P.G.W. (ed.) *Oxford Latin Dictionary* (8 vols, Oxford 1968/82)

GLORIE, F. (ed.) *Eusebius 'Gallicanus', Collectio Homiliarum* (3 vols, Turnhout 1970/1)

GLORIE, F. (ed.) *Maxentii aliorumque Scytharum monachorum necnon Ioannis Tomitanae urbis episcopi opuscula* (Turnhout 1978)

GODMAN, Peter, & COLLINS, R. (edd.) *Charlemagne's Heir: New Perspectives on the Reign of Louis the Pious (814–840)* (Oxford 1990)

GOETZ, Georg (ed.) *Corpus Glossariorum Latinorum* (7 vols, Leipzig 1888/1923)

GOEZ, W. 'Über die Anfänge der Agilulfinger', *Jahrbuch für fränkische Landesforschung* 34–5 (1975) 145–61

GOLDAST, Melchior *Paraeneticorum Veterum Pars I cum notis Melcioris Haiminsfeldi Goldasti* (Insulae ad Lacum Acronium 1604)

GRAUS, F. 'Die Gewalt bei den Anfängen des Feudalismus und die "Gefangenenbefreiung" der merowingischen Hagiographie', *Jahrbuch für Wirtschaftsgeschichte* 1 (1961) 61–156

GRAY, P.T.R. & HERREN, M.W. 'Columbanus and the Three Chapters controversy – a new approach', *Journal of Theological Studies*, new series, 45 (1994) 160–70

GRIESSER, B.   'Die handschriftliche Ueberlieferung der Expositio IV Evangeliorum des ps. Hieronymus', *Revue bénédictine* 49 (1937) 279–321

GROSJEAN, P.   'Gloria postuma S. Martini Turonensis apud Scottos et Britannos', *Analecta Bollandiana* 55 (1937) 300–48

GROSJEAN, P.   'Recherches sur les débuts de la controverse pascale chez les celtes', *Analecta Bollandiana* 64 (1946) 200–44

GROSJEAN, P., 'Notes d'hagiographie celtique' [nos 30, 31, 35, 36], *Analecta Bollandiana* 75 (1957) 185–94, 212–26

GRUBER, J.   'Bregenz', in *Lexikon des Mittelalters*, edd. Avella-Widhalm *et al.*, II.599

GUEROUT, J.   'Le testament de Ste.-Fare. Matériaux pour l'étude critique de ce document', *Revue d'histoire ecclésiastique* 60 (1965) 761–821

GULLOTTA, G.   *Gli antichi cataloghi e i codici della abbazia di Nonantola* (Città del Vaticano 1955)

GUNDLACH, Wilhelm (ed.)   'Columbani siue Columbani abbatis Luxouiensis et Bobbiensis epistolae', in *Epistolae Merowingici et Karolini Aevi I* (Berlin 1892) 154–90

GUNDLACH, Wilhelm   'Über die Columban-Briefe 1. Die prosaischen Briefe', *Neues Archiv* 15 (1890) 497–526

GUNDLACH, Wilhelm   'Zu den Columban-Briefen: eine Entgegnung', *Neues Archiv* 17 (1892) 425–9

GUY, J.-C. (ed. & transl.)   *Jean Cassien, Institutions cénobitiques* (Paris 1965)

GWYNN, A.   'The cult of St Martin in Ireland', *Irish Ecclesiastical Record*, 5th series, 105 (1966) 353–64

HAASE, F. (ed.)   *L. Annaei Senecae Opera: Supplementum* (Leipzig 1902)

HADDAN, A.W. & STUBBS, W. (edd.)   *Councils and Ecclesiastical Documents Relating to Great Britain and Ireland* (3 vols, Oxford 1869/78)

HAGEN, H.   'Iunii Philargyrii grammatici Explanatio in Bucolica Vergilii', in *Servii grammatici qui feruntur . . . commentarii*, edd. Thilo & Hagen, pp. 1–189

HAGENDAHL, H.   *La Prose metrique d'Arnobe: Contributions à la connaissance de la prose littéraire de l'empire* (Göteborg 1937)

HAGENDAHL, H.   *La Correspondance de Ruricius* (Göteborg 1952)

HALLINGER, Kassius (ed.)   *Initia Consuetudinis Benedictinae. Consuetudines saeculi octaui et noni* (Siegburg 1963)

HALM, Carolus (ed.)   *Sulpicii Seueri libri qui supersunt* (Wien 1866)

HALM, C., *et al.*   *Catalogus Codicum Latinorum Bibliothecae Regiae Monacensis* (2 vols in 7 parts, München 1868/81)

HANSLIK, R., LESKY, A., & SCHWABL, H. (edd.)   *Antidosis. Festschrift für Walther Kraus zum 70. Geburtstag* (Wien 1972)

HANSLIK, R. (ed.)   *Benedicti Regula* (Wien 1960)

HANSSENS, J.M.   *Aux origines de la prière liturgique* (Roma 1952)

HARTEL, W. (ed.)   *Sancti Pontii Meropii Paulini Nolani Epistulae* (Wien 1894)

HAUCK, A.   'Ueber die sogenannte *Instructiones Columbani*', *Zeitschrift für kirchliche Wissenschaft und kirchliches Leben* 6 (1885) 357–64

HAUCK, Albert (ed.)   *Real-Encyklopädie für protestantische Theologie und Kirche* (3rd edn, 24 vols, Leipzig 1896/1913)

HEERWAGEN [Hervagius], J. (ed.)   *Opera Bedae* (8 vols, Basel 1563)

HEIMING, O.   'Zum monastischen Offizium von Kassianus bis Kolumbanus', *Archiv für Liturgiewissenschaft* 7 (1961) 89–156

HEIST, W.W. (ed.)   *Vitae sanctorum Hiberniae ex codice olim Salmanticensi* (Bruxelles 1965)

HELBLING, B. & HELBLING, H.   'Der heilige Gallus in der Geschichte', *Schweizerische Zeitschrift für Geschichte* 12 (1962) 1–62

HELLMANN, Siegmund (ed.) *Pseudo-Cyprianus de xii abusiuis saeculi* (Leipzig 1909)

HERBERT, Máire *Iona, Kells and Derry: the History and Hagiography of the Monastic Familia of Columba* (Oxford 1988)

HERREN, M.[W.] 'Classical and secular learning among the Irish before the Carolingian Renaissance', *Florilegium* 3 (1981) 118–57

HERREN, M.W. 'Gildas and early British monasticism', in *Britain 400–600: Language and History*, edd. Bammesberger & Wollmann, pp. 65–78

HERREN, M.W. 'The stress systems in Insular Latin octosyllabic verse', *Cambridge Medieval Celtic Studies* 15 (1988) 63–84

HERREN, Michael W. (ed.) *Insular Latin Studies: Papers on Latin Texts and Manuscripts of the British Isles: 550–1066* (Toronto 1981)

HERREN, M.[W.] 'Some new light on the life of Virgilius Maro Grammaticus', *Proceedings of the Royal Irish Academy* 79 C (1979) 27–71

HERREN, M.W. 'The Hiberno-Latin poems in Virgil the Grammarian', in *De Tertullien aux mozarabes*, edd. Holtz *et al.*, II.141–55

HERREN, Michael W. (ed. & transl.) *The Hisperica Famina* (2 vols, Toronto 1974/87)

HERTEL, Gustav 'Über des heiligen Columbas Leben und Schriften, besonders über seine Klosterregel', *Zeitschrift für die historische Theologie* 45 (1875) 396– 454

HERTENSTEIN, Bernhard *Joachim von Watt (Vadianus), Bartholomäus Schobinger, Melchior Goldast: Die Beschäftigung mit dem Althochdeutschen von St Gallen in Humanismus und Frühbarock* (Berlin 1975)

HIGHAM, N.J. *The English Conquest: Gildas and Britain in the Fifth Century* (Manchester 1994)

HILBERG, Isidorus (ed.) *Sancti Eusebii Hieronymi Epistulae* (3 vols, Wien 1910–12)

HILTY, G. 'Gallus in Tuggen', *Vox Romanica* 44 (1985) 125–55

HILTY, G. 'Gallus am Bodensee', *Vox Romanica* 45 (1986) 83–115

HODGKIN, T. *Italy and her Invaders 376–814* (8 vols, Oxford 1880/99)

HOLTZ, L., FREDOUILLE, J.-C. & JULLIEN, M.-H. (edd.) *De Tertullien aux mozarabes. Antiquité tardive et christianisme ancien. Mélanges offerts à Jacques Fontaine* (3 vols, Paris 1992)

HOWLETT, D.R. 'Two works of Columban', *Mittellateinisches Jahrbuch* 28 (1993) 27–46

HOWLETT, D.R. 'The earliest Irish writers at home and abroad', *Peritia: Journal of the Medieval Academy of Ireland* 8 (1994) 1–17

HUEMER, Johann (ed.) *Sedulii Opera Omnia* (Wien 1885)

HUGHES, K. 'Some aspects of Irish influence on early English private prayer', *Studia Celtica* 5 (1970) 48–61

HUGHES, K. 'The changing theory and practice of Irish pilgrimage', *Journal of Ecclesiastical History* 11 (1960) 143–51

HUGLO, M. 'L'auteur de l'Exultet pascal', *Vigiliae Christianae* 7 (1953) 79–88

HURST, D. & ADRIAEN, M. (edd.) *S. Hieronymi Commentarii in Matheum* (Turnhout 1969)

HYLTÉN, Per *Studien zu Sulpicius Seuerus* (Lund 1940)

JACKSON, Kenneth Hurlstone 'Notes on the ogam inscriptions of southern Britain' in *Early Cultures of North-West Europe*, edd. Fox & Dickins, pp. 197–213

JACOBSEN, Peter Christian 'Carmina Columbani' in *Die Iren und Europa*, ed. Löwe, I.434–67

JAMES, E. 'Archaeology and the Merovingian monastery' in *Columbanus and Merovingian Monasticism*, edd. Clarke & Brennan, pp. 33–55

JANSON, Tore *Prose Rhythm in Medieval Latin from the 9th to the 13th Century* (Stockholm 1975)

Bibliography

JÄSCHKE, K.-U. 'Kolumban von Luxeuil und sein Wirken im alamannischen Raum' in *Mönchtum*, ed. Borst, pp. 77–130

JEMOLO, V., MEROLLA, L., PALMA, M. & TRASSELLI, F. *Bibliografia dei manoscritti Sessoriani* (Roma 1987)

JONES, Charles W. 'The "lost" Sirmond manuscript of Bede's "computus" ', *English Historical Review* 52 (1937) 204–19

JONES, Charles W. (ed.) *Bedae opera de temporibus* (Cambridge, MA 1943)

JUNGMANN, Josef A. *Pastoral Liturgy* (London 1962)

Karl der Grosse, Werk und Wirkung [Catalogue of an exhibition held at Aachen 26 June–19 September 1965] (Aachen 1965)

KELLER, H. 'Fränkische Herrschaft und alemannisches Herzogtum im 6. und 7. Jahrhundert', *Zeitschrift für die Geschichte des Oberrheins* 124 (1976) 1–30

KELLY, J.N.D. *The Athanasian Creed* (London 1964)

KENNEY, James F. *The Sources for the Early History of Ireland: Ecclesiastical. An Introduction and Guide* (New York 1929; rev. imp., by L. Bieler, 1966)

KERLOUÉGAN, François 'Le latin du *De excidio Britanniae* de Gildas', in *Christianity in Britain*, edd. Barley & Hanson, pp. 151–76

KERLOUÉGAN, François 'Essai sur la mise en nourriture et l'éducation dans les pays celtiques d'après le témoignage des textes hagiographiques latins', *Études celtiques* 12 (1968–9) 101–46

KERLOUÉGAN, François *Le De Excidio Britanniae de Gildas: Les destinés de la culture latine dans l'Ile de Bretagne au VIe siècle* (Paris 1987)

KERLOUÉGAN, F. [review of *Gildas: New Approaches*, edd. Lapidge & Dumville], *Études celtiques* 23 (1986) 332–6

KERLOUÉGAN, F. 'Une mode stylistique dans la prose latine des pays celtiques', *Études celtiques* 13 (1971/2) 275–97

KLINGSHIRN, W.E. 'Church politics and chronology: dating the episcopacy of Caesarius of Arles', *Revue des études augustiniennes* 38 (1992) 80–8

KLINGSHIRN, William E. *Caesarius of Arles. The Making of a Christian Community in Late Antique Gaul* (Cambridge 1994)

KÖRNTGEN, Ludger *Studien zu den Quellen der frühmittelalterlichen Bußbücher* (Sigmaringen 1993)

KOTTJE, R., KÖRNTGEN, L. & SPENGLER-REFFGEN, U. (edd.) *Paenitentialia Minora Franciae et Italiae saeculi VIII–IX* (Turnhout 1994)

KRILL, R.M. 'The Vatican mythographers: their place in ancient mythography', *Manuscripta* 23 (1979) 173–7

KRUSCH, Bruno, & LEVISON, W. (edd.) *Gregorii episcopi Turonensis Libri Historiarum X* (2nd edn, Hannover 1951)

KRUSCH, Bruno *Studien zur christlich-mittelalterlichen Chronologie I Der 84–jährige Ostercyclus und seine Quellen* (Leipzig 1880)

KRUSCH, Bruno *Studien zur christlich-mittelalterlichen Chronologie II Die Entstehung unserer heutigen Zeitrechnung* (Berlin 1938)

KRUSCH, Bruno 'Chronologisches aus Handschriften', *Neues Archiv* 10 (1885) 84–9

KRUSCH, Bruno (ed.) *Gregorii Turonensis opera* II. *Miracula et opera minora* (Berlin 1885)

KRUSCH, Bruno (ed.) *Ionae uitae sanctorum Columbani, Vedastis, Iohannis* (Hannover 1905)

KRUSCH, Bruno (ed.) *Passiones Vitaeque sanctorum aevi merovingici et antiquiorum aliquot* [I](Hannover 1896)

KRUSCH, Bruno (ed.) *Passiones Vitaeque sanctorum aevi merovingici* [II] (Hannover 1902)

KULCSÁR, P. (ed.) *Mythographi Vaticani I et II* (Turnhout 1987)

KURTH, Godefroid   *Études franques* (2 vols, Bruxelles 1919)

KUYPERS, A.B. (ed.)   *The Prayerbook of Aedeluald the Bishop commonly called The Book of Cerne* (Cambridge 1902)

LADNER, Gerhart B.   *Images and Ideas in the Middle Ages: Selected Studies in History and Art* (2 vols, Roma 1983)

LADNER, G.B.   '*Homo uiator*: mediaeval ideas on alienation and order', *Speculum* 42 (1967) 233–59

LAISTNER, M.L.W.   [review of *Sancti Columbani Opera*, ed. & transl. Walker], *Speculum* 34 (1959) 341–3

LAMBERT, Bernard   *Bibliotheca Hieronymiana Manuscripta. La tradition manuscrite des oeuvres de Saint Jérôme* (Steenbrugge 1969)

LAMPE, G.W.H. (ed.)   *A Patristic Greek Lexicon* (5 fascicles, Oxford 1961/8)

LAPIDGE, M.   'Columbanus and the "Antiphonary of Bangor" ', *Peritia: Journal of the Medieval Academy of Ireland* 4 (1985) 104–16

LAPIDGE, M.   'A new Hiberno-Latin hymn on St Martin', *Celtica* 21 (1990) 240–51

LAPIDGE, M.   'The authorship of the adonic verses *Ad Fidolium* attributed to Columbanus' *Studi Medievali*, 3rd series, 18 (1977) 815–80

LAPIDGE, M.   'Gildas's education and the Latin culture of sub-Roman Britain', in *Gildas: New Approaches*, edd. Lapidge & Dumville, pp. 27–50

LAPIDGE, M.   'Some remnants of Bede's lost *Liber Epigrammatum*', *English Historical Review* 90 (1975) 798–820

LAPIDGE, Michael & DUMVILLE, D.[N.] (edd.)   *Gildas: New Approaches* (Woodbridge 1984)

LAPIDGE, M. & ROSIER, J. (transl.)   *Aldhelm: the Poetic Works* (Cambridge 1985)

LAPIDGE, M. & SHARPE, R.   *A Bibliography of Celtic-Latin Literature 400–1200* (Dublin 1985)

LAPORTE, J.   'Étude d'authenticité des oeuvres attribuées à saint Colomban', *Revue Mabillon* 45 (1955) 1–28 *and* 46 (1956) 1–14

LATHAM, R.E., *et al.* (edd.)   *Dictionary of Medieval Latin from British Sources* (London 1975–)

LAWSON, C.M. (ed.)   *Sanctus Isidorus episcopus Hispalensis De ecclesiasticis officiis* (Turnhout 1989)

LECLERCQ, Henri   'Luxeuil', *Dictionnaire d'archéologie chrétienne et de liturgie*, edd. Cabrol & Leclercq, IX.2722–87

LECLERCQ, Jean   *Aux Sources de la spiritualité occidentale* (Paris 1964)

LECLERCQ, Jean   'Mönchtum und Peregrinatio im Frühmittelalter', *Römische Quartalschrift* 55 (1960) 212–25

LECLERCQ, Jean   'Anciennes prières monastiques', *Studia monastica* 1 (1959) 379–92

LEHMANN, Paul   *Erforschung des Mittelalters* (5 vols, Stuttgart 1941/62)

LEHMANN, Paul (ed.)   *Mittelalterliche Bibliothekskataloge Deutschlands und der Schweiz* I (München 1918)

LESNE, E.   *Histoire de la propriété ecclésiastique en France* I (Lille 1910)

LEVISON, Wilhelm   *England and the Continent in the Eighth Century* (Oxford 1946)

LEWIS, Charlton T. & SHORT, C.   *A Latin Dictionary* (Oxford 1879)

Lexikon des Mittelalters, edd. Avella-Widhalm, G., Lutz, L., Mattejiet, R. & Mattejiet, U. (München 1977–)

LIDDELL, H.G. & SCOTT, R. (edd.)   *A Greek-English Lexicon*, rev. H.S. Jones & R. McKenzie (9th ed, Oxford 1968)

LINDHOLM, Gudrun   *Studien zum mittellateinischen Prosarythmus* (Stockholm 1963)

LINDSAY, W.M., *et al.* (edd.)   *Glossaria Latina* (5 vols, Paris 1926/31)

LONGNON, A.   *Géographie de la Gaule au VIe siècle* (Paris 1878)

LOOFS, F.   *Antiquae Britonum Scotorumque ecclesiae* (Leipzig 1882)

LÖWE, Heinz [review of *Sancti Columbani Opera*, ed. & transl. Walker], *Theologische Literaturzeitung* 83 (1958) 685–7

LÖWE, Heinz 'Columbanus und Fidolius', *Deutsches Archiv für Erforschung des Mittelalters* 37 (1981) 1–19

LÖWE, Heinz (ed.) *Die Iren und Europa im frühen Mittelalter* (2 vols, Stuttgart 1982)

LOMIENTO, G. 'La Bibbia nella compositio di S. Colombano', *Vetera Christianorum* 3 (1966) 25–42

LOWE, E.A. *Codices Latini Antiquiores* (11 vols and suppl., Oxford 1934/71)

LOWTHER CLARKE, W.K. (transl.) *The Lausiac History of Palladius* (London 1918)

LUFF, S.G.A. 'A survey of primitive monasticism in central Gaul (c. 300 to 700)', *Downside Review* 70 (1951/2) 180–203

MAC AIRT, Seán (ed. & transl.) *The Annals of Inisfallen (MS. Rawlinson B. 503)* (Dublin 1951)

MAC AIRT, Seán, & MAC NIOCAILL, G. (edd. & transl.) *The Annals of Ulster* (Dublin 1983)

MACALISTER, R.A.S. (ed.) *Corpus Inscriptionum Insularum Celticarum* (2 vols, Dublin 1945/9)

MACARTHUR, W.P. 'The identification of some pestilences recorded in the Irish annals', *Irish Historical Studies* 6 (1948/9) 169–88

MCGANN, M.J. 'The distribution of cadences in the "De mundi transitu" of St Columban', *Archivum Latinitatis Medii Aevi* 31 (1961) 147–9

MCKITTERICK, Rosamond *The Frankish Church and the Carolingian Reforms, 789–895* (London 1977)

MCLAUGHLIN, T.P. *Le très ancien droit monastique de l'Occident* (Paris 1935)

MCNALLY, R.E. 'The *tres linguae sacrae* in early Irish biblical exegesis', *Theological Studies* 19 (1958) 395–403

MCNAMARA, Martin *The Apocrypha in the Irish Church* (Dublin 1975)

MCNEILL, John T. & GAMER, Helena M. *Medieval Handbooks of Penance. A Translation of the Principal Libri Poenitentiales and Selections from Related Documents* (New York 1938)

MACHIELSEN, J. *Clavis patristica pseudepigraphorum medii aevi* IIA (Turnhout 1994)

MAESTRI, A. 'La prima ufficiatura di S. Colombano', in *San Colombano e la sua opera in Italia*, pp. 41–55

MANITIUS, Max *Geschichte der lateinischen Literatur des Mittelalters* (3 vols, München 1911/31)

MARKUS, R.A. 'The legacy of Pelagius: orthodoxy, heresy and conciliation', in *The Making of Orthodoxy*, ed. Williams, pp. 214–34

MARKUS, R.A. 'Pelagianism: Britain and the continent', *Journal of Ecclesiastical History* 37 (1986) 191–204

MARTIN, P.E. *Études critiques sur la Suisse à l'époque mérovingienne (534–715)* (Genève 1910)

MARTINE, François (ed. & transl.) *Vie des pères du Jura* (Paris 1968)

MATHISEN, Ralph W. *Ecclesiastical Factionalism and Religious Controversy in Fifth-century Gaul* (Washington, DC 1989)

MATTHEWS, John *Western Aristocracies and the Imperial Court* A.D. *364–425* (Oxford 1975)

MAY, U. *Untersuchungen zur frühmittelalterlichen Siedlungs-, Personen- und Besitzgeschichte anhand der St Galler Urkunden* (Bern 1976)

MAYR-HARTING, Henry *The Coming of Christianity to Anglo-Saxon England* (3rd edn, London 1991)

MEEHAN, Denis (ed. & transl.) *Adamnan's De Locis Sanctis* (Dublin 1958)

MEIER, Gabriel *Jahresbericht über die Lehr- und Erziehungsanstalt des Benediktinerstifts Marie Einsiedeln für 1886–7* (Einsiedeln 1887)

Mélanges de littérature et d'histoire religieuses publiés à l'occasion du jubilé épiscopal de Mgr de Cabriéres (3 vols, Paris 1899)

Mélanges colombaniens: Actes du congrès international de Luxeuil, 1950 (Paris 1950)

MEYER, Kuno (ed.) *Hibernica Minora* (Oxford 1894)

MEYER, Kuno *Learning in Ireland in the Fifth Century and the Transmission of Letters* (Dublin 1913)

MEYER, Wilhelm *Gesammelte Abhandlungen zur mittellateinischen Rythmik* (3 vols, Berlin 1905/36)

MEYER, Wilhelm 'Poetische Nachlese aus dem Book of Cerne', *Nachrichten Göttingen* (1917) pp. 600–5

MIGNE, J.-P. (ed.) *Patrologiae [latinae] cursus completus* (221 vols, Paris 1844/64)

MIGNE, J.-P. (ed.) *Patrologiae [graecae] cursus completus* (161 vols, Paris 1857/66)

MILBURN, R.L.P. [review of *Sancti Columbani Opera*, ed. & transl. Walker], *Medium Ævum* 29 (1960) 25–7

MOHLBERG, Leo Cunibert *Katalog der Handschriften der Zentralbibliothek Zürich* I. *Mittelalterliche Handschriften* (Zürich 1951)

MOHRMANN, Christine *Liturgical Latin: its Origins and Character* (London 1957)

MOHRMANN, C. 'The earliest Continental Irish Latin', *Vigiliae Christianae* 16 (1962) 216–33

MOMMSEN, Theodor (ed.) *Die lateinische Übersetzung des Rufinus* (Leipzig 1903)

MOMMSEN, T. (ed.) *Chronica minora saec. IV.V.VI.VII* (Berlin 1892)

MOOSBRUGGER-LEU, R. *Die Schweiz zur Merowingerzeit* (2 vols, Bern 1971)

MOOSBRUGGER-LEU, R. *Archäologie der Schweiz* VI. *Frühmittelalter* (Basel 1979)

MONACO, G. (ed.) *Forma Italiae, Regio IX: Libarna* (Roma 1936)

MORELLI, M. & PALMA, M. 'Indagine su alcuni aspetti materiali della produzione libraria a Nonantola nel secolo IX', *Scrittura e civiltà* 6 (1982) 23–98

MORIN, G. 'Un écrit de saint Césaire d'Arles renfermant un témoignage sur les fondateurs des églises des Gaules' in *Mélanges de littérature*, I.109–24

MORIN, G. 'Critique des sermons attribués à Fauste de Riez', *Revue Bénédictine* 9 (1892), 45–61

MORIN, G. 'Mes principes et ma méthode pour la future édition de S. Césaire', *Revue Bénédictine* 10 (1893) 62–77

MORIN, G. 'Un nouveau recueil inédit d'homélies de S. Césaire d'Arles', *Revue Bénédictine* 16 (1899) 241–60, 289–305, 337–44

MORIN, G. 'Deux pièces inédites du disciple de Fauste de Riez, auteur des soi-disant *Instructiones Columbani*', *Revue Charlemagne* 1 (1911) 161–70

MORIN, G. 'La collection gallicane dite d'Eusèbe d'Émèse et les problèmes qui s'y rattachent', *Zeitschrift für die neutestamentliche Wissenschaft und die Künde der älteren Kirche* 34 (1935) 92–115

MORIN, G. (ed.) *Sancti Caesarii Arelatensis Sermones* (2nd edn, 2 vols, Turnhout 1953)

MORRIS, C. 'The plague in Britain', *Historical Journal* 14 (1971) 205–15

MORRIS, John (ed. & transl.) *Nennius, British History and the Welsh Annals* (Chichester 1980)

MÜLLER, W. (ed.) *Zur Geschichte der Alemannen* (Darmstadt 1975)

MUNDÓ, A. 'L'édition des oeuvres de S. Columban', *Scriptorium* 12 (1958) 289–93

MURATORI, L.A. (ed.) *Antiquitates Italicae Medii Aevi* (25 vols, Milano, 1723–1896)

NÍ CHATHÁIN, Proinséas & RICHTER, M. (edd.) *Ireland and Europe: the Early Church* (Stuttgart 1984)

NÍ CHATHÁIN, P. 'The liturgical background of the Derrynavlan altar service', *Journal of the Royal Society of Antiquaries of Ireland* 110 (1980) 127–48

NIEDERMANN, Max 'Les dérivés en *-osus* dans les *Hisperica Famina*', *Archiuum Latinitatis Medii Aeui (Bulletin Du Cange)* 23 (1953) 75–101

NIERMEYER, J.F. *Mediae Latinitatis Lexicon Minus* (Leiden 1976)

NORBERG, Dag *La poésie latine rythmique du haut moyen âge* (Stockholm 1954)

NORBERG, Dag *Introduction à l'ètude de la versification latine médiévale* (Stockholm 1958)

NORBERG, Dag *Les vers latins iambiques et trochaïques au moyen âge et leurs répliques rythmiques* (Stockholm 1988)

NORBERG, Dag (ed.) *S. Gregorii Magni Registrum Epistularum* (2 vols, Turnhout 1982)

NOTHDURFT, K.-D. *Studien zum Einfluß Senecas auf die Philosophie und Theologie des zwölften Jahrhunderts* (Leiden 1963)

Novum Glossarium Mediae Latinitatis ab anno DCCC usque ad annum MCC (Hafniae, in progress 1957–)

NUVOLONE, F. 'Le commentaire de S. Colomban sur les Psaumes rentre-t-il définitivement dans l'ombre?', *Freiburger Zeitschrift für Philosophie und Theologie* 26 (1979) 211–19

OBERHELMAN, S.M. & HALL, R.G. 'A new statistical analysis of accentual prose rhythms in Imperial Latin authors', *Classical Philology* 79 (1984) 114–30

OBERHELMAN, S.M. & HALL, R.G. 'Meter in accentual clausulae of Late Imperial Latin prose', *Classical Philology* 80 (1985) 214–27

OBERHELMAN, S.M. 'The *cursus* in Late Imperial Latin prose: a reconsideration of methodology', *Classical Philology* 83 (1988) 136–49

OBERHELMAN, S.M. 'The history and development of the *cursus mixtus* in Latin literature', *Classical Quarterly*, new series, 38 (1988) 228–42

O'CARROLL, J. 'The chronology of saint Columbanus', *Irish Theological Quarterly* 24 (1957) 76–95

Ó CRÓINÍN, D. 'A seventh-century Irish computus from the circle of Cummianus', *Proceedings of the Royal Irish Academy* 82 C (1982) 405–30

Ó CRÓINÍN, D. 'The Irish provenance of Bede's computus', *Peritia: Journal of the Medieval Academy of Ireland* 2 (1983) 229–47

Ó CRÓINÍN, D. 'Mo-sinnu moccu Min and the computus of Bangor', *Peritia: Journal of the Medieval Academy of Ireland* 1 (1982) 281–95

Ó CRÓINÍN, D. 'Introduction' in *'The Work of Angels'*, ed. Youngs, pp. 11–17

Ó CRÓINÍN, D. 'The date, provenance, and earliest use of the works of Virgilius Maro Grammaticus', in *Tradition und Wertung*, edd. Bernt, Rädle & Silagi, pp. 13–22

Ó CRÓINÍN, D. ' "New heresy for old" ': Pelagianism in Ireland and the papal letter of 640', *Speculum* 60 (1985) 505–16

O'MAHONY, HANCOCK, W.N. & O'DONOVAN, J. (edd. & transl.) *Ancient Laws of Ireland* (6 vols, Dublin 1865/1901)

O'MEARA, J.J. & NAUMANN, B. (edd.) *Latin Script and Letters* A.D *400–900: Festschrift presented to Ludwig Bieler* (Leiden 1976)

ÖNNEFORS, A. 'Die Latinität Columbas des Jüngeren in neuem Licht', *Zeitschrift für Kirchengeschichte* 83 (1972) 52–60

Ó RIAIN, P. (ed.) *Corpus Genealogiarum Sanctorum Hiberniae* (Dublin 1985)

ORCHARD, Andy *The Poetic Art of Aldhelm* (Cambridge 1994)

ORLANDI, G. '*Clausulae* in Gildas's *De Excidio Britanniae*', in *Gildas: New Approaches*, edd. Lapidge & Dumville, pp. 129–49

O'SULLIVAN, Thomas D. *The De Excidio of Gildas: its Authenticity and Date* (Leiden 1978)

OTTINO, G.   *Codici Bobbiesi nella Biblioteca Nazionale di Torino* (Torino 1890)

PALMA, M.   *Sessoriana* (Roma 1980)

PARINGER, B.   'Das alte Weltenburger Martyrologium und seine Miniaturen', *Studien und Mitteilungen zur Geschichte des Benediktiner-Ordens* 52 (1934) 146–65

PETSCHENIG, Michael (ed.)   *Iohannis Cassiani, Conlationes XXIV* (Wien 1886)

PETSCHENIG, Michael (ed.)   *Iohannis Cassiani, De institutis coenobiorum* (Wien 1888)

PICARD, J.-M. (ed.)   *Aquitaine and Ireland in the Middle Ages* (Blackrock 1995)

PICARD, J.-M.   'The metrical prose of Adomnán's *Vita Columbae*: an unusual system', *Ireland and Europe: The Early Church*, edd. Ní Chatháin & Richter, pp. 258–71

PICHERY, E. (ed. & transl.)   *Jean Cassien, Conférences* (3 vols, Paris 1955/9)

PITRA, Jean-Baptiste (ed.)   *Spicilegium Solesmense* (4 vols, Paris 1852/8)

PLUMMER, Charles (ed.)   *Venerabilis Baedae Opera Historica* (2 vols, Oxford 1896)

PLUMMER, Charles (ed.)   *Vitae Sanctorum Hiberniae partim hactenus ineditae* (2 vols, Oxford 1910)

POLARA, G. (ed.)   *Virgilio Marone grammatico. Epitomi ed Epistole* (Napoli 1979)

POLONIO, Valeria   *Il monasterio di San Colombano di Bobbio dalla fondazione all'epoca carolingia* (Genova 1962)

POOLE, R.L.   *Studies in Chronology and History* (Oxford 1934)

PRINZ, Friedrich   *Frühes Mönchtum im Frankenreich: Kultur und Gesellschaft in Gallien, den Rheinlanden und Bayern am Beispiel der monastischen Entwicklung (4. bis 8. Jahrhundert)* (München 1965)

PRINZ, Friedrich   'Columbanus, the Frankish nobility and the territories east of the Rhine', in *Columbanus and Merovingian Monasticism*, edd. Clarke & Brennan, pp. 73–87

QUACQUARELLI, A.   'La prosa d'arte di S. Colombano', *Vetera Christianorum* 3 (1966) 5–24

QUACQUARELLI, A.   'La prosa di san Colombano', in *Colombano, pioniere di civilizzazione cristiana europea*, pp. 23–41

QUENTIN, H. & DELEHAYE, H. (edd.)   *Martyrologium Hieronymianum* (Bruxelles 1931)

RÄDLE, Fidel   'Die Kenntnis der antiken lateinischen Literatur bei den Iren in der Heimat und auf dem Kontinent', in *Die Iren und Europa*, ed. Löwe, I.484–500

RATCLIFFE, E.C. (ed.)   *Expositio antiquae liturgiae Gallicanae* (London 1971)

REINERS-ERNST, E.   'Die Gründung des Bistums Konstanz in neuer Sicht', *Schriften des Vereins für Geschichte des Bodensees* 71 (1952) 17–36

REY, M. *et al.*   *Les diocèses de Besançon et de Saint-Claude* (Paris 1977)

RICHÉ, Pierre   *Éducation et culture dans l'Occident barbare IVe–VIIIe siècles* (Paris 1962)

RICHÉ, Pierre   'Columbanus, his followers and the Merovingian church', in *Columbanus and Merovingian Monasticism*, edd. Clarke & Brennan, pp. 59–72

RIESE, Alexander (ed.)   *Anthologia Latina* I (2nd edn, Leipzig 1906)

ROGER, Maurice   *L'enseignement des lettres classiques d'Ausone à Alcuin. Introduction à l'histoire des écoles carolingiennes* (Paris 1905)

RONCORONI, A.   'L'epitafio di S. Agrippino nella chiesa di S. Eufemia ad Isola (Schaller-Könsgen ICL 3449)', *Rivista archeologica dell' antica provincia e diocesi di Como* 162 (1980) 99–149

ROSSBACH, O.   *De Senecae Philosophi librorum recensione et emendatione* (Breslau 1888)

ROSSI, G.F.   'Il commento di san Colombano ai Salmi ritrovato a Bobbio in un codice della fine del secolo XII', *Divus Thomas* 67 (1964) 89–93

Bibliography

ROUSSEL, J. *Saint Colomban et l'épopée colombanienne* (2 vols, Besançon 1941–2)

RYAN, J. 'The early Irish church and the see of Peter', *Settimane di studio del Centro italiano di studi sull'alto medioevo* 7 (1960) 549–74

SABATIER, P. *Biblorum sacrorum latinae uersiones antiquae, seu Vetus Italica* (3 vols, Rheims 1743)

SAMARAN, C. & MARICHAL, R. *Catalogue des manuscrits en écriture latine portant des indications de date, de lieu ou de copiste* III (Paris 1974)

San Colombano e la sua opera in Italia: Convegno storico Colombaniano, Bobbio, 1–2 settembre 1951 (Bobbio 1953)

SCHÄFERDIEK, K. 'Columbans Wirken in Frankenreich' in *Die Iren und Europa*, ed. Löwe, I.171–201

SCHÄFERDIEK, K. 'Der irische Osterzyklus des sechsten und siebten Jahrhunderts', *Deutsches Archiv für Erforschung des Mittelalters* 39 (1983) 357–78

SCHALLER, Dieter 'Das Aachener Epos für Karl den Kaiser', *Frühmittelalterliche Studien* 10 (1976) 134–68

SCHALLER, Dieter *Studien zur lateinischen Dichtung des Frühmittelalters* (Stuttgart 1995)

SCHALLER, D. & KÖNSGEN, E. *Initia carminum Latinorum saeculo undecimo antiquiorum* (Göttingen 1977)

SCHANZ, M. & HOSIUS, C. *Geschichte der römischen Literatur bis zum Gesetzgebungswerk des Kaisers Justinian* (4 vols in 5, München 1927/59)

SCHÄR, M. 'Der heilige Columban und der Rabe', *Studien und Mitteilungen zur Geschichte der Benediktiner-Ordens* 99 (1988) 77–112

SCHIAPARELLI, L. (ed.) *Codice diplomatico Langobardo* II (Roma 1933)

SCHIEFFER, R. 'Zur Beurteilung des norditalischen Dreikapitel Schismas: eine überlieferungsgeschichtliche Studie', *Zeitschrift für Kirchengeschichte* 87 (1976) 167–201

SCHRIMPF, G., LEINWEBER, J., & MARTIN, T. (edd.) *Mittelalterliche Bücherverzeichnisse des Klosters Fulda und andere Beiträge zur Geschichte der Bibliothek des Klosters Fulda im Mittelalter* (Frankfurt a.M. 1992)

SCHUMANN, Otto *Lateinisches Hexameter-Lexikon. Dichterisches Formelgut von Ennius bis zum Archipoeta* (6 vols, München 1979/83)

SCHWARZ, W. 'Jurisdicio und Condicio', *Savigny-Stiftung, Zeitschrift für Rechtsgeschichte, Kanonistische Abteilung* 45 (1959) 34–98

SEEBASS, O. *Über Columba von Luxeuils Klosterregel und Bussbuch* (Dresden 1883)

SEEBASS, O. 'Ueber die Handschriften der Sermonen und Briefe Columbas von Luxeuil', *Neues Archiv der Gesellschaft für ältere deutsche Geschichtskunde* 17 (1892) 245–59

SEEBASS, O. 'Über die sogenannte Instructiones Columbani', *Zeitschrift für Kirchengeschichte* 13 (1892) 513–34

SEEBASS, O. 'Über dem Verfasser eines in Cod. Par. 16361 aufgefundenen Briefs, über die christliche Feste', *Zeitschrift für Kirchengeschichte* 14 (1894) 93–7

SEEBASS, O. 'Das Poenitentiale Columbani', *Zeitschrift für Kirchengeschichte* 14 (1894) 430–48

SEEBASS, O. 'Columba der Jüngere', in *Real-Encyklopädie*, ed. Hauck, IV.241–7

SELMER Carl (ed.) *Nauigatio S. Brendani abbatis: from Early Latin Manuscripts* (Notre Dame, IN 1959)

SHARPE, R. 'Hiberno-Latin *laicus*, Irish *láech* and the devil's men', *Ériu* 30 (1979) 75–92

SHARPE, R. 'Gildas as a Father of the Church', in *Gildas: New Approaches*, edd. Lapidge & Dumville, pp. 193–205

SHARPE, R. 'An Irish textual critic and the *Carmen paschale* of Sedulius: Colmán's letter to Feradach', *The Journal of Medieval Latin* 2 (1992) 44–54

SIMONETTI, Manlio 'Studi sull'innologia popolare cristiana dei primi secoli', *Atti della Accademia nazionale dei Lincei (Classe di scienze morali, storiche e filologiche)*, 8th series, 4 (1952) 341–484

SIMS-WILLIAMS, Patrick 'Thought, word and deed: an Irish triad', *Ériu* 29 (1978) 78–111

SIMS-WILLIAMS, P. 'Gildas and the Anglo-Saxons', *Cambridge Medieval Celtic Studies* 6 (1983) 1–30

SIMS-WILLIAMS, P. 'The settlement of England in Bede and the *Chronicle*', *Anglo-Saxon England* 12 (1983) 1–41

SIMS-WILLIAMS, P. *Religion and Literature in Western England, 600–800* (Cambridge 1990)

SMIT, Johannes Wilhelmus *Studies on the Language and Style of Columba the Younger (Columbanus)* (Amsterdam 1971)

SMITH, Thomas Albert 'The *De Gratia* of Faustus of Riez: a Study in the Reception of Augustinianism in Fifth-century Gaul' (unpublished Ph.D. dissertation, University of Notre Dame, IN 1988)

SMYTH, A.P. 'The earliest Irish annals: their first contemporary entries, and the earliest centres of recording', *Proceedings of the Royal Irish Academy* 72 C (1972) 1–48

SOUTER, A. 'Observations on the pseudo-Eusebian collection of Gallican sermons', *Journal of Theological Studies* 41 (1940) 47–57

SOUTER, Alexander *A Glossary of Later Latin to 600 A.D.* (Oxford 1949)

STÄHELIN, F. *Die Schweiz in römischer Zeit* (3rd edn, Basel 1931)

STANCLIFFE, C.E. [review of E.A. Thompson, *Saint Germanus of Auxerre*, and of *Gildas: New Approaches*, edd. Lapidge & Dumville], *Journal of Theological Studies*, new series, 37 (1986) 603–10

STANCLIFFE, C. 'Venantius Fortunatus, Ireland, and Jerome', *Peritia* (forthcoming)

STANTON, R. 'Columbanus, *Letter I*. Translation and Commentary', *The Journal of Medieval Latin* 3 (1993) 149–68

STEVENS, C.E. 'Gildas Sapiens', *English Historical Review* 56 (1941) 353–73

STEVENSON, J. 'Irish hymns, Venantius Fortunatus and Poitiers', in *Aquitaine and Ireland in the Middle Ages*, ed. Picard, pp. 81–110

STOKES, Whitley 'The glosses on the Bucolics', *Zeitschrift für vergleichende Sprachforschung* 33 (1894) 62–86, 313–15

STOKES, W. (ed. & transl.) 'The Annals of Tigernach. Third Fragment, A.D. 489–A.D. 766', *Revue celtique* 17 (1896) 119–263

STOKES, Whitley & STRACHAN, John (edd.) *Thesaurus Palaeohibernicus. A Collection of Old-Irish Glosses, Scholia, Prose and Verse* (2 vols, Cambridge 1901/3)

SZARMACH, P.E. (ed.) *Sources of Anglo-Saxon Culture* (Kalamazoo, MI 1986)

Thesaurus Linguae Latinae (Leipzig 1900–)

THILO, Georg. & HAGEN, H. (edd.) *Seruii grammatici qui feruntur in Vergilii carmina commentarii* III/2 (Leipzig 1902)

THOMAS, Charles *Christianity in Roman Britain to AD 500* (London 1981)

THOMAS, H. 'Der Mönch Theoderich von Trier und die Vita Deicoli', *Rheinische Vierteljahrsblätter* 31 (1966/7) 42–63

THOMPSON, E.A. 'Gildas and the history of Britain', *Britannia* 10 (1979) 203–26

THURNEYSEN, R. 'Colman Mac Leneni und Senchan Torpeist', *Zeitschrift für celtische Philologie* 19 (1933) 193–209

THURNEYSEN, R. *et al.* *Studies in Irish Law* (Dublin 1936)

TIBILETTI, C. 'Libero arbitrio e grazia in Fausto di Riez', *Augustinianum* 19 (1979) 259–85

TISCHENDORF, C. (ed.) *Euangelia apocrypha* (2nd ed, Leipzig 1876)

TOMLIN, R.S.O.   'The curse tablets', in *The Temple of Sulis Minerva*, ed. Cunliffe, pp. 59–277

TOSI, M.   'Arianesimo Tricapitolino norditaliano e Penitenza privata Iroscozzese: due piste importanti per riprendere la questione critica delle opere di Colombano', *Archivum Bobiense: Rivista degli Archivi Storici Bobiensi* 10/11 (1988/9) 9–118

TOSI, M. (ed. & transl.)   *Vita Columbani et discipulorum eius* (Piacenza 1965)

TOSI, M.   'Documenti riguardanti l'abbaziato di Gerberto a Bobbio' *Archivum Bobiense* 6–7 (1984–5) 91–172

TOSI, M.   'Il commentario di san Colombano ai Salmi', *Columba* 1 (1963) 3–14

TRAUBE, Ludwig   'O Roma nobilis. Philologische Untersuchungen aus dem Mittelalter', *Abhandlungen der philosophisch-philologisch Classe der Königlich Bayerischen Akademie* 19 (1892) 297–395

TURNER, C.H.   'The *Liber Ecclesiasticorum Dogmatum* attributed to Gennadius', *Journal of Theological Studies* 7 (1905/6) 78–99

TURNER, C.H.   'The *Liber Ecclesiasticorum Dogmatum*: supplenda to *J.T.S.* vii 78–99', *Journal of Theological Studies* 8 (1906/7) 103–14

VALLARSI, Domenico (ed.)   *Hieronymi Opera Omnia* (11 vols, Venezia 1766–71)

VOGEL, Cyrille   *La discipline pénitentielle en Gaule des origines à la fin du VIIe siècle* (Paris 1952)

VOLLMANN, B.   [review of Smit, *Studies*], *Jahrbuch für Antike und Christentum* 15 (1972) 210–14

VON CAMPENHAUSEN, H.   *Tradition and Life in the Church: Essays and Lectures in Church History* (London 1968)

WALKER, G.S.M.   'On the use of Greek words in the writings of St. Columbanus of Luxeuil', *Archiuum Latinitatis Medii Aeui (Bulletin Du Cange)* 21 (1949/50) 117–31

WALKER, G.S.M. (ed. & transl.)   *Sancti Columbani Opera* (Dublin 1957)

WALLACE-HADRILL, J.M. (ed. & transl.)   *The Fourth Book of the Chronicle of Fredegarius* (London 1960)

WALLACE-HADRILL, J.M.   *The Long-Haired Kings* (London 1962)

WALLACE-HADRILL, J.M.   *The Frankish Church* (Oxford 1983)

WALLACE-HADRILL, J.M.   *Bede's Ecclesiastical History of the English People. A Historical Commentary* (Oxford 1988)

WALLIS BUDGE, E.A. (transl.)   *The Paradise of the Fathers* (2 vols, London 1907)

WALSH, M. & Ó CRÓINÍN, D. (edd.)   *Cummian's Letter 'De controversia paschali' and the 'De ratione conputandi'* (Toronto 1988)

WALTHER, Hans (ed.)   *Prouerbia Sententiaeque Latinitatis Medii Aevi* (6 vols, Göttingen 1963–9)

WARNER, G.F. (ed.)   *The Stowe Missal* (2 vols, London 1906/15)

WARREN, F.E. (ed.)   *The Antiphonary of Bangor* (2 vols, London 1893)

WARREN, F.E.   *The Liturgy and Ritual of the Celtic Church* (2nd edn, by Jane Stevenson, Woodbridge 1987)

WASSERSCHLEBEN, F.W.H.   *Die Bussordnungen der abendländischen Kirche* (Halle 1851)

WATTENBACH, Wilhelm & LEVISON, Wilhelm   *Deutschlands Geschichtsquellen im Mittelalter* I. *Vorzeit und Karolinger* (Weimar 1952)

WEBER, Robert (ed.)   *Biblia Sacra iuxta Vulgatam Versionem* (2 vols, Stuttgart 1969)

WEINBERGER, W. (ed.)   *Boethii Philosophiae Consolationis libri V* (Wien 1934)

WERMINGHOFF, A. (ed.)   *Concilia aevi Karolini I* (Hannover 1906)

WICKHAM, C.   *Early Medieval Italy* (London 1981)

WILLIAMS, Rowan (ed.)   *The Making of Orthodoxy. Essays in Honour of Henry Chadwick* (Cambridge 1989)

WILMART, A. 'Le manuel de prières de saint Jean Gualbert', *Revue Bénédictine* 48 (1936) 259–99

WILMART, A. *Bibliothecae Apostolicae Vaticanae codices manu scripti recensiti: Codices Reginenses Latini* (2 vols, Città del Vaticano 1937/45)

WINTERBOTTOM, M. 'A "Celtic" hyperbaton?', *Bulletin of the Board of Celtic Studies* 27 (1976–8) 207–12

WINTERBOTTOM, M. 'Aldhelm's prose style and its origins', *Anglo-Saxon England* 6 (1977) 39–76

WINTERBOTTOM, M. 'Columbanus and Gildas', *Vigiliae Christianae* 30 (1976) 310–17

WINTERBOTTOM, Michael (ed. & transl.) *Gildas: The Ruin of Britain and Other Works* (Chichester 1978)

WINTERBOTTOM, M. [review of T. Janson, *Prose Rhythm in Medieval Latin*], *Medium Aevum* 45 (1976) 298–300

WOLFF, L. [review of U. Pretzel, *Frühgeschichte des deutschen Reims* (2 vols, Leipzig 1941)], *Anzeiger für deutsches Altertum* 61 (1942) 67–75

WOLFRAM, Herwig & POHL, W. (edd.) *Typen der Ethnogenese unter besonderer Berücksichtigung der Bayern* (Wien 1990)

WOELFFLIN, E. (ed.) *Publilii Syri Sententiae* (Leipzig 1869)

WOOD, I. 'A prelude to Columbanus: the monastic achievement in the Burgundian territories', in *Columbanus and Merovingian Monasticism*, edd. Clarke & Brennan, pp. 3–32

WOOD, I. 'Ethnicity and the ethnogenesis of the Burgundians', in *Typen der Ethnogenese*, edd. Wolfram & Pohl (Wien 1990), pp. 53–69

WOOD, Ian *The Merovingian Kingdoms 450–751* (London 1994)

WOOD, I. 'The *Vita Columbani* and Merovingian hagiography', *Peritia: Journal of the Medieval Academy of Ireland* 1 (1982) 63–80

WORDSWORTH, J., SANDAY, W. & WHITE, H.J. (edd.) *Old-Latin Biblical Texts* (2 vols, Oxford 1886)

WRIGHT, Neil 'The *Hisperica Famina* and Caelius Sedulius', *Cambridge Medieval Celtic Studies* 4 (1982) 61–76

WRIGHT, N. 'Gildas's prose style and its origins', in *Gildas: New Approaches*, edd. Lapidge & Dumville, pp. 107–28

WRIGHT, N. 'Knowledge of christian Latin poets and historians in early mediaeval Brittany', *Études celtiques* 23 (1986) 163–85

WRIGHT, N. *History and Literature in Late Antiquity and the Early Medieval West. Studies in Intertextuality* (Aldershot 1995)

WRIGHT, N. 'Gildas, Rufinus and Gregory of Nazianzus', in Wright, *History and Literature*, no. VI

YOUNGS, Susan (ed.) *'The Work of Angels': Masterpieces of Celtic Metalwork, 6th–9th Centuries* A.D. (London 1989)

ZAHN, T. *Forschungen zur Geschichte des neutestamentlichen Kanons und der altkirchlichen Literatur* (10 vols, Erlangen 1881/93, Leipzig 1900/29)

ZELZER, Klaus (ed.) *Basili Regula a Rufino latine uersa* (Wien 1986)

ZEUMER, K. (ed.) *Formulae Merowingici et Karolini Aevi* (Hannover 1886)

ZOEPFL, F. *Das Bistum Augsburg und seine Bischöfe im Mittelalter* (Augsburg 1955)

ZÖLLNER, E. 'Die Herkunft der Agilulfinger', *Mitteilungen des Instituts für österreichischer Geschichtsforschung* 59 (1951) 245–64

INDEX

Aachen, 101
Ad cenam agni prouidi, 258n
Adalhard, abbot of Corbie, 101
Adaloald, king, 25n
Adomnán, abbot of Iona, ix, x, 54; on
    Vergil, 279–80; *De locis sanctis*,
    166; *Scholia Bernensia*, 169; *Vita S.
    Columbae*, 2n, 3n, 7n, 152, 172,
    204n, 208, 211, 221n
Aéd, bishop of Bangor, 18n; *see also
    Aidus*
Aetius, 178, 180n
Agaune, monastery of, 203
Agde, council of (A.D. 506), 177
Agilbert, 239
Agilulf, king of the Lombards, 22, 23, 25,
    29, 50, 54, 187
Agilus, abbot of Rebais-en-Brie, 16n
Agrestius, monk of Luxeuil, 13, 238n
Agrimensores, 3n
Agripp: *see* Agrippinus
Agrippinus, bishop of Como, 23n; letter
    to from Columbanus, 24
Aidus, bishop, 9n, 17, 18n
Alamannia, 19, 20, 21, 101
Alaric, king of the Visigoths, 177
Alchfrith, anchorite, 99
Alcimus Auitus, 280n
Alcuin, works of, 99, 175n, 276, 281;
    Carmina, 253n, 277n; *Officia per
    ferias* attributed to, 272
Alcuin, pseudo-, *De psalmorum usu*, 272
Aldhelm, 48, 54, 167n, 280, 282; *De
    pedum regulis*, 278n; *De uirginitate*,
    171; *Epistulae*, 146
Alexandria, theologians of, 137n
Alsace, 20n
Altus prosator, 48
Amalgarius, *dux*, 12n
Ambrose, 118, 151, 280n; *Hexaemeron*,
    107n
Ambrosius Aurelianus, 180
Amiens, 18n
Ammianus Marcellinus, 148
Anatolius of Laodicea, 6, 66, 73

Anatolius, pseudo-, computistical works
    of, 265; *Canon paschalis*, 6; *De
    ratione paschae*, 82
Anicetus, pope, 74
Annales Cambriae, 177, 181
Annals of Inisfallen, 179n
Annals of Ulster, 3n, 4n, 5n, 7, 179
Annegray, dép. Haute-Saône, vii, 9, 10,
    206
Anthologia Latina, 31
antiphonaries: of Bangor, 5, 7n, 82, 204,
    205, 210, 211, 212, 213, 214, 215,
    247, 255, 256, 261, 262
Antony, St, 170
Apennines, 25
Aponius, works of, 172n
Apuleius, 172n
Aquileia, 187
Arator, 280n
Arbon, 20, 21
Arianism, 23, 25, 26, 175, 176, 187, 195
Arigius, bishop of Lyons, 14, 265
Arles, 113, 115, 176, 177
Armagh, Book of, 208–9
Arnobius Iunior, *Commentarii in psalmos*,
    163n
Athala: *see* Attala
Athanasian Creed, 271; *and see
    Quicunque uult*
Athanasius, *De incarnatione*, 107; *Vita S.
    Antonii*, 170
Attala, abbot of Bobbio, 17, 18, 19n, 26,
    268n
Audax es, uir iuuenis, 254
Audite omnes gentes, 246
Audite pantes ta erga, 7n
Augsburg, 20n
Augustine of Hippo, works of, 55n, 60,
    99, 102, 111, 118, 172n, 183;
    Confessiones, 133, 151; *De ciuitate
    Dei*, 151, 249n, 278n
Augustine, pseudo-, *Sermones ad fratres
    in eremo*, 106n
Augustinus Hibernicus, *De mirabilibus
    sacrae scripturae*, 152n

305

STUDIES IN CELTIC HISTORY